STRATEGY AND POWER IN RUSSIA

1600–1914

William C. Fuller, Jr.

THE FREE PRESS
A Division of Macmillan, Inc.
New York

Maxwell Macmillan Canada
Toronto

Maxwell Macmillan International
New York   Oxford   Singapore   Sydney

The Free Press
A Division of Macmillan, Inc.
866 Third Avenue, New York, N. Y. 10022

Maxwell Macmillan Canada, Inc.
1200 Eglinton Avenue East
Suite 200
Don Mills, Ontario M3C 3N1

Macmillan, Inc. is part of the Maxwell
Communication
Group of Companies.

Printed in the United States of America

printing number
1 2 3 4 5 6 7 8 9 10

Library of Congress Cataloging-in-Publication Data
Fuller, William C.
   Strategy and power in Russia, 1600–1914 / William C. Fuller, Jr.
    p. cm.
   ISBN 0-02-910977-9
   1. Soviet Union—History, Military—To 1801. 2. Soviet Union—History, Military—1801–1917. I. Title.
DK51.F85 1992
947—dc20   91-35871
                                                CIP

To Sarah

Contents

Maps

Acknowledgments

I have incurred a substantial debt to all of the institutions and individuals who have helped me in the writing of this book. Most of the research was accomplished in the following libraries and archives: Widener Library, Harvard University; the Lenin Library, Moscow; the Naval War College Library, Newport, Rhode Island; the Central State Archive of Military History (TsGVIA), Moscow; the Central State Archive of the October Revolution (TsGAOR), Moscow; and the Archive of the Foreign Policy of Russia (AVPR), Moscow. I would like to thank the librarians and staffs of all of them for the courteous assistance extended to me.

I am also grateful to those organizations, colleges, and universities that contributed to the support of my research. They include Harvard University's Russian Research Center, the International Research and Exchanges Board, The Smith Richardson Foundation, and the Naval War College Foundation. I must express most particular gratitude to the United States Naval War College. Although I began work on the manuscript long before I started to teach in Newport, in a very real sense this book has been shaped by my experience at that distinguished center for learning. The stimulation provided by students and colleagues, in addition to the encouragement given me by the leadership of the college, was simply indispensable to the writing of this work. The former Chairman of the Department of Strategy, Alvin Bernstein, was an unfailing source of advice and support. Valuable comments and penetrating questions came from Eliot Cohen,

Stephen Rosen, George Baer, David Kaiser, Bradford Lee, Douglas Porch, Steven Ross, and Brian Sullivan. I would like to thank the three Naval War College presidents under whom I have served—Admiral John Baldwin, Admiral Ronald J. Kurth, and Admiral Joseph C. Strasser—for fostering and sustaining an intellectual environment so conducive to scholarship.

Colleagues at other universities were also most helpful. Steven Schuker of Brandeis, William Wagner of Williams, Paul Kennedy of Yale, and Arthur Waldron of Princeton were kind enough to invite me to try out some of my ideas in lectures and seminars at their own institutions; I profited much from each of those opportunities. Other scholars took the time to provide critiques of all or part of the manuscript. Here I must express appreciation to Richard Pipes, Marc Raeff, David Jones, Mark von Hagen, and Jacob Kipp. Professors Daniel T. Orlovsky and Gregory Freeze provided me with particularly insightful readings of my text. I also would like to thank Professor Bruce Menning, who generously shared with me a copy of his book *Bayonets Before Bullets* prior to its publication. Finally, I must express my appreciation to Adam Bellow, my editor at the Free Press.

Until the October Revolution Russia adhered to the Julian calendar. This lagged eleven days behind Europe's Gregorian calendar in the eighteenth century, twelve in the nineteenth, and thirteen in the twentieth. For this reason, in discussing Russia's military and diplomatic relations with Europe I cite dates in both Old and New Styles. I have generally followed the transliteration system of the Library of Congress but for the omission of the hard sign ("). Names of famous Russians are spelled in the manner by which they are most familiar to readers of English. Hence Nicholas I, not Nikolai I. I have also used the standard Soviet archival abbreviations: f. for *fond* or collection; op. for *opis'* or catalogue; and d. for *delo* or file. Unless otherwise noted, all translations in this book are my own.

Introduction

"Backwardness" and Russian Strategy

It is perhaps best to begin by explaining what this book is not. It is not a comprehensive military history of Russia or an investigation of abstract Russian military theory, nor is it a study of what has been described as Russian "strategic culture." An exhaustive treatment of Russia's military past would have required not one volume, but an entire shelf. Russian military thought, while an important subject in its own right, is not my focus, concerned as I am with the realm of the practical. And the relationship between military theory and military practice, in tsarist Russia as in many other countries, was roughly similar to the relationship between political theory and politics. All too often a vast chasm intervened between them.

I make no claims for this book as an exposition of Russian strategic culture, either. Although this concept has acquired a certain vogue of late owing to the work of such people as Colin Grey and Jack Snyder, I do not find it appealing. To argue that there is (or was) one unitary Russian strategic culture is perforce to ignore or overlook exceptions, inconsistencies, competing traditions, and human agency—the very fabric of history. While some social scientists might find the concept of strategic culture congenial, because it can serve them as an analytic meatgrinder for reducing coarse and uneven historical reality to a smooth and homogeneous paste, historians have a duty to be wary of any technique that substitutes theoretical elegance for complex truth. The function of strategic culture analysis is also at odds with the enterprise of history, for it is supposed to be an instrument with predictive power.[1] Assuming past strategic culture as a constant, social scientists can invoke it to prophesy what current Soviet leaders are likely to do in the years ahead. Although one can correctly speak of a Russian military tradition, there is not now, nor was there ever, a uniform and immutable Russian strategic culture—a fact that by itself ought to raise doubts about the value of such forecasts. Still further, while history can be properly used to illuminate the present and the possible course of the future, history is abused when invoked to justify sibylline pronouncements.

This book is an interpretative study of the ways in which tsarist statesmen and governments tried to employ force or the threat of force to achieve their political objectives over the roughly three hundred years from the founding of the Romanov dynasty in the early seventeenth century to the outbreak of World War I in 1914. It is therefore a study of high strategy as the great Prussian theorist Clausewitz defined it—that is, as the connection between military means and political ends.[2] As such, it limns the Russian strategic tradition, discussing the ways in which that tradition adapted (and failed to adapt) to the challenges of geography, demographics, poverty, and technological change.

Why is this subject important? In the first place, the centrality of military power in the making and unmaking of the tsarist empire is beyond dispute. The empire was built through warfare and conquest; the military imperative left an indelible imprint upon Russian society, economy, and government. But equally, the Russian Empire collapsed as a direct result of military catastrophe. Russian defeat in the Crimea (1854–56) and Manchuria (1904–5) foreshadowed the debacle of World War I, which in turn was directly instrumental to the Russian Revolution. How and why was the Russian regime so successful in translating its military resources into power in the eighteenth and early nineteenth centuries and so unsuccessful in the very same undertaking thereafter? The answer to these questions is essential to any understanding of the course of Russian history. And even to pose these questions is to embark upon an investigation of the strategic history of Russia. Neither the rise nor the fall of the Russian Empire was inevitable; both were dependent on the results of wars. Neither Russian victories nor Russian defeats can be written off as the ineluctable consequences of macrohistorical forces or economics, for human choice played a great role in both. This brings us to the realm of strategy, because the history of strategy is quintessentially the history of choice, of options selected and options rejected. It is impossible adequately to understand the outcomes of the wars that Russia waged during this period without examining the strategic choices that its statesmen made both prior to their outbreak and during the fighting.

Another reason to study the history of imperial Russian strategy seriously is that it can cast light on more modern concerns. Many of the strategic problems that faced the Soviet government throughout its existence were strikingly similar to those with which the tsarist regime wrestled in the past. Since the October Revolution, Soviet debates—between Easterners and Westerners, between technologists and magicians, between advocates of the defense and proponents of the offense—paralleled many of the tsarist disputes this book will examine.

Then, too, during the 1970s and 1980s much misleading nonsense about the Russian military past was committed to paper by analysts eager to account for the military policies of the Soviet Union. Some attempted to explain away the huge Soviet defense effort by invoking the concept of traditional Russian "paranoia"— a deranged condition supposedly the result of centuries of invasion. Others, perhaps interested in awakening the West to the threat from the U.S.S.R., portrayed Soviet behavior as the continuation of typical, unceasing Russian aggressiveness and expansionism. Yet both schools were wrong. Paranoia is a medical diagnosis of an individual psyche. Since there is no such thing as a national psyche, it is meaningless to describe the mental processes of an entire country in terms of a psychosis. As we shall see later on in this book, at various points Russian strategists were acutely fearful. But those fears, although at times extreme, were scarcely insane. They were, rather, rational responses to an uncertain and threatening environment. It would be equally incorrect (as well as ahistorical), however, to depict Russia as eternally aggressive. At some times the Russian Empire was expansionist, at other times not. Even when Russia did expand, it usually did so in the pursuit of tangible strategic benefits, not as the result of an incontinent and mindless lust for territory. Further, although there were always some statesmen in the Imperial government who nourished secret, long-term aims of conquest, the military posture of the

Russian Empire for most of the nineteenth and early twentieth centuries was chiefly defensive. This, of course, has interesting implications for our own time. The attempt by the Soviet leadership to revise its military doctrine in 1987, to translate the idea of "defensive defense" into operational terms, was by no means the radical break with the Russian military tradition it was often represented as being.

The interrelationship between military failure and political change in the Russian past is also relevant to the origins of political reform in the Soviet Union. Under tsarism the greatest stimulus for reform was military defeat. Military fiascoes in the Crimea and Manchuria were followed by periods of strenuous reforms designed to remake not only the army but the society as well in the interests of efficient warfighting. Perestroika's initial military constituents included those who argued that wide-ranging reforms were essential if the Soviet Union was to remain technologically and consequently militarily competitive in the twenty-first century. Only social and economic renewal could ensure that the Soviet Union could participate in what the Soviet General Staff liked to term the third scientific-technological revolution in war—that is, the advent of new generations of highly precise and destructive conventional weapons. Anxiety about a presumptive future military inferiority, in addition to the very real defeat suffered in Afghanistan, may well have been instrumental in mobilizing support for Gorbachev in the early stages of perestroika.

Finally, the history of Russian strategy will help us to think about the future. The failed coup of August 1991 destroyed the *Union* of Soviet Socialist Republics. Confronted as it is by political uncertainty at home, a potentially unstable Europe, and the need totally to overhaul its armed forces, on what elements of old Russian military tradition might the central government (or what remains of it) potentially draw in the years ahead? This question can be asked with even more justice about the government of the Russian Republic. It is highly likely that we will soon witness the recreation of an authentically *Russian* army. We can confidently expect this new force to evince the keenest interest in the successes and failures of its tsarist predecessor.[3] A knowledge of imperial military history is more pertinent than ever to an understanding of the impending transformation of Russia and its military.

Strategy cannot, of course, be studied in a vacuum. Since strategy is about the marriage of capabilities and objectives, we must not ignore the environment in which it is made and the constraints on its implementation. A strategy can be brilliant yet worthless notwithstanding, without the resources necessary to execute it. For this reason this book will examine Russian strategy in its historical context. Operations and tactics obviously have a bearing on the effectiveness of strategy. But so, too, do the strengths and weaknesses of the economy and the society overall. All of these things circumscribed Russia's strategic choices and options. Where appropriate I shall therefore discuss the interconnections among economics, social structure, diplomacy, and the armed forces, both to explain why Russia adopted the particular strategies that it did and to account for their successes and failures.

A central theme of this book is the impact of "backwardness"—in its several senses—upon Russian military policies and practices. Frequently from 1600 to 1914 Russia found itself confronted by potential adversaries whose governments, societies and economies were *relatively* more modern than its own. Charles XII's Sweden, Frederick the Great's Prussia, Napoleon's France, Palmerston's Britain, and Wilhelm II's Germany can all serve as examples of states that surpassed the Russian Empire in per capita riches, in political organization, and in social development. Russia clung to serfdom until 1861, years after it had been abolished in Western and even Central Europe. And Russia remained an unbridled autocracy until the early twentieth century, a time when constitutionalism of some sort or another had supplanted monarchical absolutism in almost all other important countries.

Even when Russia fought inferior opponents, such as the Ottoman Turks throughout the eighteenth century, it had to worry lest its very military success induce a coalition of its wealthier and more powerful neighbors to intervene against it. Thus Russia could not prudently wage war against a weaker enemy without planning for the possibility that the war would widen to include adversaries stronger than itself. Russia's relative backwardness had several concrete manifestations and changed in character over time. In the seventeenth and early eighteenth centuries Russia's backwardness inhered in three areas: the material; the administrative; and the intellectual. The material dimension of backwardness was state poverty. The administrative was inadequate sociopolitical organization, and the intellectual was the inferior training and skills of the population. There were backward and forward linkages binding each of these phenomena to the others; each was potentially a source of peril to the tsarist state. The poverty of the government interfered with Russia's ability to mount and sustain a war effort against wealthier opponents. Poverty, along with geography, also helped to explain why Russia in this period was undergoverned, and consequently found it difficult to mobilize the human and material resources necessary for war. But undergovernment equally played an important part in perpetuating state poverty. At the same time, poor organization and poverty both contributed to and were in part the consequences of the relatively low diffusion of bureaucratic and military skills among the peoples that Russia ruled. Seventeenth-century Muscovy possessed some very capable bureaucrats indeed; the problem was that it had too few of them.[4] This, of course, was a serious impediment to establishing the comprehensive administrative control throughout the country necessary for a large expansion in tax revenues. Yet state poverty was itself a check on improvements in the education and training of Muscovy's bureaucrats and troops as well. In view of the barrenness of the treasury, just how large and effective a bureaucracy could Russia afford? Still further, how could Russia permanently support large numbers of foreign mercenaries or even domestic forces devoted exclusively to the mastery of the art of war?

These three dimensions of backwardness were to some extent ameliorated in the later eighteenth and early nineteenth centuries. They were not, however, eliminated. The Russian state grew relatively wealthier, but many of its potential enemies remained still richer. Administrative organization improved, as did education and skills; in key respects Russia remained inferior when measured against the standards achieved in Western and Central Europe.

After the mid-nineteenth century a new species of backwardness became increasingly important; this, of course, was the technological. Although Russia still had to fret about the other three elements of backwardness, it had additionally to worry about the military technological superiority of its opponents. During the Crimean war, the British possessed rifled naval ordnance and

Minié rifles; the Russians had neither. The steel breechloading cannon used by the Turks in 1877 and 1878 were more accurate over longer ranges than Russian artillery. The Austrian and German military railway nets consistently outclassed Russia's between the mid-1870s and 1914. And when Russia did take to the field in World War I, it was inferior to Germany in its supply of such crucial weapons as machine guns, high-explosive shells, and heavy artillery; inferior, as well, in the industrial capacity to manufacture these armaments once initial stocks had been exhausted. Throughout the history of the Russian Empire the problem of backwardness conditioned the Russian approach to strategy and to warfare in general. It had to.

During the entire period it was the task of the Russian government, like all other governments everywhere, to find strategies that both supported its external objectives and yet could be implemented with available resources. From roughly 1700 to the mid-nineteenth century Russia overall performed this task brilliantly. It is a central argument of Chapters 2 through 6 that it did so by crafting strategies and an entire military system to support them that exploited what I would like to call the advantages of backwardness. Russian successes in warfare and imperial expansion under Peter the Great and his successors were heavily dependent on Russia's ability to employ such ostensibly "backward" institutions as autocracy and serfdom to generate military power. It is in fact likely that in the absence of autocracy and serfdom, Russia's great eighteenth-century expansion might very well not have occurred. Whereas many other explanations of the rise of the Russian Empire ascribe it to "Westernization" and "modernization," I argue that Russia became a great power not so much by emulating the West as by inventing a new style of fighting that capitalized on its existing premodern political and social organization.

Until the middle of the nineteenth century, then, Russia could more than cope with backwardness, and could even derive military advantages from it. But thereafter circumstances changed. The Crimean War taught Russia an unforgettable lesson. Industrialization and dramatic changes in communication and transportation technologies had revolutionized warfare. Russian backwardness had now become not an asset but a liability, for it simultaneously enhanced the country's vulnerability and limited its capability for self-defense. Improvements in naval engineering and design left Russia's extensive coasts more open than ever to maritime attack. On land the German wars of unification appeared to demonstrate the enormous benefits that effective exploitation of railroads could confer on the offense. Thereafter, Petersburg had to live with the fear that the Teutonic powers' superiority in speed of mobilization and concentration might allow them to win a rapid and cheap victory before Russia was fully prepared to resist them. Russia's various attempts to overcome or transcend the military implications of its backwardness is a principle theme of Chapters 7 through 10. Russian strategists in this period were further confronted with underfunding, an intractable internal nationality problem, and the need to defend vast frontiers both in Europe and in Asia. As we shall see, Russia's chronic insecurity after 1855 had several important consequences. It led the empire's military elite reluctantly to adopt "magical" strategies, that is, strategies in which the élan and morale supposedly produced by Russian backwardness had to compensate for inferiority in mobilization, concentration, and munitions. For civilian officials, insecurity resulted in imprudent, reactive, and opportunistic imperialism, exemplified by Russia's advance into Manchuria, which both overtaxed the empire's resources and put it on a collision course with Japan. Finally, for both civil and military leaders alike, insecurity gave rise to a peculiar strategic pessimism, which conditioned the decisions that were made, often disastrously. Ironically enough, owing to bad policy decisions and misguided strategic choices, Russia entered World War I with a strategy that was still anchored to the premodern elements in its military tradition. Late Imperial Russia was consequently victimized by a history that it had proved unable to discard.

I

Russian Military Weakness in the Seventeenth Century

It has often been said that prior to the accession of Peter the Great, Russia was in a condition of military weakness. Indeed, to Peter himself has gone the credit for transforming Russia into a first-class military power in the course of his twenty-one-year war with the Swedes. Yet what exactly is military weakness? And how, in particular, was Muscovite Russia militarily weak? Was it chiefly a question of technological backwardness? Inadequate numbers of troops? Poor training? A social structure that could not support the army? We shall attempt to answer these and some ancillary questions by examining the history of two of seventeenth-century Muscovy's most resounding military catastrophes: the Smolensk War (1632–34) and the Crimean Campaigns (1687 and 1689).

The Smolensk War

After the death of Tsar Boris Godunov in 1605, Russia was plunged into crisis. The extinction of the original dynasty meant that there was no universally recognized claimant to the throne. The *Smuta*, a period of anarchy, civil war, and peasant rebellions, ensued. Eventually the disorder in Muscovy caught the attention of neighboring states: both the Swedes and the Poles intervened in force. Although the election of Michael Romanov as tsar in 1613 nominally resolved the domestic unrest, war with Sweden dragged on until 1617, and the conflict with Poland until 1618. Muscovy had to pay dearly for peace. Under the Stolbovo treaty Moscow ceded to Stockholm a huge swath of territory curving around the northern and western shores of Lake Ladoga. Russia was now cut off completely from the Gulf of Finland. For their part the Poles, in return for the fourteen-year Deulino armistice, exacted important lands along the western border of the state, including the strategic city of Smolensk. For the rest of the seventeenth century the government of Muscovy saw as one of its most pressing tasks the recovery of those alienated possessions. Muscovy had to choose which of its two adversaries to confront first. In the 1620s and 1630s the Polish-Lithuanian Commonwealth was viewed as the principal enemy.

There were several reasons behind Moscow's preference for a Polish war: personal, dynastic, religious, historical, and pragmatic. First, the most powerful man in the Muscovite state—the tsar's father, Patriarch Filaret—was profoundly antagonistic toward Poland, and with good reason. Arrested by the Poles in 1611, he had languished almost ten years in captivity before the Deulino armistice had resulted in his release.[1] Second, there was an important dynastic consideration. During the time of the troubles King Zygmunt III of Poland had proposed his son Wladyslaw as candidate for the Muscovite throne. Many of the most prominent boyars in the realm (including Michael Romanov) had in fact sworn fealty to Wladyslaw. On that basis the Poles refused to the recognize Michael's claim and throughout the 1620s routinely denied his title in diplomatic correspondence. From the standpoint of the Muscovite ruling elite this behavior was more than a discourtesy; it represented a clear danger to the state. The *Smuta* had been the result of contention over the right to rule, after all, and had come to an end only when all of the main political factions had agreed to respect Michael's somewhat dubious title. For a foreign power to dispute Michael's claim was a direct attack on the political compact that held the Muscovite state together and an open invitation to internal subversion and disloyalty.

Another factor in the targeting of Poland was a profound religious antipathy. To be sure, the Orthodox hierarchy of Moscow had no fondness for the Lutherans of Sweden or the Muslims of the Ottoman Empire. But Catholicism was perceived as more threatening to Orthodoxy than either Protestantism or Islam. Muscovites were particularly alarmed at the proselytizing efforts the Catholic and Uniate clergy had been making among the Orthodox Christians of the Ukraine ever since the late sixteenth century. That missionary effort was simultaneous with an increasingly onerous domination by Polish landlords in the Ukraine and carried a heavy risk for Warsaw. In the 1620s Orthodox Ukrainians began to petition Muscovy for aid against the Polish Catholics.[2] The rebellion of the Ukrainian Cossacks under Khmel'nitskyi against Poland (1648) cannot be explained without reference to the religious issue. And, in 1654, Muscovite intervention on the Cossack side (the Thirteen Years War) had the religious controversy as its backdrop.

Yet another reason for discord between Moscow and Warsaw was the very existence of the Polish-Lithuanian Commonwealth, which frustrated Muscovy's own imperial ambitions. One of the tsar's honorifics, after all, was *samoderzhets vseia Rusi,* or autocrat of all *Rus'.* Its implication was that Muscovy alone was the true successor to the old Kievan state of the ninth through the twelfth century. Some of the lands and cities of Kievan *Rus',* however, including the city of Kiev itself, lay under the sway of Poland. As Polish peace commissioners were to point out to their Muscovite counterparts in 1634, "the tsar should most properly style himself *autocrat of his own Rus'* since *Rus'* is located both in the Muscovite and in the Polish state."[3]

If all those considerations militated in favor of a war with Poland, there were eminently pragmatic motivations as well. As we shall see somewhat later, given the composition and logistics of the Muscovite army in the first half of the seventeenth century, a foray into Polish white Russia, where food and forage were readily available, had a greater chance of success than a war against Sweden, which would, perforce, be fought in the barren wastes of Karelia, Finland, or Ingria.

In any case, for Muscovy to undertake a full-blown war with any other state was hardly an easy matter in the first quarter of the seventeenth century. There was, of course, a financial problem: the time of the troubles had emptied the tsarist treasury, and many years would be required to achieve that solvency and those fiscal surpluses without which war would be unthinkable. The difficulty here was compounded by the fact that in the 1620s and 1630s Muscovy received more than three-fourths of its revenues from import duties and a tax on the sale of alcohol in the taverns.[4] It was obviously hard to squeeze more money from those sources than they already provided. Throughout the seventeenth century the Muscovite administration therefore continuously tried to find new ways of raising revenue, usually by imposing higher and (theoretically at least) more collectable new direct taxes.

Another impediment to war was the perceived inadequacy of Muscovy's indigenous military system. The Livonian wars of the late sixteenth century plus the *Smuta* itself had aroused doubts about the training, equipment, and tactics of the traditional cavalry army.[5] That army, consisting of members of the petty nobility (*dvoriane* and *deti boiarskie*) along with their armed dependents, was not a standing force. In exchange for service (and years sometimes went by between musters) these nobles received estates in usufruct or sometimes modest cash payments from the crown. Augmenting the horsemen were the so-called *strel'tsy* or musketeers, who, when not campaigning or serving in a garrison, engaged in petty trading and small-scale agriculture in the principal towns of the country. Although the Muscovite army had an artillery branch, there were few arsenals. Master gunners were in short supply. Such an army had its advantages: it was both relatively mobile and relatively inexpensive, at least by Western standards. It also had its uses in pitched battle against other cavalry formations. Indeed, this military system, which had been created for fighting Tatars, was to some extent modeled on similar Tatar military institutions.[6] Yet by the early seventeenth century this army had ceased to be an army of aggressive conquest: it did not have the power to occupy any territory *permanently*, nor was it of significant use in siege warfare.

A final check on Muscovite belligerence was the geopolitical position of the Muscovite state itself. To the northwest, west, and southwest, Muscovy shared borders with three powerful potential enemies: Sweden, the Polish-Lithuanian Commonwealth, and the Khanate of the Crimea. Those states were so embroiled in rivalry with Muscovy and with each other that Muscovy did not dare to go to war against one of them without an alliance with, or at least a promise of neutrality from, the other two. As the *Smuta* had demonstrated, Muscovy simply could not afford a two-front, let alone a three-front war. And there were many reasons for it to fear the power and intentions of each of those three states.

Muscovy had been at peace with Sweden since the Stolbovo treaty. The Swedish monarchy was satisfied with its terms and for the moment entertained no more territorial designs on Russia. But the Kremlin could not be certain that matters would stay that way. There was an anti-Muscovite party active at the Swedish court, and Sweden manifested a suspicious interest in monopolizing the proceeds of Muscovy's transit trade with the rest of Northern Europe.[7] Swedish military might, founded on its vastly profitable iron industry, its effective system of conscription, and the military reforms of the great Gustaphus Adolphus, could not be taken lightly.

For the reasons already cited, relations between Moscow and Warsaw were tense. There was growing evidence of the political decomposition of the Commonwealth, beginning in the early seventeenth century, which for the Muscovites could only be a cause for satisfaction. The monarchy, elective since 1572, was becoming progressively weaker vis-à-vis the powerful noble clans. Soon the Polish-Lithuanian state would recognize the right of *Liberum veto,* which permitted any noble delegate to the Diet (or parliament) to "explode" it, thereby paralyzing the government. The state was further afflicted with poisonous feuds between the great magnates, to say nothing of religious, ethnic, and national tensions. All this notwithstanding, with a population of more than 8 million and a land area of almost 400,000 square miles, Poland was one of the largest of European states. Then, too, although the Polish army was small (fielding no more than 60,000 men in wartime) it was formidable beyond its numbers. The Polish light cavalry was the terror of Eastern and Southern Europe: between the late sixteenth and mid-seventeenth centuries it fought outnumbered and often prevailed against Turks, Tatars, Cossacks, Swedes, Prussians, and Russians. In the early decades of the seventeenth century King Zygmunt had embarked on a series of Western-style military reforms of his own.[8]

The territory of the last great security threat to the Muscovite state, the Crimean Khanate, lay roughly 600 miles south of the city of Moscow proper. The Girei dynasty, which ruled the Khanate, was one of the last in the Muslim world that could trace itself back to Genghis Khan. Although they were nominally tributaries of the Turkish Sultan, the Gireis reserved to themselves considerable freedom of military and diplomatic action. The danger of raids upon Muscovy by the Crimean Tatars and their Nogai allies was in theory averted by the annual tribute that the tsar delivered to the Khan. Yet those bribes did not buy total protection. There were always free spirits and outlaws among the Tatars—men who mounted their own attacks on Polish, Ukrainian, or Russian territories in defiance of the Khan's orders. And given the economic problems of the Khanate (including inadequate stocks of food and overpopulation), the Khan at times yielded to the temptation to break his word and go on raids in search of plunder, slaves, and prisoners to ransom. As the Khan was able to put from 40,000 to 100,000 warriors in the saddle for a single campaign, this was no small worry. Muscovy had endured more than thirty major Tatar attacks during the sixteenth century; from 1611 through 1617 southern Russia had annually been ravaged by them. Muscovy was concerned with the Tatar danger throughout the seventeenth century and experimented with a variety of means (settlement of permanent garrisons, enlistment of the Don Cossacks, construction of fortified lines) in order to contain it.[9]

Despite all of these problems—financial, military, geopolitical—Patriarch Filaret and the people around him were bent on war with Poland. In preparing for it they took steps to overcome each difficulty. In the mid-1620s Filaret decreed a new system of direct taxation (the *dvorovaia chet'*), which enabled the government to compute taxes on the basis of the number of households in a region rather than their productivity. This fiscal measure and others permitted Filaret to restore financial stability while building up a substantial war chest.[10]

The war fund was particularly important to Filaret's plan to stockpile in advance the resources he would need for his war. Between 1630 and 1632 the Muscovite state imported more than a million pounds of iron and lead for the casting of cannon and forging of bullets.[11] Special purchasing commissions visited all the principal courts of Northern Europe in search of cannon, muskets, pistols, and rapiers.[12] Personnel were no less important. Muscovy tried to hire foreign military specialists—experts in the Western way of war—and simultaneously tried to enroll entire regiments abroad. Although the Thirty Years War was raging and it was a sellers' market for mercenaries, Muscovy's two Scottish agents, Lesly and Sanderson, were eventually able to dispatch some 3,800 troops from Germany and England to Muscovy. Their frenetic and expensive recruitment resulted in a doubling of the number of foreigners in the tsar's service.[13]

Yet Russia could not afford enough foreign mercenaries to bear the brunt of its Polish war. The "German" soldiers (as all foreigners were called, regardless of nationality) typically demanded fat salaries and substantial fringe benefits, such as lifetime pensions for their heirs in the event of serious wounds or death.[14] With a view to economy the tsarist government decided to try to train Russians to fight in the Western manner. This was the origin of the *voiska inozemnogo stroia* (troops of foreign formation). Enlisting landless *deti boiarskie*, Tatar converts, some peasants, and some Cossacks, these units began to drill under the supervision of their foreign officers in 1630. At the beginning of the war the government had eight infantry regiments (9,000 troops) of the "foreign" type on hand.[15]

Diplomatic maneuvering in Stockholm and the Crimea completed Russia's war preparations. Gustaphus Adolphus had recently intervened in the Thirty Years War as an ally of the Protestant princes and consequently welcomed Russia's proposed attack on Poland, hoping that it would secure his Livonian flank.[16] Negotiations with the Tatars, although less smooth, finally resulted in the Khanate's promise of neutrality.[17]

Confident that Russia was ready, Filaret made his final choice for war when he learned of the sudden death of King Zygmunt III in April 1632. A Poland distracted by the quarrels and intrigues of an interregnum, Filaret reasoned, would be more vulnerable than ever. Accordingly Moscow ordered the concentration of the troops of foreign formation and commanded the cavalry troops to "ready themselves for service, assemble supplies, and feed their horses."[18] *Voevody* (district military leaders) and *namestniki* (provincial viceroys) were ordered to cooperate with the recruiting officers who would shortly arrive to verify the musters of the local nobility. All those processes required time. At last, by August the Muscovite state had at its disposal 29,000 troops and 158 guns.[19] Overall command rested with the aged boyar Mikhail Borisovich Shein. Shein's qualifications for his post were his close association with Filaret (the two men hand endured Polish captivity together), his prestige as a hero of the *Smuta* and his intimate knowledge of the fortress of Smolensk (as commandant of the garrison there during the Polish siege of 1609–11).

A *nakaz*, an instruction issued in the name of the tsar, spelled out for Shein the general objectives of the war and the overall strategy he was to follow in their pursuit. Russia's goals were in fact modestly limited to the reconquest of the territories that had been lost to Poland in 1618. Russia's forces were supposed to capture Dorogobuzh and as many other frontier outposts as they could, as quickly as possible. Simultaneously, they were to issue proclamations calling on the Orthodox subjects of the Poles to rise in rebellion. Then they were to move briskly to invest and take the important town of Smolensk, some 45 miles southwest of Dorogobuzh.[20] Possession of Smolensk was critical to Muscovy's plan for the entire campaign. The lands Russia wanted to reacquire lay roughly within the oval described by the Dniepr river to the west and Desna to the east. Smolensk was located on the Dniepr at the northern end of the oval, less than 30 miles from the headwaters of the Desna.

The war began splendidly for the Muscovites. By mid-October 1632, Dorogobuzh and twenty other frontier forts were in Russian hands. On October 18, Shein and the main army arrived at the outskirts of Smolensk and prepared to besiege it.

To seize Smolensk was, however, no easy matter, for the town was protected by series of daunting natural and man-made obstacles. The core of the city was ringed by a wall almost 50 feet high and 15 feet thick. Thirty-eight bastions furthered strengthened this defense. Although those fortifications had been considerably damaged during the 1609–11 siege, the Poles had recently devoted great attention to their repair. They had augmented them by erecting a five-bastion outwork to the west of the city (known as King Zygmunt's fort), which was furnished with its own artillery and subterranean secret passages to facilitate sorties and countermining. To the north the city was defended by the Dniepr and to the east by a flooded marsh. The southern side of the city consequently offered the most promising approach for an assault, but here the Poles had build a strong, palisaded earthen rampart. The garrison, under the Polish voevod Stanislaw, was also relatively strong, comprising 600 regular infantry,

600 regular cavalry, and 250 town Cossacks. Stanislaw could rely on the townspeople to man the walls in a pinch and could also enlist the services of several hundred nobles of the local levy, who, armed and mounted, had taken refuge within the town of Smolensk at the news of the Muscovite advance.[21]

Smolensk thus confronted Shein with formidable military problems: a resolute garrison, strong fortifications, and natural obstacles. Shein's troop dispositions were commendable for prudence, economy, and foresight. He recognized that the same natural obstacles (the Dniepr, the flooded marsh) that protected the Poles to the north and east also hemmed them in, serving as natural siege works. That made a complete set of lines of countervallation unnecessary. Shein therefore deployed his troops to achieve three purposes: the possession of all tactically significant positions, such as patches of high ground around the city; the protection of his own lines of communication, supply, and retreat; and defense against potential relief columns. He ordered Colonel Mattison to occupy the Pokrowska Hill due north of the town of Smolensk on the opposite side of the Dniepr. The site was clearly the one most suitable for the emplacement of artillery batteries. Due west of the city Shein stationed the formations of Prince Prozorovskii. Prozorovskii, whose back was to the Dniepr, enclosed the rest of his camp with an enormous half-circle of earthworks (the wall alone was over 30 feet high). His purpose was both to menace the Polish ramparts on his right flank and to serve as the first line of defense against any Polish army of relief coming from the west. Between Prozorovskii and the walls of Smolensk, Shein placed van Damm's infantry and d'Ebert's heavy cavalry. Colonel Alexander Lesly, Colonel Thomas Sanderson, and Colonel Tobias Unzen, in command of the main body of Russian forces (almost nine thousand men) positioned themselves along the perimeter of the enemy's palisades to the south. To the east Karl Jacob and one thousand Russian infantry of new formation formed a screen behind the flooded marsh. Two and a half miles farther east, in a pocket formed by the bend in the Dniepr, was Shein's own fortified camp. Shein's camp protected not only the army's wagon trains and magazines, but also two pontoon bridges the Muscovites had erected across the Dniepr to secure communications with Dorogobuzh, where the reserves of food were stockpiled.

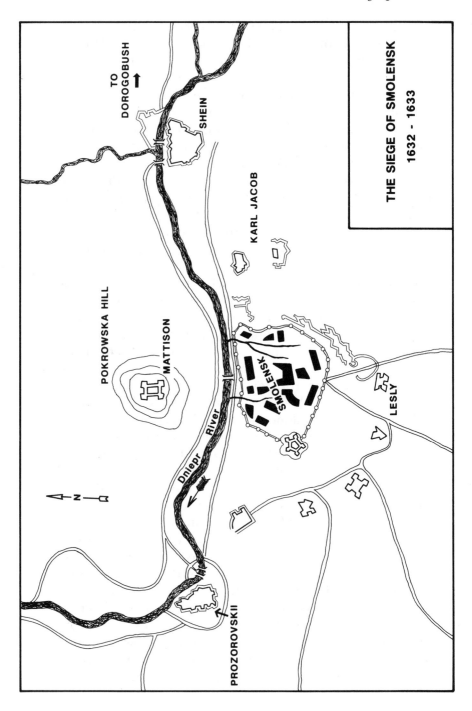

THE SIEGE OF SMOLENSK
1632 - 1633

Those arrangements were certainly intelligent, yet Shein from the beginning was incommoded by a lack of artillery. Heavy rains in the late spring and early summer of 1632 had turned the roads to mud. In the interests of surprise, Shein had decided to advance on Dorogobuzh, leaving most of his heavier guns behind. Thus the Muscovites had only seventy mostly light artillery pieces on hand in October. The rest of the field artillery was not delivered to Shein until the end of the year. It took until March of 1633 (five months into the siege) for the Russians to drag the nineteen heavy siege guns from their arsenal in Moscow to Shein's camp on the Dniepr. Part of the delay resulted from the massive size and weight of the siege pieces: more than 450 wagons were required to carry the guns, the shot, and the powder to the theater of war; the two largest guns fired projectiles weighing about 200 pounds.[22]

Without heavy guns, and siege pieces in particular, Shein was unable to effect a close blockade of Smolensk. The Poles profited hugely from this. News of the siege of Smolensk reached Warsaw by early November. Within two weeks the Diet appropriated money to put a 23,000-man crown army into the field. In the meantime the Grand Hetman of Lithuania, Prince Krzysztof Radziwill, mustered elements of the separate Lithuanian army and advanced on Smolensk himself.[23] Although Radziwill did not have enough troops to raise the siege unaided, he was able to bring Smolensk some succor. By means of two night operations in March of 1633 he broke through Shein's lines and delivered food, munitions, and more than a thousand reinforcements to the beleaguered town. That, however, was the limit of Radziwill's capability. Thereafter he withdrew from the city and engaged in guerrilla attacks on the Muscovite camps. Those attacks were more annoyances than serious threats.

By April the Russians had demolished the earthen ramparts the Poles had constructed south of the city. Shein now trained his guns on the walls of Smolensk itself in the hope of achieving a breach. Simultaneously he ordered that two mines be dug: one west from the camp of Jacob; and one northwest from Lesly's position to the Malaclowski gate. By mid-July, Muscovite gunners had reduced one section of wall almost 100 feet broad to rubble, while Lesly's sappers, under the direction of chief engineer David Nichol, had succeeded in implacing in another section a gigantic bomb of twenty-four powder kegs. On the appointed day the mine went off with such concussive force that tons of rock and timber were catapulted into the ranks of the Muscovite soldiers, who had been assembled too close to the wall for safety. In addition to the hundreds of casualties inflicted on the infantry, the blast also took the lives of thirty miners, who had been unable to scramble out of the tunnel in time. Still worse, Shein was not even able to exploit the 400-foot breach the mine had created, because the Polish defenders improvised hasty (but nonetheless substantial) barricades from the debris.[24] The Russians consequently had no choice but to break off their attack.

They never got a chance at a second assault. In part as a response to the gravity of the military emergency, the Polish and Lithuanian magnates in Warsaw had composed their differences and had chosen the son of the deceased monarch as Poland's new king. On August 23, 1633, King Wladyslaw IV arrived at Smolensk at the head of 23,000 men. From that point on the campaign was an unbroken litany of Muscovite military disasters.

On September 7 Wladyslaw launched diversionary attacks against both Mattison and Prozorovskii that made possible the conveyance of still more men and supplies into Smolensk. On September 21, despite Russian countermeasures, the Poles succeeded in smashing Mattison's defensive works to the north and west. Believing that the Pokrowska hill was now untenable, Shein ordered it evacuated.

The siege of Smolensk had effectively been lifted. The Muscovite army was now split in two; almost 10 miles separated Shein from the isolated detachments still holding positions west of Smolensk. The destruction of van Damm, d'Ebert, and Prozorvoskii was now Wladyslaw's top priority. On the night of September 27 the Poles began a series of nonstop assaults. Powerless to resist the pressure and aware that certain of his foreign troops had already deserted to the enemy, in early October Shein ordered Prozorovskii to abandon his enormous fort and retire to the main Russian camp downriver. This retreat entailed leaving tons of guns, powder, and supplies behind. Prozorovskii tried to blow up this military equipment prior to his departure, but a sudden downpour unfortunately extinguished the fuses and delivered his arsenal to the Polish king intact.[25]

Shein's only comfort was the knowledge that he had at least

reconcentrated his forces in defensible positions. He was, however, utterly surprised by the Poles' next move. A Polish column suddenly fell on Dorogobuzh, drove off the Russian garrison, and put all of the Russians' reserve stocks of food to the torch. Simultaneously, Wladyslaw marched northeast, seizing the Bogdanov dunes and the wooded hills of Skovronkovie in the rear of Shein's camp. Since the Poles had also deployed their cavalry to Shein's south, the Muscovites themselves were now surrounded and besieged. Shein made a series of unsuccessful attempts to break out of the Polish trap during October 1633. Bereft of communication with Moscow and running short of food and water, the Russian army was also tormented by the murderous bombardment of the Polish guns implaced at Skovronkovie. Shein had no way of silencing the Polish artillery, because his own guns could not be elevated high enough to fire on the Polish batteries with any accuracy. Morale in the Russian camp deteriorated, particularly among the foreigners. At one point in December Colonel Lesly assassinated Thomas Sanderson in a rage. With no army of relief in sight, Shein finally sued for peace in January 1634. The Poles were in an ungenerous mood and set harsh conditions. The Russians were to hand over all prisoners and deserters at once. They were to abandon their camp and surrender their heavy cannon and stocks of food. Foreigners in Russian service were to renounce their allegiance to the tsar and give their parole never again to make war on Poland, while Muscovites were to promise to abstain from war against the Commonwealth for four months. Shein initially balked at those terms but at last capitulated. On February 19 Shein and his fellow voevody led the defeated Russian army out from behind the palisades of the camp in grim procession. As they passed the royal entourage, each Muscovite regiment was stripped of its military banners, and Shein himself and the other Russian leaders were forced to dismount and make obeisance at the feet of the Polish king. Only eight thousand Russian troops followed Shein in his march back to Moscow. Some two thousand sick or wounded men remained behind, along with the 123 guns that Shein had had to surrender to the Poles. As for Muscovy's foreign hirelings, they either took service with Wladyslaw or prudently disbanded and made for home.

Even before the news of Shein's humiliation reached Moscow,

the ruling circles in the Kremlin had reason to be upset with the progress of the war. Since the spring of 1633 Zaporozhan Cossacks and Crimean Tatars on the Polish payroll had been conducting massive raids onto Russian territory. Partly for that reason Muscovy had found itself unable to send Shein relief or reinforcements. The finances of the state were themselves precarious. Finally, Filaret, the greatest proponent of the war, had died in October 1633. When the Kremlin finally learned of Shein's surrender, it was already obvious that Muscovy had no reasonable chance of continuing the fight. The real anxiety was that the Poles might take advantage of Muscovite defenselessness to launch a full-blown invasion of the Russian heartland. The Poles did in fact have such a plan but opted to negotiate instead, influenced by rumors that the Ottoman Sultan was contemplating a war against the Commonwealth. The peace treaty of Polianovka (May 1634), while requiring Muscovite cession of a few additional towns to Poland, essentially reconfirmed the territorial lines established by the Deulino armistice. The Russians did, however, also have to pay a substantial war indemnity to Warsaw. The only positive gain from the Russian standpoint was that in the Polianovka peace Wladyslaw did at least recognize Michael's title as legitimate ruler of Muscovy. Of course, this had less to do with shrewd bargaining than with the Polish fear of the outbreak of a major war with Turkey before peace with Moscow had been formally concluded. As for the hapless Shein, he and his lieutenants were made the scapegoats. Muscovite judges convicted Shein on the spurious charge of having been a Polish agent since 1611. He was beheaded, his property was confiscated, and his family was tortured and exiled to Siberia.

The Smolensk war had obviously been a military catastrophe for Muscovy. Yet before we turn to the reasons for the defeat it is useful to compare this botched war with two equally unsuccessful campaigns that occurred fifty years later.

Golitsyn's Crimean Campaigns

In the 1680s Muscovy's chief enemies were still Sweden, Poland, and the Crimean Khanate. Yet the relative balance of power was now different, since Muscovy was relatively stronger vis-à-vis each of those states than it had been fifty years previously. The dynastic instability and military exhaustion of Muscovy's adversaries helped to account for the shift, but so too did Moscow's patience, prudence, and guile.[26] In the period after 1634 Muscovite statesmen had tried to avoid war or defer war to the most advantageous of times. For example, when in 1637 a band of free Don Cossacks captured Azov from the Turks and offered it to the tsar, he immediately rejected the gift and apologized to the Sultan.[27] This meek behavior did not, however, mean that the Muscovites had abandoned their dreams of conquest in the south, north, or west. To the contrary, as one of Russia's greatest seventeenth century diplomats, Afanasii Ordin-Nashchokin once observed, the fundamental purpose of Muscovy's diplomatic establishment was "the expansion of the state" (*rasshirenie gosudarstva*).[28] The issue was timing. If Muscovy could wait until its enemies were enfeebled by internal struggles or foreign wars, it might be able to extract territorial concessions from them by offering an alliance or issuing threats. Alternatively, if the tsar went to war he should do so when his target was already engaged in hard fighting with someone else. Thus Muscovy made its next attack on Poland in 1654, presenting itself as the protector of the Cossacks, whose military uprising had already shaken that state to its foundations. The eventual outcome—the truce of Andrusovo in 1667—left Moscow in temporary possession of Kiev and the entire eastern (or left-bank) Ukraine.

Successful expansion brought new risks. Moscow now for the first time had a common frontier with the Ottoman Empire. The Turks were themselves emerging newly strengthened from a lengthy period of internal dissension and were looking covetously on Eastern and Central Europe. Ottoman interest in the Ukraine in particular led to a series of wars with the Poles and then to the outbreak of the first Russo-Turkish conflict (1677–81). This Chigirin war ended with the recognition of the status quo ante, for the Ottomans did not prosecute it very vigorously, preoccupied as they were with preparing for a major Central European campaign against the Hapsburg Empire.

In the summer of 1683 the Turkish Vizier, at the head of an enormous Ottoman army, marched to the walls of Vienna and invested that city. The siege, however, was raised in September when King Jan III Pobieski arrived with a Polish army of relief. As the Turks retreated east, the Hapsburgs plotted a counterattack to drive the Ottomans from Europe and break their power once and for all. Only a great western confederation, however, could accomplish that. In March 1684 Hapsburg, Polish, and Venetian diplomats signed the Holy Alliance, binding themselves to conduct a crusade against the Turks.[29] By its terms, other powers were to be encouraged to enroll as well; both Vienna and Venice were particularly eager to enlist the support of the Muscovites.

Since 1682 the titular heads of the Muscovite state had been the two boy tsars Peter and Ivan Alekseevich. Actual power, however, was in the hands of their older sister, the regent Sophia. And with regard to foreign affairs she tended to rely chiefly on the counsel of her friend and confidant, the urbane Moscow aristocrat V. V. Golitsyn. A gifted diplomatist and shrewd negotiator, Golitsyn saw no value for Russia in the Holy Alliance unless Poland could be induced to make the territorial concessions of 1667 permanent. In other words, prior to any Muscovite participation in the Turkish war, Golitsyn demanded that the Poles recognize Russian annexation of Kiev and the left-bank Ukraine. Warsaw initially balked, until military reverses and allied pressure forced it to cave in. In May 1686 Russia and Poland signed a "perpetual peace" in which Golitsyn got everything he wanted.[30] In return Russia entered the Holy Alliance and prepared for war the following year.

Although some commentators have criticized Golitsyn for having joined the Holy Alliance to serve the interests of foreign powers and to gratify his own vanity, the fact is that the signing of the 1686 peace made war with the Tatars inevitable.[31] Neither the Turks nor the Tatars were likely to accept the change in the balance of power represented by Russian annexation of the eastern Ukraine. Sooner or later Russia would have to fight, and from Golitsyn's point of view it made more sense for Russia to go war as part of a powerful coalition than on its own.

The fact of coalition had implications for Russia's war plans; it was expected to act in concert with its allies. While the Poles campaigned against the Turks in the right-bank Ukraine, while Venice attacked them in Dalmatia and Greece, and while the Holy Roman Empire dispatched its forces to the Danubian basin, Russia was supposed to assault the Khanate of the Crimea with its entire army so as to divert the Crimean Tatars from offering any succor to their Turkish overlords.[32]

Russia provoked war by means of an outrageous ultimatum to Constantinople and Bakchisarai: It demanded the total resettlement of all Crimean Tatars in Anatolia; the cession of the Crimean peninsula; and a payment of 2 million pieces of gold.[33] Those were obviously not Moscow's true war aims. Rather, Russia was going to war to secure its possession of the eastern Ukraine, to avenge insults visited on its ambassadors, and to punish the Tatars for their ongoing raids. The proclamation announcing the campaign, issued in the fall of 1686, stated that its purpose was to free the Russian lands from "unbearable insults and humiliation."[34]

The inflammatory words notwithstanding, preparations for the campaign were disappointingly slow, in particular owing to the high number of noble servitors who failed to appear at their appointed musters. Nonetheless it was an index of Russia's growing military power that the forces Moscow now assembled far exceeded those that it had been able to raise for war against Poland some fifty years previously. V. V. Golitsyn, who took personal command, had an army of more than 100,000 troops. Forty thousand of them were either *strel'tsy* or Western-style infantry. Twenty thousand others were either pikemen or Western-style cavalry.

By May 2, 1687, Golitsyn had assembled his forces on the banks of the Merlo river, not far from present-day Khar'kov. This site was to serve as the base camp for the entire expedition. Golitsyn's plan was to march southwest, crossing over into the lands of the Zaporozhan Cossacks. From here, after a rendezvous with Samoilovich's Zaporozhan army, Golitsyn proposed to move due south into the steppe and invest the fortress of Perekop, which lay athwart the narrow strip of territory connecting the Crimean peninsula to the mainland. Once Perekop was in Russian hands, Golitsyn would invade the Crimean homeland. Simultaneously the Don Cossacks were to make raids and incursions into the Khanate east of the sea of Azov while, as a further diversion, another force of Zaporozhans was to attack the Turkish forts that guarded the lower reaches of the Dniepr.[35]

The army set out on March 8. The infantry marched within the confines of an enormous moving rectangle composed of 20,000 wagons. On the right and left of the 18 million square feet enclosed by the rectangle, Golitsyn posted his cavalry.[36] The early stages of the march passed without incident; despite a couple of false alarms, there were no Tatars in the vicinity. Samoilovich's Cossacks were waiting for the Muscovites at the appointed place. Yet the rate of advance was very slow—no more than 6 miles a day. It took thirty-six days for the Russian army to cover the 180 miles that separated the base camp at Merlo from the Konskaia voda (Horse Water) River, which marked the beginning of the steppe. Perekop lay a mere 90 miles to the south. Yet it was at Konskaia voda that Khan Selim Girei unveiled his own brutally effective campaign plan. Knowing of the approach of Russian forces, the Khan had ordered his men to set fire to all of the steppe grass between Konskaia voda and the Isthmus of Perekop. On June 13 the Russians crossed over the river on pontoon bridges and entered the burned and smoldering steppe. Clouds of dust and smoke hung motionless above, befouling the air for miles around.

Within two days the effects of a march through such an inhospitable environment were making themselves felt, as men fell ill by the hundreds. The army experienced some relief on June 16, when a heavy rain settled the dust and allowed the soldiers to draw breath more freely. But by the next day Golitsyn was forced to recognize that any further advance would be folly. The burning of the steppe had eliminated the plentiful supply of fodder on which progress depended. Having had nothing to eat since June 13, the horses had become so enfeebled that they were scarcely capable of drawing the wagons. Golitsyn called a council of war, which agreed on a retreat. However, in order to mask the fact of retreat and in order to salvage something from the operation, 40,000 troops were detached to reinforce the Zaporozhan attack on the Turkish Dniepr forts.[37] Having traveled no more than 7½ miles from Horse Water, Golitsyn and the main body of the army turned tail and made for home. It was a march of hunger, thirst, and death. Possibly as many as 30,000 Muscovites perished. Golitsyn's first campaign had been an unvarnished fiasco.

Golitsyn decided to try again. This time, however, he was determined to profit by his earlier mistakes. He recognized, for example, that he had begun his campaign too late in the year. When the army had finally reached within striking distance of Perekop in June, heat and drought had turned the steppe into a vast tinderbox, which a single spark could turn into flames. Golitsyn decided to launch his attack earlier in the spring and with that in view commanded that the muster of the army be completed by February 1689.[38]

Another of Golitsyn's problems in 1687 had been a lack of bases where the sick could be left on the army's outward march and where supplies could be stockpiled against the army's return. On the advice of General Patrick Gordon, a Scottish military expert in the Russian service, it was decided to detach small bodies of men from the army every few days en route to the Crimea. Those troops were to construct camps fortified by palisades, dig wells, and gather hay. If all went as expected, the presumably victorious army would find adequate stocks of water and fodder on its journey back to Muscovy.[39]

Two final precautions taken by Golitsyn in 1689 concerned the order of march and defense against steppe fires. In 1687 the army had marched together within the protective carapace of one huge wagon barricade. In the later campaign Golitsyn used a different deployment. An advance guard led by Gordon and A. S. Shein (a descendent of the unfortunate Shein of 1633) preceded the main Russian forces, which marched behind in six separate columns. Although such an arrangement posed the risk that the Tatars might cut off and ambush one or more columns, it had advantages as well, since the advance guard could be used to screen the position of the rest of the army and to deceive the enemy about Golitsyn's intentions.[40] Finally, to safeguard against steppe fires Golitsyn sent agents far out ahead of the army in April 1689. They were to set fires of their own in the hope that when the army caught up with them the replenished steppe grass would be abundant enough to serve as forage but not so abundant (or so dry) as to make the Tatar trick of 1687 possible.

Golitsyn's army of 112,000 men and 700 guns began its advance early in March 1689. Almost at once there were problems with the weather. Golitsyn's troops were unused to winter campaigning and suffered greatly from the cold and the snow. But a huge premature thaw at the end of March brought even greater calamity. The snow turned to slush and mud, while the rivers, swollen by melting ice, overflowed their banks and swept bridges away. The flooding put a halt to the army's progress. Gordon, for instance, spent more than a week attempting to cross the Vorskla river.[41] A further complication derived from the fact that the army had taken to the field before the funds necessary for its support could be collected and delivered. At the beginning of April Golitsyn was still waiting for the cashboxes to catch up with him.[42]

Despite those trials, Golitsyn's luck seemed to have turned in mid-April. The Russians linked up with their Zaporozhan allies under Hetman Mazeppa at the Samara River. The army made good progress marching southeast on a course paralleling the Dniepr. By May 12 the army was so deep in Tatar country that it was necessary to march in battle order. Two days later a captured Tatar confirmed that this had been a useful precaution: the Khan himself had encamped a powerful army at a place called the Black Ravine (Chernaia Dolina) not 6 miles away.

It was obvious that the Khan would not permit the Russians to reach Perekop without a fight. On May 15 the Tatars attacked the advance guard on its right flank. When artillery dispersed the Muslims, the Russian cavalry set off in pursuit. That, how-ever, was exactly what the Tatars had been hoping for; a larger body of Tatar horsemen suddenly fell on the Russian wagons from the rear. In the hand-to-hand fighting that ensued serious casualties were inflicted on both sides. Eventually, however, the Russians won the upper hand by training their falconets and other light artillery pieces on the enemy. But the Muscovites were unable to exploit their victory, as the more mobile Tatar forces outdistanced their pursuers and vanished south into the steppe.

Golitsyn spent the next five days marching the 40 miles to Perekop. During this advance he had the uncomfortable sensa-tion of being completely encircled by enemies, for large bands of Tatar horsemen were constantly in view (although out of cannon range) before, behind, and on both flanks. On May 20 the Rus-sian army at last arrived at Perekop. Golitsyn was appalled by what he found there. The Tatars had strengthened the fortifica-tions of Perekop by digging a fosse that ran across the entire isthmus. The Russians would have to fight their way over this trench before they could even get close enough to the fort proper to put it under siege.

That seems to have been the final discouragement for Golitsyn. His men and draft animals were already exhausted by almost eighty days of nonstop marching; there was a critical shortage of water; and now the barriers to further advance were unexpectedly strong. Golitsyn knew he would have to withdraw. To save face he opened negotiations with Selim Girei and threatened to raze the fort of Perekop unless the Khan pledged never to raid Muscovy again. The Khan knew the threat was hollow. Russia's forces, suffering gravely from thirst and hunger, now began their retreat. The Tatars harried them on all sides, lighting steppe fires, picking off stragglers, and capturing artillery pieces in sudden attacks.[43] Upon Golitsyn's return to Moscow in June the government staged various demonstrations and services of thanksgiving in honor of his "triumph," but few were fooled. The second Crimean campaign had been almost as inglorious as the first.[44]

What Went Wrong?

One could of course assert that the campaigns just recounted are vivid proof of Russia's seventeenth-century military weakness, for Russia was unsuccessful in each of them, but such a tautological observation does not get us very far. Why specifically did Russia lose the war with Poland, and why specifically were Golitsyn's assaults on the Crimea failures? How do we distribute emphasis among the various possible causes, ranging from those that were accidental (poor weather) or situation-specific (errors in command) to those which were systemic, e.g. constituent elements of the the Muscovite military system? A good method of doing so is to examine the spectrum of potential explanations for defeat sequentially. We shall look at generalship, technology, tactics, operations, and finally endurance (including logistics, training, reinforcement, and finance).

Generalship

It is fashionable today to account for one country's victory over another in war in terms of the superiority of its military potential. A sort of relative economic, social, and institutional calculus can presumably make the detailed study of individual battles and campaigns unnecessary.[45] Material determinist analyses of this kind can be traced all the way back to Engels if not earlier.[46] Such an approach is clearly of value when applied to the history of European wars in the industrial era. It is most particularly useful in understanding the great mechanized wars of the twentieth century, although it does not have universal explanatory power even there. In the preindustrial period, however, the material determinist theory of war is often beside the point. There are too many examples of successful war waged by poor countries against richer ones. Without falling into the alternate trap of idealizing great captains and seeing military history as merely the record of their achievements, we must nonetheless note that generals can and do (and could and did) lose battles, campaigns, and wars.

There can be no doubt that decisions made by generals on both sides had an effect on the outcome of the Smolensk war and the Crimean campaigns. Simply put, Wladyslaw outmaneuvered Shein, and Selim Girei outwitted Golitsyn. Wladyslaw's great accomplishment was his surprise raid on Dorogobuzh and his simultaneous strategic envelopment of the entire Russian army, while Selim Girei was able to ruin Golitsyn's first campaign by simply converting the burning steppe itself into a weapon.

However, although beaten, neither Shein nor Golitsyn was an egregiously bad or incompetent commander. We have already had occasion to commend Shein's troop deployments at Smolensk. As we shall see shortly, he also directed the siege of that town in a modern and European fashion. As for Golitsyn, he planned his campaigns and routes of march with precision, making heavy use of the intelligence that Russian envoys had collected on diplomatic missions to the Crimea in 1680–81.[47] Golitsyn consequently possessed excellent information about where wood, water, and forage were to be found (under normal conditions) and issued each day's marching orders on that basis. The arrangements for the second expedition show Golitsyn's determination to profit from the mistakes of the first, in particular through his practice of leaving fortified outposts in the wake of his advance. It might be objected that Golitsyn's failure to develop any sound plan for the employment of his army prior to arriving at Perekop demonstrated his military incompetence, yet the objective of his campaign—a full-blown assault on the Crimean peninsula—was in a sense dictated to Golitsyn by his coalition partners. In fact, from the standpoint of the other members of the Holy Alliance Golitsyn's campaigns were successful: they did tie down the Crimean Tatars, thus preventing the Khan from offering the Sultan any support.

Shein and Golitsyn were defeated no so much through their own errors as by the novelty of the operations conducted by their opponents. Wladyslaw's deep envelopment of October 1633 was not original; such maneuvers had been conducted in Western Europe before. The Poles *had never previously* attempted it in their military history, however, and consequently Shein was caught off guard.[48] The Crimean campaigns presented similar innovations. To be sure, Muscovite troops had waged war against Tatars for generations. Yet typically the Muscovite army had confined itself to interdicting potential Tatar invasion routes or, if that failed, to repulsing bands of raiders already engaged in plunder. Muscovy's military posture toward the Crimea had therefore been chiefly defensive. By contrast, Golitsyn's campaigns represented a first effort at waging offensive war by conducting hostilities deep within the Tatar's own country. Never before had a Muscovite army marched so far south; never before had Muscovites campaigned in a steppe that was a virtual desert. Golitsyn was accordingly unprepared for Selim's burning of the steppe in 1687 and just as unprepared for his strategic withdrawal in the face of the Russian advance two years later. Both Shein and Golitsyn were consequently the victims of tactical and operational surprise. Neither displayed much flexibility when the enemy did not behave as expected.

It would nonetheless be simplistic to argue that Russia's military weakness was chiefly the function of the ineptitude of its commanders. The decisions made by Shein and Golitsyn have to be understood in the context of the resources available to them and the conditions under which they were required to operate.

Military Technology

Can part of the reason for Muscovite defeat then be found in inadequate military technology? For those who would like to portray Russia (and the Soviet Union for that matter) as the constant underdog in a series of Western-launched arms races, such an explanation has its attractions. The seventeenth century was in fact a time of considerable military-technical innovation. Improvements in gunnery had already led military engineers to redesign the fortress. The medieval style of high, thin walls was abandoned in favor of the low, thick, bastioned *trace italienne* style of fortification, which made fortress walls virtually impervious to shot. That innovation in military architecture apparently originated in northern Italy during the Hapsburg–Valois wars, was further refined during the eighty years of the Dutch revolt against Spain, and had become almost universally adopted throughout Northern, Western, and Southern Europe by the early seventeenth century. The growing importance of the fortress logically enhanced the firepower, significance, specialization, and numbers of the infantry, since infantrymen were the only troops capable of undertaking siege operations.[49] Then, too, there were improvements in infantry weapons: more and more foot soldiers were armed with firearms rather than pikes; firearms themselves became more reliable as matchlocks (cumbrous and useless in wet weather) gave way to flintlocks.[50] Those innovations stimulated the invention of counter-innovations, as European armies introduced new specialized weapons designed to respond to the changes in war. An example would be the hand grenade, which became especially important in modern siege warfare, because it allowed the attackers to clear the covered way of defenders before exploiting a breach or attempting an escalade. Gustaphus Adolphus was apparently the first monarch to employ special hand grenade troops—grenadiers—who made their debut at the siege of Ratisbon in 1632.[51]

It must be admitted that Muscovy did have difficulties in the seventeenth century in acquiring such military technologies. In particular the core of the Muscovite army remained the old levy of cavalry servitors—men who were expected to arm and equip themselves. The firearms which those part-time soldiers brought with them into the field were likely to be neither standardized nor in particularly good condition. Partly for that reason, beginning at the end of the *Smuta* the Muscovite state redoubled its efforts to produce or purchase the latest weapons for its own stockpiles. Many of its efforts were successful; throughout the seventeenth century Russia rapidly modernized its arsenal. Especially promising results were achieved with artillery. More than sixteen iron works and cannon foundries were established in Muscovy between the 1630s and 1670s. By mid-century Russia had amassed an arsenal of some five thousand guns.[52] In the same period Russia made strides toward self-sufficiency in gunpowder, while its armories became capable of an annual output of two thousand muskets a year.[53] By the end of the reign of Aleksei Mikhailovich, even hand grenades had come into general use, and Muscovy had already formed its own unit of grenadiers (*granatchiki*).[54]

These military achievements may seem modest indeed when compared with those of the most advanced West European countries. For example, as early as 1639 the Gunmaker's Company of London could by itself turn out almost 1,200 muskets a month.[55] Yet seventeenth-century Muscovy was not in military competition with either Cromwell or Louis XIV. When we compare Muscovy's military technology to that of its neighbors and rivals, we discover that it was equal or superior in all cases except Sweden's. Indeed technological parity, if not superiority, was a striking feature of the campaigns that this chapter has already examined.

Consider the Smolensk war. The matchlock, wheelock, and snaphance muskets that Russian troops carried into battle were in no way inferior to Polish models. Further, the Russian army assembled under the gates of Smolensk possessed approximately the same number of firearms as the Polish army of relief. Shein had almost 12,000 new-style infantrymen, organized into companies in which one-third of the men bore pikes and the rest muskets. Wladyslaw IV had roughly 13,000 infantrymen carrying muskets and pikes in identical proportions.[56] As for ordnance, the Russians enjoyed superiority in numbers of field pieces throughout the entire war. As late as 1650 there were no more than four hundred field cannon in the entire royal army of Poland.[57] To be sure, at certain crucial junctures Shein was incommoded precisely owing to the quantity and bulk of his guns (all together his artillery park apparently weighed more than 800,000 pounds), but the only general in Europe at the time who possessed truly mobile regimental guns was the King of Sweden.[58] What about Russian engineering and mining? On the whole Russian exploitation of those methods of war was up to the standards prevailing in Europe; mishaps such as the explosion of July 17, 1633, were in fact common whenever armies undertook a siege.[59]

If Muscovy was on the same technological plane as the Polish-Lithuanian Commonwealth in the 1630s, it was in all respects technologically superior to the Crimean Tatars against whom it fought in the 1680s. Golitsyn's forces ranged in size from 100,000 in the first campaign to 120,000 in the second. On both occasions over 60 percent of the men were equipped and trained in the Western fashion.[60] In addition Golitsyn had an impressive complement of artillery, in excess of seven hundred pieces in 1689. The Crimean Tatars were by contrast chronically short of firearms. The expense of purchasing them was often beyond the means of Tatar warriors. Manufacturing such weapons was also very difficult. Since there were no veins of ore locally available, the Crimean Tatars had to import most of their lead and all of their iron. Artillery was almost unknown.[61] That explains why Tatar chroniclers hailed Selim Girei's capture of thirty Russian cannon in 1689 as one of his finest martial accomplishments.[62] Clearly Russian military failures in 1634, 1687, and 1689 cannot be ascribed to technological backwardness.

Tactics and Operations

Perhaps the Muscovites went down to defeat because of defects in their tactical or operational skills. In testing this proposition, it is helpful to place it in the context of Western European military developments.

With the revolution in fortifications in Europe, the taking of strongpoints became the central objective of entire campaigns, even wars. New techniques of siege warfare were devised, involving the exploitation of increasingly sophisticated science and technology. Advances in mining and countermining, gunnery, and entrenchment were founded upon knowledge of geometry, physics, and geological stratigraphy. Such battles as did occur were fought between a besieging army and an army of relief, more often than not. Meanwhile, the character of field engagements themselves changed.

Although the firepower and reliability of infantry firearms increased throughout the sixteenth and seventeenth centuries, the speed with which those weapons could be loaded and fired remained low. For example, it might take anywhere from two to five minutes to reload a musket or an arquebus.[63] Military commanders consequently sought to maximize the firepower of the infantry while improving the protection afforded them during the vulnerable process of reloading. Firepower was increased in part by teaching the troops ever more complex varieties of drill, such as countermarching, which made continuous volleys possible.[64] As for protecting the arquebusiers, an initial approach was to encircle them in a forest of pikemen. Because that meant deploying the men in massive columns or squares (thus reducing firepower), however, armies gradually turned to a different expedient: field fortifications. Throughout Western Europe in the late sixteenth century, commanders shielded their musketeers in trenches, in redoubts, or behind palisades or wagons chained together. Some field fortifications grew so elaborate as to mimic the floor plans of fortresses themselves. Thus even battles took on the features of sieges, since a battle became an attempt by one combatant to storm the field fortifications of the other. Although there were a few exceptions, such as Breitenfeld, almost all the important battles of the Thirty Years War conformed to this pattern.[65]

It will be immediately obvious from the foregoing that the Smolensk war itself is a good illustration of such innovations. The goal of the entire campaign was the capture of a city that had been fortified in the Italian (or Dutch) manner. It is also fair to say that the tactics employed by the Muscovites were virtually identical to those used by Tilly, Wallenstein, or Gustaphus Adolphus. Once an investing army had encamped before a town, there were really only four practical ways of taking it. All were risky. A general could closely blockade it and hope that he could starve it into surrender before his provisions gave out or a relief army came. He could subject the town to a merciless bombardment in order to shatter the morale of the defenders and compel capitulation. Those, however, were slow methods. If a general needed to win his siege more quickly he would have to hazard using still more force. He would order a series of zigzag trenches dug in the direction of the city. When the trench system had reached a point almost within the shadow of the walls, infantry, with artillery support, could rush from the trenches and attempt to take the town by escalade (that is, using ladders). As soldiers encumbered by ladders 40 or 50 feet long had little chance of survival (let alone success) this method was seldom chosen. Finally, a general could attempt to make a breach in one of two ways. The first was to concentrate artillery fire against one or two specific points in the wall. The difficulty here was that the walls—composed of stone, masonry, timber, and earth—had been built thick precisely to make them proof against ordnance. Thus generals in the first half of the seventeenth century typically preferred to breach the walls by exploding mines under them. The dramatist John Webster was expressing the common military judgment of the age when in 1613 he put the following words into the mouth of one his characters: "We see that undermining more prevails than doth the cannon".[66]

Either on his own or at the prompting of his foreign mercenaries, Shein followed all the formal procedures of siegecraft to the letter. Indeed, he used every method of siege warfare save escalade to good effect. His blockade of Smolensk was far from perfect. Radziwill, after all, was able twice to break through Russian lines in March 1633. Yet from the time of Radziwill's withdrawal up to the arrival of King Wladyslaw in August, Smolensk was effectively cut off from outside supplies of food. Similarly Shein had been bombarding the Poles within Smolensk with every artillery piece he had since October of the previous year. At the same time he ordered the excavation of a comprehensive network of siege trenches to the southeast of the town so that his men might have a staging area from which to launch assaults after breaches had been effected. He finally did succeed in making breaches with both artillery and mines, even though he was not granted the time to exploit them.

After Wladyslaw appeared on the scene, the battles that ensued closely resembled those being waged simultaneously in Germany. The Poles seized the initiative and attempted to take the Russian strong places one by one: Mattison's works on the hills north of the Dniepr, the great earthen fort of Prozorovskii due east of the city, and the lesser redoubts of van Damm. Indeed, the final outcome of the war was determined by a siege, since the Polish king besieged Shein in his camp and compelled him to surrender with a combination of blockade and bombardment. Although Shein was eventually defeated during the campaign, his army consistently employed modern, Western tactics. In fact they were the only tactics remotely feasible in the circumstances.

Perhaps Muscovite tactics, although sound in principle, were flawed in the execution. After all, the Smolensk war was a new kind of war for Moscow. Russia had just begun to appreciate the importance of siegecraft, infantry, and field fortifications; many soldiers in its army were, moreover, foreign mercenaries of dubious loyalty. There is some truth to this. During the battles at the end of the campaign, the Russian armed forces deployed themselves deliberately, inflexibly, and unimaginatively, like an actor afraid of forgetting his lines. Still, one can make too much of the impact of such tactical (and technical) deficiencies on Muscovy's military performance, for the new style of warfare was almost as foreign to the Poles as to the Russians. Like the Muscovite forces, the traditional army of the Polish-Lithuanian Commonwealth was the gentry cavalry levy. The Poles had really only begun a comprehensive modernization of their army in the 1620s. Large-scale infantry and siege operations were therefore still a novelty for the Poles in the 1630s. The Polish infantry in the Smolensk war, just like the Muscovite, still consisted largely of hired mercenaries.[67]

In 1633–34, then, Muscovy fought a Western opponent with Western methods. Fifty years later it confronted a non-European opponent, the Crimean Khanate. Such a conflict obviously required a different operational approach. The goals of the campaign were not conquest, as in 1633, but rather booty and punishment. After marching south across the steppe, the Muscovites expected to besiege Perekop, force the isthmus beyond, and then ravage the Crimean peninsula. Thus the Muscovites were compelled to marry such traditional military practices as raiding and Tatar hunting to the newer modern European artillery, infantry, and siege tactics.

The dangers posed by the Tatar style of war complicated this problem. Although technologically inferior, the Tatars were true masters of steppe warfare. Their forces, entirely light cavalry, possessed a mobility that was the envy of all their enemies. In view of their speed the Khan's forces were capable of harassing any opposing army with devastating hit-and-run raids. Strong detachments of Tatars would suddenly appear from any quarter without warning and violently assault an enemy, then would gallop away just as the enemy was overcoming his initial shock. Such repeated onslaughts could so weaken an adversary that the main body of the Tatar army might be able to crush him in a climactic cavalry duel.[68]

The Muscovite response to such dangers was the tabor, or fortified wagon train. Although improvising field fortifications in the midst of battle by chaining wagons together was a common phenomenon of the era—it was standard Ottoman practice and was highly recommended by the great Imperial general Raimondo Montecuccoli—the Muscovites often chose to shield an army on the march within the confines of a huge moving square or rectangle of interlocked wagons. As the wagons were usually equipped with light guns, the entire tabor really amounted to a moving fortress. Such a powerful formation was in itself a deterrent to surprise attack, but if an attack came anyway the infantry could fight from cover, while the wagons could be unchained to permit cavalry sorties. It was not an impregnable system of defense: the Tatars did break into the Muscovite tabor during the engagement of May 15, 1689. Yet it must be emphasized that the tabor was the best method of advancing outnumbered into unreconnoitered Tatar country. Nor were the Muscovites alone in using the tabor. Other warriors with great experience in fighting the Tatars, notably the Poles and Cossacks, also used it.[69] There were, of course, disadvantages to the tabor. An army marching in tabor formation would obviously move slowly. Further, its general would be denied the opportunity of making his own surprise attack upon the enemy. Yet cumbrous movement with the tabor was preferable to certain annihilation without it. Muscovite tactics during the Crimean campaigns thus cannot be faulted. The only full-fledged battle of either expedition—the conflict of May 15, 1689—was won by the Muscovites precisely because of the tabor defense. We must look elsewhere for the sources of Muscovite military weakness.

Endurance

We come at last to a final set of explanations for Russia's seventeenth-century military failures, and they can be lumped together under the rubric "endurance": logistics and transport; training and reinforcement; and finance. It was precisely in those areas that the true military weakness of Russia inhered. While Muscovite technology and tactics were at a high level, deficiencies in factors of endurance prevented Russia from prosecuting war vigorously and from sustaining military operations effectively. And that in turn meant that Muscovite strategy was unworkable.

Logistical and transport problems, for instance, bedeviled the Russian army during its operations in both of the military campaigns considered here. Indeed, if one had to isolate the single most important factor in the debacles of the 1630s and 1680s, it would be this. The crucial element in the Russian defeat at Smolensk was neither the treason of foreign hirelings nor the unsteady generalship of Shein. Rather it was the failure of the Muscovites to organize the arrival of the heavy siege artillery until March 1633. That resulted as much from the virtual absence of roads and from poor weather as from the clumsy administration of the central artillery parks. Because of the delay Shein and his forces were condemned to five months of wasteful idleness outside the walls of Smolensk; without the protection heavy guns afforded, a close blockade, proper siege trenches, and even effective mining were impossible. Looked at from this perspective the real siege of Smolensk began not in October 1632 but in March 1633. By July Shein had breached the walls of Smolensk twice and was prevented from storming the city only by the untimely arrival of King Wladyslaw. Had Shein received his artillery earlier than he did, it is quite probable that he would have taken Smolensk before the advent of the Polish relief forces. The capture of Smolensk would probably have resulted in a different outcome to the war, for the Poles might have been willing to cede it in exchange for a peace treaty, fearing as they did the outbreak of hostilities with the Turks.

The logistical complications in the Crimean campaigns were different. We have already noted that the tabor formation, although slow, was indispensable. Another reason that the Russian tabors of 1687 and 1689 moved at a snail's pace was their size: More than twenty thousand wagons were involved on each occasion. In Western Europe at that time an army might have one wagon (pulled by two to four horses) for each fifteen men. In the Crimean campaign the Muscovites had one for each five, a proportion three times that common in the West. Why so many horses and why so many wagons? The answer had to do with elementary facts of geography and demography. The supply trains of West European armies actually contained only an irreducible reserve supply of food and forage; Western armies, as has been recently shown, generally tried to live off the country-side. Their ability to do so, even partially, was due to the general fertility of the soil and the generally high population density of Western Europe.[70] By contrast, the Muscovites often campaigned in territories so low in population density as to be considered virtually uninhabited and in which, also, agricultural yields were notoriously low. Further, Muscovite armies were often compelled to travel longer distances before arriving in the theater of combat than Western forces did. Hence the Muscovites had to bear with them into the field a great part of the food that would be consumed in the course of the campaign. Indeed, noble servitors who came to the muster were supposed to bring with them a personal stock of food sufficient to maintain themselves and their attendants for several months. Of course the Muscovites did try to acquire foodstuffs locally (special commissioners "for the requisition of grain and meat" accompanied every army), but there could be little confidence in such a procedure, especially when the army was required to march into an arid steppe, as during the Crimean campaigns.[71] This system of supply subjected the Muscovite army to two serious vulnerabilities. The Tatars exploited the first in 1687 and the second in 1689.

The fantastic size of the Russian wagon train meant an equally large number of draft animals. In 1687 the Russian field army probably possessed in excess of 60,000 horses and oxen. Although the beasts could haul victuals for the troops, in no way could they at the same time transport the fodder they themselves needed. Thus although the Russians could not rely on living off the land, they had to rely (as did all other East European peoples) on locally available supplies of forage. The Tatars, of course, understood that perfectly and as a result set fire to the steppe in 1687. Hundreds of Russian soldiers perished from smoke inhalation as a consequence, but what really persuaded Golitsyn to turn back was not human but equine mortality. The destruction of almost all the steppe grass—the natural forage indispensable to the survival of the draft animals—meant that any further advance would be suicidal. Without confronting the enemy, without loosing even a single arrow, Selim Girei was automatically victorious.

The Tatars were prevented from repeating this stratagem two years later. Golitsyn had anticipated them by burning the steppe himself. Selim therefore decided to exploit the other vulnerability of Russian logistics: limited capacity. As the Russian army had to transport the bulk of its food, there was an iron limit to the amount of time the army could campaign before turning back home. The Tatars decided to stretch Russia's supply capacity to the breaking point. They conducted a slow strategic withdrawal keeping in constant contact with the Muscovites. Fearing surprise attack, Golitsyn's forces marched even more slowly than usual (consuming an even greater quantity of food per mile of march than had been expected). When Golitsyn reached Perekop, stocks of food and water were already depleted. Perekop proved to be so strong that it could be taken only by formal siege, and Golitsyn knew he lacked the supplies necessary for such a long operation. Retreat was the only recourse. In both campaigns, then, the Russian army was defeated as much by hunger and thirst as by anything else. Logistical and transport problems were clearly components of Russian military weakness. Attempts at overcoming those problems were to be a dominant theme in Russian military policy for the next two hundred years.

Another weakness of the Muscovite military system was reinforcement and training, or manpower policy in the largest sense. Up until the 1690s Muscovy relied on the ad hoc mobilization of its military resources for each separate campaign. Although entire classes of hereditary warriors existed in Muscovy, dependent on the state for their sustenance (of which the *dvoriantsvo* or service nobility was a prime example), most of them were involved in agriculture, crafts, or trading for most of the time. Thus except for a handful of palace guards, garrison troops, military settlers, and Cossacks, Muscovy's forces, suspended in an emulsion of state privileges, were actually preoccupied with everything *but* the art of war. When Muscovy first began permanently to engage the services of whole companies of foreign infantry, it tried to integrate them into the preexisting military system by giving them the legal status of *strel'tsy,* which in practical terms obligated them to lay aside their arms and open shops.[72]

All of this had implications for Muscovite military power. The foreign infantry hired in the early 1630s was engaged for the duration of the Smolensk campaign only. Wladyslaw's mercenary infantry, by contrast, comprised seasoned, salaried veterans who were a standing force paid for by the Polish crown. That they outperformed their Muscovite counterparts is hence not remarkable. The native Russian troops of foreign formation, although armed and schooled in the Western fashion, similarly lacked group cohesion and esprit de corps.

There was another problem as well. When making war the Muscovite government was given to hitting the enemy with all its available forces from the very start. That procedure, the vestige of centuries of annual expeditions against the Tatars, resulted in situations in which the loss of a campaign in effect entailed the loss of the war. Since almost all military resources had already been mobilized and since there were no training depots, it was almost impossible to reinforce troops in the field. Neither during the Smolensk war nor in the Crimean campaigns was the Russian government capable of raising appreciable quantities of additional soldiers. That disability was most critical in the Smolensk war; the effort of outfitting Shein's army had stripped southern Russia of its garrisons and had left the country defenseless, which made the Polish stratagem of encouraging Tatar and Cossack attacks all the more grimly effective.[73]

A final constraint on endurance was financial. Muscovy could be defeated not only by military operations but by the length of a campaign. It did not have the money to sustain military operations indefinitely, so the state was periodically compelled to demobilize its army. Lulls in warfare, of course, were common throughout Europe; all armies, for example, went into winter quarters. Yet halts in combat were imposed on Russia not so much by the severity of the weather as by the barrenness of the treasury. Russia made war in spasms, racing to seize important military objectives before the money gave out. This, then, was the last root cause of Russian military weakness: the poverty of the state.

Seventeenth-century Muscovite Russia certainly had territorial ambitions, along with coherent strategies for their realization. What Russia did not have, however, was the military might necessary to support those strategies. Means had to be found to transcend the problems of supply and transport; manpower and training; and inadequate revenues. In short, Russia had to find the way to translate all of its resources—human, material and financial—into power. That was the problem that confronted Peter the Great. As we shall see, his unique solution was thoroughly to reinvent Russia's military system.

2

Peter the Great and the Advantages of "Backwardness"

To Peter the Great—this tall, imperious, boorish tsar—has gone credit for modernizing Russia, for dragging medieval Muscovy into the mainstream of European civilization. "Father of his country," creator of the Russian Empire, indeed the first Russian ruler to assume the Western title "Emperor," Peter did in fact alter the manners, mores, and institutions of his land. He forced the nobility to shave their beards, compelled them to adopt Western dress, and emancipated their women from the seclusion of the *terem,* thus disrupting the customary practices of boyar politics while simultaneously insisting on "European" norms for aristocratic society. The Petrine elite had no choice but publicly to adopt Western ways (or their simulacra).[1] At the height of his reign, when Peter wanted to give his new capital the air of a Western city, he regularly turned all of St. Petersburg into a public theater and its population into supernumeraries. During the weeks of carnival, the highest-ranking statesmen in the land were forbidden to doff their masks or clown costumes during the performance of official duties or even when attending funerals. And when Peter wanted to enjoy the spectacle of well-dressed throngs strolling in the public park, the beating of military drums called every nobleman within earshot to the Summer Garden for compulsory merrymaking under the threat of corporal punishment.[2]

But Peter's achievements far exceeded the mere enforcement of social conformity, for he was also more skilled in exploiting the human and material resources of the Russian state than any

previous ruler. At his command, factories were raised, metallurgi-
cal works and mines established, canals dug, roads surveyed,
schools opened. After 1714 all males of the *dvorianstvo*, or gentry,
were in principle bound to civil or military service. Peasants of all
conditions were burdened as never before. Taxes increased; tens
of thousands were drafted for the military, for industry, and for
forced labor on construction projects. The poll or soul tax, which
Peter imposed on every male peasant, became the backbone of
tsarist revenue and persisted until 1884. Even more long-lasting
were other Petrine innovations: the governing Senate (with its
mix of legislative and judicial functions) and the Holy Synod
(which supplanted the patriarchate) survived until 1917. So too
did the 1722 table of ranks, which set forth the famous equivalent hierarchy of ranks and posts for the bureaucracy, army,
navy, and court and which theoretically permitted commoners to
work their way up to nobiliary status by means of state service.[3]

This breathless list of Peter's activities is still far from a comprehensive accounting of the results of his demonic energy during
the twenty-nine years of personal rule. All of the Petrine reforms
were of course accompanied if not actually driven home by acts
of unspeakable cruelty, tyranny, and oppression. It should be
noted that Peter imported more from the West than crafty Dutch
engineers, learned Scottish mathematicians, tobacco, theories of
government, and naval technology, for instruments such as the
thumbscrews, Algerian hook, and wheel (previously unknown in
Muscovy) were also introduced by him.[4]

What lay behind it all? Here many scholars agree that an important stimulus, perhaps the *primum mobile*, of the Petrine reforms was warfare. Indeed, Peter's reign was a reign of ceaseless
wars against both internal and external foes. Astrakhan revolted
in 1705 and the Don Cossack region in 1707–8. There were wars
with the Turks (1695, 1696, 1711); there was a major war with
the Persians (1722–24); and, of course, dwarfing them all was
the Great Northern War, a twenty-one-year struggle against the
Swedes for mastery of the Baltic coast.

Some students of the period have concluded that in the main
Peter was attempting through his reforms both to attain military
victory and to establish a well-regulated police state, a state of
rules, laws, and obligations. Others have emphasized the improvi-
sational, even half-baked character of the reforms.[5] Yet both

camps concede that the unforeseen emergencies and strains of war undetermined the effectiveness of many Petrine innovations in civil life. V. O. Kliuchevskii, Imperial Russia's greatest historian, noted: "Although the [Swedish] war had caused Peter to introduce reforms, it had an adverse influence on their development and success, because they were effected in an atmosphere of confusion, usually consequent on war."[6] Thus there were several failed reforms of town administration, provincial government, and taxation. At times those failures were explained by the noncompliance of the Russian population, for so rapacious were state demands that massive flight was often the response of the beleaguered peasantry.[7] On other occasions the deportment of Peter's bureaucrats themselves explained why governmental initiatives misfired. Peter was, it is fair to say, constantly disappointed in the quality of his servitors and confidants. Much as Peter may have tried to impose the values of the "general good" and selfless state service on his bureaucracy, even some of his most distinguished statesmen and intimates—such as Shafirov and Menshikov—were not above putting their hands in the public till. And as late as 1718, Peter found it necessary to hang his thieving governor of Siberia, Gagarin.[8]

However, if some of the civil reforms of Peter the Great did not work out because of inadequate planning, popular resistance, or bureaucratic corruption, Peter's military reforms have usually been adjudged great successes. After all, Peter did win the most important of his wars, in particular his war with Sweden. Yet how exactly did Peter win the Great Northern War? How did his military system operate? How did he overcome the social, economic, even geographical features of Muscovy that contributed to the sorts of military catastrophes examined in the last chapter? To what extent *were* those problems overcome? In order to set the stage for an approach to those questions, let us begin with a brief look at the conventional explanation of how Peter the Great defeated Sweden.

The Great Northern War (1700–1721): A Conventional Account

Peter the Great nurtured expansionist ambitions from his earliest years. The enemy he initially selected for himself, however, was not Sweden but Turkey. In 1695 he dispatched a large army against the strong Turkish fort at Azov. The expedition failed almost as disastrously as had Golitsyn's Crimean campaigns of the previous decade. In the following year Peter made a second attempt on Azov and this time took that strategically important site. He immediately ordered the construction of a fleet in the Sea of Azov. When completed, that fleet would be able to debouch into the Black Sea, challenge the Turkish navy for maritime control, and disrupt communications between the Ottomans and their Crimean Tatar vassals. It was the first stage in what was obviously going to be a long and complex war. During his "Great Embassy" to the West (1698–99) Peter hunted for allies who would be willing to assist him in it.[9]

But events caused Peter to redirect his attention to the north. In 1697 the King of Sweden died, and his fourteen-year-old son was crowned as Charles XII. Shortly thereafter Peter learned that both the King of Denmark, Frederick IV, and the newly elected Polish monarch, the Elector Augustus of Saxony, were plotting to dismember Sweden's Baltic Empire. Then, too, by 1699 it was increasingly clear that most of Western Europe might shortly be plunged into war over the vexatious issue of the Spanish succession, which would preclude any aid to Sweden from its staunchest friend, France. Never had Sweden seemed so isolated, ill-led, and outnumbered. The conjunction of circumstances was irresistible for Russia's young tsar. After concluding secret treaties with Frederick and Augustus, Peter declared war on Sweden on August 9, 1700, one day after he was notified that his ambassadors in Constantinople had just signed a thirty-year truce with Turkey. Within days Peter ordered his forces to march on the Swedish fort of Narva, in Ingria. Simultaneously, the Danes inaugurated naval actions, while Augustus's Saxons made a surprise assault on Riga. Unfortunately for the northern confederates, however, Charles XII was a charismatic leader and a military genius to boot. He knocked the Danes out of the war in two weeks, maneuvered the Saxons into retiring into Germany, and then, in October, landed with an army at the port of Pernau at the apex of the Gulf of Riga. Regrouping his forces, Charles dashed 150 miles northeast to raise the siege of Narva. On November 20, 1700, the Swedish infantry made a surprise attack on the Russian forces under the cover of a sudden blizzard. Taking

THE THEATER OF THE GREAT NORTHERN WAR 1700-1721

Volga River

Lake Ladoga

Msta River

NOVGOROD

NARVA

INGRIA

PETERSBURG

PSKOV

DORPAT

ERESTFER

ESTONIA

HUMMELSHOF

PERNAU

LATVIA

REVEL

RIGA

MITAU

KURLAND

FINLAND

NYSTAD

STOCKHOLM

SWEDEN

COPENHAGEN

Baltic Sea

VILNA

LITHUANIA

GRODNO

Bug River

Vistula River

WARSAW

POLAND

Dniestr River

Danube River

SMOLENSK

Dnieper River

LESNAIA

MOSCOW

Oka River

KIEV

BATURIN

KURSK

KHARKOV

POLTAVA

PEREVOLOCHNA

advantage of the extreme length of Peter's line of circumvalla-
tion, the Swedes broke through the center and defeated the
Russian forces in detail. It was a tremendous Swedish victory and
an ignominious rout for Peter, for fewer than nine thousand
Swedes had overwhelmed 40,000 Russian soldiers. More than
eight thousand Russians had been killed, to the Swedes' thousand. Still worse, nearly all of Russia's stock of field artillery had
fallen into Swedish hands.[10]

It is usually argued that if the Narva debacle was a humbling
experience for Peter, it also had the effect of a galvanic battery
on him, for he immediately took steps to enhance Russian military efficiency and power. He ordered recruiting levels to raise
new armies, expanded the capabilities of military industry,
scoured Europe for experienced soldiers-of-fortune, and melted
down hundreds of church bells to secure metals for his artillery
foundries. Military administration was itself regularized and reformed, and army logistical arrangements were put on a sound
footing through the establishment of an impressive network of
field magazines. In short, Narva did not discourage Peter, but
rather taught him to take war seriously. Some of Peter's under-
lings were of faint heart, of course, and wanted to wash their
hands of the entire Baltic enterprise. Prince Golitsyn, Peter's
ambassador in Vienna, wrote in August 1701 that Russia should
seek just one small victory (to stifle international ridicule) before
repairing at once to the negotiating table.[11] By contrast, Peter
busied himself with building a regular army and a regular navy
capable of winning access to the Baltic even at the cost of protracted war.

Peter's confidence was not misplaced. Between the end of 1701
and 1704, Russian forces under the direction of the cautious but
able General Prince Boris Sheremet'ev chalked up important
victories. Sheremet'ev defeated the Swedes at Erestfer (December 1701) and at Hummelshof (July 1702). Russia was also fortunate in its Baltic sieges: Nöteburg fell in 1702; Nienshants in May
1703; Dorpat and even Narva in the summer of 1704. By then
Peter was master of Swedish Ingria, dominated the Neva River,
and had laid the foundations for what would eventually become
the new capital of his Empire, St. Petersburg.[12]

Peter owed the very fact that he had the breathing space for all
of these military and administrative activities to decisions taken by

his royal adversary, Charles XII. At Birsen in February 1701 Peter had renewed his alliance with the Polish King, Augustus of Saxony. Although the Swedish crown council constantly advised Charles to polish off the Russians first, his easy triumph at Narva had convinced him that Muscovy was congenitally incompetent in war.[13] Charles therefore viewed Augustus as his primary enemy and spent 1701–4 chasing him and his Saxons all over Poland, while leaving Sweden's Baltic garrisons to fend for themselves against the encroachments of Peter's armies. In the summer of 1704, when Augustus persuaded the Polish magnates to declare war on Sweden (Poland, although the main battleground, had been technically "neutral" to that point), Charles countered by convening a dummy Sejm, which deposed Augustus and proclaimed Sweden's puppet, Stanislas Leszcynski, as king. Determined to finish Augustus once and for all, Charles carried the war into Saxony itself in 1706 and in September compelled the defeated Elector to sign the treaty of Altranstadt.[14] By its terms, Augustus repudiated both his Polish crown and his Russian alliance. Abandoned by his ally, Peter was now left to confront the might of Sweden alone.

Like Napoleon after him, Charles XII planned his Russian campaign with extraordinary care. In the spring of 1707 he crossed over from Saxony into Poland with more than 40,000 troops. By the beginning of 1708 Charles had reached Grodno, and a month later Smorgoni, where he encamped some four weeks. A pattern had been set: Charles's rapid marches succeeded by several weeks of inactivity served to keep the Russians off balance about the main axis of his advance. Did he contemplate a drive on Moscow? Would he suddenly veer north toward the Baltic? But this technique was also a delaying tactic, for General Löwenhaupt, with 16,000 additional men and a vast wagon train of essential food and arms, was marching southeast from Kurland for an expected rendezvous with his king in the summer of 1708. In June Charles crossed the Berezina and shortly thereafter apparently made a radical revision in his campaign plan. Discarding his original idea (which actually had been a direct thrust at Moscow), Charles decided instead to push southeast into the Ukraine. Lowenhaupt's progress was slow, food and supplies were short, and Charles expected to replenish his stocks through the assistance of the

Ukrainian Cossack hetman Mazeppa, who had secretly agreed to defect to the Swedish cause.

At that point both Peter the Great and his newly created but robust regular army showed their mettle. While the bulk of his forces paralleled Charles's southern march, Peter rode north to Lesnaia, virtually annihilated Löwenhaupt's detachment, and captured all of his baggage on September 28, 1708. Meanwhile Peter had divined Mazeppa's treachery and had sent Field Marshal Prince Menshikov on a daring and successful attack on Mazeppa's capital, Baturin. Although Mazeppa was able to reach Charles's camp with the remnants of his forces (as had Löwenhaupt), his conspiracy had effectively been nipped in the bud, much to the disadvantage of Sweden.

Hoping for reinforcements, Charles spent the early months of 1709 appealing to the Poles, the Ukrainians, and the Crimean Tatars. Those appeals went unanswered. Charles continued his march and by May of 1709 concentrated his army on the right bank of the Vorskla River, near the small fort of Poltava, to which he lay siege. The valorous resistance of the tiny Poltava garrison bought Peter adequate time for the deployment of his own troops. That set the stage for the famous battle of Poltava on June 27, 1709, in which Charles XII was decisively defeated. While Charles and a handful of retainers fled to the Ottoman Empire for sanctuary, Löwenhaupt and the surviving Swedes surrendered to Peter at Perevolochna.

Poltava made Peter's military reputation just as surely as it destroyed Charles's. Poltava also resuscitated an expanded anti-Swedish coalition, for Russia was now joined not only by its old partners Denmark and Saxony, but by Prussia as well. In 1709 and 1710 Peter once again turned his attention to the north, occupied Kurland, and captured the cities of Riga, Pernau, and Revel. Despite military reverses, despite the growing list of his enemies, and despite foreign offers of mediation, Charles refused to sue for peace. In early February 1711 he wrote the Crown Council in Stockholm that "under no circumstances ever again consider buying a disgraceful peace with the loss of even one province."[15] For his part, Charles was determined to take advantage of his involuntary residence on Ottoman territory to stir up trouble between Russia and Turkey. A Russo-Turkish war did in fact break out and nearly ended catastrophically for Peter on the banks of the Prut River (July 1711), where the Russians found themselves trapped by overwhelmingly superior numbers of Turks and Tatars. Crafty diplomacy, territorial concessions, and sizable bribes, however, resulted in a truce, which allowed Peter to lead his army home intact. Although Russo-Turkish relations would remain shaky for a couple of years, Peter's main problem was now terminating the war with the Swedes. Peter's campaigns after that point increasingly acquired a punitive character; the object was to hurt Sweden so badly that it would have no choice but to sign a peace renouncing its Baltic possessions. Thus Peter ordered campaigns in Swedish Pomerania and drove into Finland. This period also saw intensified maritime operations. In July 1714 Admiral Apraksin's galleys defeated a strong Swedish naval squadron off Cape Hangö. The victory, as significant in its own right as Poltava, not only made the Swedish position in Finland untenable but also conferred on Peter the limited sea control he required to launch amphibious assaults on Sweden itself if need be. Peter and Frederick IV actually planned for a joint Russo-Danish invasion of Scania in 1716, but the expedition was aborted when Charles attacked Denmark's Norwegian possessions. There was a limit, however, even to Charles' obduracy. With Russia, Poland, Saxony, Prussia, Denmark, and now Britain arrayed against him, Charles acceded to a conference on Åland island in 1718, which drafted a preliminary set of peace treaties. But Charles's death in battle the following year altered the political situation; one by one, Peter's allies made their own deals with the new government in Stockholm, leaving Peter once again warring against Sweden in isolation. Undismayed, Peter set large raiding parties ashore in Sweden in 1719, 1720, and 1721 with specific instructions to burn and loot. This pressure proved impossible to resist; in 1721 Sweden and Russia signed the Peace of Nystadt, which finally brought the Great Northern War to a close. So, at least, goes the conventional version.

The conventional story of the Northern War is the tale of Peter's military education. Narva taught Peter that he could not win wars without a regular army. Thereafter, he speedily applied himself to creating one. The ensuing years saw ceaseless military improvements; the regular army and navy got better and better, finally achieving such a level of excellence that they were able to prevail against Charles's hardened veterans. In this explanation, the military prowess of Russia's army increased over the years like an upward-surging line on a graph. It is a neat, efficient, and somewhat abstract explanation. And that, of course, is the problem with it. Reality was considerably messier and more complex.

What Peter Didn't Do

We should begin by noting that Peter did not win the Great Northern War by creating a regular Russian army for the simple reason that he never succeeded in creating a regular Russian army at all. That may seem a quixotic statement on my part, since historians of all shades of opinion have generally hailed the regular army as one of Peter's signal accomplishments. Writing in 1896, the tsarist historian N. P. Mikhnevich described the regular army as the foundation of Peter's military success, a view echoed by the Soviet academician E. V. Tarle in his magisterial book on the Great Northern War. The Estonian scholar Kh. Palli declared: "From 1701 to 1704 the Russian regular army was formed and the first great successes of the Northern War were attained," while M. D. Rabinovich has asserted that a regular army was already being developed in the years *prior* to the first siege of Narva.[16]

What, however, is a regular army? As A. L. Myshlaevskii observed almost ninety years ago, a regular army is much more than merely a standing force. Russia had, after all, experimented with various kinds of standing forces for generations.[17] Rather, a regular army is a standing army that functions in accordance with rules and regulations. It possesses a rational system of recruitment, which allows it to replenish the troops in its ranks. It has received adequate training and has developed systems for imparting the rudiments of military knowledge to raw recruits. It receives pay, uniforms, food, and equipment in appropriate quantities and at the expense of the state. Perhaps as a result, it has a satisfactory level of discipline, even allowing for the general eighteenth-century laxness in this area. In short, a regular army is an institution, not an improvisation.[18] Many scholars insist that it is precisely an army such as this that Peter built for himself. To cite a typical example: "Slowly . . . in spite of innumerable difficulties . . . Peter forged his new army, organized in divisions and brigades, serviceably uniformed and munitioned and gradually tempered in fighting experience."[19]

Was that in fact the case? Let us examine each of the typical characteristics of the regular army and see how Peter's forces measured up.

We shall start with recruitment. The army that Peter raised for his initial war with Sweden was composed of the traditional cavalry levy, augmented by a motley collection of volunteers and draftees (*datochnye*), selected by means of a confusing system that inequitably distributed the obligation for supplying recruits among differing social and occupational groups.[20] The defeat at Narva, of course, dissipated those forces. Yet for a period of years after Narva, the recruiting system (or nonsystem) was virtually identical to that of 1699: volunteers were induced to enter the service with usually unkept promises of high pay, while impromptu levies of recruits were ordered most often in response to real or imagined military emergencies. To adduce merely three examples for 1703: in January 2,700 *posad* people (small traders) were collected and sent to the forces of Prince Repnin; in July one thousand men were hastily inducted to replenish the loses in Menshikov's Ingria regiment; and in October a roundup of one out of every five household serfs resulted in a levy of 10,127.[21] In February 1705, however, Peter's government unveiled a new recruiting system, which, with alterations, would remain tsarist Russia's recruiting system until 1874. By its terms, the country was subdivided into blocks of twenty households each. Each block was to supply one twenty-year-old recruit every year. If the recruit fled, died, or became incapacitated, the twenty households were to furnish a replacement for him on demand.[22] This technique for securing theoretically "immortal" recruits was vaguely based on a Swedish model. Unfortunately, it didn't work, not least because the statistical data on the number of households were more than a quarter-century old. Thus Peter was constrained to resort to additional special levies (sometimes two or more a year) to fill the ranks of his army. Indeed, so numerous and complex were the various levies that historians have ever since disagreed about just how many levies there were and about the exact number of people inducted. A document from the chancellery of the Moscow recruiting office, however, establishes the drafting of at least 205,000 men for military ser-

vice from 1700 through 1711.[23] We can also be reasonably confident that, once again as a bare minimum, 140,000 men were
called up from 1713 to 1724. It cannot be emphasized enough
that Russian recruiting methods throughout the entire reign of
Peter the Great were arbitrary, unjust, and *ad hoc* despite the law
of 1705. Additional levies would summon one person from every
fifty households in one year, and one person from every ninety-
five in the next. Sometimes entire social groups were specially
targeted, as was the clerical estate in 1721. The forcible drafting
of priests and deacons in that year depleted the Russian clergy by
almost two-thirds of its numbers.[24] That frantic and anarchic
impressment can scarcely be confused with a regular, orderly
system of recruitment.

Why did Peter need all those men? To be sure, the Russian
army expanded in size throughout Peter's reign. Peter had
40,000 soldiers under his command in 1700, in excess of 60,000
in 1705, more than 100,000 in 1709, and possibly as many as
130,000 by 1725.[25] But the enlargement of the field forces was by
no means the sole reason, or even principal reason, why Peter's
generals hungered for new levies. Service in the Petrine army
and navy was for twenty-five years—virtually for life. For most of
Peter's reign, there were two and only two ways to leave Peter's
military service: by taking refuge in the woods or by taking refuge in the grave. Thus new recruits were not generally inducted
to replace veterans who had completed their tours of duty and
were being demobilized. Rather, they were replacing those lost
through desertion or death. An official report of 1711 noted that
almost 16,000 of the 25,000 to be called up in one levy were
earmarked for replenishing regimental losses.[26] To a considerable degree Peter's policy of mass conscription was less for reinforcing the Russian army than for keeping it up to strength.
Just to stay even with regard to military manpower (let alone get
ahead) required the most intense and ferocious of efforts, owing
to scarcely believable levels of military attrition. If Peter bequeathed Russia an army of 130,000 men upon his death in 1725,
at least *a quarter of a million more* men had been mustered into that
army in the previous twenty-five years and by then were absent
from its rolls.

Attrition was the result of many things: flight, sickness, starvation, battlefield injuries. There were indeed many instances of

flight before a recruit even arrived at his unit or training depot. Military service was, for self-evident reasons, unpopular in the village. Newly inducted soldiers were sometimes led away in chains (and after 1712 were branded on the hand, for ease of identification).[27] Notwithstanding such precautions, the conscripts frequently attempted to escape from the clutches of their recruiting agents, and sometimes succeeded. On several occasions from 1703 through 1706, as much as 10 percent of a marching party was known to run away.[28]

On other occasions flight was even more substantial. In March 1705, for instance, Peter wrote to Prince Menshikov expressing astonishment at the paltry number of recruits assembled in Vilna: "There are so few of them; perhaps the other recruits have not arrived yet?" Actually, all had arrived who were going to arrive.[29] The shortfall in the numbers of recruits who reached the field was augmented by the conscripts who perished en route, which occurred fairly often, because they were herded like cattle on forced marches of hundreds of miles, crammed into leaky boats to sail on frozen seas, and fed badly if at all. In October 1713, of a party of 629 conscripts dispatched by sea from Petersburg, only 342 were healthy enough to disembark in Helsingfors. The rest were incapacitated by sickness or had drowned or died of cold.[30]

Desertion was a problem of the utmost seriousness even after the recruits had joined their regiments. In the summer of 1704, for instance, Peter dispatched an auxiliary corps of fifteen thousand troops across Poland to Saxony to provide aid for the Elector Augustus. When the latter reviewed the Russian soldiers upon their arrival, he discovered that more than one-third of them had fled.[31] Peter attempted to combat desertion by threatening military fugitives with savage and exemplary punishments. A decree of January 1705 prescribed that of every three deserters recaptured, one, chosen by lot, was to be hanged, while the other two were first to be severely flogged, then sent off to forced labor (*katorga*) for the rest of their lives. The law made little dent in desertion; laws stiffening the penalties for desertion were issued with banal regularity in almost every subsequent year. In 1707 Peter promised in yet another decree permanently to exile the relatives of a deserted soldier. That measure for deterring flight, based on punishing innocent but available people for crimes perpetrated by others who were prima facie beyond the reach of state power, does not seem to have been particularly effective either.[32] In fact its very promulgation suggests that the Russian government was experiencing real difficulties in rounding up deserters.

Of course, Peter did introduce the rudiments of military justice into Russia. Captured deserters were supposed to receive military trials before sentences were imposed upon them. Yet at times the army could dispense with even those legal niceties. On the march back across Poland from the Prut in 1711, for example, Field Marshal Prince Sheremet'ev was able to keep his army together only by erecting a mobile gallows just as soon as the troops had encamped each night. Any attempt to flee was punishable by death without trial. (To be fair, the suffering endured by the troops during the disastrous Prut campaign could hardly have been anything other than demoralizing.)[33]

Peter, however, suspected his soldiers of a propensity to desert whether the campaign was going well or ill. In an order to the army of Finland issued in the summer of 1712, Peter decreed that no soldier was to be permitted to leave a marching column for the purpose of relieving himself except under the supervision of a corporal. Presumably the tsar felt that an unwatched soldier might take advantage of the opportunity to wiggle away through the underbrush.[34] Even after the Northern War had virtually been won, high rates of desertion continued to trouble Peter seriously. A decree of 1715 actually softened the penalties for desertion, abolishing capital punishment for the crime. But interestingly, this decree explicitly recognized the phenomenon of repeat offenders:

> If a recruit runs away . . . then for the first flight he is to be beaten with rods through the ranks of the regiment one time each on three successive days, but if he runs away another time . . . instead of death he is to be beaten with the knout, his nostrils are to be slit in front of the regiment, and he is to be sent for forced labor on the galleys for the rest of his life.[35]

In the exordium of justification that accompanied this law, it was explained that the death penalty for desertion, previously the norm, had been borrowed from the usages of foreign armies. But such a penalty did not suit Russian conditions, for in foreign countries "mercenaries serve, and not [those] who are taken [into the army] by decree."[36] Those words clearly imply that although it might be fair to enforce a death sentence on a deserted mercenary who had enlisted in the ranks of an army of his own free will, it was not practical to execute a conscripted Russian peasant for the same deed. And that, of course, was a virtual admission that the compulsory character of the Russian conscription system itself was one root cause of mass desertion. The death penalty was retained, however, for soldiers who fled the battlefield in the presence of the enemy. If an entire unit fled, its members were subject to decimation.[37]

Desertion was one powerful source of military attrition, as the Petrine government itself conceded. What of other sources? Battlefield casualties should figure here, but it is probable that combat deaths did not excessively contribute to the high levels of mortality in Peter's army. The Soviet historical demographer B. Urlanis estimates that of the more than 120,000 Russian soldiers who became casualties from 1700 through 1725, only 40,000 or so were either killed outright or died subsequently of their wounds. That statistic may be too low, for Urlanis's credibility is not enhanced when he proceeds to ascribe to Sweden a number of casualties in excess of the number of all men known to have served in Sweden's armed forces throughout the entire war.[38] Yet given the typical combat pattern of the Northern War—relatively few engagements separated by weeks of maneuver or months of quiescence and spread over years—and given, also, the ratio of killed and wounded to participants in some of the better-documented battles, the 40,000 figure actually may not be far from the truth.

A greater number of soldiers probably succumbed to disease. Urlanis, in fact, estimates so-called sanitary casualties on the Russian side during the Swedish war as roughly 110,000.[39] Although the sources requisite to verify this statement are unavailable, there is no reason to presume that the experience of Peter's army was vastly different from that of the other European armies of time, in which the likelihood of dying of scurvy, dysentery, or typhus was much greater than that of dying at the hands of the enemy. Indeed, instances of soldiers' death from disease were probably more common in Peter's army than in those of Western Europe, because Peter's forces were chronically plagued by shortages of such essential supplies as uniforms and food.

A little later we shall have occasion to discuss the Petrine military economy: the system of tax collection, grain collection, establishment of magazines, opening of industrial plants, and all the rest. We should note here, however, that although the Petrine military economy doubtless contributed to Peter's success, that economy did not operate like a perfectly oiled machine. Scholars have often praised Peter for making the Russian army self-sufficient or nearly self-sufficient in food and supply.[40] That, however, is somewhat beside the point. The Petrine army was still campaigning in East European territories in which population density and agricultural productivity were low. As a result, living off the land was rarely an option. Food and equipment had to be brought to the army. At first, of course, there were problems of real scarcity of crucial material. But even after Peter's factory masters, tax collectors, and grain factors had gone to work and accumulated adequate stocks of food and equipment, nearly intractable problems of *distribution* remained. Russia's nominal capability of supplying the total requirements of its armed forces for gunpowder was irrelevant if the powder was in the Urals, the army was in Finland, and no timely mechanism for conveying the one to the other was available. Letters from Peter's field commanders constantly complain of the defective logistical system: it is not merely shortages the commanders decry but often a total lack of the most common necessities. Among the items most sorely missed were uniforms and warm clothing; without them, the soldiers's prospects of survival were low. When the Livonian nobleman Patkul took charge of the Russian auxiliary corps in Saxony in 1704, he wrote Prince Menshikov that he was appalled to find them dressed in rags. For his part, Menshikov reported to the tsar that "it was shameful for [Patkul] to command these ununiformed and almost naked men, a disgrace to the name of his Tsarist Majesty."[41] The fact that such a state of affairs was not merely a freak episode confined to the early years of the war is demonstrated by repeated calls for the dispatch of clothing to the front even after the battle of Poltava had been won. In 1712, for instance, 1,300 of the 8,600 men who constituted the Russian corps in Finland had no boots. In the spring of 1714, Admiral

Apraksin would angrily demand that the Russian Senate arrange an emergency shipment of uniforms to him "as many soldiers have entirely worn theirs out."[42]

Sometimes delays in forwarding equipment could be ascribed to the cumbrousness of the Russian administrative system. For example, the *Prikaz* of military affairs (created in 1701) was the clearinghouse for all military requests for supplies exclusive of food. Yet that institution was powerless to fill even a single order; rather, it parceled the requests out among the other administrative offices, depending upon which had either money or stocks of requisite goods at any particular time.[43] But if superfluous layers of bureaucracy frustrated the troops in the field, at other times the problem was simple transportation bottlenecks: ships, carts, or Kalmyk drivers were just not available.

The situation with regard to foodstuffs was still more critical at various key points. One might have expected rations to have been short in the first phase of the war, when Peter's forces were so heavily involved in sieges along the desolate Baltic coast. Such indeed was the case. Peter himself wrote of the "great hunger" that obtained among his troops during the siege of Narva in 1700.[44] Slightly more than a year later, in January 1702, Prince Sheremet'ev dismissed the largest party of Cossacks under his command and sent them home, explaining that he lacked the provisions to maintain them for the winter. Sheremet'ev, it should be noted, often made out rather better than other commanders in Peter's army in the struggle for foodstuffs. In a letter of October 1703, Admiral Apraksin wrote the tsar that "the horses are dying of hunger. Boris Petrovich [Sheremet'ev] has seized all of the food for himself; I don't know what for. There is no bread."[45]

Yet the crisis in foodstuffs did not abate even after the theater of war was transferred into Poland, Lithuania, and White Russia. In a perceptive memorandum of September 1706, General Hallart (one of the best foreign officers ever to take service with Peter) outlined the main defects of the Russian army and was particularly contemptuous of the food supply system. He noted that owing to the lack of any special supply corps, Russian soldiers were often compelled to carry their food on their own backs, with the result that they would sometimes "throw it aside from exhaustion."[46]

Some people have concluded that the food supply problem was largely overcome on the eve of Charles XII's invasion of Russia.[47] To be sure, daily norms for soldiers provisions laid down for 1708 and 1709 appear more than adequate—even impressive. Each man was supposed to receive 2 pounds of bread a day, in addition to meat, groats, vinegar, vodka, and beer.[48] Certainly the soldiers of the Swedish army apparently felt that their Russian enemies were eating better than they during the terrible winter of 1708. Captain James Jeffreyes, a "volunteer" with Charles's army who was actually a British agent, wrote in February 1708 that the Muscovites "have one advantage over us, that they have provision in abundance, which we suffer from want of."[49] Despite Jeffreyes's testimony, the suffering was actually mutual. In reference to the same month as Jeffreyes, Sheremet'ev wrote Peter that "the Russian forces in their march endured great need, and large numbers of both men and horses died owing to lack of food and forage."[50]

Matters did not improve much in subsequent years. Less than three weeks after the battle of Poltava, Ivan Stroev reported to Peter that stocks of food in the magazines in Moscow and throughout the garrisons of the country were low because of the nonpayment of grain taxes. He also recommended that provincial governors (voevody) who failed to collect or did not dispatch the grain allotments required of them be heavily fined.[51] Efficient distribution of food was rare even if the troops were not engaged in military operations. Admiral Apraksin warned Peter that the garrison of Narva was running out of food in the summer of 1709 and reported that the horses of the garrison were dying for the same reason the following fall.[52]

In 1713 Apraksin would still be beseeching his sovereign for food. In the following year he would call on the Senate to ship food "to support the army of Finland owing to extreme need."[53] It is thoroughly unremarkable that there was hunger in the Petrine army; after all, hunger was to some extent the common lot of every eighteenth-century soldier. What is striking, however, is the fact that at some of the crucial turning points of the Northern War it was not so much hunger as death by starvation that threatened Peter's troops.

Inadequate victuals or none at all could by itself be a powerful stimulus for soldiers to desert. Beyond that, lack of food was the breeding ground for indiscipline. Clearly the sources suggest that the Petrine armed forces teemed with disciplinary cases. Sometimes they were the outcome of alcoholic sprees. In the beginning of March 1703, for instance, a group of drunken and larcenous sailors accosted Field Marshal Sheremet'ev on the road from Moscow to Tver and would have assassinated him but for the misfiring of a pistol.[54] On many other occasions, in a more premeditated way, soldiers took to rioting and robbery to furnish themselves with the rations, equipment, and money the Russian state had promised them but had not supplied. In a letter of 1704, King Augustus of Poland complained to Peter that Russian troops were stealing even more from the peasants of Lithuania than the Swedes had when that duchy was under hostile military occupation.[55] Augustus's charges gain in credibility, because they were echoed by the Commander-in-Chief of all Russian forces in the area, Field Marshal Ogilvie. Indeed, Ogilvie exceeded all others in bluntness in explaining to the tsar the condition of discipline in his army. (He is, of course, extremely unpopular among nationalistic Soviet historians for that very reason.) In early February 1706, Ogilvie alerted Peter to "the general disobedience and absence of any discipline" among his troops.[56] Less than two weeks later Ogilvie wrote from Grodno making explicit the connections between logistic failure, indiscipline, and military ineptitude, noting that he had been abandoned

> . . . amid a collapsing force, without money, without magazines, without artillery or regimental horses; which is leading the entire army into disarray . . . it is necessary to supply the army with everything essential—men, money—and to introduce military discipline as I have frequently said and written to you.

After continuing with a description of how a certain Colonel Shtol'ts of the dragoons had lost eight men and had fled after a trivial skirmish with the enemy, Ogilvie added: "Here are the fruits of that disorder to which the dragoons have accustomed themselves. [They] only sit in the villages, don't keep adequate guard, and despoil the peasants of vodka, ham, chickens, and geese."[57]

Perhaps Ogilvie's growing ill temper can be explained in part by the fact that someone on his staff had lost the secret code book, which meant that the Field Marshal could not decrypt Peter's responses to his letters, but Ogilvie's burst of sarcasm in a missive to Peter dated February 26, 1706, was daring even for him: "Everything is fine here except that no one is obeying my orders."[58]

Was Ogilvie merely a disgruntled and bilious foreigner? The record would indicate not, since his views were corroborated by Russians. In July 1706 Prince V. Dolgorukii informed F. A. Golovin that Russian troops quartered in Lithuania were again imposing "taxes" on the local peasantry in order to give spurious legitimacy to their banditry.[59] Indiscipline and crime stemmed not only from want, of course, but also from poor supervision on the part of the officers. In fact, discipline may have deteriorated still further in subsequent years, since at the very end of the summer of 1706 Peter felt compelled to *reduce* the number of officers in each regiment from thirty-five to twenty-five in view of a dire of shortage qualified men. Certainly there are many accounts of indiscipline that relate to the later periods of the war. In January 1709 Peter even found it necessary publicly to forbid his officers to steal (in this case, horsefeed).[60] To cite one last instance (many others could be adduced) in July 1713 Admiral Apraksin wrote Major Strekalov, the principal juridical officer in the army of Finland, that the widespread brigandage by "many soldiers" had to be stopped. To aid Strekalov in suppressing it, Apraksin added, he was sending judicial reinforcements: a lieutenant and a party of horse dragoons (to arrest guilty parties), a priest (to shrive them), and an extra hangman (to string them up).[61]

Inadequate supplies, inadequate food, indiscipline, and high rates of manpower turnover—none of these could have exerted a beneficial influence on the training of the Petrine army. Indeed, it is possible that the Russian state took greater pains to train the forces that invested Narva in 1700 than it did to train any army raised thereafter up to 1714. We are informed that 3 pounds of ball were allotted to each man for practice firing in 1700, which suggests that the defeat of Narva probably had more to do with failure of nerve than bad musketry.[62] Yet most of the contemporary comments we have on the marksmanship of Peter's soldiers thereafter suggest that the level of skill attained was not very high. A passage excised from Hallart's 1706 Smolensk memorandum on the condition of the Russian army has at times been cited to argue the opposite: "Nowhere in the world is so much powder used on the training of soldiers as here." Hallart would seem to be implying that Peter's troops were simply swimming in powder and possessed more than enough for all training purposes. Yet Hallart goes on to say that "the expenditure [of powder] is useless, weapons are spoiled. It is necessary to train [soldiers] to hit the target," which strongly suggests that it was a rare soldier who could consistently shoot straight.[63] The "Instruction for Combat at the Present Time" (March 1708), a general training manual for the army that was heavily revised by Peter himself, validates this supposition; such enormous stress is laid on marksmanship that one can only conclude that it was generally deficient. In that document Peter insisted that it was essential not only for his raw recruits but even for his veterans to study "accurate and not rapid firing, good aiming, careful loading."[64] It would have been redundant nonsense to enjoin the troops to master these skills had they already possessed them. Peter, in fact, insisted that obligatory courses of training be established for all soldiers that very spring. Implementation of his demand, however, was considerably complicated by supply shortages. Only ten musket balls were allocated to each fresh recruit for target practice during the entire spring and summer of 1708 (and only five for each veteran). Indeed, no ammunition at all was issued to the men of Repnin's division until mid-April.[65] The troops who defeated Löwenhaupt at Lesnaia and crushed Charles XII at Poltava, then, were a long way from being sharpshooters.

Perhaps the training situation improved after Poltava, when the national emergency occasioned by the Swedish invasion was over. Certainly one would expect to detect signs of clear military improvement after 1709, or at least 1714. But the official history of the Semenovskii Guard regiment, one of the best and most privileged military units created by Peter the Great, observed that systematic training became possible only in 1720. "Field education [*stroevoe obrazovanie*] . . . in the course of the first twenty years of existence of the regiment not only did not improve, but gradually declined."[66] The ostensible reasons were that the "Semenovtsy" were generally thrust into the forefront of military operations without lengthy preliminary training, and that the rate of turnover was so high. Given the high attrition, the regiment was actually hollow—continuously replenished with new recruits, for whom training had to begin over again each year. In a sample test of marksmanship conducted in 1721, almost 51 percent of the Semenovskii soldiers proved incapable of hitting the target.[67]

This illustrates one of the single most important characteristics of the army of Peter the Great. That army may have been standing, but the recruits were raw every year, and training started up afresh. In fact, the greatest periods of military effort—such as 1708–9; 1712–14; 1719–21—were ones in which the army was brought up to fighting strength by inundating it with fresh recruits, as a perusal of the statistics on Peter's recruiting levies illustrates. The enormous attrition among Petrine soldiers, then, deprived his army of significant institutional continuity, and that continuity is the concealed premise lurking behind any definition of a "regular" force. But perversely, the demoralizing causes of the attrition—a brutal and oppressive conscription system, disease, nakedness, starvation, and combat—were ineluctable constants of the entire Great Northern War. Peter did not build a Russian regular army. In the circumstances, it was impossible for him to build one. Rather, his army was constantly abuilding, and just as simultaneously collapsing, like the clenching and unclenching of a fist. The army of Peter the Great was ill fed, poorly trained, often underequipped, and frequently undisciplined. Soldiers fled from it in droves and died in it like flies. Peter therefore did not defeat the Swedes because he had designed, trained, and led a finely honed, awesomely efficient fighting machine. Rather, the curious military genius of Peter the Great was that he was able to figure out how to employ an army like this and still win anyway.[68]

How Peter Did It

Given the enormous shortcomings of the Petrine army, how did Peter the Great manage to win the Great Northern War? In order to answer, we must look at Petrine economic and military innovations. The economic policies of Peter the Great were of significance because they allowed him to expand Russia's military potential, thus making possible a protracted war. Yet Peter's contributions to operations and strategy were no less important. The economic reforms and the operational/strategic practices were mutually interdependent; together they were the necessary and sufficient condition for Russian victory. We shall first examine the economic policies in each of three realms: revenue, industry, and transport. The changes in those areas permitted Peter to overcome, or at least partially to overcome, Muscovy's weaknesses in military endurance, which had proved so frustrating for previous Romanov rulers.

"Money," Peter wrote, "is the artery of war," which shows that he was aware of the connection that existed between Russia's unstable revenues and its past military failures.[69] As we have seen earlier in the case of the Smolensk war, impending bankruptcy could leave Russia's leaders with no choice but meekly to sue for peace, whether they wanted to continue or not. The emptiness of the treasury often created a situation in which the decision for war or peace was taken out of Russian hands altogether and placed solely at the discretion of Russia's adversaries. It was a trap that Peter was determined to avoid and did.

The key here was simultaneously expanding the pool of available taxpayers while increasing the tax burden generally. Muscovy's state revenues grew constantly under Peter. Amounting to roughly 1.5 million rubles in 1680, they attained 3.6 million in 1701 and 8.7 million in 1724, the year before Peter's death. Even taking into account the debasement of the coinage (another revenue-enhancing measure introduced by Peter's government), state receipts from direct taxes, indirect taxes, and other dues increased 2.7 times.[70] Up to 1720 or so, those results were attained not by rationalizing the arbitrary and capricious pattern of Muscovite tax-gathering but by intensifying that very same pattern. From the beginning of his reign Peter ceaselessly multiplied the taxes that Russian subjects were supposed to pay; taxes were slapped on glass, stove pipes, doors, beards, and bathhouses.[71] Indirect taxes on all manner of goods similarly went up. Nor did the Petrine government refrain from imposing extraordinary additional taxes of money and grain, just as it called up extra levies of recruits in addition to those inducted by the regular recruiting system. Indeed, the connection was very close between those two phenomena, since the mustering of additional recruits required additional taxes to clothe and equip them.

Extraordinary taxes were also charged to meet emergency expenses connected with the construction of St. Petersburg, to build ships, to supply the needs of troops in winter quarters, and so forth. So sizable were those extraordinary levies that they amounted to almost 60 percent of all taxes paid by the peasants of Kiev Province from 1719 to 1723.[72] Surrendering money or rye to tax collectors, whether on a regular or an *ad hoc* basis, did not mark the limit of a taxpayer's obligations to his government, either, for there were also many natural or labor duties. Even if the state did not "draft" a peasant for years of toil in construction, it could still exact short-term labor services from him. He could be ordered to do road repairs, drive loads by cart, or fell trees. Sometimes those natural services were demanded by the government regardless of the difficulty or even possibility of their fulfillment. Among the many grievances that sparked off the revolt of the town of Astrakhan (1705–6) was this: each soldier and *strelets* had suddenly been required to supply six sazhens (58 cubic meters) of firewood for the need of a nearby saltpetre works, despite the fact that there were scarcely any trees in the vicinity at all.[73]

Toward the end of his reign Peter did overhaul his tax system thoroughly. In 1718 a decree announced the abolition of most direct taxes and their replacement by the unitary soul or poll tax—an annual payment of 74 (later 70) kopecks, which was to be made by a taxable community on behalf of every male who resided in it from babes in arms to crippled old men. To enhance compliance with the act in 1724 the government unveiled the regimental district system: thirty-five regiments, quartered on the population throughout the various regions of the country were empowered both to collect the poll tax and to spend it on their own maintenance.[74]

There can be no doubt that those tax policies were effective in the end; Peter did squeeze more money, food, and labor out of his subjects than had any of his predecessors. The revenue that was harvested not only allowed Peter to continue his war but even tolerated subventions to his allies, such as the 100,000 rubles Peter promised to pay Augustus II annually in the Traktat of Birsen (1701).[75] We should emphasize, however, that there were some peculiar problems with this tax system.

In the first place, as we already observed at the beginning of the chapter, one response of the peasantry of Russia to the increasing tax burden was to run away. The number of peasant households counted by tax collectors declined by 20 percent in the first quarter of the eighteenth century, and in some provinces by as much as 50 percent.[76] What this statistic revealed, however, was not demographic collapse but massive peasant flight. It was difficult for the state meaningfully to assess or to collect ordinary taxes as a consequence, which in part explains why the government was so heavily dependent on extraordinary tax levies. Yet there was a problem here too. If peasants had difficulty paying their ordinary taxes even when they were aware of their assessment for months in advance, they had even *greater* difficulty discharging their obligations when extraordinary taxes were suddenly and arbitrarily imposed upon them. Arrears in extraordinary taxes thus mounted at a greater rate than did those in ordinary taxes. Arrears of the former type were more dangerous: extraordinary taxes were usually assessed in response to a specific need or a real emergency, which required an immediate rather than a tardy infusion of revenue. The tax system, however, produced the funds belatedly and incompletely, if at all. Money did not flow into the Muscovite treasury in a broad and constant stream. Rather, owing to peasant flight and the massive reliance on extraordinary taxes, it came in spatters and spurts, like water groaning from a rusted pipe. For most of the reign, then, the Russian government lurched from one fiscal crisis to another; the rational budgeting that might be considered indispensable in a war was virtually impossible.

To be sure, at the very end of the period the introduction of the poll tax did bring order to the tsarist fisc. But as assessment of the tax depended upon a nationwide census of taxable males, implementation of the reform took years. It was not really until 1724 that the majority of localities within the Russian Empire were operating under the poll tax system.[77] A rational system of taxation had finally been created, but the war with Sweden was long over.

Peter's exertions with regard to industry, or at least military industries, seem to have produced more consistent results than his tax reforms. One of the most successful of all of Peter's military industries was surely shipbuilding. Before Peter, Russia almost totally lacked a tradition of constructing oceangoing vessels.

In the aftermath of the successful capture of Azov, however, Peter commanded that a fleet be constructed in the Sea of Azov and a flotilla in the Caspian. Naval architecture was not, however, the preferred metier of the carpenters who built those early fleets: many vessels were constructed of green wood and used wooden pegs in place of iron nails, which resulted in their scuttling themselves.[78] Given the low level of craftsmanship indicated by such episodes, Russia's success in building up its fleet was all more remarkable. By the end of his life, Peter possessed thirty-two ships-of-the-line and sixteen frigates, all of modern design, not to speak of the scores of galleys, bomb boats, and other craft. This navy, whose Baltic presence alone surpassed that of Sweden or Denmark, bore witness to the efficiency of Peter's sawmills, boatyards, and hired British experts.[79]

Metallurgy was another area in which Russia's accomplishments were both impressive and crucial to the war effort. In 1699 work began on the large Nevianskii iron foundry in the Urals. The factory, which was handed over to the Demidov family in 1702, soon grew highly productive. By 1707 the gross weight of iron sent from the Nevianskii factory to Moscow in raw and finished form (as artillery pieces) amounted to more than 2 million pounds.[80] At Peter's death, some seventy mines and factories were devoted to the extraction and working of copper and iron.[81] The output of such establishments fed Russia's weapons industry. Although it is clear that significant numbers of muskets were imported up to 1707 or so (which probably helps to account for the fact that the Russian troops were armed with weapons of many differing calibers, making the exchange of ammunition impossible), we are told that Russian factories were capable of turning out 15,000 muskets a year by 1709 and 40,000 by 1711. Despite that, Russia still imported almost 60,000 fusils and flintlocks from 1706 through 1712.[82] Thanks in part to large reserves of saltpetre, Russia is believed to have become nominally self-sufficient in gunpowder by 1710.[83]

Other branches of industry did not serve the country or the army so well. Despite the resources allocated to them, for example, the textile manufacturing plants could never weave enough cloth to uniform the troops; the shortfall always had to be made up (if at all) through imports. There were critical shortages, too, in the output of other products of military use, such as finished leather.[84]

Important points about Petrine industry, however, still remain to be made. First, it would obviously be a mistake to exaggerate Russia's industrial progress under Peter. Although two hundred factories are said to have been opened during his reign, some of them, owned by private individuals, were clearly paper factories only—factories, launched by people eager for the special privileges and benefits Peter accorded industrialists, that produced virtually nothing.[85] A second point that bears stressing is that industrial development was lopsided under Peter. The state emphasized (and got results in) a handful of heavy industries (the building of capital ships; the casting of iron) to the detriment of lighter industries, which nonetheless made articles like woven cloth that the army needed desperately. To a large extent the favoritism toward the output of engines of war—ships, guns, muskets—was to be expected. Yet the industrial imbalance also reveals that the Russian economy could not autarkistically turn out all of the goods that the army required, which casts light on some of the supply problems identified above. Further, with a few important exceptions (iron in particular), the greatest expansion in output generally occurred either after the battle of Poltava or at the very tail end of the war when Peter's newly formed industrial and mining colleges devoted their attention to privatizing industry and making the economy grow. Although Peter's industrial policies were more rational than his tax policies, the Petrine economy was not the smoothly functioning cog in the war effort is often purported to have been.

As we have already observed, all the expansion in Russian productive capacity would have been utterly useless if the goods could not be conveyed to the army in the field. On top of that, the general agricultural infecundity of the chief theaters of the war made it impossible for the Russian army to live off the land for any length of time; it was dependent on food shipments from the heartland of the country. For those reasons, Peter's endeavors in the realm of transportation were critically important.

The geographical and climatological barriers to efficient transportation in Russia are well known.[86] Most of the river systems run north to south, not east to west, thus rendering water transport complex and expensive. Further, the inland waterways are useless for several months of the year as they ice over completely during the long Russian winter. The dramatic spring thaw clogs the rivers with ice floes and turns the dry land into a vast sea of mud. During this period—the *rasputitsa*—transportation becomes impractical. Johann-Georg Korb, an Austrian diplomat who served in Russia, noted in April 1698 that his "horses frequently sank so deep [in mud] that hardly anything but their heads could be seen."[87] This statement is, of course, a specimen of hyperbole, but it gives some sense of the difficulties involved. Only in winter was transportation relatively quick, owing to the use of sleighs and sledges; even then, however, sudden blizzards and intense cold could impede a traveler's progress.

In view of all of those obstacles, Peter made improvement in the Russian transportation network one of his highest priorities, which is why he became interested in the construction of canals quite early in his reign. The military utility of canals was never far from his mind. Indeed, an examination of the canals Peter planned gives insights into the direction he expected his campaigns to take in the future. The first canals projected by Peter's government were to have been constructed in the southern part of the country—logical enough, given Peter's expectation of sporadic war with the Turks. The English engineer John Perry was hired in 1698 to supervise the digging of a channel from the Volga to the Don. That canal would have connected the Caspian to the Sea of Azov, permitting the speedy transfer of both export goods and naval vessels from one body of water to the other. But the underfunded and undermanned project was never completed.[88] One reason for the lack of support given Perry, of course, was the shift to the north occasioned by the outbreak of the Swedish war. Peter's most immediate need after 1700 was for a water link between the Volga and the Neva river systems. In 1703 Peter ordered the construction of the Vyshnii Volochek Canal, a 2-mile passage to connect the Tversta river (an outbranch of the Volga) and the Msta (on which a transit to the Neva could be made via Lake Ilmen, the Volkhov, and Lake Ladoga). Finished in 1709, the Vyshnii-Volochek Canal doubtless facilitated the equipping and feeding of the Army of Finland and the expeditionary forces that ravaged Sweden in the last phase of the war. More than 2,100 tons of goods and grain passed through its locks annually from 1712 to 1719.[89] Although the Vyshnii-Volochek was the most successful and enduring canal built under Peter, there were problems even here. Rapids on the Msta and the inherent dangers of navigating Lake Ladoga limited the degree to which the water system could be fully exploited; ancillary canals to bypass those hazards (the Tveretskii and Ladoga) were not completed until 1722 and 1732 respectively.[90] Further, the system was not usable during the winter.

Because Peter could not rely totally on his canals to resolve his logistical dilemma, he paid great attention to organizing transportation by road from Moscow, the chief entrepôt of the country, to his dispersed military forces. Of the eight principal roads passing through Moscow, the most important in the early phase of the war was the one leading to Pskov via Tver and Novgorod. Pskov was, after all, Sheremet'ev's base of operations for the conquest of the Baltic. The Moscow-Pskov highway, more than 450 miles in length, was divided into four roughly equal sections; in each, peasants of the roadside villages were obligated to perform cartage services. In 1702 and 1703 (unfortunately the only two years for which documentation readily available) 3.8 and 4.7 million pounds of grain and flour were dispatched from Moscow to Pskov to feed Sheremet'ev's army.[91] Later, during Swedish invasion, the Smolensk, the Khar'kov, and the Kiev roads bore the heaviest concentration of military freight.

The Petrine road transport network was a magnificent accomplishment; it was not, however, perfect. The quantity of foodstuffs furnished to Sheremet'ev in 1703 may seem to be enormous, yet the entire 4.7 million pounds supplied in that year would only have provided roughly 6,000 soldiers with a daily ration of 2 pounds of bread per man. Sheremet'ev had more than 20,000 troops under his command at the time.[92] The road transport system clearly operated better in the winter than in the summer, when the demands of field work made the peasants even more reluctant than usual to fulfill their cartage responsibilities.[93] Still, even in winter there was significant evasion.

To sum up, then, Peter's fiscal and economic mobilization of his country presents a mixed picture. Revenues may have risen sharply, but delayed payment or nonpayment of taxes plus peasant flight meant that Peter's treasury could not count on a smooth influx of funds. Peter was consequently forced to finance his war without being able accurately to predict his cash flow—a very difficult task indeed. Similarly, although domestic industry eventually could supply the army with many of the commodities it needed, it was never able to satisfy all of the soldiers' demands. Certain crucial articles, such as uniforms and boots, were always in scarce supply. Further, even the most successful among Russia's nascent industries had little "surge capacity"—the capability to increase output rapidly in response to military emergencies. When Peter wrote Jacob Bruce demanding that he prepare enough gunpowder to supply 50,000 men with three hundred charges each, the latter responded (March 1705) that this "was not possible by any means, because it would require more than 828,000 pounds [of powder] and we have only . . . 54,000 pounds in all."[94] Finally, while Peter made good use of his roads and canals, the transportation system was never adequate to the demands made upon it; weather, marine hazards, and peasant stubbornness created constant bottlenecks and delays. Oddly enough, the economic and financial infrastructure for fighting the Great Northern War came completely into existence only after the Swedes had been beaten. It was only after 1721 that Russia acquired a sound tax system, experienced the greatest increase in the output of its military industries, and perfected the Volga-Neva Canal link.

All armies and all wars are characterized by logistical breakdowns from time to time. By contrast, the Petrine military economy was guaranteed to produce total logistical failures on a regular and ongoing basis. Yet despite the suffering and death that caused, Petrine fiscal and economic policies did importantly contribute to winning the war. Just enough money, food, weapons, and equipment were collected and distributed to make the difference between the barely tolerable and completely unendurable. Without Peter's tax reforms, state factories, canals, and impressed teamsters, the army could not have survived as a recognizable military force at all. Absent those Petrine innovations, Russia certainly could not have sustained so lengthy a war. The Petrine military economy, then, produced not copious abundance but rather marginal sufficiency. And marginal sufficiency was enough.

If Peter's economic policies sustained Peter's army, albeit barely, they do not account for the outcome of the Great Northern War. The economic mobilization of Russia ensured that Peter would have something to fight with, but it did not foreordain his victory. To understand how the Swedes were defeated we must look at Petrine operations and strategy. It is immediately apparent that Peter's operational practices and his strategic planning were profoundly informed by his knowledge of himself and his enemy. War, no less than politics, is the art of the possible, and Peter had a keen sense of what was militarily *possible* for an army like his and what was not.

There were three salient characteristics of Peter's operational style: fortification, mobility, and naval support. The emphasis on fortification was the outgrowth of Peter's awareness of the sources of Swedish military strength in the field.

In terms of population and resources, Sweden rated low among the states of Europe in the early eighteenth century. Sweden's 3 million inhabitants was a paltry total when compared with France's 20 million, the empire's 20 million, and even Russia's 14 million.[95] But Sweden's army was not composed of mercenaries, as were the armies of most other European powers. Rather its forces were chiefly made up of highly motivated troops conscripted from the nation at large. It was the national character of the army (and the high morale this engendered) that enabled Sweden to perfect the gå-på tactics with which its commanders regularly overcame numerically superior enemies. Unlike many other Western generals, who preferred infantry firefights, Sweden's military leaders constantly insisted on shock. Arranged in four lines, Swedish battalions would hurl themselves upon the enemy. At a distance of seventy paces the men in the first two lines would suddenly stoop over, allowing the soldiers behind to fire a blasting volley. The charge would resume with the men in the van firing their weapons at point blank range. A general mêlée would then ensue as the Swedes attempted to finish off their enemies hand to hand with bayonet and pike. Cavalry procedures were analogous. Armed with long, thrusting swords, the Swedish horse would form a flying wedge and charge pell-mell into the serried ranks of the enemy. Confronted with such ferociously aggressive tactics, the opposing army often broke and ran.[96]

Peter the Great had been given a lesson in just how effective Swedish impetus could be at Narva in 1700. Thereafter neither he nor his generals were particularly enthusiastic about confronting the Swedes in battle unless Russian forces were overwhelmingly superior. Sheremet'ev, whose numerical superiority over Schlippenback at the battle of Erestfer was almost three to one, has often been criticized for excessive caution. He was invariably averse to taking military action unless he was confident that he outnumbered his enemies by a large margin; indeed, he often delayed opening a campaign while he waited for reinforcements.[97] But Sheremet'ev's prudence was not misplaced, for the Swedes repeatedly demonstrated throughout the war that they were capable of fighting and routing superior Russian forces, as they did when they nearly annihilated Repnin's cavalry division at Holovzin (July 1708). As late as 1713, Peter the Great would himself command his generals to avoid battle in Finland if the Russian forces were not numerically much stronger than Swedish ones.[98]

Peter's solution to the problem posed by Swedish gå-på tactics was fortification. He sheltered his infantry in forts, behind field works, in trenches. So important did Peter deem the ability to improvise field fortifications rapidly that he especially trained his cavalry for that function. He commanded that over 40 percent of his dragoons carry axes, sharpened spades, and shovels. Peter stressed the benefits of fortification even to his irregular forces. In a letter of January 1707 Peter ordered Hetman Ivan Mazeppa (whom he then believed still loyal) to concentrate his Cossack forces in Kiev, recommending that he bring along with him "adequate quantities of spades and shovels . . . so that it would be possible to make fortifications with trenches at suitable places along the Dniepr and by this means bar the path of the enemy."[99]

There were many military advantages to fortifications, either permanent or hastily thrown up. In the first place, such defenses might blunt the impact of a Swedish charge while allowing the Russians to inflict numerous casualties from relative safety. That predilection for the trench, not a shortage of firearms, caused Peter after 1706 to arm one-third of his troops with pikes and halberds.[100] The sight of strong Russian field works bristling with pikes occasionally could be enough by itself to deter a Swedish attack. Jeffreyes wrote from Poltava in the early summer of 1709 that on many occasions when the Swedes advanced against the Russians, "we found them so deeply burryed in the earth that we have not been able to attack them without hazarding the loss of our infantry."[101] But when the Swedes decided that they *had* to secure a Russian position, the result could be a Pyrrhic victory. In January 1709 King Charles lost at least four hundred killed and six hundred wounded capturing the miserable little Ukrainian outpost of Veprik, where the Russian defenders poured water over the tops of their earthworks to transform them into walls of sheet ice.[102]

It is no exaggeration to say that the use of fortifications was one of the central elements in Peter's victory over the Swedes at Poltava on June 27, 1709. It was only after the Swedish army had dissipated its strength battering against Peter's famous system of redans and redoubts that the Russian army emerged from its fortified camp to give general battle.[103] Indeed, there can be no doubt that such humble instruments as the spade, the pike, and the ax were at least as valuable, if not more valuable, to Peter's soldiers as the musket. The Russian peasant may not have known how to shoot, but he did know how to dig, hack, and stab. Peter's decision to deploy his infantry behind defensive fortifications thus made excellent sense.

Peter's approach to the use of cavalry was strikingly different. Here the most desired quality was mobility, for Peter conceived of the cavalry as a force to harry, skirmish, and raid. One of the most interesting characteristics of Peter's cavalry was that it contained no heavy units—no cuirassiers or carabineers. All of Peter's cavalry regiments were organized as lightly armed dragoons. As far back as 1702 Patkul had authored a memorandum to Peter in which he expatiated on the superiority of dragoons over other kinds of cavalry units; the Livonian noted that they were "much more handy in the field and cheaper."[104] They were handy because they could be dismounted and pressed into service as infantry if the occasion demanded; they were cheaper because they did not require such expensive equipment as breastplates and pistols, which cuirassiers or reiters commonly wore. The chief advantage of dragoons, however, was their speed. They were able to make sudden surprise attacks on small enemy parties and strong points. Although the history of the campaigns of 1700–1704 is a tale of tedious Baltic sieges, what made the sieges possible in the first place was Sheremet'ev's disruption of Swedish lines of communication and retreat by means of cavalry raids, which made offensive action too risky for Charles's commanders to contemplate. When Sheremet'ev galloped into Livonia in 1703, destroying the Swedish army's magazines as he went, Schlippenback had no choice but to fall back on Revel.[105] During the Swedish invasion of 1707–8 Peter employed "frequent skirmishes of his light horse," in the words of the English Ambassador, "to ambush the Swedish army in the flanks and rear."[106]

On many occasions Peter demanded high rates of mobility not only from his cavalry but from selected infantry formations and entire armies. The speed of small cavalry parties could certainly result in successful ambushes; speedy travel by large units, however, could translate into operational surprise. Peter's war plan against Turkey in 1711 involved marching his troops to the Danubian principalities before the enemy could mobilize against him. Of course, the plan did not work, but at least Peter succeeded in moving his forces quickly. So relentlessly did he drive his army that, in the words of John Perry it "arrived on the Borders of Moldavia with an Expedition that is scarce to be credited."[107] During the Finnish campaign of 1713 Peter's army regularly performed forced marches of 15 miles a day; European armies of that time, by contrast, rarely ever traveled more than 12 miles in twenty-four hours.[108] During his war with Persia in 1722 Peter managed to top even that rate, achieving as much as 18 miles a day over nonmountainous terrain.[109] Yet such tempos of advance as those, when imposed on an entire army, could destroy it with fatigue before the enemy was ever in sight, which was one of the reasons Peter negotiated his way out of both the 1711 and 1722 campaigns.

Peter's most successful application of the principle of mobility, in fact, involved not a whole Russian army but an improvised corps of picked troops. In the summer of 1708 Peter knew that the Swedish general Löwenhaupt was advancing southeast from the Baltic in order to link up with Charles XII in the Ukraine. Peter also knew that it was vital to prevent that rendezvous. Löwenhaupt's sixteen thousand men would, of course, provide Charles with much desired reinforcements. Yet Charles needed the seven thousand cartloads of victuals and supplies in Löwenhaupt's train even more badly. On the night of September 11–12, 1708 Peter left his headquarters at Sobelev at the head of his *corps volant,* or "flying corps"—seven thousand dragoons and five thousand infantry temporarily mounted on pack horses. Sixteen days later Peter fell on the unprepared Löwenhaupt at Lesnaia and crushed him. On the morning of September 29 Löwenhaupt abandoned the all-important wagon train and fled south with the surviving third of his forces.[110] We shall return to the battle of Lesnaia subsequently, but we should note that on this occasion Peter's exploitation of mobility produced results of the highest strategic significance.

A third prominent characteristic of Peter's operational approach was his emphasis on combined arms, the use of his navy to support his ground forces. Of course, Peter had a lifelong fascination with matters nautical; his most important wars had as their objective the Russian annexation of coastlines. But Peter did not build his navy solely to gratify his vanity. He understood the mutual relationship of sea and land power more completely than did most other statesmen of his time, as he indicated in this crude but striking image: "[A]ny potentate who has only an army has one hand, but whoever has a fleet as well has both of his hands."[111] Peter learned that lesson—that a king without a navy is like an amputee—during the first serious military campaign of his reign. Peter's initial attempt to take the Turkish fort of Azov (1695) failed in part because the Turks were able to provision and reinforce the garrison from the sea unmolested. When Peter renewed the siege the following year, he brought his own flotilla of galleys along. They effectively cut off Azov from the seaward side, dispersed the Turkish relief ships, and helped induce the fort to capitulate.[112] Thereafter the value of combined land and sea operations was rarely far from Peter's mind. Sea power could have an even greater impact, Peter discovered, if the fleet suddenly intervened in an unexpected location. In August 1702, for instance, Peter transferred the bulk of his White Sea flotilla from Arkhangel to Lake Ladoga—across 150 miles of rivers, swamps, and portages—in order to support the siege of Nöteburg.[113] There are many other instances in which Peter arranged similar surprise appearances for his ships. To cite but one: in the summer of 1714 Peter ordered a wooden bridge 1.5 miles long built across the Hangö Peninsula so that his galleys could be hauled from one side to another. That measure forced the Swedish admiral to divide his fleet, which importantly contributed to the great Russian naval victory of July 26–27.[114]

Peter's most imaginative combined arms operations, however, were his Finnish campaigns of 1712–14. They depended for success on the simultaneous maneuvering of ground forces, galleys, and sailing vessels. The army was supposed to march up the southern coast of Finland, capturing important strong points: Vyborg, Forsbi, Helsingfors, Åbo, and Hangö. It was assisted in its sieges and to some extent supplied by the galley fleet, which rowed on a course parallel to the army's advance, negotiating the treacherous Finnish fjords and skerries. Farther south, and still parallel to the army, the sailing fleet operated in the deeper channels of the Gulf of Finland in order to protect the army and the galleys from Swedish naval attack. Although Russian soldiers and sailors suffered horribly during those brutal campaigns, Peter's combined arms approach did in the end enable him to achieve his goal, for he conquered all of southern Finland and capped off the achievement by defeating the Swedish fleet at Hangö. It is a measure of the importance Peter attached to the maritime component of those operations that he entrusted an admiral—F.A. Apraksin—with supreme command over all forces in the Finnish theater.[115] Indeed, it was precisely combined land and sea operations that brought the Great Northern War to a close, since it was Russia's three amphibious raids into Sweden from 1719 to 1721 that finally deprived the Stockholm government of any will to resist. During the first of those attacks, we are told, the Russian troops disembarked from barges and ships and devastated the countryside, burning villages, blowing up iron mines, and carrying off thousands of civilians as virtual slaves.[116] It is no surprise that Sweden finally caved in to that pressure. But we should stress that it was a pressure that could be applied only with the assistance of the Russian navy.

The peculiarities of Peter's operational style thus conferred several advantages on the Russian armed forces. When Russia was on the defensive, operational subtlety could be used to compensate for severe military deficiencies. Since the Russian army— ragged, undernourished, and ill-trained as it was—could not meet the Swedish army in the field on an equal footing, Peter relied on fortifications to neutralize Swedish tactics and to turn Swedish aggressiveness into a liability. The tsar could also launch cavalry raid after cavalry raid to improve the odds still further. But when Russia took to the offensive, Peter's approach to operations emphasized the quest for surprise. High mobility enabled Peter to strike powerful blows in unlikely places, as with the *corps volant* at Lesnaia. And the bold combination of land and sea forces permitted Peter to carry the war into inhospitable theaters, such as Finland, or even into the Swedish heartland itself.

In the final analysis, however, Peter's strategy was a more important ingredient in Russia's victory over Sweden than was his operational art. Despite Peter's innovations, the Swedes were almost always tactically and operationally superior to their Russian opponents. Yet the strategy of Charles XII was deeply inferior to Peter's. It was on the strategic level that Peter really defeated the Swedish monarch.

Petrine strategy had several distinctive characteristics. In the first place, it was collectively debated and collectively made in formal councils of war. Those councils, variously called *voennye sovety, konsilii,* or *konsiliumy,* took place ten to twenty times a year. (There were, for instance, twenty-two of them during that period of crisis, 1708).[117] Usually attended by Peter, his principal generals, and his ranking foreign policy experts, the councils were remarkably sophisticated decision-making institutions. The standard format was for one particular general to present a written paper in which he outlined the operational and strategic situation as he saw it and proposed a particular course of action. Sometimes the *rapporteur* would be a foreigner, such as Ogilvie or Hallart; at others, Menshikov or Sheremet'ev would be the first to address the group. After the designated speaker had been heard, lively discussion and heated criticism would follow. For example, when at the military council held on January 9, 1706, Lieutenant General Wenediger urged that the Russian army prudently retire from Grodno to Polotsk, Ogilvie raised shrill objections. He noted that in view of the lack of transport the artillery and shells would have to be left behind and would fall into Swedish hands; that a retreat would consign the three thousand men of the Grodno garrison to certain death; that the Swedes would pursue the evacuating Russians anyway; and that thousands of Russian troops would surely die if a winter march were attempted. He concluded that the very idea of a retreat was "dangerous, harmful, and also shameful."[118] After the discussion was over, a formal protocol of the meeting would be prepared for the tsar's perusal. On occasion the most prominent critics of the original proposal would then be invited to submit written memoranda expanding on the counterarguments they had originally presented orally. In any event, the final decision was taken by the tsar and the tsar alone.[119] If Peter was present, the decision might be issued quickly. If he was away, the entire dossier of proposals and counterproposals would have to be shipped to him, which was the upshot of the Grodno meeting discussed above. In a truly pressing emergency, Peter's generals might write and implore him to pay a flying visit to the army's headquarters for an extraordinary conference. It was Prince Menshikov's appeal of November 1706 that brought Peter to Zholkiev for the most momentous military council of the entire war.[120]

This system was obviously adopted originally as a heuristic devise. In the aftermath of the Narva defeat of 1700, Peter realized that neither he nor any of his native born generals had more than a shallow grasp of Western strategy. The formal military council could therefore serve as a sort of intensive strategy course, a forum in which Peter and his Russians could learn about the subject by debating Russia's most able foreign officers. Peter stuck with this method of decision-making, however, long after such people as Menshikov and Sheremet'ev had acquired the requisite conceptual sophistication; the evident benefits of the conciliar system continued to impress him.

What made the military council particularly excellent? One benefit was the intense scrutiny any proposal or plan received there. Since criticism was invited, even expected, council members did not hesitate to castigate a written memorandum for errors of fact, logic, or plausibility. The mere clash of fiercely divergent opinions, of course, does not necessarily guarantee that the truth will emerge. But heated debate can do much to expand the repertory of approaches to a problem. One of the most useful results of the conciliar method was the open consideration of multiple alternatives—not only alternatives that the Russian army might entertain but also alternative courses of action that the Swedes might themselves select. One of the greatest errors in any war is the construction of war plans for one's own country based on the false assumption that the enemy can be trusted to behave in a predictable fashion, almost if in accord with an unwritten script. But no enemy is *ever* consistently predictable. The conciliar system was thus Peter's insurance policy against the stale thinking that could lead to unpleasant surprises. A good illustration of the way in which the give and take of discussion could stimulate original insights and creativity is the military council held in Beshenkovichi in early March 1708. By that point Augustus II had left the war; there was nothing standing between Russia and the Swedish army. But what would be Charles XII's objective? What axis or axes of advance would he follow? The debate at Beshenkovichi among Menshikov, Sheremet'ev, Hallart, and Gol'ts resulted in the drafting of five plausible Swedish campaign scenarios, with detailed recommendations about how Russia might respond to each.[121]

But the conciliar system did more than facilitate clearer thinking about the enemy and his intentions, for it also gave Peter I the opportunity to correct for the personal animosities and service rivalries that otherwise could have spoiled his own war plans. For example, in the early stages of the war the Russian cavalry and infantry were not accustomed to joint operations—"the foot soldier is no comrade to the cavalry" was a contemporary saying.[112] Actually the statement might have been more accurate in reverse, for in Peter's army the horse trooper generally showed more disdain for the unmounted infantryman than the other way around. Prince A. D. Menshikov, Russia's leading cavalry general, well exemplified this sort of arrogance. He was well known for concocting projects that assigned the most central and glamorous role to the cavalry while loading the infantry with inglorious and mundane responsibilities. At Beshenkovichi, for example, Menshikov posited the following situation: Charles XII might feint in the direction of the Dniepr, then suddenly veer back into Germany for another attack on Saxony. In such a case, Menshikov advised that the Russian cavalry be split entirely away from the infantry and formed into an army of pursuit. Meanwhile Sheremet'ev should march the infantry north and attempt the siege of Riga. Sheremet'ev wisely condemned the scheme, observing that no siege would be possible without the reconnoitering and protection that only cavalry could provide.[123] The point is that Menshikov actually had some quite good ideas about cavalry raiding and strategic pursuit. The conciliar format, with its open discussion, written memoranda, and so forth, allowed Peter to draw on them while purging Menshikov's plan of its vainglorious elements by incorporating Sheremet'ev's objections.

Peter could consequently select from a range of options, or he could elect some sort of synthetic plan which combined the best of each. Indeed, Peter often went outside the military council itself for suggestions and advice about operational and strategic questions. Sometimes such input was the product of espionage coups. In the midsummer of 1708 Peter's envoy in the Hague, A. A. Matveev, wrote that he had learned by covert means that

> the Swede in view of the caution of the tsarist forces and in view also of the impossibility of attaining Smolensk, and equally because of the insufficiency of food and fodder, has taken the decision to go to the Ukraine; first, because this is a populous and rich country which has no regular fortifications with strong garrisons; second, because the Swede expects to find many adherents in the free Cossack population; and third, because proximity might allow for negotiation with the Crimean Khan to bring him into alliance, and with the Poles who take Leszcynski's part; and fourth, finally, because it will be possible to dispatch Cossacks to Moscow to stir up a popular uprising.[124]

This intelligence was an astonishingly accurate portrait of what Charles XII intended to do and why, and Peter made excellent use of it in preparing for his own Ukrainian campaign.

In certain respects the Petrine councils of war bear a resemblance to Peter's administrative colleges, those functionally discrete central institutions Peter established on a Swedish model in 1717 to regulate trade, foreign affairs, mines, manufactures, and so forth. Like the colleges, the military councils had many members, encouraged the free exchange of views, and were repositories of expert advice. But there were two important dissimilarities. The colleges were formally chartered institutions, while the councils met on an *ad hoc* basis. Still more important, the colleges took decisions (even if they had to be confirmed by the tsar) on the basis of majority vote.[125] There was no voting in the councils, for they were consultative and advisory boards only. Peter always made the final determination. Government by committee might be just barely possible; strategy by committee was inconceivable.

The conciliar system might seem to be a cumbrous and plodding technique for decision-making, yet it allowed Peter to temper his own individual judgment with the best available outside advice. At the very least it ensured that strategy would emerge as the end product of analysis. A comparison with Charles XII is instructive. To be sure, that monarch convened military councils of his own; almost all European field commanders did. But the Swedish councils usually had no more intellectual weight and significance than puppet shows or other entertainments staged in the royal camp, since Charles kept his opinions to himself and was notorious for discarding the advice of others.[126] For the Swedish King, alternately mercurial and saturnine, strategy was a matter of whim, inspiration, and improvisation.[127] By contrast, whereas almost every other institution and policy in the Petrine state might have been frantically improvised, Petrine strategic planning was not. And in the end Peter's confidence in stolid ratiocination was more justified than was Charles's faith in the "inward eye."

A second important feature of Peter's overall strategic approach was his attempt to coordinate military action and diplomacy. Peter constantly struggled to deny Charles allies and struggled even more vigorously to find allies for himself. Why was Peter so eager to participate in anti-Swedish coalitions? Coalition warfare, of course, can be both complex and dangerous: coalition partners rarely have perfectly congruent war aims, and victory itself can quickly set former allies at odds. To some extent Peter's belief in the necessity of coalitions was identical to that of his seventeenth-century forebears. Despite his military reforms, Russia was militarily weak, and Peter knew it. But another reason for an anti-Swedish alliance, Peter discovered, was that it could be used to make sure that the war would be fought somewhere other than Russia. In that regard, the deal Peter made with Augustus II at Birsen in 1701 was unquestionably Russia's most important diplomatic achievement in the entire Great Northern War. Fresh from the humiliation of Narva, Peter had traveled to Birsen as a suppliant, ready to pay almost any price to coax Augustus back into an alliance. And the price was in fact steep, amounting to pledges of heavy financial and military aid in addition to the promises (in the end unkept) that the Saxon Elector should have all of Livonia and Estonia once the final victory had been won. But, as we have already noted, the cost was worth it, because the totality of Charles's wrath now fell on Augustus.

With all of Poland as his buckler, Peter could confidently undertake his program for the incremental conquest of the Baltic. The benefit of the alliance became more and more obvious to Peter as the years passed. Charles's army might win victory after victory in Poland, but not a single one was meaningful if the Swedes could not knock Augustus out of the war. The corollary was simple: as long as Augustus continued to fight, no Swedish invasion of Russia was possible. It is because Peter grasped this fact that he made the most extraordinary efforts to prop up his ally. Peter sent a Russian expeditionary force to Saxony in 1704 to succor Augustus and occupied Grodno in 1705 in order to keep important Polish magnates loyal to him.[128] After the Treaty of Altranstadt in 1706, when Saxony did leave the war, Peter and his confidants tried hard to induce someone else to step in and play Augustus's indispensable role. Menshikov wanted Peter to arrange for yet another person to be proclaimed legitimate ruler of Poland. ("It is possible," he wrote "to select another king.")[129] And at Zholkiev in late 1706 and early 1707, Peter eagerly conspired with members of the Sandomir Confederation in the hope that they could unleash so great a civil war that Charles XII would be penned up for months in eastern Poland.[130] After Poltava, the Petrine government still welcomed the formation of enlarged anti-Carolinian alliances. Peter's immediate objective was now a rapid end to the war, and he believed a new coalition might simply frighten King Charles into signing a peace treaty. This stratagem, of course, did not work, but it came close to succeeding, as the Åland island conference demonstrated.

On the other hand, Charles XII distinguished himself by spurning allies, overrating them, or generally failing to manage them. France was Sweden's traditional diplomatic partner, yet it was in no position to lend Charles any help, embroiled as it was in the War of the Spanish Succession. With regard to Stanislas Leszcynski, it is clear that Charles's decision to depose Augustus in the former's favor was one of the worst he ever made. Unlike Augustus, Leszcynski had no independent power base outside of Poland. Stanislas was therefore a creature of Swedish foreign policy, a subordinate despite his royal crown who was always receiving more aid from Charles XII than he could ever repay. Further, by supporting him, Charles mired himself in the cesspool of Polish politics. His years of preoccupation with intrigue, treason, assassination, civil war, and the other normal features of the Commonwealth's political life hugely benefited Peter the Great. The closest Charles ever came to securing allied assistance was in his dealings with the Turks. As a "guest" of the Ottoman Empire from 1709 to 1713, Charles repeatedly tried to incite the Turks into a war with Peter's Russia. He did in fact help to stir up the Russo-Turkish war of 1711 and also had some influence in keeping Russo-Turkish relations tense for a year or so thereafter. But the Turks had an extensive foreign policy agenda of their own; they had no intention of letting a king without an army use them as an instrument of his personal revenge. Even after the death of Charles XII such meager foreign support as Stockholm could garner owed less to astute Swedish diplomacy than to Dutch and British fears about Russia's growing preponderance of power in the Baltic.[131]

A third characteristic of Petrine strategy in the Northern War was that the objectives it pursued were limited in at least two ways. They were limited in the sense that Clausewitz used the term, for Peter was never interested in total victory over Sweden. To be sure, after 1709 there were those who urged the tsar to settle with Sweden once and for all. The Danish resident at the Russian court, for example, devised an absurd scheme in 1711 for a joint Russo-Polish-Danish campaign of economic annihilation against Sweden. This campaign was to be conducted with such intensity and ruthlessness that the power of Sweden would be broken for generations.[132] But Peter habitually ignored such irresponsible, crackpot ravings. Although his war with King Charles was a war of total effort, to borrow another of Clausewitz's formulations, for him the purpose of the war was not the reduction of Stock-holm to smoldering rubble. Rather, the war was over the Swedes' possession of Baltic territories of which he wanted to despoil them. By 1704 Peter actually held the lands he had started the war to gain; for that reason he was thereafter constantly interested in a negotiated peace. He was in fact enough of a realist to offer Sweden concessions in order to clinch a bargain with it, although of course the extent of the sacrifices he was prepared to make depended on how well Russia was doing in the war. In January 1707 Peter prepared a set of draft instructions to guide his diplomats should Sweden express interest in concluding a peace. The document was written with an eye toward preventing a Swedish invasion of Russia; it represented Peter's most generous offer. In it Peter explained that Russia should try to avoid returning more than the fortress of Dorpat. However, if the Swedes proved stubborn, Russia should be ready to give all of its conquests back with the sole exception of the city of St. Petersburg ("and about giving it back there is to be no thought").[133] Peter's insistence that St. Petersburg be retained even if that caused negotiations to collapse reflected much more than his pride in his new capital, for his uncompromising stand on the issue also showed that he keenly appreciated the strategic importance of the Neva River. To hold St. Petersburg was to dominate the Neva, and to dominate the Neva was to possess an outlet to the Gulf of Finland. If Russia controlled even the narrowest corridor leading to the Gulf, it meant that Sweden's Baltic Empire was cut in half. Russia could consequently renew the war any time it chose in the future under advantageous circumstances.

That highlights another facet of Petrine strategy, the fact that it most commonly focused on the acquisition of geographically important positions. Certain nationalistically minded Russian historians have denied this, of course. Desperate to make the case for the uniqueness of Peter's military genius, they have asserted that Peter anticipated Napoleon in understanding that the enemy's center of gravity was his army. Thus such scholars have claimed that Peter *always* saw the annihilation of the Swedish field army as his supreme goal, and therefore rejected the positional warfare that was the specialty of his most illustrious contemporaries, Marlborough and Prince Eugene.[134] This, however, is to examine the Great Northern War through an acutely convex lens that grotesquely magnifies the Swedish invasion of 1707–9 while shriveling all the other campaigns into insignificance. In fact during most of the war Peter was interested in avoiding, not fighting, the main Swedish army; his military agenda was limited to the capture of towns, forts, harbors, and so forth. Russian seizure of such strategically important assets gave Peter advance bases for future operations; equally, holding them complicated Swedish communications and logistics, thereby constraining Swedish operations. Thus one purpose of the sieges of 1700–1704 was to box up Sweden's increasingly inactive Baltic army in northern Germany. Similarly, Apraksin's objective in the Finnish campaigns of 1712–14 was to cripple Swedish sea power by taking all the ports and harbors in southern Finland on which Sweden's naval operations depended. Many other examples could be adduced.

Peter was thus conducting a war of limited objectives; Charles's objectives, on the other hand, were unlimited, for he dreamed of no less than dismembering the Muscovite state. Whitworth, the British resident in Russia, reported that Swedish diplomats made the following statement about Charles's war aims in 1707:

> The king, their master, said they, would not make peace before he had entered the City of Moscow and dethroned his Czarist Majesty; that then he would divide his whole Empire into small Principalities and Provinces.[135]

That program involved undoing hundreds of years of Russian history, reversing the entire process of "the gathering of the Russian lands" under the sway of Moscow. Such a megalomaniacal delusion on Charles's part tells us a great deal about his mental image of Russia; he obviously believed that the Muscovite state was so weak, so riven by factional struggles and unrest, that one small push would bring it down like a column of toy building blocks. Charles utterly failed to know his enemy. He misunderstood Peter, underestimated Peter's subjects, and saw Muscovy not as it was, but as it had been during the *Smuta* almost a century before.[136] Charles's fundamental misperception was one of the chief factors that impoverished his strategy. By contrast, Petrine offensive strategy after 1700 was devoted to the pursuit of limited goals and based on a realistic appraisal of his enemy.

During the Swedish invasion, however, Peter adopted a new strategy enshrined in his famous plan for active defense. He developed this plan gradually and incrementally, but the first steps toward it were taken at the Zholkiev council of war. Peter arrived at Zholkiev (a small hamlet near L'vov) on December 28, 1706; most of key advisers—Menshikov, Sheremet'ev, Dolgorukii, and Repnin—had already preceded him there. A council of war was immediately convened and took up the task of analyzing the grim strategic situation. There was now a great likelihood that the victorious Swedes would cross from Saxony into Poland and march east in search of the Russian army. The issue at hand, to quote one of the few surviving sources on this meeting, "was whether to give the enemy battle in Poland, or at our frontiers."

Sheremet'ev proposed, and all agreed, "not to give battle in Poland, since such a catastrophe might take place as to make a retreat difficult and for this reason it was decided to give battle at our frontiers when inescapable need would demand this."[137] This account strongly suggests that Peter and his intimates expected an early battle with the Swedes to result in a Russian defeat. Indeed, defeat would be almost impossible to avoid, given Swedish operational superiority and the manifold weaknesses of the Russian army. Even if Peter's generals managed to flee after a defeat, they might not succeed in leading what remained of their forces back into Russia. The Prussian Ambassador, who was in Zholkiev at the time, later explained: "In the event of a defeat it would be impossible to rely on the mood of the inhabitants of Poland; while retreating [the] army might be subjected to great danger."[138] Although the fear that one or more of the private armies active in Poland might pounce on retreating Russian forces was authentic, the central reason Peter and his generals were jittery was their presumption that open battle would equal Russian defeat. As Peter later wrote in reference to the Swedish invasion, "to seek general battle is dangerous [since] all can be lost in one hour. Therefore a policy of retreat is better than limitless hazard."[139] That might sound like a coward's credo; obviously no one ever won a war by the simple expedient of running away. But there was more to the Zholkiev plan than that, for a scorched earth policy in both Poland and Russia was to complement the retreat. On January 3, 1707, Peter wrote Admiral Apraksin to arrange the following: within a zone extending from Pskov to Cherkassk and 180 miles deep, all grain and all cattle were to be hidden by early spring, so that if the enemy penetrated the region "he will not find a thing anywhere."[140] If Peter had contented himself with this he still would have been conducting a mere war of negative aim, that is, a war in which the objective was survival and survival alone. Yet Peter always expected that the campaign would end with a battle. The battle would be fought, however, only after privation and need had so weakened the Swedish army that Russia's forces could engage it with some prospects of success. The idea was to wear the Swedes down—to freeze them, sicken them, and starve them—and by so doing to reduce their military efficiency to the Russian level. At first Peter thought he might be able to take to the offensive quite early; in his letter to Apraksin he spoke of taking the Swedes from behind, apparently not too long after they had crossed the Russo-Polish border.[141] Peter shortly realized that such an attack would be premature; general battle would have to be indefinitely postponed to allow attrition to do its work.

And work it did. The Swedish army already experienced a severe dearth of provisions while still in Poland. When Charles crossed the Berezina and entered Russia proper in June 1708, the food situation grew worse. The advancing Swedes encountered ruined village after ruined village: Peter's soldiers would warn the peasants to flee, then burn everything—huts, furniture, and food—that could not be carried away.[142] Even when the Swedes reached the Ukraine they were denied any benefit from its agricultural riches. If Swedish troops dispersed to forage, the probability was high that they would be massacred by one of Peter's cavalry patrols. In September 1708, captured Swedish soldiers reported, "they have no provisions, and dare not go out for any because of the cozacks and the kalmucks; their chief diet was cabbage and turnips and that without bread and salt."[143] The supply of even these meager vegetables was precarious; most commonly they were obtained through the good fortune of stumbling across buried food hoards.[144]

Although Charles had not imagined the full extent of the victualing crisis, he had to some extent foreseen that provisions would be scarce. Löwenhaupt's mission, after all, had been to conduct an enormous wagon train laden with food from the Baltic to the Ukraine. The food under Löwenhaupt's charge— enough to sustain the entire field army for two months—was the irreducible minimum Charles needed to keep his forces together.[145] That was why the battle of Lesnaia had such strategic significance. By capturing all of Löwenhaupt's baggage, Peter the Great had ruled out the last-minute deliverance of the Swedish army from want. That, combined with the destruction of Mazeppa's grain reserve at Baturin, meant that there was no way for Charles to arrest the inexorable deterioration of his troops. Fever, dysentery, and cold now vied with hunger in tormenting the Swedes. The winter of 1708–9 was the bitterest anyone could remember; in December 1708 more than one thousand Swedes froze to death in a single night.[146]

When Charles met Peter at Poltava the following summer, he

was not in command of the same Swedish army he had led into Russia fourteen months before. In the first place, half of his soldiers were already dead. Whereas Charles's original army of invasion had numbered over 41,000, there were fewer than 19,000 on its rolls by June 1709.[147] The survivors were themselves suffering from fatigue, disease, and emaciation. There was almost no cavalry. Because so many of their horses had died, most of Charles's squadrons fought dismounted. There was scarcely any artillery either. Owing to a lack of draft power and the shortage of powder, Charles had spiked and abandoned the majority of his cannon long before. Whereas Charles had but four guns at Poltava, Peter had seventy-two. That disparity itself goes a long way toward explaining the outcome of the battle. Indeed, Charles's one bid for even partial victory (Löwenhaupt's attack on the Russian fortified camp) was lost in the smoke of artillery salvoes as Peter's batteries cut Löwenhaupt's troops to pieces.[148]

Peter's troops may themselves have been hungry and ragged, but the outnumbered Swedes they confronted at Poltava were still worse off. In order to compensate for Russian military inferiority and to give an edge to his untrained army, Peter had used Russia itself as a weapon, converting the vast distances, poor agricultural productivity, and insalubrious climate into the instruments of Charles's destruction. Of course, only a fool would accept this style of attritional warfare if there were any other choice. But the point is that Peter had no other choice, given the quality and characteristics of the army his military system had provided him. Peter knew that the typical Russian soldier could not outshoot or outmaneuver his Swedish counterpart, but perhaps he could outlast him. Even if he could not, it was no catastrophe, for he could readily be replaced, owing to the extraordinary capacity of Peter's conscription network to generate fresh drafts of peasant manpower.

Peter, of course, was not infallible. He was throughout his life guilty of numerous political, military, and diplomatic mistakes, never more so than after 1709. His total mismanagement of the Prut campaign stemmed from overconfidence and muddy thinking. And his policies toward the north German petty states in the last years of his reign were contrived, contradictory, and the source of more evil than good. But Peter did win his Swedish war, and he did it largely because he grasped the fact that Russian backwardness could be the font of tremendous military power. The very things that made Russia backward and underdeveloped by comparison with Western Europe—autocracy, serfdom, poverty—could paradoxically translate into armed might. The ruthless application of autocratic power could mobilize the Russian economy for war. The result may not have been a cornucopia of foodstuffs and goods, but it was just enough to sustain protracted war. Similarly, because rural Russia was so unfree it could be tapped for money and, most important, for men. It did not matter that the recruits were raw, that rations were short, that equipment was missing. The peasant conscripts were already inured to hardship, and there were more where they came from.

There is no reason to suppose that Peter the Great was happy about the high rate of attrition in his army. But Peter could afford casualties and desertions on a scale other monarchs could not. Mercenaries were expensive, and the kings who employed them were understandably loath to lose many of them. Sweden, of course, had a conscript army of its own, which was one reason why that small country could be so militarily formidable. But by the time of Charles XII the Swedish conscription system was operating at almost its maximum capacity, given demographic realities. Charles therefore could not tolerate many casualties either. By contrast, Peter's soldiers were dispensable as individuals; because of Russia's enormous pool of "bound" peasants, new armies could always be raised. Quantity in this case could substitute for quality. "To thyself be sufficient," says Ibsen's troll king. That might aptly be applied as a motto to Peter's entire military system, a system that could never produce overwhelming Russian military superiority, given the sparse resources that underpinned it, but *could* produce military sufficiency in the cheapest possible way.

Crucial to that sufficiency was Peter's adaptation of strategy to suit the low capabilities of his malnourished, unskilled army. In a set piece battle, entrench and make the enemy come to you. If battle must be avoided, retreat, challenge the enemy to a duel of attrition, and let him exhaust himself wandering through the expanses of barren Russia. On the offensive, use superior numbers to capture strategically important positions, thus severing the enemies lines of supply, communication, and retreat. Simultaneously, employ bodies of picked troops for surprise attacks on the enemy's flanks, or for strategic ambushes of entire enemy formations.

Peter the Great did not create the Russian regular army, but such an army was one of the most important legacies he left his successors. It was only under them that the tax, recruiting, and logistical systems started operating as Peter had initially intended. Once that happened, the Russian army improved and became truly regular. Its offensive power increased, and Russia won victory after victory. But even the regular army bore the stamp of its irregular Petrine origins. Because of Peter's success, his successors understood that autocracy and serfdom equaled military power. That, of course, impeded social and political change—who would want to tinker with something that worked? Peter did partially modernize Russia because of military necessity, but the very magnitude of his military accomplishments was a sturdy barrier against further reform for well over a century. Thus, if it is true that military policy was an instrument of progress, a motor of Russian history, it is equally true that the policy has also served as a brake.

3

Russian Imperialism and Military Power in the Eighteenth Century

Obstacles

As we saw in the previous chapter, Peter the Great defeated his enemies at the cost of nearly bleeding Russia white. Given the extraordinary human and material costs of the Petrine campaigns, it was obvious that Russia had a desperate need for peace. But such was not to be. From Peter's death in 1725 to Paul I's accession in 1796, Russia fought nine major wars. There were three wars with Turkey (1735–39, 1769–74, and 1787–92); two with Sweden (1741–43 and 1788); and three waged over Poland (1733–35, 1763, and 1795), in addition to the massive struggle against the Prussia of Frederick the Great (1757–62). This, of course, is to say nothing of the involvement of the Russian army in punitive expeditions, servile insurrections, and preventative mobilizations. Even when Russia was not at war, it lived constantly under its threat.

Russian soldiers and sailors operated across vast distances on three continents, from Alaska and the Pacific coast of Asia to the heart of Western Europe. They were deployed on the Kamchatka Peninsula, garrisoning the important Port of Petropavlovsk in Avacha Bay.[1] On two occasions, in 1735 and 1748, Russian armies marched the length of Germany from the Vistula to the Rhine.[2] And at the end of September 1760 General Totleben led the ten thousand Russian troops under his command into the city of Berlin as its conquerors.[3]

The Russian army evacuated Berlin after an occupation of only three days; East Prussia, which Russia had declared annexed, was handed back to its Hohenzollern sovereign in 1762. Russia's participation in the Seven Years War, then, did not bring it territorial benefit. But that was the exception. On almost all other occasions, Russia took advantage of its victories to engage in unprecedented territorial expansion; Russian frontiers rolled outward to the north, west, and south. Slices of Finland, Little Russia, vast lands north of the Black Sea, chunks of Poland, Bashkiria—all fell under the sway of St. Petersburg in the seventy years after Peter's death. It has been estimated that from 1750 to 1791 alone, the Russian Empire grew by 8.6 million square miles. The population of the empire, which had numbered 14 million in 1722, stood at 36 million in 1796.[4] Nor was that all. As the Russian state expanded, so too did its political and diplomatic influence over events hundreds of miles from its frontiers. During the eighteenth century the government of St. Petersburg availed itself of this influence, among other things, to impose its own candidate as King of Sweden; to win a protectorate over the affairs of the Christians in the Ottoman Empire; to mediate an end of a war between Austria and Prussia; and to form an anti-British league of "armed neutrality" during the American Revolution.[5]

The growth of the Russian Empire in this, its golden age of imperialism, was beyond question spectacular. Indeed, some scholars have been so dazzled by it that have depicted Russia's expansion in this period as an inevitable process justified by the laws of history itself—as a stately triumphal march.[6] What that sort of historical judgement obscures, of course, is the fact that Russia built its empire through a series of protracted, bloody, and hazardous struggles. To contemporaries, both in St. Petersburg and in the other European capitals, Russia's eighteenth-century expansion most definitely did not appear foreordained. Consider Catherine the Great's first Turkish war (1768–74). In hindsight that war must surely be deemed one of the most successful Russia ever waged. Yet at the time the outcome seemed in doubt. A British diplomat, William Richardson, believed in 1769 that a Russian defeat was not unlikely; in that event he anticipated a coup against the Empress.[7] And Baron de Vioménil, a military officer whom the French government dispatched to Poland to assist the anti-Russian confederation of Bar, wrote in December 1771 that Catherine would soon have to sue for a profitless peace, because the war was absorbing "too much money and too many men."[8]

There are always several "possible futures" gestating in the womb of history at any given time. The growth of the Russian Empire neither appeared to be nor was in fact inevitable. Of course, this assertion cannot be proved or disproved, but a very simple mental experiment can perhaps enhance its credibility. When considering the degree to which any historical event was "inevitable," it is useful to try to construct scenarios that lead to radically different outcomes. For example, it is extremely difficult to conceive of a set of circumstances after the start of World War I under which something akin to the February Revolution of 1917 would *not* have taken place. On the other hand, it is extremely easy to imagine conditions under which Russia's eighteenth-century growth might have been stunted or even halted: battles could readily have gone the other way; key leaders could have dropped dead; noncombatant rivals could have co-operated more efficiently to block Russian ambitions, and so forth.

Such an argument may seem to slight the influence of great impersonal forces in the rise and decline of empires. What of the correlation of economics and resources, for example?[9] In the next chapter, when we consider the reasons behind Russian success, economics will certainly receive their due. But the burgeoning economy of Russia was but a precondition, not a determinant, of the empire's aggrandizement. Economic resources (as well as all others) must be translated into power by human agency. It is therefore my contention that the expansion of Russia was not so much the product of macrohistorical forces (Westernization, modernization, absolutism, mercantilism, the Enlightenment, and so on) as the result of the actions of people themselves. Autocrats and generals, merchants and diplomats, common soldiers and peasants—what they did (and did not do) determined the fate of Russia. Mines had to be opened, keels laid down, taxes paid, armies organized, campaign plans devised, victories achieved, treaties concluded. If Russia grew almost incontinently in the eighteenth century it is because it won the wars and frequently won the peaces as well.

Russia's achievements in this period must therefore be judged all the more remarkable insofar as enormous indigenous and

RUSSIAN EXPANSION UNDER CATHERINE THE GREAT 1762-1796

B a r e n t s   S e a

White Sea

●ARCHANGEL

FINLAND

●HELSINGFORS

Baltic
Sea

●PSKOV

NOVGOROD ●VOLOGDA   ●VIATKA   ●PERM

KURLAND

Neman   TVER ●

VILNA
LITHUANIA   MOSCOW   KAZAN   ●UFA
●MINSK

PRUSSIA

WARSAW●   WHITE RUSSIA   STAVROPOL● ●SAMARA

AUSTRIA   PODLESIA   ●OREL

KIEV●
Dnieper   ●BELGOROD

Dniester   PODOLIA

JASSY ●   ●TAGANROG
ODESSA●   ASTRAKHAN●

KUCHUK   CRIMEA   KUBAN
KAINARDZHI SEBASTOPOL●   KABARDA

Black Sea   ●TARKI

THE   CONSTANTINOPLE●   Caspian
OTTOMAN   Sea

EMPIRE   ●KARS

0   200   ▨ Territory annexed by
                      Russia 1762-1796   PERSIA
Miles

exogenous constraints on Russian diplomacy, strategy, and combat effectiveness existed. The long list of such things almost compiles itself: the structure of international politics; the innate security problems of the empire; the continuous poverty of the state; the climatic, geographic, and agricultural characteristics of the theaters of war; peculiarities of the military manpower system; and, finally, the fractured, unstable, and faction-ridden governments at home. In this chapter we shall examine those formidable obstacles. Only by doing so can we appreciate the true magnitude of Russia's accomplishment.

International Politics in the Eighteenth Century

It is often alleged that war and diplomacy in eighteenth-century Europe were governed by the concept of the balance of power. In this view the European states that had cooperated so efficiently to puncture the hegemonic ambitions of Hapsburg Spain and Louis XIV's France eventually came to realize that their security was mutual and interdependent. Consequently, the significant European powers—Austria, Russia, Prussia, France, Spain and Britain—adopted a new set of tacit "rules of conduct" in international relations. Alliance systems had to be balanced off against each other to ensure a general European equilibrium so that no one state or group of states could gain the upper hand. If a state made territiorial gains, for example as a result of war, neighboring states had to be offered territorial compensation in the interest of mutual satisfaction. Vacuums of power had to filled by means of amicable agreements between interested parties. Although the powers waged war among themselves, those wars were usually limited, fought with less than total effort and waged for limited objectives. War itself became less bloody and more humane, as maneuver and siegecraft often took the place of pitched battles. What upheld the European stability, then, was the general convergence of interest on the part of the great monarchs. Coolly rational and admirably innocent of religious, national, or ideological fanaticism, those princes cooperated more often than not, swapping provinces with each other like newspaper recipes.[10] Such an interpretation of the balance, however, is heavily sanitized and excessively idealistic.

To be sure, the language of the "balance of power" was often on the lips of eighteenth-century Europeans. Political philosophers and scholars, for instance, spoke about the theory of the balance of power all the time.[11] And statesmen themselves often invoked the concept of the balance. Writing to the Austrian Emperor Joseph II in 1774, Catherine the Great characterized the recent partition of Poland among Russia, Prussia, and Austria in the following manner: it had been "inspired by the purpose of balancing all three of them by means of an equal accession to the power of each."[12] Later in the century, Prussia justified its alliance with Ottoman Turkey in 1790 "because of the prejudice which enemies have brought to the necessary and desired balance of power."[13] But such ritualistic and formulaic genuflections to the "balance of power" did not reflect a state's principled allegiance to an abstract code of international law; rather, this rhetoric usually served to cloak sordid deeds in the raiment of morality.

For the great states of Europe the balance may have been occasionally necessary, but it was rarely desired. International politics in the eighteenth century were dynamic, not static. Throughout the period states schemed constantly to rupture the balance. What is perhaps surprising is that so many of them succeeded: Britain overmastered France in the struggle for colonial empire; Russia enlarged itself at the expense of Sweden, Turkey, and Poland; Prussia despoiled Austria of the rich province of Silesia. In short, balances of power were continually collapsing and being reestablished. And what created the new balances was not the harmonious confluence of the interests of the Powers, but the collision of their greed and fear. European politics became more integrated and consequently more complex. What happened, say, in Portugal was the concern not only of the Iberian states, France, and Britain but of all the remaining governments of Europe as well.

Just as in the previous century, Russia still confronted the problem of the intertwining interests of its traditional enemies: Turkey, Poland, and Sweden. For example, Turkey declared war on Russia in 1768 in large part because of apprehensions about Russia's increasing dominance over Poland. Even after that war had been lost, the Turks remained keenly attuned to Russian activities there; as an Ottoman Ambassador noted in 1775, the claim of Russian military commanders that they were merely "guests" in Poland hardly squared with their usurpation of sovereignty in the frontier districts of the country.[14] During Catherine's second war with the Porte, Stockholm's alarm at Russian victories led to a treaty of alliance between Sweden and Turkey. The resulting outbreak of hostilities with the Swedes in 1789 aborted Russia's plans to use the Baltic fleet against Turkey in the Mediterranean, thereby forcing a rapid end to the war.[15]

But the increasing general linkage of European diplomacy now meant that Russia had to confront the ill will and animus of rivals other than its immediate neighbors. Prussia, for example, had no common frontier with the Russian Empire until later in the century, but during the war of the Polish succession (1733) Berlin at first denied a Russian siege train bound for Danzig permission to cross East Prussian territory.[16] In that case, the inconvenience was only temporary, for the Prussians eventually relented, the Russian artillery reached its destination, and Danzig fell. On many other occasions, Russia faced far more malign and determined opposition; perhaps the most important from the government of France.

During much of the eighteenth century, a standard feature of French policy was the attempt to fashion what was described as a "barrier" against Russia, composed of Sweden, Poland, and Turkey. There were a variety of reasons for the anti-Russian posture of Paris. For one, Louis XV was married to the daughter of Stanislas Leszcynski, the Pole who had briefly occupied the throne at Warsaw courtesy of Peter I's old enemy, Charles XII of Sweden. That nuptial bond tended to give France a natural *droit de regard* over Polish affairs, which was exploited most vigorously in 1733 when Paris went to war against Russia and Austria nominally in support of Stanislas's reinstatement as King of Poland.[17] Then too, a Russia in check could not meddle in German affairs and thereby spoil France's designs across the Rhine; equally, a successful barrier would prevent Russia from rendering any effective assistance whatsoever to any of France's enemies.

France therefore frequently made trouble for Russia. Paris often tried to manipulate Stockholm and Constantinople into making war on Russia, furnished those capitals with material assistance, and urged them to persevere even in defeat. For example, France helped to goad the Turks into a Russian war in 1736 and the Swedes into one in 1741.[18] In 1774, when Constantinople craved peace after six calamitous years of yet another war against Russia, France tried to pressure the Turks into fighting on anyway.[19] Thirteen years later, when hostilities between Turkey and Russia flared up anew, Paris bolstered the Ottoman forces with picked contingents of French artillery instructors and engineers.[20]

Nor was France the only West European power that Russian had occasion to fear. Russia and Britain enjoyed good relations for most of the century; indeed, Russia looked to Britain as a source for lucrative trade, superior naval technology, and unrivaled seagoing expertise. At various times St. Petersburg entrusted such British naval officers as Grieg and Bentham (Jeremy's brother) with the command of ships of the line and entire fleets. But in 1787 the government of the Younger Pitt inaugurated a policy of backing Turkey up against the Russians. London sent the Turks naval assistance, took an anti-Russian line in Stockholm, and even threatened the Russian Empire with war.[21] Whenever Russian forces were too successful in the field, whenever it appeared that Russian gains as the result of a war were going to be too large, Russia's European rivals conspired against Russia's interests. They tried to overextend Russia by creating security threats on different frontiers of the empire; proffered scarcely disinterested offers of "mediation" between Russia and its enemies; issued hostile ultimatums; and colluded to force Russia to disgorge some of what it had taken.[22]

Statesmen and generals in St. Petersburg consequently had to worry about how governments in every quarter of Europe would react to the aggrandizement of the Russian Empire; latent ill-will, if not blatant envy and full-blown hostility, had to be presumed. But Russia was not only burdened with the enmity of avowed foes and the intrigues of technical "neutrals," for it also suffered much at the hands of its friends as well. After all, the foundations of international politics in the eighteenth century were crude self-interest and the relentless struggle for power. In that environment, treachery on the part of allies was axiomatic, all the more so since for most of the period there was no state with enough strength to make a serious bid for total continental hegemony. Had that been the case, alliance partners might have been frightened into greater cooperation and cohesion as, for example, had happened when Louis XIV had terrorized Europe. But as matters stood, alliances (particularly wartime ones) were unstable, with each of the contracting parties attempting to cheat and manipulate the others for its own marginal advantage. Treaties were made to be broken.

Perhaps the most egregious violator of international agreements in the entire century was Prussia's Frederick the Great, whose disavowal of the Pragmatic Sanction—basically a solemn pledge to respect the integrity of the Austrian Empire after the death of Charles VI—plunged Europe into ruinous wars in 1740 and 1756.[23] But almost every other important monarch shared Frederick's insensitivity to international law at least to some extent. Certainly, Russia often had reason to rue the duplicitous conduct of its allies.

After the death of Peter the Great, Russia entered into a treaty of alliance and mutual support with the Austrian Empire. For a time the two courts worked well together: they collaborated during the struggle over the Polish succession and when Turkey declared war on Russia in 1736, Austria, accepting the latter as a *casus foederis,* opened a front of its own against the Ottomans. The campaign, to which we shall return later in this chapter, was enormously difficult and costly for Russia. After four years of war, however, when the Russian occupation of Moldavia was finally on the verge of compelling the Turks to capitulate, Austria sold out its ally by concluding the separate treaty of Belgrade. The abandoned Russians were consequently forced to settle for a peace much less satisfactory than the one to which they believed their victories had entitled them.[24]

Nor was that an isolated episode. Some years later the famous "reversal of alliances" of 1756 occurred, leaving almost all the important European states except Britain ganged up against the Prussia of Frederick the Great. Russia and France consequently found themselves allied against Prussia in the Seven Years War.[25] Yet from the very beginning of that struggle, Paris set itself the task of working *against* Russia's war objectives. Then, after the Seven Years War was over, Petersburg entered into an alliance with its former enemy, Berlin. The treaty was designed to be a part of the "Northern System"—a league of northern and maritime powers that Russia hoped to use to counterbalance Spain, France, and, most particularly, Austria. When Russia's policies in

Poland induced Turkey to declare war (1768), Prussia was not contractually obligated to render Russia direct military aid. Russia nonetheless had every legal right to expect Berlin to guard it against a possible surprise attack from Vienna. Frederick the Great, however, violated the spirit if not the letter of the alliance by holding secret meetings with Austrian representatives in September 1770. There he pledged himself to assist Austria in limiting Russian territorial acquisitions to the extent of promising his neutrality should Vienna make war on St. Petersburg.[26]

Yet sometimes it took the accession of new rulers to unravel Russia's alliances. In 1781 Russia signed a defensive treaty against Turkey with the Austrian Empire. Joseph II of Austria swore that he would support Russia fully in the event of a Turkish war. He also pledged himself never to conclude a separate treaty with the Turkish foe, adding that this promise would be binding on his heirs and successors.[27] When the Turks cast the Russian Ambassador into a dungeon in 1787 (the traditional Ottoman method of declaring war), the Austrians fulfilled their obligations to St. Petersburg. Although he grew privately impatient with the burden of this protracted struggle, Joseph continued publicly to play the role of dutiful ally.[28] When he died in February 1790, however, the new Emperor, Leopold, tore up the Russian treaty and led Austria out of the war.[29]

Russia's allies as well as its rivals and overt enemies could therefore prove to be sources of the gravest peril. The paradox was that the more brillant and conspicuous Russia's military victories, and the more it appeared that Russia would emerge from a war with great gains, the more likely it was that "neutral" states would intervene and that Russia's allies would betray it. That, of course, obviously hampered the effective exercise by Russia of its military and diplomatic power. Yet a no less serious constraint on Russian strategy was the inherent security problem of the empire itself.

Russia's Security Dilemma

By the early eighteenth century Russia's thousands of miles of borders were already more extensive and consequently more difficult to police than those of any other European power. The

Russian government confronted potential threats from Sweden and Turkey and also shared contested frontiers with Persia and China. Then, too, St. Petersburg had to be on guard against incursions and large-scale raids on the part of numerous tribes of steppe nomads.

This latter danger was a particularly vexatious headache. How could vast expanses of thinly populated territory be protected against the depredations of nomads whose art of war was based on mobility, stealth, and surprise?

That question haunted some of Russia's best military intellects in the period. Of special concern was the security of Russia's Ukrainian possessions, a traditional hunting ground for Crimean Tatars in search of slaves and booty. In the 1720s and 1730s the Russian state experimented with noncontinuous perimeter defenses: a loose chain of forts was constructed along the most dangerous stretches of the frontier, while the majority of the troops in the region were detailed to those forts as garrisons. Unfortunately, the Russian government discovered that such defenses were really quite permeable; the Tatar army was prevented from penetrating the Ukrainian line and irrupting into southern Russia in 1739, but only barely. Thereafter, military commanders in the Ukrainian sector of the empire tried a defense in depth. The bulk of the army was withdrawn to Kiev to serve as a reserve force, while the frontier was placed under the observation of guard posts spaced roughly 7 miles apart. Each post was equipped with three enormous pyramids of pitch-soaked wood. One signal fire was to be lit if the post learned that the enemy was approaching; two, if the enemy was in sight; and all three were to be ignited if the post was actually under attack. In that last event the ten to forty men of the post were probably doomed to be slaughtered, but it was hoped that their warning would provide the time sufficient to concentrate the forces to rebuff the Tatar invaders.[30]

All of the defenses that Russia devised for the Ukraine had one thing in common, despite their dissimilarities, for they all depended upon adequate reserves of military manpower. Moats and fosses, redans and stockades, guard posts and fortresses—none were useful unless held by enough men. Russia's military deployments illustrate just how serious the combined Turkish and Tatar threat in the south was thought to be: until 1772, twenty-seven regiments—a full quarter of Russia's active duty army—were permanently stationed in the Ukraine.[31] Nor was the Ukrainian line the only one that the Russian Empire maintained. During the 1730s and 1740s Russia's increasing sensitivity about border security resulted in the construction or upgrading of seven additional fortified lines north of the Caucasus, in the southern Urals, and in Siberia.[32] Many of those lines were still being staffed at the end of the reign of Catherine the Great, for in most cases the difference between exercising sovereignty over territories and merely laying claim to them was military occupation.[33]

Russia's successful expansion during the eighteenth century also mandated more extensive troop deployments. As Field Marshal P.A. Rumiantsev, one of Russia's most gifted commanders, noted in a memorandum of 1777, the Russian Empire had to observe the salutary rule of "possessing superiority in forces, especially in newly conquered regions."[34] In the circumstances, it is scarcely surprising that the Russian army grew in numbers. On the eve of the Seven Years War in 1756 the army of the Empress Elizabeth Petrovna comprised 172,000 field troops, a garrison force of 74,000, 27,000 members of the Ukrainian land militia, corps of engineers and artillerists totaling 12,000, and 43,000 irregulars. At that point the Russian army, stronger by 140,000 troops than it had been in 1731, was the largest in the world.[35]

Looked at from a different angle, however, the truly remarkable thing about Russia's eighteenth-century army was not that it was so big but rather that it was so small. Simply put, the army was overextended, overcommitted, and incapable of fulfilling the tasks with which it was charged despite its burgeoning size. For one thing, there were always brushfires to be stamped out within the empire itself, which placed a considerable strain on normal military deployments. For example, in 1756 more than half the cavalry in the Russian army had to be sent to Bashkiria to cope with a native insurrection there, a fact that goes a long way toward explaining why St. Petersburg was so slow to mobilize against Prussia.[36] The problem of overcommitment, an open sore in peace, became a serious infection in wartime. When Russia went to war, it could not simply denude its frontiers of troops to swell the ranks of the active army, for it would have been imprudent if not idiotic to ignore the possibility of diversionary attacks. The planning for each of Russia's three major Turkish

wars in the eighteenth century invariably began with tsarist statesmen pondering the ways in which a field army could be concentrated without leaving the borders defenseless.[37]

There were other perils connected with concentrating the
army. The local civilian bureaucratic apparatus of Russia in the
eighteenth century was weak and rudimentary. There were
fewer than five thousand full-time bureaucrats for all the provinces of the empire.[38] In a very real sense, then, the peacetime
military *was* the provincial administration of Russia, for it bore
the brunt of tax collection and was the state's only real defense
against banditry and rebellion. To accumulate forces for a foreign war meant to run the risk of leaving the empire dangerously
undergoverned. The costs of the Seven Years War for Russia
included not only blood and treasure but also the nearly total
collapse of state authority on the local level.[39] The same thing
happened again during Catherine the Great's first Turkish War,
with even direr results, for on that occasion the removal of the
army from the provinces made possible the huge peasant uprising of Emelian Pugachev, which enveloped the entire Volga basin
from 1773 to 1775. When her second war with Turkey broke out
in August 1787, Catherine told members of her Council of State
that she "had no intention of touching those regiments that were
located within the state, knowing what inconveniences had been
produced from their removal in the past war."[40] What this sample of royal understatement refers to is quite obvious: the chief
"inconvenience" that Catherine had in mind was the Pugachev
rebellion.

The Russian army, then, possessed a host of conflicting missions, and it was no easy task to resolve the tensions among them.
How to reconcile the internal and external drains on the troops
became one of the biggest themes in the military policy of the
period. Many of Russia's most talented statesmen drafted proposals for "ideal" military deployments that they hoped would strike
a balance among all those needs. Catherine's favorite, the one-
eyed lecher, amateur theologian, and brilliant administrator
Prince G. A. Potemkin sponsored exactly such a proposal in
1785.[41] Russia, he argued, should organize four armies: three to
guard against Turkey, Prussia, and Sweden, respectively, and a
fourth to serve as a reserve in the event of sudden war or domestic disturbance.[42] Rumiantsev devised his own plan in a memoran-

dum of 1777. There he spoke of the need to deploy troops "taking into account internal and external security and economy."[43] Rumiantsev's last comment introduces us to yet another problem that bedeviled Russian strategists, for Russia's ability to conduct its foreign policy or wage war was circumscribed by the barrenness of the treasury.

The Poverty of the State

Eighteenth-century Russian history affords us numerous violent and striking contrasts: between the fabulous riches of the Sheremet'ev family and the wretched penury of most serfs; between the cruel public mutilation of Volynskii and the maudlin sentimentalism of Radischchev; between the fashionable atheism of Catherine II's court and the stolid piety of the Old-Believer patriarch Andrei Denisov; between the barbaric sack of Ochakov and the courteous "occupation" of Berlin. The balls and masquerades at the court of the Empress Anna, a historian tells us, were characterized by a "mixture of luxury and tastelessness, magnificence and filth"; the lavish robes and jewels that adorned the courtiers could not always conceal the dirty rags they wore beneath.[44]

Clearly one of the greatest among those paradoxical contrasts is the fact that the Russian Empire grew so powerful on such a skimpy resource base. Russia, of course, was predominantly an agrarian country; over 90 percent of Russia's population consisted of peasants.[45] The peasants were engaged in a labor-intensive agriculture whose productivity was severely limited by inadequate tools, poor techniques of cultivation, and the vagaries of climate.[46] It has been calculated that there were at least thirty-four general or partial crop failures in the course of the century.[47] Yet it was from this precarious and chronically undernourished rural society that the Russian state had to extract its wealth.

Peter the Great, of course, had enjoyed considerable success in squeezing the peasants to the maximum. But we have already had occasion to note the results: massive peasant flight and enormous tax arrears. Peter's level of pressure on the village could not be kept up indefinitely. After Peter's death the Supreme Privy Council grew so alarmed by the excessive burdening of the peasants that it (briefly) withdrew the army from the countryside to the towns and decreed a steep cut in the soul tax.[48] On that occasion Count Osterman, the durable Westphalian who served four of Russia's rulers, demonstrated a keen insight into the relationship between military strength and rural society. Precisely because the Russian army was so essential to the survival of the state, he insisted that the state had to be solicitous of the peasantry. "When the army is so necessary to the state that it cannot endure without it, then it is necessary to be concerned for the peasants, since the soldier is joined with the peasant as the soul is with the body, and when there are no peasants, there are no soldiers."[49] Nor, he might have added, any taxes either. The hope was that the peasants, freed of the obligation to quarter troops and presented with a lower tax rate, might be more inclined to comply with the state's demands rather than resist them.

That hope, however, was not fulfilled. Throughout the entire second quarter of the eighteenth century state revenues from direct and indirect taxation showed almost no increase at all.[50] Yet arrears continued to mount. During the reign of the Empress Anna (1730–40) they resulted in an average annual deficit of 13–18 percent. Matters were still worse under Anna's successor, Elizabeth Petrovna (1741–62). In 1747, worried about the prospect of war with Sweden, Elizabeth convened a commission to investigate the fiscal health of the state. The commission's dismal findings were that although the annual state income of the Empire was supposed to be 4 million to 5 million rubles, only 3.5–3.9 million were ever collected, which meant the deficit was conceivably as high as 30 percent.[51]

Revenues did rise in the 1750s, for the government raised the soul tax and indirect tax rates and realized still other profits through a debasement of the coinage.[52] But expenses—many of them connected with war—increased still more rapidly. For example the bill for Russia's participation in the Seven Years War amounted to 31 million rubles.[53] Catherine the Great (1762–96) had the same economic headaches as her predecessors: her first Turkish war had produced a deficit of more than 9 million rubles by 1772.[54] By then the government had come to despair of most orthodox methods of balancing income and outgo; increasingly it took to financing itself with foreign loans and unbacked paper assignats, of which some 20 million were in circulation by the middle of the decade.[55] At home, Gresham's Law went into effect: the paper notes drove the intrinsically more valuable metal coins into the hands of hoarders, and a considerable inflation ensued. Russians also found that foreigners became leery of accepting the paper bills, which is the chief reason that the generals commanding Russian forces in Poland in the spring of 1770 begged St. Petersburg "not to send them assignats, but money."[56]

For all of the eighteenth century, then, the Russian government was starved for cash. The fact of Russia's financial weakness (and at times virtual insolvency) had an enormous impact on its soldiers, for it shaped the conditions of their existence in both peace and war, determining the quantity and quality of the food they ate, the weapons they fired, and the horses they rode. Often quantity was small and quality was low. For example, in 1729 Major General Kampengauzen made an inspection tour of seven regiments. He reported that the Kargopol' dragoons had had no shoes, boots, stockings, or shirts issued for the previous three years. The entire Beloozero infantry regiment, he said, was "naked and barefoot" with the result that it was incapable of marching or indeed of any other kind of work. Units that had been lucky enough to receive equipment found it to be shoddy or rotten; there were hats from which glue dripped after the slightest rain shower and sword belts that disintegrated after the first washing.[57] Doubtless corruption played a part in this state of affairs, but the largest part was played by the poverty of the state.

Poverty also helps to account for the generally dreadful condition of the cavalry in this period. The Russian government could afford to pay the regiments forage money for the purchase of hay only during the winter months. For the rest of the year the soldiers were supposed to tend to their horses' needs themselves, pasturing them wherever possible. But grass and tree bark were not as nourishing as hay. Still further, grass itself was not really abundant in various quarters of the empire, *particularly* those with a high concentration of cavalry. As a result, Russian military horses were often runty and weak—incapable of traveling as far or bearing loads as heavy as horses fed the more wholesome diet of Western Europe.[58] In 1731 Field Marshal Count Münnich proposed to outfit three of Russia's regiments of dragoons as cuirassiers. Unfortunately, a cuirrassier's equipment, including the metal breastplate, was extremely heavy. Christopher Hermann von Manstein, a Prussian officer in the Russian service, noted that "Russia itself not affording horses strong enough to remount a heavy cavalry, there was a necessity for buying them out of Holstein."[59] A year later, when Münnich wanted to convert a full half of Russia's cavalry into cuirassiers, the Russian Senate strongly objected to his plan, explaining that "in the Russian state it is so difficult to find suitable domestic horses for cuirassiers that it is almost impossible." Buying enough German horses, the Senate continued, was out of the question: they were far too expensive.[60]

Lack of money not only limited the sort of forces the Russian Empire could deploy, but also resulted in the neglect of basic maintenance. A good illustration is the decay of the Russian navy. In the later stages of the Great Northern War, Peter the Great had built or captured fifty-three ships-of-the-line, the eighteenth-century equivalent of battleships. In 1725 Russia's Baltic fleet alone included twenty-five of them. But in 1756, on the eve of the Seven Years War, St. Petersburg had only twenty-six serviceable vessels in the Baltic, and most of them were not major combatants, but frigates and smaller craft.[61]

Finances being what they were, the Russian government was not even able to guarantee that each soldier in the ranks of its army would be furnished with a musket. General Count Petr Ivanovich Shuvalov worked out a "General Instruction on the Yearly Induction of Recruits" in 1757. In it he included the following order to local military officials: "[I]n the event of an insufficient supply of real muskets give [the recruits] wooden ones."[62] That such an "event" was not all that rare even in wartime is confirmed by other sources, including a report filed by Rumianstev from Germany in January 1758 that spoke of regiments in which "there are a considerable number of people without guns."[63]

Indeed, it was the pressure of war that all too often overtaxed a financial system that was barely functional in peace. Throughout the century Russian generals would frequently have reason to complain that the money they needed to pay the operating expenses of wartime was either disbursed tardily or never at all. For example, in May 1739, when campaigning against the Turks, Field Marshal Münnich was so short of funds that he was unable to pay his officers the salaries due them for the third of the year

that had begun the previous January. As for the common soldiers, it is unclear how long it had been since they had seen any
wages.[64] The Seven Years War also provides us with other dismay-
ing illustrations of the weakness of the Russian fisc. General
Apraksin, who commanded the Russian army in 1757, required
500,000 rubles a month to buy food and forage from the Polish
peasantry along his route of march from the Russian borders to
Prussia. He was, however, provided with only 2 million rubles in
all. Although his forces began to cross the Dniepr river in February, he did not receive an an additional payment of 1 million
rubles until July. By that point, his field treasury was virtually
empty.[65] His hungry troops had no choice but to engage in whole-
sale looting to feed themselves. Sometimes fiscal distress could
produce stranger consequences still. In 1788 the Russian forces
operating in Poland were so short of funds that the Tsarist Council of State attempted to borrow the money necessary to pay for
the military occupation of Poland from Warsaw bankers.[66]

Chronic financial problems like these could not but have an
impact on Russia's foreign policy and even its troop deployments. For example, in the mid-1750s the Russian Chancellor of
State wanted to concentrate powerful Russian forces in the Baltic
districts of the country, anticipating the outbreak of a war with
Prussia. Yet that policy could not be implemented because of the
high price of foodstuffs in those regions. The same quarter of
rye that usually sold for a ruble in the vicinity of Moscow went
for 116 percent more in Kurland and Lifland. The Russian treasury could not afford those costs, which meant that a large Russian army could not be amassed in the north unless the state was
willing to see it disintegrate through starvation.[67]

The Seven Years War was doubtless the time of one of the two
or three severest fiscal crises Russia was to suffer through in the
course of the century. So great was the prospect of state bankruptcy that in November 1760 M. I. Vorontsov prepared a memorandum for Elizabeth's war cabinet in which he insisted in a
manner similar to his seventeenth-century forebears that Russia
had to have peace since it would soon simply run out of the
money necessary to continue the war.[68] Even after Russia left the
war in 1762, it continued to feel the after tremors of its fiscal
shocks. Nikita Panin, the architect of the "Northern System" to
which we have already referred, justified this foreign policy pro-

gram of the 1760s on the grounds that it would buy Russia the time necessary to repair its shattered finances. Panin's defensive confederation of northern courts was designed to preclude Petersburg's involvement, at least temporarily, in any expensive foreign policy adventures.[69] In October 1762 Panin sketched out his approach in a conversation with the French Ambassador, reassuring him that "the interests of Russia require that she occupy herself for many years only with the general reestablishment of all the parts of her internal administration which is in such a state of disorder as to demand prompt redress."[70] At that time, as well as later, an empty treasury could be a persuasive argument for a pacific foreign policy.

Given the magnitude of the state poverty and the iron necessity of maintaining a strong defense, it is hardly surprising that Russian statesmen throughout the eighteenth century preoccupied themselves with the attempt to find ways to bring the military budget into balance. We shall examine their taxation policies somewhat later, but it is useful here to pay attention to two of the techniques they tried: radical economizing and the quest for foreign subsidies. Both, it is fair to add, were fraught with dangers.

In 1727, for instance, the government established a special commission to investigate the possibility of reducing military expenditures. The committee proved unequal to the task, and a second was formed in the summer of 1730, which soon recommended that the military budget be cut by 570,000 rubles a year in peace and 360,000 rubles a year in the event of war. The proposal was adopted. The evidence does not reveal what criteria the commission used in arriving at those arbitrary figures; in any event, they were almost immediately scrapped. Military outlays actually increased in the 1730s, and there was really very little choice, given the six years of war in which Russia was involved during that decade.[71] Frugal intentions were worthless in the face of external threats. Then, too, there was always the risk that if programs of cost-slashing were strictly implemented, only false economies might result, for an underfunded, underfed, and undertrained army would probably be inadequate to the demands of battle should the empire be caught by war unawares.

The hunt for foreign subsidies presented different hazards. How could the Russian Empire conduct an independent foreign policy and still find someone to pay for it? In 1748, in exchange for substantial British payments, St. Petersburg sent 30,000 troops on a march to the Rhine. It is probably incorrect to argue that this represented the virtual "renting out" of its army by an impecunious Russian state; a strong case can be made that British and Russian interests paralleled each other on that occasion.[72] Yet this episode illustrates the fundamental problem of foreign subventions, for they came swaddled with qualifications and conditions. In July 1755 Russia opened negotiations for British financial support once again. The British promised to pay St. Petersburg £100,000 annually over the next four years to defray the upkeep of a Baltic army of 55,000 troops and fifty galleys. Should those forces be committed to war, London vowed to quintuple the subsidy.[73] What the British government expected to gain from the arrangement was a Russian commitment to defend George II's Hannoverian possessions against Prussian or French attack. The deal suited St. Petersburg as well, because Russia at the time was preparing to make war on Prussia. But in the aftermath of the Convention of Westminister and the "Reversal of Alliances," friendship bloomed between London and Berlin. When the English consequently tried to make the payment of the subsidy contingent on Russo-Prussian cooperation, Russia spurned the British treaty, being by then aligned with Paris and Vienna against Berlin. All of Russia's calculations concerning the German war had been predicated on the assumption that it could rely on English gold to cover the financial shortfall. Because last-minute diplomatic maneuvering had closed off this source of revenue, Russia resorted to fiscal improvisation in order to defray the costs of the Seven Years War.[74]

Russia's diplomats and generals continued to worry about the burden of military expenditure in later decades. In 1776, for instance, Potemkin and Rumiantsev coauthored a plan to establish military settlements in Russia populated by a substantial portion of the troops, who would feed themselves through their own husbandry.[75] Shortly thereafter Rumiantsev made yet another grandiose cost-cutting suggestion: a full third of the army, he said, should be sent home on furlough for nine months every year. Whether Rumiantsev ever thought through the problems such a system would surely engender is unclear; the logic of his explanation of the need for parsimony was, however, irreproachable: the "welfare of the service demands preparedness and exactness, but the welfare of the state in general requires that in peace every relief be given to the state and private economies, that the people be unburdened, and that the state treasury saves money."[76]

It is evident, then, that with regard to military expenditure Russia had to walk a very taut tightrope. In view of the manifold security threats it confronted, Russia felt that it could neither reduce the size of its army too much nor cut the funds appropriated for its support too steeply. To do so was potentially to leave the empire defenseless against foreign attack or domestic insurrection. The army and navy together soaked up 71 percent of all state expenditures in 1734; 63 percent in 1762, and still as much as 35 percent in 1796, when, as a result of territorial expansion and natural increase, the size of the taxable population was millions of people greater than it had been earlier in the century. After 1750 or so, Russia consistently maintained the world's largest standing army, although its revenues were probably less than 20 percent those of the French monarchy.[77] On the other hand, if Russia spent too much on defense it could also run the opposite risk of beggaring the rural society upon which its taxes, and ultimately its military power, absolutely depended. The calculus of state poverty consequently intruded itself into any Russian discussion of statecraft, diplomacy, or war.

The Costs of Campaigning in Eastern Europe

The cost of campaigning in Eastern Europe had to be counted not in currency alone, but in terms of human lives, horses, and matériel as well. We have already had occasion to disparage the popular caricature of eighteenth-century warfare as a tepid, bloodless sequence of maneuvers. Misleading enough with respect to wars on the western part of the continent (how, for instance, does it square with the butchery of Malplaquet?), it is simply preposterous to apply it to conflict in the east.[78] In Eastern Europe warfare was more sanguinary, more savage, more gruesome—in a word more costly—than it was in the West.

Sometimes the high mortality of East European war stemmed from the engagement of the religious passions of the belligerents. Russians and Turks, for example, were rarely inclined to give each other quarter or benefit of the "courtesies of war," believing as they did that the cause of religious truth itself was at stake in the struggle between Christianity and Islam. Certainly West European observers found warfare in the East rather different from what they were accustomed to. Richardson, the British diplomat, in a letter home in 1769, outlined the ways in which the ongoing Russo-Turkish war differed from warfare in the West:

> Fertile provinces rendered desolate; towns and villages in flames; numerous herds of cattle rapaciously driven away; the inhabitants butchered or carried into captivity, constitute the dreadful features of Russian and Tatarian warfare.[79]

That Richardson was not just letting a hyperactive imagination run riot is substantiated by the enormous number of undeniable atrocities the Turks and Russians perpetrated against each other. The mention of one such massacre will have to take the place of many. On December 6, 1788, Russian forces under the command of Prince Potemkin successfully stormed the Turkish fortress of Ochakov. The victorious army was allowed to loot, rape, and murder for three days. The frenzied Russian troops killed at least 10,000 Turkish men, women, and children in the course of this outrage. Even more macabre, since the suspension of discipline precluded organizing proper burial parties, most of the corpses froze solid where they lay and remained contorted in icy agony until the following spring.[80]

Religious prejudice by itself cannot explain the savagery of East European warfare, however. Even when the Russian army was not fighting Tatars or Turks, it tended to engage in pitched battle more frequently than Western armies. The casualty toll from those battles was, as a rule, higher as well. Consider the battle of Zorndorf, fought between Russia and Prussia on August 14, 1758. Here Russia lost 22,600 men—a full 60 percent of the forces it had committed. Of that number, 13,000 were killed outright. Prussia did not escape unscathed, either. More than 11,000 men—a third of Frederick the Great's army—were also slain.[81]

But the costs of war in Eastern Europe were greater than even the awesome body count from battles and atrocities can indicate, for the geographic, topographic, climatic, and demographic characteristics of the theaters of military operation there imposed substantive costs of their own. As we noted in Chapter 1, Russia had wrestled with those problems in the seventeenth century; in the eighteenth, they assumed still more dangerous proportions, precisely because Russia was attempting to *do more* with its armed forces than it had attempted in the past.

In order to get to the theater of war, a Russian army, after mustering, typically had to march hundreds of miles across desolate, underpopulated territories. And what did the terrain look like? To the south the approaches to the Crimea were guarded by 360 square miles that were, essentially, an inhospitable desert.[82] During his disastrous Crimean campaigns Prince Golitsyn had had occasion to discover exactly how arid the southern reaches of the steppe could be; in the 1730s Field Marshal Münnich actually employed camels (and regretted only that he did not have more of them).[83] The Wallachian and Moldavian plains, where Russian troops so often found themselves during Catherine the Great's Turkish wars, were transsected by numerous gorges and ravines. To the north, Finland (where most of the Russo-Swedish hostilities in the century took place) was a patchwork of lakes, swamps, and impenetrable forests. To the northwest, the Baltic lake zone impeded Russian access to Poland and East Prussia. And Prussia itself was a country pocked with rivers, marshes, and bogs.

Then there was the weather. The climates of the territories in which Russia campaigned were almost all insalubrious in one way or another. Winters, of course, were bitterly cold. Spring brought the dreaded *rasputitsa* or thaw, which turned the plains into oceans of mud. Freak rainstorms and flash floods were hazards of summer, especially in the southern theaters of war. Summer also brought burning heat, drought, and millions of swarming insects. Russian soldiers were successively forced to fight in almost every variety of unwholesome climate imaginable.[84]

The hostility of nature, the impediments of terrain, and the scarcity of population—all were constraints on Russian military operations in the eighteenth century. For one thing, bad weather could frequently impede (if not immobilize) the entire army. During the summer of 1739 Münnich had to halt his advance when sudden heavy rains caused the Dniestr to overflow, cutting his infantry off from the artillery and baggage marooned on the other side of the river.[85] Years later, General P. A. Rumiantsev ran into similar trouble at Ushpol' in Poland as a result of the *rasputitsa*. In a report of May 1757 to his superior, Rumiantsev spoke of "mud and swamps whose condition Your Excellency could not possibly imagine."[86] The Russians also suffered much from the climate during their Transdanubian campaign of 1773. They had to postpone the entire operation until May, since the spring thaw made the flooded waters of the Danube impassable. But almost at the moment the river had been crossed, rain gave way to intense heat that parched the soil and dried up even the largest of springs.[87] Rumiantsev's exceptionally successful campaign of the subsequent year (it finally forced Constantinople to sue for peace) was itself retarded by bad weather; Rumiantsev was unable to besiege the forts of Rushchuk and Silistriia until the middle of July owing, once again, to rainstorms and flooding.[88] To cite just one final example, in the late fall of 1788 General Mikhail Kamenskii's effort to disperse a strong Turkish column advancing on Bender was derailed by the weather as well; the sudden advent of below-zero temperatures coupled with a freakish blizzard took the lives of more than a quarter of his men.[89]

The underpopulation of the theaters of war or of the districts that the army had to traverse before arriving in those theaters also contributed to the slowness and inefficiency of Russian military operations. As had been true in the previous century, low population density meant that an army on the march could not readily live off the land. The fewer the peasants in a region, the less the available stocks of food. Thus the army was obliged, as in the past, to haul with it large quantities of the victuals it expected to consume en route. And that, of course, entailed gigantic baggage trains and sluggish advances, for the army as a whole could travel no faster than the sickest and most crippled ox hitched to the supply wagons.

Many contemporaries were highly critical of the size of the Russian military wagon trains. The Austrian Captain Paradies, who served with Münnich during the 1730s, disdainfully remarked of the Russians that "their army is immobilized by such an unprecedentedly large baggage train. I have never seen the army set out on march earlier than two, three, or even four hours after sunrise."[90] What Paradies was alluding to here was the time lost each morning in herding the horses and oxen, untangling wagon tongues, fastening harness, forming up the wagon train, and pointing it in the right direction.[91]

The huge size of supply trains, apparently, was not always justifiable. Russian officers on occasion encumbered the army unnecessarily by traveling with hundreds of pounds of personal baggage. Field Marshal S. F. Apraksin, the unmilitary, luxury-loving courtier who initially held command in the Seven Years War, required 250 horses to transport his personal possessions into the field.[92] Nor was his case unique. In September 1760 the Empress Elizabeth herself condemned the extravagant dimensions of officers' personal freight, noting that she had heard "with great chagrin" of "the unbelievable number of horses" that had been requisitioned to bear those superfluous loads.[93]

But much of the condemnation of the Russian baggage trains is unfounded and unfair. On the overwhelming majority of occasions, the baggage trains were large not so much because effete officers had crammed them with feather beds, clocks, and silver services as because they contained the food, water, and firewood requisite to the army's survival. Peter the Great's forces had displayed considerable mobility, but only at the expense of hunger, even starvation. In light of the locales where Russia campaigned, its baggage trains were big because they *had* to be.[94] When Münnich, that accomplished logistician, began military operations against Turkey at the end of May 1739, he was accompanied by 27,862 oxen and 6,202 drivers. That may seem at first glance to be an enormous cavalcade, but we should note that Münnich believed that he really could have used at least 10,000 more of the beasts despite the additional encumbrance that would have placed on his movements.[95]

The larger the baggage train, the slower the army. Yet perhaps this was a self-correcting problem. Surely during the course of a campaign, as food and firewood were consumed, the total weight an army hauled about with it would diminish. That sometimes happened, but it was not the desired outcome. In the first place, prudent commanders tried to replenish supplies as they were used, if possible. In the second place, it was often true that the more victories a Russian army won, the *longer* its wagon trains became. Victory itself could be an impediment to mobility. Armies that won battles, sacked towns, and seized supply depots were typically heavier than their vanquished foes, because they were laden with booty and wounded. Defeated forces obviously had no loot to show for their pains and were, moreover, often forced to abandon their wounded on the battlefield. Victories on the tactical level could thus undermine the mobility necessary to achieve strategic objectives. On August 1, 1759, the Russian army under Saltykov delivered a crushing defeat to Frederick the Great in the battle of Kunersdorf. In theory, that opened the road for a savage Russian drive on Berlin. But Saltykov did not dash to Berlin. Indeed, he did not even amble in that direction, but instead withdrew for a rendezvous with his Austrian ally, General Daun. And Saltykov's main rationale for doing so was that his army was encumbered with thousands of sick and injured men, and laden with booty besides.[96]

The relationship between the size of the wagon trains, soldiers' rations, and fodder for the animals was a kind of vicious military ecosystem that placed automatic upper limits on the well-being of any Russian army in the field. Large baggage trains entailed other consequences besides the deceleration of tempos of advance. The heavier the quantity of victuals and supplies that had to be carried, the greater the number of oxen and horses required. But large numbers of horses and oxen inevitably put great strains on locally available forage. Too many horses, and there might not be pasturage enough for them all. In that event, horses and other draft animals would become enfeebled or die, resulting in the abandonment of wagons and foodstuffs needed by the soldiers themselves. On the other hand, if a general foolishly underestimated the amount of provisions his men needed and set off with too few wagons and animals, he could lead his army into defeat by starvation before the enemy ever came into sight. In the circumstances, then, Russian military leaders usually preferred larger baggage trains to smaller ones.

The size of the Russian logistical apparatus and the nature of East European terrain thus produced chronic shortages of fodder and often of food whenever Russian armies went off to war. One reason why so many of Russia's eighteenth-century campaigns appear so irritatingly indecisive to modern observers is that although Russia might frequently take an objective, capture a city, or even conquer an entire province, it often was forced to evacuate it owing to a lack of victuals and forage. In the middle of June 1736, for example, Münnich breached the fortifications of Perekop and, for the first time in Russian history, led an invading Slavic army into the Crimean peninsula; the stunned Turks and Tatars fell back respectively on Kaffa and the Yaila mountains. Yet by the end of August Münnich had to retreat, for he had all but exhausted his own stock of food and water. He could not rely on locally obtained supplies, because his enemies had taken the precaution of burning the granaries and poisoning the wells.[97] The following summer Münnich took the Turkish fortress of Ochakov after ferocious fighting in which perhaps as much as 80 percent of the defenders and inhabitants were butchered.[98] Yet on the July 5, 1737 Münnich had no choice but to break camp and march the main Russian army away from Ochakov, this time because of a dearth of forage. The field marshal reported to St. Petersburg that 1,720 horses and 685 teams of oxen had died from the heat or from lack of fodder.[99]

Insufficient forage was a problem that dogged the Russians in other wars years later. It was most particularly acute (and damaging) during the Seven Years War, when it severely compromised many military operations.[100] P. A. Rumiantsev, then in Brandenburg, wrote to V. V. Fermor in July 1758 that he often lacked the cavalry necessary for even the simplest reconnaissance because of the undernourishment of his horses.[101] Skimpy forage often precluded decisive military action. Armchair generals have often lambasted Apraksin for his conduct after the battle of Gross Jägersdorf (August 30, 1757). They maintain that after having gained the advantage there, Apraksin should have harried the Prussians with a vigorous strategic pursuit instead of retreating. It is quite true that Apraksin did not have to retreat, but it is equally true that strategic pursuit was totally beyond his capacity in view of the condition of his underfed cavalry horses. Apraksin's inability to renew offensive action after Gross Jägersdorf did in fact provide Der Alte Fritz with the time he needed to regroup and defeat the French at Rossbach. There was little, however, that Apraksin could have done to prevent that, no matter how aggressive and offensive-minded he might have been.[102]

Indeed, shortage of forage was a problem that just would not go away. Almost two years later in the war, P. S. Saltykov explained to the Empress Elizabeth that he was organizing scavenging raids for the seizure of

> . . . as many horses and kine as possible and also provisions, as in the army of Your Imperial Majesty. . . . the baggage and artillery horses and oxen [have] fallen into extreme exhaustion because of the great heat and poor feeding.

Elsewhere in the same missive, Saltykov noted that his artillery was largely useless because it had not been resupplied with shells; that in itself was a consequence of the inadequate quality and quantity of draft animals.[103]

The adamantine laws of the military ecosystem thus forced the Russian government and its military commanders constantly to calculate and recalculate the requirements of human and equine alimentation. Sometimes an apparent good really concealed an evil. During the Swedish war of 1788, for instance, the provisioning department requested Catherine II's permission to send four hundred horses to transport food and forage to Russia's Finnish magazines and its army in the field there. Catherine referred the petition to her Council of State, where it was rejected as "deeply onerous" since "the feeding of these horses in a poor country [Finland] would increase the need of the regimental horses already there for food."[104] In other words, the possession of additional beasts of burden would actually disadvantage the army, as the liability of their food consumption would totally outweigh any benefit from their labor power.

Warfare in Eastern Europe thus naturally entailed very high rates of attrition. Distances were vast, terrain difficult, operations intense, and rations short. It was not uncommon for a regiment to ruin most of its equipment from hard use in the course of one summer campaign.[105] In August 1739 Münnich sent his prisoners-of-war back to Russia under an escort of four entire regiments. The reason for employing such a large convoy was that these regiments, in Münnich's words, "were completely without uniforms," that is, they had thoroughly worn out their uniforms.[106]

The conditions in which Russia waged war also promoted the spread of disease. The health of the troops was most definitely not furthered by the common practice of randomly appointing regimental surgeons from among the untrained peasants in the ranks.[107] Examples of astonishing military epidemics abound during the eighteenth century. In the 1722–39 period, for instance, Russia kept certain districts of Transcaspian Persia under the military occupation of 30,000 men. When the St. Petersburg government agreed to withdraw its forces, it did so more because of pathology than geopolitics. Almost 130,000 Russian troops had perished from disease while on garrison duty in Persia—a full half of all who served there—over the seventeen years.[108] The Turkish war of 1735–39 was itself a medical catastrophe. During it, as Manstein observed, the Russian army had more to fear from "hunger, thirst, continual fatigue, and marches in the intensest heats of the summer" than from the Tatars or the Turks.[109] Münnich's son, a passionate booster of his father's military reputation, nonetheless conceded that the "bad climate, combined with the unbearable heat and drought, produced many illnesses among the men."[110] Some 30,000 soldiers are said to have died in the first year of the war, chiefly from disease.[111] During the campaigning season of 1737 Russia's army suffered 25,000 deaths, 60 percent of them from disease.[112] In the following year Münnich wanted to chase the Turks into Moldavia but had to halt at the Dniester when plague broke out among the men.[113] The majority of the 100,000 Russian casualties incurred from 1735–39 were clearly traceable to sickness.[114]

In terms of both morbidity and mortality, the Russo-Turkish war of the 1730s was perhaps the worst of the post-Petrine eighteenth century. But infectious disease stalked Russian armies in later wars as well. Twelve thousand soldiers, for instance, died in one year (1757) of the Seven Years War—9,500 of them, or 80 percent, of diseases.[115] In the Turkish wars of the second half of the century, the Russian soldier's most dreaded enemy was cholera, whose outbreak in 1771 (just to adduce one example) totally spoiled Russia's planned campaign.[116]

"Action in war," Clausewitz writes in *Vom Krieg*, "is like movement in a resistant element." He continues to explain his concept of friction, those forces that in warfare grind armies down and make "the apparently easy so difficult."[117] Friction was an inescapable feature of warfare in eighteenth-century Western Europe as well. Western armies, like Russian ones, suffered from disease and logistic shortfalls. In view of the greater population density and agricultural productivity of Western Europe, however, talented commanders could minimize the effects of friction in ways their Russian counterparts could not. In the spring of 1704, for instance, Marlborough was able to march from Coblenz to the Danube while keeping his army virtually intact: he traversed populous country and made shrewd use of prepositioned magazines.[118] That justly famous maneuver could not, however, have been accomplished in Eastern Europe. As the century progressed, the disparity between West and East European warfare grew still greater, as Western commanders benefited from population growth, rising agricultural outputs, and expanding networks of roads.[119] To be sure, friction remained, but in East European warfare there was a *superabundance* of friction by comparison. Military power is after all a consumable resource, one not readily renewed. Yet the speed with which any military operation at all *devoured* power in eighteenth-century Eastern Europe represented a real constraint on Russian strategy and statescraft.

The Problems of Manpower

As we saw in the previous chapter, Peter the Great relied upon his military manpower and recruitment policies to batter down the forces of friction. Recruits were expendable and, indeed, were expended by the tens of thousands to replenish the hollow ranks of Peter's army. Yet Petrine methods worked best in special circumstances; to fight exclusively with them would eventually led to national self-immolation. Peter's successors, intuitively understanding this, were less profligate with human lives than he had been.

Russian recruitment policy continued to have virtues in the eighteenth century, and those virtues will be examined in Chapter 4. But it must be noted that the Russian recruitment system had its blemishes as well. Although the Russian state was able to tap into reserves of manpower unavailable to Western monarchies, with their mercenary armies, that benefit was to some extent counterbalanced by the extreme cumbrousness and slowness of the recruiting process. It was both cheap and expedient to summon thousands of new draftees to the colors with the simple stroke of a pen on a decree; yet the army was truly reinforced only when the recruits actually arrived. Often they were late. In July 1738, in an attempt to accelerate the process, St. Petersburg proclaimed a callup of one recruit for every 120 souls in the country. That was supposed to yield a harvest of 40,000 inductees, who, it was assumed, would have joined the army by January 1. When that date rolled round, however, barely half of the target had been reached. The army was still so short of new conscripts in February 1739 that the government radically lowered medical and fitness standards and began to accept the short, the lame, the partially deaf, and so forth.[120] Then again, with war in the offing the government announced a special recruitment in 1754 that was planned to be completed by April 1755. Yet many of the men inducted by the provisions of the 1754 act did not reach their units until 1756.[121]

Given the nature of the recruiting system and the administrative weakness of the tsarist empire, delays in transporting peasants from village to army depot were unavoidable. But another inherent defect concerned the quality of the recruits. Since recruits were taken from the peasant households of the country, the interests of the government and the landlords (in the case of proprietary serfs) were inevitably in conflict. The government wanted strong and healthy lads for its army—just the sort with whom the *pomeshchiki* were reluctant to part. As the landlords themselves had the power to nominate peasants for military service, it was not uncommon for them in appearing before the conscription board to try to palm off cripples as hale men. Even when the landlords handed the task of selecting the recruits over to the village communal authorities, as was often done, the latter were just as prone to use the recruitment system to cleanse the village of the weak, the sick, the poor, and undesirable elements.[122] Government officials railed at this practice, and although many penalties were devised to suppress it, success was never total.[123] More than thirty years later, Prince G. A. Potemkin would decry both the delay and the low standards engendered by the conscription system. In a long (and self-pitying) letter of September 1788, he wrote Catherine the Great:

> The recruits I have been given are weak and ailing; many are advanced in age—so much so that they have died in great numbers before getting here. Many parties [of recruits] have still not arrived at the army entrusted to me, with the result that the underpopulated regiments, not having been reinforced, are almost disappearing.[124]

Although we can probably dismiss Potemkin's hyperbolic last comment, there is no reason to discount the gravity of the problem that confronted him.

Desertion also troubled Russia's eighteenth-century military establishment. Under Peter the Great, of course, it had been epidemic. After Peter's death, desertion rates declined, although one modern scholar holds that 20,000 men—one-tenth of the army—deserted its ranks in 1732.[125] When Field Marshal Apraksin was appointed to command Russia's Prussian expeditionary forces in 1756, Elizabeth's cabinet, the *Konferentsiia*, enjoined him to take special pains to avert "the desertion that usually occurs from an army."[126] Whatever the real levels of desertion were (and, as we shall see later, the levels subsided considerably), the Petersburg government was always concerned about the barest *possibility* of desertion and spent much time guarding against it. Particularly vexatious was the tendency of peasants to bolt from the recruiting convoy en route to the army's camp. One technique to stop that was to organize the conscripts into artels of at least eight men each; the men could then be ordered to spy on each other in accordance with the time-honored practice of peasant "mutual responsibility" (*krugovaia poruka*).[127] In 1788 recruiting officers attached to Potemkin's army would routinely confiscate all the recruits' money to discourage desertion, an expedient that seems to have worked. Potemkin noted that because of this "flights from the road are relatively notable," that is, rare.[128]

Training

If the Russian conscription system produced its share of headaches for the Russian government, so too did the training of the troops. Military leaders in eighteenth-century Russia were constantly tinkering with the training statutes. Several of those documents have come in for criticism, especially from later nationalistic Russian historians, who have claimed that they were often flawed with an excessively servile imitation of foreign (usually German) models. Slavish copying of other armies' training and drill regulations, it is argued, stifled domestic creativity and retarded the development of an authentically "Russian" military art.[129]

But the training problem was more acute than the baleful results of ill-conceived drill regulations borrowed from abroad.
Quite simply, the Russian army was burdened with so many ancillary obligations—convoy service, labor service, and guard duty,
among others—that finding the time for effective training was
extremely difficult. One might have expected this to be true of
the garrison army, and indeed by the middle of the century the
70,000 underpaid men of that formation were widely known for
their poor training (and their rampant thievery, to boot).[130] Insufficient training, however, was a real problem even for the regular
field army. The regular troops were in fact typically trained only
during the four months (May 15 to September 15) they spent in
summer encampments; even then there were significant interrup-
tions during which the men were hired out as field hands. For the
other eight months of the year, the regiments were dispersed
among the villages of the country, and the soldiers, who were
quartered on the peasantry, became strangers to military pur-
suits.[131] For those reasons, Field Marshal Münnich, for example,
argued back in the 1730s that war would not be unwelcome, for it
"would give the troops the opportunity to train." Bestuzhev-
Riumin echoed those sentiments in the following decade, observing that a war with Prussia would enable Russia's soldiers "to
occupy themselves with the honorable exercises suitable to their
calling, in which they could never be trained enough." And a full
ten years later, Shuvalov would still be noting that the onus of
guard and convoy duty was so great that "the regiments have
been insufficiently exercised in the art of war."[132] In fact, the
issue of inadequate training would haunt the Romanov regime
through the centuries, all the way down until its demise in
1917.[133]

A Fractured Government at Home

A penultimate set of constraints on Russia's ability to formulate
strategy and to exert military power intelligently resulted from
the unique characteristics of the eighteenth-century autocracy
itself. The eighteenth century is frequently described as the "era
of the palace revolutions"; between 1725 and 1796 there were at
least eight coups or attempted coups in St. Petersburg, usually

involving one or more regiments of the Imperial Guards.[134] It was the presence of the Guards, for example, that permitted Catherine I to take power after the death of her husband Peter the Great. Equally, the support of the Guards enabled Anna Ivanovna to become Empress while spurning the "conditions of 1730"—that manifesto prepared by scions of old boyar families interested in limiting monarchical power within the state.[135] On some occasions, coups resulted in the deposal (and/or murder) of one autocrat and the elevation of another. In November 1741, for instance, the arrest of Ivan VI made possible Elizabeth Petrovna's accession to the throne. In 1762, to cite an additional example, Catherine the Great became Empress after conspirators imprisoned (and subsequently assassinated) her husband, Peter III. At other times scheming favorites launched coups designed to unseat their rivals, as Münnich did in 1740. Still other coups were financed, if not organized, by foreign governments eager for a reorientation of Russian foreign policy; one thinks here of French instigation of the failed coup of 1743 and British involvement in the successful plot against the life of the Emperor Paul in 1801. It was, of course, the political history of the eighteenth century that led to Madame de Staël to coin her famous epigram on the Russian "constitution" ("a despotism mitigated by strangulation").[136]

This political instability is supposed to have had the direst effects on state decision-making in peace and war. The Guards, for example, were known on occasion to rise up against a regent or an autocrat who proposed to employ them in an unpopular war. One reason that the Guards took part in the 1741 coup is that they feared being deployed to Finland to fight the Swedes.[137] And in 1762 Peter III's desire to use the Guards in a war against Denmark partially explains their role in his downfall.[138] The occasional predilection of the Guards for mutiny was in itself an obvious limitation on Russia's use of military force.

But their were other, less readily apparent limitations, or at least so some historians have contended. Such scholars have argued that all of the lip service paid to the "unbounded power" of the autocracy actually masked the reality of an essentially feeble state. The "all-powerful autocrat" in this view was a fictitious creation of mythmakers anxious to dupe people both at home and abroad into thinking that the Russian state was much stronger than in fact it was. Since autocrat-usurpers frequently owed their crowns, if not their lives, to the efforts of favorites and clans, the schemes and preferences of those courtiers represented a self-evident check on the monarchical will. As one historian puts it, the power of the autocracy "was in fact very narrowly circumscribed," for "the articulation of tsarist will depended upon the familial and personal patronage networks that dominated the court and the upper administration."[139] Sometimes autocrats had to purchase the continued allegiance of those networks with cash, grants of serfs, or popular policies. At the very least, any autocrat had to seek to balance all the various factions and "parties" off against each other.[140]

Clan politics and factional strife are often blamed for the lumbering inefficiency of the highest organs of administration in eighteenth-century Russia. Take the *Konferentsiia*, that war cabinet established by Elizabeth Petrovna in the spring of 1756 to unify defense and foreign policy. One reason for the incompetence of the *Konferentsiia* was the fact that Elizabeth apparently felt it necessary to appoint to it representatives of all three court factions, those of Bestuzhev, Shuvalov, and Crown Prince Peter Fedorovich. Bestuzhev favored war with Prussia and an alliance with Britain; although also hostile to Prussia, the Shuvalov–Vorontsov grouping advocated close ties to Paris; while Peter, a Prussophile, was utterly opposed to war with Frederick the Great.[141] In view of the differing visions of Russian foreign policy entertained by the factions and their mutual loathing of each other, it is not surprising that the resolutions and orders of the *Konferentsiia* were frequently trivial, contradictory, or incoherent.[142] The Instruction the *Konferentsiia* gave to Field Marshal Apraksin in October 1756 is notorious for its bumbling ambiguity. As critics have often noted, Apraksin was commanded simultaneously to move and to stay put, to take fortresses and to remain on the frontiers.[143] No faction wanted to miss taking credit for victory; but none of them wanted to accept the blame for defeat, either. The results were the cautious ellipses, qualifications, and escape clauses that studded the language of the *Konferentsiia's* official orders. Domestic political considerations—the need to appease rival groups—thus took precedence over effective strategy-making.[144]

Although almost no eighteenth-century administrative institution has received as much bad press as has the *Konferentsiia*, the *Sovet pri vyshochaishchem dvore*—the equivalent institution founded in 1769 by Catherine the Great—also has its detractors. Described by one of them as "a body in which political rivals could fight it out and neutralize each other," the *Sovet*, like the *Konferentsiia*, represented all of the various court factions and tendencies.[145] Accordingly, the Panin brothers, the promoters of the "northern system," were counterbalanced on the *Sovet* by Golitsyn, Orlov, Viazemskii, and others of their enemies.[146]

Factionalism at court is supposed to have damaged Russian interests more than by merely complicating the process of executive deliberation, for the statesmen's vicious intrigues against each other are said to have entailed ruin for Russian military and diplomatic policies on several occasions. Biron, the much-loathed German favorite of Anna Ivanovna, blocked Münnich's plan to march to Moldavia via Poland in 1737. Münnich, of course, hoped to save food, time, and human lives by taking this Polish short-cut; Biron, however, was expecting to be named Duke of Holstein soon and did not want to upset his presumptive (and nominal) suzerains in Warsaw.[147] Roughly twenty years later the Francophile M. I. Vorontsov conspired with great success against the person and policies of the Imperial Chancellor Bestuzhev-Riumin. In February 1756 Vorontsov's addendum to the Russo-British subsidy treaty, stipulating that Russia would render Britain military aid only if it was attacked by Prussia (not by France) soured relations between London and Petersburg and played a part in the "reversal of alliances."[148]

This same confusion of personal interest with the interests of state is also supposed to explain the extraordinary corruption of Russia's governing class in this century. Embezzlement, extortion, graft, the acceptance of foreign bribes—none of these practices was uncommon among the aristocratic elite. Bestuzhev was popularly reputed to have been perhaps the most venal of them all. Contemporaries often asserted (although incorrectly) that greed was the only abiding passion of his life. Frederick the Great once complained that Bestuzhev inveigled Russia into a war against Prussia for the sole purpose of avenging a private wrong: Berlin had promised him a substantial bribe of 40,000 ecus back in 1744 but had then reneged.[149] Even after the Seven

Years War broke out, Bestuzhev was not reluctant to accept quite large sums from the Prussian and British enemies in exchange for his pledge to sabotage the Russian war effort.[150] Bestuzhev, of course, had no intention of doing any such thing. If the foreigners wanted to exchange good gold for faithless vows, it was their affair. Such conduct could, however, easily be mistaken for treason, just as was Apraksin's conduct in the campaign of 1757. As noted previously, Apraksin's snail-like movement into East Prussia and his precipitous retreat from that province after the battle of Gross Jägersdorf have drawn much negative comment. And Apraksin did in fact have a hidden agenda, although it was not the Prussian cause he loved as much as his own head. Elizabeth Petrovna's health was at that time so poor that news of her death was anticipated daily. Apraksin knew that in that event the new Emperor, Peter, would most probably deal harshly with any Russian general who had been too aggressive in the struggle against his adored hero, the King of Prussia. Apraksin's cunctation was therefore his insurance policy against a change of ruler back in St. Petersburg. It was a gamble that failed, however, as the Empress made a partial recovery, dismissed him from his post, and jailed him as a traitor.[151] In this case the factionalism of the Russian government at home exerted a direct effect on the outcome of Russian military operations; the benighted Apraksin, for whom it is clearly possible to feel some sympathy, had to play to the interests and concerns of not one but several competing centers of power.

The eighteenth-century Russian autocrats themselves are reputed to have damaged the rational pursuit of national interest. They were said to have been, at times, putty in the hands of their favorites and lovers, and eager to execute their pet projects regardless of the dictates of *raison d'état*. One scholar informs us, for instance, that Elizabeth Petrovna "had no foreign policy not made for her by subordinates."[152] Catherine the Great is said to have been heavily influenced by a long procession of favorites. Toward the end of her life in 1792, certainly, the besotted Empress confounded many of her contemporaries by placing great responsibility for governmental policy, foreign and domestic, in the hands of the handsome but callow Platon Zubov.[153]

Other students of the period have argued that Russia's Emperors and Empresses were not so much the prisoners of their court-iers as the victims of their own character flaws: petulance, stupid-ity, even insanity. Catherine I's meddling in the Holstein and Schleswig questions has been ascribed from time to time to her bovine gullibility and simple-mindedness.[154] Scholars somewhat less inclined to see Bestuzhev as Elizabeth Petrovna's Svengali have nonetheless on occasion denounced that Empress for being driven by "personal hatreds and antipathies" and for nourishing an "unreasoning hatred" of Frederick the Great.[155] Peter III, Elizabeth's short-lived successor, not only pulled Russia out of the Seven Years War but signed a treaty of alliance with Prussia on the May 6, 1762, whereby he returned all of the territories captured from Berlin gratis, thus (at least according to some interpretations) defrauding Russia of important gains through an act of royal lunacy.[156]

Peter's wife, the redoubtable Catherine the Great, has come in for sharp criticism as well. Although no one would deny the fact that Russia expanded and increased enormously in power dur-ing her reign, Catherine has nonetheless been accused of mis-managing Russia's expansion. A common complaint concerns her handling of the interlocked problems of Poland and Turkey. In 1763 Catherine organized the election of one of her lovers, Stanislas Poniatowski, as King of Poland. Thereafter, Russia en-joyed an unrivaled influence in Poland. Russia's victories in the First Turkish War, however, so alarmed Austria and Prussia that Catherine had to accede to a partition of Poland in 1772 in order to provide those states with compensation. Catherine's bungling thus resulted in the reduction of Russian power in the kingdom to the west; instead of being supreme in Poland, Russia now had to share authority there with its partners in partition. That, at least, was the opinion of the British Ambassador to Petersburg, who wrote of the agreement óver Poland in 1778 that Cather-ine's policies

> . . . Had led to a treaty which nothing could ever justify and which, in addition to the ineffaceable blot it has left on her reign, has strengthened the two sole powers from whom she has something to fear, and has given them for the future an influence in the affairs of Poland equal to her own.[157]

This judgment is shared by some modern historians. One of them writes in much the same vein: Catherine's "lack of diplomatic shrewdness" permitted Austria and Prussia "to share in an influence in Poland which had never before been accorded to them."[158]

If the incompetence of Russia's sovereigns, then, represented a serious constraint on Russian strategy, so too did the incompetence of its generals in the field. In the eighteenth century, as well as later, military commands in Russia often went to men whose talents as courtiers considerably outweighed their accomplishments as captains. Military incompetence was particularly conspicuous during the Seven Years War. The rules of the Orthodox Church obliged believers to follow a regimen of rigorous fasts during several periods of the year. Armies on the march, however, had to make do with whatever stocks of food were available and were therefore routinely exempted from those requirements. Apraksin, however, declined to apply to the Holy Synod for a dispensation during the lenten season of 1757, with the result that one-fifth of his pious army, or 11,000 men, fell sick from totally avoidable malnutrition.[159] Then again, during Russia's 1760 occupation of Berlin, General Totleben was under strict orders both to demand stiff monetary "contributions" from the city's residents and to raze every military factory in the city, especially the Lagerhaus, which manufactured cloth for the entire Prussian army. But Totleben was desperate to demonstrate that the Russian army was not composed of rapacious barbarians; he not only sharply reduced the Berliners' tribute, but spared the Lagerhaus, putatively because he was gulled into believing that its profits actually supported the Potsdam Orphans' Home.[160] Many other examples of egregious Russian military incompetence could be adduced from the record of the eighteenth century, even if few of them attained this towering pinnacle of stupidity.

It is fair to say, then, that the constraints on Russian strategy in the period were both daunting and numerous. Some perhaps have been exaggerated by historians. But the majority of the fetters that bound Russian power in this period were forged not out of the papier mâché of historians' imaginations but out of the iron of material reality. Traitorous allies, rapacious enemies, state poverty, inhospitable terrain, inclement weather, a faction-ridden government, human inadequacy—all these militated against the success of Russian expansion in the eighteenth century. Yet the surprising fact remains that Russia succeeded anyway. Somehow it managed to expand despite those obstacles. Two questions naturally arise: why and how? It is these questions that the next chapter will address.

4

Russian Imperialism and Military Power in the Eighteenth Century

Why and How

What motivated Russian imperial expansion in the eighteenth century? Why did Russia's rulers undertake that risky and dangerous course? Was imperialism, in fact, a conscious policy? There have been, of course, several explanations advanced to account for Russian imperialism. Some pretend to universality and have been applied to many different forms of imperialism; others are said to be rooted in the specific gravity of Russian culture and civilization. For reasons of space we shall examine only five of them: the economic, the aristocratic, the accidental, the messianic, and the geopolitical.

Economic interpretations usually stress that Russia's leaders were acutely aware of the need to expand Russia's trade and access to markets.[1] Crude and reductionist as this style of economic determinism can be, the evidence that economic development carried great weight in the thinking of successive Russian governments is nonetheless considerable. Russian expansion into Bashkiriia in the 1730s, for instance, was in part motivated by the desire eventually to dominate the rich trade of Central Asia.[2] When the *Konferentsiia* debated Russian aims on the eve of the Seven Years War, it was agreed that Russia should seek to annex the province of Kurland compensating the Poles with slices of Prussian territory. Kurland was important because its possession would give Russia "the means to unite the commerce of the Baltic with the Black Sea and through that have in our hands almost all of the Levant commerce."[3] Later in the century Catherine the

Great's fascination with the prospects for developing the economic resources of her empire bore fruit in a multiplicity of projects for the colonization of newly acquired territory and the explanation of the reserves of minerals located there.[4]

Under the aristocratic interpretation of Russian imperialism, however, the personal contributions of individual autocrats dwindle into insignificance. This explanation, like Schumpeter's explication of the foreign policy of Louis XIV, flows directly from that theory of the "weak" eighteenth-century state to which we have already made reference.[5] In this view Catherine the Great was not the real architect of Russia's southern conquests; rather, scheming and greedy nobles—often *arrivistes*—plotted and promoted those acquisitions, for they stood to acquire the greatest share of the estates that would be carved out of them. The most extreme proponent of this interpretation writes that: "the new orientation towards the Black Sea that began in the late 1760s was a response to domestic pressures for a more extensive division of the spoils than was possible within the confines of central Russia."[6] Thus the dynamic behind the expansion of Russia was a growth in the size and avarice of the ruling class.

By contrast, proponents of what we might describe as the "accidental school" implicitly and explicitly dismiss the idea that great events can be regulated in accordance with the rationally devised plans of human beings. There is simply too much that can go wrong, they say. "Cool logic" and "reasons of state" are all too frequently undermined by frailty, obtuseness, and chance, while unforeseen (and unforeseeable) consequences inhere in every human act.[7] Such scholars criticize those of their colleagues who make the case for human purpose in history, berating them for imposing artificial patterns of their own on the randomness of the past.[8] Even historians who depict their subjects as enjoying a robust control over their own destinies are not beyond being impressed by the casual role of pure accident.[9] The extreme version of the accidental view, then, would probably hold that Russia acquired its empire as the British are said to have acquired theirs, "in a fit of absence on mind."[10]

With the messianic interpretation of Russian expansion we leave the realm of materialism for that of metaphysics. Authors of this persuasion contend that there has been a relentless drive for territorial expansion embedded somewhere in the musty caverns of the Russian soul since the dawn of time, or at least since the early sixteenth century, when the monk Filofei propounded the doctrine of the "Three Romes." That, of course, was the idea that the Russian state was the ultimate successor and inheritor of the Roman and Byzantine Empires. "Two Romes have fallen," went a popular saying, "and there will never be a fourth."[11] In this explanatory paradigm, not only Russia's autocrats and aristocrats but its merchants and serfs as well burned with the unshakable conviction that Russia's destiny was to expand. Some have even gone so far as to argue that deep-seated hegemonic urges have driven Russian foreign policy from the middle ages well into the Soviet period.[12] There are, of course, versions of the messianic hypothesis more subtle and sophisticated than this, versions which, for example, locate the Russian "will to power" in a profound cultural ambivalence and sense of inferiority vis-à-vis the West.[13] In any case messianic, or messianic *cum* psychological, explanations are often favored by those who have believed that the West needs to be awakened from its indifference to the true extent of the Russian menace.

We may call the final interpretation of Russian imperialism the geopolitical or the geostrategic—that is, the argument that the eighteenth-century expansion of Russia was chiefly the result of the rational decisions of men and women attempting to do their level best to respond to threats and take advantage of opportunities as they understood them. Although chance, human weakness, and dreams of personal gain and glory all played a part in what occurred, Russia's successful rulers, statesmen, and generals were motivated, more often than not, by an abstract sense of state interest. This is the interpretation I prefer; to demonstrate its persuasiveness, a critique of the other four is now in order.

Theories of Russian Imperialism Revisited

An elaborate refutation of the crude economic determinist argument need not detain us at this point. Its defects are too obvious to merit detailed rebuttal. It is anachronistic in that it posits the existence of a "capitalist consciousness" prior to the advent of capitalism; it is teleological because of its a priori assumption that an ultimately unprovable schema of historical development is true; and it is also reductionist in that it fails to recognize any human motivation save for greed.

This is not to deny that Russia's elites in the eighteenth century had a shrewd sense of the significance of growing trade and mercantile activity for the economy of their country. But the concept of wealth prevalent among eighteenth-century Russia's leaders was broader than that. When Russian statesmen of that time thought of state wealth, they thought first in terms not of commerce but of populated land. Uninhabited territory was not particularly useful. One might almost say that Russia already had too much of it. For eighteenth-century Russians, settled land was *the* primary form of state wealth, because of the inherent value of taxpaying and labor power of the people residing there. Count Zakhar Chernyshev wrote in 1763: "[A] state is able to support its army not through the extensiveness of lands, but only in proportion to the people living in them and the revenues collected there."[14] An astute scholar has noted that Russian statesmen later calculated the benefits that accrued to Petersburg from the Polish partitions in much the same terms.[15]

The aristocratic interpretation of Russian imperialism has more to recommend it, at least on the surface. Political clans and factions clearly did exist, did vie with each other, and did attempt to get their hands on the levers of power. Was the autocracy, however, merely the passive and docile captive of factional strife? Did Russian expansion result solely, or even mainly, from the clash of factions? More specifically, were Russia's southern annexations caused by the victory of Potemkin's party of rank-and-file nobles over the Panins' coterie?[16]

Merely to assert that this was so is to stumble into the pitfall identified by Elizabeth Eisenstein in a different context some years ago: the trap of looking for the agents of change by identifying beneficiaries.[17] Although the two groups are sometimes one and the same, they are not invariably so. Unfortunately, aristocratic explanations are often longer on assertions than on sound arguments. The assertions are sometimes bolstered with "negative proof" (since Catherine the Great was *not* deposed by her nobility she *must* have been buying them off with territorial annexations) or by invoking social science theories on the structure of ruling classes, but that does not make them any more convincing.

There are, moreover, evidential as well as logical problems with the aristocratic theory. For one, the boundaries between factions of "new men"—the *arrivistes*—and "old men" and the foreign policy preferences of each are not necessarily as clear cut as often assumed. Potemkin, we are told, favored expansion, while the Panins, representing the more established nobility, advocated the pacific northern system. One of the most important of the Panins' allies is said to have been the Chernyshev family, to whom they were tied by marriage.[18] Zakhar Chernyshev, however, frequently disagreed with the Panin brothers over questions of foreign affairs.[19] He was the author of at least two plans for the conquest of the Crimea and in 1763 wrote a famous secret memorandum in which he proposed the Russian annexation of various districts of Poland in the interest of procuring more defensible frontiers. (Interestingly enough, the lands Chernyshev recommended acquiring were approximately the same as the ones Russia actually took as a result of the first Polish partition in 1772.)[20] Similarly, although it is true that Bezborodko and the secretariat under him urged Russian expansion in the 1780s and 1790s, Bezborodko, the template of the "new man" in tsarist politics, owed his career and his prosperity to Field Marshal Rumiantsev, one of the most outstanding representatives of the "older" nobility.[21]

By presuming that the language of *raison d'état* was never any more than a verbal smoke screen, a flimsy rationalization of the private schemes of nobles eager to despoil the state, the aristocratic theory is in its own way almost as reductionist as the economic determinism propounded by vulgar Marxists. For one thing, it cannot account for historical subjects changing their minds when it was not in their selfish interests to do so. Panin, for instance, truly believed in the wisdom of his northern system in the early years of Catherine's reign. He desired strong alliances with Sweden, Britain, Prussia, and Poland; rejected expansionist policies; and hoped to avoid war, particularly on Russia's southern frontier.[22] The advent of the First Turkish War in 1768, however, altered his views on how Russia should behave in the international arena. At a meeting of the State Council on September 16, 1770, Panin, the longtime opponent of additional annexations, called for the Russian occupation of Wallachia and Moldavia as partial compensation for Russia's sacrifices in the war.[23] At a subsequent meeting of the same body, he observed that he now understood that no firm peace with Turkey would ever be possible and hinted at the possibility of incorporating the Khanate of the Crimea into the Russian Empire.[24]

Another weakness of the aristocratic theory is that it slights the authority and influence of the autocrat unduly. To point out that Russia's eighteenth-century rulers were not, in actuality, all-powerful is not to prove that they were powerless.[25] Were the foreign (as well as domestic) policies of Russian autocrats *really* "at the mercy of clashing party interests in the high administration, interests strongly influenced by foreign intrigues and money as well as by considerations of domestic patronage"?[26] Clearly, prominent courtiers and their clients played a role in the shaping of Russia's approach to foreign affairs, but the available evidence also strongly suggests that the autocrats used the parties, rather than the other way around.[27] If Bestuzhev-Riumin wanted to foment war with Prussia in the 1750s, Elizabeth Petrovna desired it no less keenly; in the end the fact that Russia actually went to war had more to do with Elizabeth's desires than with any of Bestuzhev's plots.[28] Those foreigners who believed that Elizabeth, or even Bestuzhev, could be bribed into directing Russian foreign policy in ways that contradicted their basic understanding of Russia's interests were woefully mistaken.[29] And what can be said of Elizabeth can be said with even more trenchancy of Catherine the Great. When a pacific foreign policy suited Catherine's purposes, she backed Nikita Panin and his northern system. But after she became convinced, in part because of the first Turkish war, that expansionism was attractive, she had no hesitation in jettisoning Panin and the northern league.[30] The protocols of Catherine's Imperial Council, the institution that coordinated diplomacy and military policy during almost all of her reign, provide abundant illustrations of the Empress's forceful activism in Russian foreign policies. In March 1770, to cite only one of many possible examples, we find Catherine making substantive alterations in the list of war aims the Council had prepared—not in the interest of purchasing the allegiance of the ravening bands of ambitious nobles, but out of concern for Russia's strategic position.[31]

A similar criticism can be leveled against the proponents of the "accidental theory." No one would dispute the capacity of chance or accident to frustrate human designs. It is precisely because war consists of the interaction of enemies, says Clausewitz, that it is so difficult to plan for it, discern its exact course, or foresee its end.[32] He might have applied this observation, with equal justice, to diplomacy as well. It is also true that the "inner meaning" of events tends to be clearer or at least less obscure in historical hindsight than it was to contemporaries at the time. Yet none of this precludes the necessity—as apparent to many eighteenth-century statesmen as to those of our own time—of pursuing sane, cogent, and consistent policies. In a different formulation, the mere fact that a state's foreign policy plans can be thwarted by "fate" does not mean that none of the elements of those plans can ever be realized. Nor does that fact absolve the historian from the responsibility of studying Russia's diplomatic and military *demarches* with some care; in order to assess the relations between outcomes and intentions, it is important to know what Russia's leaders thought they were doing.

The messianic interpretation is the least satisfactory of all. Even in its most sophisticated variants it is not subject to empirical verification, for it relies exclusively on the explanatory power of metaphysical or psychological phenomena, which, it goes without saying, cannot be observed. Even if we were to grant, for the sake of argument, that an urge for *imperium* resides somewhere in the Russian national character, we would still be left with the problem of explaining how that urge was ever translated into specific policies. Here messianic theorists, with their predilection for assuming that which is to be proved, are very little help. Few of them have anything concrete to say about the process of foreign policy formulation. The messianic hypothesis is, in addition, profoundly ahistorical, because it can neither discriminate between historical periods nor account for change. Clearly, on some occasions the Russian state has pursued expansionist policies; yet on other occasions it has not. What explains the difference? Finally, with regard to the eighteenth century the messianic theory is inherently implausible. This age was the greatest epoch of Russian expansionism until the time of Stalin, yet a large number of Russia's leaders were actually foreign born. Catherine I was a Livonian; Anna Ivanovna had roots deep in Holstein; and Catherine II hailed originally from the tiny German principality of Anhalt Zerbst. Many of the most important statesmen in Russia (particularly in the first half of the century)—men like Osterman,

Münnich, and Biron—were foreigners as well. All these people may have developed strong attachments to their adoptive country, but one certainly cannot argue that what they did on its behalf was the outward manifestation of the Russian national character. The "Russian soul" (if it exists) surely cannot be acquired through the consumption of vodka, *shchi*, or *kvas*.

We are therefore left with the geostrategic or geopolitical explanation for Russian expansion. Even it should not be accepted uncritically, without qualifications or reservations. Obviously, Russia's eighteenth-century statesmen and autocrats were not all masterminds, glorying in the precise unfolding of their long-range plans for dominion. Just as obviously, the cacophony of faction, the whispers of private avarice, and the bleating of idiots echoed in Russia's corridors of power during this century, just as they did in those of every other prominent European country. All of this notwithstanding if we look at the ways in which Russia's elites understood Russia's position in Europe and the world, we must conclude that generally they thought in strategic terms. To argue otherwise would be to ignore both the evidence and the salutary principle of Occam's razor.[33]

In the first place, consider the discourse of Russia's statesmen in that period. To be sure, in the communiqués of explication and vindication that Russian governments dispatched to other courts, there are endless (and clearly insincere) references to the dictates of natural law, Christian morality, and so forth. But when Russian statesmen debated among themselves, when they quarreled with each other about the sort of policies Russia ought to pursue, they generally employed the cold-blooded language of strategy and analysis. They weighed the international impact of what they proposed to do; they pondered the strengths and weaknesses of their prospective enemies; and they justified their policies in terms of the benefits they anticipated for Russian power and security. One is struck by the omnipresence of this style of reasoning in the protocols of each of the supreme instances of government during the century—be it Anna's *Kabinet*, Elizabeth's *Konferentsiia*, or Catherine's *Sovet*.

Second, policy disputes were not merely mechanical pavanes danced by unprincipled politicians whose interests lay solely in the aggrandizement of their clans. Concern for advancing the position of the family and the clan was important, of course, but was not always overriding. Policy disputes were real. Yet, as we have seen, some scholars have tried to make a case for the paramountcy of clan politics. One of them, for example, makes much of the political realignments at Catherine's court in 1762–63. There were at that time three main groupings, ostensibly divided over questions of foreign policy. The Bestuzhev faction advocated an alliance with Austria and emnity toward Prussia; that of Vorontsov was both pro-Austrian and pro-French; and the Panins, of course, supported the "Northern System." "If policy questions were by themselves decisive," this historian writes, "one should expect to find Vorontsov siding with Bestuzhev against Panin. . . . Yet with Bestuzhev's return and the sharpening of the court struggle in early 1763, Vorontsov turned right around and cooperated with Panin in negotiating an alliance with Prussia."[34] Perhaps so, but with even more justice, perhaps not, for Vorontsov's *volte face* can be readily interpreted geostrategically. This passage takes an overly restrictive view of what "policy questions" were and what they were *about*. Bestuzhev feared Prussia not because he was a paranoid, but because he was chiefly concerned with the security of Russia's Baltic possessions. Vorontsov favored an alliance with Austria as a barrier against Turkey, but *his* chief interest was the Russian position in Poland. That is why he originally looked to Paris: France was Poland's traditional protector, and Vorontsov believed Russia could do nothing there without French acquiescence. The Seven Years War, however, temporarily destroyed France's ability to influence events in Poland. By 1763 it was quite apparent to Vorontsov that it was Berlin, not Paris, that was best situated to frustrate Russia's Polish ambitions.[35] Vorontsov's cooperation with the Panins, then, should not necessarily be interpreted as the triumph of clan politics over principle. There are in fact many unambiguous examples in eighteenth-century Russian history in which opposite outcomes occurred. Aleksei Bestuzhev-Riumen, for instance, was a bitter foe of Anna Ivanovna's Chancellor, Andrei Osterman. Yet Bestuzhev supported Osterman's Austro-centric foreign policy during the 1730s and continued to adhere to it even after he supplanted Osterman in the 1740s. The reason was the Bestuzhev was firmly convinced that Osterman's system best served Russia's interests.[36]

On most occasions, the debates of statesmen were about exactly what they appeared to be about: how to satisfy the interests of Russia in the most effective manner. Since something resembling a consensus about the definition of Russian interests often existed, disputes at times concerned instrumentalities. There were disagreements about which diplomatic partners Russia should cultivate in the pursuit of its objectives; there were also differences of opinion about the prudence of risktaking. Panin's Northern System is a case in point. As we have already seen, after the Seven Years War, Nikita Panin felt that the Russian state needed to put its fiscal house back in order. But he was bothered equally by the low ratio of population to territory in the Russian Empire. Unsettled territory simply could not be defended.[37] Russia consequently also needed time to allow for natural demographic increase to take its course. It therefore behooved Russia to minimize the risk of war by avoiding foreign adventures that might rouse coalitions of powerful enemies against it. That did not mean, however, that Russia was a "satisfied power" or would necessarily be wedded to a policy of *recuillement* forever.[38]

What then did Russia's statesmen want? One subject, of course, that commanded agreement among most of them was that it was vital for Russia to hang on to the territories it already possessed. Thus Russia had to avert or preempt threats to the security of its borderlands from whatever quarter they might come. And it was this consideration that ultimately explains Russia's participation in the Seven Years War.

It is sometimes argued that Russia's entry into Kaunitz's anti-Prussian war was a horrible, irrational blunder. Frederick the Great, for one, ever after insisted (or at least feigned) that he could never understand why Russia had been so antagonistic against him as to go to war.[39] After all, Russia lost thousands of lives, wasted millions of rubles, and finally exited from the conflict with nothing to show for it. Yet was Russia's participation in this war really as irrational as that? Since the early 1740s Bestuzhev-Riumen and the Empress Elizabeth had suspected that Prussia had designs on the Baltic dutchy of Kurland. Kurland, of course, abutted the Livonian holdings, which had been taken from Sweden at enormous cost by Peter the Great. Complicating the geostrategic picture still further, however, was the fact that the sister of Frederick of Prussia, Lovisa Ulrica, happened to be the Queen of Sweden. Sweden was a power that from time to time seemed to regard the Nystadt settlement of

1721 as less than final. Stockholm had, in fact, declared war on Russia in 1741 partly in the interests of revanche. Should a Prusso-Swedish alliance take place (which was by no means impossible), and should both states simultaneously march on Russia, then Russia's Baltic coastline would be squeezed between two pincers. In short, the entire imperial legacy of Peter the Great would be in jeopardy.[40] Many of the activities of Frederick the Great were bound to heighten Russia's anxiety about the eventual intentions of Berlin. Prussia's surprise attack on Silesia in 1740 and its unprovoked invasion of Saxony (a Russian ally) in 1744 proved that Frederick was a ruthless and unscrupulous monarch who would not hesitate to violate any treaty or international agreement.[41] Considering Frederick's record, Bestuzhev asked, "is it possible to trust a prince such as this, who is so little restrained by his own most solemn promises, treaties, and formal obligations?"[42] It was, moreover, evident to St. Petersburg that Prussia was becoming stronger, not weaker. In the opinion of some of Russia's best statesmen, as long as the might of Prussia remained unchecked, Prussian aggression against Russia's Baltic provinces was always possible, maybe even probable. Bestuzhev, who was fond of characterizing Prussia as "the nearest and strongest, and consequently the most dangerous neighbor of our Empire," also wrote that "the more the King of Prussia enhances his power, the more dangerous he is for us [since] we cannot predict what will arise from such a powerful, light-minded and inconstant neighbor."[43]

This then was what worried both Bestuzhev and Elizabeth: were Prussia to succeed in dominating Central Europe, sooner or later Russia itself would be threatened. Chancellor Bestuzhev consequently justified Russian support for Austria in the following terms: "If my neighbor's house is on fire, I am obliged to help him extinguish it for the sake of my own security."[44] Note that for Bestuzhev the reason for the fire-fighting is not altruism but self-protection. When Russia declared war on Berlin in 1756 with the avowed goal of "weakening the King of Prussia," its government believed that the hostilities were in the best interests of the Russian state.[45]

After several years of war, after Russia failed to achieve almost any of its objectives, it was naturally easy to deride Russia's war effort as unreasoning and ill-conceived. Here court politics very definitely did play a role. In 1762 the Panins persuaded the superannuated Count Münnich, who had scarcely unthawed from his years of Siberian exile, to author a pamphlet condemning the pointlessness of the Seven Years War in those very terms.[46] The Panins, of course, did want to enhance their own power by unseating Count Bestuzhev, but they wanted no less ardently to promote a new foreign policy, and there was no better way to do so than by heaping scorn and obloquy on the old. In the 1740s and 1750s, however, Russia's animosity toward Prussia was quite definitely justifiable in terms of *raison d'état*. Certainly, Elizabeth Petrovna hated and feared Frederick the Great, but she had sound reasons for doing so, at least by her own lights.

If Russia's statesmen desired to retain control over the potentially vulnerable border provinces, then, many of them were no less attracted by the concept of defensible frontiers. As we have seen, Russia's borders were vast in extent and also quite permeable to nomadic attack. That being so, as we have also seen, the Russian government expended vast sums on the organization of defensive lines against the peoples of the steppe. Given the political and economic instability of the nomadic world, however, the logic of defense could easily be understood by St. Petersburg as requiring an offensive extension of Russia's frontiers farther to the east and southeast. That policy was in fact traditional and dated back to the period of Ivan the Terrible, if not before. In support of "defensive expansionism" against the nomads, eighteenth-century governments employed a variety of techniques. One, of course, was the time-hallowed method of *divide et impere:* Russia could exploit the hostility between different tribes of nomads to play them off against each other. The Russian conquest of Bashkiriia in the late 1730s was facilitated by manipulating rivalries among Kazkhs, Kalmyks, and Bashkirs.[47] Another of St. Petersburg's expedients was the attempted resettlement of nomadic groups into territories where they might be watched or controlled more easily. An example is the case of the Yedisan Nogais. These nomads, tributaries of the Crimean Khan, inhabited lands to the northwest of the Black Sea. In the summer of 1770, however, Russia was able to arrange a treaty whereby an independent Nogai state was proclaimed in the Kuban region on the sea of Azov, hundreds of miles away from their traditional pasturages.[48]

Nor did the idea of aggressive defense occur to Russian statesmen only when they contemplated the nomad problem. In the Seven Years War, for instance, the scheme of conquering Royal Prussia, then swapping it with Poland for Kurland and Semigalia, was founded in part on commercial considerations; yet lying behind it was also the desire to obtain a defensive buffer between Russian Livonia and northern Germany.[49]

A similar concern for defensible frontiers through the elimination of salients and the establishment of buffer zones helped shape Russia's thinking about its relationship with Turkey in the eighteenth century. In fact, Russian objectives toward the Porte were surprisingly consistent throughout the period.[50] In 1737 Anna Ivanovna's foreign adviser, Count Osterman, drafted secret instruction to guide Russia's peace negotiations with the Turks. In that document—more fanciful than realizable in view of the poor progress of the war—Osterman stated that Russia needed frontiers on the Kuban and Dniester rivers. Ideally, Russia's border with the Turkish Empire should be advanced to the Prut; Wallachia and Moldavia should be made independent principalities; and Russia should annex the Kuban and the Crimea.[51] The defensible frontier argument cropped up again in General P. A. Rumiantsev's 1765 memorandum "Military and Political Observations." Rumiantsev pointed out that Russia's then existing border with Turkey could be defended only under two conditions: Russia would have either to deploy enough troops totally to occupy the frontier line or to build a much more elaborate network of strong points than it currently possessed. Owing to economic and demographic realities, however, Rumiantsev stressed that it would be impossible for the Russian Empire to do either. For that reason, he advised that Petersburg should entertain the long-term goal of extending the frontier south to the Black Sea coast and west to the southern reaches of the Bug; the Crimean Khanate, as well, should be absorbed into the Russian state.[52] In fact the Russian state fulfilled almost all of Rumianstev's program through the peace of Kutchuk Kainardzhi of 1774. Osterman's designs were more grandiose, but most of what he had wanted was achieved by the 1790s. In 1783, Russia annexed the Crimean peninsula, and in 1792, with the Jassy treaty, Russia acquired the lands between the southern reaches of the Bug and Dniester, the Kuban, and a chunk of the northern Caucasus as well. In the middle of Catherine's Second Turkish War, the State Council would call for the independence of Wallachia and Moldavia, just as Osterman had done more than fifty years previously, so that "the extensive barrier formed in this way between both Empires" could guarantee a stable peace.[53] Eventually Russia realized even that ambition, although it had to wait until 1829 to get its way.

In addition to the issue of defensible frontiers, however, there was the matter of Russia's response to geostrategic opportunities. The two were often intertwined. As Poland continued to crumble during the eighteenth century, Russia's statesmen believed that St. Petersburg could tolerate neither anarchy nor a vacuum of power on its western border. The one condition might pose a danger of spilling over into Russia proper; while the other might excite the cupidity of other neighboring states. At the very beginning of the 1730s, Münnich had advocated expansion into Poland in view of that country's turbulent weakness.[54] In November 1760 Count Vorontsov tried to test the international waters by provocatively observing to the French Ambassador Breteuil that Poland was a country that "within the next fifty years ought to be divided among its neighbors."[55] And we have already alluded to Zakhar Chernyshev's prescient note of 1763, calling for Russia to take advantage of the anarchic interregnum in Warsaw by acquiring a stronger bulwark "against Europe." Annexation of all the territory up to the Dniepr and Dvina rivers plus the lands that lay between them would, in Chernyshev's opinion, definitely further Russia's "interests of state" (*gosudarstvennaia poleznost'*).[56] But equally, after the middle of the century the Russian elite was generally in agreement that a Poland made robust again by national regeneration would not be in Russia's interests either. A resurgent Poland with an absolute monarchy would most probably be hostile to St. Petersburg. Even in its decay Poland had been able to complicate Russia's strategic problems considerably during the Turkish wars, or so the State Council believed.[57] Thus in the eighteenth century Russia used force against Poland both to suppress anarchy and to promote it there. In 1767 Russia intervened in Poland to crush a private army of anti-Russian dissidents, but in 1792 and 1795 it invaded to quash political reforms that might have resulted in a strong and viable Polish state.[58] There were some in St. Petersburg who held that the eventual "solution" of the Polish question—the destruction of the Polish state with the final partitions of the 1790s—was too extreme.[59] Yet almost every prominent Russian statesmen agreed that Russia could not refrain from meddling in Poland's domestic affairs; Russia's *raison d'état* demanded it. The Second and Third Partitions of Poland were therefore not accidents. That they happened exactly as they did owed a great deal to the vagaries of chance, diplomacy, and war, but they were not unplanned. In fact, Russia's policy toward Poland since mid-century had been pregnant with an outcome such as this.[60]

Of course, when dissecting the motivations of Russia's empire-builders, as in discussion of all human motives, it is never simply a question of either/or—that is, *either* strategic considerations drove Russian expansion, *or* commercial considerations, *or* dynastic ones. Disparate goals can happily come together and be served by the same policy. But the predominant goals, the ones that persisted over time, from reign to reign, were strategic. Eighteenth-century Russia possessed a set of well-articulated strategies. And given the fact that geography informed strategy in Russia (as indeed it had to), it is no surprise that so many different statesmen in so many different decades of that century reviewed Russia's international position and came to much the same conclusions.

The "How" of Russian Imperialism

If Russia possessed reasonably coherent strategies, then, how did it implement or attempt to implement them? To answer this question we must examine the institutional contexts in which Russia's strategies were made; the quality of its strategists' ideas; the economic and financial underpinnings of its military power; the operational and tactical practices of its commanders; and the morale and performance of its troops in the field. For Russia's strategies to be realized, or even partially realized, as a bare minimum it had to have relative efficiency at each those levels of activity.[61]

Strategy-making Institutions

Of great importance in the implementation of strategy was the development in Russia of higher governmental institutions that could attempt to coordinate military and diplomatic policies in both peace and war. Three of those bodies in the post-Petrine period were most noteworthy: the *Kabinet* (1731–41); the *Konferentsiia* (1756–62); and the *Sovet pri vysochaishchem dvore*, or State Council (1768–96).[62] The first was the council of advisers that Anna Ivanovna appointed in the aftermath of the "constitutional crisis" of 1730, which served her throughout her entire reign. The second was a council hastily created by Elizabeth Petrovna when war was on the verge of breaking out in Central Europe. The third was an improvisation that nonetheless persisted. Called into being by Catherine the Great at the start of her First Turkish War, the council endured until the end of the Empress's life. It is true that those councils had a role to play in the domestic politics of Russia. They almost invariably included the leaders of the chief clans and court factions, thus allowing the autocrat to referee among them and keep watch on them all. But it should not be forgotten that those people were often also best-educated, most insightful, and shrewdest statesmen the Russian Empire possessed. The debates among those men were in fact a great enforcer of strategic realism, much as the heated discussions in Peter I's military councils had been. Further, as the capabilities of Russia's generals and diplomats improved over the course of the century, so too did the performance of those higher governmental bodies.[63] Each of them was superior to its predecessor.

The war cabinets contributed to the success of Russian strategy in at least three ways. First they evaluated, emended, and approved the operational plans for campaigns and entire wars. During the Turkish war of the 1730s, for example, Münnich would prepare an operational proposal for the coming campaign season every winter. That detailed project was then submitted to the *Kabinet* for scrutiny. If accepted by that body, it would then be passed to the Empress for her imprimatur.[64] During the Seven Years War, the *Konferentsiia* had similar responsibilities. Almost all the instructions sent out to Russia's field commanders were issued in its name.[65] It has, of course, been charged that the *Konferentsiia* was overzealous in that regard, attempting to regulate even the most petty matters and attempting to foresee everything. The charge has some substance. As the members of the *Konferentsiia* wrote of themselves in 1761: "Almost from the very beginning of the current war we have thus issued our instruc-

tions and even plans of operations." They continued by observing that they had tried to envision all possible situations that
could arise, "proposing for each of them special arguments and
orders."[66] Yet in all fairness, as one scholar has recently noted,
the *Konferentsiia* was the sole institution in Russia with the "will
and authority" to make war.[67] Further, both the *Konferentsiia* and
the empress Elizabeth became wiser as the war proceeded and
allowed greater scope for the discretion of individual commanders in the field.[68]

Catherine's *Sovet* was the clearinghouse for military planning
for most of her reign as well. Asked by the Empress to devise a
program for the Turkish war in November 1768, the Council
came up with a three-year operational plan that included four
variants for the first campaign depending upon what the Ottomans did.[69] This council was, however, more sophisticated than
the two war cabinets that had preceded it, at least in part as a
result of its exploitation of the institutional memory of Russia's
increasingly competent central bureaucracy. The Council began
its deliberations about the First Turkish War, for example, only
after making a detailed study of the archival records on Münnich's
campaigns of the 1730s. Deliberations about proposed courses of
action in 1787 were informed by an elaborate historical analysis
of what had gone right and wrong in the previous wars with the
Porte.[70]

The war cabinets additionally played an important part in tem-
pering the excessive ambitions of some of Russia's commanders
and in guarding against strategic megalomania. The process of
reassessment was constant, as the cabinets evaluated and reevalu-
ated the relationship between Russia's war objectives and the
probable costs of their realization. Münnich's initial plan for the
Turkish war was, for example, ridiculously overoptimistic. In it,
he prophesied that Russia would take Azov and the Crimea in
1736 and the Kuban in 1737. In 1738 "without the slightest risk
[sic] the Belgorod and Budzhak hordes will be subordinated to
us [and] the Greeks will be saved under the wing of the Russian
eagle. In 1739 the banners and standards of Her Majesty will be
hoisted . . . in Constantinople."[71]

Several years of war, however, demonstrated just how unrealistic Münnich's dreams had been. After consultation with her
Kabinet, the Empress Anna wrote in the fall of 1738: "We cannot

by ourselves entirely destroy or ruin the Turkish state, and our army has shown this fully this current year, as men and horses have fallen; even if the army were to be reinforced next year, all of the recruits would be raw."[72] For those reasons, Anna and the *Kabinet* decided to pare down Russia's list of war aims and to seek a negotiated peace. The cabinets imposed a sense of limits in later wars as well. During the time of Catherine the Great several people concocted fabulous plots for the partition of the Ottoman Empire.[73] Perhaps the most famous was the "Greek Project" of the 1780s, Bezborodko's scheme to butcher a new Byzantine Empire out of the prostrate carcass of Turkey. To this day there is a debate about how seriously Catherine (or anybody else) took this project.[74] One thing, however, is certain. During the Turkish War of 1787–92 there was little talk of the "Greek Project" in Catherine's *Sovet pri vysochaishchem dvore*. There, discussion focused solely on war aims that were realistically attainable. If Catherine really wanted "to drive the Turks from Europe," the deliberations of her council reveal that it was to be done not at once, but by degrees.[75]

In the second place, these cabinets were also the nerve centers for Russia's conduct of coalition war. It was in the meetings of those bodies that Russia's statesmen selected allies prior to war and coordinated strategies with them during it. Anna's *Kabinet,* for instance, was the scene of fierce debate in the early 1730s about the relative virtues of alliance systems founded alternately on Vienna or Paris.[76] The war cabinets also discussed the means of bamboozling and manipulating Russia's alliance partners. If Russia had to endure much at the hands of its allies in the eighteenth century, it was also capable of repaying them in kind. Osterman, the *de facto* head of Anna's *Kabinet,* was notorious for his opaque and impenetrable discourse even in conversation with ambassadors from friendly countries. A contemporary wrote of him that

> . . . he had so strange a way of talking that very few people could ever boast that they had succeeded in comprehending him. Very often foreign ministers, after a conversation of two hours with him, found on leaving his room that they knew nothing more than when they entered.[77]

For all its many failings, the *Konferentsiia* must be deemed to have managed Russia's alliance with Paris skillfully. Even France's most masterly diplomats found their relationship with Petersburg one-sided and frustrating: Elizabeth's *Konferentsiia* was adept at extracting concessions from them without, however, giving up anything substantive in return. France's foreign minister irritably wrote in the beginning of 1759 that "the experience of the last two years has made clear to us that we must not count upon the Russians. It is necessary, then, to use them and to draw from them all that we can for immediate operations against England."[78] Unfortunately for Choiseul, he was to be no more successful in wrangling a declaration of war on Britain from Petersburg than the previous incumbents of his office had been.[79] In its turn, Catherine the Great's Council carefully supervised Russia's alliance with the Austria of Joseph II during the Second Turkish War.[80]

There was one final contribution made by the war cabinets, for the cabinets were the bodies that sought to understand the "big picture"—that is, the impact that Russia's wars had on its relations with the nonbelligerent great European powers. It is fair to say that Russia's success in aggrandizing itself during the eighteenth century had as much to do with the wars its cabinets were able to divert as with the ones its generals waged and won. The cabinets worried endlessly (and with justice) about the possibility of a hostile country's taking advantage of the fact that Russia was tied up in one war by launching another; they consequently did everything they could to discourage this. When they managed to prevent other powers from attacking an already embattled Russia, they rendered invaluable services to their country.

One way to scare off a prospective additional enemy was to make capital out of Russia's victories in the field. During the Turkish war of the 1730s, for example, the *Kabinet* was concerned lest Sweden also declare war. Osterman and the *Kabinet* therefore took pains to encourage an exaggerated view of Russia's military prowess in Stockholm, exploiting Russia's victory at Stavuchany especially shrewdly for this purpose.[81] Hostilities with Sweden were consequently postponed until the war with Turkey had ended.

Another technique was to attempt to modulate Russia's military operations in the field with the goal of producing a particular impression on potentially belligerent foreign states. In the fall of 1761, for instance, the *Konferentsiia* wrote Generals Rumiantsev and Buturlin that they had to take the fortress of Kolberg without delay. Russia's war effort seemed to have bogged down to such a degree that there was a danger that other states (presumably Sweden and Turkey) "seeing the protracted conduct of this war and not foreseeing its conclusion [might] intervene in it and fish in troubled waters by adhering to the camp of our enemies."[82]

Of all of the three institutions, it was Catherine's *Sovet* that was most alive to the complexity of waging war in the environment of contemporary international politics. Meetings regularly began with a reading of reports addressed to it from Russia's ambassadors in London, Paris, Warsaw, Stockholm, Copenhagen, and Berlin.[83] That was natural, because the Council took over the direction of Russia's diplomacy in wartime, when diplomacy is expected to support war. But the Council equally employed war to support diplomacy, for it waged war with the attitudes of the other powers constantly in mind. If Russia suffered too many reverses or defeats, coalitions of additional enemies might assemble against it. Unfortunately, too many Russian victories might have the same effect. Such concerns framed the orders the Council issued to Russia's armies. Whether a general should be encouraged to press forward for still greater victories or should be commanded to acede to negotiations was firmly grounded in the context of international politics.

In early 1772, for example, the Council fretted over the possibility of an Austrian attack and discussed ways in which a rapid campaign might be conducted to force the Ottomans to an immediate peace, a discussion that later bore fruit in Rumiantsev's lightning offensives.[84] During the second Turkish War Russia had to cope not only with the Ottomans but with the Swedes, whose king marched on Russian Finland in 1788. When, at that very moment, the Prussians threatened to declare war also, the Council went into emergency session. Should Russia radically scale back its territorial demands to bring the Turkish war to a close? In that event,

> ... given the internal and external situation, we would have extricated ourselves relatively satisfactorily from our

current troubles as, freed from one powerful enemy, we would be able in the event of need to turn our principal forces jointly with the Austrians against the King of Prussia. We certainly do not think that we should wish or seek a war with that sovereign, but our attention must be fixed on the attempt to end the war with Sweden gloriously and profitably and on the restoration of our influence in Poland, which has lately been reduced.[85]

Alternately, the Council argued, Russia might give Joseph II of Austria permission to make a separate peace with Turkey so that he could deal with the threat posed by Berlin.[86] What eventuated was a stepup in the tempo of Russian military operations in the south. That, in combination with the accession of the Danes to the war against Stockholm (partially negotiated by the Council), was enough to keep Prussia neutral—at least for the moment.

In 1790 the Council continued to worry about the growing possibility of foreign intervention on the part of both Prussia and England. Prussia was readying an army of 40,000 for operations against Russia, and Britain was backing Prussia's unctuous proposal for "mediation" between Russia and the Porte that, if accepted, would have prevented Russia from realizing any gains at all from the Turkish war.[87] In view of the parlous international situation, the Council ordered Russia's best field commander, General Suvorov, to limit the scope of his forthcoming campaign, a restriction under which that eccentric genius evidently chafed.[88] The inimical attitude of Berlin and London was still a problem in 1791; the ambassadors of those two powers presented Russia with an ultimatum demanding immediate peace with Turkey. The Council advised playing for time and drafted the Empress's affable (but opaque) note of response, but eventually concluded later that summer that owing largely to the distractions posed by the French Revolution there was litle risk of a sudden attack.[89]

This brings us to the final means that the Council used in order to keep additional enemies at bay: territorial compensation. Russia's great expansion to the south in the eighteenth century directly and almost irresistibly brought the partitions of Poland in its train. The Council fully recognized that the interests of Poland and Turkey were inextricably intertwined. Turkey would not allow the Polish state to fall under the sway of Russia without a fight; the Ottomans had no affection for their traditional Polish enemies but felt they needed Warsaw as a shield against Russia. It was Russia's military occupation of Poland that caused the Ottomans to declare the Balta massacre a *casus belli* against Russia in 1768.* Similarly, if Russia were at war with Turkey, the Poles were apt to avail themselves of that opportunity to wriggle away from St. Petersburg's unwelcome embrace in the direction of greater independence.[90] For those reasons, at the very beginning of Catherine's First Turkish War the Council included in its list of Russian war aims demands for the rectification not only of the Turkish but also of the *Polish* frontiers.[91]

When Russian victories aroused the envy of Austria and Prussia, Russia found it had no choice but to assuage those sentiments with the August 1772 partition treaty.[92] The idea of the partition may have originated in Vienna and Berlin, but Russia's statesmen—even Nikita Panin—came to perceive the impregnable logic of the agreement too.[93] Giving shares of Poland to the two German monarchies was the necessary price that had to be paid if Russia wanted to retain its southern conquests. The balance of power was not thereby restored; rather, Petersburg bribed Prussia and Austria into overlooking the fact that Russia had just overturned it. Russia was relatively stronger vis-à-vis both Vienna and Berlin *after* the partitions than before; the Turkish annexations of the eighteenth century were to be the foundation of the power of the Russian Empire in the nineteenth.

The first division of Poland meant, however, that Russia's future freedom of action in what remained of the Commonwealth was necessarily mortgaged to Russia's German accomplices. When the Council plotted Russia's 1792 invasion of Poland in response to the promulgation of the consitution of the May 3, it insisted that Austria and Prussia had to be consulted:

> To be confident of our success we must be no less confident in the agreement to this [the invasion] on the part of Poland's neighbors, the Vienna court, and most particularly the court of Berlin.[94]

---

*In pursuit of a small Polish force, a band of Russian Cossacks crossed over into Turkish territory in July 1768, slaughtered the inhabitants of Balta, and burned that town.

That invasion is what led directly to the Second Partition of 1793. Russia's easy triumph over a bankrupt and enfeebled Poland plus its remarkable though costly victories against the Porte led Frederick William of Prussia to balk at continuing his own war with Revolutionary France. To appease the Prussian King (thus keeping the struggle against France going), Russia had to serve him additional slices of the Polish ham. The Third Partition was, from Petersburg's point of view, no less logical: the rebellion of Kosciuszko had convinced Catherine that even a rump Poland could never be stable; still further, there was still the greed of Vienna and Berlin to consider.[95] The partitions of Poland may well have been immoral, cynical, and shameful deeds that blatantly transgressed even against the prevailing lax norms of international behavior. But they were also strategically necessary to St. Petersburg.

Strategic Planning and Geography

Eighteenth-century Russia thus developed war cabinets that were sensitive enough to the nuances of international politics to manage friends and thwart foes. Despite all its wiles, however, Russian diplomacy would have been useless without effective military performance. In that regard, Russia's strategists often distinguished themselves throughout the century by crafting prudent and sound operational plans, profoundly informed by a knowledge of geography.

Some scholars, perhaps taking Napoleon's great campaigns of mobility as their standard, have complained that Russia's wars with Turkey in this period all too often degenerated into static and bloody sieges. Such quibbling misses the point, however. Although they were miserable for all parties—famine and disease were the usual lot of both besieger and besieged—sieges were unavoidable in the context of eighteenth-century warfare, not only in Eastern Europe but in Western Europe as well.[96]

Fortresses and strongpoints occupied a central position in the security policy of all the important states of the age. In the first place, fortresses served as barriers: they protected the frontiers, stood at the confluence of seas and waterways, and commanded the narrows of the principal rivers on which military communication and supply depended. An adversary who rashly attempted to bypass an important enemy stronghold automatically put his army at the risk of having its logistical lines severed. For that reason, the capture of such a fort was often the essential precondition for any field operations at all in a region. Russia's inability to take Ochakov in 1787, for instance, impeded the movements of its armies during that entire campaigning season.[97] In the same way, the fortress of Stettin served Frederick the Great as a durable bulwark against Russia throughout the Seven Years War.[98]

Second, fortresses usually contained the administrative bases and war arsenals of the powers that maintained them. The stocks of uniforms, food, powder, ball, and shell warehoused in the fortresses were the indispensable sinews of both defense and offense. The supplies stored in Magdeburg or transshipped through that fort were vital for Frederick II's war in Saxony.[99] At times the loss of a fort could imperil an entire province, or even make the difference in the outcome of a war. Kolberg (by way of an example) was the key to northern Pomerania; when Rumiantsev captured it in December 1761, Prussia's position on the Baltic coast became precarious.[100]

Constantinople, of course, depended on its fortresses even more than Berlin. Turkey's strongholds on the Don, Bug, Dniestr, Prut, and Danube protected the northern marches of its empire like the fingers of a mailed hand, guaranteeing its possession of the entire northern and western littorals of the Black Sea. Azov, located near the mouth of the Don, overlooked the Sea of Azov and preserved Ottoman communications with Transcaspia. Ochakov dominated both the lower reaches of the Bug and the 30 miles of Dniepr estuary opposite Kinburn. It was the *sine qua non* of Ottoman rule in the territory between these two rivers and, together with Kinburn, ensured the Porte's access to the Crimean peninsula.[101] On the Dniestr, Khotin and Bender were the two most important fortified towns. The former covered the junction of the Dniestr and the Prut, while the later upheld Constantinople's domination over its Budzhak Tatar vassals.[102] Of the Prut strongholds, the most notable was Jassy in the north. Jassy linked the Nogai horde to the body of the Turkish Empire and barred enemy access to Moldavia.[103] For its part, Izmail on the Danube was the *place fort* that maintained Turkish sway over the delta of that river and the northwestern Black Sea.

The impressive network of fortresses, then, defined the cockpit of Russo-Turkish conflict throughout the century. Each of the forts was linked to its fellows in a system of mutual support determined by interior lines—a fact that imparted the characteristics of a complex geometrical puzzle to Russia's campaigns in this theater. It was of course occasionally possible to secure the capitulation of one or even more of those strongholds by defeating a Turkish field army. Münnich's annihilating victory over Veli Pasha at Stavuchany, for instance, led directly to the surrender of Khotin by its craven governor in August 1739.[104] After Suvorov, with the aid of the Prince of Coburg, won the battle of Focsany in the summer of 1789, the Turkish forts on the Dniester all rather quickly opened their gates to Russian forces.[105] And, in what was probably one of the most spectacular martial feats during the century, Rumiantsev dashed across the Danube in 1774, cutting off all of the Turkish forts to the northeast from the body of the Ottoman Empire—an operation that by itself forced Turkey to accede to the peace of Kutchuk Kainardzhi.[106] The Turks, however, usually tried to avoid being caught out in the open and cut to pieces. They retired on their fortresses, giving Russian commanders no recourse but the siege.[107]

Confronted with such Turkish behavior, Russia's commanders and strategists in the eighteenth century developed a rather distinctive style of warfighting. Most Russian campaigns against Turkey in the period are strikingly similar in design, for most involved simultaneous two-pronged attacks, either north and south or east and west. Those attacks, sometimes supported by riverine flotillas or oceangoing fleets, were designed to spread the Ottomans thin by making them deploy their forces in two places hundreds of miles apart. The goal of at least one of the attacks was the acquisition of a specific, strategically important Turkish stronghold, in the interest of carving the Turkish network of fortresses into halves, thirds, or quarters. Sometimes this might be accomplished by garrisoning a captured fortress and using it as a *point d'appui* to create havoc with Turkish communications and logistics; on other occasions the Russians might elect to demolish it, for as Münnich once wrote, "there is an old military rule that . . . an enemy position that has no linkage to [one's own] borders and which the enemy can always approach and attack at leisure, ought not to remain in one's hands after having been seized."[108] There was certainly some wisdom in Münnich's adage, for a stronghold captured in one campaigning season could often be lost in the next.

In 1736, for instance, Lacy's successful assault on Azov complemented Münnich's invasion of the Crimea.[109] The following year, it fell to Lacy to raid the Crimea, while Münnich invested Ochakov. After he took it (a Russian bomb fortuitously exploded the powder magazine, and the Russians took that opportunity to storm the city from the seaward side), he described the exploit as "a splinter in the enemy's foot."[110] In a later missive to the Empress Anna his tone was less jocular. "I consider Ochakov," he wrote, "to be the most important fortress that Russia has ever conquered, for Ochakov cuts the connection between the Turks and the Tatars, between the Budzhak and the Crimea." Perhaps indulging in fantasy overmuch, he added that "if one had a fair wind, one could get from this place to Constantinople by sea in five or six days."[111] In 1738 Lacy was once again supposed to pin down the Crimean Tatars while the German Field Marshal was to cross the Dniestr and try to blockade Bender into submission.[112] The plan for 1739 involved a thrust at Khotin in Moldavia, with auxiliary operations against the Turks and their tributaries in the Crimea and the Kuban.[113]

The two Turkish wars of Catherine the Great also featured the same sort of double attacks that Münnich and his generals had pioneered. In 1769, the first year of the first war, Rumianstev was instructed to march on Perekop, while Peter Panin besieged Bender. A year later Rumiantsev's First Army operated in Wallachia and Moldavia, while the Russian Second Army covered his flanks and rear to the east. St. Petersburg utilized dual offensives in a similar vein for the campaigns of 1771, 1773, and 1774, when a siege of Ochakov was conjoined with a drive on the Danubian forts of Rushchuk and Silistriia.[114] In the second war (provoked by Russia's annexation of the Crimea and its offer of "protection" to Georgia) St. Petersburg's methods were usually the same, with Ochakov as the focus of the main Russian blows in the early stages of the conflict and Izmail in the later.[115] Russia's custom of organizing its campaigns around sieges does not therefore illustrate its strategists' poverty of imagination; rather, this strategic tradition was a sensible and hard-headed adaption to the realities of geography, logistics, and friction.

The Economics of Protracted War

But siegecraft inevitably meant protracted war. Even Suvorov, whose reputation for speedy and decisive operations was well deserved, thought in terms of war of at least three years' duration.[116] And protracted war is, of course, expensive. What then of money, Peter the Great's "artery of war"? As we have already seen, the poverty of the Russian state was an undeniable constraint on the ambitions of the government of the empire. Nonethless, St. Petersburg managed to bear the costs of numerous of major wars during the eighteenth century. How was that done? The answer lay in the state's ability to take advantage of expansion in Russia's population and economy.

Although the weakness of post-Petrine Russia clearly emerges from any per capita comparison of its wealth with that of its Western neighbors, its population grew strikingly in this period, as did the output of its economy. As we have already observed, while in 1722 there were some 14 million people subject to the Russian crown, in 1744 there were 18 million, and in 1796 36 million. Some of the increase, roughly 9 million or so, was the result of Russia's conquests and annexations; most of it, however, was traceable to the radically higher birthrate after mid-century.[117] That population explosion naturally had a dramatic impact on the economy. In the first place, although there was no substantial improvement in labor-intensive techniques of cultivation, there were more people to till the soil, with the result that agricultural output grew. With the exception of years of poor harvests, that meant the richest farming regions of the country increasingly produced surpluses that could be sold on the internal market or exported. It has been calculated, for example, that even in times of moderate harvests, the Central Black Earth region regularly amassed a surplus of 10,000 quarters of grain a year.[118]

Then, too, more food and more people provided a foundation for a surge in Russian industrial production. Helpful as well in this regard was the unconscious economic stimulation the Russian government provided until 1762 essentially by tolerating the merchantry's ownership of serf factory labor.[119] After that date, the government's emancipation of the nobility from the obligation of state service and its gifts to that class of additional lands, serfs, privileges, and immunities were stimuli to its entrepreneurial efforts as well.[120] Perhaps as a result, the number of factories and mines operating in Russia increased sharply. At the end of Peter's life there were only two hundred of such enterprises in the country. By 1767, however, that statistic had more than tripled to 663, and by 1799 it had almost doubled again (1,200).[121] Russia's output of iron shot up from 10,000 tons in 1720 to more than 162,000 tons in 1800, by which point Russian production was on a par with the British.[122] It is not surprising therefore that Russia's exports also increased: from 4.6 million rubles in 1742 to 5.9 million a decade later, to 12.8 million in 1762, and to more than 43 million rubles in 1793.[123]

The state was natually interested in siphoning some of this burgeoning wealth off into its own hands and adopted several means for doing so. First, Petersburg found it possible to manipulate the indirect tax rate on common commodities, like vodka and salt, for which the demand was relatively inelastic. Although Russia's needy peasants were likely to resist paying new direct levies, they could sacrifice neither the boon of salt nor the benediction of alcohol, whose taxes were secreted in the purchase price. Thus the Imperial treasury could profit from the demographic expansion of Russia regardless of how destitute its teeming inhabitants were. It was Petr Ivanovich Shuvalov, the great financial and ballistics expert, who was behind the upping of the taxes on vodka and salt in 1750 that resulted in annual enhancement of state revenues by 1.5 and 0.7 million rubles respectively over the following decade.[124] That expedient remained in the financial repertoire of the Romanov dynasty until the revolutions of the twentieth century.

The state was also able to capitalize on the expansion in the volume of Russia's foreign trade by elevating tariffs on both imports and exports. By 1796, 33.7 percent of the government's total income was derived from the soul tax, 28.6 percent from the alcohol tax, 7.1 percent from the salt levy, and 8.7 percent from foreign tariffs.[125] Real state revenues more than doubled from 1749 to 1760 and more than doubled again by 1795, when they attained 56 million rubles.[126]

Of course, none of this should be taken to suggest that the imperial goverment was wallowing in a capacious trough of specie. If revenues increased, so too did outlays, and at an even more rapid rate. We have already had occasion to discuss the desperate steps the tsarist fisc adopted to cover its deficits: the debasement of the coinage, the issuing of paper banknotes, the hikes in the soul tax, and the floating of loans abroad. Financial crises were in fact epidemic during the reigns of each of Russia's rulers during the eighteenth century. Then, too, some of Peter's successors seem to have been less concerned about the relationship between manufacturing and military power than he had been. Catherine the Great's government, for example, did not decree anything remotely resembling a military-industrial census until 1789.[127] Yet despite the fiscal problems that attended each of its wars, Russia's growing revenues generally did not lag too far behind the growing scope of its military activities. Indeed, the proportion of revenue allocated to the support of the army and the navy actually declined, particularly in the second half of the century.[128] The emperors and empresses who came after Peter were able, like him, to raise sufficient resources to wage war and support armies. Unlike him, they managed to do it without nearly destroying Russian society in the process.

The Contribution of the Commanders:
Operational and Tactical Innovations

As we have already had occasion to observe, however, economic resources do not by themselves win war. All they can do is undergird the general and armies on whom victory in the end ultimately depends. And Russia, it is fair to say, was fortunate in the quality of both its troops and many of its military leaders through the course of the eighteenth century. Several outstanding commanders served Russia during the period. Three, however, especially distinguished themselves: Burchard Christoph von Münnich (1683–1767); Petr Aleksandrovish Rumiantsev (1725–96); and Aleksandr Vasilievich Suvorov (1729–1800). Those three gifted generals radically differed from each other in background, character, and personality. There were nevertheless striking resemblances in the military-operational practices of each.

Münnich, who had been born in the German state of Oldenburg, originally settled in Russia as an engineer in the employ of Peter the Great.[129] Although he did important work during Peter's lifetime (he was the director of construction for the Ladoga

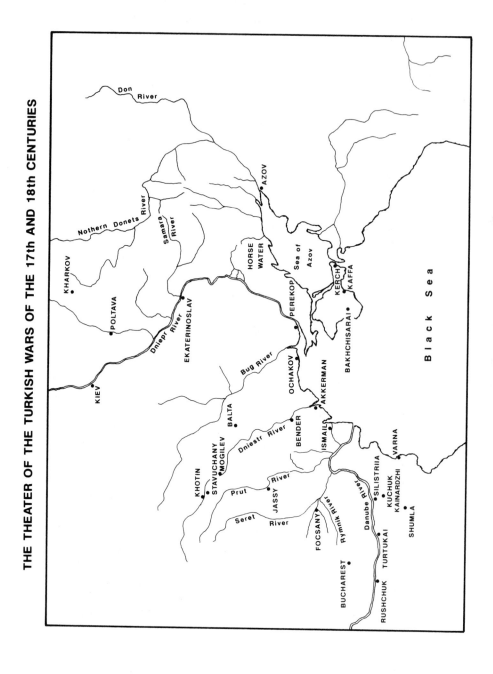

THE THEATER OF THE TURKISH WARS OF THE 17th AND 18th CENTURIES

canal), it was under Peter's heirs—particularly the Empress Anna—that Münnich rose to the heights of prominence within the state. Appointed vice president of eighteenth-century Russia's ministry of defense (the College of War) in 1727, he became the chief inspector of the Russian artillery two years later. In 1732 Anna promoted him both to Field Marshal and to the presidency of the War College. From that vantage point he virtually controlled Russia's military policy in both peace and war for the next nine years.

Münnich's German origins have occasionally provoked attacks on him by Russian historians, who deem him one of the most prominent members of the Teutonic cabal that is supposed to have brought Russia so much grief in the "dark age" of the Empress Anna. His management of the Turkish war of the 1730s has also been savagely attacked, not in the least because of the extraordinarily high death toll of the Russian forces that took part in it.[130] Yet the criticism that Münnich was biased in favor of his fellow foreign soldiers of fortune will not in fact stand up; as President of the War College, Münnich founded a school to improve the military education of the indigenous Russian nobility and, still further, actually equalized the pay of native-born officers and foreign mercenaries.[131] Münnich did, however, have his share of character flaws. He was deeply proud and vain—so much so that after capturing the crimson caparisoned *telega* of the Crimean Khan in 1736, he insisted ever after on being hauled around in that two-wheeled carriage like an Oriental potentate, even when on campaign.[132] He was also thoroughly ruthless. In 1739 he personally ordered the murder of the Swedish diplomatic courier Major Sinclair, who was caught in Silesia (en route back from a trip to Constantinople) and dispatched by Münnich's assassins.[133] Of course, he burned with personal ambition; indeed, his involvement in a grab for power in 1741 led directly to a suspended death sentence and more than twenty years of exile in the frigid Siberian hamlet of Pelim, a punishment from which only the accession of Catherine the Great reprieved him.[134] Münnich was, however, a great military engineer and a superior military organizer and planner whose achievements against the Poles, French, Tatars, and Turks during the 1730s brought him European fame. Frederick the Great, to cite only one of his admirers, described him as "the Prince Eugene of the Russians" and as "a true hero of the Russian state."[135]

Rumiantsev, by contrast, was born into a family of petty Russian nobles who owed their rise to the favor of Peter the Great. Indeed, Rumiantsev himself actually may have been Peter's bastard son.[136] His military career spanned more than half a century. After becoming an officer at the age of sixteen, Rumiantsev served in the St. Petersburg guards regiments. In 1748 he accompanied Repnin on the latter's famous march to the Rhine. When the Seven Years War broke out, Rumiantsev held command over cavalry regiments, infantry brigades, and, eventually, entire divisions, distinguishing himself at Gross Jägersdorf, Kunersdorf, and Kolberg. Later, Catherine the Great made him the Governor-General of the Ukraine. In the First Turkish War his exploits as commander of the First or Danubian army brought him a marshal's baton and a title ("The Transdanubian") from a grateful Empress, not to mention 100,000 rubles, 5,000 peasants, and a diamond-encrusted sword. After another decade as viceroy of Little Russia, he returned to the field army during the second war with Turkey as commander of the auxiliary, or Ukrainian, army. After the signing of the peace of Jassy, he lived in nominal retirement in Kiev until 1794, when, despite his poor health, he was recalled to active duty for operations in Poland. It was to be his last command. When he died two years later, he had survived Catherine II by only thirty-two days.[137]

Rumiantsev has fared better than Münnich at the hands of Russian and Soviet historians. The latter, in particular, have hailed the Field Marshal as the torchbearer of the vital native military tradition, in contradistinction to the supposed sterile Prussianism of the court Germans.[138] Of course, Rumiantsev also had his unattractive side; he was vainglorious, arrogant, and a brutal disciplinarian, though not a martinet. Still, he was concerned for the well-being of his men; for example, he showed an all-too-rare interest in the cleanliness of their hair. The troops' pigtails might be the usual repositories of lice and filth in other generals' commands, but not in his.[139] Rumiantsev was, moreover, a talented strategist as well as a tactician whose stature as a Russian national hero is deservedly secure.

We come to the most brilliant but, oddly, the least influential of the three leaders, A. V. Suvorov. Suvorov's life was full of paradoxes and ironies. Plainspoken and disdainful of court etiquette, Suvorov acquired a reputation as an eccentric buffoon, much to the irritation of the autocrats he served and much to the consequent detriment of his career. Tormented by poor health for most of his life, he was also so astonishingly accident-prone that one must wonder whether there wasn't something wrong with his balance.[140] Yet despite his ridiculous antics off the battlefield (dressed only in a shirt, he would sometimes serenade his troops by imitating a rooster's crow) and despite the physical and emotional ills that plagued him, Suvorov was undoubtedly the single most dazzlingly successful military commander eighteenth-century Russia ever produced.[141] Deeply religious and highly educated (he spoke at least seven foreign languages, including Turkish and Finnish), he began to make his military name during the First Turkish War, consolidated it with the spectacular victories of Rymnik and Focsany in the Second, and capped his achievement with his fabled conduct of the Italian campaign of 1799. Yet never once did he bear the main responsibility for overall strategy in any war; he was always the executor of other people's plans. Although many years after his death his collection of canny maxims ("The Art of Victory") was touted as a work of genius, his most lucid reflections on military education and the techniques of command were contained in a lengthy letter he wrote to his three-year-old godson in 1793.[142] Although he later becamse such a cult figure for Russians that Stalin was even moved to create a decoration in his honor during World War II, he died in ignominious disgrace.[143]

Despite all the differences among these three great commanders, the campaigns of Münnich, Rumiantsev, and Suvorov may be said to epitomize the best in an evolving Russian style of military operations in the eighteenth century. The exigencies of war with Turks helped shape that style more than anything else. Consider, for example, the consequences of the Turkish wars for Russian infantry musketry.

It is often correctly assumed that most of the prominent eighteenth-century armies were heavily influenced by the military practices of Frederick the Great, most particularly with regard to marksmanship. Early in his reign, Frederick became convinced of the superiority of the tactics of firepower. He later wrote: "Battles are decided by the superiority of fire. Except in the attack on defended positions, a force of infantry which loads speedily will always get the better of a force which loads more slowly."[144] What that meant in practice was that Frederick drilled his army to load and fire their muskets as fast as humanly possible. Well-trained Prussian troops were said to reach a rate of six rounds per minute in peacetime conditions. Speed of fire was everything, aiming nothing. Indeed, Frederick even *forbade* aimed fire. It did not matter than Prussian soldiers might occasionally discharge their muskets into the earth, or load and fire their ramrods, since it was the quickness and the intensity of the infantry volleys that was supposed to shatter the morale of the enemy and drive him from the field.[145]

Frederick's example carried weight in Imperial Russia; the Infantry Statute of 1755, for instance, was clearly inspired by a Frederickian model, emphasizing as it did the quantity rather than the accuracy of fire.[146] Yet Münnich, Rumiantsev, and Suvorov, contrary to prevailing fashions, were known for insisting on *aimed* fire. The most likely reason they did so was that they were all veterans of Turkish and Tatar warfare. Whenever a Russian commander led an army off into the steppe or into the Balkans, he could usually be certain that he would be fighting an enemy superior, sometimes even vastly superior, to him in numbers. If the Russian general was to win, he had somehow to overcome that fundamental disadvantage in manpower. Yet this difficulty was often overcome. Rumiantsev noted of himself, with characteristic immodesty: "to defeat large forces with small numbers is art and profound glory, but to be victorious owing to superior strength— this is not extraordinary."[147] One of the features of this "art," then, was a general's insistence that every infantry ball be loaded, aimed, and fired with precision. Given the difficulties of supply, the nature of the terrain, and the size of the enemy, it was unthinkable to condone the wasting of even a single shot.

Münnich was an enthusiast for training his troops to aim, and partly ascribed his victory at Stavuchany in August 1739, when he crushed a Turkish force of more than 80,000 with only 48,000 men of his own, to his emphasis on aimed fire.[148] Even at the time of the Seven Years War Rumiantsev insisted that aimed firing be taught his men and proscribed utterly the practice of unaimed volleys at great distances—techniques that would serve him well in his later Ottoman wars.[149] As for Suvorov, he was also a great believer in making his ammunition count. During the Second Turkish War he expressed his incredulity that the troops of his Austrian ally, the Prince of Nassau, had never been drilled in firing at targets. In a letter of 1788 he advised his subordinate, General N. A. Chirikov, "to conserve bullets (although I have 100 cartridges [per man] here, this is for three days of battle); he who accurately levels his musket at the chest or the guts will always shoot his man."[150]

Another Russian military practice characteristic of the age was a concern for improving the mobility, speed, and killing power of the field artillery. In the previous century, Russian generals had typically relied on the concentrated fire of small artillery pieces to stop mass attacks of Turks and nomads, thus preventing the army from being overrun. That technique persisted decades later. Münnich, for instance, used it on several occasions during his Turkish war (although he usually followed it up with a vigorous counterattack).[151] And in the Seven Years War the Russians exploited the technical innovations of their artillerists—such as Peter Shuvalov's "secret howitzer"—and the skill of their gunners to offset "the failing of the cavalry and [their] general lack of mobility."[152]

As the century wore on, however, the best of Russia's commanders became more adept at employing field artillery in support of offensive operations. The gun crews had to learn how to service their field pieces with greater efficiency and dispatch; equally they had to become more rapid in the entire process of limbering and unlimbering the guns. After the Russian victory at Larga (1770), Rumiantsev praised the performance of his artillery units on that field, reporting that "wherever the field artillery was used, successes were obtained everywhere in the shortest possible time."[153] Many historians have subsequently concurred that the deft management of the artillery was one of the key elements in the operational achievements of Rumiantsev during the entire First Turkish War.[154] In the Second, Rumiantsev was known to dispense with limbers altogether, moving his artillery instead by means of ingeniously designed wheels fastened to the traces of the pack horses that could be attached or removed from the underside of the gun carriages in a matter of minutes. Thus his field guns could readily be shifted to new positions and could commence firing almost upon their arrival there.[155]

Then, too, throughout the century the more able of Russia's generals came to display the same sort of creativity in dealing with logistical problems. This is not to deny that logistical nightmares abounded—there were many of them, as we have already seen. But the sort of total logistical failures that had scuttled Golitsyn's Crimean campaigns in the 1680s and that had caused the deaths of tens of thousands of Peter's soldiers became increasingly rare, if we except the first three disorganized years of the war with Prussia. Münnich deserves much blame for the losses his army suffered from disease and hunger in 1736.[156] But it is difficult to judge his conduct of the campaigns of later years harshly, for he planned the logistics of his offensives meticulously, trying to find the equilibrium in the military ecosystem by reducing unnecessary weight and by making his equipment and his draft animals do double or triple duty. He carried his water, for instance, in enormous wooden casks, which when empty could be used to construct pontoon bridges. After the 900 pounds of provisions loaded on each cart had been consumed, the oxen that pulled it were, in accordance with his plan, slaughtered and eaten, while the cart itself was broken up for firewood.[157] Rumiantsev and Suvorov were also known for their keen attention to logistics, although in the Second Turkish War of Catherine the Great they received enormous assistance from the masterly administrator Prince G. A. Potemkin, who turned the Ukraine into the granary of Russia's armies, storing the food he requisitioned there in an enormous network of forward magazines he constructed on the Dniepr and the Bug.[158] Supply always remained a major headache for the Russian army in the eighteenth century (as indeed it always is for any army at any time). Yet insofar as the supply picture did get better, it was the consequence of the partial success of Westernization in Russia, for this improvement, even if marginal, represented the triumph of applied mathematics, a rationalized bureaucracy, and diligence over frenetic improvisation, slipshod government, and sloth.

Another quality that Münnich, Rumiantsev, and Suvorov all shared was an appreciation that the differing characteristics of Russia's enemies and of the theaters in which Russian confronted them required radically different tactics. It was of course an old problem, for the special skills and methods needed for steppe warfare were useless for warfare in Europe, and vice versa. Muscovy, of course, had tried to cope by organizing what were in effect two armies, for, as we have already seen, Moscow raised European-style troops of new formation in the 1630s designated for offensive combat with the Poles or the Swedes while still maintaining the traditional cavalry levy for defense against the Tatars. The vestiges of that bifurcated military organization survived into the eighteenth century embodied by the active field army on the one hand and the Ukrainian land militia on the other. To develop an offensive capability in the south as well as the north, and also for reasons of expense, however, St. Petersburg gradually fused its two military organizations into one in this period. By mid-century the active army had swallowed up the Ukrainian land militia, which ceased to exist as an independent formation. Yet if the resulting military amalgamation were to prevail regardless of where it fought, it had to develop great tactical flexibility; Russia's generals had to learn to tailor their tactics to setting and circumstance. Münnich observed in an appeal for pardon he addressed to Elizabeth in 1749: "The *metier* of war has its rules, but as the cases that exist in it are infinite the rules and maxims are infinite also; the maneuver of observation against the Swedes will not have the same effect against the Turks or the Persians."[159]

In Western Europe infantrymen were customarily arrayed in linear formations in order both to maximize their firepower and to facilitate maneuvering them. Indeed, quite intricate tactical maneuvers were possible with lines, of which Frederick the Great's "refused wing" and "oblique attack" were probably the most notable.[160] When Russia went to war with Western Europe, it usually deployed its men into lines as well. And although Russian lines were often more sluggish than those of their opponents, Russia's commanders were at times capable of pulling off tactical coups with linear formations, as Fermor did at Kunersdorf in August 1758, when he rapidly reversed his front from north to south to prevent being caught from behind by the Prussians.[161]

Linear (or columnar) deployments, no matter how brilliantly handled, were completely ineffective when Russia's foes were Turks or Tatars, however. Worse still, they were positively suicidal, for the Muslims, taking advantage of the mobility and numbers of their cavalry, could readily encircle and annihilate a Russian army so arranged with flank and rear attacks. Russian armies in the south were therefore usually formed into squares—both on the march and in battle. Yet as Golitsyn had discovered during the previous century, squares often imposed unacceptable, even calamitous costs in terms of slow movement and tardy reaction. The solution of Russia's best military leaders in the post-Petrine period was constantly to reify and improve on the principle of the rectilinear formation, decreasing the size of the squares and dispersing them in ever more complex patterns of mutual support. The ascendant curve of this trend is evident in the tactical dispositions of Münnich, Rumiantsev, and Suvorov.

During the 1736 campaign, for example, Münnich had formed his army into not one but five great squares. There was no novelty in this; after all, Golitsyn had employed a six-square formation back in 1687. But Golitsyn had moved his squares along a single route of advance, while Münnich assigned each of his a route of its own on one bank of the Dniepr or the other. The result was a more rapid convergence of his army on Perekop than would have been possible otherwise, not in the least because his squares were not in competition for forage. Münnich displayed a similar inventive use of his squares on the battlefield. At Stavuchany, he maneuvered the three squares of his army independently, using one to feint at the Turkish right flank while the others assaulted the Turkish left.[162]

As for Rumiantsev, his disciple, the future General of Infantry A. Khrushchev once characterized him as the man who "taught us how to construct a front against the Turks."[163] And Rumiantsev's front was constructed out of smaller building blocks than Münnich had used, for he reduced the size of the squares still further, whittling them down to the proportions of a division.[164] Rumiantsev's speed at reforming his marching columns into divisional squares and his deft exploitation of the resultant fighting formations often garnered him credit for several important Russian victories, including that of Kagul in the summer of 1770.[165] Suvorov improved on even those tactics, winning at Focsany and Rymnik with battalion squares of infantry deployed in chessboard fashion with units of cavalry serving as diagonal links.[166]

Of course, when at war in Europe, Russia's most gifted generals could also be ingenious in solving the special tactical problems that emerged in that theater as well. Some of their techniques either anticipated or paralleled the tactical innovations of the most important Western armies. The Austrian and the Prussian forces in the Seven Years War, for instance, relied to some extent on jägers—dispersed infantry sharpshooters and skirmishers who were supposed to mask an army's approach, picking off as many men as possible in the opposing lines before the battle was formally joined. But Rumiantsev also created special jäger units and employed them himself during the same conflict.[167] Rumiantsev similarly experimented in 1761 with attack columns of the kind that would be recommended by postwar French military reformers and that would be used with such enormous efficiency by the armies of the revolutionary Republic.[168] Later in the century, Suvorov would also try out his own version of *tirailleurs* and small attack columns.[169]

There were, however, other practices of Russia's generals, whether on campaign in the south or in the west, that were rarely, if ever, attempted by their West European counterparts: night marches and attacks through wooded areas and marshes. French and German generals eschewed those maneuvers not so much because of the inherent difficulty of performing them as because of the risk of mass desertion they entailed. Movement after sunset or over difficult terrain inevitably degraded the officers' control over their troops; in those conditions, the mercenary soldiers of mid-eighteenth-century West European armies were apt to run away en masse. Such was not the case with Russian armies.

During the 1730s, despite the grotesque weight of his baggage train, Münnich attempted a few night marches.[170] On several occasions in the Seven Years War, Russia's generals routinely led their men through forests and swamps, even in the midst of battle.[171] And Rumiantsev was famous for the night operations he regularly ordered to deceive and surprise the enemy. In June 1770 he crept around the Muslim fortified camp at Riabnaia Mogila at night and occupied the heights behind it.[172] He did the same thing at the battles of the Larga River and Kagul.[173]

A final set of military-operational innovations reposed in the cultivation of speed and shock. In view of the size of the baggage train, it might at first seem absurd to include the words "speed" and "Russian army" in the same sentence. Truly rapid movement was of course an impossibility for an army with the logistical apparatus of the Russian. But such an army could still be trained up to a relatively faster rate of progress. And smaller picked formations could achieve almost astonishing rates of speed, just as Peter the Great's *corps volantes* had. One way to attempt this was to lighten the equipment the troops carried. Up until Münnich's era, for instance, Russian soldiers marching into the steppe had borne with them long and cumbrous pikes to ward off Tatar cavalry charges. But Münnich discarded the pikes, replacing them with *chevaux de frise,* or "Frisian horses"—prefabricated barricades studded with spikes—which were transported in wagons and not on the soldiers' backs.[174] Soldiers freed from the weight of their pikes were now available for offensive action, pursuit, and so forth. It was this consideration that governed Rumiantsev's attitude towards the *chevaux.* Although he did not leave his base camp without them (he later wrote that he feared incurring the reproaches of those whom custom had prejudiced in favor of these barricades), he originally declined to deploy his men behind them.[175] His reason was that the use of *chevaux de frise* presupposed an entirely defensive style of combat. In contrast, Rumiantsev wanted to win quickly and decisively by means of an attack. "It is not *chevaux* but fire and sword that are our defense," he is popularly reputed to have said.[176] Suvorov, of course, was even more offensive-minded. He emphasized the enormous importance of celerity in war with the Turks and the Tatars ("In a land campaign against the Muslims what is needed is unceasing movement!" he wrote in 1788) and inured his men to rapid forced marches.[177] On July 17, 1788, he rendezvoused with the Prince of Coburg at the Seret River, having led four thousand Russian troops almost 50 miles in the preceding thirty-six hours.[178]

The classroom of Russia's southern campaigns was also where Russia's generals learned to appreciate the value of shock. Stealth and speed were supposed to gain the Russian army the advantage of surprise, but surprise was no good unless the Russians could drive their startled opponents from the field. Accurate marksmanship might help to do that, it is true, but it would have been the acme of folly for any Russian general to have expected to win a battle solely by exchanging musket fire with his more numerous Muslim adversaries. It was to compensate for Turkish manpower superiority that Russian generals became accustomed to ordering their troops to fire, then charge, close, and fight it out with cold steel. The impetus of such a ferocious hand-to-hand assault could so demoralize the Turks (especially if they were being attacked from an unexpected quarter) that they might well break and run. All of Russia's most important victories from 1760 to the end of the century—Larga, Kagul, Kinburn, Focsany, Ochakov, Rymnik, Adda—conspicuously featured at least one great bayonet charge.

We arrive, finally, at Suvorov and the cult of the bayonet. The great Field Marshal's slogan ("*pulia duraka, no shtyk molodets,*" "the bullet is a fool, but the bayonet is terrific") is often taken as as illustrating Suvorov's puerile derision of firepower.[179] Actually, as we have already noted, Suvorov had a high regard for fire, especially if it was well aimed. He did not, however, think that it could by itself win battles; rather, only infantry charges could be decisive. Although slavish adoration of Suvorov and bayonets would have the most baleful consequences for Russian military operations in the next century, there was much to be said for the infantry charge in the context of the Turkish wars of the eighteenth century.[180] Russia's commanders in this period relied on the shock of infantry assault not because they were sadistic voyeurs or connoisseurs of carnage, but because that tactic was deemed to be effective. The purpose of the charge, after all, was neither to chalk up enormous Russian casualties nor to exterminate the Turkish defenders to the last man; rather, the charge was designed to break the morale of the Turks and to propel them into flight. If that happened, Russian generals could often achieve victories against overwhelming odds with the *least possible* sacrifice of Russian lives. And happen it did. At Stavuchany (1739), Münnich lost no more than seventy men to the Turks thousand, while driving more than 60,000 Turks and Tatars from the field.[181] At Rachevskii Forest (1769) Golitsyn took six hundred casualties while inflicting several thousand.[182] Rumiantsev's forces suffered ninety-one dead at Larga and possibly as many as a thousand at Kagul, but routed the enemy on both occasions, killing more than 20,000 of them.[183] At the end of the first Turkish war in the battle of Yushemlu, Suvorov slew three thousand Turks at cost of only seventy-five of his own soldiers. In the Second Turkish War, Suvorov defended Kinburn; his losses were less than three hundred, while the Turkish ones were more than ten times as high.[184] Many more examples could be cited. Some of these martial feats were immortalized in folk songs that Russian peasants would still be singing generations later. The popular ballad "The Capture of Khotin," first published in 1877 but believed by folklore experts to date back to the late eighteenth century, gives an account of Russian tactical success against the Turks under Catherine the Great:

> Uz kak nachali streliat'—
> Turki proch' ot nas bezhat
> Bombadiry ocherchali,
> Vse v ogoniu pobezhali;
> Gde odin soldat bezhit—
> tut piat'-shest'turok lezhit
> A gde korpus-to bezhit—
> Tut kak most turok lezhit

[As soon as we began to fire/ the Turks simply ran from us,/ the bombardiers got angry,/ and everyone took off in pursuit,/ and where one soldier ran/ there five or six Turks lay,/ and where the corps ran/ there the Turks lay like a bridge.][185]

Tactical innovation in the eighteenth-century tsarist army, then, did not originate in the avid perusal by Russia's commanders of Western military treatises. Those innovations were formed in the crucible of Russia's Turkish wars. They resulted from the practical efforts of individual tsarist generals to think through the problem of fighting and beating a particular enemy in a specific theater of war. The exploitation of aimed infantry fire and mobile field artillery; the use of intricate squares and stealthy maneuver; the stress on speed and shock—none of these things, unfortunately, crystallized into the general military statutes and service regulations of the time.[186] Those techniques were closely associated with the commanders who had pioneered them. Yet they were remembered notwithstanding, and all became part of a distinctive Russian military operational style. Decades later, future commanders would attempt to employ them without modification in Western theaters of war, often with indifferent results. But when used on the southern frontiers of the eighteenth-century Russian Empire against the enemies who had inspired them, these tactics could succeed brilliantly.[187]

The Quality of the Instrument: the Final Military Component of Russian Imperialism

We must be careful, however, not to exalt Russia's great eighteenth-century captains overmuch. They may have planned and conducted extraordinary campaigns that concluded in dazzling victories, but their achievements were finally dependent on the excellence of the troops they led. The "quality of the instrument"—the toughness, morale, discipline, and enthusiasm of the Russian army—was in large measure responsible for eighteenth-century Russia's military prowess; it was obviously also a necessary condition for the triumph of Russian imperialism in the age.[188]

Take, for example, the risky maneuvers (night marches and so forth) that were routine Russian military practice. That Russia's generals would attempt them so regularly indicates that they were confident, unlike their Western opposite numbers, that their armies would not disintegrate through desertion. Their confidence was in fact well-founded. Although desertion had been the cancer of the army under Peter the Great, after his death the levels of desertion subsided almost to insignificance. Of the almost 14,000 soldiers called up in the draft levy of 1730, only 177, or barely more than 1 percent, are recorded as having fled.[189] Eighteen years later, during Repnin's march to the Rhine, scarcely eight hundred of his 30,000 troops deserted.[190] Desertion was also infrequent among the Russian soldiers who served in Germany and Pomerania during the Seven Years War.[191] At the end of the century, less than 1 percent of the 200,000-man Russian army of Finland ran away in 1792.[192] In fact, so rare was desertion from the ranks that foreigners who took service in the Russian army were frequently dumfounded, leaving a record of their astonishment in the pages of their diaries and memoirs. The German officer Manstein, who held a Russian commission for more than a decade, wrote in the 1740s that, "as to desertion, it is a thing unknown in the Russian armies."[193] Count Langeron, a Frenchmen who held a Russian colonelcy in the 1780s, also noted that desertion was much less common in the Russian army at that time than it was in the armies of Prussia or France.[194]

Perhaps that trustworthiness was not all that it seemed to be.

Could not the apparent loyalty of the Russian troops be explained away as the product of linguistic isolation or the desire for self-preservation? After all, illiterate Russian serf-soldiers who deserted might well have difficulties making themselves understood in mid-eighteenth-century Germany, let alone finding a safe haven. Then, too, the hostile environment of the southern front of war might well in itself have deterred flight, for the risks of hunger, thirst, and massacre at the hands of Tatar renegades or Turkish patrols could possibly have convinced a potential deserter that his best chance of survival lay in marching with the army rather than away from it. There may be something to such an explanation, but it is far from complete. In the first place, many of post-Petrine Russia's campaigns were set in the same theaters— Poland, Finland, Bessarabia—in which Peter the Great had fought. If desertion was inhibited *only* by linguistic ignorance and the accidents of geography, one would then have expected Peter's soldiers to have refrained from flight when on duty in those territories as well. But that, of course, was not the case. Soldiers deserted the ranks of Peter's army by the thousands no matter where that army was deployed. Still further, to exclude moral factors from the explanation of the Russian soldier's small propensity to desert (at least after 1725) is to ignore two other salient qualities that those troops displayed: bravery and endurance. In fact, those characteristics of the Russian soldiers impressed not only their enemies but their own generals as well.

Münnich, for instance, was effusive in his praise of his men's valor in the report he sent Anna Ivanovna after the battle of Stavuchany.[195] The Field Marshal from Oldenburg was no less amazed by their fortitude. In a letter of reproof of 1739 to one of his former Austrian allies, Münnich expatiated on all the miseries his troops had overcome during the Turkish war, concluding: "I assure you, sir, that there is not an army in Europe, except the Russian one, able to endure such fatigues."[196] One may perhaps accuse Münnich of hyperbole, but it must be admitted that at least he had a standard by which to judge, since he had served in three different European armies before coming to Russia.

Yet was Münnich merely boasting? Russian troops exhibited exceptional bravery and endurance in many other eighteenth-century wars. Frederick the Great, for example, came to regret the fact that he had underestimated the Russian infantry prior to the

Seven Years War; it later galled him to recollect that he had been warned against that mistake by the Scottish General Keith, himself a veteran of nineteen years with the Russian army.[197] The tenacity of the Russian soldiers during the battle of Zorndorf (August 1758) led the despairing Prussian king to cry out: "It is easier to kill these Russians to the last man than conquer them."[198] The 21st Apsheron Infantry Regiment, which had held its position at Zorndorf although bespattered with blood, ever afterward wore red-topped boots in remembrance of that heroism.[199] Nor was the Russian performance at Zorndorf unique; in large measure, the Russian army captured the fortress of Kolberg in 1761 by dint of outsuffering its Prussian garrison.[200] Indeed, Russia's military achievements in the Seven Years War helped establish a high reputation for the Russian infantry abroad. The British diplomat William Richardson was merely expressing the commonly held opinion when he wrote to a friend in 1769: "I need not inform you that the Russian army is reckoned inferior to none in Europe."[201]

Of course, in the European wars in which Russia participated in this century its army fought defensive engagements more often than not, thus giving rise to the erroneous view that Russians made stolid and stoical troops, best suited for the defense. The Turkish wars of Catherine the Great, however, demonstrated that their aptitude for the offense was equally great. In both wars, as we have seen, they often defeated forces vastly larger than their own. Rumiantsev informed Catherine that "the army of your majesty does not ask how big the enemy is; it only wants to find out where he is."[202] In both wars, as well, they took by storm fortresses and towns previously deemed impregnable. In the summer of 1771 the Russians succeeded in scaling the walls of Perekop despite the murderous fire of the Tatar defenders; although their ladders were too short, they literally clawed their way to the top of the ramparts with the help of their bayonets.[203] In 1790, despite its miles of walls and 50-foot moat, Izmail fell under the pressue of six separate Russian attack columns, one of them led by a regimental priest who rallied the men with his crucifix after all the officers had fallen.[204]

What motivated such astonishing martial deeds? To be sure, the prospect of booty could be a powerful stimulus to valor, especially if a general had signaled his prior permission for looting in the event of victory. Suvorov, for one, had the following standing order for his men: "Take a camp and everything is yours; take a fortress and everything is yours."[205] George Bernard Shaw could have been speaking of the Russian army when he wrote of Napoleon that the French infantry conquered Italy "not because each soldier [carried] a marshal's baton in his knapsack, but because he [hoped] to carry at least half a dozen silver forks there the next day."[206] When offered a chance to plunder, Russian soldiers needed no encouragement to take full advantage of it. After the sack of Ochakov in 1738, for instance, we are told that they bore away with them "whole hatfuls" of Turkish gold.[207] Potemkin, who was scarcely tender-hearted, is said to have been reduced to tears by the three-day pillaging of Izmail.[208] And even Russian nationalist historians have admitted that the spoliation of Praga by Suvorov's men during the Polish war of 1792 was both savage and extremely thorough.[209]

Then, too, it was possible for an eloquent general to whip up the zeal of his troops for battle by means of impassioned oratory. Ritual exhortations of an army by its leader have been common, of course, since the time of Caesar, if not before. Several of Russia's eighteenth-century military leaders seem to have been peculiarly gifted in this regard. As one might expect, Suvorov had a genius all his own for rousing his men; it is not for nothing that he subtitled one section of "The Art of Victory" "*Razgovor s soldatami ikh iazykom*" ("a conversation with the soldiers in their own language").[210] In short, direct, but nonetheless cadenced sentences, Suvorov goaded the troops to exert themselves unsparingly. On the day of the storming of Izmail he is quoted as having said: "Two times the Russian army besieged Izmail and two times withdrew; it remains for us this third time either to conquer or die with glory!"[211] Those sentiments may seem hackneyed, but the army evidently responded enthusiastically to them.

Suvorov and many of his fellow generals also appealed to the men's religious beliefs, depicting the struggle against the Turks in the terms of a religious crusade, and reminding them that even the worst fate that could befall them—death on the battlefield—would be requited with heavenly immortality.[212] Indeed, that religious faith helped to sustain morale in the ranks of the army is beyond question.[213] The devotion of the men to Orthodox fasts even while on campaign has already been noted.[214] Some might also argue that national feeling also partially explains the military virtues of the Russian infantry. The mercenary soldiers in Western armies were very often foreigners. Only 50,000 of the 133,000 men in the Prussian army in 1751 were native Prussian subjects, and only 70,000 of 160,000 in 1768.[215] By contrast, almost all of the soldiers in the Russian army were Great Russian peasants. The state subjected few of the subject nationalities to conscription, usually imposing a tribute (*iasak*) in its stead. Even when conscription was extended to the Ukraine and Belorussia, the recruits called up there were normally placed in auxiliary units, not combat units of the line. Clearly, the Russian government believed that the ethnic and cultural homogeneity of its army was beneficial. Writing in 1764, the special military commission stated that the foundation of the army's strength was "a common language, faith, set of customs, and birth." Yet although rudimentary national feeling, the tug of ethnic identity, and even a strong abhorrence for the foreign may have flourished among the Russian soldiery, it would of course be anachronistic to apply the word "nationalism" to those mental and emotional phenomena.[216]

One is nonetheless left with the disquieting feeling that there is something absent from the picture. The allure of plunder, the consolation of religion, and the adduction of ethnic solidarity, even taken all together, do not appear (at least to me) fully to account for the military qualities that Russian private soldiers displayed in the eighteenth century, especially when the ugly features of military life are factored in. After all, service in the ranks of the tsarist army was brutal, degrading, and oppressive. The men recruited into it were effectively removed for life from their homes and their families. After the Second Turkish War, the length of service was reduced to twenty-five years, but it amounted to the same thing.[217] Discipline was harsh, punishments cruel, pay irregular, and ill-treatment common. Why should any men fight so hard for an institution that used them so cruelly?[218] The historical evidence on this score is naturally fugitive. Still, we may propose an explanation, if only a tentative one. Surely one of the most remarkable features of the Russian army, as observed by a freshly drafted recruit, must have been the degree to which military society was a complete world sufficient to itself, separated from the outside by an impassable chasm. Although soldiers in prereform Russia were, ironically enough, juridically free men—induction was legally an act of manumission from servile status—they were members of a corporation from which there was virtually no escape. Even if a soldier were to desert, how could he reach his native village? Even if he did, how could he spend the remainder of his life hiding? His landlord, whether a serf-owning human being or some entity like a factory or a mine, or else an institutional abstraction, such as the state, the church or the crown, would certainly be keen to recapture him and send him back. Further, what was there for him in the village? To a peasant community, recruitment was a species of civil death; as the eighteenth century wore on, it became the custom to mourn the departure of the draftee with *plachi,* the ceremonial dirges that were sung at real funerals.[219] The mere fact of being drafted obliterated completely the property rights a peasant had previously held within his family. It was as if he had never been born. His wife (if he had one) had no independent status within his family after he had joined the army; she had to subsist on the grudging charity of his relatives and occasional handouts from the village council.[220] Indeed, on some occasions she was even ordered to remarry by the local landlord, despite the fact that this was forbidden by the laws of both church and state.[221] If a soldier survived his twenty-five years of service and tried to return to his old home (there were a few such cases) it is no surprise that he was received there as an unwelcome interloper.[222]

But if induction was a kind of death, it was also a kind of rebirth, for the recruit now found himself a member of a regimental family. What doubtless aided him in accustoming himself to his new circumstances was his assignment to one of the many *artels* into which his regiment was divided. The *artels,* company-size cooperatives, had many important functions, including economic ones, for each *artel* had four treasurers who collected between a half and a third of the soldier's pay, the payments for the soldiers' winter victuals, and other emoluments, such as might, for example, be realized by hiring out some of the men as private labor. Those monies might be used to buy the soldiers treats (such as fresh meat) when on summer maneuvers. Usually, however, they went to buy horses and carts, which the men collectively owned. It was not uncommon for a soldier to discover within a few years that he had eight to ten rubles to his account with the *artel;* Langeron, the French officer who served with the

Russian army during the late eighteenth century and knew it well, argued in his memoirs that the *artel* system meant that the Russian soldier, unlike any other soldier in Europe, possessed property. And that fact, he continued, was a powerful discourager of desertion.[223] There were also sub-*artels*—comradely associations of eight to ten men. In essence, the *artels* and the sub-*artels* were the primary building blocks of the Russian army. The men of the *artels* pooled their resources, worked together, ate together, and fought together. If a soldier died, it was generally his comrades who inherited his share of the communal property. In short, the *artels* paralleled and performed the same social, economic, and organizational functions as the village communes to which the drafted peasants no longer belonged. The *artels* were therefore the chief means of socialization within the army, and as such, may well have fostered the small-group loyalty on which, as modern researchers tell us, tenacity under fire ultimately depends.[224] After some years, the now veteran recruit might find that the authorities might condone or at least tolerate his taking up with a woman. The offspring of such unions constituted an entire social category known in late-eighteenth-century Russia as *soldatskie deti,* or soldiers' children.[225] In fact there were knowledgeable contemporaries who argued that the soldier's lot was not really all that bad during peacetime conditions. One such person was Count Langeron, who wrote:

> The [Russian] soldier in a regiment whose commander is not a hangman is the happiest soldier in Europe. He is well dressed, excellently fed by the peasants during the winter, and in the summer in the camps.
> He is a little tsar in the village [where he is quartered].[226]

Langeron, of course, may be spinning a reactionary fantasy here, airbrushing the ugliness out of his portrait of Russian military life, although we should say in his defense that he fills many pages of his work with unrestrained descriptions of cruelty and oppression in the military milieu. Nonetheless, his depiction of the lot of Russian peasant soldiers shows little insight into their feelings. Even if a Russian soldier was materially better off than his Prussian counterpart in some ways, what possible consolation could that be for him? He had not the slightest idea what military conditions were in Potsdam. Surely the comparison that must have mattered to the peasant soldier was the one to be drawn between his military life and the life in the village he had left behind. After all, rural existence was hard too. And, given the impossibility of returning to civil life, is it fanciful to speculate that the recruit's affinity for the military environment might have grown strong even as his attachment to his previous civilian life weakened? We do have evidence suggestive of this, for Russian soldiers did come to show a clannish (if churlish) loyalty to each other, especially when clashes with civilians were involved. The regimental historian Dirin informs us that on holidays in St. Petersburg full-blown melées between the soldiers of the garrison and the burghers and peasants of the town were routine occurrences. Some of them attained gargantuan proportions, with two thousand combatants engaged on each side.[227] It seems probable, therefore that the conscription system—a much-loathed innovation under Peter the Great—eventually came to be regarded by the Russian peasants as normal and legitimate. After the death of Peter the Great his improvised army calcified into an institution, and the peasants of the empire, both within its ranks and without, became accustomed to it as such. Indeed, implementation of recruitment would have been impossible in eighteenth-century tsarist Russia without the collaboration and complicity of the peasant *obshchiny*, the communes themselves; as one gifted ethnographer has noted, the communes were able to *use* the military draft system, despite its burdensomeness, to enforce norms of behavior in the village and to support the traditional patriarchal power structure there.[228] Whether the explanation advanced here is right or wrong, however, there can be no doubt that the high quality of the troops was the bedrock of Russian military power; coherent strategy, let alone imperial expansion, would have been impossible without it.

Conclusion

Imperial Russia grew enormously in territory, power, influence, and wealth during the eighteenth century. Its growth was neither foreordained nor easy. The climate of international politics did not favor it: Russia had to cope with hostility and envy from avowed enemies, declared neutrals, and foresworn allies. Russia was embarassed throughout the century as well by well-nigh insuperable problems of frontier defense, and was limited by the poverty of its state treasury. At times it found itself unable adequately to equip its army and had to drill its peasant soldiers with wooden sticks instead of fusils. Almost all the time, in order to fund its military operations, it had to hunt for foreign subsidies, issue unbacked paper money, debase its metallic currency, or plead with foreign bankers for loans. The territories in which Russia campaigned (and through which its armies marched en route) were man-killing wastelands where intolerable heat, famine, and pestilence stalked its soldiers. The titanic baggage trains such campaigns required impeded the mobility of its forces, while the laws of the military ecosystem imposed additional costs in men and beasts alike. Many of Russia's ministers were venal, many of its generals inept, many of its junior officers both ignoble and incompetent. Its local administration was weak, and its central administration was beset by the intrigues of factions and clans. The roster of obstacles was so long as almost to beggar the imagination.

Yet Russia succeeded in aggrandizing itself despite everything. That it did so was not solely or even chiefly accidental, but had much to do with the conscious decisions and planning of its most skillful statesmen and rulers, who concurrently were driven by the desire for security and a lust for geostrategic advantage. Those were the men and women who crafted the national strategies of Russia, strategies that were founded on an appreciation of the dynamics of international politics and the resonances of Russia's wars abroad. Military strategies were developed with an equally keen attention to the realities of geography, logistics, and climate. Underpinning the entire effort was the frantic exertion of the state to keep its financial capabilities in step with Russia's appetites and ambitions. Then, too, the state was fortunate enough to locate and promote a handful of brilliant commanders whose operational and tactical innovations evolved in the direction of an authentically "Russian way of war." Ultimately, however, as much, if not more, depended on the social dimension of Russian strategy as on the political, diplomatic, economic, or operational ones. It was in the end the readiness of the peasant soldier to take part in suicide attacks, storm fortresses, endure forced marches, and accept death that transformed the strategic ideas of the government and the generals into the reality of Russian conquests. The expansion of the Russian Empire in the eighteenth century testified profoundly to the extraordinary adaptability of the Russian government and its people in the face of the challenges of war and the uncertainties of peace. Russia's eighteenth-century history also demonstrated just how dangerous it could be to underestimate Russia. If Napoleon Bonaparte had had anything more than a smattering of that history, had he really understood the peculiar strengths of the Russian military system, he might not have launched his march to disaster of 1812.

5

The Baleful Consequences
of Victory

Russian Strategy and the War of 1812

As we have already seen, the eighteenth century was on balance a time when the power of the Russian Empire waxed considerably. Russia owed the growth in its might in large measure to the skill its policymakers evinced in the crafting and implementation of strategy. In the early part of the nineteenth century, however, Russia's strength was to be tested in the maelstrom of wars with revolutionary France, of which the most decisive was the Napoleonic invasion of 1812. Indeed, Russia's great victory over Napoleon's Grand Armée is truly one of the most dramatic events in world military history. It was, as well, a watershed in the Napoleonic wars themselves, for not only did it explode Bonaparte's reputation for military invincibility, but it also resulted in catastrophic losses of treasure, matériel, and, most important, trained men. The very magnitude of the French defeat induced several of Bonaparte's most important allies to desert him and laid the foundation for the Fifth Coalition, which would finally succeed in utterly destroying the French Empire.

But the outcome of the war of 1812 was as decisive for the fortunes of Russia as it was for those of France. Russia, of course, had secured its position as a Great European Power prior to the outbreak of the French Revolution in 1789. After 1815, however, it seemed to many that Russia's relative strength vis-à-vis its neighbors had only benefited from the lengthy contest with Napoleon. It was as if the Napoleonic wars had finally educated Petersburg as to the full extent of the power actually at its disposal. Russia came to be regarded as the premier land power on the Continent, and the Russian autocracy and its army of 800,000 troops, as the arbiter of European order, the bulwark of legitimacy, conservatism, and stability.

Given the profound military, political, and even economic and social consequences of the war of 1812, it is no surprise that much ink has been spilt on studies of the war itself. Yet despite the enormous volume of scholarship thus engendered, it is hard to sort out the events of 1812. In the first place, for a variety of reasons the contemporary evidence is actually quite murky. For example, the motivations and plans of the Russian side are obscured by the extraordinary rancor that poisoned relations among the leading statesmen and generals of the day. The two principal Russian generals at the outbreak of hostilities, Barclay de Tolly and Bagration, were consumed with mutual loathing. The latter, in particular, never passed up an opportunity to impugn the former's ability, courage, and motives.[1] But both were united in their contempt for Field Marshal Kutuzov, to whom the supreme command over them was eventually given.[2] For his part, Kutuzov both hated and intrigued against Barclay.[3] Kutuzov also despised Chichagov and was in turn detested by the Emperor Alexander I himself, who employed the influential English envoy Wilson to spy on the activities of his Field Marshal.[4] The nobility and dignity of the monuments[5] to the heroes of 1812 is thus belied by the written record; the reports, correspondences, and reminiscences of many of them are tainted with pettiness, spleen, and slander—a fact that greatly complicates the effort to arrive at the truth.

There is, however, an even more serious difficulty in writing about Napoleon's invasion of Russia: the pervasive, reductionist (and contradictory) mythologies that purport to account for the outcome of the war. In the main there are three such myths. The first is that of the "accidental defeat," the view that the Grand Armée was defeated not so much owing to any mistakes of its own, but rather because of the impersonal forces of nature as represented by the unyielding Russian winter. The second is the myth of inherent defeat: that Napoleon's enterprise in Russia was somehow doomed to fail from the very beginning, owing to the innate problems of command, control, discipline, logistics, and distances, which even the Emperor's genius for warfare was incapable of surmounting. Both of those interpretations absolve Napoleon and his forces from blame for the Russian debacle— the first completely, the second partially. Both of them also give very little if any credit to the Russians for what happened on the soil of their country in 1812.

Whether consciously or not, those two exculpatory explanations of the events of 1812 have obviously had a soothing effect on the national pride of the largely French and German commentators who have popularized them. Yet there is a corresponding (and equally pernicious) myth about 1812 that has long occupied an important position in Russian culture. That is, of course, the celebratory vision of the war as a supreme expression of Russian nationalism. Accounts in this vein hold that victory over Napoleon was achieved by omniscient strategists presiding over the Herculean efforts of the united Russian people. Unfortunately, however gratifying they may be for individual national sensibilities, none of the three explanations can adequately account for what occurred in 1812. The accidental explanation is little more than a boldfaced lie, originally concocted by Napoleon himself. While the view of "inherent defeat" has somewhat more merit, what caused the Napoleonic invasion of Russia to fail was, as we shall see, more than the scale of the undertaking alone. Russia's government and armies made great contributions to the destruction of the Grand Armée. At the same time, as I shall also show the third, triumphalist version of the "Fatherland War" is deeply flawed too.[6]

It is clearly the third explanation, however, that is most important in the history of the Russian art of war. The triumphalist myth, which began to be propagated in educated Russian circles in the immediate aftermath of the war of 1812, had at least two insidious consequences for the development of Russian strategy. In the first place it tended to confirm a unidimensional theory about the root causes of war in general and security threats to the Russian Empire in particular. The false premises underlying that theory were to inform Russian military and diplomatic policy for decades after the Congress of Vienna. Second, the celebratory vision of the war of 1812 also encouraged complacency and unrealism about the authentic limits of Russian military power— two attitudes that were also very much in evidence in the court of the Emperor Nicholas I.

Yet before we examine either the real reasons for the failure of Napoleon in Russia or the individual deficiencies of each of the three explanations, we must first recount the prehistory of the war of 1812 and the course of the invasion itself.

Franco-Russian Relations, 1789–1811

Like most other capitals in Europe, Petersburg was both surprised and alarmed by the outbreak of the French Revolution in 1789. Yet rather quickly Catherine the Great came to the conclusion that by crippling the French state and distracting its nearest neighbors, the revolution actually represented a tremendous opportunity, a chance for Russia to make further encroachments against its traditional eighteenth-century victims, Poland and Turkey. For example, the Empress took advantage of the preoccupation of Berlin and Vienna with France to invade Poland in 1792, speciously justifying herself with the claim that she was acting solely to crush the Polish "Jacobins."[7] Despite her personal fears of the contagion of revolution, which found its vent in the persecution of such figures as the writer Radishchev, Catherine remained aloof from the first coalition formed in 1793 to combat the revolutionary French. While British, Dutch, Hapsburg, Spanish, and Imperial armies marched against France, Catherine contented herself with organizing the Second and Third Partitions of Poland.

It was Catherine's son, the neurotic Prussophile Paul I (1796–1801), who brought Russia into the war.[8] The circumstances under which he did so were rather peculiar. In 1797 Napoleon Bonaparte, then one of the principal generals in the service of the French Directory, embarked 38,000 French troops in four hundred ships for an attack on Egypt, an attempt to strike an indirect blow against Britain's possessions in India. En route he captured and occupied the island of Malta in the eastern Mediterranean, which he hoped to use as a French naval base. Up to that point Malta had belonged to an ancient Catholic crusading order, the Knights of St. John. Representatives of the Knights of Malta, now dispossessed and eager to enlist one of the Great Powers in defense of their interests, induced Paul I of Russia to accept the mastership of their order toward the end of December

1798. The world was accordingly afforded the bizarre spectacle of an Orthodox sovereign accepting the leadership of an organization technically subordinate to the Pope. There were several reasons why Paul assumed the mastership of the Knights of St. John, including a dreamy enthusiasm for the romantic history of the order and a more down-to-earth concern over the French advance into the Ionian islands. But in addition, we must not rule out Paul's appreciation of the strategic advantage that a naval base on Malta might afford Russia.[9] When Bonaparte declined to cede Malta to its new overlord, Paul declared war on France.

Russia now allied itself with Britain, Austria, and Turkey (!) to form the Second Coalition. Russian fleets operated around Naples, besieged Corfu, and supported a joint Anglo-Russian amphibious landing in Holland. On land, Suvorov marched west and conducted his famous campaigns in Italy and Switzerland. Yet Paul's enthusiasm for the war soon began to wane. In particular, he was enraged at what he regarded as the duplicity of his principal allies, Austria and Britain. As he saw it, Austria had been insufficiently supportive of Russia's Italian operations. Still worse, however, was the conduct of the British, who had wrested Malta away from France in 1800 but had then refused to hand it over to its Russian Grand Master. Paul's response was to place an embargo on the import of British goods. When that failed to persuade the English to change their minds, Paul withdrew from the coalition and concluded a secret anti-British alliance with Napoleon, who by then had overthrown the Directory in a military coup. Paul's new Foreign Minister, Rostopchin, was also quick to point out the advantages of collaboration with the French First Consul: his support would be invaluable as Russia reverted to its traditional policy of aggrandizing itself at the expense of Ottoman Turkey.

Paul's warming relationship with Bonaparte probably accelerated his murder, for it seems that the conspiracy against him was ripened with liberal infusions of English gold.[10] In any event, dissatisfaction with Paul's domestic program was itself a sufficient pretext for the assassination. In March 1801 a band of aristocratic officers burst into the Engineer's Palace and strangled Paul; the crown of Russia was inherited by his son, Alexander I. Alexander moved immediately to heal the rift with Britain, canceled all military operations against it, and countermanded his father's chimerical order for 22,000 Cossacks to ride east for an attack on India. Russia was once more at peace.

The peace was not to be of long duration. Preoccupied as he was with issues of internal reform, Alexander nevertheless could not ignore the dangerous growth of Napoleon's power. By 1803 France had annexed the Low Countries and the left bank of the Rhine, and held an increasingly dominant position in northern Italy. Still worse, Napoleon's actions by then had made it apparent that he respected no law other than that of brute force. In the spring of 1804 French agents seized the Duc d'Enghien in the German state of Baden, spirited him across the French frontier, and had him shot (purportedly to punish him for his involvement in plots against the life of the First Consul). Alexander's wife was a princess of the House of Baden, so outrage at the French crime was particularly acute in Petersburg. During the autumn, while Napoleon was busying himself with preparations for his coronation as Emperor of the French, Alexander dispatched his friend and confidant Novosil'tsev to London to negotiate with Pitt for a treaty against France. The upshot of the Novosil'tsev mission—the convention of St. Petersburg (April 11, 1805)—laid the foundation for the Third Coalition.

Britain and Sweden took responsibility for the naval aspects of the war, while Russia and Austria undertook to prosecute it on land with all of their available forces (in return, of course, for British monetary subventions). But the land war was brief. In December 1805 Napoleon overwhelmed the combined Austrian and Russian armies at Austerlitz. Although Russia was able to extricate its shattered forces from Central Europe by means of an armistice, the Austrians were compelled to sign the humiliating Peace of Pressburg. In 1806 Prussia, which had previously stood on the sidelines, declared war on France. It, too, was quickly defeated in the twin battles of Jena and Auerstädt; King Frederick William evacuated Berlin, which was swiftly occupied by the French. War was renewed the following year, as the advancing French fought a series of bloody engagements with the Russians and what remained of their decimated Prussian allies. After the decisive French victory at Friedland (June 1807), however, it occurred to many in the Tsar's entourage that it really made very little sense for Russia to continue to prosecute the war.

Since most of Prussia was in the hands of the French, any assistance that that kingdom could furnish Russia could only be meager. Russia had no other Continental allies. As if that were not bad enough, since 1806 Russia had been involved in a war with Turkey over the future of the Danubian Principalities of Wallachia and Moldavia.

Alexander accordingly appealed to Napoleon for a truce, and the two emperors met, dramatically enough, on a raft in the middle of the Neman river, which delimited Russia's western border. During the meeting, Napoleon apparently tantalized Alexander I with the vision of a Europe partitioned into French and Russian spheres of influence. By the terms of the peace of Tilsit (July 1807), France promised Russia diplomatic support in its efforts wrest Finland from Sweden and the Danubian Principalities from the Ottoman Empire. For its part, Russia declared itself a French ally and vowed to join the continental system, Napoleon's scheme for economic warfare against his one remaining enemy, Great Britain, by barring imports of British goods to the European Continent.

It seems clear that Alexander I never considered the peace of Tilsit to be a permanent arrangement. To be sure, one outcome of Tilsit was the appointment of a new Foreign Minister, N. P. Rumiantsev, a Francophile who was an ardent advocate of a friendship with Paris. Yet Alexander used his ministers as instruments and did not hesitate to change them when he wanted to signal a change in his policies.[11] When his mother wrote him a letter of reproof for abasing himself before Napoleon at Tilsit, Alexander responded that he had signed the Tilsit peace only "to have the possibility of a certain amount of time to breathe freely and to increase in the course of this most precious time the resources and strength of Russia."[12]

In the following years both parties to the peace of Tilsit had much reason for dissatisfaction with the bargain they had made. From the vantage point of St. Petersburg, the French alliance was the source of dynastic, economic, and geopolitical harm to Russia. Such haughty French actions as the annexation of the Duchy of Oldenburg (whose Duke was Alexander I's uncle) were perceived as direct affronts to the dignity of the house of Romanov. More important, however, was the economic problem. Adherence to the continental system and the French alliance structure immediately put Russia in a formal state of war with the British. And that was devastating for Russian commerce, since prior to 1807 Britain had been one of Russia's most significant trading partners. Before 1807 the English had typically purchased over 70 percent of Russia's hemp and iron exports and almost 90 percent of its flax. Now there was almost no market for these products. Even more crippling was the blow to Russian agriculture. Whereas Russia had exported more than 1 million quarters of wheat total from 1801 to 1805, in the ensuing five years the volume of exports fell by almost 80 percent, chiefly because of the official rupture of trade with Great Britain.[13]

Yet the geopolitical consequences of the peace of Tilsit worried Russian statesmen the most. To be sure, Russia was able to avail itself of the alliance to wage a victorious war with the Swedes (1808–9), ending in the annexation by Petersburg of Finland and Åland Island. But the war with Turkey dragged on. Not only were the leaders of the Russian Empire irritated by Napoleon's conspicuous failure to provide the support he had promised at Tilsit, but they also had solid grounds to suspect that Bonaparte was in fact secretly encouraging the Turks to keep the war going.[14] Of all the grievances Russia had against Paris, however, there was none more serious than the challenge posed by Poland. In the aftermath of his defeat of Prussia, Napoleon had cobbled together the Grand Duchy of Warsaw from the chunks of Poland that Berlin had acquired in the partitions of the eighteenth century. Russian statesmen could only regard the existence of this newly created Polish state as an obvious security threat to the Russian Empire, for the Duchy would inevitably act as a magnet for the aspirations of the hundreds of thousands of Poles who chafed under Russian rule. Napoleon himself was apparently wont to describe the Duchy as a "pistol" with which he could intimidate his unreliable Russian ally.[15] When Napoleon enlarged the Duchy again with a slice of territory taken from defeated Austria in 1809, there were those in Petersburg who feared that the French Emperor's eventual purpose was the restoration of the Polish kingdom as it had been prior to the First Partition in 1772.

From the French perspective, there were dynastic antagonisms that arose in the post-Tilsit period as well. In his quest for legitimacy, Napoleon had divorced his wife Josephine in the hopes of marrying into a prominent European royal family. His first choice fell on the house of Romanov, but Alexander skillfully frustrated Napoleon's efforts to wed his sister, the Grand Duchess Anna Pavlovna. Although Bonaparte contented himself with an Austrian match, that slight was not one that he was willing to forgive.

Also important in the worsening relations between Paris and Petersburg was what Napoleon regarded as Alexander's duplicity as an ally. When war broke out between France and Austria in 1809, for instance, Alexander in theory was bound to supply Napoleon with military assistance. But the Tsar purposefully delayed his help. Napoleon had already taken Vienna (12 May) before the Russian auxiliary force of 33,000 had even crossed the Bug River. Still further, Alexander had informed the Austrians that his army would not engage in any active military operations against them, even if it were to arrive in the theater of war before a decision had been reached.[16] As might have been expected, Alexander was unable to keep his promises to the Hapsburgs secret from his enraged French ally.

The Russian attitude toward the continental system, however, was the single greatest irritant to Napoleon. Ever since defeat at Trafalgar had deprived him of his fleet, Bonaparte had had no weapons against the British save economic ones. The continental system was supposed to effect the economic strangulation of the British Isles. Napoleon hoped that by depriving the British government of the revenues of trade and denying it crucial imports of grain and naval stores, he could in the end cripple that government's commitment to the war.[17] Yet Alexander I's compliance with the system from the beginning had been lukewarm at best. In December 1810 the Tsar dropped all pretenses and legalized the importation of British goods into Russia on neutral ships. Simultaneously, he established a high tariff barrier against imports of French wares. That was more than a repudiation of the continental system; it was a virtual Russian declaration of economic war.

Indeed, during 1810 Alexander had already begun to prepare his empire for a renewal of armed conflict with France. The new Minister of War appointed that year, Barclay de Tolly, began a program of vigorous military reforms, basing his work chiefly on French principles. Within two years the Russia army had more than doubled in size, attaining a strength of 480,000 men.[18] Nor did Alexander's government neglect its diplomatic preparations. In the spring of 1812, through a series of adroit negotiations, Russia was able to secure both its northwest and its southwest flanks in expectation of a new contest with Napoleon. In May the peace of Bucharest finally ended the Turkish war. In the same month Russia signed an alliance with the Swedes, thus extinguishing the fear that a vengeful Stockholm might side with France.[19] In expectation of a positive outcome to these acts of diplomacy, in April Alexander's government presented Paris with an ultimatum that demanded the dismantlement and reversion to Prussia of the Grand Duchy of Warsaw. Napoleon had expected this demarche, however; since the summer of 1811 he had been making intense military preparations of his own. Huge quantities of stores and wagons were accumulated; troops were raised in every quarter of the empire and from every one of the allies—Holland, Italy, Poland, Spain, Austria, and Germany. Napoleon had in fact assembled one of the largest armies the world had ever seen: 368,000 infantry, 80,000 cavalry and more than 1,000 guns. Only half of the soldiers were French.[20] On June 24, 1812, the Grand Armée started to cross the Neman River, thus inaugurating the invasion of Russia. It did not begin entirely auspiciously, however. On the previous day the Emperor had been thrown from his horse, an event taken by many as an portent of evil.[21]

The War of 1812

Although the Russian government had originally contemplated advancing to intercept Napoleon in Poland or even Germany, in the end it was decided to wait for the Emperor of the French on Russian soil.[22] The Prussian émigré Karl Maria von Phull was responsible for preparing the initial Russian strategic plan. It involved separating Russia's forces into four components. The first army (130,000 men), under War Minister Barclay de Tolly, was to cover the approaches to St. Petersburg. The second (45,000) under the command of the flamboyant P. I. Bagration, was to guard the road to Moscow. The third or reserve army, under Tormasov, would meanwhile screen the Ukraine from the

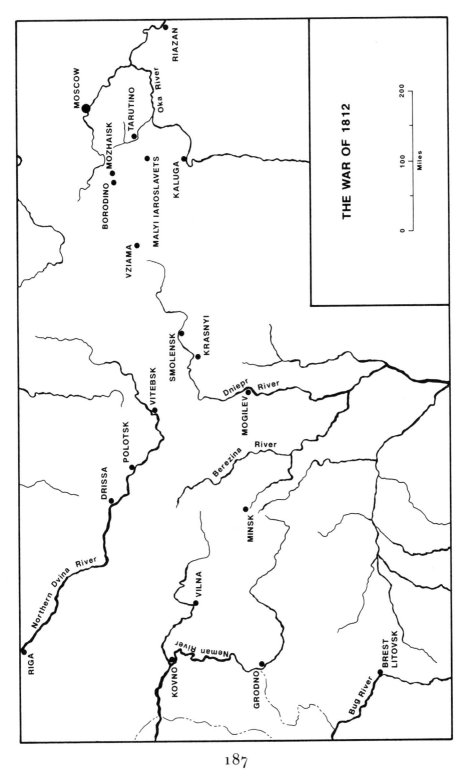

THE WAR OF 1812

Miles

0   100   200

RIGA
Northern Dvina River
KOVNO
Neman River
VILNA
GRODNO
BREST LITOVSK
Bug River
MINSK
DRISSA
POLOTSK
VITEBSK
Berezina River
MOGILEV
Dniepr River
SMOLENSK
KRASNYI
VZIAMA
MALYI IAROSLAVETS
BORODINO
MOZHAISK
TARUTINO
KALUGA
Oka River
MOSCOW
RIAZAN

enemy. In addition, the Russians constructed an enormous fortified camp at Drissa, near the Dvina river in Belorussia. Phull
supposed that Napoleon's ultimate objective would be St. Petersburg. He therefore intended to use the first army as bait to lure
the Grand Armée towards Drissa, where the second and third
armies would rendezvous and smash into its flank and rear.[23]

For his part, Napoleon was counting upon a rapid campaign.
He expected to force the Russian army or armies into a decisive
battle or a set of decisive battles as near as possible to the frontier
zone, perhaps near Vilna, perhaps near Drissa, but certainly no
farther east than the city of Smolensk. Once Russia's forces had
been annihilated, Napoleon was confident that he could induce
Alexander I to sue for peace. If Russia's army somehow managed to elude defeat and withdrew in the direction of Moscow,
the French Emperor then considered that the war might have to
be extended for another year, because his own forces would have
to go into winter quarters in Lithuania before delivering the
decisive blow in 1813.

Napoleon's initial operational goal was therefore to profit
from the dispersion of Russia's forces into four relatively weak
forces by defeating them piecemeal. His prime target was Barclay's first army. But sensing that the French were maneuvering
to cut him off from the Dvina River, Barclay fell back on Drissa,
while Bagration simultaneously retreated to the Berezina. It was
at this point that Barclay strongly urged the Emperor to discard
the entire Drissa plan. He advanced three reasons for such
course of action. First, the Drissa plan had been predicated on
the erroneous assumption that Napoleon's army of invasion
would consist of no more than 200,000 troops, whereas the actual Grand Armée was more than twice as large. Russia's four
much smaller forces were accordingly all the more vulnerable.
Second, Barclay argued that Phull had also misunderstood Napoleon's operational intentions: Bonaparte's purpose was not the
capture of Russia's capital but rather the destruction of its armies. It therefore followed that any continuation of the attempt
to "entrap" Napoleon at Drissa might well result in the entrap-
ment of the Russians themselves. In view of those considerations,
then, Barclay insisted that all of Russia's forces immediately recombine. But finally, owing to Napoleon's superior strength, not
to mention his extraordinary military talents, the Russian forces

should retreat into the depth of the country, refusing battle until the combined attrition of hunger, disease, and guard duty had reduced Napoleon's forces to Russian levels.

Alexander I was moved enough by Barclay's advice to adopt it at least in part. He ordered the First and Second Armies to retire once more and unite at Vitebsk. Napoleon, however, arrived at Vitebsk almost at the same time Barclay did and ahead of Bagration. Once again avoiding encirclement, the Russians now retreated in the direction of Smolensk. Although Napoleon at first considered wintering in Vitebsk, his belief that he had to win at least one major victory before bringing the campaign of 1812 to a close led him to resume the pursuit. Because his lines of communication and logistics were lengthening, and because small Russian auxiliary forces (the Western, Danubian, and Finnish armies, in addition to Wittgenstein's corps) were pressing on his flanks, he detached five corps to protect his supply routes. Bonaparte then pressed on toward Smolensk, but with only 185,000 men.

At Smolensk the First and Second Russian armies were finally able to link up, forming a combined force of 110,000. But the Grand Armée itself quickly turned up on the scene. Disregarding Barclay's arguments in favor of a continued retreat, Bagration insisted on standing and fighting, heedless of Napoleon's numerical superiority. The upshot was the battle of Smolensk (August 16–17, 1812). Protected by Smolensk's complex but decaying set of seventeenth-century fortifications, the Russians initially repulsed all French attempts to take the city by storm. But when Barclay, who had reasserted his primacy, learned that the French were beginning a flanking movement against Russian troops still in the field, he slipped out of Smolensk, leaving behind some demolition teams to explode the powder magazines. In the fighting at Smolensk, the Grand Armée had incurred casualties of at least 20,000. Once again Napoleon toyed with the idea of making Smolensk the terminal point of his 1812 campaign. Yet the Russian army was still more or less intact, and his appetite for a substantial victory had not yet been satisfied. Napoleon therefore decided to *force* battle on the Russians by marching all the way to Moscow, if need be. No Russian commander, he reasoned, could afford to decline a battle at the very gates of Moscow. The Russian army would have to stand its ground, and that would furnish him with the opportunity to demolish it that he had been seeking in vain all summer. Bonaparte confidently predicted to his staff that the Grand Armée would cover the 280 miles from Smolensk to Moscow within a month; within six weeks, he said, a defeated Alexander would be groveling for peace.[24]

At this point Emperor Alexander made a rare concession to the growing hysteria of the nobles of Moscow and Petersburg. The Russian army's policy of continuous retreat was increasingly inexplicable to such people, among whom Barclay de Tolly was disparaged with the punning nickname of *"boltai da i tol'ko"* (roughly, "all mouth and nothing more").[25] Then, too, there was the matter of Barclay's ethnicity. A Livonian of Scots descent, Barclay's foreign-sounding name did not inspire much confidence in a Russian society experiencing a renaissance of patriotic feeling. Alexander accordingly demoted Barclay and replaced him (much against his own inclinations) with General Mikhail Illarionovich Golenishchev-Kutuzov.[26]

At first glance Kutuzov did not seem to a very promising candidate for the supreme command of the Russian armies. Advanced in age, blind in one eye (the result of a Turkish bullet), enormously corpulent, and in chronic ill health, at that point the sixty-seven-year-old general occupied the obscure post of supervisor of the Petersburg militia. Yet his reputation as a protégé of Suvorov and as a hero of the Turkish wars of Catherine the Great accounted for his popularity.[27]

The new commander's first idea was to draw back to Moscow and regroup, for he was under the mistaken impression that reserve formations totalling 100,000 men awaited him there. Despite his disappointment when he learned that this was not so, Kutuzov resolved to make a stand against the Grand Armée at the approaches to Moscow. He chose and prepared a position for defense about 12 kilometers west of Mozhaisk near the tiny hamlet of Borodino. Here on September 5–7, Napoleon's 135,000 troops met 125,000 Russians in combat. Borodino was one of the single bloodiest engagements of its time. The frontal assaults ordered by both sides led to vicious hand-to-hand fighting and enormous levels of casualties. On September 7, after having discharged 90,000 artillery shells and more than 2 million rounds of ball, the French had gained a kilometer and a half of territory. As the Russians withdrew, leaving the French in possession of the field, the latter were the nominal victors at Borodino. But the success held little consolation for Napoleon. In the first place, appreciating that victory was as much a psychological as a material state, the French Emperor measured the decisiveness of any battle in terms of the numbers of enemy soldiers who surrendered to his forces. Borodino yielded only 800 POWs, thus proving to the Emperor (and his army) that the morale of the Russians was still intact. Second, after disengaging from the battle, Kutuzov still had some 90,000 troops under his command.[28] Napoleon could only conclude that his Russian campaign was far from over.

But the Russians had a dilemma of their own. Halfway into the battle of Borodino, Kutuzov had reported it as victory to Alexander I. In premature gratitude the Tsar had bestowed the rank of Field Marshal upon him in addition to other valuable rewards. But Kutuzov soon realized that it was time to silence the triumphal pealing of the church bells of Petersburg. The Russian army had had to retreat from Borodino; further, it was still outnumbered by Napoleon's forces. Should he offer a second battle in the hope of saving Moscow? On September 1 (13), in the village of Fili, Kutuzov convened a council of war to address this very question. Opinions were divided, with five of the generals attending favoring fighting, and four (led by Barclay) recommending retreat. Kutuzov sided with the latter group.[29] He observed that "by preserving Moscow, we do not preserve Russia" and that "it is better to sacrifice Moscow and buy time."[30] On September 4 (16) Kutuzov wrote the hardest letter he would ever write, a justification to Alexander I of his decision to abandon Moscow to the enemy. In words similar to those he had uttered at Fili, the Field Marshal explained to his soveriegn that the French occupation of Moscow was not the same as the subjugation of Russia, as long as Russia's army remained intact.[31] The French had already marched into the city one day before.

To the intense surprise of Napoleon, who had been expecting to be greeted by a delegation of ermine-clad boyars, there was no official welcome. Moscow was almost entirely deserted, for the Governor-General, Prince Rostopchin, had successfully organized the evacuation of most of the city's population of 300,000. Almost at once the energies of the Grand Armée were distracted by the need to combat the fires that flared up in almost every quarter of the town. The fires were not the result of any master plan. Some were the by-product of drunken looting, since Rostopchin had released all of the convicts from the city jails on the eve of his departure. Some were impulsively set by nobles, who preferred to put their mansions to the torch rather than allow the French to bivouac in them. Finally, still others were calculated acts of arson, efforts by Russian agents to destroy stocks of grain, powder, and ammunition that might be of military value to Napoleon.[32] Yet since the city was constructed almost entirely of wood, and since the winds were high, the fires spread rapidly, consuming between one-half and two-thirds of the town before they could be controlled.

Despite his shock at the burning of Moscow, Napoleon came to believe that his mere occupation of that city would somehow force Alexander I to sue for peace. What made that belief all the more remarkable was the fact that Russia still had powerful and growing field forces. Kutuzov had swung southwest of the city to Tarutino, a position that commanded access to the great armament factories of Tula in addition to the richest agricultural zones in the Empire. Alexander I would have no talk of peace and rebuffed each of Napoleon's three efforts to open negotiations. Napoleon briefly contemplated marching on Petersburg to bring Alexander to his senses but discarded that option in view of the mammoth problems of communications and logistics it would entail.[33] At the same time, it was obvious that wintering in the city was out of the question. At the time the French had entered Moscow, there had in fact been large quantities of foodstuffs and forage in its warehouses. But much fire and pillaging had intervened since then; not enough victuals remained to sustain the Grand Armée until the spring of 1813.[34] Besides, the French lines of communication and supply, stretching back hundreds of miles to Smolensk, Lithuania, and Poland, were strained to the maximum. Also disrupting the supply equation was the organized guerrilla war the Russians were conducting against French outposts, garrisons, and convoys.

Napoleon consequently came to the realization that his army would have to retreat. Scholars have frequently pointed out that during this period Napoleon's unfounded expectations of Russian capitulation, in addition to his weird dispositions for the retreat, indicated just how far he had drifted away from reality. For example he commanded that forage for two months be accumulated and 20,000 horses purchased. Yet Russian guerrilla operations made foraging practically impossible, and sellers of horses were nowhere to be found.[35] Finally on October 7 (19), after tarrying in Moscow for thirty-three days, Napoleon began his retreat. At that point Bonaparte's forces mustered in at roughly 100,000 men. He needed speed, but his army was burdened with loot. He needed good intelligence, but so many horses had died during the sojourn in Moscow that much of his cavalry was dismounted. He also urgently needed food, for his army was marching with only a fifteen-day ration. That was why he first marched south in an attempt to travel to Smolensk via the road through Kaluga. But Kutuzov was waiting for him there. After a small but bloody encounter at Maloiaroslavets, Napoleon veered north to the direct Smolensk road, which he knew the Russian scorched earth policy and guerrilla war would have left almost devoid of provisions. He took this decision, uncharacteristically, in order *to elude* battle, for by this stage he was convinced that if he had to fight his way out of Russia mile by mile, the result might be the destruction of his entire army. He definitely preferred a hungry army to no army at all.

As Napoleon proceeded west, Russian forces by now numbering more than 300,000 engaged in marches parallel to his flanks, while partisans and guerrillas harassed the rear guards and massacred stragglers. As a result of those actions, in addition to the effects of hunger, fatigue, and disease, only 60,000 men remained in the ranks of the Grand Armée when it reached Smolensk on October 29 (November 7). The men had been told that once they had attained Smolensk their sufferings would be over, but they discovered that the city did not hold even sufficient rations for an army as reduced in size as theirs. Le Comte de Segur, present during the campaign of 1812, noted that when the troops learned just how scarce provisions in Smolensk were,

[they] scattered through the streets, their only hope now being in pillage. But the carcasses of horses cleaned of meat down to the bone lying everywhere indicated the presence of famine. The doors and the windows had been torn out of all the houses as fuel for the campfires, so the men found no

shelter there. No winter quarters had been prepared, no wood provided. The sick and the wounded were left out in streets on the carts that had brought them in. . . . From that time on the strong plundered the weak, stealing from their dying companions by force or by stealth their food, their clothing, or the gold with which they had filled their knapsacks instead of provisions.[36]

As this grim account makes clear, to a large degree the Grand Armée had already begun to disintegrate as an organized military force. Efforts made by Napoleon to rally his men at Orsha were unavailing. It was during that stage that the first snows came, and with them the first days of subzero temperatures. And there was still the danger of the enemy to contend with. Cossack raids alternated with larger assaults and sometimes full-fledged battles, such as the three days of fighting near Krasnoe on November 3 (15) to November 7 (19). Two weeks later the shattered remnants of the army crossed the Berezina River over inadequate bridges and under hostile enemy fire, which cost them possibly as many as 30,000 casualties. Shortly thereafter, pleading political necessity, Napoleon abandoned his army and hurried back to Paris incognito to try to reestablish his authority before the full magnitude of the disaster became known. The army limped on to Vilna and from there to Kovno and the borders of the Russian Empire. Of the more than 400,000 whom Napoleon had led into Russia, scarcely 40,000 emerged alive.

Causes of Defeat:
Problems of Climate and Scale

How can we account for a military catastrophe on such a scale? One explanation put out by the French was that the defeat had been an accident, a particularly grisly one to be sure, but an accident all the same. In this view the French had been defeated during their retreat not by the Russian armies but by the very weather itself. This interpretation of the events of 1812 actually originated with Napoleon himself, who informed the French

Senat upon his return to Paris in December that "my army has had some losses. . . . but this was due to the premature rigors of the season."[37] It is an interpretation with which we may rapidly dispense.

In the first place, winter came rather later to Russia in 1812 than was normal. In fact, Napoleon's forces enjoyed exceptionally fine weather for all but one of the twenty-one days it took them to march from Moscow back to Smolensk.[38] Yet, as we have seen, the Grand Armée was already in the throes of decomposition by the time that it arrived at Smolensk, a process that obviously cannot be blamed on the weather. After that, to be sure, it turned colder. The sufferings of the French forces were considerable. Larrey, the French Surgeon General during the campaign, left behind unforgettable descriptions of the horrors of frostbite and the gangrene that succeeded it when afflicted soldiers tried to warm themselves too close to the campfires.[39] Yet if the French fell victim to the freezing temperatures, so too did the Russians. The troops of Alexander I had no greater immunity from the vicissitudes of the climate than did the troops of Napoleon. Finally, the most severe temperatures (-18 to -24 Reamur) were recorded in December *after* the murderous crossing of the Berezina had all but effected the extermination of the Grand Armée.[40]

If the role of the weather in Napoleon's downfall in Russia has been exaggerated, what then of the the view that his defeat was somehow inherent in the very scale of the enterprise? Some who have taken this view have argued that the Grand Armée despite its size was still too small a force with which to dominate the vast land mass of Russia. Napoleon was accordingly compelled to advance on a very narrow axis, which inevitably resulted in vulnerable (if not untenable) lines of supply, communication, and retreat. We should note, *inter alia,* that this interpretation was popular with Hitler and the Nazis, who sought to overcome what they regarded as the flaws in Napoleon's resources and strategy by employing three enormous army groups to invade the Soviet Union on broad fronts.[41] Others who have pondered the relationship between Napoleon's objectives and the resources at his disposal have looked at the issue somewhat differently. In their view, the Grand Armée's problem was not that it was too small but that it was too big. The size of the force (not to mention its multinational composition) created insoluble difficulties with command and control of the troops, given the available technologies of the day. The predictable result was massive indiscipline, which led to indiscriminate looting on the road both to and from Moscow, which in its turn resulted in the destruction of the army's logistic system. And owing to that indiscipline, the Grand Armée literally starved itself to death.[42]

There is something to recommend both interpretations, although neither is complete. It is true that the Grand Armée was simultaneously too small and too large—too small adequately to control the vast territories through which it passed, and both too large and too polyglot for the effective maintenance of discipline. By advancing as deeply into the heart of Russia as he did, Napoleon indeed assumed the risk that the enemy might raid or cut off his operational lines. The almost universal indiscipline among the troops was also a great evil. The dispatches of the generals in command (in addition to their memoirs) leave no doubt about the execrable condition of army discipline. In his order for the day of September 15, for instance, Victor spoke of the "blameworthy excess" his troops had manifested in despoiling the local population of foodstuffs, noting that the officers up until then had been incapable of stopping it.[43] Caulaincourt, to cite just one additional example, wrote that after the soldiers began their march east from Smolensk, pillaging was practically uncontrolled and uncontrollable, because army authorities were incapable of issuing regular rations.[44]

The marauding by the French troops had two unsavory results. In the first place, the rapacity of the Grand Armée alienated the Russian peasants, causing them to bury or burn their food and abandon their villages.[45] That, of course, greatly complicated the efforts of French officers to organize a system of planned requisitions. But indiscriminate looting also led to much waste and in addition to obvious inequities in distribution. Davout noted that thieving soldiers "destroy in a quarter of an hour the resources of many days."[46] That this was not merely an inconvenience is shown by the case of the food stockpiled in Smolensk. Apparently the main reason the retreating Grand Armée found meager provisions in Smolensk was plundering of the magazines by the soldiers left behind to garrison the town.[47]

Reasons for Defeat:
The Russian Contribution

Interpretations of the War of 1812 that stress the inherent difficulties of geography, logistics, and discipline may well be necessary to explain Napoleon's defeat; they are not, however, sufficient. We have already had occasion to observe that war is an interactive process. To understand its outcome we must take into account the errors and accomplishments of both combatants. Theories of Napoleon's innate defeat discount or disregard the Russian side's contributions to the destruction of the Grand Armée. Three contributions were most conspicuous: the political leadership of Alexander I, the Russian military recruitment system, and the strategies adopted and successfully pursued by the Russian military leadership after Napoleon's occupation of Moscow.

Clausewitz teaches that victory in war inheres in achieving one's political objectives by imposing one's will on the enemy. Sun Tzu might add that this process generally occurs in the mind of the enemy. If an enemy capitulates anywhere short of utter annihilation, it is because he has become convinced that the war is no longer worth fighting, that the costs of the conflict outweigh any conceivable political benefit that he might extract from it. Prior to 1812 the overwhelming majority of Napoleon's victories in war had followed that pattern. These wars had been limited wars of limited objective, not unlimited wars of total conquest. Napoleon won when the political leadership in the country or countries opposing him concluded that further hostilities would be useless, opened negotiations, made concessions, and signed a peace treaty. For that to happen, Napoleon had to have at least some insight into the personality and character of the monarch with whom he contended. With regard to Alexander I in 1812, Napoleon's intuition utterly failed him.

It is fair to say that Napoleon was always baffled by Alexander.[48] Indeed the Tsar, one of the most consummate actors of his age, continually perplexed his contemporaries. He duped Bonaparte (as he was latter to dupe Metternich) into thinking that he was simple-minded, shallow, slightly mad, or all three. It was upon that inaccurate estimation of Alexander's frailty that Napoleon reposed his psychological strategy for the War of 1812. As he explained to his former Ambassador to Russia, Caulaincourt, the French invasion of Russia would so terrify the great land-lords about the security of their estates that they would mob the Emperor and petition him to make peace. Since Alexander's objective in the war—the elimination of the Grand Duchy of Warsaw—was one about which most Russians cared nothing, the feeble Tsar would swiftly bow to the wishes of his richest and most influential subjects. The entire war would be over in two months.[49] Caulaincourt responded that the scheme showed a misunderstanding of both the Tsar and the nobility of Russia. He reported to Napoleon that prior to the break in diplomatic rela-tions Alexander had told him that "if the fighting went against me I should retire to Kamchatka rather than cede provinces and sign in my capital . . . treaties that were really only truces."[50]

From the very beginning of the war Alexander's conduct showed that he had spoken those words in earnest. Although he privately had moments of doubt, in public he never wavered from the oath he had sworn at the outset of the hostilities: to continue the struggle until the last invader had been expelled from Russian soil. What accounted for his resolve?

There were two probable reasons. First, far from whining for peace, the overwhelming majority of the nobility of Moscow and Petersburg was so consumed with hatred for the French that Alexander had reason to believe any attempt to negotiate a settle-ment to the conflict might precipitate his assassination. In Sep-tember 1812, on the anniversary of his coronation, Alexander rode through the streets of Petersburg in a closed carriage, not on horseback, as was customary, out of concern for his personal safety. Alexander was unpopular with the *dvorianstvo* of the city because they blamed him not for the *fact* of the war but for waging it badly.[51] A second and more important consideration that steeled Alexander to stand up to Napoleon was his convic-tion that the real purpose of the invasion of Russia was the extinc-tion of the Romanov dynasty. He simply refused to believe that the French war aims were limited, despite all the communica-tions he received from Napoleon to the contrary. Indeed, Napo-leon himself may have been uncertain about his own war aims, for he made contradictory remarks about them to his aides. On some occasions he indicated that the war was merely an act of chastisement designed to drive Alexander back within the fold of the continental system. For that purpose a swift battlefield success conjoined with a peace treaty enlarging the Polish state would be sufficient. Yet at other times he mused aloud to his entourage about putting an end to Russia's position as a European Power and driving it "back into the ice from which [it] had come."[52] Convinced that Napoleon was in pursuit of the latter objective, Alexander construed the war as a struggle for the survival of the Russian Empire and the Romanov dynasty. That belief lent the Tsar the courage of desperation. *Pourparlers* with Napoleon were out of the question, no matter how bleak the military situation. And Alexander's iron refusal to deal with Bonaparte even after the occupation of Moscow in the end would necessitate the disastrous French retreat. In that respect Alexander's fortitude, whatever its motivations, was an important element in Russia's victory in 1812.

Yet another element was the Russian recruitment system. In June, at the very beginning of the war, Alexander I had sent his Minister of Police, A. D. Balashov, on a mission to warn Napoleon that there would be no negotiations as long as foreign troops remained in Russia. Napoleon received Balashov on June 19 and treated him to a rambling discourse on the causes of the war and the inevitability of a French victory. In passing, Bonaparte boasted about the comprehensiveness of his intelligence concerning the Russian Empire:

> I know everything and I have calculated everything. I know that you have called up recruits and that you will call up still more of them [but] what is to be said of your recruit? He is not a soldier and you will not have time enough to make him one.[53]

As this passage indicates, Napoleon had at least some insight into the way the Russian command system of recruitment worked, but he supposed that he would be able to crush the Russian field armies before the growing Russian military manpower could be brought to bear on the battlefield. To some extent Napoleon was right: many of the peasants called to the colors in 1812 never saw service in that year, but instead reinforced the army for the German campaigns of 1813 and 1814.[54] He was also correct when he prophesied that there would not be sufficient time for the army to make full-fledged soldiers of those conscripts who joined front-line regiments during 1812. Napoleon's assessment of the likely influence of the Russian recruitment system on the course of the war, however, was wrong on three counts. In the first place, Napoleon clearly underestimated the population resources of the empire and consequently could not conceive of the scale of the recruitment drive that would be mounted by Russia in 1812. As we have already noted, in the late eighteenth and early nineteenth centuries the Russian Empire experienced a demographic explosion. The population of male peasants, who were of course the source for recruits, increased from roughly 12 million in the early 1780s to approximately 17.5 million in 1812.[55] Since men could be drafted as early as age fifteen, this increase of almost 32 percent obviously represented a tremendous expansion in the available military manpower pool. The recruiting policies of Alexander's government took full advantage of the population growth. Between 1801 and 1812 Petersburg decreed seventeen separate recruit levies, with the three of 1812 alone (totaling twelve men for every five hundred male peasants in the Empire) producing an intake of at least 400,000 soldiers.[56]

Secondly, because he was overly sanguine about an early victory in the war, Napoleon did not foresee that time would in fact suffice for the incorporation of large numbers of freshly inducted troops into the ranks of Kutuzov's armies. The largest quantity of reinforcements was acquired during the month when the French were in possession of Moscow. Whereas Kutuzov had arrived at Tarutino with 80,000 soldiers, he found himself in command of 130,000 thirty-three days later.[57] Although approximately one-half of the increment consisted of Don Cossacks regiments, which had been mobilized in July and August and were only now joining the army, the other half—25,000 men—were peasant recruits dispatched to the Tarutino camp after rudimentary training at Arzamas and Kaluga.[58] Since the highest estimate for the numbers of the marching parties that reached Napoleon during the stay in Moscow is 15,000, the arrival of reinforcements in September and October 1812 at last gave the main Russian army numerical superiority over the French. Napoleon was to receive no more men, but fresh detachments of conscripts continued to stream to Kutuzov and other generals in the field from October until the end of the year. Because they were operating within their own territory and because of the nature of their military draft, Russian forces had been able to afford more casualties than the Grand Armée even prior to the occupation of Moscow. Thereafter the imbalance was even more disadvantageous to Napoleon. Unlike Napoleon, Kutuzov was able to replace the soldiers he had lost. Not that those casualties were inconsiderable: by one estimate 48,000 men of Kutuzov's army were killed, were wounded, or succumbed to disease during the marches from Tarutino to the border of the empire.[59] Still further, Kutuzov's plentiful and growing strength enabled him to confound the enemy by deploying entirely new formations against him. Sir Robert Wilson, attached to Kutuzov's headquarters for most of the campaign, was often openly contemptuous of many aspects of the Russan war effort. But he was awestruck by the success with which the Russian government inducted and mobilized its recruits in 1812.[60]

Finally, although he was properly dismissive of the martial qualities of Russia's new recruits, Napoleon failed to allow for the potential deterioration of his own army. As we have already seen, the material (and moral) strength of the Grand Armée declined steeply during the retreat from Moscow. The situation was similar to that of Charles XII's Ukrainian campaign more than a century before. Alexander's half-trained recruits, like those of Peter the Great before them, would have been no match for well-fed, disciplined, and confident enemy regulars. But a ragged, starving, and diseased enemy army was something else again. The conscripts of 1812, however poorly drilled, were equal to the task of harrying Napoleon's forces all the way back to the Polish frontier. The recruitment system created by Peter the Great, which had delivered a margin of victory to him in his contest with the Swedes, proved just as important in Alexander I's triumph over Napoleon.

The third important element contributed by the Russian side to the destruction of the Grand Armée was strategy. We shall confine ourselves here to the strategies pursued by Kutuzov after the battle of Borodino. There were several, corresponding to different phases of the war. With the French in possession of Moscow, Kutuzov's first purpose was to keep them immobilized there as long as possible to buy himself time to rebuild his strength at Tarutino. With that in mind, the Russian Marshal received Napoleon's envoy Lauriston in his camp on September

23. On that occasion Kutuzov pretended that both he and his army were eager to conclude an armistice; he promised that the Russians would lay down their weapons as soon as couriers could travel to St. Petersburg and return with Imperial permission to do so.[61] That subterfuge helped Kutuzov to keep Napoleon hopeful and off his guard for several weeks.

As his strength increased, Kutuzov's next objective was to induce a French retreat from Moscow. The most important means he had for doing so was the skillful organization and exploitation of partisan warfare. Although there had been some partisan activity earlier in the campaign, the real explosion in partisan activity came after Borodino. Most accounts agree that the first articulate proponent of partisan war was Colonel Denis Davydov of the Akhtyrsk Hussar Regiment, who approached Bagration on the eve of the battle of Borodino to suggest that light cavalry detachments be organized to disrupt Napoleon's lines of supply and communications. Kutuzov initially had his doubts about the idea but relented in the end and gave Davydov one hundred men (evenly split between Hussars and Cossacks) to conduct an experiment.[62] The splendid results of Davydov's early operations soon made of Kutuzov a convert; many more partisan detachments were rapidly organized. By late September 1812 partisan units, comprising both regular and irregular cavalry, ringed the city of Moscow, with exceptionally heavy concentrations to the south and east.

The partisan commanders of 1812—men like Davydov, Zeslavin, and Figner—have long been celebrated in Russia as national heroes. There was, of course, a darker side to their story. Some of them committed revolting acts of cruelty. Even contemporaries questioned the sanity of A. S. Figner, notorious for his policy of murdering prisoners.[63] Yet overall the partisan captains of 1812 were responsible for invaluable services to their country. Guided by general directives from Kutuzov, the partisans performed two main functions during Napoleon's occupation of Moscow. First, by means of constant hit-and-run raids they made foraging beyond the city limits virtually impossible for the French.[64] Second, on several occasions they succeeded in interdicting all road communications between Moscow and the west, thus demonstrating to Napoleon just how exposed his army's position in the city was. In late September partisans cut the road to Mozhaisk. The first units sent by Napoleon to reopen it (several squadrons of chasseurs and dragoons) were captured.[65] Somewhat later, partisans surprised and slaughtered all the French troops in the town of Vereya. Finally, on October 6 (18) came news of the engagement at Vinkovo, in which partisans had defeated and driven off a strong formation of French cavalry.[66] Soon afterward, Napoleon took the decision to retreat.

In the last phase of the campaign, as the Grand Armée slowly moved west, it was Kutuzov's intention to grind it down principally by means of barring its access to food. He employed both his regular forces and his partisans for the purpose. As the French army retreated, Kutuzov engaged in parallel marches on both of its flanks in order to restrict it, as far as possible, to the road. As a result, foraging became extremely hazardous. If the French attempted to break out, they were met with stiff resistance. On one occasion Napoleon did in fact succeed in forcing his way through the Russian columns surrounding him. But the French Emperor's victory at Krasnoe (November 3–7 [15–19]) was paid for with heavy casualties and at least 20,000 prisoners.[67] At the same time, partisan detachments of light cavalry and Cossacks raided enemy encampments, looted baggage trains, and killed stragglers.[68] French efforts to take precautions against surprise attacks, especially at night, proved unavailing. Victor, for one, noted ruefully that his soldiers were notoriously slack when it came to performing guard duty.[69] It would be straying from the truth to suggest, as Napoleon himself once did, that Russia owed all its successes in the war to the operations of its cavalry partisans.[70] Still, conjoined with the maneuvers of the regular army the exploits of the partisans were of the highest significance in conducting the Grand Armée to its doom.

Mythologies of Victory

The political leadership, military system, and strategies of the Russian Empire must not be slighted in any balanced discussion of the reasons for Napoleon's defeat. Yet equally the victory of 1812 was not the great and perfect triumph of generalship and nationalism that generations of Russian historians have represented it to be. There are at least two reasons for stating this. The first has to do with the nature of Russian strategy during the war, and the second concerns misleading assertions about the nation in arms.

Long before the outbreak of the War of 1812 there had been many highly placed Russians who had recommended that Russia adopt a Fabian strategy should it ever again have to try a passage of arms with the French Empire. Count S. R. Vorontsov, the Russian Ambassador in London, had pointed out that Russia was sure to be victorious if its armies retreated while conducting a tenacious defense. "If the enemy pursues us he will perish, because the farther he proceeds from his stores of provisions, his arms and munitions depots, the farther he penetrates a land without passable roads or provisions which he could seize, the more pitiful will be his condition."[71] As far back as 1807 Barclay himself had apparently proposed luring an enemy army into the depths of the country, if war with Napoleon should be renewed.[72] This idea was also the cornerstone of the note that Barclay presented to Alexander I in early 1810 on "The Defense of the Western Borders of Russia."[73] After the war had broken out and the Russian armies began to fall back, French intelligence reported that the explanation given the troops was that the retreat had been planned as a ruse to draw the enemy onward to destruction.[74]

Nothing, of course, could have been farther from the truth. The Russian retreat of 1812 was a spontaneous response to the pressure of superior forces. In fact, in view of the way Alexander I had structured the command of his armies, the distinguishing characteristic of the Russian Empire's initial approach to the conduct of the war was incoherence. Nominally, Alexander had reserved for himself supreme authority over the military. But the chain of command was hopelessly confused. As War Minister and general in charge of the largest army, the First, Barclay de Tolly bore responsibility for military operations in the western and northwestern quarters of the Empire. But Bagration was simultaneously subordinate and *not* subordinate to Barclay, for he enjoyed the right of personal report to the Emperor. In addition there was the headstrong Admiral P. V. Chichagov, chief of the Danubian Army, who had his own ideas about how to wage war against Napoleon, which he rarely deigned to share with his colleagues. The result was extraordinary strategic confusion. Although in theory the Phull plan was supposed to provide general guidance for Russian operations, in practice each of Russia's generals in the field pulled the war effort in his own direction, like children tugging on a blanket. Adding to the chaos were the unceasing advice and orders that originated with the Emperor.

There was, however, one common element in the thinking of all of Russia's generals in the initial phase of the War of 1812: all of them anticipated offering Napoleon a major battle before the summer was over. Perhaps the most flamboyantly aggressive was Admiral Chichagov. At the end of June (O.S.), he had written Alexander that his Danubian Army should stage diversions against the French-held territories of Dalmatia and Illyria. Once those provinces had capitulated, Chichagov said, he would then swing southeast and march on Constantinople itself. Fortunately for Russia, the Tsar had the good sense to veto Chichagov's harebrained scheme. Because of Napoleon's numerical superiority, Russia could not afford any risky foreign military adventures; it had to keep all its troops available for use at home. Besides, to attack Constantinople meant widening the war by bringing the Turks in as Napoleon's allies—obviously something to be avoided.[75]

As for Bagration, as we have already observed, he found Barclay's policy of retreating in the face of the Grand Armée incomprehensible if not actually craven. He complained bitterly of Barclay's decision to abandon Smolensk, asserting that he had been on the point of conquering Napoleon until Barclay began to meddle.[76] And in a letter of August 14 (26) (seasoned with much profanity about Barclay), Bagration expressed his view that the only proper way for the Tsar of Russia to fight was offensively, not defensively.[77]

Even Barclay, despite his innate caution, by no means originally imagined that the Russian retreat would last as long as it did. To be sure, in his plan of 1810 he had envisioned drawing the enemy into Russia, but no farther east than the defensive line he proposed on the western Dvina and the Dnepr. By that point he expected Napoleon's forces to be so softened up by hunger and fatigue that the Russian army would have a good chance of inflicting a defeat upon them.[78] Once the invasion began, to Barclay's credit, he recognized the necessity of retreat more quickly and completely than did Bagration, Phull, or Alexander.

But he had no idea how long it would be necessary to retreat, or what the terminal point of the retreat would be. From time to time he grew despondent about the way the war was going. Shortly after the withdrawal from Smolensk, he wrote, with apparent sincerity, that the only hope for the salvation of Russia lay in a general battle.[79] In retrospect it is lucky that he changed his mind, for a general battle in August would only have played into Bonaparte's hands.

Emperor Alexander, although a proponent of defensive war at the outset, all the same wanted to see his forces go over quickly to the offense. In his correspondence with Barclay, the Tsar made no secret of his disappointment with the absence of offensive action. In his letter approving Barclay's request to retire to Smolensk and unite with Bagration, Alexander wrote that "although for many reasons and circumstances at the beginning of military operations it was necessary to abandon the borders of our land, the fact that this withdrawal had continued to Smolensk itself can only be regarded with shame."[80] Alexander's enthusiasm for offensives did not abate even after the defeat of the Russian army at Borodino, when he sent Kutuzov a plan for a frontal assault on the Grand Armée that was supposed to prevent the loss of Moscow.[81] By the time Alexander's couriers had reached him, however, the council of war at Fili had already taken place; Kutuzov had resolved to cede the city to the French.

Why all the interest in offensives on the part of Alexander and his generals? Several considerations had weight with them. First, retreat entailed abandoning territory to the enemy, driving off cattle, and destroying stocks of grain. Such a scorched earth policy obviously inflicted grave harm on the very country Russia's leaders were sworn to protect. The "Scythian strategy" could be the recourse only of an army that had no other choice. Given the magnitude of the catastrophe the retreat was visiting upon Russia, it was always tempting for Russia's generals to think that there *had* to be another choice, another way of expelling the invader without resigning themselves to the ruination of the countryside. Second, by retreating and depriving the enemy of resources, Russia's generals were depriving themselves of resources as well. It was possible to get along without Lithuania and Belorussia; those impoverished regions had never furnished the Russian military with much in the way of munitions, grain, or recruits anyway. But the farther east the enemy advanced, the closer he came to the Great Russian heartland, whose factories, estates, and populous villages were the very fabric and texture of Russian military power. Russia's military resources were vast, but they were not limitless. Serious questions had to be asked about the amount of territory Russia could prudently afford to sacrifice in the interest of wearing the enemy down.[82]

There was one other problem with retreating. To be sure, a strategy of trading space for time had an honored place in the Russian military repertoire; Peter the Great had employed it with brilliant results in his war with Charles XII. Yet the Russian army had grown more self-consciously "European" since Peter's day. Such glory as that army had won had been acquired through bold and daring offensives. Ceaseless retreat was a repudiation of that tradition. It was also an obvious confession of military inferiority. It seemed somehow unmanly and un-Western, not to mention costly in lives. The very expression used to describe the retreat both at the time and later—*skifskaia strategiia* (a Scythian strategy)—was almost a reproach, drawing a linguistic distinction between accepted European military practices and Asiatic ones. Small wonder that Russia's military leaders were reluctant to embrace the necessity of withdrawal. Intellectual, cultural, and institutional reasons, then, militated against the crafting of a master plan for retreat in the first months of the campaign of 1812. In the end, of course, the Russian armies did fall back all the way to Moscow. That was probably the only course of action appropriate under the circumstances, but it was not prearranged, but rather improvised in stages.

A second, even more insidious misrepresentation of the victory of 1812 is its depiction as the template of national war, the inevitable triumph of the aroused nationalism of the Russian people over the hated foreign invader. This, of course, had been a stock interpretation of many Soviet scholars who have written about the history of the war. Tarle, for one, wrote of the "popular character" of the conflict, describing how the depredations of the French awoke the "pitiless fury" of the Russian peasants. He asserted that "the entire war against the invader was from start to finish a national war."[83] More recently, P. A. Zhilin has reaffirmed the "decisive role" of the popular masses in Russia's victory.[84] Indeed, many contemporaries themselves thought there was an equation of some kind between Russian nationalism and the destruction of the Grand Armée. A young infantry officer, Aleksandr Chicherin, made the following entry in his diary for March 1813: "[T]his campaign demonstrates, more than any other, that if a people is worthy of a name distinguishing it from other European nations, then it is dangerous for an enemy to invade the territory of such a people, regardless of how powerful he may be."[85] For Chicherin the Russian people, by their stalwart services in the war, had redeemed their claim to the dignity of nationhood. Denis Davydov, in his memoir of his partisan service, made a similar point when, alluding to the treatment the peasants accorded French foragers and stragglers, he wrote that those soldiers died in a vain and unequal struggle "with the entire nation."[86] In a conversation of August 1812 with his friend the architect J. A. Erenstrem, Alexander I himself explained that one of the reasons he had favored a defensive rather than an offensive war was to awaken the national passions of the Russian people and to rally them around their government. Allowing Napoleon to invade the country had had the desired result, the Tsar continued. "The spirit of people . . . is superb. The majority of them are ready to render the greatest sacrifices for the fatherland. Bonaparte is relying, perhaps, on the sympathy of a certain part of the Russian population for himself, but he has miscalculated, since all classes of society are savagely opposed to him and to the French."[87] Alexander was expressing his confidence that even if Napoleon were to try to exploit the class divisions in Russia (perhaps even by issuing a decree emancipating the serfs), he would still be unable to quench the ardor of the united Russian people for the defense of their native land. As the events of the war unfolded, they seemed to bear out the Emperor's prediction.

There are problems both with the versions of the national awakening purveyed by historians and with the contemporary evidence itself. Tarle, for instance, completed his book during the early years of World War II. For that reason, he consciously designed it to serve as a work of monumental history (in Nietzsche's sense of the term)—a piece of scholarship that would employ the example of 1812 to embolden the citizens of the Soviet Union in their struggle against the Nazi aggressors. In and of itself, that need not necessarily disqualify Tarle's views on the mass rising of 1812. Yet as we read on, it becomes apparent that he has borrowed extensively from the literary genre of the epic in fashioning his depiction of the war. At times he sings a jarring and anachronistic paean to Soviet patriotism in addition to Russian nationalism. "The national minorities," he insists, "were not a whit behind the Russian population in their desire to defend their Fatherland," and here he heaps special praise on the Don Cossacks, Bashkirs, Tatars, Ural Cossacks, Transcaucasians and Jews—an all-inclusive litany that frankly seems incredible.[88] Zhilin's description of the nationalism of 1812 inspires no greater confidence. He takes the heroism of the masses as an unquestioned article of faith, not susceptible to ordinary historical analysis. To Zhilin, the emphasis by Soviet historiography on the popular role in Napoleon's defeat proved its superiority to prerevolutionary scholarship on the question. "One of the primary tasks confronting Soviet historiography," he writes, "was the comprehensive illumination of the heroic struggle of the Russian people—the decisive force in the destruction of the Napoleonic army of invasion."[89] A little later on, however, he confesses that the task still has not been completed and adds that the "comprehensive exposure of the participation of the popular masses in the war, their decisive role in the victory is the central scholarly problem of the history of the war of 1812."[90] This passage is notable for its circular reasoning, its assertion of that which is to be proved. The doubts of even a credulous reader are certain to be aroused when Zhilin proceeds to explain why the exposure of the participation of the masses in the war by that date had been less than comprehensive: a dearth of archival materials on the subject.[91]

What, then, of the contemporary testimony? There are difficulties here, too. Lieutenant Chicherin's diary (which was not intended for publication) might appear to be a disingenuous and consequently reliable source. It is indeed a good source, but of value more for reconstructing Chicherin's thoughts and inner emotional state than for soberly analyzing the objective reality of his time. A bookish young man, Chicherin was an avid reader of sentimental novels, such as those of Laurence Sterne. His diary consciously reflects those literary influences, hence it becomes the record not so much of his life as his fantasy life. As a result it represents both the author and Russia not necessarily as they were but as he wished them to be. In the passage on the dignity of the Russian people, cited above, what Chicherin is really saying is that Napoleon's defeat on Russian soil was *prima facie* evidence that the Russians were a great *European people*. Chicherin assumed that national consciousness was a prime feature of modernity and Westernization, so he asserted that the Russian masses in fact possessed it. That is not surprising, for Chicherin, like a good many other cultivated and progressive noblemen of his generation, wished Russia to be regarded as a Western country. But the voicing of desires and the ventilation of prejudices does not in fact constitute proof of an explosion in popular nationalism during the War of 1812.

Similar problems becloud the statements of Denis Davydov. Davydov, like Chicherin, viewed the War of 1812 as a national triumph. He was originally moved to write up his war experiences in response to the publication of Napoleon's memoirs, which, in his opinion, slighted the the partisan movement and defamed the Russian national character as well.[92] But unlike Chicherin, who was killed in 1813, Davydov lived on into the reactionary era of Nicholas I. Perhaps for that reason, he felt he had a special obligation to serve as custodian of what he regarded as the authentic, progressive, and liberal significance of the war. The War of 1812 and the ensuing campaign of 1813 and 1814 were wars of liberation, pitting freedom-loving Russians against the oppressive French Empire. It was therefore very important for him to maintain that in 1812 Napoleon met with resistance on the part of the entire Russian nation. Yet, although he provides invaluable information on the activities and stratagems of the partisans, he is suspiciously short on details about the national insurrection against Bonaparte. As we shall see somewhat later, some of the evidence that he does provide actually undermines the case that a general insurrection actually occurred.

Alexander I, in his discourse with Erenstrem, offers a blanket insistence on the universal allegiance of his subjects to himself. He speaks like a man trying to convince himself of something solely on the strength of intoxicating rhetoric. In fact, there appears to have real concern on the part of many landowners that Napoleon's invasion would unleash peasant rebellions *against them*. Rostopchin was fairly typical. His letters of 1812 are so full of insipid and irrelevant anecdotes about the loyalty and patriotism of individual lackeys and serfs that one can only conclude that he was padding his correspondence with them to conceal a latent anxiety.[93] Of course, the serfs did not rise up against their masters in 1812. For one thing, there was very little point in their doing so. As a monarch and essential social conservative, Napoleon never had any intention of publishing a decree manumitting the Russian peasants. But the absence of a servile jacquerie is not evidence for the boundless loyalty of the masses to the Tsar, let alone for their nationalism or their enthusiasm for the Russian war effort. Although Alexander himself was later convinced that the patriotism of the Russian people had paved the way to victory, his conviction, once again, does not necessarily mean that it was so.

None of the foregoing should be construed as a denial of the fact that there was a national awakening in Russia during the War of 1812. There was such an awakening, but among the privileged classes of the empire. Insofar as there had been any Russian national consciousness at all previously, it had been the property of the educated and literate. The intense shock occasioned by the war and the dramatic reversals in fortune that it brought in its wake caused many among the Russian elite to ponder the question of their national identities with renewed seriousness.[94] We can actually see the process at work in the pages of Chicherin's diary.[95] The birth of national feeling is, of course, also anatomized with acute insight by Leo Tolstoy in *War and Peace*. It is said that the trauma of 1812 was instrumental in planting the seeds for the national ideology advocated by the Slavophiles in the succeeding reign. Yet the ideology of intellectuals is a far cry from mass nationalism.

If the authentic nationalism engendered by the War of 1812 remained closely confined by the boundaries of class and education, that does not mean the Russian peasantry played no role whatsoever during the struggle with the French. Some peasants did actively engage in the fight, but they were not motivated by nationalism, and their contribution to the war effort was decidedly minor. Their participation was less heroic and less universal than it has often been portrayed as having been.

In the early stages of the campaign, the resistance of the peasants is best described as passive. In many localities they retired into the forests after burning or burying stocks of food.[96] Later, during the Tarutino period, when organized partisan war had begun, at least some peasants served as scouts and guides to those cavalry detachments.[97] Still later in the fall, emboldened peasants often did ambush, plunder, and murder unfortunate soldiers who had fallen behind their marching columns.[98] Robert Wilson, among others, has left behind a grim account of the plight of such men, who became "the sport and victims of the peasantry."[99] There are also a handful of documented instances in which armed bands of peasants apparently gave assistance to regular army units.[100]

When and why did peasants did take up arms against the French? Upon his departure from Drissa on July 6 (18), the Emperor Alexander I had issued a proclamation calling on the people of Russia to rise up in armed struggle with the invaders. The proclamation, however, appears to have had little success in rousing the masses.[101] For one thing, the villages were largely quiet throughout the summer. Serious peasant resistance was a phenomenon of the fall and winter. At that time the most important motivation appears to have been the bad treatment the peasants had already suffered at the hands of the Grand Armée. Ermolov, a Russian officer of acute perception, later wrote that "the brutality and crimes" of Napoleon's forces aroused the hatred of the people against them. If the French army had instead treated the peasants well (for example by paying generously for provisions instead of simply seizing them), Ermolov speculated, then army might have won many of them over.[102] That assessment was shared by Caulaincourt, who observed that "the disorder and pillage which inevitably followed our forced marches had caused the initial damage and alienated the peasants."[103] It also seems to have been the view of Kutuzov himself. On the mission to the Tarutino camp, Napoleon's Ambassador Lauriston had been instructed to reprove the Russians for the barbarous cruelty Russian peasants were visiting upon French soldiers. Kutuzov's reply was that peasants "consider this war to be just like an invasion of the Tatars."[104] This episode, so often cited by Soviet historians as illustrating the Field Marshal's insight into the patriotic ardor of the masses, actually does nothing of the kind.[105] Kutuzov's point was that the peasants had come to detest the French not as the foes of the Russian national idea, or even of Russia itself, but rather because they considered them personal enemies. Such feelings are far more elemental and less abstract than nationalism.

At least some peasants fought the French because partisan detachments had organized, armed, and ordered them to do so. Davydov provides many accounts of his own efforts along those lines, at the village of Takarevo in early September, for example. After driving off a band of French marauders who had been preying on the villagers, he supplied them with weapons and urged them to welcome other bands of Frenchmen in and then murder them at night.[106] The role of the partisans in stimulating peasant resistance makes good psychological sense. Although already primed to fight, they had little incentive to do so if they felt that Napoleon was firmly in control of their province and winning the war. A surprise visit by a detachment of Russian partisans, apparently able to operate freely behind enemy lines, might be exactly what was needed to encourage them to translate their hatred of the French into action.

A final motivation that may have been of weight with some peasants was a complex set of religious grievances. It was widely rumored throughout rural Russia that the French were desecrating Orthodox churches and icons as a matter of policy. Tales were told of the stabling of horses in the Kremlin cathedrals and the burning of sacred icons. The clergy of Russia itself preached a holy war against the invader Napoleon, whom they reviled as a "forerunner of the Anti-Christ."[107] The governing council of Russian Orthodoxy, the Synod, formally anathematized the French Emperor.

Whatever the reasons for peasant resistance, it is important not to exaggerate it. Peasant antagonism actually played very little part in the downfall of Napoleon in 1812. In the first place, as we have seen, those peasants who armed themselves did so only after the French occupation of Moscow and consequently had no influence on the earlier phases of the campaign.[108] Even after armed resistance had begun, it was chiefly defensive; what the peasants did more than anything else was protect their own villages and fields from the raids of small parties of French troops who had wandered off from the Grand Armée in search of food.[109] Such operations obviously could have had very little impact on the course of the war. Nor could the (admittedly numerous) episodes of the torture and murder of French stragglers during the late fall and summer. Separated from their comrades, alone in a hostile and inhospitable country, such men would soon have perished anyway from disease or starvation. What of the *opolchenie,* or popular militia? The Russian government did try to build one up during the War of 1812. Militia regiments were established in towns and rural provinces. Although there may have been some peasant volunteers, the majority of the recruits appear to have been sent into the militia by their landlords.[110] Most of the militiamen, however, were armed only with pikes and axes. Even more tellingly, the government did not even bring the militia into the field until the very end of December 1812. By that point, of course, what was left of the Grand Armée had already left Russia.[111]

If the participation of the peasants in the war was not decisive, neither was it universal or uniformly enthusiastic. For one thing, in certain areas under nominal French control, there appears to have been a significant amount of collaboration. When Denis Davydov later wrote down his reflections on partisan warfare, he indicated that one of its most important functions had been to lift the spirit of the civil population behind enemy lines and to deter treasonous intercourse with the enemy.[112] Had all the peasants of Russia (and their lords) been indomitably and implacably opposed to Napoleon, there would have been no point in mentioning such a function.

It might be argued that the serfs showed the most serious commitment to the struggle only when they were in uniform. Evidence abounds that the peasant soldiers of 1812 fought with conspicuous bravery on many occasions. Once again, however, the actual record presents a mixed picture. Did peasant volunteers stream to the colors, burning with fervor to fight the French? Clearly some did. But just as clearly, others did not. One is struck by the extraordinary inducements both the government and private individuals at times felt were essential to attract volunteers. For example, Alexander's sister, Duchess Catherine of Ol'denburg, tried to raise a regiment at her own expense in Tver' Province during the late summer and early fall of 1812. To fill the ranks, she was obliged to promise the recruits on her own estates that they would be mustered out of the army just as soon as the war was concluded, with their short-term service counting as a full twenty-five year term—an extremely advantageous deal that would exempt their extended families from the burden of furnishing recruits in the future. She also vowed to exempt any veterans of her regiment from the payment of *obrok* (quitrent) for life.[113] Such generosity on Catherine's part would obviously have been superfluous if her serfs had been Russian patriots to the last man.

Other evidence also hints at a reluctance, at least on the part of some, to perform military service during the Fatherland War. To my knowledge, only one printed memoir by a peasant who fought in the ranks of the Russian army in 1812 exists. As is to be expected, the circumstances of its composition were unique. Pamfil Nazarov from Korchusk District (also in the Province of Tver') enlisted in September 1812. After a twenty-four-year military career he retired, took the tonsure, and joined a monastery. There he learned to read and write, and drafted a history of his life. His memoir is fascinating on many counts, not in the least because of the portrait it gives of the sorry lot of the common Russian soldier in the first quarter of the nineteenth century. It is a dreary chronicle of misery, beatings, and disease. Yet in the context of the present discussion it is most interesting for the insight it provides into the circumstances surrounding Nazarov's enlistment. There is no mention of patriotic motives and high ideals. Nazarov admits that as a bachelor he joined up to spare his older married brothers from being drafted. Nazarov does not hide the anguish he felt at being forced into the army (as he saw it) by family pressure. Far from showing any zeal for combat with the French, Nazarov recalls that he went nearly insane with grief as he was marched away to the recruiting depot, which distressed emotional state enabled his comrades to steal his spare clothes and all of his money from his knapsack.[114]

Nazarov, obviously, is an exceptional case. His literacy, longevity, and biographical interests clearly differentiate him from thousands of serfs who served in the army of that time. Yet we cannot be certain that his attitude toward the War of 1812 was not shared by other peasant soldiers. Other items in the contemporary record also strongly suggest that he was not alone in his aversion to the struggle. For one thing, if French military intelligence is to be believed, there were considerable numbers of Russian troops who deserted, particularly in the early phases of the war.[115] Yet another sign that desertion was serious is the fact that in September the Russian government increased the penalties both for the deserters and for those who harbored them.[116] As we saw in the previous chapter, desertion typically had not been a grave problem for the late-eighteenth-century Russian army in either war or peacetime, but the crisis of 1812 was so acute, and so many peasants were drafted both prior to the war and during it, that it is likely that the traditional military institutions that built small-group loyalty and inhibited flight (such as the army *artel*) were simply overwhelmed.

The conduct (or misconduct) of other Russian soldiers also casts doubt on the War of 1812 as a great national struggle. If the motivation and discipline of the troops had been high, and if they had been well led, there would have been little reason to worry that they might run amok in the Russian countryside and loot the villages they were supposed to be defending. But there *was* reason to worry, for on many occasions that appears to be exactly what they did. Alexander I himself was concerned enough to instruct Barclay in July to take all steps to prevent his troops from "robbing, injuring, and despoiling" the civilian population of the empire.[117] But criminal attacks by Russian soldiers upon Russian peasants remained a reality throughout the entire war. On September 12, no less a personage than Kutuzov sent a circular message to all of the governors in central Russia warning them "that . . . pillaging on the part of the army is increasing and has even spread to provinces far removed from the theater of war."[118] In early October Lieutenant General Shepelev, military commander of Kaluga, noted that Russian military units in the province "are carrying off everything, exactly as if they were in the enemy's country."[119] Documents prepared in the province in October, November, and December prove that the destruction did not abate even in the final phase of the war, for they contain extensive inventories of the houses, livestock, windmills, barns, and taverns that the Russian soldiers had looted.[120] Small wonder that peasants sometimes responded by assaulting small groups of troops themselves.[121] That helps make sense of Davydov's recollection that when he first began his partisan operations, he and his men were often fired upon by Russian peasants, even though his troopers, attired in Russian uniforms, had loudly identified themselves to the peasants as Russian soldiers and defenders of the Orthodox faith. Later the villagers would typically offer the implausible excuse that they had mistaken Davydov's partisans for Frenchmen.[122] It is more likely, however, that the rapine by the troops on both sides had taught the peasants to regard all soldiers as enemies, no matter what insignia they wore. If that is so, the state of national unity in Russia during the Fatherland War of 1812 was far from ideal.

The Russian Empire did prevail in the war. The Russian government, Russia's generals, and its people all deserve credit for that. The victory of 1812 was neither accidental nor foreordained. The resolve of Alexander I, the skill of Barclay and Kutuzov, and the intrepidity and initiative of the regular partisans all were instrumental in Napoleon's defeat. But Russia's triumph had not been perfect. Months of bumbling had intervened before the army was able to improvise a workable strategy. The commitment of the masses of the population to the war effort had been variable. Some of the common folk were authentically devoted to the extermination of the French, but others tried to shirk their duty, enrolled in the army reluctantly, deserted in the face of the enemy, or turned to banditry and despoiled the countryside.

Napoleon's downfall in Russia had been so dramatic and complete that it was far too easy for educated Russians (and other Europeans, for that matter) to exaggerate the military prowess of the Tsarist Empire, to see the 1812 war as proof of Russian invincibility. As time passed, it also became more difficult to remember precisely how victory had been achieved, at what cost and with what effort. A conscious or unconscious process of self-delusion was at work, and it propagated the mythology of national unity and popular insurrection in 1812. The tsarist government, in particular, wished to believe in the correctness of its policies and the magnitude of its power. The myth of the popular insurrection supported both those beliefs.

If it had occurred, surely it demonstrated that the Russian people were fanatically loyal to their fatherland and their Emperor. Liberals and radicals, of course, could interpret the "insurrection" differently. To them, the uprising was occasioned by nationalism and patriotism, not monarchist zeal. That equally fallacious understanding of the mentality of the peasantry may well have helped deceive the Decembrists (and their successors) into thinking that the country was ripe for a violent revolution. On the other hand, returning to the government's perspective, the "popular insurrection" could be taken as proof that the

sources of Russian military strength had nothing to do with reform or modernity. In a generation of warfare with Revolutionary and Napoleonic France, almost all the major European powers had suffered severe defeats. The armies of disgruntled and
dispirited mercenaries whom they put into the field were inferior to the spirited and motivated French forces. The obvious
conclusion drawn in Berlin, Vienna, and the lesser German capitals was that to beat the French in battle, you had to emulate
them at least to some degree. That implied certain concessions to
the forces of liberalism and nationalism. Thus Prussia emancipated its serfs, the Rheinish states enacted constitutions, and
even the stolid Hapsburg monarchy gingerly embraced the cause
of reform. From the standpoint of conservative tsarist statesmen,
however, such steps were deadly errors. Liberalism was not a
fount of military power but a source of contaminating evil that
could give birth to revolutionary states zealous to overthrow the
order established by both king and God. Liberalism and revolutionary nationalism were the enemies of stability and legitimacy.
Prudent sovereigns had to keep alert to such movements and be
ready at any moment to nip them in the bud. An almost exclusive
preoccupation with the liberal-revolutionary paradigm of vulnerability is central to understanding the foreign policy and even
much of the military posture Russia adopted for the next forty
years.

Liberalism was not only dangerous, it was unnecessary. The
serfdom and autocracy of Russia had proved equal to overthrow-
ing one of the greatest of generals and the largest army ever
assembled in the history of Europe. Such reasoning, at the time,
was difficult to contest. Under Peter the Great, Russia had become a European Power by paradoxically capitalizing on the
strength of its backwardness. In 1812 the Russian military effort,
as it were, reverted to its Petrine roots and did in fact succeed.
But for the last time. The complacency engendered by 1812,
which blinded much of the Russian elite to the military implications of the Industrial Revolution, would be shattered forever on
the Crimean peninsula.

6

The Policy and Strategy of
Nicholas I

The thirty years between 1825 and 1855 were a time of extraordinary consistency in Russian policy. The period was indelibly marked by the character, temperament, and intellect of one man, the Emperor Nicholas I. Nicholas reveled in the exercise of his autocratic power; he believed it was his duty to rule, not merely to serve as a figurehead for ministers who governed in his name. He consequently sought to involve himself in all the facets of the policies of his empire. He surrounded himself with advisers notable not only for their personal loyalty to him but also for thinking just as he did.

Nicholas has been much misunderstood both by contemporaries, who feared him, and by later historians who have tried to come to terms with him. An unabashed militarist, he sought to avoid wars, yet waged many. Lampooned by West Europeans as "the gendarme of Europe," Nicholas did in fact intervene abroad to suppress revolution, but often with reluctance. Derided as a boorish reactionary, he nevertheless carefully observed the forms of the Polish Constitution until 1831. Suspected of harboring a lust for European domination, he actually was of the opinion that the Russian Empire was a satisfied power and needed no new territories. How do we account for the difference between the way Nicholas was perceived and the man he was? To put the question somewhat differently, why was there such a gap between the intentions that drove Russian policies and the outcomes of those policies?

The question is of particular interest because of the fundamental coherence of Russian policy and strategy during the period. Nicholas's foreign policy goals, his strategic ideas, and his military system were mutually supportive and self-contained. With regard to foreign policy Nicholas presumed an equivalence and an interconnection between external and internal security threats. In other words, his commitment to domestic order impelled him to to support the principle of legitimacy and to oppose revolution abroad. In pursuit of international stability Nicholas naturally availed himself of all of the diplomatic means at his disposal. But to a certain extent he had to rely on his military forces, although chiefly as an instrument of deterrence and intimidation. Intimidation, however, was not always successful. If war broke out, Nicholas's approach to strategy was linear and geometrical, influenced by the experience of the War of 1812 and by the mythologies to which that war had given life. As for the army itself, as suited a military establishment whose *raison d'être* was to threaten, not necessarily to fight, it was supposed to be large and formidable in appearance, but simultaneously as cheap as possible. Unfortunately, internal consistency is no guarantee of success. Nicholas failed to achieve his objectives; at the very end of his life he led Russia into its greatest nineteenth-century humiliation, the Crimean War. Before attempting to anatomize the reasons behind those failures, we must consider the relationships among Nicholas's goals, his strategic outlook, and his army.

The Foreign Policy and Security Objectives of Nicholas I

When examining Nicholas's foreign policy objectives, a good place to start is the obvious contrast between his personality and that of his predecessor, his elder brother Alexander. Alexander I (1801–25) was mercurial and headstrong, a man easily carried away by his enthusiasms. Not surprisingly, ambivalence and moodiness were features of his foreign policy. The contradictions were many. On the one hand, Alexander was capable in all sincerity of proposing the Holy Alliance of September 1815, a messianic plan for world order based upon the subscription of all European monarchs to a common set of Christian principles.[1] On the other hand, during the negotiations among the victors at the Congress of Vienna, Alexander indulged in such devious intrigue over the Polish question that Austria and Britain became convinced that he was scheming for European hegemony.[2] In fact, so tortuous was Alexander's policy that even figures in *Russian* diplomatic circles were confused about what the Tsar was up to—whether he meant to promote or suppress liberalism, for example.[3]

Where Alexander was flighty and complex, Nicholas was a man of stolid simplicity. Unlike his brother, whose policies were a bizarre mishmash of noble (if naïve) idealism and sordid cunning, Nicholas was exclusively devoted to framing his foreign policy in terms of his calculus of the Russian national interest.[4] Nicholas started from the assumption that the Russian Empire had all the territories it needed. In a political note of 1830 the Emperor wrote that "the geographical position of Russia is so happy that it makes her almost independent with respect to her own interests of that which transpires in Europe . . . her frontiers are sufficient for her."[5] To be sure, in the aftermath of war Nicholas could occasionally be induced to annex small swaths of territory in Asia and the Near East, but such action was against his natural inclinations.[6] More territory meant more territory to defend. When Poland rose up in rebellion against Russia in 1831, Nicholas even toyed with the idea of renouncing all Russian interests in that country and contracting the Russian frontiers to the Vistula and Narew once the Poles had been crushed militarily. Honor would consequently be satisfied, while the intrinsic danger to Russia of possessing hostile Polish territories would be lifted.[7] Although the project of cutting a chastised Poland loose from the Russian Empire was soon abandoned, it illustrates that Nicholas was no rapacious proponent of imperial expansion.

Yet if Russia was a satisfied power and contemplated no aggressive foreign wars, that did not mean it could afford to neglect the international environment. Russia obviously had to be concerned about the possibility that foreign states might combine to attack it. No matter how much the odds might favor Russia in such a struggle, Nicholas did not view war with equanimity. Like most other statesmen who had lived through the Napoleonic period, Nicholas was alive to the enormous destructive forces unleashed by war. That feeling was reinforced when he took up a personal command during the 1828–29 Turkish conflict and was apparently nauseated by the carnage he witnessed on the battle-field.[8] Then, too, Nicholas was aware of the grievous harm that the War of 1812 had inflicted on the fiscal health of the state: a special commission had informed him in 1828 that the economic dislocation of the "Fatherland War" had not been overcome; Russia was still wrestling with the problem of massive tax arrears.[9] All those considerations helped make Nicholas a firm advocate of peace; there is no reason to doubt his honesty when, in frequent audiences with foreign ambassadors, he expatiated on his pacific intentions.[10]

But how was war to be avoided? One way might be for Russia to have weak, possibly even dependent, neighbors on its frontiers. A desire to bring about that situation accounted for the Turkish policies of Russia throughout the entire reign. N. K. Nesselrode, Nicholas's Foreign Minister, wrote to his sovereign in February 1826 that Turkish control of the straits and Constantinople actually benefited Russia. As a feeble power, Turkey was susceptible to Russian pressure. In particular Russia might be able to coerce the Turks into closing the straits (and consequently the Black Sea) to the warships of any other foreign power. On the other hand, if the Ottoman Empire collapsed, it was likely that a hungrier and more aggressive state would seize the Bosphorus.[11] Three years later Nicholas appointed a secret commission to study Russia's long-term policy toward the Ottomans. It unanimously concluded "that the advantages of the preservation of the Ottoman Empire in Europe outweigh the disadvantages and that, as a result, its destruction would be contrary to the interests of Russia." If, owing to circumstances beyond Russian control, the Turkish Empire fell apart anyway, Russia had to be able to ensure that the entrance to the Black Sea did not fall into the hands of any other major power.[12] The decision of the commission of 1829 was endorsed by the Tsar and became the foundation of Russia's foreign policy with regard to the "Eastern Question" for much of the ensuing thirty years.[13]

When the Egyptian Khedive Mehmet Ali revolted against Constantinople in 1833, Nicholas posed as Turkey's protector, extracting its promise to bar foreign warships from the Black Sea in exchange. Although the strong protests of the other powers voided that Unkiar Skelessi Treaty, the Straits Convention of 1841 established the principle that no foreign warships were to pass through the straits as long as the Ottoman Empire was at peace. Nesselrode gloated (prematurely) that the latter document had secured Russia "henceforth against any naval attack."[14]

But Turkey (and Persia) were in the end special cases. Russia also had to worry about its European neighbors. In Nicholas's opinion, instability and potential revolutions in Europe posed direct threats to the safety of the Russian Empire, for he believed revolution was in and of itself a source of war. It might be possible to live in peace in a Europe ruled by conservative kings, but the very maintenance of peace was in doubt if dynamic revolutionary regimes superseded those monarchies. For Nicholas it was important at all costs to prevent the recurrence of a French-style revolution anywhere in Western Europe. Had not the French Revolution produced Napoleon, and had not Napoleon dragged Europe down into more than twenty years of calamitous wars?

His fixation on the French Revolution led Nicholas to consider revolution the sole source of the most serious and catastrophic wars. But he saw that foreign revolutionary activity threatened the Russia state in yet another way, for it went hand in glove with domestic subversion. That conclusion resulted from the shattering impact the Decembrist conspiracy of 1825 had upon him.

In the ten years following the signing of the peace treaties in Vienna, Southern and Southeastern Europe had been afflicted with revolutionary disturbances of varying gravity. Russia at first had seemed to be immune. Although overt opposition to the autocracy or the regime was conspicuously absent, however, such opposition was already in gestation. Beginning in 1816 or so, progressive-minded army officers, eventually to number in excess of five hundred, had held secret political meetings to debate the future of the Russian Empire. Over time those groups coalesced into two discrete bodies, the Northern Society (in Petersburg), and the Southern Society (in the Ukraine). Eventually some of the officers crossed the line from discussion to conspiracy. Unlimited autocratic authority, they argued, was corrupt and oppressive. It was time to change Russia's system of government. Alexander I's death in 1825 gave them an opportunity to act.

Since Alexander had no son, the crown originally should have gone to the eldest of his younger brothers, the Grand Duke Konstantin Pavlovich. But Konstantin had contracted a morganatic marriage and had accordingly agreed to relinquish his claim; documents naming the next brother, Nicholas, as heir presumptive had been secretly filed away. Because the new arrangements had not been made public, when the news of Alexander's death reached Petersburg there was initially confusion in that city about who was the legitimate successor.[15] Capitalizing upon this interregnum, Decembrist ringleaders led some three thousand soldiers under their command down to the Senate Square in St. Petersburg on the morning of December 14. There they denounced Nicholas as a usurper and ostentatiously swore their allegiance to Konstantin in the manifest hope of sparking a military insurrection against the autocracy. The standoff lasted all day, until loyal troops were able to rout the Decembrists with cannister shot. The insurrection had failed, as did a similarly ill-coordinated rising by the Southern Society the following week. The result was the arrest, interrogation, and trial of the participants. One hundred and sixteen of them received sentences of exile or harsher terms of penal servitude. Five were hanged.

Although Nicholas disparaged the significance of the revolt in conversations with foreign envoys, he actually was of the view that the Decembrists had all been part of a monstrous international plot directed against himself and his Empire.[16] In the ensuing years the revolts and rebellions that afflicted Western and Central Europe did nothing to disabuse Nicholas of this notion. The 1830 revolutions in France and Belgium, the Polish insurrection of 1830–31, the Cracow rebellion of 1846, and the great revolutions of 1848, which threatened monarchs throughout Europe from Italy, through the Germanys, to France, were all taken by Nicholas as demonstrating the existence of a sinister international conspiracy of liberals devoted to the destruction of the established order. Nicholas and his closest associates also regarded many of the riots and rebellions as posing a direct threat to Russia for two distinct reasons. In the first place, upheaval abroad might provide an unfortunate example to the disaffected at home. Among the disaffected, the Poles came immediately to mind. When Nesselrode described the revolutions of 1848 as a "devastating crisis which menaced our internal tranquility," it was clearly the impact of the revolutions on the disgruntled Poles he had in view.[17] Indeed, when Nicholas finally decided to lend aid to the beleaguered Austrian Emperor by marching into his dominions in 1849 to crush the Hungarian revolution, he did so out of a conviction that the Hungarians were collaborating with the Poles. Nesselrode wrote of the "Hungro-Polish revolution" as having become "just as dangerous for Russia as for the Austrian monarchy itself."[18] Nicholas, in a letter to one of his most prominent military commanders, justified the intervention by observing that "in the Hungarian rebellion there are clearly visible the forces of a general conspiracy against all that is holy and against Russia in particular, since the heads of the rebellion and its chief instruments are our eternal enemies, the Poles."[19]

The other reason Nicholas was concerned about foreign revolutions was a different, indirect sort of threat they presented to his Empire. A successful foreign revolution might bring to power an aggressive regime whose belligerence could touch off war that would sooner or later involve Russia. To Nicholas's mind, the country where the greatest danger of that existed was France. Nicholas harbored a lifelong distrust of France, which he viewed as a hotbed of instability, truculence, and ambitious politicians. The three changes of regime that occurred in Paris during Nicholas's reign tended to validate Russian suspicions. The revolution of 1830 swept the Bourbon King Charles X away and replaced him with Louis Phillipe. In 1848, revolution once again engulfed France, and Louis Phillipe's monarchy was supplanted by the Second Republic. Finally, in the 1850s the Republic gave way to the Third Empire of Napoleon III. The *bouleversements* of French politics (plus memories of the depredations of the first Napoleon) led Nicholas consistently to exaggerate the malignity of French intentions, just as he overestimated French capabilities. In 1831, for instance, Nicholas gloomily speculated that French designs on Belgium might make a general war inevitable.[20] In 1840, during the second Mehmet Ali crisis, Nicholas interpreted French support for the Egyptians as part of a deeply laid plot to reconquer the left bank of the Rhine.[21] On both occasions, the Emperor failed to anticipate that the French would back down. Another telling index of Nicholas's excessive anxiety about the French menace was the fact that whereas the military intelligence collection effort generally was rudimentary throughout his reign, the chief exception to this pattern was France, about whose armed forces he evinced an insatiable curiosity.[22] Nicholas's Francophobia was shared by all his closest counselors. Even after Nicholas's death, Nesselrode warned the new Tsar Alexander II against any effort at a rapprochement with France, "a country which since 1815, despite all European guarantees, has been the theater of three revolutions, each more violent and more democratic than the other and in which we have seen two dynasties which had the appearance of being more solidly established than that of Napoleon vanish in twenty-four hours."[23] These were sentiments with which Nicholas, of course, would have heartily concurred.

Foreign revolution, then, threatened Russia with both internal subversion, particularly on the part of the Poles, and possible involvement in a war. The belief that Russia had to avoid both perils in very large measure set the foreign and domestic policy agenda of Tsar Nicholas I.

In the first place, Nicholas and the men around him felt that it behooved Russia to support (at least in qualified form) the doctrine of legitimacy, the concept whereby states and provinces were recognized as belonging only to rightfully established dynasties. Respect for the principle of legitimacy was the anchor of Nicholas's policy toward Europe, but it also affected his thinking about Russia's relationship with Eastern countries. After Russia had successfully crushed the Persians in 1827, the issue arose of what territorial indemnities, if any, St. Petersburg ought to demand of Teheran. General Paskevich recommended Russian absorption of Azerbaidzhan, noting that the province might serve as a barrier against the penetration of Russia's Transcaucasian possessions by Shiite Muslim fanatics from Iran. Nicholas declined to acquire Azerbaidzhan, despite his general's protestations, at least in part because it bothered him to annex the property of the legitimate Shah.[24] Similarly, although there were geopolitical considerations also involved, Nicholas's support of the Sultan against the Egyptians in the two Mehmet Ali crises also stemmed in part from his distaste at the spectacle of even a Muslim vassal's trying to humiliate his legitimate overlord.

The principle of legitimacy, however, was not absolute. It did not, for example, commit Russia to work toward a restoration of the international order as it had existed prior to 1789. The goal was more modest: to conserve, if possible, the structure of international politics that had been fashioned at the Congress of Vienna in 1815. In 1830 Nesselrode expressed the position of the Russian government in a succinct letter to Austrian Chancellor Klemens von Metternich: "The old Europe has not existed for more than forty years; let us take it as it is today and try to preserve it lest it become something much worse."[25] An attempt to turn the clock back might be fraught with unanticipated dangers. For example, one condition of the restoration of the Bourbon dynasty in France had been its acceptance of a limited constitution, the so-called Charter. The effort of that unreconstructed absolutist, Charles X, to abrogate the Charter led directly to his deposal through revolution in 1830. Although Nicholas I was a personal believer in untrammeled monarchical authority, as the confrontation between Charles and his subjects intensified he repeatedly advised the French King to respect the terms of the Charter. After the revolution had triumphed and Charles had fled, Nicholas did not hesitate to lay the blame for what had happened on Charles's "illegal acts."[26] Clearly neither Nesselrode nor Nicholas was a blind reactionary.

But it was also true that certain parts of the world political order of the post-Napoleonic era were less important to Russia than others. For example, during the negotiations that led up to the treaty of Unkiar Skelessi in 1833 Nesselrode emphasized to one of his envoys that while Russia would engage itself to defend Turkey proper against direct Egyptian attack, Petersburg would do nothing to protect or recover Turkish provinces in Africa from Mehmet Ali. The French conquest of Algiers, he hinted, had to some extent delegitimized Turkey's nominal sovereign rights in North Africa.[27]

There were also occasions when principle had to give way to pragmatism. Distasteful as it was to him, Nicholas I eventually decided that he had no choice but to make obeisance to reality and recognize the government of King Louis Phillipe of France, despite the fact that that regime was the spawn of revolution.[28] In 1830 it simply was not feasible for Russia, alone among the Powers, to treat a country as important as France as a pariah.

The doctrine of legitimacy is thus best construed as an ideal rather than a practical objective of Nicholas I. On a more realistic and immediate level, the regime had two chief concerns. First, it was necessary to protect Russia from the contamination of harmful Western ideas. Second, it behooved Petersburg to do all in its power to maintain the European equilibrium, both through a system of alliances and through the deterrence or containment of revolution abroad.

It was, of course, the Decembrist uprising that awoke Nicholas to the danger of exposing uncorrupted Russian minds to the liberal and radical thought of the West. The arrested Decembrists were obliged to give evidence about the sources of their ideas. Many obligingly delivered themselves of copious testimony; some of their confessions explicitly stressed the influence that Western ideology and recent history had had upon them.[29] How could Russia be protected from the poison of Western revolutionary principles? One could, of course, place restrictions on foreign travel. Personally convinced that trips to such countries as Italy, Germany, and France exposed impressionable Russian travelers to ideas inimical to the stability of his regime, in early 1826 Nicholas commanded his ambassadors to undertake what he described as a "stern surveillance" over the activities of all Russians abroad.[30] Yet spying on Russian travelers was deemed not sufficient to protect the empire against harmful ideas. At home the task of ferreting out and exposing disloyalty fell to the lot of a reformed and expanded police force, which became known after 1826 as the Third Section of His Majesty's Personal Chancellery. It was the job of the Third Section to promote correct thinking while combating dissent. The Third Section was responsible for much of the extensive persecution of authors, students, and intellectuals that characterized the Nicholaevan period.[31] The shock and terror engendered at court by the revolutions of 1848 induced the Tsar to intensify repression: he placed further restrictions on the universities and foreign travel, while strengthening press censorship.[32] Foreign Ministry officials noted ruefully that 1848 had proved that even the Western and Southern Slavs were not immune to the contagion of revolution; some came to advocate a policy of virtual isolation vis-à-vis the rest of Slavdom as the most reliable prophylaxis against radical ideas.[33]

If the defense of the empire against the subversive influence of foreign ideas was primarily a question of police work, the preservation of a benign international order was the task of the diplomats. In the main Nicholas and his foreign ministry were most attracted by collaborative approaches to the problem of European security. To an extent the precedent for that had been set during the latter stages of the reign of Alexander I. In the first few years after the conclusion of the Napoleonic wars, the five Great Powers (Britain, Prussia, Austria, Russia, and France) had periodically convened international congresses to address issues of European stability. In practice the congresses were all concerned with the suppression of revolution. For example, at Troppau in 1820 discussion centered on crushing the revolution in Spain; the armies of Bourbon France eventually received authorization to do so. The Congress of Laibach, held the following year, sanctioned Austrian military intervention to put down revolts in Naples and Piedmont.

The formal congress system was short-lived. At the last congress, that of Verona (1822), the British announced their opposition to renewed intervention by the Great Powers either in Spain or in Spain's rebellious colonies across the Atlantic. That event is usually taken as marking the demise of the unified concert of Europe. Although Alexander I at first tried to revive it in order to mediate the Greek war of independence against Turkey, by the last days of his reign he had given up the task as hopeless.[34]

Nicholas came to power, however, believing that it might be possible to build allied unity over the intertwined issues of Turkey and Greece. At first he enjoyed some success. The Petersburg protocol of 1826 and the London treaty of 1827 committed the British and the French to the Russian position on the need to intimidate the Turks into granting Greece autonomy.[35] But discord and self-interest soon broke down the relationship of St. Petersburg with Paris and London. By 1830 Nicholas had become convinced that authentic partnership with either Britain or France was not a serious option. Both countries were liberal and quasi-democratic, and *ipso facto* unreliable in Nicholas's eyes. As we have already seen, the Orleanist regime that ruled France in the 1830s and 1840s was to Nicholas's mind compromised from the beginning, because King Louis Phillipe owed his crown to a revolution.

In his effort to maintain a European order favorable to Russia, Nicholas began in 1830 to cultivate relationships with the two conservative German monarchies, Prussia and Austria. While not fully absolutist, those two states were considerably closer in their values and preferences to Nicholas's autocracy than were Britain or France. Then, too, Nicholas already had familial ties to the court of Berlin through his Prussian bride. All three Eastern conservative regimes had something else in common, for each had shared in the Polish partitions of the previous century. In an annual report, the Ministry of Foreign Affairs noted that special ambassadors had been dispatched to both Berlin and Vienna in the summer of 1830 to work for the establishment "of the closest union of the three states, which is the only guarantee of universal peace."[36] The warming trend in Petersburg's relations with the two Germanies culminated in 1833. In September of that year the convention of Münchengrätz bound Russia and Austria to defend the Turkish Empire in its weakened state and similarly pledged them to support the status quo in partitioned Poland. The following month, through the Convention of Berlin, the Prussians joined in as well.[37] The Convention of Berlin also included articles about mutual military assistance between the signatories in the event of serious domestic revolt. Obviously a response to the Polish insurrection of 1830, these articles stipulated that if one of the three powers was afflicted with an internal rebellion, it might invite either or both of the others to come to its aid with an auxiliary corps of 20,000 men.[38]

Thereafter the system of conservative alliances with Berlin and Vienna was the cornerstone of Russia's European policy. The alliances were supposed to serve as a defensive bulwark against radical changes in the political map of Europe. That did not mean Russia thereafter would ignore Britain and France. When action had to be taken over such sensitive issues as the Eastern question, Nicholas I and his diplomats always attempted to secure the cooperation of London at least in order to diminish the threat of a general European war. During the first Mehmet Ali crisis, for instance, it was received wisdom at Nicholas's court that any unilateral Russian action against the Egyptians, unsupported by either the British or the Austrians, might lead to a war between Russia and all the rest of Europe.[39] During the second Egyptian crisis of 1839–40, Nesselrode was both exultant and relieved when Russia succeeded in inducing the British to array themselves on its side, describing this as "one of the most important transactions of modern times."[40]

The Policies of Nicholas I: Military Instrumentalities

Diplomacy by itself would not always suffice to bring about the international outcomes Petersburg desired. In that event it would be necessary to rely on Russia's armed forces. The regime of Nicholas I used those forces both to threaten war and to fight it. Of the two courses, the former was considered preferable. The idea was simultaneously to influence events abroad and to avoid a war by threatening to wage one. Indeed, a crude principle of coercive deterrence was the key to Nicholas's military policy. In the 1830 note in which he had observed that Russia needed no new conquests, the Emperor had gone on to argue that Russia's "*defensive* position ought to be so imposing so as to make any aggression impossible."[41] Nicholas maintained such an enormous army and navy precisely because of the imposing impression he hoped they would make on Russia's enemies at home and abroad. The mobilizations, maneuvers, naval demonstrations, even parades of the Nicholaevan era were all scenes in a theater of intimidation that Nicholas staged for the benefit of his foes. If matters were adroitly handled, military deployments could be used to communicate Russia's displeasure (and its overwhelming strength) to its potential adversaries. For that reason, Nicholas often made the deployments with a maximum of publicity and ostentation. Throughout the reign, when Nicholas decreed a concentration of infantry forces on the frontier or a voyage by his men of war, it was usually done to browbeat a foreign government, not to put Russia's forces in an advantageous position from which to open hostilities.

In the late 1820s, for example, Nicholas tried to use naval demonstrations in the Black Sea and the Mediterranean to cow the Turks into bowing to his will over the Greek revolution.[42] When that failed to work, he announced that his forces would occupy the two Danubian principalities of Wallachia and Moldavia in the hope of sending an even stronger and more efficacious signal to Constantinople. The idea, of course, was to scare the Turks into capitulating without inciting them to start a new war with Russia.[43]

Nicholas also relied on military intimidation when confronted by problems of domestic order. After the Polish insurrection of 1831 had been crushed, the Emperor instructed Paskevich, his most trusted commander, to waste no time in constructing a strong citadel on the outskirts of Warsaw. The fort was built not in anticipation of defending the Polish capital against foreign aggression but to frighten and demoralize the Poles out of their rebelliousness. Nicholas wrote of the Warsaw citadel that "from the moment of the erection of its walls all hope of the Poles of ever wrenching themselves free of Russian power will collapse—and then they will tremble!"—a prospect to which he obviously was looking forward with unconcealed glee.[44]

During the crisis of 1833, when Nicholas felt it prudent to support the Sultan against the Egyptian Khedive, he turned again to military intimidation. He organized a menacing demonstration by a Russian flotilla in the Constantinople roadstead, complete with a troop landing.[45] When the revolutions of 1848 broke out in Western, Southern, and Central Europe, Nicholas once more had recourse to his military to threaten, not to fight. The mobilizations Nicholas conducted in that year were designed to dampen any possible enthusiasm on the part of foreign revolutionaries and foreign revolutionary governments for an armed clash with Russia. The Russian military maneuvers of 1848 were decidedly not the prelude to the opening of a counterrevolutionary military crusade. As Nesselrode expressed it: "[L]et the other countries manage as they can, we shall let them alone as long as they do not touch us."[46] The next year, after Nicholas had reluctantly decided that he would have to help his Austrian ally combat the Hungarian insurrection, he secretly hoped that the very magnitude of the military preparations he made would be enough to terrorize the Hungarians into surrendering before Russia ever had to fire a shot. Paskevich later recalled that "it was decided to assemble 150,000 men so that the Hungarians would see the impossibility of the success of their schemes."[47]

Military threats were also a feature of the Russian policy that led up to the outbreak of the Crimean War. When the breakdown of negotiations over Russia's right to "protect" the interests of Christians in the Ottoman Empire resulted in the suspension of diplomatic relations between Petersburg and Constantinople in the spring of 1853, Nicholas once again decided to occupy Wallachia and Moldavia as a means of pressuring the Turks.[48] Intellectual justification for that operation was provided by Paskevich in a memorandum of March, in which he observed that the occupation would probably persuade the Turks to honor their treaty obligations.[49] When the exasperated Turks failed to act as expected and declared war, Nicholas still clung to his original plan. He ordered his troops in those two Balkan provinces not to cross the Danube under any circumstances, evidently reasoning that the Turks (who might be bluffing) could perhaps still be persuaded to back down if Russia avoided giving them any more military provocation.[50]

During his tenure as Emperor of Russia, then, Nicholas rarely deviated from the practice of planning military maneuvers and even initial operations in terms of their value as deterrents or threats, not as preliminaries to actual fighting. Almost the only exception to this pattern came in 1830. In the late summer of that year, almost fatalistically convinced that a general European war could not be prevented, Nicholas ordered four corps onto a war footing.[51] What made that order so uncharacteristic was that Nicholas was adamant about keeping the military preparations secret, so as not to arouse "the suspicions of either our enemies or our allies."[52] Ordinarily, as we have just seen, Nicholas insisted on making military preparations so obvious and open that neither enemies nor allies could fail to take note of them. It was his way of telegraphing his intentions, inhibiting his adversaries, and signaling his resolve.

Despite all the skill of his diplomacy and military threats, however, war might still come. Nicholas's efforts to deter or avert it did not always work. Repulsive as he found war to be, Nicholas nonetheless believed that two things were worse: dishonor and *general* war. Nicholas's idea of honor will come under discussion later in this chapter. Here we shall consider his ideas about how Russia should try to prosecute a war should it have the misfortune to become involved in one.

In the first place, Nicholas believed that Russia could really afford to fight only localized wars. Russia might of course operate with the assistance of allies, but at all costs it had to avoid entering a war in which a coalition of powerful enemies was arrayed against it. The crisis in the Low Countries of 1830 provides an example of such thinking. When Belgium revolted against the authority of King William of Holland, the latter appealed to Nicholas for military assistance. William's son was Nicholas's brother-in-law, and Nicholas regarded William's cause to be just, but he was at first extremely reluctant to do anything to help.[53] Nicholas thought that if he were to make the first military move in the crisis, he might well find himself at war with France and Britain simultaneously. In any event, if London and

Paris were to unite in support of the Belgian rebels, Nicholas was of the opinion that Russia had the power to protest but not much more.[54]

Second, given the nature of Russia's international objectives, Russia's purpose could only be to fight limited wars in Clausewitz's sense. Russia was a conservative power; it sought no great new expanses of territory anywhere in Europe or in Asia. Its purpose in waging war, therefore, could not be to overthrow sovereign states or dynasties. When it waged war, it did so in the interests of preserving the established order, enforcing treaties, repelling invasion, or inflicting reprisals. Regardless of their scale, the wars of Nicholas I were almost always conceptually akin to punitive operations.

It was the Emperor's desire that such wars be fought and won as quickly as possible. That, obviously, necessitated speedy offensive operations. Nicholas's voluminous wartime correspondence with his generals in the field is peppered with reprimands for their slowness, indecision, or hesitation. General Ermolov, who was unfortunate enough to be in command in Transcaucasia when the Persians invaded in 1826, was severely condemned by his sovereign for insufficient aggressiveness in his conduct of operations, even though he had only 10,000 troops with which to engage the Persian army, monitor the Turkish frontier, and maintain internal order, all at the same time.[55] When the Tsar removed Ermolov and replaced him with Paskevich, he informed the latter that his duty was to "compel the Persians to a rapid peace."[56] In 1831 General Dibich was the target of the imperial wrath; Nichlas reproved him for his failure to suppress the Polish insurrection swiftly despite the numerical superiority of his forces over those of the rebels.[57] The reason for his insistence on quick victory was no doubt Nicholas's appreciation of the rate at which active military operations consumed military power. Money, equipment, and, most important, human lives were sacrificed by any state that went to war. Once expended, such resources were difficult to replenish. Nicholas also realized, just as his eighteenth-century predecessors had, that the typical theaters in which Russia went to war made the attritional effects of campaigning on the Russian army immoderately high. Just as in the past, this was attributable to the influence of climate and terrain factors (in addition to poor logistics and military medicine) on the health and well-being of the troops.

During the last four months of the Turkish war of 1828–29 alone, more than 60,000 Russian soldiers perished, almost half of them in military hospitals.[58] Certain military operations during the reign of Nicholas I came down to races against changes in the weather and the seasons. In the midsummer of 1849, for instance, Nicholas committed to paper his ardent wish that "military actions [against the Hungarian rebels] could be conducted as quickly and as decisively as possible so that they might be ended prior to the time of bad weather and bad roads." If not, the Emperor added, Russia could expect to lose up to one-half of its expeditionary force in Hungary to disease.[59] Here, however, a paradox emerges. Although Nicholas typically exhorted his generals to achieve quick successes (and berated them if they failed to do so), in certain special circumstances he worried that Russia might win a victory so quick and decisive that an unintended and undesired consequence might be the utter collapse of an enemy government. Sometimes the need for quick victory ran counter to Russia's long-term political interests.

This was a particular worry in the case of Turkey. In 1853, when the Tsar and his advisers considered a possible war with the Ottomans, they paid attention to a bold proposal prepared by Nicholas's son, the Grand Duke Konstantin, a noted naval officer and reformer in the subsequent reign. Should there be a Turkish war, Konstantin advocated ending it with one decisive naval and amphibious attack on Constantinople. While Konstantin admitted that such an operation would probably cost Russia at least five ships and the lives of several thousand sailors, he insisted that those losses would be small compared with those incurred in a one- to two-year ground campaign "in which the troops [would suffer more] from the hardships of the march, fevers, and cholera than from the enemy himself."[60] Despite the fact that the plan was endorsed by Prince Paskevich, it was decisively rejected by both the Naval Minister and the Tsar. Nicholas apparently concluded that Konstantin's plan posed grave risks, whether it failed or succeeded. If it failed, Russia would have squandered military resources without gaining anything. If it succeeded, there was the possibility that the Turkish Empire would simply cave in. Nicholas's preference was for no war at all, both because he shared his son's concern for the ruinous effect of the climate of the Balkans on the health of the troops and because "of the indeterminate goal which we may have to appoint for our forces, if we wish of course to avoid the overthrow of the Turkish Empire."[61] In other words, since Russia could not afford to deliver an annihilating blow against the Turks it might have to protract a conflict with them unnaturally, should one erupt.[62]

A final exception to the rapid war scenario would occur in the unhappy event that Russia found itself faced with the prospect of overland invasion from Central Europe. Yet the plans for such a contingency were extremely rudimentary. The Ministry of War hoped to rely on the shield of the Polish fortresses of Novogeorgievsk, Ivangorod, and Brest to buy the army the five or six months that would be needed for a total mobilization.[63]

In the majority of wars either planned or waged by Russia during the period, however, the operational approach endorsed by the Emperor was consonant with the goal of rapid and limited conflict. Nicholas and his generals were all keenly alive to the problem of supply. Although they realized that shortages of food and ammunition would inevitably plague any Russian army in the field, they were also aware that there was nothing like a total breakdown of logistics to prolong a campaign. As living off the land during a Balkan war was no more realistic for a Russian army of Nicholas's time than it had been fifty years earlier, the Tsar's commanders made strenuous (although not always successful) efforts to operate within the bounds of the logistically possible. Sometimes that entailed extravagant preplanning, or even the cooperation of foreign states. For instance, after the failure of the overly ambitious campaign against European Turkey in 1828, Dibich made his logistical preparations for the campaign of 1829 with a great deal more care; thousands of camels were used to haul foodstuffs, ammunition, and other supplies from central Russia to the theater of war.[64] Paskevich's intricate design for operations on the left bank of the Vistula in the spring of 1831 envisioned supplying the field army from a stockpile of more than 200,000 quarters of grain and forage, to be amassed with Prussian help in the fortress of Thorn.[65] Indeed, Paskevich, whose talents lay more in the field of military administration than in generalship, was widely known for his pithy maxim, "He who does not think of food will get no benefit from victory."[66]

Operational objectives were similar to those that Russia's eighteenth-century armies had pursued. Typically the Emperor's commanders were instructed to catch the enemy in the open, divide him, and then destroy him in a general battle. Nicholas's generals expended much intellectual energy on elaborate operational plans, which required maneuvers by Russian forces along interior geometrical lines so as to entrap the enemy. Nicholas I himself took the keenest interest in the design of the plans. The sheer volume and geographical detail of the proposals, orders, and suggestions that he sent his generals suggest that he must have devoted many hours to their composition with compass and map.

Yet a general battle might not always be possible. The enemy might act otherwise than had been expected. And when he retreated or fell back on his strong points, the Russian military resorted to its traditional siegecraft. Because Nicholas was almost always desirous of rapid victory, however, he placed strong emphasis on the speediest possible reduction of forts. They were to be taken by mining or by storm—not merely starved out.

A final point about the Nicholaevan approach to the conduct of war was that it was informed by memories of Russia's military practices in 1812. The great interest of Nicholas and his generals in augmenting the operations of regular forces with partisan raids obviously stemmed from that source. During Paskevich's Polish campaign of 1831, for instance, light cavalry detachments of Hussars and Cossacks were used to guard the rear of the regular army and to protect Russian lines of communication, while simultaneously attacking those of the enemy.[67] During the Hungarian intervention of 1849, Nicholas himself strongly urged the use of cavalry raids "to seize the initiative from the enemy and strike fear into him."[68] On the very eve of his death, in a note of February 1, 1855, Nicholas showed his continued fascination with the military paradigm of 1812. Worried that Austria was about to declare war on Russia, thus joining the already formidable Crimean coalition, Nicholas sketched out a plan for the defense of Poland against an anticipated attack of 300,000 Austrian troops. Partisan operations against the enemy's flank and rear played a prominent role in the plan.[69] In the event of a dire need, the Nicholaevan military establishment was also prepared to fall back on an 1812 scorched earth policy. An example was the August 1853 proposal by Vice Admiral Serebriakov that the 13th Infantry Division be transferred to the eastern shores of the Black Sea in order to devastate all of the lands between the mouth of the Kuban and the valley of Adogum in order to complicate an enemy landing in the territory.[70]

The Army of Nicholas I

Whether as a deterrent or as a combat force, then, the army played a central role in the foreign policies of the regime of Nicholas I. Indeed, it is impossible to think of the reign of Nicholas I without thinking of his army, for Nicholas's boundless devotion to even the minutiae of military life has become a historiographic cliché. So pervasive was militarism under Nicholas I that some have depicted the Russia of his time as a gigantic garrison state, an armed camp under the rigorous supervision of an autocratic drillmaster. Although this picture may be overdrawn, Nicholas's love of the military is beyond dispute.[71]

That is somewhat surprising in light of the fact that it was the army that had produced the Decembrist conspiracy, the only truly serious domestic challenge to the Tsar's authority. Nor could the Decembrists be dismissed merely as a small band of juvenile dreamers; among the persons implicated in the plot were sixteen colonels and two major generals.[72] Of course, in public statements about the case, most particularly in discussions with foreign ambassadors, Nicholas tried to downplay the military character of the revolt. The majority of the army, he insisted, was deeply devoted to both himself and his house; the very fact that the rebellion had been so quickly suppressed, he said, supplied the proof.[73] Privately, however, the Decembrist conspiracy left Nicholas with considerable doubts about the loyalty of his military officers. When the Tsar established his secret police, the Third Section, one of its principle functions was the collection of evidence about political thinking and attitudes within the Russian officer corps. In his very first report of 1827, General Benkendorf concluded that many officers were indeed disaffected for reasons ranging from poverty and boredom to liberalism.[74] Nicholas's anxiety about potential subversive activities on the part of his officers resulted in his planning of secret agents within the regiments to keep an eye on what the officers were saying and thinking.[75] That anxiety also underpinned his command, after 1831, that the officers of the Warsaw garrison be rotated frequently, presumably to prevent them from identifying with the cause of the Poles. "It is the moral contagion," the Emperor wrote, "that I fear the worst of all."[76]

If Nicholas was tormented with fears about the reliability of his army, why did he rely upon it so much? At least one scholar has suggested that the militarism of Nicholas must be seen as an excrescence of his psyche. Neurotically timorous, Nicholas was obsessed with military regimentation, discipline, and hierarchy, which served him as some sort of a psychological defense mechanism. Nicholas thus used his vast autocratic power to create an external environment that would allay his deep-rooted insecurity and dread.[77]

There obviously is something to this view, for there is abundant evidence about the aberrant psychological makeup and bizarre phobias of the Emperor. Yet in my opinion to explain the military system of Nicholas I exclusively in terms of the Tsar's deformed psyche is to overlook the functional hypothesis. Neurosis may have played a role in the sort of military system that the Emperor created, but so too did rational (if mistaken) calculations about the nature of the international environment and the directions in which Russia wanted to shape it. Nicholas relied on the army because it was the only institution in the Empire that could be used to achieve his foreign objectives. And, more than this, despite its manifold flaws the army of Nicholas I was logically suited to serve the aims for which Nicholas intended it.

For example, the immensity of the Nicholaevan army is readily understandable when we remember that it was the Tsar's intention to use that army in a deterrent capacity. The reign of Nicholas witnessed a slow but impressive expansion in the size of the army. If in 1826 there were roughly 729,000 soldiers present and accounted for, by the 1850s the army had grown to more than 930,000 regulars plus 240,000 irregulars.[78] For comparative purposes, two of the other major Continental armies, the French and the Austrian, numbered roughly 275,000 men and 250,000 men respectively in 1840.[79] To be sure, as we shall see shortly, Russia did have problems bringing all that vast manpower to bear in wartime. Because one of the main purposes of the army was precisely to be imposing, to overawe foreigners, the regime of Nicholas I was hardly inclined to publicize those difficulties. Certainly the Russian government did nothing to correct the errors of those travelers who, like Haxthausen, falsely estimated that if Russia had gone to war in Western Europe in 1848 it could have dispatched 355,000 regulars and 400,000 irregulars for such a campaign without much trouble.[80] The distribution of those forces—chiefly on the perimeters of the Empire—further enhanced their deterrent value. Up until the mid-1840s, Russia deployed four of its eight infantry corps in Poland. Obviously those troops were in part an army of occupation. Yet they were also designed to be an ostentatious threat to Western and Central Europe. The V corps was stationed on the Black Sea and was thus theoretically available for operations either in Transcaucasia or in the Balkans. The VI Corps, near Moscow, was a reserve formation that could reinforce either the Polish or the southern forces, while the Corps of Guards and Grenadiers, billeted in Petersburg and Novgorod, watched over the Baltic and the Swedish frontier.[81]

Nicholas's army did have its serious defects, which cannot be ignored in any attempt to make an assessment of it. Yet it would be equally inaccurate to picture the army of Nicholas as strictly a matter of appearances, outward forms, and spit-and-polish. In the first place, the army retained its traditional strengths. One of these was the platoon *artel*. Writing in 1833, the expatriot Polish officer Joseph Cánski had noted that the "the interior of the regiment is the true fatherland for a Russian soldier."[82] As we have previously suggested, this was so because the literal impossibility of rejoining civil life caused the soldiers to adjust to their new environment by accepting the *artel* as a substitute family. The soldiers' *artel*, with its unique arrangements for the sharing of work, food, and property, had helped to account for the reliability and superior combat performance of the Russian army since the middle of the eighteenth century. Baron August von Haxthausen, who traveled extensively in Russia in the 1830s and 1840s, describing the military *artel* in his famous volumes on the Russian Empire, hailed the contributions it made to esprit de corps.[83] Russian soldiers continued on many occasions to fight with conspicuous gallantry throughout the reign of Nicholas I. The heroism of the troops in battle received the plaudits of foreign observers during every war in which the Russian army took part, from the conflict with Persia in 1826 to the defense of Sevastopol in 1854. Insofar as such praise was valid, it testified to the ongoing efficacy of the *artel* in building small-group loyalty and morale.

Second, in certain small but important ways, the regime also sponsored military reforms that led to notable improvements in army efficiency. Some of them concerned military administration. In 1831 General Chernyshev drafted a note advocating the subordination of the Main Staff (*Glavnyi Shtab*) to the Ministry of War. Up to that time the Staff had served, in effect, as a quasi-independent component of the Imperial suite, a sort of relic of the decentralized and personalized military decision-making of the eighteenth century. Chernyshev's proposal resulted eventually in the issuance in 1836 of a new statute for the Ministry of War, which provided that ministry with a modern bureaucratic organization.[84] Another important reform, this time affecting military education, was the foundation of the Military Academy (*Voennaia Akademiia*) in 1831. That higher military school, created partly on the advice of General Jomini, was the first approximation of a general staff academy in Russian history. Many of the most distinguished military reformers and intellectuals during the reign of Alexander II received their first serious exposure to military science within its walls.[85]

In a move designed to ameliorate the lot of the common soldiers while providing Russia with a pool of trained reservists, Nicholas also instituted procedures for leaves without term in 1834. Soldiers who had completed fifteen years of "flawless" service were eligible for furlough from the army's ranks. Although those men could be recalled to the colors in the event of emergency, they were for all intents and purposes released back into civilian life. Between 1834 and 1850 more than 17,000 men on average were put on such indefinite leaves each year; by the outbreak of the Crimean War there were more than 200,000 of these reservists.[86]

A final and often overlooked improvement for which Nicholas's government deserves full credit lay in the area of horse breeding. Extensive state investment and management of stud farming literally revolutionized the Russian cavalry. The runty horses—ponies, really—that Russian troops had ridden in the seventeenth and eighteenth centuries were replaced by high-bred beasts, fully as large and strong as those in West European cavalry formations.[87]

The army of Nicholas I, then, was large in size and formidable in appearance—just as it was meant to be. One other feature of Nicholas's military policy deserves attention: its parsimony. Nicholas was interested in maintaining the largest army possible at the lowest possible cost. Of course, soldiers' pay in Russia remained both sporadic and negligible. But when multiplied by the hundreds of thousands of men in the ranks, the total military wage bill amounted to a formidable sum. Much more expensive was the cost of equipping the troops—supplying them with uniforms, firearms, and munitions. And the most costly item in the debit column of the military ledger was foodstuffs and forage. In the effort to establish control over those costs, Nicholas had a preexisting instrument ready to hand: the notorious system of military colonies.

Although the practice of settling peasant smallholders along defensive lines had been standard in Russian history for centuries, the formal military colony system originated with a proposal made by Count A. A. Arakcheev to Tsar Alexander I in 1814. Arakcheev's idea was to station certain military units permanently in specific regions and provinces. Those territories, and all of the peasants already residing there, would come under direct military administration. The soldiers who entered the colonies were to occupy themselves with drill and with agriculture, so that they might grow the food for their own support. They would be encouraged to marry, and their children, known as cantonists, would be predestined for military service themselves. The colonies therefore had several purposes simultaneously. First, as has often been remarked of them, they represented an attempt at social engineering, an effort to bring discipline, order, and hygiene to the Russian countryside. Second, by creating a hereditary class of potential recruits in the cantonists, the system might alleviate the burden of conscription on the villages of the rest of the empire. Finally, the farm labor of the soldiers themselves (and the additional taxes levied on the peasants who lived in their midst) could be used to reduce the amount that the state had to pay for the army's maintenance.

The first settlements were created for infantry units in Novgorod Province in 1816. In the following year the state established colonies for cavalry regiments in the Ukraine. By 1826 more than forty regiments, half each of infantry and cavalry, had been settled in the colonies, which then had 160,000 soldiers,

54,000 children, and 374,000 peasants on their rolls.[88] Initially at least, the system of colonies resulted in significant economies for the tsarist treasury. For example, the savings on food alone in 1822 was calculated to have been in excess of 3.5 million rubles.[89] Nicholas I continued the system of the colonies, which are said to have contained a full third of the Russian army in the early years of his reign.

Nicholas's concepts of statecraft, strategy, and military policy were thus almost too neatly intertwined. Revolution had to be averted both at home and abroad, because revolution was the source of calamity and war. To prevent revolution (and consequently general war), Russia needed a strong military deterrent. That meant military forces that could pose a plausible threat to Russia's neighbors while representing the least possible burden to the treasury.

Yet, as has frequently been observed, the reign of Nicholas I was a catastrophic failure in both domestic and foreign policy. The Tsar's foreign policy goals were both unrealized and unrealizable. His strategic ideas were impoverished. And his army was inadequate for the purposes he set for it, as it was at once too weak to wage a war successfully with Europeans and too frightening not to antagonize them. The responsibility for all of this must rest mainly with Nicholas himself. Unfortunately, the premises that informed both his diplomatic and his military policies were false.

The Foreign Policy Goals of Nicholas I: A Critique

Again, Nicholas put such a high priority upon the thwarting of foreign revolution because he believed that a stable international order was indispensable for the domestic security of his own empire. That policy had many serious intellectual defects. In the first place, the Tsar overestimated the threat posed to Russia from foreign liberals and radicals. He had a firm but erroneous belief that all of them were linked together in one great international revolutionary organization. Nicholas thought such subversive activities of this supposed organization as could be detected and thwarted were as nothing compared with those that remained covert. Europe, in his view, was honeycombed with furtive conspiracies, all of them centrally directed. This meant that while monarchical governments might appear to be solid, they were all actually in dire peril. Outward strength only masked inner weakness. In reality, although liberals and nationalists in many countries entertained sympathy for each other's causes during the Restoration period, no such international radical network ever existed. Nicholas's faith in its existence, however, meant that a central goal of Russian policy during his reign was chimerical, involving as it did shadowboxing with a nonexistent opponent.

Nicholas's ideas about the appropriate methods for fighting radicalism were also flawed. The Tsar suffered from an extreme case of the idealist fallacy, the view that the motive force behind history is almost always thought and thought alone. Nicholas's idealism (in the philosophical sense) skewed his understanding of the origins of political instability and revolution. In his opinion, the process of revolution worked something like this. First there was the spread of harmful ideas among the educated and literate. Those disgruntled intellectuals—the hosts for the revolutionary bacillus—then set to work to confuse the masses and lead them astray. Without such malevolent intervention, the masses by themselves would never rise up in a serious challenge to the established authority. Ergo, all that was really necessary to prevent revolution, was to quash the dissemination of subversive ideas. Of course, this theory was reductionist and simplistic. Although various strains of liberalism and nationalism were genuinely destabilizing influences in post-Napoleonic Europe, they did not make revolutions all by themselves. Rather, revolutions such as those of 1830 and 1848 resulted from the synergistic combination of ideology *and* such material conditions as poverty, oppression, economic dislocation, and so forth. Nicholas never recognized the contribution of material environment to revolution. Even if he had, the living conditions of peasants and artisans in Europe were completely beyond his power to change. It was, of course, still possible to fight radical ideas, but it was a very difficult task even at home, not to mention abroad. In the end, how does one combat an idea? A policy of indiscriminately executing all known or suspected radicals is one possibility. Nicholas, however, although a tyrant, was not an unscrupulous murderer. His solution was censorship, stultifying control over education, and secret political denunciations.

Still, it has proved hard even for twentieth-century dictators with vastly greater resources to police that which is in the mind. Despite the ferocity of Nicholas's repression—in fact, probably *because* of the resentment it inspired—it is evident that many "harmful" ideas circulated in the Russia of his time. Clearly the serious revolutionary movements that burst upon the scene in tsarist Russia of the 1860s had roots that extended back into Nicholas's reign.

A final problem connected to Nicholas's obsession with revolution is that he was excessively literal-minded. Nicholas's belief that the horrors of the French Revolution and Napoleon were lurking in the wings, ready to make a reappearance on the historical stage, demonstrates the degree to which he imposed the patterns of the past on the present and the future. Nicholas was not alone in doing so. For generations there have been statesmen so fixated on one or another past evil that they have made preventing its recurrence (however improbable) their top priority. That sort of intellectual rigidity naturally enough bars people from thinking seriously about the implications of change. Revolutionary France was possible only in a particular place at a particular time. The relative distribution of power in Europe of the 1830s was strikingly different from that of the late eighteenth century. But Nicholas, who apparently did not understand this, was so concerned with the threat from Paris that he overlooked more proximate hazards. One, of course, was the threat from Vienna, a threat founded not upon ideology but upon the divergence between Austrian and Russian interests.

Nicholas's goal of suppressing revolution abroad was therefore unattainable largely because of the Emperor's defective understanding of the nature of the revolutionary process. But another of his objectives—the avoidance of war—could not be attained either. The reasons that was so were partly outside the Emperor's control, for Nicholas inherited problems that had been created by the policies of his predecessors.

One of those policies was Russian expansion into the Caucasus and Transcaucasia. Paul I had annexed central Georgia to the Russian Empire in 1801. Alexander I stepped up the pace of conquest in the Caucasus. Between 1801 and 1825, Ganzhiia, Imeretiia, Abkhazia, Karabakh, Kubin, Derbent, and Daghestan were some of the principalities and khanates that fell under Russian domination. Acquisitions in the southeastern Caucasus gave

Russia a common frontier with Persia for the first time. Not unnaturally, Persia found the Russian encroachment obnoxious. Border incidents increased in gravity and intensity throughout the early 1820s and finally culminated in 1826, when a Persian force of 60,000 invaded Armenia and Karabakh, touching off a year and a half of war.[90]

Russia's forward movement in the Caucasus also confronted it with serious problems of internal pacification. By 1820 Petersburg had had to organize a separate 50,000-strong army of the Caucasus for that purpose. The Georgian military road, cut through the mountains from Vladikavkaz to Tiflis, served as the lifeline connecting this army to the main body of the empire. Networks of fortresses and blockhouses, punitive expeditions, and raids were the initial expedients adopted by the Russians in their struggle with the hostile Muslim tribesmen of the region. The situation was particularly critical in Daghestan. There the influence of muridism (a type of sufism) on the indigenous mountaineers primed them for a Holy War against St. Petersburg. In Imam Shamyl they found a charismatic leader of genius who in the mid-1830s unleashed a savage guerrilla war against the hated Russian occupiers. The war dragged on for more than two decades, costing the Russians scores of thousands of lives.[91]

Another difficulty that Alexander had bequeathed his brother was Poland. Claiming that he wanted to redress a historical injustice, Alexander had insisted at the Congress of Vienna on the reestablishment of a Kingdom of Poland with himself as monarch.[92] Unlike autocratic Russia, Poland was to be a quasi-constitutional state with an elected Diet. It was to have its own currency, its own schools, and its own army. The Poles, along with the Finns, thereby became the most privileged of Russian subjects. That was not, however, sufficient, for many Poles would be satisfied with nothing less than complete independence. Although Nicholas I was careful to respect the formalities of the Polish constitution, in December 1830 the Poles unexpectedly rose in a war of liberation against the Russians. Russian forces were engaged in military operations in Poland into October of the following year.[93] In the aftermath of the Russian victory Nicholas cracked down on Poland. The Organic Statute of 1832 replaced the Polish Constitution, the Polish army was perma-

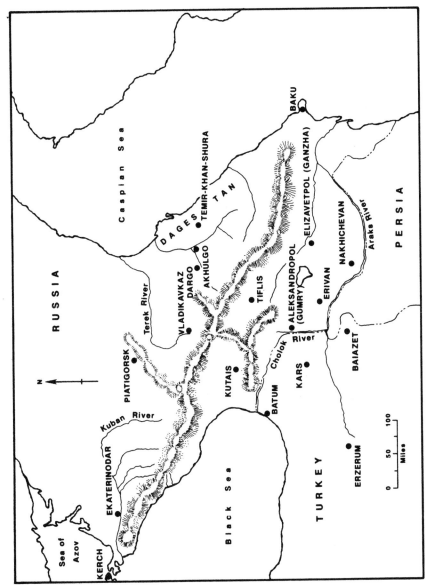

THE CAUCASUS IN 1853

nently disbanded, and other repressive measures were carried out. Punitive action, however, scarcely enhanced Polish allegiance to Russia. The Poles remained sullen, and Poland itself was a potential flashpoint for Russian military action.

If some of Nicholas's wars were not the Emperor's fault, others were. There is, after all, no guarantee of peace with bellicose and determined opponents other than capitulation. Nicholas, while not truculent, was not noted for his malleability or willingness to compromise either, particularly when he felt an issue affected his personal honor and by automatic extension the honor of his empire. The misunderstanding and blunders whereby Russia became enmired in the Crimean War owed a great deal to the Emperor's sense of affronted honor. In an unusual tone of admonition, Nesselrode wrote to his master after the war had begun that "honor does not oblige us to hurl ourselves into a bottomless abyss."[94]

So Nicholas's goals of averting revolution, supporting stability, and avoiding war were unrealized. Beyond that, the diplomacy he used in pursuit of those interests was itself deficient. The centerpiece of Russian foreign policy since the 1830s had been the system of conservative alliances with Prussia and Austria. In the opinion of Nicholas and his Foreign Minister, Russia simply had no choice in the matter of allies. Austria, Prussia, and Russia were united in their common opposition to Polish nationalism. Then, too, as Nesselrode wrote, in opting for alliances with the German powers Nicholas was "yielding of necessity . . . to the exigencies which had created His own self-interest of conservatism," for Prussia and Austria were no less antipathetic to revolution than was Russia.[95]

It is true that on certain occasions the Austrians and particularly the Prussians had been helpful to Russia. For example, during the early phases of the Russo-Polish war Frederick William III had supported the Russian cause by interdicting arms shipments to the rebels.[96] Russia also granted favors to its alliance partners. Nicholas I had every reason to believe that by intervening in Hungary in 1849 he reinforced his friendship with the court of Vienna.

The difficulty was that the German alliances encouraged false confidence and complacency on the Emperor's part. In fact, neither Prussia nor Austria was in a position to provide Nicholas with much in the way of effective military help either in Asia or in Europe. In the first half of the nineteenth century Prussia was relatively weak militarily. Austria was enfeebled by ulcerous problems with its subject nationalities. Both powers had reason as well to resent an alliance in which Russia was so clearly the dominant partner. Besides, Austria's interests in the Balkans and the Near East were by no means identical to Russia's. In particular it suspected Russia of wishing to aggrandize herself at Turkey's expense. Yet an important reason that Nicholas bungled into the Crimean War (in addition to his misunderstanding of the British) was the excessive reliance he placed on the solidity of his alliances during his negotiations with Turkey and France. As Nicholas boasted to the French Ambassador during the summer of 1853, "I can count on Vienna and Berlin."[97] The Emperor's confidence was unfounded. Neither during the buildup to the Crimean War nor during the war itself did either of the German states furnish Russia with moral encouragement or material support. In fact, Austrian actions during the war were openly inimical to Russia. When Austria coerced Russia into evacuating its forces from Wallachia and Moldavia in the summer of 1854, Austrian troops promptly marched in. St. Petersburg suspected that Austria had done so at the prompting of the French and the British. In any event, the Russian government was seriously concerned about the military implications of the loss of the principalities. A Foreign Ministry document stated that the move would allow the French, British, and Ottoman forces that had been immobilized in Turkey "to fall en masse upon our Asian and European littoral in the Black Sea."[98] Later in the war, of course, Vienna became still more hostile to Petersburg. The Austrians threats and ultimatums of December 1855 and January 1856 were finally decisive in forcing St. Petersburg to sue for peace. Vienna thereby fulfilled the famous prophesy of Schwarzenberg, who after the Russian intervention in Hungary had written that "Austria will astound Europe with the extent of her ingratitude."[99] The Crimean War, far from being "accidental and transitory," as Nesselrode once called it, was a national humiliation of the first order. To many thinking people, the debacle of the war seemed to illustrate the bankruptcy of Nicholas's alliances and indeed of his entire regime.[100]

The Strategic Errors of Nicholas I

The diplomacy of Nicholas I, then, all too often consisted in using inadequate means to try to reach the unattainable. Nicholas's approach to the use of his military power was also faulty. Consider, for example, his practice of using his army as an instrument of deterrence and intimidation. It is always risky to stage such threats; instead of cowing one's enemies into submission, they may galvanize them into action. Such was often the case during the reign of Nicholas I. His blustering against the Turks, for instance, led them to declare war on Russia first in 1827 and again in 1853. The bellicose posturing of the Russia was also counterproductive in its relations with the French and, most particularly, the British. The Tsar's conversations with the British Ambassador in early 1853, when he had suggested the need for an agreement with London in advance about how to fill the vacuum of power that would occur should the Ottomans collapse was misinterpreted by the British as evidence of Russian annexationist designs.[101] The Russian destruction of the Turkish fleet at Sinope the following November—which the Tsar had intended to use to force Turkish capitulation—inflamed British public opinion against Russia and set the stage for the British declaration of war.[102] Nicholas's practice of trying to bully and intimidate his neighbors with his military might often backfired, much as similar Soviet efforts did under Brezhnev in the 1970s and early 1980s.

Still further, mobilizing the army to send signals or to make military demonstrations was often fundamentally detrimental to Russia if war broke out. Deploying forces as a signal could make the prosecution of a real war much more difficult. The requirements of intimidation and the requirements of warfighting at times radically diverged. Take, for instance, Russia's occupation of the Danubian principalities in 1828 and 1853. On the former occasion Russia marched into the principalities, despite the fact that Turkey had already declared war, in the hope of scaring the Porte to the bargaining table. Not only did the gesture fail to achieve its purpose, but it also complicated the execution of the Russian campaign plan, as the occupation of the principalities subtracted 20,000 men (almost one-third of its strength) from the ranks of the army.[103] Nor was Russia any more successful in 1853, when as before it seized the principalities and then stopped. That action both antagonized the Austrians and provided the Turks with a breathing space of several months in which to organize their defenses.[104] In international relations, no less than on the street, it can be perilous to draw a gun if one does not really intend to use it.

Once shooting war broke out, Nicholas's ideas about how to wage it also had harmful results. In the first place the Tsar, who had a grotesquely distorted opinion of his own military talents, meddled far too much in the military planning and operational decision-making. The letters and memoranda he showered on his commanders analyzed the military options available to them in excruciating detail. The Tsar's gratuitous advice and exhortation naturally enough hobbled his generals, stifling even what little initiative they had.[105] Some of Nicholas's military recommendations were simply boneheadedly wrong, as the proposal he seriously made in February 1854 for a suicide naval attack should the British and French fleets enter the Black Sea and anchor off Feodosiia.[106] Further, the Tsar's constant insistence on the need for speedy victory, although founded on a shrewd estimation of the limitations of Russian power, often resulted in spreading forces too thin or incurring unacceptable risks. During the Turkish campaign of 1828, for instance, Nicholas ordered simultaneous sieges of three Turkish forts—Varna, Silistriia, and Shumla—despite the intelligent counsel of General Wittgenstein that it would be better to concentrate all effort on merely one objective.[107] As Wittgenstein had foreseen, Russia did not have the forces with which to capture all three fortresses at once. Shumla and Silistriia successfully resisted Russian sieges, and although Varna fell, it took eighty-nine days to do so, principally because of the minuscule resources the Russian army was able to devote to investing it. Nicholas's decision here was clearly one of the capital blunders of the campaign.[108] Although his purpose had been to accelerate the progress of the war, arguably he only succeeded in protracting it. Nicholas's demand for rapid results was not much of an asset to the Russian army during the war with Shamyl in Transcaucasia, either. It inclined at least some commanders to reckless haste, such as Viceroy Vorontsov, whose forces Shamyl trounced at Dargo in 1845 for that very reason.[109] It took Nicholas too long to grasp the fact that pacification of guerrilla tribesmen in the extraordinarily difficult terrain of the Caucasus would perforce have to be accomplished gradually and slowly.[110]

A final flaw in Nicholas I's appreciation of warfare was the pernicious influence upon it of the image of the War of 1812. As we saw in the previous chapter, a considerable gap existed between the reality of the Fatherland War and the myth. The Fatherland War had not in fact seen the forging of unshakable national unity. Nicholas thought that it had. He considered its chief lesson to have been that the Russian army was invincible when in defense of its own territory. That was a dangerous belief for the Tsar to hold, for it engendered overconfidence no less than his erroneous reliance on alliances with the German Powers. Unrealistic expectations befogged the Emperor's mind during the Crimean War. It was as if he expected his troops to be able to compensate for every advantage the enemy possessed by dint of gallantry alone. That gallantry, although evident on many occasions, was inadequate to the task.[111]

Weaknesses in the Armed Forces

Nicholas's use of military forces to gain his objectives often misfired. Part of the trouble lay in the quality of the military instrument itself. Grave inadequacies in the army, many stemming from Nicholas's preference for using it to threaten, not fight, crippled the execution of Russia's wartime strategies.

Of all of the problems of the Nicholaevan army, perhaps the most severe was that of manpower. Nicholas's army was larger on paper than it was on the parade ground or in the field. In every war waged by Russia throughout the reign, its generals were chronically embarrassed by a shortage of troops. During the Turkish War of 1828–29, for instance, the Second Army mustered only 65,000 men, roughly half what it was supposed to contain by statute. Adjutant General Vasil'chikov, entrusted by the Tsar with drafting a report on the failure of the 1828 campaign, concluded that it had occurred in large measure because of insufficient military manpower. Ninety thousand men, he wrote, were simply too few with which to occupy Wallachia and Moldavia, block the Danubian forts, and conduct the sieges of

Brailov, Varna, and Shumla.[112] Three years later, during the Polish war, the situation was no different. The initial contingent of Russian forces earmarked for field operations consisted of only 120,000 men, and it required two months to assemble even that number.[113] When Paskevich begged for reinforcements in August 1831, Nicholas replied that only 10,000 infantry men were immediately available and that there would be no more at least until the spring.[114] Still later in the reign, when Russia went to war against Britain, France, and Turkey, it experienced grave (and notorious) difficulties in bringing its military power to bear in the chief theater of conflict. Out of total military forces that were supposed to amount to 1.4 million soldiers, fewer than one hundred thousand were initially available for the defense of the Crimean peninsula.[115] Indeed, Russia's military effort in the Crimea would be crippled throughout the two and a half years of war by inadequate numbers of troops.

What explains the fact that in Nicholaevan Russia, the outbreak of any war was immediately attended by a crisis of military manpower? Several factors were responsible. In the first place casualties were always high whenever the Russian army embarked on a campaign, and for the traditional reasons: miserable weather, bad hygiene, and inferior military medicine. During the Persian campaign of 1827 Russian losses from heat prostration (temperatures hit well over 100 degrees F. that July) so weakened the army that the siege of Erivan had to be postponed.[116] During the subsequent Turkish war, disease in combination with extreme cold during the terrible winter of 1828 resulted in the loss of 40,000 men, virtually half the army.[117] Operations in Poland in 1831 were stymied by an epidemic of cholera, which carried off the Tsar's Viceroy and his commander-in-chief along with thousands of common soldiers.[118] Excessive mortality and morbidity were also features of the campaigns in the Caucasus. Conditions of service in the Black Sea forts that Russia built to blockade the coast were so harsh that a soldier's life expectancy there was estimated at three years.[119] D. A. Miliutin, who was a participant, remarked that the rapid spread of sickness among the Russian soldiers during the siege of Akhulgo in 1839 was the result of "prolonged encampment in the same positions, on sunparched cliffs and in air poisoned by corpses."[120]

We should note, *inter alia,* that poor hygiene and bad food plagued the health of the troops in peace as well as in war. The Ministry of War admitted, for instance, that dysentery "was a frequent, even common" ailment suffered by the troops every summer.[121] Official statistics indicate that more than 16 million cases were treated in military hospitals and clinics from 1825 to 1850.[122] Over the same time period, whereas 30,000 Russian soldiers perished in combat, more than 900,000 succumbed to diseases of all kinds.[123]

Another strain upon available military manpower in war was the widespread use of military units to perform a variety of non-military services within the empire. During the first twenty-five years of Nicholas's reign some 2,500 battalions of troops were at some time employed in state works for the Ministry of Finance, the Ministry of Communications, the Engineers, or the military colonies.[124] Elements of the Russian army performed such essential tasks as the road repair and bridge-building.[125] A still more serious headache for military planners was the deployment of large numbers of troops as permanent garrisons throughout the empire for the maintenance of internal order. In addition to the fifty battalions of the Internal Guard, troops were also stationed in quantity for this purpose in Finland, Orenburg, and Siberia.[126] During the Crimean War forces detached for internal duty (and consequently excused from combat) may have numbered as many as 500,000.[127] Also complicating the manpower problem during 1853–56 was the need to deploy troops in auxiliary and potential theaters of war other than the Crimean peninsula. The struggle against Shamyl's murids tied up the entire 200,000-man army of the Caucasus; 300,000 soldiers were emplaced in the northeast to defend against possible attacks on the Baltic coast; and Paskevich insisted on retaining sizable forces in Poland to deter potential Austrian intervention.[128]

A final limitation on military manpower inhered in the defects of recruitment. Throughout the reign of Nicholas, Russia continued to replenish its armed forces on the basis of the old Petrine conscription system. In times of peace the state decreed levies of from two to three soldiers per 100 taxable men in the empire. The system was naturally burdensome to the Russian economy, and Nicholas, for one, was troubled by that fact. Although early on he rejected the idea that the military colonies should be enlarged so as eventually to create a captive pool of manpower equal to the army's entire annual needs, he was keenly interested in reducing the strain of recruitment on the population of his empire. He experimented with various reforms, including dividing the country into halves from which conscripts would be taken only in alternate years.[129] Yet none of his reforms came up to the Tsar's expectations, principally because the system as it was almost guaranteed that the quality of recruits would be poor. To be sure, selection of recruits by means of lotteries, which was gradually made mandatory for state peasants (*gosudarstvennye krestiane*) under Nicholas, was a reasonable safeguard against the tendency of that segment of the population to defraud the army of quality men.[130] But for the majority of peasants—the proprietary serfs— selection of recruits was still in the hands of local landlords and village communes. Both the landlords and the communes still had every incentive to fob the dregs of the village off on the army. Because the conscription laws were often quite slackly enforced during peacetime, the consequence of the system was that the Russian army began each of the wars it fought under Nicholas seriously under strength. When the Turkish war broke out in 1828, for instance, the army was undermanned by no less than 40 percent.[131] Since Nicholas almost never foresaw the outbreak of any war (expecting his military bluster to prevent it), the army was always severely short of men at the precise moment when operations began. The government therefore had no choice but to institute draconian recruitment procedures, including a doubling or tripling of the conscription levy, in order to fill the ranks of the army as quickly as possible. Yet despite all of the emergency efforts of the recruitment officers, numbers of recruits dispatched to the theater of war always lagged behind army requirements. The forced marches the new recruits endured, in addition to their almost total lack of training, seriously impaired their military value once they arrived on the battlefield. During wartime, in Nicholas's words, the regiments "either did not receive reinforcements or received naked, unshod, and exhausted recruits; the regiments melted away, perished, and behind them stood nothing."[132]

It was precisely because he was alive to this problem that Nicholas had tried to overhaul the recruitment system by introducing provisions for "unlimited furloughs" in 1834. As already noted, the purpose of the reform was to build up a supply of trained reservists who would be available for recall to the army in the event of a crisis. After fifteen years of blameless service, a demobilized soldier was assigned to a reserve battalion that was in turn linked to an actual field regiment. On one level the "unlimited furloughs" were doubtless a boon to the Russian army, for having reserves was clearly preferable to having none. For example, in 1848 and 1849 the state succeeded in calling up more than 175,000 men in this category.[133] Unlimited leaves were probably beneficial to army morale as well. Surely the prospect of an early discharge from the ranks was a powerful incentive for good behavior.

But the "unlimited furlough" system imposed costs on the state as well. In granting up to 17,000 men a year indefinite leave, the Russian government in effect created a legally anomalous and impoverished new class. Where, after all, were these discharged men to go? State peasants on indefinite leave might rejoin their communities, but for the majority of men on leave, former proprietary serfs, there was no welcome at home. Now legally free, they had nonetheless lost all of their claims on land or property within the village the moment they had entered the army. If they tried to rejoin their families, the latter were burdened with feeding them and paying their taxes.[134] Thus neither their relatives nor their former landlords, for that matter, wished to see them return. The result was that many apparently took to begging, vagabondage, or crime.[135] The plight of those miserable outcasts properly ought to have been a matter of grave state concern; in actuality, the Russian government was even more worried lest the former soldiers prove to be an unstable element in the villages and towns where they took up temporary residence. One prominent general warned Nicholas that "a man who is not attached to society by either property or family ties, wandering without work or goals, easily gets involved in disorders."[136] The head of the political police himself reported to the monarch in 1842 that in his opinion indefinite leaves had produced "an undesirable change in the morals of the Russian soldier."[137]

In any event, the reform of 1834 was a palliative, not a solution. Although it was able to provide the army with enough reservists to undertake the punitive expedition into Hungary in 1849, the program was too small in scale to satisfy the army's need for reinforcements in case of a major war. All the 200,000 reservists on the books had been called up within the first year of the Crimean War. As that number was insufficient, the government once again had to resort to *ad hoc* emergency levies, which inducted possibly as many as 800,000 men into the ranks of the army during the conflict.[138] Even that quantity proved in the end to be too small.

Problems other than inadequate manpower sapped the combat strength of the Russian army. The omnipresent evils of corruption and peculation are an example. On all too many occasions, officers devised ingenious methods for robbing both the state and the soldiers under their command. They ranged from outright theft, to doctoring the books, to substituting inferior goods for state supplies and pocketing the difference. To be sure, soldiers themselves stole as well. Then, too, as one scholar has recently emphasized, in view of the haphazard issuance of pay, the snail's pace of logistical deliveries, and in general the relatively small state resources expended on its maintenance, the Russian army could not even have survived without some corruption.[139] Still, egregious thieving could not but be detrimental to the morale of the troops. Some colonels were known to have syphoned off as much as 60,000 rubles from the regiments in a single year.[140] It was not uncommon for soldiers to be deprived of such necessities as rations and firewood because of the criminal greed of their commanders. Abuses like those, a War Ministry report of the 1850s commented, "have a harmful effect on discipline"—an understatement if there ever was one.[141]

Bad consequences arose also from what has been termed the "*platz parad*" (parade ground) tradition during the reign of Nicholas I. The tradition has often been portrayed as more dysfunctional than it actually was: goose-stepping and meticulously executed drill really did make the army look fearsome and imposing, which is how the Emperor wanted to look to potential enemies abroad or potential dissidents at home. Still, as was the case also with military deployments, drill that served the interest of military intimidation often did not prepare the troops for war. At inspections and exercises troops were required to observe petty rules: ranks had to be perfectly dressed; intervals between each man had to be identical; and boots had to be polished just so. Failure to measure up could incur many blows of the stick.[142] In general, disciplinary measures were brutal. Army authorities meted out harsh punishments (including often fatal sentences of running the gauntlet) for quite trivial offenses.[143] Although better off than common soldiers, officers themselves were not spared the rigors of Nicholaevan discipline. One young officer complained in his diary that as he found it physically impossible to fulfill all of his service obligations, he was under intolerable mental strain, fearing that any moment he might be visited with summary punishment for dereliction of duty.[144]

In any event, contemporaries often bemoaned the deleterious effects of this rigorous and punctilious training on the health of the troops. Tight uniforms and incessant parading are said to have born fruit in disease.[145] Parade ground exercises also wreaked havoc with military equipment. The manual of arms, which required a soldier to slam his musket violently onto the ground, often dislocated the firing mechanism, which could later result in the breech exploding in his face when he tried to take a shot. At least one commander placed such an emphasis on the smartness of his unit when on parade that his men's gun barrels were actually worn thin through excessive burnishing.[146]

Drill can obviously be of great military use. It can teach civilians to think of themselves as soldiers and can help build confidence and esprit de corps. There can, however, be too much drill. Pushed too far, as it was under Nicholas I, drill contributed little to preparing the soldiers for battle. Still worse, if soldiers attempted to perform in the field as they had been trained to on the Champs de Mars, the results could be disastrous. Intelligent young officers assigned to the Army of the Caucasus during Nicholas's reign quickly discovered that it behooved them to forget everything they had learned on the parade ground—that is, if they wished to remain alive.

A final set of difficulties stemmed from the state's efforts to economize on the maintenance of its army. Take, for example, the military colonies. One of the principal reasons for establishing them was the desire of the government to keep the military budget under control. Yet despite the fact that the colonies allowed (and indeed encouraged) soldiers to marry and raise families, both the soldiers and the peasants settled in the colonies regarded them as little more than hells on earth. Count A. A. Arakcheev, the driving force behind the colonies, was a sadistic martinet, and the administration of the settlements bore the imprint of the deformities of his character.[147] Every aspect of life and behavior in the colonies was regimented; each colonist was attired in military uniform; hours of drill were demanded on top of backbreaking agricultural labor; discipline was both harsh and capricious. Conditions in the colonies, frankly unendurable, resulted in high incidences of suicide and eventual rebellion.[148] In 1831 military colonists in Novogord suddenly rose up in revolt and massacred more than two hundred bailiffs, nobles, and officials; 3,600 men and women implicated in the atrocities were tried and punished.[149]

The rebellion forced the state to ameliorate the regimen that existed within the colonies. In the immediate aftermath of the 1831 uprising many of the colonists were reclassified as "farming soldiers." That relieved them of the responsibilities of military drill and placed them more or less on a par with the state peasants. Their children were no longer automatically enrolled as cantonists.[150] Those reforms, however, represented a retreat from the principle of squeezing the colonies to provide food, money, and conscripts for the army.

Although Nicholas's regime was unquestionably militaristic and although the Tsar personally was devoted to his army, the fact remained that the state simply did not possess enough revenue to support its armed forces or its ambitious military policies. Despite all the efforts of the Ministry of Finance, the state ran a budgetary deficit almost constantly during the reign of Nicholas I. Although the army continued to claim a high proportion of total governmental outlays, the bad harvests of 1839–41 compelled St. Petersburg to cut even its military spending.[151]

Financial pressure had obvious consequences for military preparedness. Nicholas I was, for instance, very interested in constructing or improving fortifications along the western perimeters of his empire from Åland Island to Aleksandropol. Yet while Nicholas started nine large-scale fortress-building projects during his reign, he completed few. Of the three forts deemed indispensable for the defense of Poland—Novogeorgievsk, Ivangorod, and Brest—only the first had been finished when Nicholas died.[152]

Revenue problems were still damaging to the armed forces during the 1840s and after. During that time Russia's European competitors increasingly adopted advanced (and expensive) military technologies.[153] Impoverished Russia lacked the money with which to compete. The navy was the first to suffer. In the early years Nicholas had been concerned with upgrading and improving his fleets. Indeed, sea power had served Nicholas well at Navarino in 1827 and at Constantinople in 1833, to mention but two occasions.[154] Yet when the transition from sail to steam began, the Russian navy lagged behind. Russia did not acquire its first steamship until 1848. When the Crimean War began, there were only ten small paddle-wheelers in the entire Black Sea fleet, and they were completely outclassed by the French and British ships-of-the line, driven by their screw propellers.[155] Russia was to suffer for that naval inferiority throughout the entire war. It was the reason that Russia felt it had to detach such a high proportion of troops to guard its Baltic coast in the 1853–56 period. It also meant that certain Russian possessions had to be abandoned. In December 1854 the Grand Duke Konstantin Nikolaevich ordered the governor-general of Eastern Siberia to evacuate all Russian troops from the island of Kamchatka in view of the impossibility of defending it against an amphibious invasion.[156] Technological inferiority was also a great problem for the army. The smoothbore muskets and cannon employed by the defenders of Sevastopol were no match for the rifles and improved ordnance of the enemy. French and British guns could fire faster and farther than Russian ones. The allies, moreover, were more abundantly furnished with ammunition; during the siege the French and the British fired at least 400,000 more shells on Sevastopol than the Russians were able to fire back.[157] There is something in the end pathetic about Nicholas's requests during the war that captured enemy rifles and shells be brought to Petersburg for his personal inspection; he was making an all too belated acquaintance with the implications of nineteenth-century technological progress.[158] Allied technological superiority was in the end to be decisive in the Crimean War.

The Crimean War

As Russia interpreted them, the terms of the Peace of Kuchuk Kainardzhi of 1774 gave it special rights to protect the interests of Orthodox Christians living in the Ottoman Empire. In 1850,

however, the government of France began to pressure Constantinople to grant it exclusive rights over the Churches of the Holy
Sepulcher and the Nativity, in Jerusalem and Bethlehem respectively. Those demands were advanced even more forcibly after
1852, when, by means of a coup d'état, Louis Napoleon had
swept away the Second Republic and proclaimed himself Emperor of the French. As Emperor, Napoleon III was eager both
to enhance his international prestige and to curry favor with
Catholic opinion in France by posturing as the most devoted
defender of the Roman Catholic faith.

Napoleon's negotiations with the Turks put Nicholas I in a
difficult position. While the Holy Places *per se* were of little concern to him, he was unwilling to be perceived as backing down in
the face of the French. Then, too, he believed that Imperial
France was about to embark on a revolutionary policy, designed
to win influence in Turkey at Russia's expense.[159] After much
abortive negotiating, Nicholas finally dispatched his Minister of
Marine, Prince Menshikov, to Constantinople as his personal em-
issary. Menshikov's mission was to demand that the Turks recon-
firm the special privilege of the Russian Tsar to protect the status
of the 12 million Orthodox believers who were Ottoman subjects.
Regarding this as tantamount to a surrender of sovereignty, the
Turkish government rejected the demand, counting on the support of both France and Britain.[160] Napoleon III was only too
glad to oblige. And the coalition government of Lord Aberdeen,
which included the Russophobe Palmerston as Foreign Minister,
was increasingly inclined to view Russia's activities as a prelude to
an aggressive assault on the Near Eastern balance of power.

After the fiasco of the Menshikov mission Nicholas I attempted to threaten the Turks, as we have previously seen, by
staging an invasion of Wallachia and Moldavia, two provinces
under the nominal suzerainty of the Sultan. The Turks, however,
were not inclined to give way. When a last-minute attempt at
mediation by the Austrian Chancellor, Count Buol, also failed,
Turkey declared war on October 4, 1853.[161]

Although Russia intended to stand on the defensive against
the Turks on land, it undertook offensive naval action early. In
November its Black Sea fleet caught a Turkish naval flotilla in the
Black Sea port of Sinope and sent it to the bottom. Fearing that
Turkey was now in danger of toppling, France and Britain sent

naval squadrons into the Black Sea and shortly thereafter (March 1854) declared war themselves.

Although the Russians had successfully repulsed Turkish attacks in the Balkans and the Caucasus during the first months of the war, the correlation of forces was now different. In September 1854, under the cover of the Royal Navy, an Anglo-French expeditionary force landed on the Crimean peninsula roughly 30 miles north of the strategic fortress of Sevastopol. On September 20 combined French, British, and Turkish forces ran into a Russian detachment of 36,000 men at the Alma River. The battle of the Alma, which featured senseless frontal assaults on both sides, resulted in a costly victory for the allies. The Russians were forced to retreat into the fortress of Sevastopol itself, reinforcing the 20,000-man garrison.

The Russians now made extensive preparations for the defense of the city. Under the direction of the brilliant engineer Colonel Totleben, Russian troops constructed an intricate system of earthworks and fortifications on the southern or inland side of the town. Those works were so formidable that the allies hesitated to risk an assault on them. Finally, in early October 1854 the allies launched the first of their attempts to take Sevastopol. The allied fleet bombarded the seaward side of the fortress with more than 40,000 rounds, while siege guns dragged into positions inland hammered at Totleben's fortifications. The struggle, however, proved inconclusive, for if many of Sevastopol's guns were silenced, several allied warships also took heavy damage.

But food and ammunition supplies were running low inside Sevastopol. Precisely because of powder shortages, Menshikov, the commander of the garrison, now ordered a Russian counterattack in the hope of raising the siege. The Russians selected as their target Balaclava, the site of a great concentration of British food and stores. The upshot was the Battle of Balaclava (October 12, 1854). The Russian 12th Division under Liprandi early on captured four Turkish redoubts on the British right flank. It soon appeared that the entire battle would turn on the British efforts to retake them. This was the engagement that witnessed the notorious Charge of the Light Brigade. Misunderstanding its orders, which were to harass the Russians on Causeway Heights, Cardogan's light brigade instead attacked directly into the massed Russian artillery, with predictably catastrophic results. Despite wholescale carnage on both sides, Balaclava was also curiously indecisive. Although the Russians had failed to break through the allied lines, their military position actually improved after this defeat, for they shortly received a large number of reinforcements.

On October 24 Menshikov once again tried to break out of the allied encirclement by assaulting the forces of the British right flank on Inkerman Heights. Initially hard pressed by the Russian assault, the British troops were saved by the timely arrival of French troops from Bosquet's corps of observation. The Russians were once again rebuffed, taking 11,000 casualties—roughly 40 percent of the men they had committed to the battle.

The war now settled into the dreary pattern of siegecraft, bombardment, and sorties. But time was not on the Russian side. Finally, after losing the suicide engagement at Black River (August 4[16], 1855), the Russians decided that Sevastopol had to be abandoned. The outgunned and outnumbered Russian soldiers and sailors began the evacuation; Sevastopol fell to allied forces at the end of August. Russia was now at the point of exhaustion. It was fighting a coalition composed of France, Britain, Turkey, and Sardinia. Sweden was growing increasingly hostile. When the Austrian government presented its ultimatum, demanding that Russia negotiate or face war, the new Emperor, Alexander II, felt that he had no choice but to agree.

The Crimean War represented the death knell of the Nicholaevan system. That system, and much of what it stood for, was thoroughly discredited. The Crimean defeat put into motion a process of reassessment that eventually resulted in such important reforms as the abolition of serfdom in 1861. Efforts by Russian diplomats to undo the humiliating Peace of Paris, which ended the war, were to occupy them for years afterward. But the impact of the war on the Russian military establishment was no less momentous. For more than a hundred and fifty years, the Russian military system with its impressed peasant army had proved equal to almost any challenge that could be brought against it. The Russian army had been an extraordinarily reliable instrument of the state's grand strategy. But the Crimean War demonstrated that this was not necessarily the case any longer. The old military system was no longer of value under the changed conditions of warfare. That system now had to be reinvented—taken apart and replaced with something else that would permit Russia to be victorious on the battlefield once again. The problem was complex. What new sort of military system ought Russia to have? How could Russia integrate modern military technologies into its armed forces? Finally, how could it pay for it all? In one way or another, those questions continued to bedevil Russian statesmen for the next eighty years, until Stalin finally and conclusively resolved them in the 1930s. But a first attempt to answer them came in the reign of Alexander II. It is to this subject that we must now turn.

7

From the Treaty of Paris to the Congress of Berlin, 1856 - 78

Russia and the New Vulnerability

At the very end of 1867 Russia's Foreign Minister, Prince Gorchakov, addressed a memorandum to Tsar Alexander II summarizing Russian foreign relations over the previous eleven years.[1] Gorchakov began by recalling the circumstances that had led Russia to sue for an end to the Crimean War. By early 1856, a nearly bankrupt Russian Empire was simultaneously fighting France, Britain, Turkey, and Piedmont yet was incapable of offensive action against any of them. And the list of powers arrayed against Russia was growing. Austria was treacherously threatening to take up arms, and if Sweden, Prussia, and Persia had followed suit, Gorchakov pointed out, Russia would then have confronted a "coalition without parallel in history."[2] The danger was obvious: as the coalition grew, so too might its war aims, and "Russia, having on the extent of all her frontiers and all of her extremities provinces which had been conquered in barely a century and which she had not time to assimilate nor to attach to the center via a solid line of interests and communications (Finland, the Baltic provinces, Poland and the Polish provinces, Bessarabia, Transcaucasia and Armenia), would then be exposed to territorial losses which would undo all her history and which would drive her back for a considerable time outside the European continent."[3] In Gorchakov's melancholy estimation, once despoiled of territory to the north, south, and west, the Russian Empire would be degraded from its status as a major Western power to that of an

Oriental backwater. Indeed, Russia's military ineptitude during the Crimean War suggested even to its own statesmen that this was what it might truly be, for it had demolished the myth of its martial prowess. P. A. Valuev, later Minister of Internal Affairs, wrote in 1855 that "in waging war with half of Europe it was impossible any longer to hide behind the curtain of official self-congratulations to what degree and precisely in what areas of state power we lagged behind our enemies. It turned out that our fleet lacked exactly those ships and our army exactly those weapons needed to equalize the combat."[4] Gorchakov himself insisted that another powerful inducement to make peace had been the light that the Crimean War had cast on the causes "of the weakness inherent in the situation of the Empire, the causes having been hidden for forty years by our system of conservative alliances."[5]

Under the terms of the Peace of Paris (March 1856), Russia lost southern Bessarabia, was deprived of any future influence in the Danubian principalities of Wallachia and Moldavia, and, most humiliatingly, was forced to accede to the neutralization of the Black Sea. That last clause forbade Russia (and for that matter Turkey) to maintain any serious naval forces in the Black Sea.[6]

It would be hard to underestimate the influence of the Crimean catastrophe upon Russian diplomacy and strategy over the next twenty years. In the first place, the Crimean defeat presented the Russian Foreign Ministry with a new set of primary objectives. For more than a decade, Russia's diplomats became obsessed with obtaining a revision in the clauses of the Paris Peace that concerned Bessarabia and, most important, the Black Sea. That foreign policy effort was not undertaken merely to salve St. Petersburg's wounded pride. Of course, the Peace of Paris was naturally perceived by educated Russians as a galling disgrace. One historian has noted that Russia's enemies would not have imposed such conditions on any state that they regarded as truly European.[7] But from the Russian point of view there were essential issues of security that underpinned the desire to rip up the treaty of 1856. Although that document had technically closed the straits to the warships of any nation, St. Petersburg did not believe in the good faith of either London or Paris. In a crisis, with the Sultan's connivance, a powerful British or French fleet might come steaming through the Dardanelles and Bosphorus, subjecting Russia's weakly defended Black Sea coast to naval bombardment or amphibious attack. Thus the people and commerce of the southern coast of Russia were the permanent hostages of the Western maritime powers—at least as long as the Paris treaty remained in force.

The Crimean War had therefore created a new paradigm of vulnerability for Russia, one to supplant the fear of revolutionary war and land invasion that had been a legacy of the struggle against Napoleon. The new paradigm held that Russia was particularly endangered by coalitions, especially coalitions of wealthier and more industrialized states. Russia therefore had to prevent the formation of coalitions against it at all costs through careful and nonprovocative policies. If those efforts failed, and Russia was confronted by a hostile coalition either in peacetime or in war, it would have to do all it could to dissolve the alliance. If it failed to do so and was forced to wage lopsided war, the result might be not defeat but catastrophe. As Russia's statesmen interpreted it, the treaty of Paris, although odious, had nonetheless been a narrow escape from a potentially worse fate. According to Gorchakov only Russia's timely acquiescence in the treaty had averted the loss of every territory it had acquired since the time of Peter the Great. Of course, such an outcome objectively had not been very likely. The mutual suspicions and rivalries of Russia's Crimean adversaries would have precluded their colluding in the total demolition of the Russian Empire. But Gorchakov calculated that the Russian Empire had been in real danger of collapse in 1856. Although such expressions as "the undoing of Russian history" might in retrospect seem hyperbolic, they reflected authentic anxieties.

Russia's generals also began to adopt an apocalyptic vocabulary in the post-Crimean era. Precarious as Russia's security may have seemed to Russian diplomats, it looked still worse to Russia's military leadership. Although the diplomats were agreed on the necessity of avoiding war, their fears of what might happen to Russia if war broke out were less numerous and less specific than those which haunted the army and navy. The nightmares of the military were far more vivid. It was the duty of Russia's generals and admirals to prepare for war, after all, and to think through the problems of waging it even in the most unfavorable international and domestic conditions. While the diplomatists calculated the external threat to Russia on the basis of political probabilities, the generals measured it exclusively in terms of military capabilities—a line of thought that could only intensify their apprehensions. For most of the reign of Alexander II, fear underpinned the processes of military reform, weapons acquisition, and strategic reassessment no less than it informed the diplomats' concept of a dangerous international environment

Gorchakov's Diplomacy in the 1850s and 1860s

For more than a generation after the Crimean War, the steward of Russian foreign policy was Prince A. M. Gorchakov. This vain, hypochondriacal grandee, who padded his letters to the Emperor with constant references to chills, lumbago, and stomach cramps, among other symptoms, possessed the virtues of shrewdness and caution.[8] Yet offsetting those admirable qualities were others less appealing. His appetite for flattery was, for instance, almost insatiable. Perhaps Gorchakov's greatest failing was the fact that his mind and temperament had been thoroughly formed by the ultraconservatism of the previous reign of Nicholas I. To be sure, he did grasp that a new era of mass politics was dawning in Western Europe, an era in which nationalism, plebiscites, public opinion, and popular unrest were likely to be more important than traditional monarchism and legitimacy. In 1860 he wrote the Tsar that "the thing which makes the situation in Europe dangerous is *above all* the formidable social questions which complicate it."[9] Yet he did not have the imagination to anticipate the economic, territorial, and political changes that were already looming in the West. Moreover, when change occurred, his usual posture was to deplore it rather than frame policies to cope with it or profit by it. In that respect Gorchakov's instincts were more those of a moralist than those of a statesman. Unfortunately, it was an age dominated by such unscrupulous politicians as Louis Napoleon, Camillo Cavour, and Otto von Bismarck, men who were thoroughly at home with the new mass politics, whose devious behavior at least partly stemmed from their desire to co-opt, deceive, and manipulate public opinion at home. Gorchakov scorned any compromises with public opinion, either foreign or domestic. To take even such feeble Russian public opinion as there was into account during the crafting of policy would be to dilute the principle of autocratic authority. That would also pose the risk that passion might unseat reason in the councils of state. This, of course, is precisely what Gorchakov believed was happening in the West. In a rare reflective mood, he once lectured the Tsar:

> Constitutional governments have this enormous advantage. When a Palmerston[10] commits infamous political acts, he takes refuge behind public opinion, majorities. If he passes a measure, the country can disavow its author and retain the profits. But the country is not dishonored, because it shields its honor behind the rampart of minorities, much like Sodom and Gomorrah from which God only demanded forty virtuous men. An autocratic sovereign is responsible for his least acts, and he leaves to his successors the example of his entire political life.[11]

To Gorchakov, then, Western governments were tainted by their responsiveness, however slight, to popular opinion. Such regimes were at best unpredictable and at worst underhanded. Since autocratic policies had to be consistent and consequently honorable, it was impermissible for Russia to go down that path.

If there were ethical constraints on how Russia conducted its foreign relations, Gorchakov held that there were material constraints on Russian foreign policy as well. As a general rule successful diplomacy relies on the fulcrum of power, whether economic or military. Russia, however, was precariously short of either commodity, and its foreign rivals understood that well. The Crimean War had resulted in a deficit of almost 800 million rubles.[12] The war had, as well, exposed many serious defects in Russia's military system. Gorchakov therefore believed that Russia needed to enter upon a lengthy period of self-examination and reform. "The first duty of Russia is to accomplish the work of her internal reorganization, which contains the germ of her destiny in the future," he wrote.[13] Nor was Gorchakov alone in thinking so. Indeed, the period of Alexander's reign from 1856 to 1874 became known as the "era of the Great Reforms" owing to the numerous legislative acts the regime sponsored in those years to ameliorate and transform Russian society. In 1861 serfdom was abolished; in 1864 new civil and criminal codes (prescribing trial by jury) came into effect. Also in 1864 the government established elected rural councils (*zemstva*) to deal with problems of public health and education; urban counterparts (town dumas) followed six years later. Censorship was eased, and greater autonomy was granted to the universities.[14] Russian diplomacy had to foster the process of internal reform by shielding the country from distractions from abroad. Russia consequently needed a careful, risk-adverse foreign policy compatible with its internal preoccupations. The Russian approach to foreign relations under Alexander II came to be known, appositely enough, as the policy of *recueillement*, from Gorchakov's famous quip: "*La Russie ne boude pas, mais se recueille*" (Russia does not sulk, but rather contemplates herself).[15]

But the policy of *recueillement* (self-contemplation or, perhaps better, self-absorption) did not connote total inactivity abroad. The Ministry of Foreign Affairs set several goals for itself. First in importance was shattering the old Crimean coalition in order to ensure that the anti-Russian alliances of wartime did not perpetuate themselves in peace. To that end Gorchakov helped to engineer a rapprochement with Napoleon III of France, who had begun to hint at a wish for warmer relations with St. Petersburg even before the Paris Peace Conference was over. By means of the entente of Stuttgart (so called because of the meeting between the French and Russian Emperors that occurred there in September 1857), Gorchakov hoped at one stroke to extricate Russia from its diplomatic isolation; to drive a wedge between Paris and London; and to garner French support against Austria over the questions of Bessarabia and the Black Sea. Only the first of those hopes was realized, and that only temporarily. Napoleon III had no intention of allowing the Russians to poison his relationship with England. He wanted to use them to keep Austria and Prussia in check, while promising Russia nothing very concrete in return. For its part, St. Petersburg became markedly colder to France when it was realized with disgust that Napoleon's involvement in Italy, his partnership with Piedmont in a war against Austria (1859), and his patronage of the newly formed Kingdom of Italy were not traditional great power politics but rather the politics of revolution.[16] Napoleon's outspoken advocacy of the cause of the rebellious Poles during the anti-Russian insurrection of 1863 finally ruptured the entente with France. Prussia's sympathy and support during that crisis was one reason why Gorchakov's policy thereafter began to tilt in the direction of Berlin.

Another task of the Russian Foreign Ministry was to monitor developments in the Ottoman Empire carefully while avoiding any overt intervention there. Gorchakov himself never doubted that Russia had some great, if undefined, destiny to fulfill in the Near East at some unspecified time in the remote future. The Ottoman Empire contained millions of Slavic Christians, who increasingly chafed under the strictures of Turkish rule. Many of them openly looked to St. Petersburg for aid in the struggle for liberation. The Balkan Christians had their partisans in Russia, including friends within the Russian Ministry of Foreign Affairs. N. P. Ignat'ev, a notorious Pan-Slavist, used his vantage point as Ambassador to Constantinople (1864–74) to advocate Russian efforts to destabilize the Turkish Empire.[17] Gorchakov, however, was unmoved by Ignat'ev's pleas. In the first place, protestations of friendship and anticipatory gratitude on the part of the Bulgarians or the Serbs might well be insincere. Who, Gorchakov asked, could really believe in the authentic sympathy of the Balkan Slavs for *autocratic* Russia?[18] Were Russia to intervene on behalf of the Slavs against their Turkish overlords, it would in fact be championing the dangerous and reprehensible forces of nationalism, forces that it behooved Russia to keep at bay both at home and abroad. "An Emperor of Russia," Gorchakov insisted, "cannot conduct a revolutionary policy."[19] In fact Gorchakov, like Nesselrode before him, frequently emphasized just how useful a decrepit but still extant Turkish Empire was for Russia. "In its state of real weakness Turkey was the most convenient neighbor we could desire," he wrote in 1867. Nine years later he repeated this thought in a letter to Russia's Ambassador in London, noting that Russia needed for the straits to be in weak hands, which would not close them to its trade or threaten its security. "Turkish possession fulfills this program."[20]

In any event, Russian meddling in Turkey, or even the perception of meddling, could lead to a general war from which a Russia engaged in internal reform could only lose. What then of the plight of the Christians in the Ottoman Empire? Here Gorchakov counseled patience in the expectation that sooner or later something he described as "the natural decadence of Islam" would result in Christian dominance in the European parts of the Turkish Empire without any direct Russian participation in the process or, indeed, any violence at all.[21]

Gorchakov's foreign policy program in the 1860s contained one more notable element. While avoiding foreign complications and entanglements that might distract Russia away from its course of internal regeneration, it should "insofar as possible . . . keep watch so that in the meanwhile there do not occur in Europe modifications in territory, equilibrium, or influence which would cause serious injury to our interests or to our political position."[22] Those were, of course, already empty words when Gorchakov penned them in 1867, for the history of Europe in the 1860s was a history of precisely such dangerous modifications. By means of three limited wars—in 1864 against Denmark, in 1866 against Austria, and in 1870–71 against Napoleon's France—Bismarck unified the German states into an Empire ruled from Berlin. That event conclusively overturned the balance of power in Europe, making Germany the predominant political and military force on the Continent.

Even if the Russian government had perfectly foreseen the consequences of the unification of Germany, Petersburg would have been hard put to postpone or forestall it, given the inescapable reality of Russia's economic and military weakness. Throughout the period of German unification, the Russian government was probably at least as afraid of the escalation of Bismarck's wars into general European war as was Bismarck himself.[23] In fact, insofar as Russia played an active role during the period of German unification, it was as Prussia's sympathizer and not its adversary. From St. Petersburg's standpoint Prussia appeared to be inimical to Austria, just as Russia was. As for the French, their policy was ambitious and fickle. In the circumstances, Gorchakov believed that German unification might be a boon for Russia, because a German Empire might prove to be a sturdy counterweight to France. The "creation of a strong political and military power interposed between us and France under the direction of an anti-Polish Protestant state long allied to Russia offers us real advantages," the self-deluded Russian Chancellor wrote the Tsar.[24] Gorchakov's mistake of overestimating the French and underestimating the Germans was by no means unique to him. For the majority of European statesmen in the late 1860s, France was still invested with the military reputation that Bonaparte had acquired for it. It was accordingly regarded as the paramount military power, the power to be feared. The general consensus in 1869 was that France would crush Prussia handily should war break out, while the general apprehension was that, having done so, France might then exploit its victory to annex the Rhineland, Belgium, and Luxembourg. Few dreamed that Prussia and its south German allies would defeat the French armies so quickly, that France would in the end be so utterly humbled as to accede to German seizure of its provinces of Alsace and Lorraine, or that the war would entail the collapse of the French monarchy and the restoration of the republic.

Military Policy After the Crimean War: Sources of Weakness

While Gorchakov fretted over his agenda, Russia's generals and admirals worried about their own. Russia had been beaten on the Crimean peninsula, and the military feared that it would inevitably be beaten again unless steps were taken to surmount its military weakness. From the standpoint of the Ministries of War and Marine, that weakness arose from the formidable synergy of systemic defects in the Russian military system with international isolation, an inferior transportation network, and the geographic position of the empire. Although the military flaws might be repaired by administrative reform, the isolation overcome by skillful diplomacy, and the transportation system corrected with time and money, the problems that stemmed from Russia's size, location, multinational character, and resources were iron and impassible barricades to military progress.

The Crimean War had laid bare many of the systemic defects. First, it was obvious by 1856 that the Russian military system was too centralized to be responsive to the friction of local circumstances. Although various persons had served as Commander-in-Chief of Russia's Crimean forces, to a large extent the war had been fought from St. Petersburg. The Tsar's prior approval had been necessary for any changes in the campaign plans; the Crimean army could not even requisition local stocks of forage, food, or medicine without lengthy correspondence with St. Petersburg. Second, as we saw in the previous chapter, Nicholaevan militarism had clearly been insufficiently attentive to technological innovation. At the beginning of the war, less than 4.5 percent of Russia's soldiers had been armed with rifles; even as late as February 1856, only 13.5 percent possessed them.[25] The remainder were equipped with smoothbore muskets, whose effective range of roughly sixty paces was no match for the Miniè rifles of the Anglo-French troops, sighted in at two hundred.[26] Similarly, although Russian gunnery on the whole had been excellent, skillful gun-handling by itself could not compensate for the inaccuracy and low range of the Russian bronze smoothbore cannon. The battles of the Alma and Inkerman had conclusively demonstrated the superiority of the allies's rifled artillery.[27] The backwardness of Russian maritime technology was another crippling disadvantage. Russia's Black Sea Fleet was inferior in both quantity and quality to the maritime forces London and Paris committed to the Crimean War.

Perhaps the gravest systemic defects the war revealed, however, were connected with Russian recruitment practices. In the first place there was a problem with quality. Traditional conscription procedures almost guaranteed that landlords would try to send misfits, idlers, and the sick off for military service. By the time of the Crimean War the army's tolerance for such conscripts had been worn away. After that war, as the army struggled to assimilate new military technologies, quality recruits became an even higher priority. Training had become more important, as had specialization, for a larger proportion of the army was to consist of engineers, artillerists, and the like. In those conditions the armed forces needed a recruitment pool superior in quality to that traditionally available to them. Without totally new conscription procedures, based on a different principle of selection, it was difficult to see how that could be done. The emancipation of the serfs in 1861 did not fundamentally alter the system. Choosing conscripts now devolved upon the rural communes, which perpetuated the old practices. In 1867 instructions for the recruiting officers were still warning them against accepting into the ranks of the sharpshooters "people with eye diseases, in particular weak vision, also myopia, those with hollow or badly developed chests, and those with organic deformations of the liver, spleen, or mesentery glands"—an injunction that provides some insight into the physical condition of the annual recruit levy even at that late date.[28]

Other difficulties impaired efforts to supply the armed forces with reserves. The regime of Nicholas I had tried to solve the problem of reserves by granting long-term leaves (*otpuski*) to meritorious soldiers who had served ten to fifteen years. This, as we have noted was unfortunately no more than a half-measure. By the end of the first year of war, when almost all of the *otpuskniki* had been called back to the colors, the Russian army had reached the limit of its manpower. Panic action on the part of the government—including quadruple conscriptions at various points during the war—did not ameliorate the situation much, since the time to train and equip the new recruits fully was lacking. Exacerbating the crisis was the fact that Russia's forces had been spread too thin. Although the main theater of the war had been the Crimean peninsula, there was an auxiliary theater against Turkey in Transcaucasia as well as two potential theaters (the Baltic coast and Poland) in which Russia expected military operations to begin at any time. Two hundred thousand Russian troops were tied down in Transcaucasia through the entire Crimean War, both to observe the Turks and to continue the struggle against Shamil's murids. In view of the weakness of the Baltic fleet and the absence of shore defenses, the Russian government deployed three hundred thousand more in the Baltic provinces to guard against an Anglo-French naval attack and to defend the approaches to the capital city of St. Petersburg. Meanwhile, Field Marshal Paskevich had strong forces under his command in Warsaw, a precaution against a surprise entry into the war by either of the two Germanic powers. Finally, internal security requirements led to the stationing of thousands of troops more at various bases and outposts within the empire.[29] Decisions about the distribution of Russian forces reflected the fact that the Crimean War was a coalitional war, a war in which Russia's enemies were capable of distracting it with diversions, attacking simultaneously in different places, or shifting the focus of the struggle from one theater to another. Russia's vulnerability to coalitional war overtaxed its military manpower system in the first place, promoting the lack of trained reserves from a nuisance to a calamity.

Nor did the perception of vulnerability abate after the fall of

Sevastopol. For years to come the Russian military would still have reason to disperse, rather than concentrate, its armed forces, since the most probable war scenarios would involve Russia in a struggle with some sort of coalition. At first the fear was of a resuscitated Crimean coalition taking up arms against Russia. By the late 1860s Austria and Britain, perhaps assisted by Turkey and Sweden, were seen as the most likely potential enemies.[30] An even more extreme version of this threat assessment posited the adherence of France and Italy to that already formidable coalition, in which case, it was argued, Russia would have to anticipate ground invasions from Bukovina or Moldavia in addition to "potential landings anywhere on our coast from Akkerman to Kerch."[31] Throughout the 1860s and into the 1870s, planning for any of those contingencies had to take into account the indispensability of large garrisons to ward off trouble on the Persian and Central Asian frontiers.

The problem was that Russia could not be sure of whom or where it might have to fight next; prudence therefore counseled Russia to prepare to meet "worst case" situations. Even in a best case scenario—war against just one other European power— Russia would be outmatched if that power possessed a system of trained reserves. In 1870 the Russian War Ministry concluded that security requirements in Asia and the Caucasus left at most 600,000 men for a war in Europe, "which cannot be considered sufficient to protect the state from the invasion of an army of a million men, which can now be raised by Germany alone, even without other allies."[32] It went without saying that Germany's ability to do so without beggaring itself was the result of its short-term universal conscription and the enormous pool of reserves thus created.

Russia had extensive frontiers to defend and inadequate manpower to defend them. But compounding those interlocking problems was the deplorable state of Russia's transportation and communication infrastructure. During the Crimean War it had proved easier and quicker for London to convey troops to the battlefield than for Petersburg in view of the abominable condition of Russia's roads and railways. Improvements in the transport network were slow in coming even after the war. In 1860 Russia could boast of but 1,600 kilometers of railroads. Ten years later it possessed 10,700 kilometers to France's 17,900 and Germany's 18,700. Russia was at a disadvantage even when compared with Austria, since its rail net was by no means as dense.[33] The situation with regard to paved military roads was scarcely better; in 1870 there were merely 7,600 versts of them in the entire Empire.[34] It did not help much that the inadequate military maps of the time did not even accurately depict the transportation network, such as it was. As late as the early 1870s, it was not uncommon for marching parties of recruits to be ordered down nonexistent routes to billets in villages that weren't there.[35] Poor transportation undermined the well-being of the army and military preparedness, while limiting Russia's strategic options. Just as in the past, lack of transportation complicated and sometimes foreordained the ruin of military logistics, especially for those units stationed in the more distant regions of the empire. The Commander of Orenburg Military District (which then included Russian Central Asia) reported a sickness rate of almost 50 percent among his troops in 1871, ascribing it to the climate and to "the impossibility of regularly supplying the men with fresh and varied food and drink; the absence not only of good but even of potable water."[36] The impossibility he alluded to resulted from insufficient transport.

Such difficulties were the traditional burdens that bad transportation imposed on the Russian army. After the Crimean War, however, the defects of the transportation network, like those of the conscription system, had to be viewed in a new light, because they crippled Russia's ability to defend itself, let alone use its military power to give weight to its voice in European affairs. In 1859, for instance, Russia had promised to assist Napoleon III in his Italian war by concentrating four army corps on the Galician frontier in order to pin down as many Austrian troops as possible. Yet the value of that gesture was slight, for France had already won the war before the five months necessary for Russian deployment had elapsed.[37] In 1870 it was the same thing all over again. In August of that year, Alexander II secretly commanded the Russian army to mobilize as an insurance policy against the escalation of the Franco-Prussian conflict into a general European war. The War Ministry was required to furnish the Emperor with weekly reports on the army's readiness. Yet by the time the alert was suspended in March 1871, its original purpose had long since been overtaken by events. The chief lesson of the episode was the extraordinary sluggishness that attended any effort to go over to a war footing. Well into 1871, some of the troops of Russia's westernmost military district were still without rifles.[38]

Lacking a sufficient network of railroads, Russia was hard put either to mobilize its troops or to concentrate them where they were needed. That was particularly disturbing because Russia's westward neighbors, particularly Germany, had inaugurated large-scale programs of military railway construction. Prussian triumphs over Austria and France in 1866 and 1870 were viewed as demonstrating the need to integrate the railroad into operational planning.[39] Throughout the 1870s Prussia found emulators in most of Western Europe.

But Russia was poor in railroads and was to remain so for a long time. That had important strategic implications. Because Russia could not easily move troops from one quarter of the empire to another, responsibility for the conduct of military operations (whether defensive or offensive) in any potential theater of war had to reside with the troops who were already in place. Speedy reinforcement would not be a viable option. In August 1875, for instance, Alexander II decided to approve General Kaufmann's request that additional military units by sent to Central Asia in view of his impending expedition against Kokand. The War Ministry informed Kaufmann of its favorable response to his appeal but warned him that he could not expect to see any of the additional forces in Tashkent until the summer of the *following year.* The reason for that enormous time lag was obvious: the troops were going to have to *walk* from Europe to Asia.[40] As we shall see somewhat later, the feebleness of Russia's transportation and communications was to engender a veritable obsession in the higher echelons of the army with the prepositioning of troops in anticipation of military emergencies, both probable and improbable.

A final set of military liabilities inhered in the geography of the Russian Empire. As had been true since the days of Peter the Great, the climate and terrain of the regions into which Russia dispatched military forces imposed inordinate strains on the health and endurance of the troops. The Commander of Orenburg Military District complained in 1866 that most of his troops were accommodated in temporary barracks. Those structures were unsuitable for the climate, he wrote, because they were "in the main small, nasty, cold, and in general [did not satisfy] hygienic conditions for the support of health"—sentiments that could have been (and were) echoed by military commanders in many other regions of the country.[41]

The geographical encumbrance to Russian military power that was perceived as the most serious after the Crimean War was the distribution of populations within the empire. Russia was a multinational state, yet its non-Russian minorities lived overwhelmingly in borderlands on its northern, western, and southern peripheries. Many of the ethnic and national groups under the Russian crown were openly restless—contemptuous of Russian rule and eager for independence. Shamil's Caucasian mountaineers waged guerrilla war against St. Petersburg for more than twenty years. Even after Shamil surrendered in 1858, Russia still had reason to doubt the allegiance of its Muslim populations, so long as independent Islamic khanates continued to exist in Central Asia. In the mid-nineteenth century, however, St. Petersburg still regarded the Poles as the most dangerous, disloyal, and indigestible of all of the empire's subject populations. In 1830 the Poles had fielded armies in a full-blown war against the Russian state. Thirty-three years later, Poland rose in revolt once again and was pacified only with the greatest of difficulty. Indeed, in later decades this Polish rebellion of 1863 became the archetypal national insurrection in the minds of Russia's ruling elite. What if a foreign enemy had taken advantage of Russia's preoccupation with the revolt to launch an attack? There had in fact been sufficient concern at the time about a possible French amphibious attack in the Baltic to stimulate military preparations to thwart it.[42] Should an invading army have crossed the frontier into Poland in 1863, the tsarist government had little doubt that it would have been greeted as liberators. The conviction that Russia's potential Western adversaries would find allies in armed Polish traitors never wavered over the rest of the century.

Thus when Russia's military elite contemplated a war in Europe, it had to plan for the simultaneous defense of the Polish theater against threats both from within and from without. But the demands of foreign and domestic security were sometimes incompatible. Until 1876, for instance, artillery ammunition in the Warsaw Military District was not distributed to the batteries but locked up in the fortress of Novogeorgievsk; the object was to prevent those stocks from falling into Polish hands in the event of another popular rebellion. That practice further lengthened the process of mobilizing the forces in Poland in the face of a foreign crisis. To convey shells to the 4th Foot Artillery Brigade in Ostrov could require as many as twenty-one days.[43] Thus the very measures taken to alleviate one sort of security problem could magnify another.

In any event, the sullen mood of the subject populations not only in Poland but in the other borderlands was an additional argument for the dispersal of Russia's armed strength. The stress of foreign war might well ignite nationalist rebellions in any or all of the extremities of the empire. The only way to deter revolt would be through the deployment of formidable standing garrisons—a policy that could subtract from the number of troops available for battle in the main theater of the war. But Russia's nationality problem also made perimeter defenses highly desirable. Were Russia to be attacked, it could not respond with a strategic withdrawal into the heart of the country without grave apprehensions. The Russian military elite believed that the most likely political objective of a hostile power in the event of a war would be to deprive Russia of one or more of its frontier provinces. In other words, possession of the borderlands, and most probably Poland, would be what the war would be fought about. A withdrawal (like that of 1708 or 1812) would consequently entail abandoning the frontier provinces to the enemy, surrendering the chief political stake in the war without firing a shot. Still worse, a Russian army that had regrouped and reinforced itself after such a withdrawal could find merely dislodging the invader from the borderlands insufficient to retake them. Thorough reconquest and pacification might be necessary. Unfortunately, to avoid being forced into a withdrawal, Russia's forces had to be sufficiently strong at the point of an attack to repulse the invader decisively. The problem was that there were too many potential points of attack; to attempt to be strong everywhere was to be strong nowhere.

What finally complicated postwar Russia's security dilemma was acute pressure for reductions in the military budget, which of course had been caused by the war itself. The Crimean War deficit had been so enormous that the Ministry of Finance was able to insist plausibly on at least temporary cuts in all categories of state expenditure, including defense. In 1864, as a money-saving measure, the government reduced the size of the army by 232,000 men. The budget approved for the War Ministry was 25 million rubles less in 1865 than it had been in the previous year. The state went on to shave 9 million rubles more from the Ministry in 1866.[44]

The impediments, then, to the reconstruction of Russian military power in the aftermath of the Crimean War were numerous and daunting. Overcentralized administration, inferior munitions, and the manpower crisis resulting from the antiquated conscription system enfeebled the defense effort. At the same time the War Ministry's obligation to prepare for the possibility of simultaneous conflicts in multiple theaters, each poor in roads and railways, each separated from the others by hundreds, if not thousands, of miles—all of this severely taxed the ingenuity of Russia's strategists, who also had to keep Russia's precarious financial position in mind.

Architects of Reform: Konstantin Nikolaevich, Miliutin, Obruchev

Despite those obstacles, the military leadership of Russia in the 1860s and 1870s did develop a set of plans for the renovation of the armed forces. The plans involved executing a wide range of reforms—administrative, bureaucratic, technical, educational—all intended to support newly crafted land and sea strategies. Although many statesmen took part in the work, the contribution of three men was particularly significant: Grand Duke Konstantin Nikolaevich, General D. A. Miliutin, and Colonel N. N. Obruchev.

Konstantin's father, the Emperor Nicholas I, had ordained a naval career for him from birth. Educated under the supervision of naval officers, Konstantin took command of his first ship in 1843, when he was scarcely seventeen. Within a few years he would become an important functionary within the Imperial Ministry of Marine. Upon the accession of his brother as Alexander II, he was elevated to the head of the ministry. He would occupy that position until 1862. Liberal-minded (at least in the Russian context) Konstantin Nikolaevich was active in many branches of state affairs other than defense. His administrative restructuring of the

Naval Ministry would serve as the template for the reorganization of several other ministries. He played an influential role in several of the "Great Reforms" of the period, most notably the abolition of serfdom in 1861.[45] The gifted protégés he attracted, trained, and sponsored would eventually make their mark in the highest reaches of the tsarist government. Yet Konstantin Nikolaevich's first love was the navy, of whose cause he was a tireless promoter. Because of his enthusiasm and his Imperial birth, the Grand Duke's influence on naval policy remained strong for decades after he had left the Ministry of Marine for other assignments.[46]

Konstantin's great counterpart at the Ministry of War, D. A. Miliutin, was, by contrast, the product of an obscure and penurious family of the petty nobility. First in his class at the Imperial War Academy, Miliutin had distinguished himself as both soldier and scholar before becoming Minister of War in 1861. Surviving portraits show a man whose hooded eyes and dull expression masked keen intelligence and unceasing industry. One of the greatest statesmen of the entire reform era, Miliutin, like Konstantin Nikolaevich, was concerned with issues of reform apparently far beyond the purview of his own ministry. One reason for that, of course, was Miliutin's understanding that the army of any country mirrors the strengths and weaknesses of the society that gives birth to it. In Miliutin's opinion it followed that no aspect of state policy, and no feature of Russian life, could be matters of indifference for a responsible War Minister. We must hasten to add that Miliutin's commitment to reform derived also from his abstract belief in the need to turn Russia into a *Rechtsstaat,* a state founded on the impartial and consistent administration of the laws.[47]

The oddest and most enigmatic of all the figures who had influence on tsarist military policy in this era was N. N. Obruchev. At the same time that Konstantin Nikolaevich and Miliutin were taking charge of their respective ministries, Obruchev, a young army captain, was committing acts of high treason against the tsarist government. Closely associated with the radical literary critics Chernyshevskii and Dobroliubov, Obruchev helped to found the seditious Land and Liberty conspiracy in the early 1860s and was a frequent contributor to Herzen's illegal publication *The Bell,* authoring articles that, *inter alia,* urged peasant soldiers to mutiny if ordered into the countryside to suppress rural disorders.[48] Yet within a decade, as a Colonel of the General Staff, Obruchev would become one of Miliutin's closest and most trusted collaborators. He would play a crucial role in the redesign of Russian strategy attempted by the War Ministry in 1873 and would have a decisive impact on Russian planning for the Turkish war of 1877–78. As Chief of the Main Staff in the 1880s and 1890s, his thinking about Russia's preparations for war in the West would be instrumental in forging the Franco-Russian alliance. No single individual would be as important in the making of Russian military strategy during the entire second half of the nineteenth century as he.[49]

Army Reform in the Reign of Alexander II

Miliutin's goal as war minister was a thorough overhaul of the Russian army: to change the way it was recruited, the manner in which it was trained and disciplined, even the physical environment in which it performed its duties. Miliutin's reforms in such areas as military education (to open an officer's career to talented non-nobles) and law (the introduction of a Western-style legal code and the abolition of corporal punishment in peacetime) need not detain us here. Of greater importance to the themes we are exploring are the reforms that were supposed to produce direct and immediate improvements in the combat strength of the Russian army.

One technique for doing so was a program of weapons modernization. From the beginning, Miliutin made the acquisition of rifled weapons a high priority. Unfortunately, the third quarter of the nineteenth century was a period of rapid advances in small arms technology. Thus it was that the War Ministry found that the percussion cap, muzzle-loading rifle model 1858 was obsolete before the army could be totally equipped with it. The Karlé rifle (with a firing mechanism similar to that of the famous Prussian needle gun) was adopted in 1867 but was supplanted two years later by the Krnk rifle, with its unitary metal shell. Finally, in 1870 the War Ministry approved the smaller caliber (10.67 mm), breech-loaded Berdan rifle no. 2. By the time the Russo-Turkish war broke out, sixteen of the forty-eight infantry divisions in the army had been equipped with the Berdan.[50]

Improvements in the artillery came still more slowly. The Russian army acquired its first rifled ordnance in 1860. These bronze muzzle-loaded guns were the norm until 1866, when the army began to test prototypes of breech-loaders. In the 1870s increases were made in the absolute size of the artillery forces. The number of batteries per brigade was raised from four to six, then eight, while the number of artillery brigades grew to fifty-five, significantly enhancing the firepower of the ordnance arm.[51]

Another facet of Miliutin's reforms was the reorganization of military administration. Miliutin was well aware of the overly centralized decision-making procedures that had so crippled the war effort in the Crimea, which compared unfavorably with procedures in the considerably more autonomous Army of the Caucasus, where he had served as chief of staff in the late 1850s. Centralization did more than stifle the initiative of local commanders; with the poor state of communications and transportation in Russia, the obligation to consult with St. Petersburg even over small issues often led to administrative paralysis. Miliutin's solution was the creation of the military district. During the 1860s the empire was divided into fifteen quasi-independent districts, each headed by a powerful commander, each with a staff organization that replicated that of the central War Ministry. The district commanders enjoyed considerable autonomy in such matters as military logistics and supply, and were made responsible for intelligence collection, threat assessment, and eventually even defense planning for the territories and troops under their control.[52]

While concerned with streamlining provincial military administration, Miliutin nonetheless did not neglect the central institutions of his ministry. He restructured the main administrations (*glavnye upravleniia*) into which his ministry was divided. The most important of them, by virtue of the breadth of its functions, became the Main Staff (*Glavnyi Shtab*). Established in 1865, the Main Staff was supposed to supervise personnel, recruitment, training, and mobilization.[53] Two organizations subordinated to it were particularly noteworthy: the Military Education Committee and the Mobilization Committee. Despite its innocuous name, the Military Education Committee became the closest analogue to a Prussian-style general staff that mid-nineteenth-century Russia was to have. From its absorption by the Main Staff in 1865 until its abolition in 1903, it served as the sole repository of all military intelligence in the Russian Empire. Each of Russia's military attachés abroad funneled his reports on foreign armies to it, as did the chiefs of staff of all of Russia's frontier military districts. Eventually, after Obruchev took it over, the committee was to concentrate most of Russia's central war planning in its own hands. After June 1875 it was assisted in the latter task by the Mobilization Committee, chartered "to collect material relating to the transfer of forces to a war footing and to study general questions relating to military preparedness."[54]

Miliutin's final important reform was the introduction of a universal military service obligation (January 1874). The decree did not institute universal conscription, for the army did not have the resources to train all the empire's young men, but it did subject most of them to what was in effect a draft lottery, irrespective of social origins. Since the early eighteenth-century, Russia had conscripted its soldiers almost exclusively from among the peasants. But now the pool of potential recruits was enlarged: merchants were forbidden to buy substitutes, and even noblemen could technically be called up for service in the ranks. Miliutin had to fight hard to win Imperial consent for this measure. Conservative opponents both at court and in the press had bitterly opposed the plan in view of its likely social implications. They correctly understood that the law was an overt attack on the traditional privileges of the gentry and were worried as well by provisions in the act for awarding reductions in the term of a recruit's active duty on the basis of his education—even for a peasant who could merely display a certificate of attendance at a grammar school. Furnishing such powerful inducements to peasants to value learning might well threaten Russia with the democratization of its society. That, of course, was exactly what Miliutin intended.[55]

But the War Minister also had military objectives very much in mind. By reducing the years of active service to a maximum of ten (which dropped later in the century to four) while simultaneously increasing the annual intake of recruits, Miliutin hoped to build the cadres of trained reservists who were alone the answer to Russia's military manpower problem. Miliutin anticipated that within a few years Russia would be maintaining a peacetime army of 736,000 men, expandable to more than 1.6 million in the event of war.[56]

Military Strategy Under Alexander II

The military and naval reforms of the 1860s and 1870s were impressive achievements, but in the end they would not have been worth much had not the Ministries of War and Marine also tried to integrate them into coherent and realistic strategies. Although ambitious strategies may be valueless without the forces to implement them, it is equally true that neither advanced weaponry nor numerous and well-trained armies can compensate for the absence of plans for the effective use of military force to fulfill prescribed political ends. It is to the credit of the reformers at the Ministries of War and Marine that they understood this and took pains to reexamine Russian strategy even as they purchased munitions, overhauled their bureaucracies, and developed a new system of conscription.

The navy's problems were less complex than the army's. One of Konstantin Nikolaevich's first acts upon taking office as Minister of Marine had been to order an extensive study of the following question: "What in general is the goal and the purpose of the fleet in Russia, and what as a result ought to be its size and composition?"[57] It was obvious that there were certain *a priori* constraints on the way in which the question could be answered. Russia traditionally was not a maritime power; it possessed neither a large seaborne commerce nor any distant colonies that had to be defended by a strong oceangoing fleet. Then, too, there were geographical limits on the ways in which Russia could employ the naval power it possessed. The Paris Peace severely restricted the number of warships Russia could legally maintain on the Black Sea.* Even had Russia been allowed to rebuild a large Black Sea fleet, Turkey could at any time deny it access to the Mediterranean by simply closing the straits. Russia's Scandinavian and German neighbors could imprison the Baltic Fleet in the same manner by shutting down the Sound. The Caspian was, of course, an inland sea, while Russian ships in the White Sea and the Pacific had to operate out of ports that were icebound for much of the year. It followed that Russia could not count on

---

*To get around these restrictions, the government eventually established a dummy "Russian Steamship Company," whose ostensibly commercial vessels could be quickly armed in the event of war.

concentrating its naval assets in one place in the event of crisis or war. Barring exceptional circumstances, each of its fleets and flotillas had to operate on its own, without help from any of the others. That meant it was hopeless for Russia to try to match France or Britain—the two first-rank naval powers of that time—in a naval competition. Russia's maritime forces were permanently divided. By contrast, France and Britain (either singly or together) could unite their fleets, and by choosing the time and place of the attack could invariably assure themselves of naval superiority over Russia. In view of all of this, Konstantin concluded "that our fleet ought to be such that we will always be stronger than our weak neighbors, and such that the first-time naval powers, in the event of a war between them, will prize our alliance or neutrality, and such that our shores will be secure from sudden attacks by several ships . . . since the outfitting of powerful squadrons requires large-scale preparations and efforts and cannot be done in secret."[58]

The strategy for the Russian navy laid out here might well be described as minimalist and defensist. In Konstantin Nikolaevich's opinion, Russia could not win a naval arms race with London or Paris, no matter what sums it decided to lavish upon it. It should not aspire to be a great naval power but should content itself with the maintenance of a small but excellent set of fleets and flotillas. Those should be sufficient in strength to outclass the naval assets of such countries as Turkey, Sweden, and Persia. The Russian navy should also be powerful enough to deter surprise attacks even by France and Britain. If either of those states decided to attack Russia with their total fleet, of course, there could be no question of surprise; Russia would have adequate warning during the time it took the enemy to assemble its expeditionary forces. In that event, it would be the duty of the navy to put up the best possible fight until army units could be brought into position to deal with a potential amphibious invasion. Konstantin's ideas were approved by Alexander II and served as the intellectual foundation for Russia's naval program over the next twenty years.

Konstantin thus embraced a strategy of calculated naval inferiority, whose goals were both prudent and realistic. That does not mean Konstantin was uninterested in eventually building an offensive capability for the Russian navy that could divert a potential enemy from attacking Russia in its home waters. At various points he promoted (albeit unsuccessfully) the acquisition by Russia of foreign naval bases and coaling stations.[59] We should also note that Konstantin meanwhile made extremely modest claims about the potential contributions the navy could make to national security in the absence of such an offensive capacity. In Konstantin's opinion, circumstances might arise in which the navy could not even guarantee the defense of Russia's coasts against maritime attack without the army's assistance. The army, of course, had no such luxury. The army could not afford to limit itself to one or two threat scenarios but rather had to consider an entire kaleidoscope of them. Still further, the army was supposed to develop plans to prevail in each.

Throughout the 1860s strategic thinking in the Russian army was in a period of transition. Almost exclusively oriented toward defense, Russian land strategy tended to be reactive and situation-specific. Given the imperatives of internal military reform and the fundamental instability of European and domestic politics in that decade, Russian strategists felt it was premature to draft unitary, long-term programs for the national defense. Nonetheless, certain themes and concerns emerge even in the transitory plans that were adopted—themes and concerns that would remain important for years.

As we have already seen, War Ministry officials were virtually unanimous in their belief that Russia would have to ready itself for war against a coalition. In the 1860s it was assumed that the most likely power to lead such a coalition would be Austria, perhaps aided by Turkey and Sweden; most planning was based on that contingency.[60] In that event, Austria would have three possible routes of invasion to choose from. Two were in the south. Should the Austrians irrupt into Russia, the Dnestr River would offer them a logistical base that could support either operations from Moldavia and Bukhovina into Bessarabia and Kherson or an attack from Galicia northeast into the provinces of Kiev and Podolia. Were Austria to select either of those options in wartime, the Russians proposed to fall back on Bender, accumulate forces, and prepare to maneuver against the Austrian left or right flank.[61] The third variant was, however, even more frightening, for it might be feasible for the Austrians to lunge north from Lemberg toward Lublin or even Warsaw, thus cutting Poland off from the body of the Russian Empire. Enhancing that apprehension (and complicating any scheme for defense against it) was the fact that the only railroad linking Poland and Russia ran from Warsaw northeast to Petersburg.[62] The majority of the reinforcements and supplies needed for the Polish theater would therefore be dependent on road transport from the southern and central regions of the empire; the chances were that they would arrive too late.

If Austria was seen as the most likely opponent, the War Ministry regarded the threat from Britain as only slightly less plausible. The Russians did, of course, recognize that Britain's strength resided in its navy. London would therefore be most dangerous to Russia if it were to act in concert with Continental allies. Yet, whether allied or not, Britain and its maritime power were not to be despised, particularly in view of the vulnerability of Russia's numerous coasts. The problem was that as a land power Russia had almost no means of retaliating against Britain or British interests. Proposals to sanction privateering expeditions against British commerce should war break out (some still current in the mid-1870s) were obviously slipshod and desperate expedients.[63] Of course there was always India, but no responsible tsarist statesman from the 1860s until the Russian Revolution ever believed it realistically possible for Russia to launch a war of conquest from Central Asia against the British possessions in India. In fact, the real concern in St. Petersburg was that Russian gains in Central Asia might arouse British suspicions, leading to the very rupture with London that had to be avoided at all costs. There were Russian statesmen, such as the irrepressible N. P. Ignat'ev, who were unabashed apologists for Russia's Asian expansion, a cause that also had a more or less permanent lobby in the Asiatic department of the Ministry of Foreign Affairs. But Ignat'ev and his colleagues must be regarded as belonging to the lunatic fringe of Russian autocratic politics. For most government officials, Russian activities in Central Asia had to be weighed against the potential harm they could do to relations with London.

Decentralized Strategy: Russia in Central Asia

Despite the reluctance with which it was usually contemplated in Petersburg, Central Asian conquest was a dramatically constant feature of the reign of Alexander II. The cities of Turkestan and Chimkent fell in 1864, Tashkent in 1865, and Samarkand in 1868. In 1873 the khanates of Khiva and Bukhara both surrendered and became Russian protectorates. Kokand was annexed in 1876, and encroachments were made against Geok-Tepe, the last stronghold of the Turcomans in Transcaspia. Those advances were not motivated by such economic considerations as the search for captive markets or the need for cheap supplies of raw cotton.[64] Equally, they were not deliberate chess moves in some sinister geopolitical plot. Rather, the reason for Central Asian imperialism during the 1860s and 1870s was the quest for defensible frontiers on the one hand, conjoined with the excessive ambition of unruly local commanders willing to gamble that euphoria over easy victories would expunge the consequences of insubordination. Gorchakov's circular of November 1864 to the Great Powers, although invoking the *ex post facto* justification of "civilizing the heathen," nonetheless reflected the authentic views of the Russian government when it stressed that the advance into Central Asia was being forced on Russia by strategic requirements. Every time a tribe was pacified, Russia was exposed to attack from the peoples who lived on the other side of the new frontier cordon.[65] The strategic argument for expansion was made even more explicit in the internal report of General Kryzhanovskii, Commander of Russian forces in Orenburg and Turkestan, who wrote in early 1865 that "by not subordinating Tashkent . . . and placing it in a position of direct dependency upon us, we have subjected our frontier to ceaseless bandit invasions and have placed our troops in the unsatisfactory position of a border guard, constantly expecting attacks from all directions and at all times."[66] Miliutin had to agree, however grudgingly, with the logic of those remarks. As Minister of War he understood that it was the duty of a commander to shield his troops from unnecessary risks. He clearly understood as well that Kryzhanovskii was right in pointing out that the failure to subdue Tashkent confronted the empire with continuous security hazards, particularly since the Russian military manpower crisis meant that Russia did not have the troops to police every verst of its vast Asiatic borders. In such circumstances, the Russian government was constrained to approve cautious imperial expansion. The expansion, however, had to be measured and controlled, with prior diplomatic efforts to

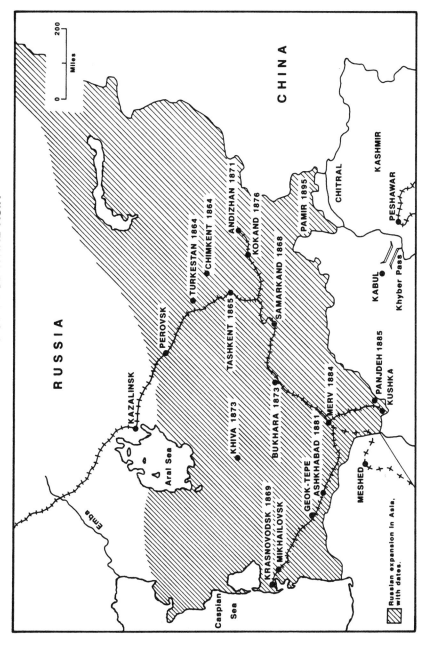

RUSSIAN EXPANSION IN CENTRAL ASIA

limit damage in London. Characteristic was Gorchakov's emphatic order in August 1872 that Russia's Ambassador to Britain exert himself to prevent a souring of relations over Russia's forthcoming expedition against Khiva.[67]

Upsetting those calculations were the poor communications between the capital and Central Asia, which gave truculent commanders an excuse for their disobedience. Try as it liked, St. Petersburg had constant difficulty in curbing the Central Asian generals. Even such events as Miliutin's removal of the popular General Cherniaev (1866) served neither fully to reestablish ministerial authority in Asia nor adequately to reassure England about the benignity of Russian intentions there.[68] Gorchakov revealed a keen insight into the situation when he confided to the Tsar that he "feared the action of our distant [military] chiefs, who, having the local circumstances exclusively in view, do not sufficiently ponder the influence that their acts could have on general policy."[69] The fact was that what Russia chose to do or not to do in Asia could have an impact on its standing in Europe and visa versa. Russia's security problems in the late nineteenth century were interconnected, just as they had been two hundred years before. After 1870 it seemed to the Russian War Ministry that the time had come to establish some consistent priorities for the national security. Russia's response to military crises and threats throughout the previous decade had been *ad hoc,* poorly coordinated, and badly planned. Such extempore strategy could no longer be tolerated in the future. The first wave of military reforms had almost been completed. Rearming the troops was well on its way, and the empire had been organized into military districts. Then, too, the foundation of the German Empire had presented Russia with a novel and particularly dangerous security threat.

Russian Policy in the Aftermath of German Unification

Russia was, at least at first, a collateral beneficiary of Germany's victory over France, for it took advantage of the confusion it engendered to issue a circular of October 1870 that unilaterally denounced the Black Sea clauses of the Treaty of Paris. Despite heated British objections, the London conference of January

1871 acceded to the abrogation of the clauses, cloaking its inability to do anything about the Russian *fait accompli* behind the figleaf of a "unanimous" agreement of the Great Powers.[70]

But if the Ministry of Foreign Affairs could be proud that it had not allowed this opportunity to pass, it could be no more sanguine about Russia's position in Europe after 1871 than it had been before. The fact of the matter was that Russia was still isolated. Vienna and Constantinople were still hostile, principally over Balkan disagreements, while relations with London were deteriorating, owing in large measure to British suspicions of Russian expansionism in Central Asia. In St. Petersburg, France was seen as weaker and less stable under the Third Republic than it had been under the Empire; Russian statesmen consequently deprecated the worth of any true understanding with Paris. Further, Berlin was decidedly cold. What now frightened Gorchakov and his aides, however, was the possible emergence of a solid Austro-German block, which by the nature of things would be directed against Russia. Russian apprehensions played into the hands of the German Chancellor, Prince Bismarck, who was determined at all costs to keep France bereft of Continental allies. When Alexander II learned that William I and Franz Joseph intended to meet in September 1872 in Berlin, he insisted on inviting himself.

In Berlin the foreign ministers of the three empires exchanged vague guarantees and platitudes. Bismarck assured Gorchakov of German friendship; Austria, he said, was permanently on the defensive and harbored no wishes for territorial expansion into the Balkans. Gorchakov told his Austrian counterpart, Prince Andrassy, that "a strong Austria is in our interest; if she didn't exist it would be necessary to invent her."[71] For his part, Andrassy expressed his government's satisfaction with the status quo in the Near East. The Berlin meeting was not, however, devoid of undertones of menace. Bismarck did his utmost to unsettle Gorchakov by hinting to the latter (untruthfully) that Andrassy had offered Berlin an offensive/defensive alliance directed against Russia.[72]

It was chiefly fright, then, that pushed Russia into the so-called League of the Three Emperors (Dreikaiserbund) of 1873. Based on the Convention of Schönbrunn between Austria and Russia of May–June 1873, a document to which Germany subsequently adhered, the League was a dynastic agreement pledging the three sovereigns to uphold legitimacy, order, and the monarchical principle. Additionally there were indefinite promises of military assistance in the event of an attack by any fourth party on one of the contracting three. The Russian government had few illusions about the Three Emperors' League, from which it had not really acquired much. It was impossible to mistake this ambiguous vow of royalist solidarity for a treaty authentically enhancing Russia's security. The Convention of Schönbrunn did nothing to resolve any outstanding disputes between Petersburg and Berlin, let alone between Petersburg and Vienna. St. Petersburg suspected Austria of having designs on Bosnia and Herzegovina, two Turkish provinces with a largely Serbian population. Russia also suspected Germany of harboring a desire for total Continental hegemony.

In 1875 the French government's law on increasing the size of its army led Bismarck to provoke a war scare through the medium of the German newspapers. Rumors of a preemptive German attack on France, spread in part by the French themselves, alarmed the British, who responded with strong protests. But the Russians were no less frightened. Gorchakov and the Tsar once again scurried to Berlin to warn Bismarck that Russia would not tolerate a new German campaign against the French. Bismarck protested that his intentions were pacific, but privately he was livid, accusing Gorchakov of attempting to pose "as the savior of France." The Reich Chancellor himself dated the origins of the Russo-German antagonism to this very incident.[73] There had in fact been little real likelihood of war. The French were unprepared for it, while Bismarck's intention had been to bully France, not to attack it. Still, the Russian reaction was understandable. Russia could not afford *not* to go to war, if the alternative was to see France crushed once again, perhaps even driven from the arena of European politics. Were that to happen, Germany might well become the undisputed arbiter of the Continent. Gorchakov had come to realize that Europe needed a strong France to counterbalance German power.[75] Yet equally, given the condition of its economy and its army in 1875, Russia could not afford *to go* to war with Germany or with anyone else. Convinced that the peace of Europe was truly in jeopardy, Gorchakov's tactless posturing in Berlin, his substitution of a bluff for the reality of military power, was the best course of action open to him under the circumstances as he understood them. Within a scant two years of its conclusion, the Three Emperors' League was already proving to be a league of mistrust.

"Wiped from the Earth by History": *The Strategic Conference of 1873*

Russia's generals were even more alarmed by the burgeoning power of Germany than was the Foreign Ministry, since, unlike the latter, they had no confidence in diplomatic accommodations. The magnitude and speed of the German triumph in the French War had shocked the Russian military establishment no less than that of every other power in Europe. Miliutin became converted to the idea that a revolution in war had taken place, that had placed Russia in a position of exceptional jeopardy. Determined to convince his ministerial colleagues of this as well, he organized the strategic conference of 1873—the first attempt in Russian history to commit the entire Russian government to a long-term plan for the defense of the empire. In preparation for the conference he commanded each of the district staffs of the empire to prepare extensive studies of all potential security threats in their particular sectors of the frontier. The job of collating all of this material and wielding it into a coherent whole fell to Obruchev, who had finished his memorandum "Considerations on the Defense of Russia" by early January 1873. That document set the agenda for the security conference.[76]

"Preserving peace," wrote Obruchev, "all prepare for war. Therefore we also must urgently take steps for the defense of the security of the Empire, all the more so, since now the transition from peace to war is accomplished, so to speak, instantaneously."[77] Obruchev went on to point out that the political, economic, and technological changes that had recently occurred in Europe had combined seriously to imperil Russia should war break out in Europe in the immediate future. Russia would be most likely to face a coalition of enemies, including as a bare minimum Austria-Hungary and Germany. Although the total number of forces Russia could eventually field in war outnumbered those of its potential Teutonic adversaries, and although it had made cuts in the amount of time necessary for its own mobilization since the mid-1860s, the German powers still had a considerable edge in mobilization and concentration speed. It would require 54–58 days for Russia fully to ready itself for war with Germany, and 63–70 days to prepare against Austria. The Germans and Austrians, would, by contrast, be capable of opening full-scale military operations on M+20 and M+30, respectively.[78] The reason for the difference, not surprisingly, was the superiority of the Austrian and German railway nets over the Russian.* For example, Russia had only four lines running to the German frontier, whereas the German army could use ten to deploy against Russia. That meant Russia would face the gravest dangers in the opening period of a campaign, when Berlin and Vienna could take advantage of their temporary superiority in numbers and mobility to conquer vast territories of the Russian Empire at very little risk to themselves. Obruchev estimated that by the thirtieth day after the proclamation of mobilization the Germans could overrun most of northern and central Poland plus Lithuania. As for the Austrians, Obruchev believed that they would be capable of seizing southern Poland and northwestern Volynia in the same period. The Polish salient, its undefended flanks offering a tempting opportunity for enemy combined operations, was the single weakest point in the Russian Empire's western defenses. The situation was so bleak that the conclusion was inescapable: in Obruchev's words, "the armed forces of Russia in their present condition [were] insufficient for the defense of her security."[79]

The conference convened by Miliutin to discuss the issues Obruchev had raised started its deliberations on the last day of February and concluded them on the last day of March 1873. Working under the personal chairmanship of the Tsar, the conferees consisted of the Ministers of War, Marine, Foreign Affairs, and Internal Affairs; two field marshals (Berg and Bariatinskii), ten military district commanders; and five Grand Dukes, including the heir to the throne. Debate revolved around the package of measures Obruchev and the War Ministry proposed to overcome the threat to Russia's security in the west.

---

*It may be useful here to draw a distinction between mobilization and concentration. Mobilization time refers to the period necessary to call up the reserves of a particular unit or military district, in order to bring it up to full combat strength. Concentration time is time necessary to transport the troops to their preplanned deployments on the frontiers. M+20 is the twentieth day after the declaration of mobilization.

First, the ministry wanted a crash program of military railway construction, requiring an outlay of 250–300 million rubles over a ten-year period. Five thousand versts of roads were to be built. One thousand (within Poland) would provide Russia with three lines to the Vistula plus a set of links between its defensive positions on that river and the fortresses of Ivangorod, Brest, Warsaw, and Novogeorgievsk. The remaining four thousand versts of lines would connect the Polish, Volynian, and Lithuanian advance theaters with the Russian heartland.[80] Second, Miliutin and his aides advocated the appropriation of 44 million rubles (also to be disbursed over a decade) for fortifications within Poland. Fortresses for the protection of the northern and southern Polish flanks were to be built at Grodno, Osovets, Kovno, and Dubno, while defensive works between the Bug, Narew, and Vistula would turn that entire region into a base for the protection of Warsaw.[81] To increase Russia's complement of trained reservists, the War Ministry urged that the law on universal military service obligation be enacted without delay. Finally, because the German and Hapsburg empires would continue to possess the advantages of speedier concentration and mobilization for some time to come, Russia's military strategists proposed a partial redeployment of the army to plug the most obvious holes and gaps in the empire's western defenses. They simultaneously recommended increasing the size of the active army by eight divisions; the newly raised units would all be stationed in Poland.[82]

The plan implicitly conveyed how the Russian War Ministry perceived the shape and character of a future war. It also provided information about the manner in which the ministry preferred to fight it. Before discussing the outcome of the strategic conference, it is worth pausing for a moment to consider those features of the plan.

The War Ministry recognized, of course, that the Russian Empire faced potential security threats on all its extremities. Yet central to the argument it made in 1873 was the premise that the strategic situation in Central Europe was so ominous that all other dangers had to take a back seat. That did not mean the integrity of Russia's frontiers in Central Asia, the neglect of coastal defenses in the south, or the rumblings of nationalism in the Balkans were no longer of concern. But the Russian Empire could not deploy forces in strength everywhere, nor could it draft foolproof plans for every contingency. In the opinion of the War Ministry, it was better to arm thoroughly against the most serious of the threats that confronted Russia than to dissipate its defense effort among a number of theaters. It should be noted that technical rather than political considerations lay at the basis of this threat assessment. The War Ministry was not making political judgments about what sorts of wars were more or less probable than others. Instead, it was predicating its recommendations about Russia's future defense effort on the comparative offensive capabilities of Russia's potential enemies. In Miliutin's view, Austria-Hungary and Germany were the states with the ability to do the greatest harm to Russia. It did not matter whether Berlin or Vienna was currently plotting a war against Russia or not.[83] The fact was, if they ever opted for war they had the power to defeat Russia. The consequences of a potential defeat in Central Europe were particularly grave because if Russia lost there it might lose everywhere. Overwhelmed militarily by Germany and Austria, humbled by defeat, Russia would be unable to prevent its other neighbors from pressing territorial claims against it. In that event, the empire might collapse utterly. In view of this, the War Ministry felt that Russia had to concentrate the bulk of its attention on the single European war scenario while downplaying all others. As we shall see, that style of thinking would later have serious implications.

The Obruchev–Miliutin plan also contained prescriptions about the manner in which Russia would wage this European war. Because the war would begin with a foreign invasion, Russia at first would be on the defensive. It would be, however, a defense of a particular kind. Rather than follow the traditional expedient of withdrawing into the heartland of the country, as Peter I and Barclay de Tolly had done when confronted by superior attacking forces, Russia would meet the enemy in its border provinces, relying on the defensive power of modern technologies to stem the enemy attack. The War Ministry's proposal of 1873, with its requirements for high-priced railroads and fortifications, did not envision Russia's engaging in an offensive arms race with the Teutonic powers. Instead Russia would employ the technology it was purchasing to compensate for its initial numerical inferiority. Fortifications and defensive works would sap the momentum of the enemy's offensive if he attempted to attack them directly. If he tried to bypass them, the Russian High Command could use them as staging areas for thrusts at the enemy's flanks and rear. Meanwhile, the expanded network of railways would shift troops rapidly to any threatened point, while also bringing in reservists and reinforcements by the thousands from the heart of the country. Once the balance of forces was more equal, Russia would engage in a battle or set of battles to defeat the enemy armies in detail. Only after that had been achieved would Russia embark on offensive operations of its own. Since the War Ministry supposed that Austria and Germany would be committing almost all of their available troops to the invasion of Russia, once those armies had been destroyed the roads to Budapest, Vienna, and Berlin would be open. With the capture of any of these cities, the war would come to an end.

A final assumption undergirding the plan of 1873 was that the war would be short. It is sometimes argued that Prussia's rapid victories in 1866 and 1870 so deluded the General Staffs of the European Great Powers that they prepared ever after exclusively for short wars, blind to the possibility of a protracted struggle. In reality, the reasons for the interest in the short war were both more rational and more complex than that would suggest. Of course, in view of the horrors of war, a short victorious conflict is objectively more desirable than a long one. In the opinion of the Russian War Ministry the purpose of Austrian and German efforts to speed up mobilization was to eliminate uncertainty. The temporary preponderance of power they would enjoy before Russia could bring all of its strength to bear might, if properly employed, enable them to win rapidly. That was indeed what German military planners had in mind in the event of a war with Russia.[84] "It became clear to all," Obruchev wrote somewhat later, "that overwhelming success goes to him who mobilizes his army more quickly, concentrates it more quickly, and strikes his still unprepared opponent with mass."[85] The preference of the Teutonic powers for a short war, then, derived from the fact they clearly found the prospect of victory in a longer one less certain. In effect, the Russian generals agreed with that analysis; unless it took steps to prevent it, Russia was in real jeopardy of being quickly defeated by the German powers. But what was the best way to respond to the German threat? If Russia sought to frustrate the German plan by merely trying to drag the war out, it courted hazards of another sort. If it were to execute a strategic withdrawal into the interior, it would lose Poland, a disaster that might ignite nationalist conflagrations in every other border district of the empire. Further, a strategic withdrawal from the Transvistula provinces might not even be possible, as Russian forces within the Polish salient might be enveloped by coordinated German and Austrian thrusts from the north and the south. Nor did it do Russia any good to place its hopes on the transformation of Poland into an impregnable fortress capable of repulsing enemy attacks indefinitely. In the thinking of the Ministry of War, a protracted defense of that sort, even if it could be maintained, was no solution. Such a posture, while warding off Russian defeat, was no guarantee of Russian victory. It followed that the best method of waging war against the Central Powers—the least expensive, most cost-effective, and most promising—was to accept the enemy's short war scenario and defeat it head on. Were Russia to slow the invading forces down, reinforce, and crush them, it would not only have denied its adversaries a quick victory, but would have achieved one for itself. After the obliteration of the German and Austrian armies in the east, Obruchev estimated, Russia could be in Vienna or Berlin within a month.[86]

The ins and outs of the sessions at the strategic conference of 1873 do not concern us here. Although Miliutin had to confront some criticism of his proposal on strictly military grounds, in the end the conference accepted it virtually in its entirety, albeit only in principle. Implementation of the proposal was deferred until the money to pay for it could be found.[87] Unfortunately, the money to pay for it was not going to be found, largely because the Minister of Finance, Count Reutern, was unalterably opposed to large military expenditures. In a secret response to the Miliutin–Obruchev proposal, drafted prior to the strategic conference, Reutern complained that too much was already being spent on the army. The state, he asserted, could not afford to provide much more, adding that "the destruction of the monetary system, the insolvency and consequent liquidation of banks, economic enfeeblement and the disarray of the finances were the consequences of the Crimean War . . . our finances even now have not entirely recovered." Reutern went on to argue that prosperity, fiscal solvency, and a well-developed infrastructure were more beneficial to the national security than the possession of large arsenals of weapons, especially if they were acquired through deficit financing. Once again he tried to bolster his point by referring to the Crimean War: "If, in the period prior to the war, the annual savings of the people had not been exhausted unproductively by deficits but had been used for transport, communications, and the development of industry, trade, and agriculture, then the outcome of this war would have been different in the financial and, it is possible to presume, even in the military respect."[88] That was, of course, a disingenuous analogy, because the bulk of the money Miliutin was now requesting was precisely earmarked to improve Russian communications and transportation. Even the Ministry of Transport and Communications had agreed that Miliutin's proposed railways were desirable from a commercial as well as from a strategic point of view.[89] Reutern's position, however, was firm. He was determined not to raise taxes, which would further burden the empire's population. He made the Ministry of War a top offer of only 174.29 million rubles for 1874, to be followed by a payment of 179.29 million every year from 1875 through 1878.[90]

Toward the end of 1872, War Ministry personnel had released into limited circulation a report comparing Russia's and Germany's defense expenditures to the detriment of the former. The War Ministry evidently hoped that the document would strengthen its hand both during the strategic conference and in the budgetary process to follow. Reutern ordered his subordinates to prepare a formal rebuttal. In it they accused the War Ministry of falsifying its statistics, invoked Russia's glorious defeat of Napoleon in 1812, and concluded by observing that "history can testify that the Russian people do not stint their sacrifices or spare their strength when the minute to defend the Russian cause arrives." A war of pamphlets ensued when the Main Staff responded to Reutern's paper with a counterblast of its own.[91] Even allowing for its partisanship, this latter document's justification of large defense outlays provides additional insight into the Ministry's conception of the gravity of the security crisis. Military expenditure, the Main Staff wrote, had always been a burden to nations and peoples. But there were circumstances under which such a burden could not be avoided, most particularly "when powerful neighbors arm themselves, furnish themselves with improved arms, build fortresses, provide themselves with strategic railway lines, and become capable of hurling armies of millions of men against a foreign country." If Russia shirked the burden of a proper defense when faced by those challenges, it could well be "wiped off the earth by history." The Main Staff was particularly contemptuous of Finance's attempt to use the War of 1812 to suggest that high levels of defense spending were not really necessary. In fact the Finance Ministry's references to the Patriotic War provided an irresistable rhetorical opening:

> Perhaps from the point of view of financial management it is more convenient to wait to expend revenues on state defense until that fatal moment when the enemy, passing over the Berezina and through Smolensk, is burning Moscow, covering the entire country with fire and destruction . . . he who truly wishes to defend the Russian cause must, before all else, preserve both the people and the state precisely from that fatal minute which would demand from them the burning of the towns and the capital, the destruction of all the productive forces and villages of Russia. Neither an army, nor weapons, nor military ammunition can be created in minutes. Time is necessary for these things . . . when the people themselves begin to defend the Russian cause on the ashes of their homes, it is already too late to apply to the state treasury for credits.[92]

But the Minister of Finance and many of the other delegates to the strategic conference were not as convinced as the War Ministry that Russia needed to take emergency action to prop up its security. Perhaps many of them believed, as did Foreign Minister Gorchakov, that Russia could negotiate some sort of agreement with Germany and Austria that would at least temporarily reduce the danger in Central Europe. The elderly Prince was already at work on what would become, within a few months, the Three Emperors' League. Perhaps other conferees felt Reutern was correct to emphasize that an incontinent expansion in military outlays could derail the internal reform and development that was so cherished a part of the government's program. The protocols of the conference have not survived, so we cannot be absolutely certain about why the delegates took the decision that they did. Miliutin, however, knew that he had been defeated. Of what use was his defense program without the revenues to fund it? Still worse, later in 1873 Reutern succeeded in imposing a cap on the growth of the War Ministry budget, in theory binding until the end of the decade.[93] The last entry in Miliutin's private diary for 1873 testified to his despair: "[A]fter the sad outcome of the secret conference on military matters held in the beginning of the year and with the establishment of a normal military budget for the War Ministry, it became impossible for me to attend to the affairs of military reconstruction with that independence and energy with which I had conducted them in the previous eleven years."[94]

An Interim Strategy for Russia: Technologists into Magicians and the Horse Against the Machine

The discouragement of the War Minister, however, did not excuse him from his obligation to defend the Russian Empire. Miliutin, Obruchev, and the Main Staff had to try to develop the best strategy they could despite the limited resources available. In order to understand the decisions taken, we must view them against the backdrop of the then current debate about Russian military power.

One of the most interesting controversies in Russian military thinking for the past 20 years has been that between a group that might be termed "the technologists" and another that might be called "the magicians."[95] The technologists, who made their debut after the Crimean war, were military intellectuals who held that Russia's traditional style of warfare—based in large measure on the expendability, endurance, and courage of its peasant conscripts—was no longer adequate to the demands of modern warfare. In the view of the technologists, if Russia was to win wars against first-class European opponents in the future, it could do so only if supplied with a sufficient stock of modern armaments. Russia could no longer afford to ignore or deprecate advances in military technologies, for technological mastery was, increasingly, a precondition for victory on the battlefield. By contrast, magicians held that Russian soldiers possessed compensatory qualities that might allow them to fight with inferior equipment yet prevail notwithstanding. During the *ancien régime,* those qualities were variously identified. Some pointed to the fervent religious faith of the Russian soldiers, while others, later influenced by social Darwinist thinking, would laud the inherent "racial characteristics" of the Slav. After 1917 Soviet magicians, for their part, would emphasize the motivational power of Communist ideology. Regardless of the different talismans the magicians believed in, they were united in arguing that wars were won by men, not by machines. That being so, Russia was in fact blessed, because its soldiers were superior to those in other armies. Owing to the magical properties of faith, ideology, or "race," Russian soldiers were capable of outsuffering, outlasting, and outfighting any other soldiers in the world. General M. I. Dragomirov, tactician, military psychologist, and magician par excellence of the 1860s and 1870s, wrote: "able to suffer, able to die—this is the foundation of the martial prowess which is peculiar to the Russian soldier in the highest degree."[96]

Obviously it would be inappropriate to press this distinction too hard. Russian military history does, of course, afford examples of some figures who drew inspiration from both quarreling camps, or who defected from one to the other, in the course of their careers. Each approach did have something to recommend it: the increasing technological complexity of warfare did not in fact make the question of a soldier's morale and motivation irrelevant. Yet in their extreme form, of course, neither view was satisfactory, since both were reductionist and devalued strategy to boot. Technological enthusiasts in effect could substitute technology for strategy, while pure magicians could put tactics in strategy's place. Yet the two categories provide a useful way of conceptualizing some of the most important polemics and trends in Russian and Soviet military policy since the Crimean War. If Dragomirov was a magician, Leer was a technologist. During World War I, Nikolai Nikolaevich, Russia's first supreme commander, belonged to the first group, while General Alekseev, the Emperor's eventual chief of staff, adhered to the second. There are many illustrations of similar pairings in the Soviet period as well: Frunze and Trotskii; Budennyi and Tukhachevskii; Sokolovskii and Gareev.

Miliutin and Obruchev were both technologists by temperament and conviction. The plan that they developed and promoted in 1872 and 1873 was a technologist's plan, predicated on the acquisition by Russia of sophisticated armaments, fortifications, and a strategic railway network. But absent the money to pay for those things, the plan could not be executed. By the time Alexander II was assassinated in 1881, *none* of the railroads proposed by the Ministry of War in 1873 had been built, save a small stretch between Bender and Galats that had been constructed during the Russo-Turkish war.[97]

What was the Russian army to do? Clearly, some sort of interim strategy had to be found until the Ministry of War could succeed in wresting sufficient appropriations from the tsarist state to make the preferred strategy—that of 1873—workable. An initial expedient was a redeployment of the artillery and infantry in the frontier zone. Since Russia was going to have to accept inferiority in mobilization and concentration indefinitely, it made sense to withdraw those units from the immediate vicinity of the border. Because their mobility was limited and because a rapid reinforcement had to be ruled out, the infantry battalions and artillery batteries would most certainly be overwhelmed by the invading tides of Germans and Austrians were they to continue to be stationed along lines that closely paralleled the contours of the frontier. A new dislocation scheme, approved in April 1874, mandated the deployment of the bulk of the infantry and artillery in the western military districts behind the natural barriers of the Narew, Bobr, Bug, and Vistula rivers.[98]

That measure was a palliative, not a solution. Obruchev's original goal had been to check the onslaught of the invader with fortifications and troops rapidly concentrated by railroad. Now he had neither fortifications nor railroads, and something had to be found to make up for their lack. After agonizing over the problem, the War Ministry finally decided to try to employ the Russian cavalry to achieve the results that railroads and fortresses had been destined to play in the event of war. Accordingly, the War Ministry detached a sizable proportion of its cavalry deployed in the west, moved it up to the border areas, and entrusted it with a new mission. If war between Russia and the Germanic powers broke out, the Russian cavalry was immediately to gallop across the frontiers and fan out into Galicia, East Prussia, and Moldavia, burning down railway bridges, attacking troop trains, and demolishing military depots. The raids would have a dual purpose. First, the cavalry could collect tactical intelligence about the precise strength of the enemy forces and their axes of advance, thus permitting Russia to make prudent counterdispositions. Second, and more important, the mounted raiders were supposed to cripple the German and Austrian concentration, disrupt the calculations of the invaders, and by so doing *buy the Russian army as much time as possible* to complete its own mobilization and concentration. It was, in short, an attempt to pit the horse against the machine.

Thus Miliutin, Obruchev and their associates, all originally technologists, found themselves perforce transformed into reluctant magicians embracing a strategy that substituted horseflesh and daring for revetments and locomotives. Their strategy was taken with the utmost of seriousness; every effort was made to prepare to execute it. Beginning at the end of 1873, some of the most talented of the students at the General Staff Academy were enlisted to help articulate the plan.[99] The new cavalry dispositions were rushed into effect. By 1880 Russia had deployed sixty-four squadrons of cavalry on the 1,000 versts of its German frontier and an equal number on the 800 versts of its common border with Austria-Hungary.[100] This amounted to almost 40 percent of all the cavalry in the Russian army. In fact, for the next thirty-five years there would always be Russian cavalry units stationed in the western marches of the empire, constantly training for the moment when they would be summoned to dash off into Germany or Hungary on spoiling raids against enemy mobilization.

This interim strategy still envisioned the climatic battles of a future European war being fought close to the border, rejecting a strategic withdrawal for the same reason that the optimal strategy of 1873 had: the fear of losing Poland. But it was different in at least one key respect from its predecessor. The 1873 strategy purported to offer Russia the means to fight and win a Central European war quickly. By contrast, that of the mid-1870s posited that Russia could not succeed in any war in Europe that was not a protracted conflict of between six months and a year in duration. Assuming that Russia's relative backwardness in railway transportation would not be overcome any time soon, Obruchev recognized that Russia required more time than ever to mobilize and concentrate the forces it would need to have any chance whatsoever of containing, let alone repulsing, the invading armies. In view of the paucity of the resources on which the War Ministry could count by the mid 1870s, a short war would be, by definition, a war that Russia would lose. But that did not mean Russia could be confident of winning a long war either. There was no pledge of eventual victory built into the interim strategy, only the modest promise that if it worked, Russia might avoid an early defeat. In sum, the interim strategy was not for winning a war but for not losing one.

It was also possible, of course, that the interim strategy might collapse. There was no real guarantee that the forays of Russian dragoons and cossacks would be sufficient to retard German and Austrian concentration by weeks or even days. Conceivably, Russian cavalry might be neutralized by the enemies' own horse. Then, too, the damage done by cavalry raiding might turn out to be superficial and easily repaired. Even if the damage was deep and abiding, few in the Russian Main Staff had any delusions about what the fate of the cavalry troopers committed to those operations would be: they would be riding to annihilation. That in turn might eventually bear bitter fruit, because the bloody sacrifice of the cavalry in the beginning of the war might deprive the army of the means to collect intelligence or screen its maneuvers later.

The Main Staff and the War Ministry did not freely select the interim strategy from a range of alternatives; it would not be too much to say that the force of circumstances virtually imposed that strategy upon them against their wishes. Given its inherent riskiness, the interim plan was, naturally enough, a source of great strategic anxiety and pessimism. Although the army's mobilization committee concluded in early 1876 that there was *as of then* little danger of a rapid invasion of Russia by an enemy, it was widely recognized that, unless Russia constructed more strategic railroads, the chances of successfully implementing even the interim strategy were growing dimmer every year, for there was no letup at all in the Austrian or German railway building program.[101] Thus it was that the Russian Ministry of War, already Eurocentric in orientation by the early 1870s, became still more passionately Eurocentric as the decade passed. The Central European threat grew to dwarf all others in the thinking of Russia's professional strategists. They neglected to plan for other contingencies or to prepare other theaters, obsessed as they were with salvaging as many resources as they could for the defense of the western portions of the empire. Although thoroughly understandable, this was to some degree unfortunate, since long before Russia would ever confront the Germanic powers it would take up arms against Turkey in the last major war fought on the Continent of Europe in the nineteenth century.

Russian statecraft on the eve of the Turkish war of 1877–78 was characterized by the same caution and hesitation that had marked Russia's conduct of international relations since the signing of the Peace of Paris. Russia's plans for the war demonstrated the evolution in War Ministry thinking over the past twenty years. The Ministry's approach to the conflict was informed by the spirit of the Miliutin reforms insofar as it was alive to the social and economic implications of warfighting. Russian strategy for the war, very much shaped by Obruchev, reflected the tension between his innate strategic pessimism and the involuntary strategic optimism he had been forced to assume as a newly baptized magician. Russia's military performance in the war illustrated both the strengths and the weaknesses of the Miliutin reforms. Finally, the outcome of the war led to the overlay of new paradigm of vulnerability upon the old.

Background to War

Although Greece was independent, and Rumania, Montenegro, and Serbia were autonomous, in the third quarter of the nineteenth century the Ottoman Empire still controlled much of the Balkan peninsula. The nationalistic and religious passions of Turkey's Christian subjects there finally exploded in 1875, when the Bosnians, and eventually the people of Herzegovina as well, rose up in revolt against their Ottoman overlords. That event reopened the dormant Eastern Question. In the Balkan provinces there was considerable hope that Russia might intervene against the Turks to protect the interests of Christianity and Slavdom. Yet St. Petersburg was as wary now as it had been in the past. To be sure, there was sympathy in the tsarist government for the plight of the oppressed Slavs, but that sympathy was balanced by a strong disinclination for any unilateral Russian military involvement. The Ministries of War, Finance, and Foreign Affairs were unanimous in agreeing that war was undesirable. In the first place, the army was not yet ready to wage one. Then, too, a Balkan conflict with Turkey might well undo the process of internal reform and consume the surpluses of the treasury. Finally, Prince Gorchakov cowered at the prospect of arousing the other powers of Europe into another anti-Russian coalition.

The new Eastern crisis alarmed statesmen in the other capitals of Europe as well. Bismarck feared for the survival of the Dreikaiserbund should the crisis produce a rupture between Austria and Russia. It was precisely such a rupture that Disraeli was hoping for, as he followed the traditional British policy of backing up the Turks as a bulwark against the Russians. To the statesmen in Vienna, the potential weakening or collapse of Ottoman Turkey was viewed with terror. If Russia were to grow stronger at Turkey's expense, Vienna would feel threatened, just as it would by the creation of independent Balkan states whose very existence might inflame Slavic nationalism within the Dual Monarchy itself.

From the Russian point of view it was vital that Russia not be perceived as acting alone. Over the next two years the goal of its policy was to organize a common démarche by all of the Great Powers to force Turkey to grant meaningful reforms. To a certain extent, Germany and Austria shared the Russian desire for joint management of the Eastern crisis; London, however, did not. The latent opposition of the British, the intransigence of the Turks, and the frustration of the Balkan Slavs conspired to defeat any attempts for a diplomatic resolution of the Balkan problem. The Andrassy note of December 1875, prepared by the Austrian Foreign Minister in consultation with the Russians, would have obliged Turkey to promise civil equality for its Christian subjects, in addition to programs of land and tax reform. Although the Porte accepted Andrassy's proposal, the Bosnian rebels condemned it as too little and too late. In April 1876 the crisis deepened when the people of Bulgaria joined the insurrection. The Berlin memorandum, a cooperative attempt by Bismarck, Andrassy, and Gorchakov to restate the demands of the previous year, failed owing to political instability in Constantinople and its repudiation by the British. In June and July the principalities of Montenegro and Serbia declared war on Turkey. Much to the embarrassment of St. Petersburg, thousands of Russian officers resigned their commissions and entrained for Belgrade to offer themselves as volunteers in the Slavic cause. Prince Milan of Serbia even entrusted command of his army to a Russian general—the overrated conqueror of Tashkent, M. Cherniaev.

By the early summer of 1876 many in Europe believed that they were finally witnessing the death agony of the Ottoman Empire. Turkey seemed to be on the verge of total decomposition. Its finances had been ruined by excessive foreign borrowing and corruption; its Sultan, Murad V, was clinically insane; and its military efforts were now overtaxed by the dual burden of defeating the Serbian army and pacifying Bosnia, Bulgaria, and Herzegovina. Russia and Austria hastily concluded the Reichstadt Convention in July, a treaty promising each other modest territorial concessions in the Balkans once the Turkish Empire had collapsed. Russia was to acquire the chunk of southern Bessarabia it had lost in 1856, while Vienna was to seek compensation in northern Bosnia. The agreement was, however, premature. Contrary to most predictions, the Turks quickly crushed the Serbian forces. In September Russia felt constrained to impose an armistice by threatening war, and backed up its threat by mobilizing forces in Odessa, Khar'kov, and the Caucasus military district.[102]

In Bulgaria Turkey's irregular Circassian troops (the Bashi-Bazouks) suppressed the rebellion by waging war on the entire civilian population, looting, raping, burning, and slaughtering possibly as many as 10,000 noncombatants. The massacres outraged public opinion throughout Europe, but the reaction was particularly strong in Britain. There the great Liberal leader W. E. Gladstone authored a best-selling pamphlet (*The Bulgarian Horrors and the Question of the East*) that stimulated popular revulsion against Disraeli's policy of support for Turkey.[103]

When Turkey rejected yet another round of reform proposals at the end of 1876, Gorchakov began to make diplomatic preparations for war. The first task was to secure Austrian neutrality. By the Budapest Convention of January 1877, in return for its pledge of neutrality, Russia tendered Austria the right to occupy Bosnia and Herzegovina, if it so chose. St. Petersburg further promised Vienna that it would not create any large Slavic states in the Balkans in the aftermath of a victorious war.[104] Gorchakov then turned around and negotiated transit rights for the Russian army across Rumania. Finally he schemed to outmaneuver the British. N. P. Ignat'ev convinced Britain to subscribe to the London protocol of March 1877, another program for Turkish reforms. If the Turks rejected it (as in fact they did) a Russian decision for war could be explained as a last attempt to force Turkey to comply with the demands of all the Great Powers, not just Petersburg alone. The explanation might not be accepted by everyone in London, but along with the political controversy raging over the Eastern question, it might be just enough to inhibit a strong British response to the outbreak of a Russo-Turkish war.[105]

Strategy for War

Miliutin and his colleagues at the War Ministry observed the early stages of all of those Balkan crises with alarm, hoping that diplomacy might somehow obviate the necessity of war. In a meeting with Gorchakov on November 9, 1875, for instance, Miliutin emphasized that it was a matter of the highest importance to resolve the rebellion in Bosnia without recourse to military intervention.[106] But as the months went by, it became increasingly apparent that war might come whether desired by Russia or not. Preparations began in earnest in 1876. The War Ministry was able to persuade the Tsar to approve an appropriation of 1.4 million rubles to hire the services of seventeen southern railway lines should war break out.[107] The Ministry also elaborated the first series of tentative war plans. In May 1876 Colonel N. D. Artamov of the Military Education Committee prepared such a plan, buttressed with an elaborate historical analysis of what had gone right (and wrong) in all previous Russo-Turkish wars since the late eighteenth century.[108] Major General Levitskii followed that in October with an even more operationally detailed memorandum of his own.[109] N. N. Obruchev's series of notes (February–April 1877) to the Emperor and Miliutin, however, proved to be the definitive statements of the initial strategy for the conflict.

While recognizing the war could be "truly a great disaster for us," Obruchev denied that Russia needed peace at any price. At issue was Russia's prestige and security. If Russia was excessively

THE TURKISH WAR OF 1877-78

SCUTARI
CONSTANTINOPOL
SAN STEFANO
Sea of Marmora

Black Sea

VARNA

SILISTRIIA

SHUMLA

ADRIANOPOL

RUSHCHUK

BUCHAREST

TYRNOVO

SHIPKA

ZIMNITSA
SISTOVA

FILIPPOPOL

PLEVNA

Danube River

SOFIA

VIDIN

accommodating, offered extravagant concessions, or watered down the demands it had made on Constantinople, then the other powers of Europe would have reason to suspect Russia of weakness. Should that happen, Russia could "within a few months be dragged into a decisive war but under completely different, incomparably worse circumstances."[110] In other words, if Russia declined to fight Turkey now, the other European powers, interpreting this as a confession of impotence, might combine against Russia later. Even if a general European war did not occur, the consequences for Russian foreign relations might be serious. In his memorandum of February 13, 1877, Obruchev stressed that Russia could not afford to disperse the troops it had mobilized the previous year until it had resolved the Balkan crisis. In Obruchev's opinion, Turkey had to be compelled to make concessions to the Christian provinces of its Empire. If Russia demobilized its forces without achieving them, this would "almost correspond to a second lost Crimean campaign" in terms of the decay of Russia's international standing that might result.[111] As Obruchev saw it, the costs of war (high as they were likely to be) were still lower than the costs of refusing to fight.

But how should Russia fight? Here Obruchev supplied some prescriptions. In the first place the war had to be won quickly. Obruchev revealingly observed:

> We have no choice. We are not free to pose the question: is it possible or impossible to end the war in one campaign? It must be ended in one campaign, as we do not have the resources for a second, and moreover, because then we would have to fight not only Turkey but with all of those who are only waiting for our exhaustion. It is necessary quickly to put an end to the matter and suppress the Turks, while we still preserve the entire extent of our strength and have not revealed our weakness.[112]

Thus precisely because Russia was feeble, it had to achieve an early victory, both in order to husband its resources and to prevent its potential West European enemies from understanding and exploiting that feebleness through military threats or declarations of war.

But was there any sure-fire way for Russia to defeat the Turks rapidly? Obruchev was convinced that there was. First, the out-break of the war had to be carefully timed; diplomacy had to cooperate with strategy. Obruchev expected the war to open with a Turkish rejection of a Russian ultimatum. The ultimatum should be issued to the Turks either in early March or at the very end of April to facilitate the immediate invasion of the Turkish Empire, because the Danube was impassable for much of the third and fourth months of the year, when its annual flooding occurred.[113] Second, the war had to come as a surprise to the Turks. Although Russia could not concentrate its forces for war as swiftly as its western neighbors could, a significant proportion of troops—some 546,000—had been mobilized and held at the ready since 1876. Those units, available at once, should be the spearhead of a sudden and unanticipated Russian attack that would catch the Turks off guard, accustomed as they had be-come over the past twenty months to specious warnings and protracted negotiations. Finally (and most importantly), Russia had to choose a single strategic objective and focus all of its energies upon it. That objective would be the Turkish capital, Constantinople. "In order to attain decisive results the goal of our strategic operations, more than ever, must be Constantinople itself," Obruchev wrote in April. "Only on the shores of the Bosphorus is it possible to smash the domination of the Turks and obtain a firm peace once and for all settling our quarrel with them on behalf of the Balkan Christians."[114] Obruchev recog-nized that what he proposed was hazardous. Russia's forces would have to cross the Danube, contend with strong Turkish fortresses, traverse the Balkan passes, and then defeat the large Constantinople garrison. Yet he maintained that it was *not* absurd to dream of capturing the Turkish capital; it was highly feasible, he argued, if Russia's commanders were sufficiently bold and energetic to drive into the heart of European Turkey before Constantinople's defenses could be strengthened or the English could declare war and land troops. Obruchev was in effect pro-posing to refight the war of 1853, getting it right this time.

Operationally, Obruchev recommended dividing Russian forces in Europe into two armies. The first army, comprising 100,000 to 120,000 men, would make a dash on Constantinople just as soon as it had passed over the Danube. That army should make every effort to cover the 500 versts between the Danube and the Bosphorus in four to five weeks. It should consequently by-pass Turkish forts, refuse battle with independent Turkish columns, and, most dangerous of all, make no effort to guard its lines of communication, supply, or retreat. The task of covering the rear of the first army in Bulgaria would fall to the second army, comprising eight infantry divisions, four cavalry divisions, and ten to twelve regiments of Cossacks. As a bare minimum, those units would have to take Rushchuk, since that town was the terminus of the rail link from Russia via Rumania to the Danube; it might also be necessary to capture Shumla. In the Caucasian theater, Obruchev advocated a mere holding operation using the smallest possible number of troops.[115]

If Obruchev was clear about the scope and direction of Russian operations, he was far less so about the political or territorial gains that Russia should seek if the plan worked as intended. Obruchev later denied that Russia had entertained any objective in the war other than the emancipation of Bulgaria. Because the mere Russian seizure of that country would not be enough to coerce the Turks into granting it independence, a Russian campaign against Constantinople had been necessary. Russia never intended, he explained, to annex Constantinople or lay claim to the straits.[116] To be sure, Obruchev's memorandum of April 1877 does contain some evidence that might support such an interpretation of limited Russian intentions: there he speaks of the occupation of Constantinople and the straits "in the military sense" and implies that such occupation would be temporary.[117] Yet the two notes of February suggest that Obruchev's aims were considerably more ambitious than the relief of the downtrodden Bulgars alone. In one of them he spoke of "smashing" the Turkish dominion—presumably everywhere in Europe. And in the other he stated that a "rapid, swift success of our army could strongly influence European opinion and evoke from Europe such concessions about which it is impossible even to think at present."[118] It would appear that Obruchev was as eager as his greater contemporary, Moltke, to allow the ebb and flow of battle to dictate policy.

The Emperor entrusted his brother, the Grand Duke Nikolai Nikolaevich the elder, with the supreme command of Russia's Danubian army. As Obruchev received neither a field nor a staff command, he had no say in the subsequent evolution of the war plan. Nikolai, who was somewhat more cautious than Obruchev, estimated that it would require five to six weeks for Russian troops to march from the Danube to Adrianople, let alone Constantinople.[119] Nikolai and his entourage were to introduce still more modifications in the plan as the war progressed. Yet the general design for the war had been Obruchev's.

While an exhaustive analysis of Obruchev's war plan is not necessary here, several of its more conspicuous defects are noteworthy. First, the plan contained no allowance for friction. It ignored or underestimated the uncertainty that is always an inescapable condition of warfare. Logistics might break down, the weather might be uncooperative, or the enemy might do something unanticipated—and any of those complications (and others besides) might ruin the Russian timetable. If the Russian *coup de main* failed or could not be executed, Obruchev had no fallback position. He admitted himself that if Russia was stopped short of Constantinople or the straits, the only way to end the war would be through "the complete destruction of the land possessions of Turkey in Europe and Asia"—a dubious undertaking that St. Petersburg would be unwise to attempt and unlikely to accomplish.[120]

Second, by demanding such rapid tempos of military advance, the plan placed operational and physical requirements on the troops that probably could not be borne. The unwritten assumption here seemed most definitely to be that of a magician: that Russian soldiers were capable of enduring and achieving anything. Artamonov, Levitskii, Obruchev, and Nikolai Nikolaevich all argued that the forced marches they contemplated would actually save lives, for they would prevent the overexposure of the troops to foul climatic conditions and poor hygiene. That argument was unrealistic, however, because it disregarded human exhaustion, an exhaustion rendered all the more likely given the rough, lightly populated country through which the army would have to pass.

In the third place, the plan was so open-ended about war aims that it is fair to say that its framers had not adequately thought through the problem of war termination at all. Even if Russia surprised Turkey, crushed it quickly, and occupied Constantinople before the other Great Powers woke up to it, why would they necessarily agree "to such concessions about which it is impossible to think at present"?

Finally, the audacity of Obruchev's strategy was the consequence of his estimation of the threat, not from Turkey, but from the Great Powers of Europe. It was a strategy firmly anchored in the dread of anti-Russian coalitions, with which Obruchev and every other tsarist statesman had lived since the conclusion of the Peace of Paris. According to Obruchev, if Russia cravenly backed down from a Turkish war, its western European neighbors would most probably band together to defeat or humiliate it. But equally, a Russian failure to beat the Turks quickly would also expose it to the peril of a new "Crimean coalition," and against such a coalition Russia could not hope to prevail. Obruchev proposed to steer between those two dangers by showing resolve and by winning an implausibly swift victory. Yet Obruchev's strategy for war with Turkey, like his strategy for war in Europe, may have concealed yet another set of assumptions. It is implausible to speculate that the former revolutionary might have internalized the radical theory about the instability of Russian state power? In the 1860s and 1870s the radicals with whom Obruchev had once associated believed that autocratic power in Russia was as fragile as an eggshell. One more serious reverse either at home or abroad might be enough to topple the tsarist empire. Obruchev's near obsession with concealing Russia's weakness from its potential enemies was consonant with that belief. In other words, Obruchev's preference for perimeter defenses in a European war and his unrealistic plans for a quick triumph over Turkey may have stemmed from an inordinately pessimistic assessment of the true strength of Russia. In any event, the failings of the war plan of 1877, just as an intellectual exercise, go a long way toward explaining what went wrong with it in practice.

The Russo-Turkish War: Plan and Reality

The Russian decision for war was made, with much soul-searching, by the Emperor Alexander II. Although both revulsion at Turkey's treatment of its Christian subjects and the clamoring of the Russian press influenced him, it is highly probable that Obruchev's argument that war was *strategically* necessary to defend Russian prestige and to hide Russian weakness also had weight with him. Turkey's rejection of the last ultimatum of the

Powers (the Shuvalov protocol) led to a Russian declaration of war on April 12 (24), 1877. Simultaneously, as had been prearranged, the first Russian units crossed into Rumania. The Turks' initial objective was to check the Russian advance on the banks of the Danube. At first they had every expectation of success. The northern and central reaches of the river were protected by the powerful fortresses of the quadrilateral—Rushchuk, Silistriia, Varna, and Shumla—in addition to Vidin. Also guarding the Danube was the Turkish riverine flotilla, considerably stronger than the Russian. Finally, even the weather seemed to be favoring Turkey; the exceptionally severe Danubian flooding of 1877 persisted into June, thus dashing any Russian hope of bridging the river in the late spring.

But Russia did not waste time. Russia's own Danubian flotilla, although small in size, made skillful use of pole charges to clear the river of Turkish vessels and protected the region of the crossing between Zimnitsa and Sistova by floating hundreds of mines at either end. Once the entire army had struggled over the pontoon bridges and reassembled on the right bank of the Danube, it split into three parts. That, of course, was a divergence from Obruchev's plan. Nikolai Nikolaevich had been unhappy with Obruchev's scheme for an immediate assault on Constantinople by the first army, being of the opinion that it might easily be cut off from its rear bases. In accordance with Nikolai's new dispositions, 70,000 men under the nominal command of the heir to the throne, the future Alexander III, moved east and attacked the fortress of Rushchuk. General Krüdener, leading the 85,000 men of the western detachment, marched on Plevna—strategically important because it was the crossroads of almost all lines of communication in northeastern Bulgaria. Simultaneously, an advance guard of 12,000 men under General Gurko penetrated the Balkans and seized the Shipka Pass. With Rushchuk captured and Plevna in the Russian hands, all of northern Bulgaria would be clear of Turks, while the supply lines back through Rumania into Russian Bessarabia would be secure. At that point, Russian forces, assisted by Rumanian regulars and Bulgarian auxiliaries, could recombine and cross the Balkan mountains, availing themselves of the route that Gurko had opened for them.[121]

Within a few weeks of the passage of the Danube, however, the Nikolai–Obruchev plan began to break down. Turkey's most competent commander, Osman Pasha, outraced Krüdener to Plevna and immediately set about fortifying that town. Krüdener attempted to storm Plevna twice in July but failed on both occasions, incurring heavy casualties. Plevna's successful resistance ruined the prospect for a rapid campaign. As long as Osman held out, the bulk of the Russian forces could not follow Gurko into the Balkans because of the threat posed by the unsubdued Plevna garrison to the army's western flank. In the south, Gurko, denied the reinforcements on which he had been counting, was forced back into the mountains by Sulieman Pasha's superior forces. Suleiman's 27,000 troops now effectively besieged the five thousand Russians holding the high ground in the Shipka Pass. From August 9 to August 11, Gurko's men repelled from ten to fourteen Turkish assaults a day, on many occasions raining heavy stones and boulders down on the enemy in order to conserve their ammunition. By the third day the Shipka defenders were entirely encircled. Annihilation seemed imminent when help materialized in the person of General M. I. Dragomirov, whose successful relief of Gurko at the head of the 14th Infantry Division demonstrated that he had the practical qualities of a soldier in addition to those of a military theoretician.[122]

Meanwhile, both the Russians and the Turks at Plevna had received reinforcements. On August 30, Nikolai Nikolaevich's 84,000 men made their third assault on Plevna's garrison of 36,000. The date had been selected because it was the Emperor's name day. It was an unfortunate choice: heavy rains turned the fields around Plevna into muddy bogs, which greatly complicated the Russian attack. Third Plevna was just as unsuccessful a battle as its two predecessors. Moreover, it was even bloodier; in the attack on the Grivitskii redoubts alone, Russia took 4,000 casualties. At that point the Russian High Command realized that without sufficient preparatory and supporting artillery bombardment, any future attempts to storm Plevna were likely to be futile. Russia's military leadership now decided to change course: Plevna was to be totally blockaded and starved out. The aged General E. I. Totleben, hero of Sevastopol, came down in person from St. Petersburg to supervise the Russian field works. The policy was slow to produce results. Still, by mid-October the Turkish garrison was already on half rations. A month later, with almost all stocks of foodstuffs exhausted, Osman Pasha understood that he had to either break out of Plevna or surrender. When his attempt to fight his way out of the Russian encirclement failed on November 28, Osman immediately capitulated.

After the capture of Plevna the Danubian army was able to resume its southward advance. Unfortunately, it was now winter. Should the Russian army hazard a passage of the Balkans through the snows or wait until the spring to resume operations? To the astonishment of many Western experts, St. Petersburg adopted the former course. On December 27, 1877, Sviatopolk-Mirskii and Skobelev took the key Turkish fortified town near Sheinovo, at the southern end of the Shipka pass, and the route into Turkey proper was opened to Russia's forces. Turkish armies to the south, demoralized by the news that Russia had managed to pierce the protective carapace of the Balkan mountains, now began to disintegrate. By early January 1878 the Russians had reached Plovdiv, and by January 8 [20], Adrianople. Meanwhile the Russian cavalry advance guard had reached the shores of the Sea of Marmora. With the Russian army at the very gates of Constantinople, the Sultan sued for an armistice, which was granted to him on January 19 [31].

As was to be expected, other European capitals—Vienna and London in particular—followed Russia's successes with dismay. Already on January 11 [23], Disraeli's Cabinet had ordered Admiral Hornsby to take Britain's Mediterranean fleet from its anchorage at Smyrna to Constantinople. In response, Russia seized the village of San Stefano, just 6 miles from the capital. On January 30 [February 11] Alexander II telegrammed Nikolai Nikolaevich that in the event of a British landing the Danubian army was immediately to enter Constantinople.[123] Shortly afterward Nikolai learned that a British force of five ironclads had in fact entered the Sea of Marmora. Four days later Miliutin counseled the Tsar to change his mind about the occupation of the city, observing that "obviously England is seeking a pretext for a rupture with us; perhaps war is in any event inevitable, but all the same in my opinion it would be better were we not to provide the pretext that the Queen and her Prime Minister desire."[124]

But the Tsar was not easily dissuaded. News of the peace terms that Russia imposed on Turkey at San Stefano on February 20 [March 3], 1878, did nothing to allay British or Austrian fears.

The Treaty of San Stefano recognized the political autonomy of Bosnia and Herzegovina. Serbia, Montenegro, and Rumania (which had in varying degrees participated in the war as Russian allies) were to receive complete independence. In addition, an enormous Bulgarian state, comprising the old province of Bulgaria plus Dobrudja, Macedonia, and Eastern Rumelia, was to be established under the protection of Russia. For its part, Russia was to receive southern Bessarabia (a foreign policy objective since 1856) and the important Transcaucasian fortresses of Batum and Kars. In Vienna, Foreign Minister Andrassy expressed the feeling that the "Big Bulgaria" violated the terms of the Budapest Convention and urged an immediate Austrian mobilization.[125] Britain now openly began to prepare for war. Alexander II became so convinced of the imminence of war that on March 18 [30] he wrote to urge his supreme commander to press Turkey either to ally itself with Russia against Britain or to declare neutrality. If Turkey were to stand with Russia (however improbably), Alexander wanted it to transfer control of its Bosphorus fortifications on the European side to the Russian army, while immediately entering into negotiations with Nikolai about the coordination of military efforts. If, however, it considered itself too weak to enter the war, it should still surrender the fortifications to Russia prior to demobilizing its army. The only touch of realism in that bizarre missive came in the last paragraph, where Alexander conceded that in either event Russia did not really need to occupy Constantinople, just a few points on the bank of the Bosphorus in order to prepare in-depth defenses.[126] For all his bellicose posturing, Alexander knew that another war was beyond Russia's strength and had come around to Miliutin's position that he ought to be careful not to provoke one. Russia's treasury was empty; its field army encamped outside Constantinople was ravaged by typhus and dysentery.[127] The upshot was that Russia agreed to accept the mediation of Bismarck. Representatives of all of the powers who had signed the 1856 Peace of Paris accordingly assembled in Berlin in the summer of 1878 to review the terms of Russia's treaty with Turkey.

By the decision of the Congress of Berlin a Bulgarian principality was in fact created, but one much smaller than the one Russia had planned. Territories that Russia had designated as Bulgarian at San Stefano were parceled out to other states. Rumania received Dobrudja; Eastern Rumelia was made an autonomous province; and Macedonia was to remain within the Ottoman Empire. Austria would now garrison Bosnia, Herzegovina, and the Sanjak of Novibazar, the swath of formerly Turkish territory that separated Serbia and Montenegro. The other Powers were of course happy with this outcome. Britain was relieved that a Turkish Empire still existed. Both Vienna and London were reassured by the whittling down of Bulgaria from the enormous Russian puppet state they feared to a modest little principality they could tolerate. Austria's new military position in the Balkans allowed it to stand watch over the forces of south Slavic nationalism.[128] Russia, however, felt misused. It had fought for ten months, spent a billion rubles, and incurred more than 200,000 casualties. St. Petersburg considered itself cheated of the fruits of victory it deserved.[129] It emerged from the Congress of Berlin not only angry with Britain and Austria but resentful of Germany, too. Although Bismarck had billed himself as "the honest broker," the diplomat whose task it was impartially to mediate the differences between the Powers, many Russians, who had expected more from him, thought his support against Vienna and London had been intentionally inadequate. News of the terms of the Berlin arrangement naturally enough infuriated Russian Slavophiles, who interpreted it as a betrayal of the Slavic cause. But it also enraged *zemstvo* liberals, who angrily noted that the Bulgarian state was to have a constitution, whereas Russia itself still lacked one. Finally, it breathed new life into the activities of the revolutionary left, which viewed Russia's diplomatic defeat as an opportunity to open a campaign of assassination against state officials.[130]

Eventually the St. Petersburg government came to execrate the Congress of Berlin for translating a glorious Russian victory into an ignominious defeat. The Congress was a turning point in European diplomatic history. Less than a year later, although the Dreikaiserbund was still in full force, Bismarck concluded his Dual Alliance with Austria-Hungary, which included a secret military convention directed against Russia. Although Bismarck may not have intended that treaty as an irrevocable choice, in retrospect it clearly furthered the process of polarization that was to make two armed camps of Europe by August 1914.[131]

War, Military Policy, and Strategy: Some Assessments

It has long been popular among Soviet historians to characterize the Russo-Turkish war as historically progressive, even though autocratic Russia was the nominal victor, because it resulted in the defeat of still more backward Ottoman Turkey and the independence of Bulgaria.[132] Equally popular with both Soviet and Western historians has been the argument that Russia's military performance in the Balkan war validated the military reforms accomplished in the empire in the 1860s and 1870s.[133] It is true that Russia fought better in 1877–78 than it had in the Crimea a generation previously, but it is also true that the Balkan war exposed serious shortcomings in military reforms, military practices, and Russian strategy. Some of them were by no means the fault of the reformers themselves, but others, particularly in the strategic arena, most definitely were.[134]

Take, for example, the issue of rearmament. The process of acquiring modern rifles and cannon for the Russian army, which took more than twenty years, unquestionably enhanced Russian military power. Yet the frequent changes of emphasis during the rearmament program—one rifle being adopted only to be discarded for a newer model—left the Russian soldiers of 1877 without a standard infantry weapon. Some troops were furnished with Krnks, some with Berdans, some with Karlés, and none of those rifles' ammunition was interchangeable with any of the others. Further, good as the new rifles were, they were inferior to those the Turks possessed. The Peabody-Martini rifle of the Turkish forces, sighted in at 1,800 paces, outclassed either the Krnk or the Berdan with their effective ranges of 1,200 and 1,500 paces respectively.[135] What was true for rifles was true for artillery as well. Turkey's Krupp-made steel breech-loaders both fired farther and were more durable than Russian ordnance.[136] The Turkish technological edge was amplified by the fact that Russia's officers had not generally assimilated the tactical lessons of the U.S. Civil War or the Franco-Prussian War. They did not understand that the primacy of the rifle had invalidated the tactics of the first half of the century, which emphasized frontal infantry assaults and close-range fighting with cold steel. They consequently drove their troops forward in closed formations under murderous fire and took thousands of unnecessary casualties—as the bloody mire of third Plevna testified.[137]

The war revealed that there were problems with some of the reforms of military administration, as well. The central Main Administrations, in particular those in charge of medicine and provisions, had great difficulty adapting themselves to the demands of a wartime environment. Logistical and sanitary horrors abounded. At one point the field army entrusted the acquisition of its victuals in Rumania and the Balkans to contractors whose only qualification was their willingness to accept promissory notes, with predictably dismal results.[138] On another occasion, bottlenecks on the Moscow–Riazan railway line resulted in a stack-up of four thousand carloads of troops lasting for several weeks.[139] Although military medicine had improved since the Crimean conflict, morbidity and mortality from sickness remained shockingly high. The sickness rate in the Danubian army was over 140 percent; in the army of the Caucasus it was almost 500 percent.[140] Hygiene was so poor that by May 1878 almost half the army at San Stefano was ailing from fevers.[141] By contrast the military district system seemed to function much better. The mobilization of 1876, carried out by three of the southern districts, had been a success. But the practices of the military districts during the war (and right after it) should have provided food for sober reflection. There was in the end as much risk from excessive decentralization as from centralization. Built into the district system, as we have already seen, was an implicit decentralization of the processes of threat assessment and war planning. That helps to explain the fundamental incoherence and paralysis with which the War Ministry attempted to cope with the possibility of war with Austria and Britain immediately after the signing of the San Stefano agreement: every military district in the northwest, west, and south clamored for reinforcements; each was obsessed with the potential threat to itself to the exclusion of all others.[142] The shadow general staff (the Military Education committee) was to remain just that—a shadow—for a long time.

The conscription system of 1874 had proved undeniably effective. Owing in large measure to it, Russia was able to deploy almost a million troops in the course of the war, including 554,000 in the Balkans and 315,000 in the Caucasus.[143] The war was popular, draft evasion low, and morale high. To the amazement of the tsarist Ministry of the Interior, there were episodes in which enthusiastic recruits covered 100 versts—more than sixty miles—on foot in two days to reach their mobilization depots.[144] The willingness of the troops to endure hardships and sacrifices imposed upon them (often by the blunders of their own commanders) caused some to conclude that Miliutin's dream of a patriotic citizen-soldier was already a reality. For years afterward, "magicians" would cite the fortitude and bravery of the Russian soldiers of 1877 as evidence in favor of their doctrines. But the conclusion was premature and the evidence ambiguous. The war was popular with the masses of peasant recruits because they understood it to be a quasi-holy struggle, almost a crusade, to rescue fellow Christians from the heathen Turk. There was no guarantee that piety could be harnessed so effectively to any war effort in the future. The culture of citizenship, moreover, had not yet come to Russia. Miliutin had hoped that the great reforms would defuse social tensions, dissolve distinctions between the estates, and promote the concept of citizenship, crucial to the maintenance of Russian military power in an era of nationalism and mass armies. But the realization of that program was beyond Miliutin's capabilities. The Great Reforms, admirable as they may have been, proved to be half-measures. In the reign of the next monarch, Alexander III, they were diluted to a great extent by a wave of counterreforms. The social dislocation that resulted from Russia's rapid industrial modernization later in the century would create an urban working class itself increasingly alienated from the tsarist regime. Since an army obviously reflects the strengths and weaknesses of the society behind it, none of those developments boded well for the future performance of Russia's soldiers on the battlefield.

As for the navy, the performance of the Danubian flotilla (in particular its imaginative use of mines), to be sure, had been splendidly innovative. Yet the prudent strategy of Grand Duke Konstantin Nikolaevich had remained unimplemented, owing in part to a shortage of funds. By 1877 Russia possessed 223 ships in its six fleets. Many of them, however, were small vessels, or antiquated wooden ones.[145] The navy was not, in fact, even up to the task of defending the Russian coast. When hostilities with Turkey broke out, Russia's Black Sea fleet consisted in the main of two floating batteries (*popovki*), four elderly wooden corvettes, and a handful of steamboats.* As a consequence the Ministry of War had to deploy 73,000 men throughout the war to guard the Black Sea littoral.[146] Nor was the situation in the Baltic much better. An exhaustive study prepared in 1878, when war with Britain seemed likely, drew the conclusion that Russia did not have the naval assets adequate to protect Finland, and painted a bleak picture of enemy fleets blockading ports, ravaging coasts, destroying port facilities, and temporarily occupying seaside towns.[147]

Insufficient revenues and the promise of an indefinite future of insufficient revenues—the legacy of the conference of 1873—had had important implications for land strategy as well. As I argued earlier in this chapter, the emergence of the German threat coupled with Russian technological backwardness placed Russian strategists in a quandary. Technologists by preference, they were forced to become magicians by necessity. If war came in Central Europe, it had to be protracted by magic. If it came anywhere else, it had to be won quickly by magic, in order to prevent the Germans (and possibly others) from coming into it. In other words, precisely because the overall strategic situation was so gloomy, because Russia was so vulnerable, it had no choice but to take risks. The Turkish conflict taught just how unrealistic the belief in magically quick peripheral campaigns could be. The lesson was not entirely learned. But another lesson was perhaps learned too well—a lesson concerning the nature of victory. The Russo-Turkish war awoke the Russian military elite to a truth long known to any serious student of Clausewitz, namely, that there is really no such thing as purely military victory. Russia had waged war against Turkey determined to avoid all of the mistakes of 1854–56. And it had, in fact, avoided them. With the involuntary aid of the Turks themselves, Russia had managed to isolate Turkey from 1875 to 1877. It had succeeded in fighting the Porte without raising up a coalition of European powers against itself. It had, moreover, won all the significant battles in

---

Popovki were the brainchild of Admiral Popov, who originally supposed that these monstrous circular ironclads, displacing 2,500–3,500 tons, would be maneuverable gunboats of great power. Unfortunately, since they demonstrated an alarming propensity to go about in circles instead of moving in straight lines, they were turned into floating batteries instead.

1877 and 1878. Yet how much difference did it make? Despite all its successes, Russia had failed to achieve the political objectives expressed in the treaty of San Stefano. To the extent that it had failed to achieve them, it had *lost*, not won, the Russo-Turkish war. There was, of course, nothing intrinsically wrong with the Russian Ministry of War's new interest in the issue of war termination. In the abstract, such an interest reflected a salutary intellectual maturity on the part of Russia's military planners. The problem was the way in which those planners conceptualized wars coming to an end, their near fixation on only one means of terminating a war: the international conference. The fear of the Crimean coalition was waning, to be replaced by what we might term "the Congress of Berlin syndrome." That syndrome, and the fears that it engendered, were to haunt Russian statecraft and strategy for years to come.

8

Alliances, Squandered Opportunities, and Self-Inflicted Wounds

Russia Between Two Wars, 1878 – 1903

History never exactly repeats itself, but the parallels between the events that framed the 1878–1903 period and its immediate predecessor are almost uncanny. As had been the case after the Crimean War, Russia in 1878 once again found itself contemplating a military setback, ruined finances, and diplomatic isolation. Russia's military and diplomatic leaders scrambled to extricate Russia from its predicaments, vowing never to repeat the errors of the past, just as they had a generation previously. Yet despite all of their good resolutions, by 1904 Russia was on the verge of a war with Japan that was as least as unnecessary, unwanted, and unplanned-for as the conflict with Turkey had been.

Here, however, the similarities end. The 1878–1903 period was in fact rich in developments that augured well for improvements in Russia's defense posture. First, after the economic dislocation of the Turkish war had been overcome, the Russian economy entered a period of sustained and, in the 1890s, spectacular growth. The economic expansion, if well managed, promised sooner or later to transform the Russian Empire into a state more powerful in every respect, including the military. Second, in response to the military and diplomatic lessons of the 1880s, Russia succeeded in escaping from isolation through a treaty of alliance with France (1892). Russia's leaders had good reason to hope that the Franco-Russian alliance might serve to deter aggression on the part of the Teutonic powers. If a general European war were to break out notwithstanding, the formal relationship with France could improve Russia's chances of winning it, since the Russian War Ministry cynically intended to exploit the French alliance for the sole purpose of making Russia's preexisting plan for an offensive against Austria workable again.

Russia's relative military potential, however, did not substantially improve over this period. Indeed, in key respects it actually deteriorated, especially on the western front. These years saw the emergence of a full-blown arms race in Europe. Russia's ability to keep up with its neighbors was hobbled by the tight-fistedness of its own Ministry of Finance, which prevented the army from profiting greatly from the improving economy of the empire and the concomitant burgeoning revenues of the treasury. The central military leaders perceived such fiscal constraints as an evil, but they viewed the rash Asian imperialism undertaken by Russia at the end of the 1890s as a catastrophe. The turn toward Asia, sponsored at various points by the Ministries of Finance and Foreign Affairs, in addition to the court itself, resulted in the construction of the Trans-Siberian railroad, the seizure of Port Arthur, and the occupation of Manchuria. Those events, combined with maladroit diplomacy, impelled Russia toward a violent confrontation with the Japanese Empire. Still worse, the demands of eastern adventurism starved the Ministry of War of the resources to improve Russia's western defenses. Making the army's financial crisis all the more acute was the fact that by the end of the period military and political considerations had convinced both the generals and the Emperor that Russian security was increasingly dependent on the maintenance of the alliance with France. For that reason it was deemed essential to redraft Russia's war plans to conform to French expectations. The tsarist military now concluded that Russia had to be ready in the event of war to launch dual offensives against Austria-Hungary and Germany. Unsurprisingly, that meant the army had a need for even higher appropriations. But the revenues were not forthcoming. Because of overcommitment, bureaucratic politics, and opportunistic imperialism, in 1904 Russia was ready for war neither in Asia nor in Europe. It had squandered its opportunities and by so doing had left itself more vulnerable than ever before. By the turn of the century Russian strategy for war in Europe far exceeded the empire's military capabilities. It was a strategy of bluff, and the Russian military leadership knew it.

Russia and External Menaces, 1878–1890

In the aftermath of the Turkish war Russia faced the gravest internal problems. The war deficit of more than a billion rubles had obviously disrupted the country's finances. Political problems were, however, even more acute. The People's Will (*Narodnaia volia*) conspiracy, formed in 1879, had resolved to topple the autocracy by means of a terrorist campaign whose chief objective was the murder of the Emperor himself. The government's responded to the terrorist *attendats* by beefing up the police, proclaiming martial law, and finally establishing a temporary military dictatorship under Prince Loris-Melikov. Yet key members of the People's Will party managed to avoid detection and eventually (March 1881) succeeded in assassinating Alexander II with dynamite bombs. That brutal attack stimulated popular revulsion, and the People's Will conspiracy swiftly disintegrated under the reprisals of the new Tsar, Alexander III. However, for almost two and one-half years after the conclusion of the peace, the entire Russian government felt itself to be in a state of siege.

Nor could that government find any consolation in the international environment. Relations with Britain remained poor. In the minds of many prominent Russian statesmen, war with England was still possible, despite London's apparent satisfaction with the outcome of the Congress of Berlin.[1] On top of that came the news of conclusion in 1879 of an alliance between Germany and Austria. At least initially, St. Petersburg was unaware that the secret military convention appended to that document was defensive only. In a confidential memorandum, the Russian Foreign Ministry wrote of the new treaty that it "had all the appearances of an offensive and defensive alliance against Russia."[2] Nor did intelligence intercepts allay Russian fears. In November 1879 Bismarck met with the French Ambassador to Berlin on the subject of the Austro-German alliance; the Frenchman's aide-memoire of the conversation fell into Russian hands. As they read it, Petersburg officials were appalled by the emphasis that the German Chancellor placed on the exclusively anti-Russian character of the new alliance. Other recorded comments by Bismarck were also unlikely to inspire Russian confidence in the sincerity of his personal (and oft-expressed) friendship for Petersburg. The Chancellor had regaled his French guest with a string of gratuitous insults about the chief figures in the Russian government and the Tsar personally ("this prematurely aged man, worn out and enervated by aphrodisiacs, this autocrat without control, the toy of favorites and generals of the boudoir").[3]

Therefore, when Bismarck began to sound Petersburg out about the possibility of renewing the Three Emperors' League, the tsarist government was suspicious. N. K. Giers, soon to be Russia's Foreign Minister but already a power in the formulation of foreign policy, complained to the Tsar that the Chancellor's proposal was grotesquely one-sided: Germany would acquire almost total security, while Russia would be forced into an odious partnership with Austria.[4] But eventually Giers realized that Russia was not in a strong bargaining position. A conference held on December 18, 1879, at the Ministry of Foreign Affairs resolved that Russia had no choice but to accept the German offer, precisely because the Austro-German alliance contained "an eventual menace" against Russia. If Russia refused to join a revived Three Emperors' League, the hostility of Germany "and of all our other adversaries" would surely increase.[5] Russia needed diplomatic ties to Berlin and Vienna, if only to manage the threat posed by the new treaty between the German powers.

Bismarck had thus succeeded, just as he had hoped, in frightening Russia back into a nominally friendly posture. Eventually he was able to manipulate the Austrians as well, and agreements establishing a new Dreikaiserbund were signed in the summer of 1881. The three empires pledged to each other their neutrality in the event of an attack on one of them by a fourth state; Austria gained the right eventually to annex Bosnia and Herzegovina; and Berlin and Austria-Hungary committed themselves to the principle of the neutrality of the straits.[6]

The real beneficiary of the Dreikaiserbund of 1881 was, of course, Bismarck. In the decade of diplomatic activity remaining to him, Bismarck spun a complex web of treaties building upon both it and the Austrian alliance of 1879. Russia, however, harbored no illusions about the good will of either of its nominal allies. In Petersburg, the Three Emperors' League was seen as an impermanent phenomenon, a particularly nasty-tasting draught of medicine that Russia had to take temporarily to ensure itself "the repose of which she has the most imperious need."[7] The secret instructions Giers issued to Russia's Ambassador-designate to Berlin in 1884 stressed the latent dangers of the League. Germany, could, for example, exploit it to attack and destroy France, while Austria might be able to pursue "morally and materially a policy of encroachment on the Balkan peninsula."[8] In either event, the League would guarantee neither peace nor Russian interests. The key to Alexander III's policy, Giers explained, was to buy time—years of calm and status quo—in the expectation that the accession of a new Emperor in Germany might provide Russia with the opportunity to uncouple Berlin from Vienna.[9]

The Russian foreign policy approach in the early 1880s, then, echoed that taken by Gorchakov in the early 1860s: on both occasions Russia sought to avoid overt clashes with the other Great Powers and equally tried to employ diplomacy to paper over military weakness. After the Crimean War, the undeniable need for internal reform, including military reform, had momentarily rendered Russia incapable of waging war. In the early years of Alexander III, fiscal austerity had the same effect. Russian military expenditures—more than 255 million rubles in 1881—had fallen below 200 million by 1884.[10] In the same three-year period, the standing army was reduced from 863,000 to 756,000 men.[11] The potential hazards of such troop cutbacks and such underfunding became increasingly evident over time. As the souring foreign relations, diplomatic crises, and war scares of the 1880s demonstrated, the Dreikaiserbund was too weak a buckler to protect Russia even from its Austrian and German allies, let alone the British.

Russian offical policy toward London throughout the 1880s was driven by the alternating sentiments of frustration and fear. The near clash with the British at the end of the Turkish war had reconfirmed the Russians in their belief in the implacable enmity of Britain. As before, Russian statesmen felt encumbered by impotence to strike back at London in any meaningful way. How indeed could the elephant exert pressure on the whale? The only expedient was to adopt a forward policy in Central Asia, which might alarm the English about the security of India. In the winter of 1881–82, a Foreign Ministry official, Charykov, urged the Imperial government to accumulate as much intelligence as possible about British India, not in order to prepare for a war of conquest but to acquire "an important means of political pressure."[12] The problem was that St. Petersburg simultaneously wanted to persuade London that its suspicions of Russian ambitions in the East were groundless. The fundamental contradiction in Petersburg's mingling of threat and mollification naturally served to keep English Russophobia alive. That Russophobia stiffened British responses to Russia's Central Asian activities, which led in turn to escalating Russian counterresponses.[13]

In 1878, with a crisis brewing in the Bosphorus, the Imperial government made a hostile maneuver against London by dispatching Major General N. G. Stoletov to Kabul with orders to secure an anti-English treaty with the Emir of Afghanistan. Sher Ali's signing of an agreement to that effect provoked the outrage of the British government, which construed Stoletov's presence in Afghanistan (really no more than a petulant gesture) as evidence of a serious Russian conspiracy against India. The Stoletov mission led directly to the second Anglo-Afghan war. Although that war resulted in the reduction of Afghanistan to a tributary of the British Empire, Britain blamed Russia for the two years of bloody campaigning and observed Russian activities in Asia for years afterward through the prism of that episode.[14] Petersburg meanwhile predictably misinterpreted the British invasion of Afghanistan as the preliminary stage in a policy of encroachment against Russian Central Asia. In particular, the Russian government believed that Britain would exploit its victory to enhance its influence first in Persia and then among the bellicose Teke Turcomans north of the Persian frontier. Russia decided to respond by attacking the Turcoman stronghold at Geok Tepe. Although the first Russian expedition (1879) suffered a humiliating rebuff at the hands of the Turcomans, in 1881 Skobelev took Geok Tepe by storm; the entire Akhal Teke oasis region was swiftly absorbed into a newly created Russian province, Transcaspia. When Persia recognized the legitimacy of this conquest, Russia acquired for the first time a fixed border with Iran. Three years later, in 1884, the strategically important oasis of Merv peacefully submitted to the authority of the Russia crown, an event that alarmed the British once more, in view of the proximity of Merv to Herat.

Given Russia's concern for its security in Europe, on no account could it risk the outbreak of a war in Asia. In 1881 Russia had considered it prudent to cede the Tien-shan passes back to Beijing to avert war with even so weak an opponent as China.[15]

As Britain was a far more dangerous potential enemy, it was all the more necessary to appease it. A special conference on the Russo-Afghan border issue held in Petersburg in December 1884 had recommended making concessions during the negotiations "in the interest of general policy not to arouse alarms in the British government through the occupation of points too close to Herat."[16] Upsetting that plan, however, was the border incident at Panjdeh (March 1885), which quickly escalated into an open battle in which Russian troops routed Afghan forces.

Gladstone, once again Prime Minister of Britain, denounced the clash as an inexcusable Russian provocation; for his part, the Russian commander on the spot claimed self-defense. Foreign Minister Giers tried to repair the damage by means of a formal explanation to the British Ambassador. Unhappily for Giers, Ambassador Thornton's report of this conversation to London was picked up by Russian intelligence and transmitted to the Tsar. Giers's description of the Panjdeh battle as an "unhappy accident" infuriated Alexander III. "This proves how careful one has to be with expressions. It is insulting to Russian honor!" the Emperor wrote in great heat.[17] For a moment it seemed as if Russian Foreign Ministry's policy of reassuring Whitehall had collapsed, a victim of the Imperial temper. Indeed, Alexander's sense of personal insult made the risk of an Anglo-Russian war very real in the spring of 1885, for he stubbornly insisted that his government repudiate any apologies or explanations for the Panjdeh events. Negotiations with London were suspended. As Gladstone appealed to Parliament for war credits, Alexander began to make military preparations of his own. So serious was the Tsar about war that he instructed Giers to demand that Russia's partners in the Dreikaiserbund use their influence to force Turkey to neutralize the straits. Bismarck's response showed that the promises underpinning the Three Emperors' League were valueless. His assertion that it was "untimely" to put pressure on the Sultan revealed that neither Germany nor Austria intended to give Russia any help.[18] Eventually, as the Tsar cooled down, the danger of war receded. The Russo-Afghan frontier was regularized, with compromises on both sides, by a treaty in September 1885, to which the British gave diplomatic assent two years later.

The crisis of 1885 left a bitter aftertaste. Convinced that Berlin and Vienna could not be trusted to stand by the obligations of the Dreikaiserbund, the Imperial government concluded at the very end of that year that Russia had to acquire the means to close the straits itself at any time. Eight million rubles' worth of credits were appropriated. The 13th and 15th Infantry Regiments in Odessa district were to be strengthened and trained so that an amphibious assault on Constantinople could be launched without warning. For its part, the navy was supposed to acquire warships, troop ships, and a stockpile of mines for the creation of a barricade at the Bosphorus.[19] As subsequent events proved, Russia never became strong enough to undertake a surprise attack on the straits, but the consistent interest over the next twenty years in purchasing such a capability indicated how vulnerable Russia continued to feel about the prospect of English naval blackmail.[20]

Nor was Russia at ease during the 1880s about its relationship with the Germans and the Austrians. The highly protectionist tariff that Bismarck had erected against Russian agricultural products in 1879 was but one irritant to St. Petersburg. Another was the fulsome interest (from the Russian perspective) that Berlin now began to manifest in Near Eastern affairs. I. S. Dolgorukov, whom Alexander III occasionally employed as a personal envoy, reported in 1882 that "the presence in Constantinople of military instructors and of a number of German personnel charged with the administration of finances prepares the ground slowly for the predominant influence of Germany in the Danubian basin, the Bosphorus, and the Dardanelles."[21] That theme—Germany as a potential rival of Russia in the Levant—was continuously reiterated and embroidered by the conservative publicist M. N. Katkov, whose newspaper *Moskovskie vedomosti* became the bellwether of anti-German sentiment during the period.[22]

Russia's real rival in the Balkans, however, remained Austria-Hungary. The flashpoint of conflict between Petersburg and Vienna in the 1880s was Bulgaria. Bulgaria had, of course, become independent as a direct result of Russia's defeat of Turkey in 1877–78. In part for that reason, the Russian government expected Bulgaria to behave as a docile satellite of St. Petersburg. Yet the Prince of Bulgaria (and nephew of the Tsar), Alexander of Battenberg, was too proud and ambitious to act the role of an obedient puppet. Courting popularity via appeals to domestic nationalists, Alexander presided over Bulgaria's effective absorption of the province of Eastern Rumelia (1885), oblivious to Russian protests. Eventually Alexander's unwillingness to take St. Petersburg's dictation drove the Imperial government to launch a series of plots to unseat him. The ins and outs of Russia's blunders in Bulgaria in 1886 and 1887—including the attempted kidnapping of Alexander—do not warrant retelling here.[23] Alexander was at last induced to abdicate. The new Prince elected in 1887 by the Bulgarian parliament, Ferdinand of Saxe-Coburg, however, was even less acceptable to Russia than his predecessor had been because of his Austrian connections. To Russia, the only tangible political gain of the Turkish war—predominant influence in Bulgaria—appeared to be slipping away. Petersburg accordingly warned Sofia that it might mount a military intervention.

But Austria issued counterthreats to Russia. At various points in 1886 and 1887 it appeared as if the two eastern empires might soon be locked in war. Indeed, during those two years it seemed that all of Europe could be engulfed in war, for paralleling the Bulgarian crisis was the Boulanger affair in the West. In 1886 General Georges Boulanger, a fire-breathing advocate of a war of revenge against Germany, became the French Minister of War. Bismarck responded by introducing legislation to increase the size of the German army. The French and German press vied to outdo each other in nationalist vituperation and abuse.

However, as had been true in 1875, neither Germany or France was actually willing to go to war, a fact of which Russian military intelligence was well apprised.[24] If information from Paris had a soothing effect on the nerves of tsarist statesmen, that collected in Vienna had the direct opposite effect. During much of 1887 Russian intelligence indicated such extraordinary military preparations on the part of the Austro-Hungarian Empire that many came to the conclusion that Russia was in imminent danger of attack. In Petersburg it was noted with alarm that work on strategic railroads in Galicia had been accelerated, that large numbers of transport trains and locomotives were being concentrated between Neu Sandec and Kashits, that several million portions of rusks were being concentrated at Lemberg, and so forth.[25] Kiev Military District reported in January that the Austrians had come to consider war with Russia inevitable and "that it would start very soon, perhaps no later than the beginning of next spring."[26] Although the Russian military attaché in Vienna reported that the head of the Austro-Hungary General Staff, General Beck, had insisted to him that the preparations had exclusively defensive purposes, unsettling dispatches about Austrian war readiness continued to pile up on Obruchev's desk (and the Emperor's) for several months.[27] At the very end of March 1887 War Minister P. S. Vannovskii summarized what had been learned of the suspicious Austrian military activity in a memorandum for his sovereign. Work on the Membits-Tarnow railway line, so indispensable for operations toward the Vistula, had sped up; increased stocks of food and forage were being amassed in Lemberg, Tarnow, and Cracow; Vienna had placed rush orders for 300,000 uniforms, coats, and pairs of boots; and 240 temporary barracks had been constructed in Galicia, presumably to accommodate a large influx of troops preliminary to the invasion of Russia.[28] As late as May the War Ministry would turn to the Ministry of Foreign Affairs for help in confirming or refuting the rumor that Vienna intended to conduct a clandestine mobilization of the VII and XII Army Corps.[29]

The war scare of 1887 blew over, just as that of 1885 had. But it, too, had its unpleasant consequences. In the first place, Alexander III's government now repudiated the Dreikaiserbund, then up for renewal. Bismarck moved to fill that void by proposing what became known as the Reinsurance Treaty of 1887. The treaty, with a term of three years, obliged Germany and Russia to be neutral in the event either of them was attacked by a third power. In 1890, however, the government of the new German Emperor, William II, declined to reaffirm the Reinsurance Treaty. Russia was considerably alarmed at that, despite verbal promises by the Germans that all would go on as before.[30] Thus by 1890 Russia found itself once again alone and without allies. Many potential grounds for war with Britain over Asian disputes still existed. And in Europe, the Russian government felt itself confronted with a maleficent Austria and a more devious (but scarcely less hostile) Germany.

Prospects were all the more ominous because the crisis of 1887 had forced Petersburg to come to terms with harsh truths about the military balance. Russian diplomacy had very nearly failed during the crisis, almost forcing Russia to rely exclusively on its military power. In the Russian government's pessimistic assessment of its own military preparedness, Russia in 1887 was not even strong enough to resist an invasion *by Austria, acting independently of its German ally.*

That assessment was in fact far too pessimistic. At the height of the crisis, the Austrian General Staff wrote the Emperor Franz Josef that Austria was in no condition to make war on Russia without German support.[31] The Russian elite, however, was unaware of that Austrian view. Somewhat later, in 1891, Russia's military attaché in Vienna, Colonel Zuev, reported to St. Petersburg that General Beck had called him into his office to protest against Russia's strengthening its forces on the Galician frontier. On his copy of Zuev's report, Alexander III scrawled: "Thank God that they are still afraid of us!"—a remark that stands as an authoritative confession of self-perceived Russian military weakness.[32] How had Russia managed to neglect its defenses to this (ostensible) degree? The answer must emerge from a brief examination of Petersburg's military policy and strategy in the 1880s. Deliberate fiscal austerity had a heavy influence on both. War Minister Vannovskii wrote in a note to himself of 1887: "[We are] supposed to be ready to prepare weapons, rations, and food, and they don't even give us kopecks for these things."[33]

"Our Borders Are Completely Open": Military Policy and Strategy in the 1880s

After 1881 it was increasingly the Minister of Finance to whom the new Emperor Alexander III listened most attentively. By nature fiscally conservative, Alexander was worried about the continued economic distress that had been one consequence of the Turkish war. The war had been followed by an economic slump, which persisted until the late 1880s. The finances of the country were in disarray. The budget was unbalanced, and the national debt stood at over 4.9 billion rubles. In those circumstances the Finance Ministry had little difficulty convincing the Emperor that the only possible remedy was the immediate slashing of state expenditures. The cuts were hard on every ministry, but most particularly on the Ministry of War, which had traditionally enjoyed a 30 percent share in the Imperial budget. Army outlays, more than 255 million rubles in 1881, had fallen to 203 million two years later and had not worked their way back up to 225 million until the end of the decade.[34]

The fiscal crisis of the 1880s put pressure on the military in several respects. For one, it made it impossible for the Ministry of War to modernize the army's weaponry, a major concern at a time when all the other European Great Powers were beginning to introduce magazine rifles. But equally, the downward pressure on the state budget meant that work on a system of railways and macadamized roads in the western frontier zone was indefinitely postponed. By 1888 construction had begun on only three of the eleven railroad lines that the Ministry of War had identified as strategically indispensable back in the early 1870s. The Main Staff concluded that, with regard to railroads, "the task of 1873 is farther away than ever" and appealed for a crash program of railway building. The Staff's request for an immediate commitment to build 959 versts of new lines and to doubletrack 602 versts was rejected out of hand by a special conference held in the beginning of December 1888.[35]

The situation with regard to macadamized roads was no better. Roads were needed both to permit the troops to march quickly from one part of the defensive line to another and to connect front-line units with their secondary magazines in the rear. Alexander III himself had approved a plan for a net of 2,655 versts of them in 1881. By 1888, however, scarcely 1.5 percent of the plan had been realized; only 40 versts had been built.[36] When Obruchev (by now Chief of Staff) provided Giers with a survey of the strategic landscape in 1883, he laid particular stress on the imbalance in military transportation between Russia and the Teutonic Powers. In Obruchev's opinion, Poland—that enormous salient protruding into Austrian and German territory—had been placed "in a state of unconditional siege" owing to the density of the rail nets of the Dual Alliance. "There is no doubt," he continued, "that Germany and Austria-Hungary are incomparably stronger than we and can mobilize and concentrate their armies on the frontier much more rapidly than we. Our borders are completely open."[37]

Yet, as has been often observed, despair is not a strategy. It fell to Obruchev, War Minister Vannovskii, and their colleagues to develop plans making the best use of what they had. The strategic plan of January 1880 was an important step in that direction.

THE 1880 DEPLOYMENT PLAN

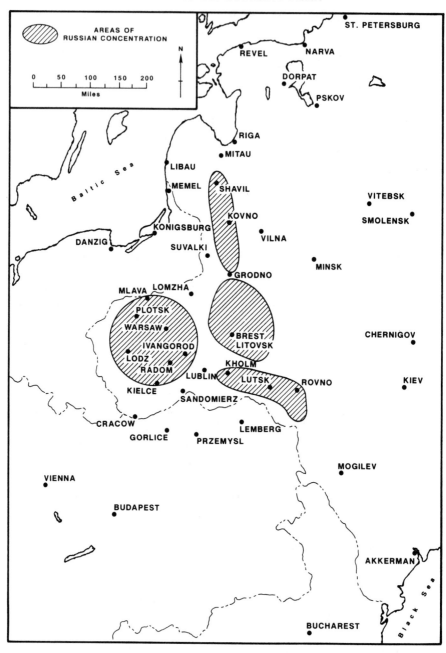

Its preamble stated that "in view of the superiority of enemy forces [at the opening of the campaign], we must recognize as least risky for ourselves the employment of a concentrated defense in the center of our western borders so that the distribution of our armies will reliably defend access to the interior of the Empire and so that we will be able to meet the blows directed against us from different quarters with the largest possible concentration of our forces."[38] The basic plan required Russia to divide its forces into four armies. The first, consisting of 140 battalions and 90 squadrons of cavalry, would hold a line on the Neman on a front between Polangen and Avgustov. Its task would be to protect Lithuania, the Baltic states, and the road to Petersburg. The stronger second army, with 232 battalions, 128 squadrons, and 678 guns, would be positioned in Poland on a line extending between the Bug, Narew, Vistula, and Veprezh rivers. The third or southern army (148 battalions, 108 squadrons) would defend Volynia, Podolia, and the other provinces of southern Russia from its initial deployment on a front from Lutsk via the Styr River to the Prut. Finally, the main (*glavnaia*) or reserve army would concentrate its 244 battalions, 157 squadrons, and 798 guns in eastern Poland, from Belostok to Pruzhany. This large force was, naturally enough, to serve as a general reserve for the other three.[39]

Unlike the documents of 1873, which had merely adumbrated a general strategic concept, those of 1880 represented a fully articulated mobilization and deployment plan. The plan of 1880 was in fact so influential that it served as a template for its successors of 1883, 1887, and 1890. Plans issued all the way up until the outbreak of the Russo-Japanese War would also have many features in common with it. Like the concept of 1873, the plans of the 1880s all continued to rely on an initial cavalry raid of more than 120 squadrons in order to disrupt Austrian and German mobilization.[40] Obruchev was also as insistent in the plans of the 1880s on the need for forward defenses as he had been in 1873. Strategic withdrawal in the face of invasion was not an option for the Imperial government, unless it was willing to renounce its grasp on Poland forever.

There were several differences between the plans of the 1880s and the defense concept of 1873, and they stemmed from a new approach to the problem of Russian technological backwardness.

The initial cavalry raid (even if it worked perfectly) would not be enough to even the odds in a war between Russia and the Central Powers. Russia had to cultivate additional methods of compensating for the lack of efficient military transportation. Obruchev decided that from then on Russia would always have to be in a higher state of military readiness than its western neighbors. Further, it would have to train itself to fight smarter than its potential enemies—through the use of foreign espionage.

A higher state of military readiness implied that Russia would have to keep a greater proportion of its regular army on continuous active duty in the western regions of the empire. To the thinking of the Ministry of War, that was the only way in which Russia might be able to diminish the impact of the superiority in manpower that Germany and Austria would enjoy in the early phases of the war owing to their rapid mobilizations. Concomitantly, the closer the units in the western military districts were to full combat strength in peacetime, the less would be their dependence on slow-moving shipments of reservists from the interior of the empire once war broke out. The process of raising the number of troops permanently assigned to the Kiev, Warsaw, and Vil'na military districts began in 1881 and acquired irreversible momentum in 1887, when Obruchev came to the depressing conclusion that it would be "unrealistic" for the army to count on the state to supply it with much more in the way of strategic railroads.[41] Thus, whereas in 1883 Russia had only roughly 227,000 troops in the three westernmost districts, ten years later it maintained over 610,000 there, about 45 percent of the active army at that point.[42] There were both costs and risks associated with the venture. Obviously, the state now had to foot the bill for the construction of new barracks, stables, warehouses, and the like. In addition, there was also the danger that Vienna and Berlin might misread the redeployment as a gesture of hostility or, still worse, as a prelude to Russian aggression. But the Imperial government apparently believed that such a risk had to be run, for the consequences of not redeploying the army—rapid defeat should war come—were unacceptable. It might be argued that by incurring that risk the Imperial government revealed a myopic incapacity to see itself as others saw it. Yet, despite occasional lapses, Russia's attentiveness in this period to its image in Berlin, its attempts to avoid provoking the English, testified to an acute awareness of the international repercussions of its military preparations and activities. With regard to Central Europe, Petersburg's resolve to proceed with the redeployments despite the anticipated German and Austrian objections was hardened by both knowledge and belief: the knowledge that Russia had no bellicose designs against the Teutonic Powers, and the belief that Vienna and Berlin knew it. When Bismarck had earlier warned the Imperial government that the Prussian General Staff saw "a sword of Damocles" in the concentration of the Russian cavalry in Poland, the Main Staff dismissed his words as empty and egregious bullying.[43] Obruchev wrote: "[W]ho can really compare the offensive power of cavalry with the offensive power of railroads? Just as steam power exceeds horse power, in modern strategy offensive force is determined not by the relative deployment of cavalry squadrons in peace, but by the quantity and speed of those trains which will bear the troops from all quarters to their points of concentration on the frontier with the declaration of mobilization."[44] The tsarist Ministries of War and Foreign Affairs thus held that it had to be privately clear to Germany and Austria that Russia's forward deployments were defensive regardless of what their governments might say in public.

There was more to elevated military readiness than a higher number of regiments stationed in the west. Military preparedness was also a quality of mind. The Russian military leadership had to be intellectually prepared to fight a war that would begin for it under extremely disadvantageous conditions. For that reason, the Ministry of War introduced the concept of shadow commands. Experimented with in the 1880s, the system of shadow commands was formally instituted in 1890 by the Field Ordinance for War (*Polozhenie o polevom upravlenii voiskami v voennoe vremia*). The regulation provided that a shadow command structure for each of Russia's wartime armies would be established in peacetime and secreted within the existing military district system. When mobilization was proclaimed, the commanders of the Vil'na, Warsaw, and Kiev districts were immediately to become generals-in-chief of the First, Second, and Third Armies respectively. The peacetime staffs of those districts would also assume staff responsibilities for those armies at once.[45] The principle was very simple: the existence of a hidden command structure was meant to facilitate and accelerate the transition from peace to war. Thus the key officials of the westernmost districts were simultaneously to discharge two jobs. While fulfilling all of the demands of their peacetime positions, they were also supposed to evaluate intelligence, construct plans, and constantly train themselves for future war. After 1890 the government continued to refine and amplify its ideas about strategic anticipation and preplanning. Secret interministerial working groups prepared lists of provinces, cities, and ports that were to fall under direct martial law on the very first day of mobilization. That was to be done in defense of internal security, for the localities involved (including the entire Baltic coast, Poland, and Transcaucasia) were the ones "closest to the western frontier of the state which represent the greatest difficulties in maintaining calm among the populations."[46] Those powers of martial law were also supposed to assist the staffs in supplying the armies with food and equipment by giving them control over the economic resources in what became known as the rear regions (*tylovye raiony*).[47]

At that same time, the Russian War Ministry also began to place an ever increasing emphasis on the collection of reliable intelligence about its potential enemies. In the view of the Main Staff, espionage was yet another tool with which to compensate for Russian backwardness. A most important source of intelligence was the reporting of Russia's military attachés abroad. Those general staff officers were charged with the collection of as much information as possible about the military posture of the host country. They were to work openly—reading newspapers, pursuing social contacts—and covertly, by developing networks of paid or unpaid informants.[48] Meanwhile, the commanders of the frontier military districts, both in Europe and in Asia, mounted intelligence efforts of their own, frequently dispatching members of their staffs on clandestine excursions across the frontiers.[49] Other ministries of state also had a part to play in the accumulation of data, notably the Gendarmes and the Okhrana (both under the Interior Minister), and the Minister of Finance's Frontier Guard.[50] In retrospect, the intelligence system of Imperial Russia is better classified as massive than as well-organized: decentralization, overlapping responsibilities, and poor coordination inevitably produced confusion and redundancy. There was, however, a central clearinghouse for intelligence, for sooner or later all reports of military significance reached the Military Education Committee, which in turn funneled them to the Chief of the Main Staff. Indeed, the Military Education Committee occasionally underwrote intelligence collection efforts of its own, as in 1892, when it remitted 1,000 rubles to the Russian political agent in Bukhara to hire agents to go spying in Afghanistan.[51]

What varieties of intelligence appealed to the Main Staff? To a certain extent that depended on the country involved. For example, the Russian War Ministry was extremely curious about the long-term trends in birthrates within Austria-Hungary, believing that the rapid growth of the Slavic population would inevitably enfeeble the Dual Monarchy.[52] Appositely enough for a military establishment fearful of technological inferiority, a high premium was placed on information about inventions with military applications. The December 1880 instruction to military attachés required them to supply reports on all such subjects, not omitting "even trivial details."[53]

Given Russia's apprehensions about the sluggishness of its own mobilization, interest in data about the mobilization of the Central Powers was also keen. Intelligence about the capacity and capability of German and Austrian railways in the frontier zone had a high priority, as did that about any changes or alterations in the mobilization schedules of the Dual Alliance. Acquisition of the mobilization plan of the 95th Austrian Infantry Division (1893), for instance, revealed that the I, X, and XI Galician Corps would actually be instructed to mobilize six days before Vienna announced a general mobilization, apparently owing to concern about the disruptive effect of Russian cavalry raids.[54] Most crucial, however, was the procurement of the enemy's actual order of battle along with the concomitant war plans. Russia was notably successful in this type of espionage against Austria-Hungary. After 1890 Russia's secret agents supplied it with copies of every general war plan devised by the Austrian General Staff. Even if intelligence collected about the Germans was paltry, Russia could attempt to look through the window of Vienna to pry into the secrets of Berlin. Although the Germans were by no means entirely candid with their Austrian allies, intercepts of letters between high officials, reports of interallied conferences, and an analysis of the operational assumptions built into the Austrian plans themselves could provide some inkling about what the Germans might be up to—or so the Russians hoped.[55]

Would Austria concentrate the bulk of its forces near Cracow or farther to the east? Would there be a coordinated Austro-German drive against Poland in the early phases of a war? Did Germany intend to attack Russia with the majority of its available corps, only detaching a few as a shield against France? Answers to such questions were obviously of great moment to any Russian planner. Indeed, it would not be too much to say that intelligence collection was one of the motors that drove Russian war planning from the 1880s until the outbreak of World War I. On the basis of clandestine information, the Main Staff altered the deployment of battalions and squadrons in each redaction of the plan to solder together vulnerable junction points between the three westernmost armies and to reinforce sectors in which intelligence indicated that the enemy was likely to be stronger than previously expected. One version of the 1887 plan, for example, transferred the I, X, and XV Corps from the southwestern army to that of the Vistula, to stem an anticipated German assault in that region. A few years later, when intelligence data suggested that the heaviest German blow would originate even farther to the north, the plan of 1890 redistributed troops from the Warsaw military district to defensive lines on the Narew from Lomzha to Zegrzha.[56] The problem, of course, was that since Russia's military posture was largely defensive and reactive, Russia's military plans were usually at least one step behind those of its western rivals. The redeployments in each new Russian plan were ordered to counter German and Austrian deployments. By the time those changes had been made, Berlin and Vienna had typically learned of them and had inaugurated yet another wave of new troop dispositions. When Russian intelligence in turn picked up those, the entire cycle would start again, but with the initiative, once again, in the hands of the Teutonic Powers.

There is another point about the way Russian employed intelligence in this period: intelligence can be used and just as easily abused—all the more so because it is rarely, if ever, complete. The tsarist military establishment was prone to prejudge the intelligence it collected as validating its own strategic pessimism. Intelligence materials were selectively interpreted, evidence about the growth of Austro-German military power and belligerence being highlighted, while contrary evidence indicating the weakness or irenic intentions of Vienna and Berlin was filtered out. For example, when the Main Staff obtained a copy of a letter by the Chief of the German General Staff to Austrian Emperor Franz Josef (May 1895), it was taken as confirming Austrian designs for an offensive in eastern Galicia; tsarist officials disregarded those sections in which Alfred von Schlieffen warned of the potentially disastrous consequences of any European war.[57] Thus enemy capabilities were almost always confused with enemy intentions, a practice that promoted anxiety, not repose, within the Russian Ministry of War.

A final shared characteristic of the war plans of the 1880s was their inclusion of provisions and contingencies for some offensive operations even in the beginning of the war. Despite the manifold problems they had in conceptualizing even strictly defensive operations, the Russian military planners of the 1880s showed an interest in offensives for two reasons. In the first place, they felt that in certain circumstances they might *have to* conduct an offensive. Appreciating the uncertainties of war as they did, they recognized that there was a possibility that a defense alone might not be sufficient to save Poland, for the enemy might prove capable of overwhelming Russia's forces in several places, thus puncturing the line. If the Austrian and German armies succeeded in exploiting such breakthroughs, Russia's troops might be hurled back beyond the Neman, Shara, and Styr rivers, and all of the Transvistula provinces would be effectively lost. If Russia were able to respond to the Austro-German invasion with a counteroffensive, however, the enemy's need to revert to the defensive at least in the threatened sectors might throw his own forward drive into disarray.[58]

A second reason that Russian generals began to regard an initial offensive as a serious option was that they managed to convince themselves that it might be *possible* to conduct one in certain circumstances. Reverting to the traditional theme that Russian strength inhered in Russia's weakness, several influential figures on the Main Staff now argued that Russia's size, poor soil, and climate constituted powerful defenses all by themselves. Obruchev put this best in 1880 when he wrote that "the breadth of our country, its poverty, its low population density and lack of roads are a defensive force before which an invading army must think twice and which could possibly free more of our troops for an offensive."[59] In other words, bad roads, mud, and the limited availability of food and forage might so retard the advance of the aggressor that Russia might be able to get by with a thin and crusty defense, while using the forces thus released for an attack.

If Russia were to stage an offensive, however, where would it occur? The Germans were expected to be too strong along the front from Grodno to the Pripet marshes for an offensive to have any hope of success. To attack on a front from Kovno to Insterburg would be equally dangerous, because it would have to advance in a narrow band between the Baltic and the marsh/forest belt. The left flank of any Russian army operating in that region would be vulnerable; such an army could be cut off too readily from the body of the Russian Empire and encircled with its back to the sea. The most promising choice—dictated by geography more than anything else—would be for Russia to attack in Austria-Hungary in Galicia, on the enemy's extreme right.[60]

The plan of 1880 actually contained two variants: defensive and defensive/offensive. The first, or automatic, variant obliged Russia to defend against both Teutonic Powers with three forward armies relying on an enormous Polish reserve. If the second variant was used, forces from the reserve army would be transferred to the Volynian army, to strengthen it for the invasion of Austria-Hungary. The plan of 1883 replicated that arrangement, as did that of 1887 (which did, however, provide for a Russian suicide attack against German forces in the Bobr-Narew-Bug region if Germany appeared to be on the verge of smashing through to the general Russian reserve). By the time mobilization schedule 14 came into effect (1891), the alarming growth of German offensive capabilities had required additional alterations in the variants. In variant one, Russia would mount a powerful defense against Germany with its northwestern and western armies, stripping the southwestern force down to a mere screen against Austria-Hungary. Positing that a significant number of German troops would be distracted by France, the second variant provided for the reduction of the Russian northwestern army to the status of a corps of observation; the plurality of Russia's forces would then be allotted to the Volynian army for offensive operations.[61] Those dispositions were extreme—almost parodic—versions of their predecessors, but the family resemblance between the plan of 1891 and that of 1880 is still unmistakable.

In the case of all of the plans of the 1880s, the selection of which variant to pursue was to be based on the operations of the Germans. If, on the eve of a war, Russia had acquired reliable intelligence that Germany would assault Russia with all of its strength, then the defensive variant would determine the Russian mobilization. If Russia knew that Germany intended to split its forces (some going east, some west), then the second variant would come into play. Yet what if, as is usually the case, intelligence data were incomplete? In that event, the Russian Ministry of War would automatically adopt the defensive deployment, switching to the other if the German mobilization (or the early phases of an Austro-German invasion) indicated that it was possible to do so. Thus if, even after war had been declared, the Main Staff determined that Germany was not launching a strong attack, or if that attack, however strong, was perceived to be bogging down, then the Russian army was supposed to change its mobilization *in midstream,* transferring newly mobilized battalions from the northeast to the south in preparation for a flanking maneuver against the Austrians in Galicia.

It almost goes without saying that the assumptions undergirding this dual-track system of plans were unrealistic, if not ridiculous. To require the Russian army to prepare simultaneously to implement either one of two radically different variants in the plan saddled it with well nigh insupportable administrative, intellectual, and logistical burdens. Still worse, it was preposterous to suppose that Russia's forces would be capable of gliding effortlessly, like a corps de ballet, from one variant to the other amid the turbulence of war.

Why then did Russian strategists formulate such plans? They did so out of their conviction that they had no choice, in view of Russian military weakness. Because Russia was so weak, it had to be ready for every contingency. Since a strictly defensive strategy might not work, the Russian army had to prepare to launch spoiling attacks—regardless of the chaos that might ensue for command, control, and logistics—and expect a miracle. Unfortunately, to expect a miracle was to commit to the position of the magicians, a position with which many generals were already uncomfortable. Military feebleness and uncertainty imposed that sort of magical reasoning upon them. Many of the magicians of the 1880s were as reluctant as those of a decade before. As a Main Staff memorandum of 1883 soberly noted, given the paucity of metalized roads and railways in the western regions of the country, "there is no plan of action that could promise us true and reliable success at all."[62]

A final source of disquiet was this: since Russia did not have any allies, it had no way of managing or narrowing the spectrum of threats to which it was potentially exposed. If Germany and Austria were menaced by no other powers, they would hold all the strategic cards in the event of war between one or both of them and Russia. They could, for instance, elect to attack simultaneously with all they had, in which case Russia's prospects for mounting a credible defense, let alone an offense, were not good. Russia's chances against Austria-Hungary alone would be better, of course. Yet Russia could not be confident that a war against Vienna could be localized. An initially uninvolved Germany could always abjure its neutrality and fall on Russia at a critical moment. The Main Staff believed that the odds would be still more favorable (although hardly optimal) if Germany were distracted away from the conflict in the east by military threats on its western frontiers. That was the rosy assumption that informed the second variant of the war plan of 1890. But in the absence of allies, Russia had no means of shaping events so that this would come to pass. Those, then, were the strategic problems that were the subtext to the conclusion of the Franco-Russian alliance. As we shall see, the role of the Russian Ministry of War in the creation of the treaty (and its interpretation) would prove decisive.

Russia and the French Alliance, 1890–95

Ever since the late 1870s, if not before, France had been seeking some sort of close political and military relationship with Russia.[63] That was very logical from the French point of view. Prussia and its allies had humiliated Paris militarily in 1870 and in the aftermath of victory had stripped it of the provinces of Alsace and Lorraine. There were those in France who had been dreaming of revanche ever since. Yet how could France embark on such a war of revenge by itself? Alone it was no match for the might of the German Empire. If it could ally with Austria or Russia, it might be able to overcome its German enemy in a two-front war. The

Austro-German treaty appeared to eliminate Vienna as a potential alliance partner, so after 1879 aggressive-minded Frenchmen
came more and more to look to St. Petersburg. Those who wished
to retaliate against Berlin and recover the lost provinces felt that
an alliance with Russia was France's only hope.

An even more elemental and persuasive reason for wooing
Russia was to preserve French security. The French government,
isolated by Bismarck's adroit diplomacy, realized as the years
went by that Germany regarded any improvement in France's
military capabilities with suspicion and distaste. In Paris it was
feared that the German General Staff had developed a doctrine
of preventative war that would counsel a surprise attack on
France if it ever seemed to become too strong. In such an unequal contest France would confront defeat, perhaps even extinc-
tion as a political entity. A Franco-Russian alliance might be an
essential insurance policy to deter the Germans from taking any
rash steps in the midst of a crisis.[64]

Petersburg was only slightly less disturbed by the prospect of
another German defeat of France than was Paris. That was not
impartial solicitude but self-interest, for a Europe without France
would be a Europe unsafe for Russia. As we have already seen,
alarm on this score had goaded Gorchakov into diplomatic action on France's behalf during the "war-in-sight" crisis of 1875.
Several years later the Minister of Foreign Affairs would instruct
Russia's Ambassador to Germany that Alexander III had no wish
to see France "disappear from the European scene under the
blows of Germany or in the convulsions of anarchy."[65]

Yet the Russian diplomatic establishment, as well as the court,
had strong reservations about an alliance with France. At the
beginning of 1880 an internal Foreign Ministry document had
referred to "the established fact of the total impossibility of any
entente with the French government."[66] Why was the "impossibility of any entente" taken as an article of faith? In the first place,
Russia's flirtation with Napoleon III in the early 1860s had
ended badly. But second, and more important, after 1871 France
had become that most hideous of political abominations, a republic. In the eyes of the Russian autocrat and his servitors, republics
were prima facie faction-ridden, unstable, and unreliable. Russia
could do business with the French, but it would have to hold its
nose and keep its distance while doing so. An alliance was out of

the question. If the French came to their senses and restored the monarchy, however, it would be a different matter.[67]

By contrast, the highest ranks of the Russian military in the early 1880s did contain at least some advocates of cooperation with France. General M. I. Dragomirov, who attended the French military maneuvers of 1883, evoked the rebukes of Berlin for the voluble and expansive sympathy he expressed on that occasion for the Third Republic.[68] Dragomirov was, however, known to be eccentric, excessively enthusiastic, and a lover of the bottle. Level-headed generals were more ambivalent about the utility of an alliance with France, in part owing to doubts about the quality of the French armed forces. Typical was the reaction of the Russian delegation at the French maneuvers of 1879. While praising the cleanliness they encountered in the barracks (an observation that by itself speaks volumes about Russian standards of military hygiene), they also reported their disgust at the indiscipline and poor motivation of the common soldiers.[69]

By the late 1880s, however, changing circumstances had induced Russia's diplomats, soldiers, and Emperor to rethink the issue of a close relationship with France. Alexander III, as we have already seen, was a principled opponent of republican institutions. What, then, persuaded him to choke back his distaste and authorize an approach to Paris? Strategic concerns evidently played little part in his decision. Alexander's grasp of political and military strategy was weak, arguably inferior even to that of his son and successor, Nicholas II. In fact, Alexander's approach to foreign policy was not so much cerebral as emotional. Although not impervious to the arguments of his advisers, his conduct of Russia'a foreign relations was determined by his notions of personal honor and dynastic dignity. In 1885, once again as previously noted, his sense of outraged honor over the Panjdeh incident nearly brought Russia and Britain to the brink of war. We must therefore look to his anger rather than his intellect to understand his approbation of the Franco-Russian alliance. In essence, Alexander began to favor the alliance at that moment when his anger at Germany started to outweigh his contempt for France.

In considering the Tsar's growing rancor against the Germans, two factors stand out. The first was the influence of his Empress, Mariia Fedorovna. The Empress, born a Danish Princess, had never forgiven Bismarck or Prussia for the abasement her native country had suffered at their hands during the Schleswig-Holstein war of 1864. While not discounting the Empress's Germanophobia, however, the clinching point in Alexander's thinking seems to have been the refusal by the German government to renew the Reinsurance Treaty in 1890. Alexander saw in that German demarche an affront perpetrated against himself and his house by the bumptious new German Emperor, William II. His commitment to explore more friendly relations with Paris, then, was in large part an act of vengeance against his imperial colleague in Berlin.[70]

For the Ministries of Foreign Affairs and War, however, issues of political and military strategy were paramount. The Minister of Foreign Affairs, N. K. Giers, throughout his career had been a consistent proponent of cordial Russo-German relations. Yet Russia's growing international vulnerability had come to perturb even Giers and his associates at the turn of the decade. By that time an isolated Russia confronted the Triple Alliance of Germany, Austria, and Italy. Then, too, there were disquieting indications, to quote from a Russian Foreign Ministry document, "of the more or less probable adhesion of the British to the plans" of the Triplice.[71] From the standpoint of Giers, the enormous agglomeration of power represented by the Triple Alliance, with or without the adherence of England, obviously threatened the stability of Europe and the security of Russia. The disparity in force between Russia and the German-led grouping enhanced the risk of war in and of itself. At worst, military preponderance might someday tempt Berlin to unleash a war against Petersburg, a war in which the latter's chances would be slight. Even at best, the Triplice might be able to establish a *droit de regard* over Russia's international behavior through military intimidation. A friendly understanding with Paris therefore became attractive to Giers as a means of rectifying the imbalance of power. The mere existence of such an arrangement might deter German aggression; failing that, it could ensure that Russia would not have to fight alone.

Vannovskii, Obruchev, and the Main Staff regarded a potential Franco-Russian alliance in a different light. In 1890 German military policy was in transition. Alfred von Schlieffen would soon replace Moltke as Chief of the General Staff. And Schlieffen, unlike Moltke, thought it might be possible for Germany to achieve total rather than limited victory in war with Russia and France.[72] Yet even before Schlieffen was firmly in control the Main Staff had already come to believe that the Triplice was actively and purposely plotting war with a view to annexing Russian Poland.[73] In conformity with that assumption, the Russian military establishment was interested in a French alliance not as a guarantee against the outbreak of war but as a guarantee against defeat once war broke out. Russia's war plan of 1890 did project victory in a war with the Central Powers, but the projection was based upon a suspension of disbelief and an invocation of "magical" arguments. Cold scrutiny revealed just how specious those were. In fact, the only way the plan could plausibly be made to work would be if Russia could forge a military alliance with France. From the standpoint of the Ministry of War, France had a virtually indispensable role to play in a preexisting war plan, for the participation of France was the missing ingredient that alone could make the difference between a relatively low and a relatively high probability of success. The differing opinions at the Ministries of Foreign Affairs and War about the purpose of a Franco-Russian alliance therefore explains why each of them strove to shape an agreement in conformity with its expectations.

It was Giers who set the process in motion. In July 1891 he held a series of meetings with Laboulaye, the French Ambassador, in which he suggested that it might be in the interest of France and Russia to explore a formal rapprochement. Draft agreements were prepared, exchanged, and modified by both sides. In the end mutually acceptable language was found: an exchange of notes in August ratified the promise of the two governments "to coordinate measures" in the event either of them was attacked by another power.[74] But Ribot's government wanted something more substantial than those vague words (what did a pledge "to coordinate measures" mean, precisely?) and almost immediately proposed that the contracting powers follow up the notes with a military convention. The French draft convention (also of August) would have required both France and Russia to initiate total mobilization the moment that Germany announced a mobilization of its own. In addition, were either France or Russia to be attacked by the Triple Alliance, or by Berlin alone, both states would then deploy all of the forces not absolutely indispensable elsewhere against Germany.[75]

As soon as Giers had read this document, he dashed off a strong letter of protest to the Emperor. Russia, he wrote, should go no farther with France than the agreement of August 1891. That agreement "fully protected Russia from the danger of being isolated in the event of war." As an added benefit, the public announcement that France and Russia had combined to form "a counterweight" to the Triple Alliance had put a damper on the bellicosity of the latter. Russia needed no more. To sign this military convention would be to assume definite military obligations toward Paris, and that could not be done without compromising Russia's freedom of action in the future. Particularly worrisome to Giers was the article in French draft that required Russia to stage an immediate and complete mobilization if the Germans did so. Such action might well be the escalatory prelude to a general European war. In any event, were the convention signed, it might be impossible to localize any future war between two of the Great Powers.[76]

The Ministry of War was no less convinced of the virtues of a military convention than Giers was of its vices. The Ministry's most talented intellect, the ubiquitous Obruchev, accordingly authored a defense of the military convention, which was distributed to both the Emperor and Giers in early May 1892. Obruchev began by denying that Russia could ever afford to construe a German mobilization as a diplomatic signal. Since faster mobilization and concentration ensured a higher probability of victory in the first battles (and indeed in the entire campaign), the announcement "of mobilization can now no longer be considered as if it were still a peaceful act; on the contrary, it is the most decisive act of war."[77] For that reason, if Germany mobilized, the only prudent course of action for Russia would be to assume that Berlin had made the choice for war. By promising the French that it would countermobilize in that event, Russia was not therefore surrendering its diplomatic flexibility, as Giers had supposed, but rather was taking unavoidable military precautions.

Obruchev was equally dismissive of Giers's thoughts about the localization of war. Given military tensions in Europe, it was difficult to see how any serious war could be localized for long; sooner or later all of the Great Powers were bound to be dragged in. Nor was that necessarily a bad thing, from the Russian point of view. If one of Russia's enemies managed to sit out part of a war while Russia was preoccupied with others, that foe might acquire the upper hand when it did come in. That was so because the war would "end with a general congress, and at this congress the side will have the greatest weight that has the greatest strength. The victor will not be so much the one who has exhausted all of his forces, as he who, conserving his forces, can threaten a new war advantageous to himself."[78] A few sentences later, Obruchev made his fixation on the events of 1878 even more explicit. Arguing that it would be dangerous for Russia to delude itself with the thought that it could wage an isolated war, he wrote that "the Congress of Berlin was a sufficient lesson for us in this regard, and it taught us whom we ought to consider our more dangerous enemy—he who clashes directly with us or he who awaits our exhaustion in order then to dictate the terms of the peace."[79]

Obruchev's memorandum contained more, however, than a mere amplification of the reasoning the French had already advanced for a military convention, for he took issue with one of the points in the draft most dear to Paris: the one that would commit Russia to deploy the bulk of its forces against the German Empire. On the contrary, Obruchev insisted that once a war had begun Russia had to reserve full freedom of action to decide both how and where it would use its armies. In certain circumstances, to be sure, it might be most logical to deliver the main blow against Germany, "the most powerful and dangerous enemy." Yet, in Obruchev's opinion, it might be even more advantageous to hit Austria-Hungary the hardest at first, in order to knock it completely out of the war.[80] Obruchev's words left no doubt that he meant for Russia to preserve its freedom of action regardless of any promises it might make to the French.

The Obruchev memorandum, then, provides striking insight into the specific reasons the Ministry of War had for backing a Franco-Russian alliance. By the end of the 1880s a combination of technological underdevelopment, low budgets, and international and domestic political requirements had backed the Russian military establishment into the corner of devising a war plan that could not be implemented. Only through a treaty with Paris could Russia's military leaders be rescued from that hopeless situation, for it conferred at least three discrete benefits upon them. First, it enabled them to contemplate a European war with greater confidence, since the alliance might somehow offset the disadvantages of slow Russian mobilization and concentration. The treaty would surely result in Germany's siphoning off at least part of its forces for use against France. The evening of the odds on the eastern front that would result would thus serve as a compensatory mechanism for Russia's inferior transportation in its western theater.

Second, a treaty would further decrease the uncertainties attending such a war by reducing the number of possible war scenarios to one: an unrestricted contest between the two alliance groupings. The war would be a general European war from the very beginning, which is what the Russian Ministry of War wanted it to be. That desire on the part of the Russian military might appear at first glance to be tinged with fatalism or irrationality. Who would really prefer to fight multiple enemies if it was possible to wage war against one alone? But the Main Staff rejected the idea that such a localized war would be possible. Russia's military leadership was strongly of the belief that even if Russia were to be attacked at first just by Austria-Hungary, it would be incapable in the end of avoiding a clash with Germany also. The same thing would be true if St. Petersburg and Turkey became embroiled in a conflict: when the moment was propitious, the Central Powers would intervene against Russia. Making any European war general would deprive Germany and Austria of the benefits of the initial repose that could make them even more formidable antagonists for Russia later on. This argument betrays Obruchev's obsession with the timing of military operations, which traces back through all his work on the war plans of the 1880s, through his preliminary designs for war with Turkey in the mid-1870s, to his first analyses of the problem of Central European war in the early years of that decade. It also reveals Obruchev's concept of the primary lesson of the war of 1877–78: that a nation had to prepare to win the peace as well as the war. Because the peace had to be won within the setting a Pan-European conference of all the Great Powers, there really could be no such thing as a safely localized war.

The third benefit of the Franco-Russian alliance would be that it might facilitate early Russian offensives in the event of war. The reasons behind the Main Staff's attraction to offensives have already been discussed, the prospect of shortening the war and saving Russian lives and money among them. More precisely, an alliance would empower Russia to conduct exactly those offensives its military had been dreaming of throughout the 1880s: offensives against Austria-Hungary in Galicia. A treaty with Paris would make possible a Russian attack on Vienna, not on Berlin, as the French supposed. It was of little concern to Obruchev and his colleagues that by swearing to do one thing secretly preparing to do another they would be deceiving their alliance partner *ab ovo*. They believed that Russia, like any other power before or since, should seek to make an alliance serve its own particular interests. From the standpoint of the Main Staff, it was in Russia's interest to use the French to salvage its preexisting war plan.[81]

Giers was not persuaded by anything in the Obruchev memorandum. Since a formal Franco-Russian military convention would limit Russia's room for maneuver in a future crisis, it was prima facie still unacceptable to him. He immediately made his opinion known to both the Tsar and Minister of War Vannovskii in notes of May and June 1892. There was one concession Giers was prepared to consider, however. If the convention were to be understood as merely an nonbinding exchange of views between the French and Russian staffs, and were it to be held in strictest secrecy, Giers was prepared to waive his objections to the document. Alexander III backed Giers on this point, so Vannovskii and Obruchev had no choice but to go along as well. When the French Chief of Staff, Boisdeffre, came to Petersburg in the summer of 1892, the Emperor would confirm the draft convention only as a "project," not a treaty.[82]

It would thus seem that Giers had succeeded in imposing his vision of the Franco-Russian alliance upon the Emperor he served: while the treaty of August 1891 usefully extricated Russia from its diplomatic isolation, Russia should not put itself under any encumbering military obligations to Paris. Yet within a year, the War Ministry would make a nullity of Giers's cautious policy, for Obruchev's version of the relationship with France would prevail. That happened as the direct result of an Imperial *volte face*, which was itself caused by events in Berlin.

In late 1892 the German Chancellor, Caprivi, introduced a bill in the Reichstag designed to increase the size of the German standing army by more than 70,000 men. If enacted, the measure over time would also obviously result in huge increases in the number of trained reservists available to Germany, despite the fact that it also reduced the term of active service from three years to two. The conclusion drawn by the French General Staff (and seconded by the Russian) was that the law represented "an augmentation of the offensive power" of Germany—positive proof of the belligerence of that state. Boisdeffre, who had requested amendments in the "military convention project," used the passage of the German military bill in July 1893 to stress the need for a binding military arrangement between Petersburg and Paris. In September 1893 he transmitted a proposal on the subject to Giers, who duly passed it on to the Tsar, then vacationing in Copenhagen. "The speed with which Germany can today start a campaign," Boisdeffre wrote, "now more than ever excludes all possibility of our concerting our efforts at the last minute. The accord which was established last year between the General Staffs of France and Russia ought to be all the more precious a pledge for the maintenance of the peace and security of the two countries." Next to these sentences, Alexander III penned but one marginal comment: "True."[83]

Russia's top military chiefs endorsed the French argument unreservedly. In a series of letters to Giers and the Emperor in September, Vannovskii placed stress on "the extraordinarily offensive goal of this law," noting that it was fully consonant with other hostile military steps recently taken by Germany. Vannovskii also reminded Giers and Alexander that during the Reichstag debates on the bill, some of its supporters had justified it as necessary to the fulfillment of the Moltke strategy of 1879, which posited an initial German attack on Russia. The War Minister closed by once again making the link between the need for a firm military alliance and Russian military technical backwardness (in this case an insufficient stock of field guns in addition to an inadequate rail net).[84]

Issues of domestic politics, in addition to questions of strategy, are what really drove the German government to increase the size of its army. Still further, insofar as strategic issues were involved, the strategy the law was supposed to underpin was not the original Moltke plan of 1879 but the new anti-French approach that is immortally connected to the name of Alfred von Schlieffen.[85] Petersburg was unaware of this. The Russian Ministry of War and eventually the Emperor himself interpreted the

German military act of July 1893 as irrefutable evidence that Berlin was bent on war with Russia. That "evidence" was what overcame Alexander's resistance to a formal military alliance with France.[86] In late November the Emperor approved the dispatch of a letter to the French Ambassador, Montebello, adopting the French redaction of the military convention without alterations. Montebello responded in the name of the French government, and Alexander's acceptance of that response (December 24, 1893 [January 5, 1894]) constituted an official ratification of the convention.[87] Russia and France committed themselves to total and simultaneous mobilizations in the event that the Triple Alliance mobilized first. Further, should either of the signatories be attacked by any members of the Triplice, France vowed to take the field against Germany with 1.3 million troops, and Russia with 800,000 by M+14.

The Franco-Russian alliance has always provoked controversy. After the guns were silenced on the western front in November 1918, an entire school of historians (many with pro-German sympathies) emerged to represent it as a fateful act that almost by itself foreordained the bloody carnage of trench warfare. That interpretation, which fell into disrepute as a result of World War II, has recently been resurrected by a noted American scholar and diplomat.[88] Despite the distinction of its proponents, the interpretation is hard to sustain, as we shall argue later. Without anticipating too much, we should merely not that there was nothing irrevocable about the alliance. Indeed, on several occasions it came close to falling apart altogether.

But the alliance was not uncontroversial even for knowledgeable contemporaries. In 1896 Sergei Popov, a veteran diplomat and former Ambassador to China, sent his Emperor a short treatise on international relations in which he roundly condemned the policies that had led to the alliance. The Russian government, he argued, had consistently misunderstood its Central European neighbors. German outrage at the intemperate Germanophobia of Slavophile journalism was in fact understandable, not proof of a Teutonic military conspiracy directed against Russia. By turning its back on Vienna and Berlin, Popov wrote, Russia was truckling to domestic public opinion and betraying all the honorable traditions that had guided its international statecraft with such success in the past. We should note in passing that Popov's reference to domestic public opinion was calculated to have maximum impact on the new Emperor, Nicholas II. Throughout his reign (1894–1917) Nicholas was to be morbidly afraid of even appearing to do anything at the behest of public opinion. Indeed, it became part of the mythology of his court that his grandfather had been influenced by public opinion in his decision to opt for war with Turkey. Since the war had emboldened revolutionary terrorists, Nicholas believed, by giving in to public opinion Alexander II had put in motion the events that would lead to his own assassination. Although Popov's memorandum was carefully preserved, Nicholas II was still not convinced by it.[89]

Popov's denunciation of the Franco-Russian alliance remained very much a minority view. Although the ratification of the military convention had been a setback for Giers, eventually the majority of high-ranking Foreign Ministry officials came to regard it as something of a diplomatic triumph. The Ministry's secret review of Alexander III's foreign policy, composed soon after the death of that autocrat, spoke of the Franco-Russian alliance in a tone of self-congratulation: Russia had wisely made its deal with France in order to counterbalance the power of Germany and its allies, "and thus the power of the Triple Alliance was paralyzed, or at least the possibility of its launching an attack [against us] was made much more difficult."[90] The Ministry of War was, naturally enough, even more elated by the outcome of the negotiations with Paris. The Russian military elite viewed the French alliance not as a constraint but as an act of emancipation. From the standpoint of the General Staff, Russia had received much while giving away little. To be sure, there was always the risk that Russia might be dragged into a war as the result of a colonial dispute between France and Britain, but that risk was small. In the words of the War Minister, "hostilities are much more likely to begin on the Balkan peninsula than in Africa."[91] Despite what had been said in the military convention, the Russian army made no effort to conform to its terms in any of the remaining plans that it crafted during the 1890s. Except for the initial cavalry raid that remained a feature of all of the plans, the posture of the Russian War Ministry toward Germany in a hypothetical war remained defensive. Indeed,the War Ministry began to modify its plans to accommodate some of the promises Russia had made to Paris only after regular conferences between the Russian and French Chiefs of Staff began in 1900. The treaties with France, then, had rescued the entire process of Russian war planning, by granting it a foothold in the world of the feasible.

Foreign Affairs and Defense in the Later 1890s: "An Honorable and Consistent Policy"?

In the aftermath of the signing of the Franco-Russian military convention, it appeared that Russia had acquired an opportunity—a fresh chance, as it were—to approach the problem of its international security seriously, consistently, and with renewed hope. Nor was this merely because of the successes of tsarist diplomacy, for the striking improvements in the tsarist economy in the last decade of the nineteenth century could only be taken as encouraging by statesmen concerned with the national welfare, both domestic and international.

The period between 1888 and 1904 was a time of an unanticipated and unprecedented economic boom within the Russian Empire. In no area of the economy was the boom as remarkable as in industry, which attained a growth rate of 8 percent per annum.[92] The reasons for the economic transformation were complex. First, of course, there were the economic stimuli provided by the Ministry of Finance under such redoubtable leaders as Vyshnegradskii and Witte: the establishment of a favorable balance of trade (in part through the promotion of high levels of grain exports); the creation of a convertible ruble backed by gold; the erection of protective tariff barriers; and massive investments in the ever expanding state-controlled railroads. In part because of those policies, Russian industry became increasingly successful at attracting foreign capital. Total foreign investment in Russian stocks and banks may have increased by as much as 600 million rubles from 1890 to 1900.[93] Indeed, the Franco-Russian alliance itself may have contributed to improving the inflow of foreign capital. Between 1890 and 1900 French investment in Russian corporations had increased more than threefold; in that latter year only Belgium had larger investments in Russia than did France.[94] Nonetheless, as recent scholarship has demonstrated, the role of domestic savings and investment in fueling economic growth and industrial expansion was at least equally important if not more important than the conscious economic policies of the tsarist state.[95] It should not be overlooked that Russia was not the only country to experience great economic expansion in that period. The spectacular economic boom in Germany in the 1890s kept it well ahead of Russia.[96] In any event, the growth of the Russian economy was attended by a remarkable growth in state revenues and consequently state outlays as well. Government revenues went up by more than 100 percent between 1888 and 1900, while expenditures nearly doubled in the same period, from roughly 900 million to 1.8 billion rubles.[97]

As the ostensible financial health of the government improved, the Ministry of War had every expectation that it would be allowed to share in the bounty. Although the Ministry of Finance did everything in its power to prevent that from happening (by saddling the army with the so-called maximum budgets of 1888–1903, for example), and although the relative share of the military in the overall tsarist budget continued to decline, absolute army outlays increased in the 1890s from roughly 240 million rubles at the beginning of the decade to almost 380 million at the end.[98] Owing to those increases, the Ministry was able to fund two discrete rearmament programs: the acquisition of magazine rifles (the Mosin three-line rifle, patent 1891), and the introduction of the first quick-firing field artillery piece (the 3-inch gun, patent 1900).[99]

Complementing the gradual defense buildup, at least in the early and middle part of the decade, was a renewed commitment on the part of both the military and the diplomatic leadership to Europe as the empire's primary security concern. The Ministry of Foreign Affairs, as was its tradition, stressed the need to eschew provocative gestures that might alarm Russia's neighbors, particularly those in Asia. The willingness to compromise that Russia manifested in the Pamirs "crisis" of 1892–93 was but one illustration of this approach.

During the early 1890s Russian explorers, acting on their own authority, had penetrated the Pamir mountains, a disputed territory between Afghanistan and China. The British government was fearful lest that expedition represent an attempt to secure access to the passes through the Hindu Kush, and from there into

Kashmir. Although the Governor General of Turkestan at first responded to British, Afghan, and Chinese protests by sending in a military detachment to uphold Russia's claims to the region, the Imperial Government ordered a rapid evacuation of the Pamirs in late August 1892, when it realized how upset London and Beijing truly were. Expanding Russia's frontiers to the borders of India was simply not worth antagonizing the British.[100]

Solicitude for the British continued to manifest itself throughout the decade. In 1898 the new War Minister, A. N. Kuropatkin, invited the commentary of the Foreign Ministry on the potential international repercussions of an overhaul of military administration he had in mind. In brief, he wanted to unite the Governor-Generalship of the Steppe with Irkutsk military district, while merging Transcaspia into the Turkestan district. Kuropatkin explained that the reorganization would involve no troop increases but would still enhance the empire's Asian defenses by enlarging the pool of soldiers on which each of the two principal Asian military commanders could draw. The Ministry of Foreign Affairs lost no time in vetoing Kuropatkin's proposal: reorganization was superfluous, because Russia was not threatened by attack from China, Persia, or British India. Still worse, "such a fusion would be in all respects pernicious" since Britain would regard it as a Russian preparation for aggression and would feel obliged to retaliate. Speaking for the Foreign Ministry, Lamzdorff followed up his official letter by summoning Kuropatkin for an informal conversation in which the latter was curtly told that "immoderate development of military forces in our Central Asian territory would hardly facilitate the preservation of calm and peace necessary for Russia."[101] Then again, toward the end of the subsequent year the Ministry of War wrote the Ministry of Foreign Affairs for guidance about Anglo-Russian relations: was there any truth to the rumor recently passed along by the military attaché in London that Britain might soon resort to military pressure against Asiatic Russia in a quest for diplomatic advantage? Lamzdorff's response was as direct as the one he had provided a year before. In his view, the rumor was groundless, yet because of the current political situation it was still "essential to be vigilant and very careful, avoiding clashes with England in all places where our interests come into conflict."[102]

With few exceptions, the leadership of the Russian army in the

1890s found itself in agreement with the proposition that the best policy in Asia was a quiet one. As had been true under Alexander II, the majority of the generals thought Russia had to concentrate its attention on the security situation in Europe. Even Cherniaev (of all people!), who had been an irresponsible booster of Central Asian imperialism twenty years before, now admitted as much in a private letter to the Minister of War.[103] The principal dissenters from that received wisdom were, as might have been expected, the local Central Asian commanders themselves. The security of the Central Asian frontier naturally appeared more precarious from Tashkent than it did from Petersburg. Then, too, it was in the institutional interest of such personages as the Turkestan Governor-General to inflate the threat in the east in order to justify requests for more money and more men. It is therefore unsurprising to discover that Governor-General darkly asserting in 1892: "As is known, for the past several years Great Britain . . . has been preparing for war with Russia in Asia," or to find his successor in that office gloomily contrasting British strength with Russian weakness on the borders of Afghanistan in 1898.[104]

Yet there is no better way of grasping the actual place that Central Asia occupied in the defense priorities of the Ministry of War than by an examination of the war plans against Persia, Afghanistan, and China prepared by the staff of Turkestan district in 1900. Those contingency plans for the unforeseen required offensive action against each of those three Asian states: the seizure of the Persian border provinces of Khorosan and Astrabad; the capture of Herat, Mazar-i-Sharif, and Kabul; and advances to Kuldja and Kashgar. Yet the resources that could be allocated for those ambitious undertakings were no more than skeletal. For example, in an attack on Afghanistan, Tashkent estimated that the Russian invaders would be outnumbered two to one by Anglo-Indian and Afghan forces, while only 14,000 troops in all would have to suffice for the invasion of the western provinces of China. Although the Turkestan District Commander huffed that there were "significant chances of success" despite those odds, it had to be obvious even to him that the forces of which he disposed sufficed only for the launching of temporary expeditions, not wars of permanent conquest.[105]

Given the importance of defending Russia in Europe, Ministry of War officials were not inclined to devote more resources to

Central Asia than they had to. For that reason they typically turned a deaf ear to the demands for reinforcements that thundered to them every year from that quarter. To be sure, Kuropatkin, who had once commanded Transcaspia himself, at first showed greater interest in the security problems of Central Asia after he became War Minister (1898) than had Vannovskii. But he rapidly became persuaded that Europe had to come first in the thinking of his Ministry, and thereafter he acted accordingly.

In retrospect the Imperial government can only have regretted that it had not been as wise in other matters as it had been with regard to Central Asia. The alliance with France had relieved the pressure on the empire's diplomats and strategists. An improving economy and a uniformly cautious set of foreign policies might have provided Russia with the means and the time for the further development of its defenses. Yet such was not to be. As the decade of the 1890s proceeded, Russia became ever more prone to take bold, if not insane, risks in foreign affairs.

The dismal catalogue of errors began in 1895 with the conclusion of the Sino-Japanese War. Quickly defeating China, Japan had imposed upon it the Peace of Shimonoseki, which involved Japanese annexation of Formosa and the Liaotung peninsula. Alarmed by those Japanese gains, Russia immediately enlisted Germany and France to force a revision in the treaty. The scenario of 1878 repeated itself, with Russia this time taking the role of Bismarckian Germany: Japan was forced to disgorge much of what it had acquired through the war, Liaotung included.[106] That Russian interference left even more resentment in Tokyo than the German meddling of 1878 had left in Petersburg, and it gave birth to a broad-based nationalist movement with the slogan "Gashin shotan" (suffer privation for revenge.)[107] Russian diplomats, however, did little to effect a reconciliation with the Japanese. In the following year the Russian government organized the Russo-Chinese bank. While the bank, capitalized largely by the French, was nominally private, no one could fail to see that its true purpose was to serve as an instrument of Russian policy in China. Beijing was eventually induced to grant it a concession to build and operate the so-called Chinese Eastern Railway in northern Manchuria. That saved Russia millions of rubles, for it completed the Trans-Siberian Railroad with a direct shortcut across Chinese territory. To protect its interests, the Imperial government dispatched regular troops to Manchuria masquerading as a railroad police force. Japan and the European powers could not but regard those activities as another stage in an evolving Russian imperialism.

The Far East was not the only casino in which Russia was willing to gamble. In 1897 the population of Crete rose up against Turkish rule, demanding union with their fellow Greeks on the mainland. Turkey and Greece went to war; Britain made noises about sending a fleet to Constantinople. In the midst of the Cretan crisis the Imperial government came within a hair of of ordering a surprise attack for the seizure and permanent annexation of the Bosphorus. Russia in the end did benefit from the crisis, for it was against its backdrop that it negotiated an agreement with the Austrians to respect the status quo in the Balkans for the next ten years.[108] A Russian expedition against the Bosphorus in 1897, however, could easily have touched off a general European war.[109]

If the act of imperialism in the Mediterranean was aborted, Russia's Pacific imperialism was unrestrained. In 1898 Petersburg responded to the German lease of Kiaochow by proclaiming the virtual annexation of the Liaotung peninsula, with its two important coastal cities of Dal'nyi (Dairen) and Port Arthur. Two years later Russia sent a small army into China to help suppress the Boxer Rebellion.[110] After the Boxers had been crushed, Petersburg maintained a formal military occupation of all of Manchuria for several years, ostensibly as a guarantee of Chinese good behavior. At the same time Russia also appeared to be establishing itself in Korea, enhancing its influence in that feeble kingdom through railroad and timber concessions. By the early twentieth century there could be little doubt that Russia's movements in the Far East had greatly enhanced the prospect of war with Japan. Although Nicholas II complimented Lamzdorff in 1901 for following "an honorable and consistent policy" in foreign relations, Russian actual policies in Asia conspicuously diverged from that description.[111] They were contaminated with recklessness and consequently devoid of either consistency or honor.

How, then, can one account for the allure of Far Eastern imperialism to Russia? What induced the Imperial government to abandon its caution and take risks? Many theories have been

THE RUSSIAN EMPIRE AT THE TURN OF THE CENTURY

advanced. Popular at the time was the erroneous view that Russian expansion in Asia was the unfolding of a deeply considered master plan.[112] Among more recent scholars of the problem, some have stressed the economic and psychological motivations behind Russian imperialism, while others have explained it as the accidental by-product of the bureaucratic politics of an increasingly disunited and incoherent Imperial government.[113] As we shall see shortly, although there is something to each of these interpretations, none is by any means complete.

In order to understand Russia's East Asian advance, it is best to begin with the court. In 1894 Russia had a new Tsar in Nicholas II. Young, dreamy, and ambitious, Nicholas had been a believer since his youth that Russia would someday become the greatest empire on the face of the earth. Those vaguely messianic ideas were fed by his cousin, the German Emperor William II, who (for self-interested reasons) constantly reminded him that Russia's future lay in Asia. Characteristic was the letter of April 26, 1895, in which William promised to "guard the rear of Russia so that nobody shall hamper your action towards the Far East!" and concluded with the observation that "[it] is clearly the great task of the future for Russia to cultivate the Asian continent and to defend Europe from the inroads of the great yellow race."[114] As the years went by Nicholas, was also increasingly inclined to heed such courtiers as A. M. Bezobrazov and Aleksei Abaza, who urged forward policies in Korea and China upon him, justifying them with specious economic and strategic arguments.[115] Delusions of national grandeur, a platitudinous sense of destiny, and bad advice thus combined to cause Nicholas to smile on East Asian imperialism. For example, he responded to the news of the seizure of Port Arthur with the following telegram to Admiral Dubasov: "I rejoice in the fortunate conclusion of the landing and the occupation of an ice-free port on the Pacific."[116] There was, however, yet a third element: racism. Nicholas was no friend of the Japanese. Indeed, he had nearly been murdered by a demented Japanese policeman during a tour of the islands he had made while Crown Prince.[117] The trauma of that incident reinforced Nicholas's contempt for the Japanese, whom he persisted in underestimating until the military catastrophes of 1904–5 showed him otherwise.

But Nicholas did not make Russia's Far Eastern policy all by himself. All of his biographers agree he was a weak man and easily led.[118] It required pressure from some of the most powerful ministries in the state to commit the Emperor to Asian imperialism. A most important figure in this regard was Count S. Iu. Witte. Witte, the Minister of Finance, 1892–1903, rapidly became the most influential of all Nicholas's Ministers in the early part of his reign. He used this position to promote an entire financial and economic agenda, in which the Pacific and Asia played an integral part. Witte was the prime mover behind the scheme for the economic penetration of China. The Trans-Siberian and Chinese Eastern railroads would allow Russia to establish a monopoly over the resources and markets of Manchuria; he hoped that the profits realized could be plowed back into domestic economic development.[119] Despite his ignorance of the realities of warfare and foreign relations, and regardless of his *ex post facto* excuses, Witte was obviously aware that his economic program had military and diplomatic implications. Yet by the time he realized just how dangerous the situation in Asia was, he was too politically weak to do much about it.[120] Even though the total responsibility for the Far Eastern catastrophe cannot be laid at his door, he nonetheless deserves substantial blame for it.

Nicholas favored a bold foreign policy in part because of his inchoate longing for glory, and Witte, because of his desire for a flourishing economy. Both men consequently stressed the benefits that could accrue to Russia from imperialism. But for every argument that highlighted the potential rewards of international aggression there were many others that emphasized the probable losses that Russia would suffer if it *failed* to act. In fact, the most common rationale given for imperialism by turn-of-the-century Russian statesmen was founded upon fear that time was not on the side of Russia; that if Russia was not decisive enough it might lose opportunities that would never return; and that the consequences of inaction could be worse than those of audacity.

That style of thinking underlay, for example, the various schemes for an attack on the Bosphorus. In 1897 the crisis in Crete had once again provoked anxiety in Petersburg about the rapid decomposition of the Ottoman Empire. Were that to happen Europe would enter a period of explosive danger, for the Balkan states and the Great Powers were certain to squabble over the remains of Turkey. Still further, if Turkey did dissolve into anarchy it would doubtless lose control over the straits. It was the old worry all over again. If Russia did not then take control over them, some other power hostile to Russia might. And that, of course, resurrected the prospect of naval attacks on Russia's weakly defended Black Sea coastline. So worried was Vannovskii about this danger that in early January he was able to persuade Nicholas II to endorse a contingency plan to deal with it. In the event that large European naval squadrons moved on Constantinople, Russia was to make an amphibious landing in the upper Bosphorus and occupy territory up to Beikov on the Asiatic side and Kirech-Burnu on the European. The purpose of the operation, according to the Ministry of War, was exclusively "to maintain our security in the Black Sea."[121] No attack was contemplated against Constantinople, nor any against the Dardanelles. In other words, the reason for the Bosphorus expedition was not to ensure that Russia could get out of the Black Sea in the future at will; it was, on the contrary, supposed to prevent other Powers from getting in.

Fear also accounted for the Ministry of Foreign Affairs' qualified support for the plan. During a report to the Emperor of March 26 Lamzdorff said the following:

> Is it possible actually to seize at once the upper Bosphorus, to establish ourselves there, and truly cut off the entrance to the Black Sea? Everything depends on this main, vital question. If the Ministries of War and Marine can vouch for the successful fulfillment of their task, diplomacy can guarantee a peaceful outcome of the undertaking. Actually controlling the passage into the Black Sea . . . we could let the European powers and the Balkan states divide the Turkish inheritance and fight over it as it suited them.

Lamzdorff, however, went on to warn Nicholas II that an expedition should only be launched if the chances of seizing and holding the Bosphorus with one surprise attack were overwhelmingly favorable. If Russia could not establish an impregnable position on the Bosphorus, "then this unsuccessful and hare-brained attempt would inevitably lead to war and to countless miseries for us."[122] If Lamzdorff displayed a sensitivity to the dangers of undertaking this mission, he was also alive to the perils of not doing so. He told the Tsar later that summer that "circumstances might suddenly force us into essential action with extreme speed or deprive us forever of the chance to resolve our historic tasks in a sense corresponding to our interests, thus forcing us to bear a terrible responsibility before our posterity."[123]

Lamzdorff's point was simple: if Russia did not avail itself of this opportunity to take the Bosphorus, it might never have another. If another strong Power got there first, then all of southern Russia might be permanently threatened. In the end there was, of course, no expedition, either in 1897 or in 1899. The main reason was that after close study the Ministry of War found it impossible to be confident of rapid victory. The Main Staff had calculated that a surprise attack would require at least 30,000 troops and 104 guns. The naval assets at Russia's disposal would not permit the embarkation and transport of more than 20,000 troops over any two-week period; those numbers were insufficient to guarantee a Russian *fait accompli*.[124]

If the calculus of fear lay behind the planned but unexecuted attack on the Bosphorus, it was no less evident in the very real East Asian imperialism of the regime of Nicholas II. In the east, no less than in the Levant, Russia felt that it was face to face with yet another crumbling empire. Were China to fall, and if other Powers got the lion's share of the spoils, the damage to Russia could be incalculable. With the exception of Witte, then, most of the proponents of eastern expansion accentuated the negative (that is, the costs of inaction) as much or more than they did the rewards of aggression. One example was Lieutenant Prince Vol'konskii. Vol'konskii had been a member of the delegation, headed by Prince E. Ukhtomskii, that Nicholas II had sent to China and Siberia in the summer of 1897. Upon his return to the capital, Vol'konskii authored an influential secret memorandum for the Emperor—a mini-treatise on Russia's position in Asia. Russia's failure to acquire any suitable military bases in China, he noted, had already deprived the Russian people "in the future of all the countless advantages connected with rule over millions of people and countries rich in territory." But Vol'konskii had an even more immediate and compelling reason to urge such a policy: Japan and the European Powers were on the march in the Pacific. If Russia declined to play the game of imperialism in Asia, it not only needlessly impoverished its future, but also risked eventually losing such Asian territories as it already had. This was a variation on a familiar strategic justification for imperialism: without new territories and bases, the old one cannot be adequately protected. Russia's lethargy in Asia was hazardous, for "if this continues for many more years then Vladivostok [will be] threatened with the fate of Sevastopol."[125]

Russia's Asian imperialism in this period was thus driven more by reactive desperation than by ebullient opportunism. Lamzdorff, to provide another illustration, in November 1897 gave the Emperor the following reasons why Russia had to acquire a Chinese port. Germany's seizure of Kiaochow would inevitably induce a new wave of imperial competition in China in which Russia had to take part. If Russia could not take a Chinese port for its own at this very moment, it had to renounce the idea once and for all. "If not we," he argued, "then within days England will appear in Port Arthur."[126] After the occupation of Port Arthur Lamzdorff continued to embellish that theme. In a report to the Emperor of January 7, 1898, responding to charges from certain high-ranking naval officials that Russia had acted too hastily and that Port Arthur had serious technical defects as a naval base, he offered the excuse that at the time "the acquisition of some port or another [*kakogo-libo porta*]" had been "unconditionally essential."[127]

An identical sense of urgency permeated the memorandum on Korea that the Grand Duke Aleksandr Mikhailovich presented to the Emperor scarcely two years later. The Grand Duke Aleksandr, the Tsar's brother-in-law, had long been a staunch proponent of increasing Russia's influence within the Hermit Kingdom. Hostile to both Witte and the Foreign Ministry bureaucracy, Aleksandr has usually been depicted as a witless and callow booster of Asian imperialism. Yet in his note of 1899 he defended a forward posture in Korea much as Lamzdorff had defended the seizure of Port Arthur. Russia had to become dominant in northern Korea, he wrote, to prevent Britain and Japan from taking over the entire country. At the same time Aleksandr advocated a deal with Tokyo over Korea almost amounting to an informal condominium. If Russia temporized and Japan, Britain, or both gobbled up all of Korea, that outcome would be more than an opportunity forgone: Russia's possessions south of the Amur would thereafter be in danger. Russia consequently had to advance in Korea out of a concern for self-defense. Simultaneously it had to seek an accommodation with Tokyo to preclude a war with Japan for which it was unprepared.[128]

The reasons that Russia embroiled herself in the Far East were many. There was the desire to compete with the other Great Powers, there was the Emperor's vision of national greatness, there was the half-baked economic program of Witte. But a decisive component underpinning the Asian imperialism was anxiety. The key moments in the Asian expansion, including the seizure of the Liaotung peninsula and the occupation of Manchuria, were impulsive acts spawned by fear. The Imperial government pursued an aggressive course in the East without thinking through the probable consequences in advance and, as it transpired, without considering what the costs of imperialism would be. Russia had carelessly acquired a new Eastern empire but lacked the manpower and revenue to maintain it. Attempts to encourage Russian colonization in Manchuria were unsuccessful. Witte's expectations about the monetary gains Russia would realize from its special position there also proved illusory. Despite all the efforts that Petersburg made to make Manchuria a captive market for Russian goods, Russia still continued to run a huge trade deficit with China, amounting in 1903 to more than 26 million rubles.[129] Nor did Manchuria prove to be conspicuously fertile soil for Russian industrial enterprise. The Staff of the Priamur Military District observed in early 1903 that Russia had failed utterly to integrate the population of Manchuria into its economy; since Russia had gotten involved in the provinces, only two Russian factories had been started there, and those were distilleries that produced liquor mainly for the Russian army of occupation.[130]

The problem was that Russia did not feel it could back down from the position into which it had blundered. Factiousness and intrigue back in St. Petersburg were no help to the pursuit of consistent Far Eastern policies. The creation of special institutions to cope with the Eastern problem (the Viceroyalty of the East and the Special Committee on Far Eastern Affairs, both in 1903) only heightened the confusion. The danger of war with Japan seemed to be increasing with every year, and the Imperial government could not decide whether to seek to avoid war through appeasement or to try to prepare for it with a crash program for Asian defense. Appeasement would risk national self-abasement before the despised Orientals, while war preparations, requiring massive expenditures, were scarcely more palatable. The upshot was that the Imperial government never fully accepted or fully rejected either alternative. By the end of 1903 Russia had neither tried hard enough to preserve peace nor prepared sufficiently to wage war.

Of course, St. Petersburg did not lack enthusiasts for war with Tokyo. They were people who ignorantly supposed that the easy victory Russia was sure to achieve would establish it as the undisputed hegemon of East Asia. Some courtiers even went so far as to prepare drafts of the peace treaty that Russia would impose on Japan after its defeat. One such document of 1903, for instance, stipulated limitations on the size of the postwar Japanese army and navy; the annexation of Tsushima island; a heavy war indemnity; and repudiation of the treaty of 1875 by which Russia had recognized Japan's international equality with itself.[131] Shortly after the war had begun, Nicholas himself informed a horrified Lamzdorff that Russia ought to insist on the total neutralization and disarmament of Japan as the principle condition of peace.[132]

Anyone who knew anything at all about modern warfare, however, realized that defeating Japan in the Far East would by no means be easy. The Ministry of War concluded in 1900 that Russia would "in all likelihood" have to go to war with Japan in the near future and found little comfort in the prospect.[133] In the first place, the Main Staff believed that such a war would have to be fought on the Asian mainland, because the Russian Pacific fleet, incapable of policing both the Yellow Sea and the Sea of Japan simultaneously, would be unable to prevent a Japanese landing in Korea.[134] In view of the distribution of forces, then, the war would begin with Russia at a terrible numerical disadvantage. The Chief of Staff estimated in 1901 that within forty days of the start of hostilities, Japan could advance through Korea an army of 96 battalions of infantry, 90 squadrons of cavalry, and 504 guns to within 180 versts of the border of southern Manchuria. Russia would be able to muster forces only one-third as strong to oppose those of Japan in the same amount of time.[135] Russia's Far Eastern generals would accordingly be obliged to retreat until reinforcements could be brought in from Central Asia and European Russia itself—a process that might take as long as six months. Questions about the availability of such reinforcements surfaced almost at once. How many troops could Russia prudently dispatch to the fields of Manchuria without imperiling its western defenses? To draw down military strength in the westernmost districts of the Empire might provoke an attack by the Triple Alliance. After the conclusion of the Anglo-Japanese alliance of 1902, there were more worries still. If Britain took the side of Japan in a war with Russia, the troops of Turkestan Military District might not be available for combat in the Far East, for it might be necessary to keep them where they were to put pressure on India.[136] Further complicating the task of Russia during the initial stage of the war would be the fact that the two main objects Russia would have to defend—Port Arthur and Vladivostok—were more than 1,500 versts apart. The position of Port Arthur would be particularly dangerous. If the Japanese army succeeded in driving up the Korean peninsula and irrupting into southern Manchuria, Port Arthur could be cut off from the main body of Russian forces, its garrison abandoned to shift for itself.

None of those problems in conceptualizing a Russo-Japanese war had been adequately thought through when the war broke out. That was not only because of their technical difficulty, but because the entire system of decentralized military planning militated against coherent war preparations. During the five years that preceded the conflict, Kvantung oblast, Transamur province, the Viceroyalty of the East, and the Main Staff itself all competed in the design of plans, many wildly inconsistent with the others.[137] When the Japanese began their surprise bombardment of the Russian Pacific fleet (February 1904), Russia's war plans were as rudimentary as its fortifications at Port Arthur were incomplete.

The Ministry of War was clearly at fault for failing to devise sound plans for a war with Japan. But that Ministry was not responsible for creating the imbroglio in the Far East in the first place. High-ranking officials of the Ministry had not sought dominion in Manchuria. Kuropatkin in particular was notorious for his opposition to Far Eastern adventurism; he had argued for years that his Ministry had not been provided with the resources to defend Russia's European frontiers, let alone its Asian ones. To be sure, Kuropatkin was either optimistic or unimaginative enough to predict that Russia would prevail against Tokyo despite all the defects in Russia's military posture in the Pacific. But he believed that the bill for that unnecessary victory would be excessive. At a special conference in March 1903, Kuropatkin advocated the reestablishment of friendly relations with Japan, estimating that a Russo-Japanese war would cost the empire at least 50,000 lives and 800 million rubles—"sacrifices that will be too large to be borne, given our complete lack of desire for a war."[138] To the Ministry of War the Far East was an infuriating distraction from Russia's chief security problem, Central Europe. The drain of resources to the east meant that there was less to spend on military readiness where it really counted: in the Baltic, in Poland, and in the Ukraine. The Chief of Staff complained to the Emperor in March 1903: "It is essential to give priority to the main danger over others. And this menaces Russia from the powers of the Triple Alliance. They threaten Russia with the greatest loss, having the capacity . . . to deliver a blow against the very center of our might."[139]

1900 and After: Russia Takes Stock of the Strategic Situation

In March 1900 War Minister Kuropatkin delivered a lengthy report to his sovereign. This remarkable document was no less than an analysis of the ways in which Russia had used its military power over the preceding two hundred years and a series of predictions about the sorts of military challenges Russia might have to face in the twentieth century.[140] *Inter alia*, the War Minister offered a *tour de horizon* of Russia's strategic position around the globe in addition to a shrewd assessment of the limitations of military force. Russia, he argued, neither needed nor desired war with any of the other Great Powers; it simply had nothing to gain by it. Even if Russia were to win a war with Germany, territorial compensation would not profit it. Were it to annex East Prussia, as it had tried to do during the Seven Years War, for example, it would acquire a subject population that, owing to its nationalism and its superior culture, would never adapt itself to Russian rule. Further, Germany was a great nation that would never reconcile itself to the loss of such a province and would eventually unleash a new war against Russia to recover it.[141]

What was true of Germany also held for Austria-Hungary. It would be imprudent in the extreme for a victorious Russia to strip Vienna, say, of Galicia. The Slavs of the Hapsburg Monarchy, Kuropatkin noted, did not want to become Russian subjects. They wanted to create independent states. If Galicia were taken, it could become "an Alsace-Lorraine for us" by providing a constant pretext for the renewal of hostilities, much as Germany's occupation of those two French territories had created a permanent risk of war in Western Europe.[142]

In the interests of security, Kuropatkin continued, Russia should also eschew conquests in Asia. Russia needed no rectification of the Central Asian border, had no designs on Afghanistan, and coveted no portions of India. Although Russia had to be plausibly capable of attacking India as way of influencing the British government, Petersburg should seek a peaceful resolution of its disputes in Asia with London. War with Great Britain was definitely undesirable.[143]

To be sure, Kuropatkin had to concede, Russia was not a satisfied Power. In a report addressed to Nicholas II he had no choice but to endorse the continued economic exploitation of Manchuria, the expansion of Russian influence in the East, and an expedition against the Bosphorus at some time in the future. He nonetheless urged moderation on his Emperor: Russia should annex no territories in either Persia or China.[144] Indeed, his disapproval of imperialism in general was evident in the warning he gave Nicholas about the hazards it might engender:

> However just our attempts to possess the exit to the Black Sea, to acquire an outlet to the Indian Ocean, and to obtain an outlet to the Pacific, these missions touch so deeply on the interests of almost the entire world that in pursuit of them we must prepare for a struggle with a coalition of Great Britain, Germany, Austria-Hungary, Turkey, China, and Japan. These powers are frightened not by the fact itself of Russia's movement toward one or the other of these exits but by the consequences which would ensue if the movement succeeded. Possession of the Bosphorus and the exit to the Mediterranean ocean would give us the possibility of decisively acting in the Egyptian question in order to internationalize the Suez canal. Access to the Indian Ocean

will create a constant threat to India. But the most important thing that has to frighten the more cultured peoples of
Europe and America, supplying the entire world with the
products of their factories and plants, is Russia's entry into
the struggle with them for world markets. Holding in her
hands the railroads connecting the Pacific Ocean and the
Baltic Sea and having her tentacles in the Bosphorus, Russia, with her inexhaustible natural resources, could create a
frightful industrial competition for the powers of the entire
world.[145]

Kuropatkin was thus arguing that Russia had to be very careful
to consider how its international behavior was perceived. Unchecked Russian imperialism might well incur enmity on the part
of every important Power on the face of the earth. Despite the
hearty optimism that he was almost required to feign elsewhere
in his report, Kuropatkin insisted that Russia was unprepared
for war against a global coalition.[146]

The general was of course a child of his time; many of the
intellectual systems popular at the turn of the century influenced
his thinking. The passage cited above, for instance, contains obvious traces of McKinder's geopolitics, Social Darwinism, even
Marxism (in its pointed reference to "the struggle for markets").
Yet despite those lapses in cogitation, the preparation of the
report of March 1900 was the first occasion in Russian history in
which a statesman had tried to commit to paper a synoptic vision
of Russia's political and military strategies in the past, present,
and future. It was a masterly effort and inspires admiration.

On a more mundane level, however, the report repeatedly
emphasized a theme of great concern to the Ministry of War: the
negative consequences of Russia's preoccupation in the Far East
for the security of its western frontiers. "To the delight of Germany," Kuropatkin wrote, "in directing our attention to the Far
East we are giving her and Austria a decisive preponderance in
forces and materiel over us." The main task of the Ministry of
War in the twentieth century could be none other than the development of Russia's defenses against the Triple Alliance.[147]

From the standpoint of the Main Staff, it was Asian expansionism that explained why Russia remained so militarily weak in
the west. The political necessity of meeting some (but by no

means all) of the demands of the security of Manchuria entailed a corresponding diminution of Russia's security in Europe. Although the Chief of the Main Naval Staff himself insisted in 1903 that Russia needed a defensive, not an offensive, naval strategy and a fleet composed chiefly of torpedo boats and submarines, not battleships, Far Eastern imperialism almost inevitably resulted in an expansion in the size of Russia's blue-water navy.[148] That could be paid for only by increasing the share of the navy in Russia's overall defense outlays, an expedient that caused irritation in the Ministry of War. Whereas the navy's budget had been less than 13 percent that of the army's in 1883, by 1903 it amounted to over 35 percent.[149] Competition with the navy was only one of the many headaches that the Russian position in Manchuria engendered for the War Ministry. In 1898, in order more readily to satisfy eastern security requirements, Nicholas II had commanded a *total halt* in the growth of Russia's armed forces in the western theaters.[150] What was true of manpower was also true of railroads. "The diversion of the financial resources of Russia to the construction of the Siberian railroad almost stopped the development and improvement of our net of railways in the western half of the country," went one ministerial complaint.[151]

As the highest leadership of the army saw it, the Russian government was in effect freezing defense expenditures in the west at the very time that they needed to be increased. By the turn of the century the concern of the Ministry of War was not so much with improving Russia's western defense posture as with arresting its deterioration. The worldwide arms race had not abated but accelerated in the final quarter of the nineteenth century; states vied with each to acquire the new military technologies: machine guns, field mortars, smokeless powder, and so forth. Russia's relative poverty in comparison with many of the other Great Powers disadvantaged it in its effort to keep up. One solution proposed by Kuropatkin was arms control. In 1898 he suggested to the Ministry of Foreign Affairs that Russia negotiate with Austria-Hungary a ten-year moratorium on the acquisition of offensive quick-firing artillery. According to Kuropatkin, an agreement on that point might save Russia as much as 120 million rubles. But the trial balloon came to nothing, for, as its critics pointed out, a treaty that did not also limit German acquisition of advanced artillery was valueless, all the more so since Germany already had quick-firing field guns in its arsenals.[152] Kuropatkin's enthusiasm for improving the financial position of his ministry by means of arms control treaties was, however, undiminished. In the following year he helped persuade Nicholas II to call the first ever international disarmament conference at the Hague. The real purpose of that initiative was to reduce the pressure on the Russian military budget.[153]

The Hague conference proved a disappointment for the Ministry of War. Although it did adopt resolutions prohibiting the use of poison gas projectiles and expanding bullets in warfare, opposition from the German delegation prevented any consideraton of limiting or reversing the arms race. Given the intransigence of Russia's neighbors, arms control could not serve as the financial panacea Kuropatkin had hoped it might.

The strain of Far Eastern imperialism, then, was tipping the balance of power against Russia in the west. The growing disparity of railway development was, characteristically, the trend that disturbed the Main Staff the most. By 1900 Germany had seventeen railroad lines (six double-tracked) to the Russian frontier; Austria had ten lines and twelve tracks; Rumania, then considered a likely ally of the Triplice, had two. Russia had but eleven tracks extending to the borders of those potential enemies.[154] According to the estimates of the Main Staff, Germany had the capability of running 552 trains a day to the frontier, and Russia, only 98.[155] By 1903 the Ministry of War had concluded that with respect to railroads the Triple Alliance had achieved "total superiority over us."[156]

Almost every highly placed figure in the Russian army agreed about the potentially deadly consequences of the transportation gap. The chief of the Warsaw district, for example, noted that because of the railway disadvantage in the initial stage of a war the troops under his command would "have to endure the blows of an enemy two or even four times stronger" than themselves. If the Imperial government could not build up its own rail net, he implored it at least to appropriate money for the completion of the fortresses of Warsaw, Zergrzh, and Novogeorgievsk.[157] In 1898 the commanders of each of the westernmost military districts emphasized that the preparation of the most likely theaters of war was completely inadequate owing to the insufficiency of railroads.[158] In a top secret communiqué Kiev district complained that the position of the army it was supposed to field in wartime (the army of the southwest) was becoming

> ...more unsatisfactory every year. At a time when our neighbors accelerate the concentration of their armies on our frontiers, lay down new railways and perfect the existing ones, almost nothing is being done to speed up the concentration of the southwestern army.[159]

The central War Ministry itself reiterated the warnings of the district commanders: the railroad superiority of the Powers of the Triple Alliance would create for Russia "a critical period lasting from 14 to 35 days after the declaration of war. During this period, Austria-Hungary and Germany might employ coordinated attacks to smash Russia's still concentrating forces."[160]

Nor were railroads the only category of transportation in which Russia was deficient. The commander of Odessa district pointed out in 1900 that the contingency plan for an amphibious attack against the Bosphorus and Constantinople was still completely unworkable. He wrote that the only vessels he had to ferry the strike force across the Black Sea were "three old ships, which had previously served the volunteer fleet for ten years and were then transferred to the navy for the needs of the expedition."[161] Those rusting tubs were both too few and too unsafe to be of any use in an emergency. Since the employment all alternative means of transport (the main battle fleet and commercial steamers) would not even suffice for the movement of the first echelon, the Odessa commander appealed for the construction of a class of modern troop ships in the Black Sea.[162] The Caucasus district sounded the same theme, highlighting the problems that poor transportation created for its war planning. Referring to the paucity of railroads and steamships in his district, the Caucasus commander warned that Turkey might be able to concentrate more troops than Russia could in the first thirty or forty days of a war.[163] A secret War Ministry report submitted to the Tsar in 1903 asserted that Russia was "insufficiently prepared for defense not only against Germany, but even against Austria-Hungary."[164]

What made that conclusion all the more dismal was the fact

that the international environment was increasingly conducive to war. In his 1903 report Kuropatkin informed the Emperor that if corrective measures were not taken the likelihood of a European war would be greater within five years than it was at present. The feebler Russia appeared to be, the more probable it was that its enemies, Germany in particular, "with her barely concealed desire to occupy a position of global hegemony in the near future," would launch an attack. The War Minister explained that he was troubled by the recent unrest among the students, workers, and peasants of the Russian Empire; if those phenomena could not be halted, the Triple Alliance would doubtless construe them as signs of Russian decadence. That problem was small, however, when compared with the drain on resources that stemmed from Russia's forward policy in East Asia. The outlays in the east had weakened the western defenses of the empire, and if the process continued much longer it would without question encourage Germany to meddle in Russia's most vital interests by making "demands on us in both the political and economic arenas."[165]

Increasing uncertainty about the war plans of the enemy also fueled the anxiety of Russia's strategists at the turn of the century. Intelligence about the war dispositions and order-of-battle of Austria-Hungary remained excellent.[166] But Russia had failed to collect reliable information about what its most formidable adversary, Germany, intended to do. The 1901 special conference on western defense confessed that "to determine the number of German corps earmarked for deployment against us is not possible." "In all probability" the journal of the conference continued, "Germany has prepared two plans of concentration: one based on the deployment of the main forces against France, and the other against Russia. The choice of one or the other of these plans will take place at the moment of the declaration of war, depending on the general political situation."[167] The vacuum of intelligence about Berlin left Chief of Staff Sakharov equally perplexed, ruing his inability to predict whether Germany would deliver its main blow in the west or in the east.[168] The Ministry of War considered that question unanswerable without reliable espionage, because all other clues about potential German intentions were ambiguous. The Germans were, for example, making significant investments in defensive works on both their eastern and their western frontiers, which would be consonant with offensives in either direction.[169] Germany's highly developed transportation network could also, in the Main Staff's opinion, support offensives against either France or Russia equally well. Russia had no comparable flexibility. It therefore followed that the only prudent course would be for Russia to anticipate the worst case scenario and make its plans on the presumption that the main German onslaught would fall in the east. At a special conference held in Warsaw in March 1902, Nicholas II himself commanded that henceforth all Russian war planning be based on the assumption of a massive German attack.[170]

Another reason that the military leadership felt that Russia had to prepare for a nightmare attack by eighteen German corps, in addition to the entire Austrian army, was a disturbing shift in French military policy. The radical administration of Waldeck-Rousseau had come to power in Paris in 1899 determined to purge the French officer corps of monarchism and clericalism. The reforms of Waldeck-Rousseau's Minister of War, General André, included a reduction in the term of conscript service to two years, an attack on the privileges of the officers, and the employment of a network of informants within the corps to spy on the political reliability of officers considered for promotions. Those measures demoralized the French army and arguably reduced its efficiency.[171] Such at least was the perception in St. Petersburg. Throughout 1902 and 1903 the Minister of War worried that the deterioration of the French army might offer yet another inducement for Germany to strike at Russia first. The weaker the French army became, the greater the temptation for Berlin to think it could postpone settling military accounts with Paris until later. Still worse, there was the possibility that military debility might induce a future French government to opt out of the alliance with St. Petersburg altogether. In that event, Russia would have to confront the full power of the Triplice by itself, a prospect that was completely unthinkable.[172]

Giving the changing strategic circumstances—the increasing risk of war, the presumption of massive German attack, and concerns about the reliability of the French—did it not now behoove the Russian government to rework its military deployments on strictly defensive lines? Nicholas II, for one, thought so. In October 1902 he inquired of his War Minister about the possibility of an initial Russian withdrawal to Minsk in the event of a Teutonic invasion. Such a move would permit Russia to concentrate its forces in safety deep within the country. Still further, because Germany and Austria would still have to deal with the Russian fortresses in the rear areas, they might find it more difficult than they had expected to consolidate their position in Poland.[173]

But the Main Staff was flabbergasted by the Emperor's suggestion. Ministerial functionaries there, believing that a defensive withdrawal like the one Nicholas was advocating would be a catastrophe, immediately prepared a comprehensive report designed to explain why. The report (really a crash course in strategy for the Emperor) resurrected all the arguments against an initial Russian pullback that had been current since the early 1870s. A withdrawal would mean ceding Poland, with its agricultural and industrial resources and its population of 16 million, to the enemy without resistance. Such a move would hearten the Austrian army and bolster the morale of its Slavic regiments. It would simultaneously discourage Bulgaria and Serbia from entering the war on Russia's side. Still further, all the money that had been devoted to the preparation of the Polish theater of war would have been spent in vain. Finally, a withdrawal to a depth of 300 versts would be impossible without the construction of an entirely new network of bases and depots, for which the bill could exceed 200 million rubles.[174] But the Main Staff also came up with a new justification for the forward deployment of the Russian army. This, of course, was the Franco-Russian alliance itself.

As one of his first official acts after the death of his father, Nicholas II had reaffirmed Russia's adherence to the French alliance in a personal note to Casimir Perier, President of the Republic.[175] He had done so despite the strident protests of William II of Germany, who had hoped that the accession of a new Emperor in Petersburg would give him an opportunity to pry Russia away from France. The German Emperor wrote his Russian cousin in characteristically quaint English: "[I]f you are allied 'for better, for worse' with the French, well then keep those damned rascals in order and make them sit still, and if not then don't let your men who go to France make the French believe that you are allied and get reckless and turn their heads until they lose them and we have to fight in Europe instead of for it against the East!"[176] Even if it disregarded the opinions of the Kaiser, the government of Nicholas II initially looked on the Franco-Russian alliance much as Obruchev had—as a treaty whereby Russia had gained much and had given up little. The alliance guaranteed Russia succor in the event of war with the Triplice without hobbling it with any obligations toward Paris that could not be repudiated if necessary. Lamzdorff, for example, gloated that the chief advantage of the military convention was that it was vague.[177]

But that lax view of the alliance on Petersburg's part would change. In the summer of 1899 France's Foreign Minister Theophile Delcassé visited Russia. The alliance partners once again reaffirmed their commitment to each other with an exchange of notes. Delcassé's mission resulted in more than empty ceremonies of reassurance, however, for he was able to persuade the Russian government to agree to annual strategic conferences between the Chiefs of Staff of the two sides.[178]

In those staff conversations, the first of which occurred in 1900, Russia was forced to share more information with Paris than it had ever done before. It was required to discuss and defend its thinking about the probable nature of a future war. Finally, Russia pledged to undertake certain specific military operations at the behest of France. The Franco-Russian alliance was thus becoming more concrete, and Russian freedom of maneuver was diminishing correspondingly.

At the 1900 conference, for example, France predicted that Germany would attack in the west with the bulk of its forces. Chief of Staff Sakharov acknowledged that to be the most likely possibility but insisted that Russia had to entertain the contrary hypothesis of a main German attack in the east, in view of Germany's need to support its Austrian ally and of the extraordinary offensive capability of the railroads that Germany had been laying down in Silesia and East Prussia. In that event Russia would confront sixteen German and fourteen Austrian corps, and at least at first would have to go on the defensive. If the situation proved to be otherwise and France was the principle target of German aggression, Russia would be ready to attack the Triple Alliance with 700,000 men by M + 28. Sakharov's French counterpart, General Delanne, objected that if Russia did not take the offensive until four weeks into a war, it might be too late. Both

France and Germany, he said, expected that there would be climactic, decisive frontier battles from ten to eighteen days after the outbreak of hostilities. Were France to be defeated in those battles, Germany would be able to employ its interior lines of communication to transfer possibly as many as eight additional army corps to the eastern front by the twenty-eighth day. Delanne therefore urged Russia to launch spoiling attacks with as many forces as it had available as early as possible. Sakharov grudgingly had to agree.[179] At the next staff conference, held in Petersburg in 1901, the French were even more specific about what they wanted Russia to do; they demanded that Russia invade Germany with infantry no later than M + 14. Sakharov, once again, responded that he would give the matter his most serious consideration.[180]

Russia made still other pledges during the staff talks of 1900 and 1901. For instance, it promised France that it too would mobilize "to oppose, with force if necessary, an aggrandizement of Germany at the expense of the integrity of the Austro-Hungarian monarchy."[181] Were France to be attacked by Britain, Russia agreed to make a diversionary attack in Afghanistan, both to prevent the British army from drawing reinforcements from India and to preclude British assaults on any of France's Asian colonies. In 1901 Sakharov said that as soon as the Orenburg to Tashkent railway line was complete, Russia would be capable of moving 300,000 troops to the Afghan border within three weeks.[182] Should Britain attack Russia, France's offer of a diversion—simulation of invasion preparations through the deployment of 150,000 men on the English Channel—was clearly unequal. Russia, after all, was giving its word to fight the British, and France, merely to stage mock threats.[183] All those promises considerably diverged from the original Russian interpretation of the alliance with France. In 1892 Russian statesmen would have angrily rebuffed any attempt by the French to dictate what Russia's wartime strategy ought to be, yet by 1900 the Russian Chief of Staff was complacently enduring French lectures on that subject. Similarly, it would have been unthinkable in 1892 for Russia to obligate itself to enter a war against Britain over colonial conflicts between London and Paris, and even more unthinkable for it to consent to fight to defend the integrity of Austria-Hungary, one of its most implacable enemies. By endorsing "the substance" of the staff talks of 1900 and 1901, however, this was precisely what Nicholas II did.[184]

Of course, it was always possible for Russia to foreswear itself and go back on its promises to Paris when war came. If Germany attacked France first, Paris expected its Russian ally to respond with an offensive in East Prussia. Russia could, however, decline to do so. Taking advantage of Germany's western distraction, it could redeploy its forces to the southwest in the expectation of knocking Austria-Hungary out of the war—the course of action Obruchev had recommended most strongly in the early 1890s. That plan still had its adherents in 1900, as a report originating in Odessa Military District made clear.[185] But Russia's military leadership was increasingly convinced that it could not fecklessly disavow the obligations it had assumed toward the French. The reason was the security crisis that Asian imperialism had engendered on the western borders of the empire.

Simply put, Russia's Manchurian adventurism had made Russia much more dependent upon France than it had been a decade previously. In 1892 France had been the suppliant, Russia the party wooed. By 1900 the situation had been reversed, and France held the preponderant position with the alliance. In view of the widening gap between the military power of Russia and that of its Teutonic adversaries, the assistance of an ally, even ally whose only military power was in decay and whose wartime army might "manifest the qualities of a militia," could not be scorned. In fact, paradoxically, the weaker France seemed to be, the more Russia felt the need for it.[186] The Russian Pacific advance therefore revitalized the alliance between Paris and Petersburg, transforming it from a one-sided association favoring Russia into a relationship authentically binding on both signatories. In the early 1890s military leaders in Petersburg had promoted a treaty with the French as a way of making a hopeless strategy workable and of buying time for a defense buildup on the German and Austrian frontiers. But the opportunity had been lost. Inspired by a sense of false confidence, key Russian decision-makers had continued to neglect the western defenses of the empire while simultaneously overextending themselves in Asia. The upshot was that Russia was even less capable of prevailing alone in a war with the Triplice than it had been when the first military convention had been signed. France had to be retained as ally at any price, even if that price included extravagant promises and a serious determination to honor them.

This, then, was the conclusive argument that the Main Staff used against a strategic withdrawal into the Russian heartland: the sanctity of the Franco-Russian alliance. As the Chief of Staff expressed it, that alliance

> . . . obligates us to render [France] powerful support, support which is expressed in the fact that either we will take upon ourselves the main forces of the Germans, or, by a rapid transition to an offensive, force the common enemy to think about the defense of its own territory, perhaps its own capital, and in this way, weaken or even deflect the blow prepared against France. For this latter purpose we must concentrate not in the depth of the country, but close to the border, in order to cross the borders of our enemy earlier than he can destroy our ally. In a word, our obligations in relation to France do not permit us to organize our strategic concentrations any farther away. In the opposite case it would be necessary to declare to France that we were not capable of giving her essential support in the first period of the campaign, which would lead to the collapse of our alliance.[187]

Chastened by that reasoning, Nicholas II made haste to withdraw his suggestion.

Yet, as the passage quoted above reveals, the Ministry of War felt that the Franco-Russian alliance did more than merely rule out a Russian pullback were Russia to be invaded by overwhelming forces. It also committed Russia to attack Germany as soon as it could be determined that Germany had definitely opted for an aggressive campaign in the west. For some time, as we have already seen, the Main Staff had been arguing that Russia needed an offensive, in addition to a defensive, capability for European war. Without the power to strike offensively against the enemy, Russia had no way to bring the war to an end. That view had been developed since the 1880s, and the Main Staff saw no reason to repudiate it now.[188]

By the turn of the century the Ministry of War had identified another reason for an offensive: it might be logistically necessary. This assessment was based upon calculations that had been performed by the Main Intendancy Department. The Russian army would initially concentrate in the ten provinces of Poland, in addition to Volynia, Lifland, Kurland, Grodno, Vil'na, Podolsk, and Bessarabia. As the average annual harvest of those territories would not suffice to feed the civilian population in addition to 2 million troops, it was obvious that grain and other foodstuffs would have to be shipped in from the center of the empire. There were several difficulties with that. The approved methods for victualing the army (the subcontracting and commissioner systems) were so cumbrous that it might require three months to build up a one-month supply of food.

If that were not bad enough, transportation resources would constrict the distribution of even such food as there was. To supply an army of 2 million men and 6 million horses with the 619 million pounds of food and forage needed each month would involve sending thirty-eight trains a day to the front. The Intendancy had the capability of running only twenty food trains a day. It might consequently take as many as fifty-seven days to move one month's worth of foodstuffs. Owing to difficulties in procurement and transportation, the Intendancy concluded that "the first shipments of food under the most favorable conditions would reach the theater of military operations only in the end of the fifth month or even in the sixth month of the war." By that point locally obtainable foodstuffs and the troop's iron rations would both have been exhausted; the army would be in a condition "of absolute need."[189] The Intendancy did offer several remedies to ease the anticipated crisis, including a streamlined food acquisition process, the sequestration of all food designated for export on the first day of mobilization, and the establishment of food committees to be staffed by members of the rural zemstvos and town dumas (which was actually done during World War I). Yet it occurred to some that the best way of averting food shortages might be by means of an offensive, by crossing the borders of the enemy and living off his lands.

The Intendancy may seem in retrospect to have been excessively conservative in its estimates about the speed with which food could be collected and distributed in wartime. Yet its report, which was adopted in its entirety, clearly reinforced the conviction of those in the War Ministry who were believers in the offensive. If Russia adopted an exclusively defensive posture, the war in Europe would be protracted. If the war lasted as long as six months (and the Intendancy was correct), the Russian army might be in danger of decomposing through starvation.[190]

In the past, however, Russia had made plans for a serious offensive only against Austria-Hungary. Even if Germany were to deploy a mere four to five army corps in the east, offensive operations against it were to be limited to cavalry raids, both to screen the concentration of Russia's troops and to impede the disembarcation of German forces on the Vistula.[191] In 1901, however, the Ministry of War came to the conclusion that Russia had to begin a war by initiating attacks against both Austria and Germany if possible. The offensive against Austria could not be abandoned. After all, it was the best means of replying to the invasion of Russia that Austria was expected to unleash. Further, owing in part to the extensive intelligence it had compiled about the military plans of Vienna, the Ministry felt that an offensive into Galicia would have at least a reasonable possibility of success. If Russia achieved early and dramatic successes, those might demoralize the Austrian army or, more desirable still, cause a large proportion of Vienna's Slavic troops to defect to the Russian side. The happy result might be the rapid collapse of the entire Austrian war effort. As a Main Staff document of 1901 expressed it, the "political situation and the internal position of the Austro-Hungarian monarchy demands that we strike precisely this enemy with the swiftest and strongest blows possible."[192] But in addition, if the commander of the Russian northwest front determined that Germany had left only token forces in the east, he should be instructed to undertake an offensive of his own. It was the political necessity of supporting France that made such an offensive unavoidable. The special conference on western defense spelled that out explicitly. If reconnaissance indicated that Germany's main attack was in the west: "Then the First and Second Armies must invade Germany, an offensive that corresponds to the wishes of the French General Staff, which requests that by means of a forward offensive we hold the East Prussian forces on the spot, not permitting them to be transferred to the western frontier for use against France."[193] The dual offensive plan was enshrined in mobilization schedule 18 of

1903 and in the secret instructions Nicholas II issued to the future commanders of the northwest and southwest fronts in the same year.[194]

By the early twentieth century, then, Russia's dispositions for war in Europe had been influenced by uncertainty, Slavophilism, and the politics of the Franco-Russian alliance. Because it was uncertain about the direction in which Germany would mount the chief thrust, Russia had to be ready both to defend and to attack. The problem was that it was ill-prepared to do either. Part of the reason was what the Ministry of War considered to be insufficient investment by the tsarist state in transportation and communication. But the provisions for simultaneous offensives against Austria and Germany should Germany march west also clouded the prospect of success. As opposed to preparing to do the ostensibly most logical thing—attacking just one enemy and defending against the other—by 1903 the Ministry of War had been boxed into a plan for two offensives. To attack Germany alone meant to risk the Austrian penetration of Poland, a possible uprising of rebellious Poles on the behalf of Vienna, and the creation of an extremely attenuated and vulnerable left flank. Simply to attack Germany would also be to renounce any early chance of exploiting disaffected Slavic nationalism within the ranks of the Austrian army. It could also so discourage the Balkan states that Russia might afterward have great difficulty reestablishing its position as the natural leader of Slavdom. But to defend against Germany and attack Austria was no solution, either. Merely preparing to do so could prove disastrous; if the French caught wind of it, they might repudiate the Russian alliance. Even if they never managed to learn that Russia intended to strike solely against Austria prior to the outbreak of a war, when they realized once a war had started that this was what Russia was in fact doing, they might seek a separate peace with Germany. In the opinion of the Ministry of War, a Russia bereft of its French ally was almost certain to be defeated.

As it subsequently turned out, in August 1914 Russia did mount weak offensives against both the German and Hapsburg empires. The First and Second Russian Armies did invade East Prussia (with horrible results), and the forces of the southwest front did advance into Galicia. Students of World War I have often wondered why that happened. There have naturally been many attempts to make sense of those apparently mysterious Russian deployments. They have been explained variously in terms of "cults of the offensive," bureaucratic politics, even psychological analyses of leading tsarist political and military figures. Overlooked in these theories, however, is the impact of Far Eastern imperialism. Because Russia's expansion in the East led to a deterioration in its capability to fight effectively in the west, it became so dependent upon its French ally that it felt it had to do anything to keep Paris satisfied. That entailed burdening its strategy with provisions for an attack on Germany in addition to the traditional prescription for an offensive in Austrian Galicia. Thus, paradoxically enough, because Russia was overextended in Asia, it was forced into a posture of overextending itself in Europe as well.

The war plans that Imperial Russia adopted in 1903 were by no means etched in stone. Indeed, as we shall see shortly, in later years there would be a serious attempt by several high-ranking military leaders to rethink and redesign Russian strategy for war in Europe thoroughly. That was itself the result of another consequence of Russia's Asian imperialism: the Russo-Japanese War and the controversies to which that catastrophe in its turn gave rise.

9

The Quest for Exits

Russian Strategy, 1904–14

The military catastrophe that Russia suffered in Manchuria was a watershed in the history of the Imperial State, for it touched off the revolution of 1905, which in turn resulted in the establishment of the Duma and the transformation of the autocracy into a quasi-constitutional monarchy. Nicholas II still insisted that military and foreign policy were his personal perogatives, not subject to legislative scrutiny, but the Duma and the increasingly active press put constraints on what the Tsar could do independently even in those fields. In particular, the regime had to become ever more attentive to public opinion.

As the Russo-Japanese War caused changes in the way policies were made, it also provoked renewed discussion about what the content of those policies should be. After the conclusion of the Peace of Portsmouth, the Foreign Ministry was convinced that Russia had to do everything in its power to avoid getting entangled in an armed conflict in Europe. As in the late 1850s, Russia needed time to lick its wounds and gather strength. But Russia's foreign-policy-makers were also worried about the damage the military defeat had done to the empire's international standing. The Manchurian debacle had shaken Russia's alliance with France and had undermined its influence among the Balkan Slavs. Not only did the foreign-policy-makers believe that Russia could afford no more humiliations, they also felt that Russia needed some diplomatic victories, if only to restore its prestige. Those two needs were not congruent; in fact they diverged. The quest for peace obliged Russia to pursue the relaxation of international tensions, for which purpose some sort of understanding with Germany seemed the most promising course. The need for diplomatic victories, on the other hand, entailed risks, for it could involve Russia in a dangerous process of coercive bluffing. One response to a bluff is to call it, in which case Russia could be forced to back down. Hence the pursuit of diplomatic successes could perversely result in Russia's setting itself up for an intolerable international pratfall.

The Russo-Japanese War also led to an upheaval in tsarist military policies. In the first place, the battlefield ineptitude exposed in the war spurred familiar calls for substantive military reforms. Russian culture and society (even military culture and society) were now much more sophisticated than they had been after the Crimean War. The debate over military reform was now carried on openly in the public press, as well as in musty bureaucratic memoranda. Certain extreme reformers (the Military Voice group, in particular) even called the army's relationship to the Tsar into question when they proclaimed that the military owed its highest loyalty to the nation. In addition, their appeal for the mass mobilization (and patriotic indoctrination) of the entire Russian population was an implicit endorsement of an agenda for political and social reform that was too radical for the state to stomach. Complicating the struggle for reform was the fact that the "lessons" of the Russo-Japanese War were extremely obscure. They could be invoked in support of countless contradictory operational, tactical, educational, and organizational theories.

Thanks to the Duma and the journalists, military grievances and abuses now received an amount of publicity previously unimaginable. The Manchurian defeat also provoked vigorous secret debates about the future and direction of Russian strategy. Russian statesmen unanimously agreed that the Russian Empire was dangerously overextended. Russia did not have the resources to defend itself should it be engulfed in war in Europe and Asia simultaneously. Because such a two-front war was prima facie unwinnable, it followed that Russia had to work to simplify the international security environment; diplomacy would have to defuse the threat to Russia in one of those theaters so that Russian arms would have a chance of victory in the other. Easterners and Westerners disagreed, however, about where Russia would next have to fight and about the sort of war Russia should prepare for. In brief, Easterners argued for a total redeployment of the Russian army, a shift in its center of gravity from Poland to the basin of the Volga. Several considerations lay behind that recommendation, the main one being the expectation that a renewed war with Japan in Asia was more probable (and consequently more hazardous) than a conflict in Central Europe. Should Russia continue to neglect its Pacific defenses, when the Japanese attacked again the outcome was likely to be dismal: Vladivostok would suffer the fate of Sevastopol, and Russia might even be driven as far west as Lake Baikal.

Westerners took a different view. In their opinion, the military threat from Austria and Germany remained paramount. It therefore behooved Russia to strengthen its French alliance; it should seek accomodations with the British and the Japanese and should beef up its western defenses.

Many of the twists and turns in Russian foreign and military policy in the decade before the World War are explicable in terms of this debate. The entente with Britain (1907) was clearly a victory for the Foreign Ministry and the military Westerners. After Russia was embarrassed in the Bosnian crisis of 1908–9, however, the new Foreign Minister tried to reorient Russian policy toward Berlin. If tensions in Europe could be relaxed, Russia could then acquire the time and resources to concentrate on its Asian problem. Paralleling that diplomatic shift, the military redeployment plan of 1909 envisioned the introduction of a territorial system of recruitment and the transfer of a large proportion of Russia's forces from the western borders to the heartland. If it had been fully implemented, that plan would have amounted to a unilateral repudiation of the French alliance, for it would have precluded Russian fulfillment of its military obligations to Paris should a European war come. After 1912, however, the Westerners regained the ascendancy. Austro-Russian tensions over the Balkans festered, and Petersburg increasingly worried about the growth of Turkish naval power (not to mention the growing influence that the Germans now appeared to wield in Constantinople). Defense outlays went up; spending was heaviest in the western frontier zones and on the needs of the Baltic and Black Sea fleets. The effects of those erratic zigzags in defense and foreign policies were all felt during the July crisis of 1914. Fear of another diplomatic humiliation provoked the Council of Ministers to take a firm line against Vienna. Fear about Germany's relative mobilization advantage (which had actually grown greater as a result of Russia's contradictory deployment programs of 1910 and 1912) induced Russia's generals to insist on early mobilization. Plan 19 altered, with which Russia took the field in 1914, contained many defects, some stemming from the old 1900 defense concept, some from the strategic incoherence of the interwar period. Russia's pessimistic generals were in the position of trying to implement an outrageously optimistic and ambitious plan. The opening battles of World War I showed up the profound limitations of the "magical" tradition in Russian strategy.

The Russo-Japanese War

Late at night on February 8, 1904, a force of ten Japanese torpedo boats slipped into the Russian naval roadstead at Port Arthur under the cover of dense fog. Shortly before midnight they launched a surprise attack on Russia's naval squadron at anchor there. The battleships *Retvizan* and *Tsetsarevich* took severe hits in the rudder and the stern, respectively, while the torpedo that struck the coal bin of the cruiser *Pallada* ignited the adjacent powder magazine. Although all three vessels began to ship water rapidly, their crews managed somehow to maneuver them to the very entrance of the harbor, the Tiger's Tail, where they were put aground. Early the following morning, Admiral Togo's main battle fleet arrived and began to bombard both the port and the remainder of Russia's squadron. The siege of Port Arthur had begun, and with it the Russo-Japanese War.[1]

Back in Petersburg there was outrage in government circles. The Japanese had broken off relations with Russia less than twenty-four hours before they opened hostilities. Further, Tokyo had attacked without bothering to issue a declaration of war. Nicholas II himself told his Foreign Minister that after such an insult Russia had no choice but to wage a war to the death.[2] Unfortunately, Russia's forces in the Far East were too weak at that juncture to undertake offensive action against the enemy. They were, in fact, so outnumbered and outgunned that defense was the only option. When the Japanese melinite torpedos exploded at Port Arthur, Russia possessed but 98,000 soldiers, 168 field guns, and 8 machine guns in Eastern Siberia and Manchuria to confront the entire 280,000-man Japanese army and its 400,000 reserves. Still worse, after the battleship *Petropavlovsk* collided with a mine while returning from a sortie in early April, its sunken hull effectively blocked the last egress from Port Arthur into the open sea. Russia's naval assets were bottled up and consequently useless; the Japanese fleet was at complete liberty.

It soon became evident to the Russians what the Japanese objectives would be. Within ten days after the Port Arthur attack Japanese transports steamed into the port of Inchon and offloaded Kuroki's First Army. That expeditionary force, which immediately started to drive up the Korean peninsula, was obviously intended to attack Russia's communications and administrative centers in Manchuria at Liaoyang and Mukden. Meanwhile the blockade and shelling of Port Arthur left no doubt that Tokyo had scheduled that fortress for reduction.

In attempting to thwart those Japanese operations, Russia's generals labored under severe obstacles, many of which they themselves had foreseen in years prior to the war. Almost total Japanese command of the sea, which had been predicted in a Russian staff memorandum of 1899, meant that Russia had no means of either lifting the Port Arthur blockade or interdicting Japanese ground reinforcements.[3] Japanese naval dominance in the east also meant that Russia's army had to depend on the Trans-Siberian Railway as its exclusive lifeline. But that railway, running 5,500 miles from Moscow and terminating in spurs at Vladivostok and Port Arthur, was single-tracked and consequently limited in freight capacity. Railway traffic on the line was, moreover, extraordinarily vulnerable to sabotage and disruption, as the War Ministry had pointed out early in 1903.[4]

The crafting of Russia's own war plan fell to General A. N. Kuropatkin. Kuropatkin, who had served as Minister of War since 1898, was now appointed commander of Russia's Far Eastern Armies and abandoned the comforts of his forty-room palace on the Moika for the fields of Manchuria. As we have seen, Kuropatkin had long warned of the dangers of imperial expansion in the east. He had nevertheless devoted considerable time to thinking through the problem of waging war against Japan if one should become necessary. Recognizing that the Japanese

THE THEATER OF THE RUSSO-JAPANESE WAR 1904-1905

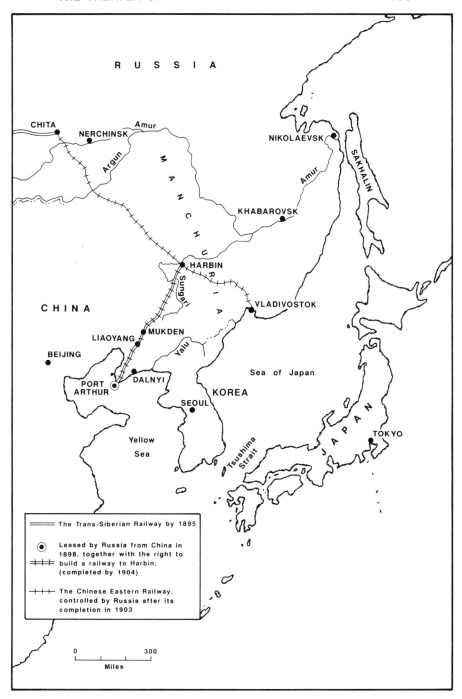

RUSSIA

CHITA
NERCHINSK
Amur
Argun
NIKOLAEVSK
SAKHALIN
Amur
KHABAROVSK

M A N C H U R I A

HARBIN
Sungari
VLADIVOSTOK

CHINA

LIAOYANG MUKDEN
Yalu
BEIJING
Sea of Japan
PORT ARTHUR DALNYI
KOREA
SEOUL

Yellow Sea
Tsushima Strait
J A P A N
TOKYO

The Trans-Siberian Railway by 1895

Leased by Russia from China in 1898, together with the right to build a railway to Harbin; (completed by 1904)

The Chinese Eastern Railway, controlled by Russia after its completion in 1903

0   300
Miles

would have initial numerical superiority, Kuropatkin's idea was to deny Tokyo an early victory by alternating tenacious holding actions and strategic withdrawals in order to gain the time needed to bring in thousands of additional troops from European Russia. "Insofar as possible," he wrote, "our forces must avoid decisive engagements in order to escape being defeated in detail prior to the concentration of forces sufficient for the defeat of the Japanese."[5] Kuropatkin expected that sooner or later the Japanese would succeed in invading Manchuria. He also anticipated that Port Arthur would be besieged. Yet if those Japanese movements could be slowed through skillful defensive measures, eventually three army corps could be moved from Great Russia to Harbin. This, he believed, would give him the margin he would need to take the offensive.[6]

From the beginning however, everything went wrong. Despite his undeniable intelligence and administrative talent, Kuropatkin was not gifted with the decisiveness of character requisite for a field commander. Furthermore, he committed the fatal error of underestimating his enemy. Highly motivated and trained, and led by capable commanders, the Japanese army was more than a match for Russia's Far Eastern forces. At the very beginning of May, a Russian column under General Zasulich was defeated at the Yalu River, and the Japanese began to cross over from Korea into Manchuria. Shortly thereafter, another Japanese army landed near Dalnyi and invested Port Arthur from the land.[7] General Stessel', commander of the fortress, had more than 40,000 soldiers and 500 guns at his disposal for the defense. He was opposed by the 80,000 troops of Nogi's Third Army. Nogi's objective was to break through the 13-mile ring of fortified hills and lines that surrounded Port Arthur from the north and west, and he launched assault after assault in order to do so. Finally, at the end of November, by dint of ferocious combat that cost them at least 10,000 lives, the Japanese succeeded in capturing 203 Meter Hill. Heavy 11-inch siege guns, dragged up to that position, now subjected Port Arthur and what remained of the Russian fleet in the harbor to a pulverizing bombardment. The mounting artillery casualties, the growing sick list, and the shrinking stocks of food, in addition to the apparent impossibility of any relief columns getting through, finally induced Stessel' to surrender the fortress to Nogi on December 29, 1904.

In central Manchuria the Russian cause had been faring no better. In August and early September, Oyama engaged Kuropatkin at Liaoyang. On September 2 the Japanese appeared to be on the verge of overrunning the Russian left, and Kuropatkin abruptly broke off the engagement and retired behind the Sha-ho River.[8] Russian attempts at counteroffensives failed. Mishchenko's cavalry raid from the Sha-ho to the sea was a disappointment, for it appreciably disrupted neither Japanese communications nor Japanese logistics. And the January 1905 attack at San-de-pu, which Kuropatkin had counted on to envelop the Japanese forces, also misfired. By February three Russian armies totaling 330,000 men occupied entrenched positions on a 95-kilometer front just south of the city of Mukden. Although slightly inferior in numbers of men and guns, the Japanese immediately took the offensive initiative. The great battle of Mukden, which raged until March 10, foreshadowed the combat of World War I in its scale, carnage, and inconclusiveness. In the end, having lost almost 100,000 men killed, wounded, or captured, Kuropatkin disengaged once more and fell back on Harbin.

Back in St. Petersburg the Tsar quickly convened a council of war to discuss Kuropatkin's fate. Although some were of the view that Kuropatkin should keep his command, Nicholas II was swayed by the outspoken General Dragomirov, who made the case for Kuropatkin's dismissal by noting that "up to now General Kuropatkin has already cost Russia 200,000 lives and probably a billion in money. Your Highness, do we really have to wait for him to cost us another 200,000 men and another billion?"[9] Kuropatkin was relieved, and Linevich was appointed in his stead.

But the government had more to worry about than inadequate generalship in Manchuria. Early on, St. Petersburg had appreciated that its central strategic problem was its lack of sea power in the Far East. With the defeat of the final attempt at a naval sortie from Port Arthur and with the destruction of the Vladivostok squadron, both occurring in August, the Japanese had acquired total sea control in the theater of war. Indeed, the Manchurian war taught Russia (and the entire world) a crucial lesson about the interdependence of land and sea power.[10] How could Russia bring additional naval assets to bear in the Far East? It might be possible, of course, to buy a battleship or two abroad. Nothing, however, came of an effort to purchase the one ship of the line in Argentina's navy.[11] There was always Russia's Black Sea fleet. The Russian admiralty suggested that the Sultan be asked to permit three battleships to pass through the straits en route to the Pacific, but the Foreign Ministry was strongly opposed. Such an action would violate international treaties on the closure of the straits to warships; London had repeatedly warned Constantinople that if it allowed any armed Russian vessels into the Mediterranean, the response would be a British naval blockade of the Dardanelles.[12] There remained the Baltic fleet. In October 1904 Nicholas II commanded Admiral Rozhdestvenskii to sail that fleet around the world to confront the Japanese navy in its home waters. This expedition began with a blunder and ended in disaster. While steaming through the North Sea, the Russians improbably mistook some British fishing trawlers for Japanese gunboats and blasted them with naval gunfire. This Dogger Bank incident quite naturally infuriated the British, who demanded an apology and compensation. For a moment it appeared that Russia and Britain might go to war. Britain had been allied with Japan since 1902, and Nicholas suspected that the Japanese had moved against Russia in Asia with London's tacit backing. But, owing in part to French intercession, Nicholas finally decided to give the British what they wanted.

Russia's naval troubles had only begun. After an eight-month voyage plagued by mishap and hardship, Rozhdestvenskii encountered Admiral Togo's fleet in the Tsushima Straits, the corridor separating southern Korea from the Japanese islands. In the battle of Tsushima (May 28), Togo used the superior speed and armament of his vessels to inflict an annihilating defeat on the Russians. The bulk of Russia's Baltic fleet went to the bottom, while the rest was captured or dispersed.

Long before the catastrophe at Tsushima, however, the tsarist government had already begun to come to terms with two unpleasant problems. In the first place, Russia was running short of the resources needed to wage war. The Manchurian army was on the cusp of a food crisis. In part, that was the result of transportation bottlenecks on the Trans-Siberian Railroad. For that reason, for instance, not a one of the 680 loads of foodstuffs scheduled to arrive in Harbin in the six weeks between mid-January and March 1, 1905, actually made it there. Because the Manchurian army was growing even as the territory under its control contracted, it was not possible to rely on supplying the army from locally available resources. The War Ministry estimated that by the late spring of 1905 the Manchurian army would have exhausted all its reserves of victuals. Thereafter, the army would have to "be fed from day to day."[13]

Worse than the headache of army provisions, however, was the somber realization of the costs that the war was imposing on Russia. There were many of them, of which the most serious was erosion in the writ of governmental authority. The string of seemingly endless defeats that Russia's forces suffered on land and sea during the war debased the prestige of the autocracy and helped to focus popular discontent.[14] The liberal Union of Liberation campaigned for political reform; factory workers were increasingly inclined to strike; and revolutionaries launched hundreds of terrorist attacks against state officials both prominent and obscure. On Bloody Sunday (January 9, 1905), when the government responded to a peaceful workers' demonstration in St. Petersburg with repeated volleys of live ammunition, social unrest metastasized into open revolution. A massive wave of strikes spread through urban Russia, while agrarian disturbances swept through the rural districts of the empire.

Soon disturbing backward and forward linkages developed between the struggle against the revolution and the Manchurian war. The Imperial government lacked a reservoir of trained men adequate to prosecute both simultaneously. Troops detained in Europe to suppress disorder obviously constricted the effort that the regime could mount in Asia. But equally, the 800,000 soldiers committed to the Eastern conflict were not available for repressive service in Central Russia, Poland, or the Caucasus. The very process of military recruitment during the war had stimulated considerable domestic discontent. Throughout 1904 the Russian High Command continuously failed to gauge what its true manpower requirements would be. Whereas Kuropatkin had believed that at most six army corps would be enough for a Russian victory over the Japanese, by early 1905 St. Petersburg had already had to deploy twice that number. To flesh out and replenish those units, the government had recourse to nine separate partial mobilizations of the reserves.[15] In theory the partial mobilizations were supposed to allow Russia to wage its Eastern war with the least possible disruption of its defensive posture in Europe. Yet in practice, since the partial mobilizations often called up older reservists and married ones (while sparing bachelors), in the villages the entire procedure was regarded as rankly unfair. The outbreak of revolution further aggravated the manpower problem. By March 1905 the Tsarist Ministry of the Interior had come to the conclusion that unrest was so bad that further mobilizations would be impossible in thirty-two of the fifty provinces of European Russia. In any event, were any additional mobilizations to be declared, they would have to be conducted in the presence of armed military units so as to deter rioting at the recruiting depots.[16] Of course, to detach regular troops for that purpose would improve the army's manpower problem not at all.

The strain of waging the Manchurian war also created the predictable havoc with Russia's defensive posture in the western quarters of the empire. Although William II of Germany expressed voluble sympathy for Russians as they combated the "yellow peril," military circles in St. Petersburg continued to mistrust the Central Powers. What would happen if they took advantage of Russia's eastern preoccupations to launch a surprise attack of their own? By early 1905 fully 20 percent of the infantry and artillery that were supposed to be deployed in the west were either already in the Far East or earmarked to go there. Still worse, much of the best equipment and technology had been stripped away from the forces that remained in the western theater for assignment to Manchuria.[17] Since many officers had also been seconded to the Far Eastern armies, there could be no doubt that command and control would be totally inadequate in the event of a military emergency in the west.[18] The only ray of hope in the gloom was provided by Russian military intelligence. At the end of 1904 a Russian spy in Vienna (doubtless Colonel Alfred Redl) had supplied Petersburg with Austrian staff documents indicating that the Hapsburg monarchy viewed the current situation as propitious for an attack on Italy, not Russia. Conrad von Hötzendorf, Chief of the Austrian General Staff, called for the diversion of defense resources away from the potential northeast—Russian— front to the southern, or Italian.[19] Russian strategists could only be relieved to learn that Vienna was (at least temporarily) regarding Rome, not Petersburg, as the primary enemy.

Finally, the Japanese war was creating difficulties for state finances. The Minister of Finance noted in March 1905 that Russia had begun the war in a relatively strong financial position, with a budget surplus of 185 million rubles on hand. After that sum had been exhausted, it had been possible to cover war expenses with half a billion rubles of foreign loans. Now, however, still more money was needed. Unfortunately, military defeat and revolution had shaken the confidence of the world financial community in Russia's political order. As the value of Russian state paper was falling, more and more foreign capital markets were closed to Petersburg. Although Russia could float an internal loan, it could not expect to realize more than 150 million rubles from it, owing in large measure to capital flight. That 150 million would not defray the expenses of the Manchurian army for more than two and a half months.[20] After that, in Kokovtsov's estimation, the Imperial state would be nearly bankrupt; with an empty treasury it would impossible to continue the war, even if the government wanted to.

When the war first broke out, of course, most people in the government had been confident of a rapid victory. Even the initial defeats of 1904 had not shaken that belief. For example, throughout the year, Russian military intelligence had specialized in collecting data that suggested that the Japanese were on the verge of collapse—yet another example of the way in which preconceptions can skew the process of intelligence.[21] Yet by early 1905 the congeries of disasters the war had spawned finally muted enthusiasm for the war in the highest circles of the Russian government. The problem was to find a means of extricating Russia from the war with at least some vestiges of pride and honor intact. On February 22, 1905, with the battle of Mukden still unresolved, Nicholas II confided to his Foreign Minister that just as soon as its armies had achieved one respectable victory, Russia should begin to press for a negotiated settlement.[22] With Kuropatkin's defeat at Mukden, however, the prospect of a prestige-enhancing military success seemed farther away than ever.

At that stage some officials began to argue that it would be in Russia's best interest simply to cut its losses in the Far East. The most influential spokesman for this position was Russia's Ambassador to France, A. Nelidov, who made the case for ending the war in a trenchant memorandum to Emperor in March. Nelidov pointed out that even if Russia somehow managed to reconquer Manchuria, it would have achieved nothing tangible. Given the open hostility of China to Russian occupation of that northern province and the continued enmity of Japan, Russia's position in the Far East would remain untenable. To be sure, Nelidov recognized that to sue for peace now would be costly to Russia's military reputation. Yet he insisted that it would be still more costly to go on with the war in the hope of decisive victories. What made it costly was the impact the war was having on public opinion abroad, particularly in France. Nelidov did not equivocate about the consequences of continuing the war: "Our alliance with France, already shaken by our defeats, would finally be sundered."[23] Nicholas II was impressed enough with Nelidov's argument to order him to seek French mediation for an end to the conflict.

Nicholas's conditions for the negotiations, effectively requiring Japanese acceptance of the status quo ante bellum, were, however, unacceptable to Tokyo. The one remaining hope of the Russian government was a naval triumph over Japan once Rozhdestvenskii's Baltic Fleet had arrived in the Pacific. That hope, of course, did not survive the battle of Tsushima. When President Theodore Roosevelt of the United States proposed to mediate between the belligerents, his offer was accepted. Domestic revolution and the prospect of bankruptcy had made Petersburg eager to end the war. As for the Japanese, they were reaching the limits of their own military and financial strength.

Peace was concluded in the town of Portsmouth, New Hampshire, on August 23 [September 5], 1905. Russia's plenipotentiary, Count S. Iu. Witte, managed to get the best possible terms. Although he was compelled to agree to Japanese acquisition of half of Sakhalin island in addition to the Liaotung peninsula, Witte succeeded in denying Tokyo any war indemnity.[24] That consolation was, however, too modest to outweigh the enormous damage the war had inflicted upon Russia. Four hundred thousand soldiers had been killed or wounded; a quarter of a billion rubles in naval assets had been lost; and two and a half billion rubles had been spent in the course of hostilities.[25] Besides, the problem of the revolution had yet to be resolved.

On October 17, 1905, under pressure from a massive general strike, Nicholas II promulgated the famous October Manifesto.

The document announced the intention of the government to respect the civil rights of its subjects and, as well, promised the creation of a parliament, or Duma, with significant legislative powers. Despite that concession, revolutionary violence not only continued but even grew worse. Throughout the rest of 1905, through 1906, and into 1907, tsarist police and soldiers were involved in a desperate struggle to reimpose order in the country. Military units were dispatched to render aid to civil authorities more than eight thousand times. Troops were used both to crush revolutionary disturbances with force and to cow potential rebels into submission through armed demonstrations, marches, and guard duty. Those actions were attended by a considerable upsurge in civil-military tensions, for repressive duty was unpopular with many officers in the army, including some of the top War Ministry officials.[26] Alarming clusters of military mutinies in late 1905 and the summer of 1906 considerably complicated the task of combating the revolution.[27]

Diplomacy and Military Policy After 1905: Changes in the Decision-making Environment

The promise of the October Manifesto was at least partially redeemed in April 1906 when, the Imperial government issued the Fundamental Laws, a set of written constitutional guidelines. By their terms, supreme control over the military and foreign policy of the empire was vested in the Tsar. The Duma was supposed to have no oversight whatsoever with respect to the organization, structure, and planning of the armed forces. That did not, however, mean that all went on as before in the realms of foreign relations and military affairs. The institutions that the revolution had created exerted influence, both direct and indirect, even on the formulation of tsarist high policy. That was most particularly true after the third Duma, elected on a much restricted franchise, assembled in Petersburg in late 1907. In the first place, although the Duma was not permitted to reject the state-sponsored military budget, it could appropriate monies for the needs of the army and navy—a right that validated its examination of military affairs in debate. The Tsarist Ministry of War saw an opportunity here, for a tacit partnership with influential

Duma delegates might prove useful in wresting more funds from the Ministry of Finance.[28]

Second, although the ministries were responsible solely to the Tsar, the Duma did have the authority to interpellate them. In theory the ministries could ignore the Duma's request for a formal defense of their policies; in practice, they found it generally expedient to comply. Finally, since Duma delegates could not be prosecuted for what they said from its rostrum, the regime had in effect created a legal forum in which it could be subjected to rigorous criticism.

In a strange way, it was the tsarist regime's new attentiveness to foreign public opinion that made it take its own domestic public opinion much more seriously. The Russo-Japanese War had reminded the tsarist government just how important it was for Russia to project an image of strength and resilience abroad. If Russia was perceived as weak, that might at worst hearten its potential enemies. Even at best, if foreigners received the impression that Russia was disunited, suffering from intractable domestic problems, there could be the most serious consequences for the empire's credit.

Of course, none of this induced the Russian government to accept meekly the guidance of either the newspapers or the Duma. The Duma was frequently insulted and domestic opinion overriden. Nicholas II, who came to loathe the Duma, never understood the importance of opinion, either foreign or domestic. But certain of his key ministers did. As they crafted their policies, they had to keep the possible impact on opinion in mind. Some were concerned to insulate themselves from criticism; others wanted to cultivate allies in the Duma; still others were interested in the manipulation and co-optation of the press. Such practices amounted to prima facie constraints on the formulation and execution of policy.

Military Reform After 1905: Successes and Limitations

Not unnaturally, the defeat in the Japanese war provoked ferocious debate in Russia about what had gone wrong. In the past, of course, there had been disputes about the wisdom and direction of military reform. But the *glasnost'* and press freedom of the constitutional era that had now dawned in Russia resulted in a debate conducted in the glare of unprecedented publicity. Scores of retired and active-duty officers committed to paper their thoughts about the military shortcomings the war had exposed. While they pointed the finger at many specific abuses, progressive officers were increasingly prone to view the central Russian failing in the war as a problem of morale. Japanese troops had been able to use tactical offensives to prevail despite the horrendous casualties that modern armaments had inflicted upon them, a fact that testified to their superior motivation.[29] The Japanese soldier had strongly identified with the goals his government had been pursuing in Manchuria. By contrast, his Russian counterpart had typically been confused or apathetic about the reasons that St. Petersburg was waging war in the remote Far East. Many reformers deduced from this that Russia's chances of military victory in a future struggle depended upon the mass mobilization and motivation of its population. A future war would have to be national in character, and that would have to be understood by every recruit. Some radical reformist officers, such as those associated with the *Military Voice* newspaper and the subsequent *Military Encyclopedia,* went so far as to assert that the army should owe its primary allegiance to the nation, not the autocracy.[30] Such sentiments, however patriotic, could only be viewed with alarm in the highest councils of the tsarist state.

While disturbed by the politicization of elite Russian officers, the tsarist government itself became committed to substantive military reform in the aftermath of the Japanese war. A major defect of the war effort, it was believed, had been the lack of coordination between the army and the navy, which had drafted their plans in mutual isolation. Disunity had been a problem even within the army. There had been far too many generals ignorant of the capabilities of the branches of service to which they did not belong. Critics charged, with some justice, that General Stessel's defense of Port Arthur had been so unsatisfactory in part owing to his insufficient understanding of artillery and military engineering.[31] Nicholas II supposed that the remedy for this was organizational change. In the summer of 1905 he created the Council of State Defense (*Sovet gosudarstvennoi oborony*) under the chairmanship of his uncle, the Grand Duke Nikolai

Nikolaevich. In a simultaneous effort to enhance the status of strategic planning, the Tsar split the General Staff off from the Ministry of War, granting it autonomy.

The purpose of the Council of State Defense was to bring unity and coherence to the military and defense policies of the Russian Empire. Members were to include the Ministers of War, Marine, and Foreign Affairs, in addition to the Chief of the General Staff. A premium was placed on the open and free exchange of information, for the Council was to be the venue for the collegial evaluation of Russia's military potential, the threats that confronted it, and the strategies it might adopt to combat those threats.[32]

Yet the Council would not be able to do its job unless the entire Russian military system could be regenerated. For that purpose, other reforms were essential. The War Ministry established the Higher Commission on Performance Reviews in 1906 in order to purge the army of incompetent commanders, of whom more than two thousand were "retired" within two years.[33] Considerable thought was also given to overhauling military education— staff education in particular—and a special secret poll was conducted among Staff Academy graduates about the most desirable curricular improvements.[34] Still other reforms affected the material conditions under which the officers and men served. The government raised the common soldier's pay, improved the officers' pension program, and instituted streamlined procedures for regimental purchasing.[35] The Ministry of War was at the same time interested in re-equipping the army with the best and most sophisticated weaponry. The Ministry's official report for 1905 observed that the Japanese war had conclusively demonstrated that Russia's armed forces needed more howitzers, mountain guns, machine guns, and field telephones, as well as other highly developed technologies.[36] The navy was as avid for new technology as the army. Not only had it lost both its principal fleets in the war with Japan, but Britain's launching of the first Dreadnought in 1906 had made all other battleships obsolete. The Admiralty projected constructing a new Baltic squadron of four battleships and a force of fourteen destroyers for the Black Sea.[37] Twenty-seven submarines were to complement those surface combatants.[38]

Sweeping as all of those reforms may have been, they had their limitations. Some of them were outright failures, in part because of the structure of the autocracy. The key to tsarist ministerial politics had long been secrecy in the defense of institutional interests. In view of this, it is perhaps not surprising that the Council of State Defense did not live up to expectations. Far from candidly sharing information, members of the Council often sought to keep their colleagues in the dark about the programs and intentions of the departments under their control. That, of course, had ludicrous consequences, especially in relations between the Ministry of War and the General Staff. The General Staff was supposed to be the brain of the army, the War Ministry the executive agency that prepared the army for combat. Because the Chief of Staff was not inclined to furnish the War Minister with precise details about the planning process, the Minister had considerable difficulty performing his duty. Indeed, Chief of Staff Palitsyn frequently made decisions of the greatest importance for Russia's defense posture without notifying the Council at all, as in 1908, when he ordered an automatic mobilization of Russian forces in the Caucasus if Turkish army formations on the other side of the frontier reached a certain density.[39] Neither could deliberations in the Council overcome mistrust between the navy and the army. The rancorous squabbles over resources that occurred there between the admirals and the generals bespoke antipathy, not cooperation.[40] Nicholas II recognized that his experiment had not been a success; in the summer of 1908 he abolished the Council, and shortly thereafter he reincorporated the Staff into the Ministry of War. He announced that from then on general state security policy would be coordinated in small, *ad hoc* committees under his personal supervision, which meant, for all practical purposes, that issues of defense would not be coordinated at all.[41]

Autocratic political culture was responsible for the defeat of still other reforms. For example, the Emperor Nicholas personally intervened in the work of the Higher Commission on Performance Reviews in order to protect officers whose devotion to his throne outweighed their lack of military talent. The results may have been satisfactory to him, but they were obviously less than optimal when viewed from the standpoint of military efficiency. Then, too, despite all of the efforts to stamp it out, corruption in the disbursement of money and supplies and in the awarding of contracts could never be totally extirpated. For a small but by no means minuscule proportion of tsarist officers, to hold a commission was to enjoy the traditional right of augmenting one's pay by means of peculation. Episodes of misprision and venality abounded in the commissariats.

The condition of the treasury also played a part in the fate of military reform. Reconstructing the Russian armed forces was difficult in the absence of the revenue to pay for it. As we have already seen, the Russo-Japanese War had placed tsarist finances under a nearly intolerable strain. Throughout late 1905 and into 1906, the state teetered on the chasm of bankruptcy. In view of the near insolvency of the state, many reforms were underfunded. The Ministry of Finance discarded others altogether.

Looming over everything, however, was the monumental task that the army confronted in putting down the revolution. Because of the need to suppress and deter disorders, military units were dispatched all over the country, often hundreds of miles from their bases, throughout 1905–7. Those deployments wreaked as much havoc upon Russian military preparedness in the west as had the Japanese War itself. By the end of 1906, more than forty-six battalions of active-duty troops had been temporarily transferred from the westernmost military districts to trouble spots in the Caucasus or in the interior.[42] Troop training was obviously impossible in those conditions.[43] Heavy involvement in the pacification of urban and rural unrest also deprived the army well into 1907 of the ability to conduct a complete mobilization should an international crisis make one necessary. It was clear that recovery from the ravages of the war and revolution would be a long process. It was just as clear that until the recovery was complete, Russia would lack the military power to defend its position in the world. As the Minister of War wrote, "at the present moment after the war and the current upheaval the condition of our armed forces is such that it is extremely desirable for us to avoid foreign entanglements for some time to come."[44]

The Strategic Picture 1905–8

Russian weakness was fraught with implications. For one, it opened the possibility of a substantive realignment of European politics. Such at least was the view from Berlin. William II, as we have already seen, had long exerted his influence and charm to persuade his Imperial cousin Nicholas of the virtues of a forward Russian policy in the Far East. The German Emperor was immoderately delighted with the outbreak of the Russo-Japanese War. He reasoned that he might be able to use the conflict to make Petersburg dependent on Berlin. In particular, he was interested in rupturing the Franco-Russian alliance. If he could forge a link with Petersburg, perhaps even the French would be forced to come to terms with him. Should that happen, Germany would become the dominant partner in a Continental coalition directed against England. Twice, in 1904 and 1905, William raised the issue of an alliance with the Russians. The second time he came close to success.

In July 1905 William's yacht, the *Hohenzollern,* came to anchor near the Tsar's pleasure boat, the *Polar Star,* in the roadstead outside the Baltic port of Björkö. In a private interview with the Russian monarch, William induced him to sign a defensive alliance committing each empire to resist an attack by any European power on the other. Nicholas II apparently subscribed to the treaty because he was swept away by the Kaiser's eloquence and because he nourished hostility toward Britain, whose 1902 alliance with Japan had in his opinion made possible the Manchurian war.[45] Back in Petersburg, however, high officials were flabbergasted by this *coup de main* against Russian foreign policy. Witte and Lamzdorff convinced Nicholas that the Kaiser had manipulated him: the treaty, they told him, violated the spirit, if not the letter, of the Franco-Russian alliance; implied German hegemony in Europe; and was therefore contrary to Russian interests. William's plot was foiled when Nicholas agreed in essence to repudiate the Björkö treaty.[46]

If the Japanese war gave rise to unexpected warmth on the part of Russia's putative foes, it also seemed to cause a certain coolness among Russia's traditional clients and allies. Disturbing messages from Russia's Minister in Belgrade suggested that the Serbs were reevaluating their connection to Petersburg; a Russia convulsed by military defeat and internal disorder might not be in a position to give them much help in a dispute with Vienna.[47] More worrisome even than this, however, was the trouble that the Eastern war had caused in the relationship with the French.

In 1904, just two months after the Japanese attack at Port Arthur, French Foreign Minister Delcassé had fashioned the entente cordiale with Great Britain. That agreement, a solution of the outstanding colonial disputes that had divided the two countries, produced a growing closeness between London and Paris. The Russo-Japanese War, however, brought in its train the possibility of a clash with the British, who were, after all, allied to the Japanese. Given Paris's new friendship with London, what would France do in that event? Could it be relied upon to honor the terms of its treaty with Russia if the British should attack? That question continued to bother Russian statesmen even after the Japanese war was over, most particularly because Petersburg came to believe that the French were divulging Russian military secrets to London.[48]

Petersburg was eqully perturbed by the possibility of a French reassessment of Russia's own worth as an alliance partner. Russia's Ambassador to Paris voiced that concern when he pointed out that "our defeats in the Japanese war and our internal shocks could not but tell upon [French] confidence in our power and in our ability under current conditions exactly to fulfill the obligations we have assumed by the treaty of alliance."[49] Many of the leading tsarist officials agreed that it was vital to preserve the special arrangement with Paris. In the first place, Russia needed access to French capital markets if it was somehow to extricate itself from its fiscal crisis. Still more important was the impression that only the French alliance stood between Russia and the malodorous and stifling embrace of Germany.

To bolster French confidence in Russia, St. Petersburg made haste to offer Paris tokens of its reliability. In 1905 Germany had sought to challenge the special privileges the entente cordiale had granted to Franch in Morocco by posing as the defender of Moroccan independence. At the international conference on the Moroccan question held at Algeciras in 1906, contrary to Germany's expectations, Russia gave firm support to the French position. As all the other Great Powers with the exception of Austria did likewise, Germany's bid to humble and dominate the French came to nothing.[50]

St. Petersburg was equally concerned with reassuring France that its military power remained adequate to the challenge of a general European war. For that purpose even deceit was permissible. During the Franco-Russian staff talks held in Paris in April 1906, General Palitsyn consistently (and fraudulently) minimized the harm that the Japanese war and the revolution had caused Russia's defense posture. He made the bogus claim that the Russian army had suffered smaller losses of matériel during the Far Eastern war than was commonly supposed. Even now, he insisted, the Russian army was capable of a mobilization in the west. The lies Palitsyn fed the French during those discussions made the rankest hypocrisy of his private complaint about their lack of "frankness."[51] In any event, the French were not taken in by Palitsyn. For one thing, their military attaché in Paris was furnishing them with much more accurate (and depressing) estimations of the condition of the Russian armed forces.[52]

The fact of the matter was that while Russia was unequal to making war, there were potential menaces looming against it on two continents. It still had reason to fear Austria and Germany in Europe, while in the East there was the possibility that Japan might reopen hostilities against it at any time. Petersburg was of the opinion that Japan's representatives had been disappointed in the outcome of the Portsmouth peace negotiations; Japan, it was felt, had by no means achieved all of its ambitions in Asia. Finally, there were the ancient conflicts with Britain over Afghanistan and Persia—disputes that were more fraught with danger than ever. Owing to its debility, however, Russia found it next to impossible realistically to prepare for even one war, let alone two or more. The General Staff's December 1906 logistical plan for the resumption of war with Japan required moving twelve pairs of trains a day between the Volga basin and Vladivostok. To accomplish that, 690 locomotives would have to be shunted from European Russia to Asia, which would leave the western quarters of the empire almost defenseless.[53]

The new security problems could not but give a new direction to Russia's conduct of foreign relations. In rare unanimity, all the principal ministers of state now agreed that the cure for Russia's overextension was moderate and realistic diplomacy. The new Chairman of the Council of Ministers, P. A. Stolypin, observed: "Our internal situation does not permit us to conduct an aggressive foreign policy."[54] He was seconded by the new Foreign Minister, A. P. Izvol'skii, who emphasized that Russia must renounce "fantastical" schemes for imperial expansion.[55]

Yet it was also the obligation of Russia's diplomats to try to diminish the ranks of Russia's potential enemies. Russia had to achieve a relaxation in tensions on its borders either in Asia or in Europe, if not both. Although the Tsar at first winced at the idea, the most promising expedient here seemed to be a rapprochement with Great Britain.[56]

Such a deal would have several advantages. In the first place, ever since the signing of the entente cordiale, France had been working hard to bring London and Petersburg together. Fruitful negotiations with Britain would please the French and might help to re-cement Russia's ties to Paris. Second, as Izvol'skii pointed out to his colleagues, friendship with Britain might contribute to a Russo-Japanese reconciliation, which in its turn would provide Russia's Far Eastern possessions with essential security.[57] It was also true that to defuse Asian tensions with the British was really just a ratification of reality. Russia did not have the military or financial means to vie with London for influence in such places as Persia or Afghanistan. Kokovtsov, the Minister of Finance, decried the folly of a policy of rivalry with Britain in Asia: "[I]f in the past putting pressure on England was beyond our strength, then at present it is completely impossible."[58] The Ministry of War itself cautioned that, absent an understanding with the British, "peace and tranquility" on Russia's "weakly defended Central Asian frontier" could not be guaranteed.[59] The Russian government fully expected that it could make a British deal without paying the price of worsened relations with Berlin. The Germans, it was assumed, were certain to understand that a British arrangement was not directed against them. The upshot was the conclusion of the Anglo-Russian entente of 1907.

Like the entente cordiale, which it resembled, the agreement of 1907 was an amicable settlement of colonial conflicts. Both powers agreed to the neutralization of Tibet, while Russia renounced all interest in Afghanistan. The most important provisions of the treaty concerned Persia. That nominally independent state was divided into three parts: Russian and British spheres of influence in the north and south of the country, respectively, were to be separated by a neutral zone. A complimentary arrangement was then signed with Japan, defining the interests of the two powers in Mongolia and Manchuria.[60]

Prime Minister Stolypin hailed the two treaties as palpable

victories of Russian diplomacy.[61] St. Petersburg regarded the entente with Britain as a centerpiece of its foreign policy and was committed to upholding it. Almost at once, however, its determination to do so was put to the test. The Shah's abrogation of the Persian constitution led to anarchy and civil disorder in his country. The unrest was serious enough to endanger the lives of Russian representatives in Persia. There were, in addition, cross-border attacks into the Russian Caucasus by hostile Persian bands. Evidence also existed of collaboration between Persian rebels and domestic Azeri revolutionaries involving the exchange of explosives.[62] Russia's response to the crisis was tempered by its concern about the British entente. Although the Russian Ambassador in Tabriz demanded massive military intervention, the Council of Ministers authorized only a tiny expeditionary force as a way to signal to London Russia's lack of aggressive intentions toward Persia. "The very insignificance of these forces," Stolypin wrote, "will be the best proof of the fact that Russia does not nourish any plans to occupy, let alone annex, Persian possessions."[63]

By means of the rapprochements with Japan and Britain, Russia both had overcome the risk of strategic encirclement and had enchanced its prestige with its French ally. To Foreign Minister Izvol'skii, however, it was not enough merely to lance the boil of insecurity. He believed that Russia needed to achieve some sort of diplomatic triumph in order to demonstrate to the entire world that it was still a first-class power. The sticking point was Russia's military feebleness, which rendered it incapable of backing up any threats with force. If Izvol'skii was going to get away with some sort of international coup, he would have to do so by bluffing.

Izvol'skii's first effort in that direction involved opening the question of the Åland islands. Although Russia was their proprietor, the Paris Peace of 1856 had forbidden their militarization. The Foreign Minister felt that if he could win recognition of Petersburg's right to fortify the islands he would have usefully reaffirmed the principle of Russian sovereignty. But Izvol'skii's efforts to bully Sweden (the state most vitally concerned) into acquiescing to his scheme were rebuffed when the other Great Powers unexpectedly took Stockholm's part.[64] Izvol'skii now began to consider whether it might not be possible to alter the status of the straits in Russia's favor. The outcome of that was the Bosnian crisis of 1908–9, an excruciating blunder that caused a change of course in Russian foreign policy and accelerated an alteration in military strategy as well.

The Bosnian Crisis

By a treaty of 1897, Russia and Austria had pledged to uphold the status quo on the Balkan peninsula. In Vienna the new (and reckless) Foreign Minister, Aloys von Aehrenthal, was unsatisfied with that arrangement. It was his intention to annex the two nominally Turkish provinces of Bosnia and Herzegovina, which had actually been under Austrian occupation since 1878. Aehrenthal's goal's were several. The Young Turk revolution of 1907 had brought a nationalist government to power in Constantinople. Aehrenthal was consequently interested in fully incorporating the provinces into the Hapsburg Empire to thwart any Turkish effort to reclaim them. He was equally concerned to enhance Austria's prestige, while simultaneously delivering a blow to that of Serbia, which had dreamed of eventually absorbing those provinces itself. When Aehrenthal sounded the Russian government out about the two provinces in an exchange of notes during the summer of 1908, Izvol'skii saw an opening.

The two Foreign Ministers secretly met at Buchlau in September. Izvol'skii declared that Petersburg would accept Vienna's acquisition of Bosnia and Herzegovina if the Austrians were to provide adequate compensation, which would include an Austrian evacuation of the Sanjak of Novipazar, recognition of full independence for the Kingdom of Bulgaria, and some trivial concessions to Serbia, Bulgaria, and Montenegro with regard to river traffic on the Danube. Most important, however, Austria would have to promise to help Russia secure a revision in the rules governing the straits. By the terms of the Berlin Treaty of 1878, the straits were to be closed to the warships of all powers; the Sultan was supposed neither to permit armed Russian vessels to exit the Black Sea through them nor to allow those of any other power to pass in the opposite direction. Izvol'skii wanted Austrian support in coercing Turkey to open the straits to the Russian navy and the Russian navy alone. Aehrenthal obligingly gave his word and committed himself to obtaining German assistance as well.[65]

Izvol'skii, who had been acting on the Tsar's authority, immediately sent an encrypted telegram to his sovereign informing him of these results. Izvol'skii's assistant back in Petersburg, Charykov, reported that Nicholas was "extraordinarily pleased."[66] The peripatetic Russian Foreign Minister then journeyed to Munich, where he discussed his Austrian negotiations with German State Secretary Schoen, who gave them Berlin's conditional blessing.[67] Up to this point none of the other tsarist ministers of state had been let in on the secret. Izvol'skii, however, anticipated no opposition from them; once they were informed, he thought, they would at once accept the rigorous logic of his approach to the Bosnian problem.

From Izvol'skii's standpoint, Russia had no way to prevent formal Austrian annexation of the two provinces, mainly because Vienna already occupied them. In his opinion, his real coup had been to persuade Aehrenthal to give Petersburg something in exchange for a largely meaningless approval of Austria's impending act. The beauty of it all was that Vienna would end up shouldering all of the blame. Aehrenthal's unilateral declaration of annexation would be a violation of the Treaty of Berlin. France, Britain, and Turkey were sure to be outraged. There would be calls for an international conference, and at that conference, Izvol'skii wrote, "Austria will appear in the character of the accused, while we will appear in the role of the defenders of the Balkan Slavs and even Turkey."[68] Russia would then both have its cake and eat it. It would retain the moral high ground while sharing in the spoils of overturning the 1878 agreement among the Powers.

To be sure, there was a risk involved. If the details of the Buchlau deal became known, it might appear to some that Russia had sold out its Slav clients and Serbia in particular. But Izvol'skii thought the danger could be minimized if the Russian Foreign Ministry took appropriate pains to neutralize domestic public opinion in advance. "Once more with special emphasis," he wrote Charykov, "I consider it my duty to call your attention to the necessity of preparing public opinion and the press."[69] Some editors and journalists could be won over with interviews and flattery; others might have to be bought with appointments and money. Izvol'skii also instructed Charykov to canvass prominent Duma politicians, such as the Octobrist A. I. Guchkov and the Kadet P. Miliukov.[70]

Almost all the assumptions behind Izvol'skii's reasoning were, however, fallacious. In the first place (when they finally learned of it) Buchlau elicited not compliments but fury from the other prominent tsarist ministers. They demanded that the Buchlau agreement be repudiated. The Ministers of Finance, Interior, War, and Marine concluded that "without making the annexation a *casus belli*, we must give clear proof to Turkey and the other Powers that we are not participating in the violation of the status quo and that, if the annexation takes place, then it does so without our consent and at Austria's own risk."[71] At the direction of the Council of Ministers, Charykov was forced to rewrite the aide-memoire on Buchlau that he had been readying for dispatch to Vienna. The document that resulted was as internally inconsistent as the Russian government was disunified. While retaining all the clauses about Austria's obligation to help Russia over the issue of the straits, it simultaneously denounced the annexation of Bosnia and Herzegovina in the strongest terms.[72]

In the second place it apparently had never occurred to Izvol'skii that Austria could foil all his schemes through the simple expedient of publicizing the content of the Buchlau meeting. When Austria proclaimed the annexation of the two provinces on October 6, that is precisely what it did. Despite Charykov's assurances that "the press is sufficiently in our hands," Austria's maneuver (and Russia's apparent complicity in it) provoked a firestorm of public opposition. Papers of all political persuasions united in condemning the Russian government for its sordid violation of international law and its "plundering" of the Slavs.[73] Petersburg's public and private denials of the Austrian version of the Buchlau events were not believed. Russia's efforts to convene an international conference to resolve the crisis were unavailing.

Of course, Russia could make its new-found opposition to the annexation more credible if it wished to issue a threat of war. Petersburg had little stomach for hostilities, however. Izvol'skii stated at a late October meeting of the Council of Ministers, "to wage war for Bosnia and Herzegovina isn't worth it."[74] Yet there was a dismal prospect that war might be forced on Russia anyway. Russian intelligence had detected heightened military activity on the part of Austria stretching back to the summer of 1908. By the end of September Austria was massing forces on the Serbian frontier and was preparing for a mobilization in Galicia.[75] To be sure, it was known in Petersburg that the Austrian General Staff was of the view that the armies of the Dual Monarchy would not be ready to fight until the middle of March 1909, at least.[76] The problem was that Russia was even less prepared for war than was Austria, most particularly if the latter was assisted by its German ally. Russia's army was feeble and its navy no better off. The Admiralty had concluded in late summer that the Baltic fleet was not even strong enough to protect the capital.[77]

As it also soon became clear that Russia would not be able to count on much in the way of French support, the outcome of the Bosnian crisis hinged on what attitude the Germans would adopt. If Germany abstained from intervening on Austria's behalf, the result might be an Austro-Russian standoff. On the other hand, if Germany backed Vienna, Russia would either have to accept the annexation of the provinces or go to war.

In Berlin Chancellor Bülow decided to give Austria succor. He did so to preserve Germany's alliance with Vienna, but also because the warming relations between London and Petersburg in recent years had come to alarm him. In his eyes the Franco-Russian relationship was either already or soon to be converted into a tripartite pact. The Bosnian crisis might therefore be an opportunity to break the Triple Entente. German support for Austria would cause France to distance itself from Russia, thus raising doubts in Petersburg about French reliability. At the same time Bülow took it upon himself to stir up French apprehensions about Russian trustworthiness by spreading a rumor that the German government had received assurances from Petersburg that Russia would remain neutral in a Franco-German war.[78] Finally, in March 1909 Germany sent Russia a note insisting on immediate Russian acquiescence to the annexation.[79]

To the tsarist elite in Petersburg the timing of this note seemed to coincide ominously with the conclusion of Austrian military preparations for an invasion of Serbia. Russia's attaché in Vienna had also informed his government that the Germans had agreed to send forces of their own into Galicia, so as to hold the tsarist empire in check.[80] If Russia either accepted the annexation or idly tolerated the destruction of Serbia, it would lose honor and dignity. In those circumstances war became a more attractive option. But at the emergency meeting of the Council of Ministers resulting from the Berlin note, War Minister Rediger declared that Russia's armed forces were not even capable of repelling a foreign invasion, let along taking any offensive action.[81] Russia had no choice but to accept Austria's absorption of Bosnia and Herzegovina.

The Bosnian crisis was an international humiliation of the first water for Petersburg. Coming so soon on the heels of the Manchurian defeat, it tended to confirm the decay of Russia's moral and material influence in the affairs of Europe. It also put an end to Izvol'skii's ministerial career. Slightly more than a year after the resolution of the crisis, he resigned his office and departed for Russia's Embassy in Paris.

It was well understood in Petersburg that the principal reason for Austria's triumph had been the firm support of Germany. If Russia wanted to avoid a painful repetition of the events of 1908–9 it therefore had to take the path of appeasing Berlin. As the new Foreign Minister, S. D. Sazonov, would later observe, "it was essential for the Russian government to placate German hostility for a long time to come by means of all possible concessions in the economic sphere."[82] The unhelpful attitude of France during the Bosnian crisis was another reason for a pro-German turn in Russian policy. Changes of top-level personnel in Germany also aroused Russian hopes. Petersburg was satisfied that the new Chancellor, Bethmann-Hollweg, and the new Foreign Minister, Kiderlin-Wächter, were not particular partisans of Austria. In November 1910 Nicholas II and Sazonov visited Potsdam for discussions with the German Emperor. There a bargain was struck. The Russians agreed to drop their opposition to Germany's pet scheme of a Berlin-to-Baghdad railway. Still further, they offered to connect that line to their own Caucasus-to-Teheran railroad, thus opening up all of northern Persia to German economic penetration. In return, Bethmann promised Sazonov that Germany would not be a party to any more Austrian *"dispositions agressives"* in the Balkans.[83] Two years later, during another state meeting of the two sovereigns at Baltic Port, Bethmann reiterated his vow to restrain any possible Austrian adventurism in southeastern Europe.[84] As was to be expected, Paris viewed Russia's submissiveness to Germany with suspicion.

But still more suspicion was aroused when the French became aware of the strategic implications of Russia's military reorganization of 1910.

The Reorganization of 1910: Russian Strategy Changes Course

The origins of the strategic reorientation of 1910 dated back to the aftermath of the Russo-Japanese War. Russia's defeat in the Far East reopened the old question about whether Europe or Asia would be the most probable theater of future conflict. Since Miliutin's time, Russian military planners had emphasized the primacy of Europe; now, however, that assumption seemed open to doubt. What if Japan wanted to make itself the undisputed master of Asia? In that case the Peace of Portsmouth would prove to have been only an entr'acte preceding another burst of Japanese aggression. Russia was even less capable of defending itself in Asia after the termination of the Manchurian war than it had been before. In an enormous secret memorandum of 1906, A. A. Abaza painted a gloomy picture of what another conflict with Japan might be like. Basing themselves in Port Arthur, Southern Manchuria, and Korea, the Japanese would sever the Trans-Siberian Railroad, thus isolating Vladivostok. They would then seize control of Russias entire Pacific Maritime Province. That would force the Russians "under very difficult conditions to attempt to reconquer our own territory or to retire to Lake Baikal."[85]

Other responsible people shared Abaza's worries about Russia's Pacific security. General Unterberger, the Commander of Priamur Military District, sent repeated warnings to Petersburg on this score from 1907 through 1909. Russia, he said, should have no confidence in its détente with Japan. Since Japan had failed to drive Russia from the Pacific, neither the Japanese government nor the population had been satisfied with the Peace of Portsmouth. Unterberger therefore confidently prophesied that another war with Japan was inevitable.[86] In this war the Japanese objectives would be to "establish hegemony over the eastern shore of the Asian mainland . . . and to paralyze any development by us of the lands lying east of Lake Baikal and to reduce them to a colonial position."[87]

Those dire scenarios were not just the febrile imaginings of self-interested parties. After Portmouth, the Russian military elite was inclined to take the potential threat from Japan very seriously. Many of Russia's most prominent "Westerners" were now in fact converted into "Easterners"—a process doubtless assisted by a longing for revenge. A. N. Kuropatkin provides a good example of the intellectual shift. Prior to 1904 Kuropatkin and been one of the most ardent proponents of building up Russia's strength in the west. Military investments in the east were a dangerous diversion of resources away from the continent where they were most needed. By 1906, however, Kuropatkin had reversed himself. Also convinced that war with Japan would flare up again, he argued for a reorientation of Russia's defense priorities toward the Pacific. In a multivolume work published in 1910, he sounded the same theme. Russia should distance itself from European affairs in order to gather strength to combat the "yellow peril."[88] All of that was, of course, a striking repudiation of all of the ideas he had been championing before the Manchurian war.

Central military planners were themselves alarmed about the possibility of a new Japanese war and pondered deeply how Russia might cope with the challenges that would present. Russia simply did not possess the resources to fight major war simultaneously in both Europe and Asia. Yet war could conceivably break out in either theater, and Russia consequently needed to become capable of a prompt military response in either. Was there not something lopsided, in that case, about Russia's current defense posture, with its heavy forward deployment of troops in the western districts of the country? Grand Duke Nikolai Nikolaevich, Chairman of the Council of State Defense, in a note of December 1907, advocated concentrating a larger proportion of Russia's forces in the heart of the country so that they could be used either in Europe or in Asia. While he wanted to screen the western frontiers with an improved network of fortresses, he insisted that "all state military organizations serving and feeding the army ought to be located in the safest and most central place. Such a place is the Volga basin."[89]

General Palitsyn, the Chief of Staff, fleshed out the thinking of his patron Nikolai in a memorandum drafted one month later. The army had to be redeployed so as to make possible the dispatch of troops "against any of our potential enemies and their coalitions in Europe or Asia."[90] That meant that "the current grouping of our forces . . . is justified neither by the contemporary development of our railroad net nor by politico-military conditions."[91] "Our [current] deployment," Palitsyn continued, "was developed with war with the powers of the Triple Alliance in mind and the need, resulting from this, for the swift concentration of our troops on the western frontiers. But after the distribution of forces had already taken form there arose in the Far East a terrible military power which could open hostilities against us at any minute."[92] Those words clearly reveal that the Russian General Staff continued to fear a conflict with Tokyo despite Foreign Ministry assurances that successful negotiations with both Britain and Japan in 1907 had made that possibility remote. Palitsyn did include some additional justifications designed to garner the the support of civilian ministers for his plan. He insincerely argued that redistributing troops toward the center of the country would ease the problem of quelling domestic unrest should any more of it flare up. He also stressed that redeployment would entail a reallocation of military spending to the benefit of the Russian population and to the detriment of the Poles and the Jews.[93] Yet the key motivation behind his entire plan was unquestionably his desire for strategic flexibility.

In specific terms, Palitsyn envisioned transferring 138 battalions away from the westernmost military districts to eastern Russia, the Caucausus, and Siberia. The three districts most radically affected would be Vil'na, Warsaw, and Kiev. Vil'na would lose twenty battalions, Warsaw forty-four, and Kiev forty-nine. That would result in the reduction in troop strength in these districts by 11, 17, and 28 percent, respectively.[94] Although Palitsyn insisted that his proposal would not substantially reduce Russia's military readiness in the event of a clash in the West, such a redeployment would obviously have the most profound consequences in any future Russian war with the Central Powers.[95] In the first place, the reconcentration would actually make it easier for Russia to mobilize. Then, as in the Soviet Union today, in peacetime most military units were maintained at less than full strength. The process of mobilization was a matter of reinforcing the regiments so as to put them on a war footing. Reservists were called up and dispatched to preassigned military units. However, since over 40 percent of Russia's forces were massed on the western frontiers, mobilization involved shunting some 200,000 men from the more densely populated central provinces of the Empire to the periphery.[96] If a significant proportion of battalions were transferred back into the heartland, as Palitsyn desired, they would be closer to the sources of their wartime manpower. It followed that the time necessary to furnish the army with its full complement of men would be significantly reduced.

Yet if the Palitsyn plan would speed up the mobilization of Russia's forces, it would also retard their *concentration* in the event of a war in the west, for now many of the mustered battalions would have travel considerable distances to arrive in the frontier zone. That would increase Germany's and Austria's advantage in the opening stages of any war. It would, moreover, seriously constrain Russia's ability to honor its commitments to its French ally. In the end, however, financial difficulties, in addition to the dismantling of the Council of State Defense, prevented the Palitsyn plan from getting much beyond the talking stage.

That was not, however, the end of the matter. In December 1909 the new War Minister, V. A. Sukhomlinov, unveiled an entire package of military reforms in which the Palitsyn deployment concept played a prominent role. Sukhomlinov was interested in increasing the size of the Russian army, both in peacetime and in war, without, however, placing new burdens on the treasury. He ingeniously argued that this could be done by means of a total overhaul of the procedures governing conscription and reserves. Shortening the term of active service from four to three years in the infantry and from five to four in the cavalry would eventually enlarge the pool of Russia's reservists by one-fourth. The introduction of a "secret cadre" system would allow Russia to take maximum advantage of the increased manpower. When mobilization was declared, the cadres would be detached from each unit; they would serve as the core for 560 additional battalions, which would be built up around them using reservists.[97] The savings gained by this, in addition to the money saved by abolishing various other categories of troops (such as fortress infantry), which Sukhomlinov considered superfluous, would be used to increase the size of Russia's peacetime field forces by 13 percent. The number of active peacetime battalions would go up from 1,110 to 1,252 without costing the state one extra kopek.[98]

A thorough redeployment of the Russian army would complement those changes. Like Palitsyn, Sukhomlinov wanted to shift the Russian army's center of gravity to the east. Warsaw and Vil'na districts were to lose 91 and 37 battalions respectively, which would permit the establishment of a general reserve of 320 battalions in Kazan Military District.[99] Sukhomlinov asserted that this arrangement would confer many benefits on the Russian army. It would now, for example, be possible to go over to a territorial system of recruitment: the territories within which the military units were billeted would henceforth supply them with the bulk of the conscripts they needed. But the key reason Sukhomlinov advocated the redistribution of forces was identical to Palitsyn's: the need to respond to potential Asian threats. Like Palitsyn, Sukhomlinov did not share the Foreign Ministry's belief that Russian diplomacy had neutralized Japan in 1907.[100] He had also been enormously impressed by the Unterberger's description of the peril in the Far East.[101] According to Sukhomlinov the rise of China and the awakening of Japan meant that "we cannot concentrate our exclusive attention on the West any longer; we also have to ready ourselves for a serious struggle on our farflung eastern borders."[102]

Sukhomlinov's plan diverged from Palitsyn's in two controversial respects. First, Sukhomlinov wanted to abandon Russia's network of fortresses in the west altogether. As we have seen, both Palitsyn and Nikolai Nikolaevich wanted to upgrade the fortresses so as to provide a shield behind which Russia could concentrate its divisions. In Sukhomlinov's opinion, however, the expenses connected with remodeling the antiquated fortresses would be excessive and wasteful. The money could be better spent elsewhere. Still further, for the fortresses to have even a minimal chance of withstanding Teutonic onslaughts, they would require enormous garrisons. Apportioning troops for that purpose would subtract from the strength of Russia's field armies, which was unacceptable.[103] But there was an additional consideration. In the event of the outbreak of a western war, Palitsyn had wanted to mobilize in the east and concentrate on the frontiers. Sukhomlinov, on the contrary, preferred that both mobilization *and concentration* be conducted in the heartland. "The concentration of our forces," he wrote, "must inevitably be transferred into the depths of the country, so as to have the chance of completing it without impediment and also so as to determine the grouping of forces of the enemy, who, unfortunately being better prepared, will have the initiative. Then, going over onto the offensive with massed forces, [we shall] inflict a decisive defeat on our enemies."[104] Sukhomlinov's meaning triumphed over his tortuous syntax: if war with the Central Powers erupted, Russia would at first abandon vast regions in the west to the German and Austrian invaders while gathering strength for a knockout blow. Such a vast strategic withdrawal was in effect a rejection of the principles that had guided Russian war planning since the days of Miliutin.

What lay behind the Sukhomlinov defense concept? Its intellectual underpinnings were not in fact the creation of the War Minister himself. There appear to have been two principal sources behind Sukhomlinov's new direction in Russian national security policy, one relatively well known, the other much more obscure.

The first source was a note about changing Russia's wartime deployments by Colonel Iu. N. Danilov of the General Staff in late 1908. If war with the Central Powers broke out, Danilov recommended concentrating Russia's forces not on the Vistula and the Narew as was the current intention, but farther to the east, within a diamond defined by Sventiiany-Grodno-Brest-Baranovichi. That would involve trading territory for the time necessary to complete the safe assembly of Russia's forces. It also presupposed that Germany would invade Russia in force as early as possible, reflecting the morbid fear of the German army from which Danilov suffered throughout his entire professional career.[105]

The second source was the Vitner report of February 1909. In late 1908, while still Chief of Staff, Sukhomlinov had commissioned a study of the fortress issue by Major General Vitner of the Engineers. Vitner was a technologist, an Easterner, and a strong proponent of mobile warfare. For those reasons he was harshly critical of Russia's *western* fortresses. Since a potential enemy could not strike everywhere simultaneously, Vitner estimated that no more than 10 percent of the forts would play a role even in a major war.[106] For that reason, and also because of their rapid obsolescence, the military value of the fortresses did not justify their upkeep. Vinter used his attack on the fortresses as a platform from which to call for a comprehensive reassessment of Russia's defense priorities. Poland, he argued, would prove to be indefensible in the early stages of any war with the Dual Alliance. In view of the initial numerical superiority they would derive from their dense railnets, Austria and Germany would launch simultaneous offensives into the Polish salient. Russia's forward-deployed forces would inexorably face encirclement and would be compelled to withdraw. If it were wise, Russia would recognize the inevitability of its loss of Poland and would plan to concentrate its armies somewhere east of the Vistula.[107]

Vitner had a further point to make. In his view, there was simply no reason for Russia to go to war with Germany in the first place. The only conceivable way in which one could arise would be if Franco-German hostilities had already begun and Russia wished to intervene to help Paris. To Vitner it would be folly for Russia to involve itself in war in order to assist an ally. "Can we really acknowledge that any one of them is so sincere, and so reliable, that it would be worthwhile for us to get mixed up in a war, which, under contemporary conditions, would demand such frightful sacrifices?"[108] That, of course, was an obvious allusion to France's unsupportive behavior during the Bosnian crisis. What then of the danger of French military collapse and German domination of the Continent? "I am far from indifferently looking on," he wrote, "if our neighbor wishes to strengthen his might at the expense of another. But calm neutrality and a veto at the decisive moment is completely sufficient to prevent this from happening."[109]

Vitner's emphasis on "calm neutrality" made it apparent that he wished for Russia to disengage itself from the affairs of Europe. But, as befitted an Easterner, he was passionate about the need to improve Russia's defense capability in what he described as "our most sensitive frontier"—the Pacific. While deprecating investment in western strongpoints, he demanded that the fortifications of Vladivostok be made sufficient to the demands of a three-year siege.[110] Vitner concluded his memorandum with a call for the reallocation of Russian defense resources. Battleships were, to his way of thinking, just as redundant as the western fortresses. If Russia razed the fortresses and declined to build any more large surface combatants, it could put the money saved to much better use by developing its railroads and purchasing torpedo boats, submarines, and airplanes.[111] Sukhomlinov appropriated almost all of the ideas of Danilov and Vitner. The same month he read the Vitner memorandum, Sukhomlinov announced the abolition of the western fortresses.[112] The thinking of both men profoundly informed the War Minister's December 1909 report.

We are now in a position to see Sukhomlinov's defense plan for what it truly was. Whereas Palitsyn had wanted a deployment flexible enough to meet military emergencies in either Europe or Asia, Sukhomlinov's priorities were clearly biased toward the east. The War Minister held that war was more likely on the shores of the Pacific than on the banks of the Vistula. It was in Asia as well that Sukhomlinov evidently would have preferred to fight a war. Of course, he did not ignore the possibility of a war with the Teutonic Powers. But the western strategy implied by his redeployment was strikingly different from the strategies of his predecessors. Sukhomlinov's new strategy was enshrined in mobilization schedule 19. This document, largely Danilov's work, was approved by the Tsar in 1910. The war would begin with the *de facto* concession to the enemy of a great deal (almost ten provinces) of Russian Poland. That would permit the secure mobilization and concentration of Russian troops. Thereafter, as in earlier plans, the dispositions of the enemy would dictate Russian actions. If Germany and Austria were preoccupied with other enemies, Russia might attempt an offensive. But if Russia was their principal target, it would have to organize a stout defense. Although the original plan 19 envisioned earmarking more Russian forces for "active measures" against Germany than against Austria-Hungary, the new eastern concentration that underpinned it, conjoined with Sukhomlinov's decision to raze such fortresses as Warsaw and Ivangorod, clearly signaled the War Ministry's intentions with regard to the Franco-Russian alliance.[113] If plan 19 were to be implemented strictly, France's expectations of military assistance could not be fulfilled at the beginning of a war. If Russia eventually took offensive action against Germany, it would not even begin to happen earlier than the twentieth day after the declaration of mobilization. From the French point of view, that would be too late to be of much use.[114] Whether or not Sukhomlinov expected the French to grasp this,

THE 1910 DEPLOYMENT PLAN

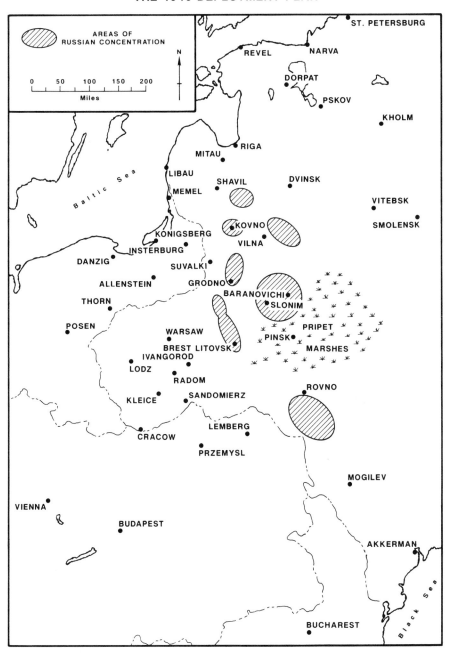

he certainly hoped the Germans would. It would not be too much to describe his defensist strategy as a plot against Russia's traditional foreign policy, for the strategy clearly subverted the alliance with Paris. Easternism was (at least temporarily) in the ascendent.

The Strategic Shift of 1910: Controversies

From the very beginning Sukhomlinov ran into difficulty in putting his plan into effect. There were, for example, some technical problems, of which the worst was the shortage of housing. There simply were not enough barracks available in the heartland of the country to accommodate the units being transferred back from Poland. The dearth of quarters was particularly acute in Kazan Military District, where the War Ministry had to resort to the eighteenth-century practice of billeting the troops among the population. Although it retarded the implementation of the redeployment, the housing question did not arrest it.[115]

Much more serious was the opposition presented by other Ministers, by certain circles within the army, and by the Duma. Sukhomlinov's efforts to defuse criticism were by no means entirely successful. When the Chairman of the Council of Ministers raged that "without the knowledge of our allies we had no right to reshuffle our cards," Sukhomlinov tried to placate him with the ineffectual lie that the redeployment and fortress demolition plans were theoretical only, devoid of practical significance.[116] It was easier for the War Ministry to neutralize military detractors of the new defense concept. Dubious members of the Military Council could be cowed into acquiescence.[117] At least some officers who were tactless enough to commit their objections to print could be reprimanded and retired.[118]

But there were certain military critics who could not be silenced. Grand Duke Nikolai Nikolaevich, the Tsar's uncle, headed a patronage network of his own within the army that (in part for tactical reasons) was consistently hostile to the destruction of the fortresses.[119] It was likewise impossible for the War Minister utterly to stifle Duma criticism. Those pressures constrained Sukhomlinov to compromise on the fortress issue: he agreed to spare Novogeorievsk—the fortress that guarded the railway bridges over the Vistula—even though in the event of war the main armies would be assembling more than 200 kilometers to the east.[120] Sukhomlinov also proved powerless in the end to prevent the appropriation of monies to preserve several other forts.[121] But demolition crews were active in Poland throughout 1910 and 1911; still further, by early 1912 the eastward redeployment of the Russian army had been completed.

All this had a predictable impact on Petersburg's relationship with Paris. Although Zhilinskii reassured Dubail at formal staff talks in 1910 and 1911 that Russia remained unquestionably loyal to the terms of the alliance, the French found the new Russian war plan deeply troubling.[122] Lieutenant Colonel Janin, whom the French *État-Major* sent on a fact-finding mission to Petersburg, sent back disquieting reports suggesting that Russia's 1910 strategy for western war was modeled on that of Peter the Great and Alexander I.[123] To many Frenchmen, the Russo-German agreement at Potsdam and the new military arrangements were all part of an ominous pattern. A spate of anti-Russian articles appeared in the French press. Certain influential Frenchmen, such as former Foreign Minister Delcassé, reproved Russian emissaries for the "deterioration" of the Franco-Russian alliance.[124] French newspapers continued to condemn Russia's redeployment into late 1912, prompting Russian diplomats in Paris to inquire whether Petersburg had given satisfactory explanations about the matter to the President of the Republic.[125] The French obviously feared that Russian appeasement of Germany would sooner or later entail an open rupture with Paris. They would have been even more suspicious had they been aware of the conversation between the Russian and German Prime Ministers at Baltic Port in 1912, in which the former affirmed that Russia's defense reorganization of 1910 was proof of its pacific policy towards Berlin.[126]

The Pendulum Swings Again: The Renewed Interest in Europe

Less than two years after the the defense reorganization of 1910, Russia's statesmen and generals were forced to admit that at least one of the premises behind it—the paramountcy of the Japanese threat—had probably been erroneous. By 1912 it seemed that the most serious potential trouble spots were in Europe and the Near East. In part that resulted from the unintended consequences of Russian diplomatic initiatives themselves.

Worried about Austrian interest in the Balkans, and terrified lest Austria try to humble Serbia (and consequently Russia) again as it had in 1908–9, Russia for a long time had been promoting an alliance between Belgrade and Sofia. Such an agreement was signed in March 1912; when Greece adhered to it later in the year, a bilateral alliance was transformed into the Balkan League. Russia had desired to create the Balkan League so as to counterbalance Vienna in Southeastern Europe.[127] The League, however, was not a malleable instrument. Bulgarian, Serbian, and Greek leaders soon found an aggressive purpose for their confederacy.

The Young Turk revolution had once again (as so often in the past) seemed to herald the imminent collapse of the Ottoman Empire. Emboldened by the internal instability in Constantinople, in 1911 Italy declared war on Turkey to compel it to recognize the Italian annexation of Tripoli. The three Balkan states saw in the Tripolitan war an opportunity to despoil Turkey of the rest of its holdings in Europe. In October 1912, on the very day the Italians and Turks finally signed a peace, the first Balkan War broke out. Much to the surprise of the Great Powers, the Balkan allies quickly achieved dramatic victories. Mediation (and threats from Vienna) eventually resulted in the settlement of the conflict by means of the London Treaty of May 1913, which deprived the Turks of most of their remaining European provinces. But the erstwhile allies soon fell to squabbling among themselves. Because Austria had prevented Serbia from acquiring lands in Albania that would have given it an outlet to the Adriatic, Belgrade wanted Sofia to compensate it with a larger slice of Macedonia. That led directly to a Bulgarian sneak attack upon Greek and Serbian forces, which touched off the Second Balkan War in June 1913. Greece, Serbia, Turkey, and Rumania now ganged up on Bulgaria and overwhelmed it in a month. In the ensuing peace treaties, all four states profited at Bulgaria's expense.

Although the Great Powers had managed to localize the Balkan wars, there was no reason for complacency about the stability of Southeastern Europe. Belgrade's relative success on the battlefield had given a strong boost to the forces of Serbian nationalism, which left Vienna more convinced than ever that it would soon be necessary to settle accounts with that upstart state. The Serbs were aggrieved at the Austrian insistence on independence for Albania, which they felt had unfairly cheated them of their due. If the open quarrel between Belgrade and Vienna festered, Russia had to worry about becoming entangled in it. Austria's concentration of five army corps on the its Serbian border in the first half of 1913 had produced anxiety in Petersburg about the imminence of war.[128]

Adding to Russia's woes was the behavior of the Germans. In conciliating William II and Bethmann, Sazonov had hoped to drive a wedge between Austria and Germany—at least insofar Balkan issues were involved. But the backing the Germans had furnished the Austrians during the Balkan crises of 1912–13 indicated that the policy had failed. Russia had to assume that if war erupted between itself and Austria, Germany's armies would augment those of the Hapsburgs.

Indeed, Germany's policies in the Near East were increasingly obnoxious to the Russian government. The Young Turk coup d'état of January 1913 had paved the way for the expansion of German influence in Constantinople. Especially sinister from Petersburg's point of view was the growing prominence of the role played by German military advisers in Turkey. At the end of October 1913 Russian's Ambassador in Constantinople reported having learned that a German military mission headed by General Liman von Sanders was soon expected to arrive. The German officers in Sanders's entourage were all to receive commands in the Turkish army; it was rumored that Sanders himself would be named commander of the Turkish I Army Corps. Since that corps was entrusted with the defense of Constantinople and the Bosphorus, to Russian eyes Sanders's appointment would be tantamount to German acquisition of full control over the straits.[129] The Russian government regarded the situation as intolerable and loudly protested to Berlin. Germany's cavalier dismissal of Russia's complaints only aggravated the crisis. Yet if the Germans would not budge, perhaps the Turks could be induced to do so. In December Sazonov called a special conference to review options for pressuring Turkey, which ranged from the suspension of diplomatic relations to military action. The news of Sanders's promotion to Turkish Field Marshal finally relaxed the tension in January 1914. An officer with that lofty rank was ineligible to command an army corps. Petersburg's relief was mitigated, however, by the unpleasant fact of Sanders's simultaneous elevation to the post of Inspector General of the entire Turkish army. Russia still had reason to dread German machinations in the Ottoman Empire.[130]

By 1912 the Russian military elite was also expressing renewed concern about Turkey. Unlike the Ministry of Foreign Affairs, the Ministry of War assumed that Turkey would cooperate closely with Austria and Germany should a general European war break out.[131] The problem was not Turkish land forces. The paucity of railroads in the Ottoman Empire would impede any Turkish mobilization against Russia.[132] But Turkish naval power was another matter altogether. Russia had been powerless to prevent Turkey's closure of the straits to commerce during the Tripolitan War. Although they had swiftly been reopened, the episode reminded the Russians about how vulnerable they were to economic strangulation; almost three-quarters of Russia's exports passed through the Bosphorus. Still worse, the tempo of Turkish naval modernization raised serious questions about the security of Russia's own Black Sea coast. In a Black Sea naval arms race Turkey possessed all the advantages. While it could purchase battleships abroad and add them to its fleet, the international treaty on the closure of the Dardanelles to warships precluded Russia from doing so. Russia could augment its Black Sea squadron only with vessels it constructed itself in its own limited-capacity Black Sea boatyards.[133] By the summer of 1913 Foreign Ministry officials were describing the naval situation in the Black Sea as "dire."[134] If Russia took no effective countermeasures, it was estimated that Turkey would possess naval supremacy in the Black Sea by 1916; in the opinion of the Naval General Staff, that would constitute "a serious threat to the integrity of the Empire."[135]

The parlous condition of Russia's security in Europe had to be addressed. The response of the St. Petersburg government was to increase military spending. Defense outlays had already been raised with the adoption of the "Small Program" of 1910. That had allocated authorized above-budget expenditures of 715 rubles by the army and 550 million by the navy over the ensuing decade. The Small Program, however, had been part of the general national security reorganization of that year and had consequently placed a high priority on the defense of the Far East.

That priority now had to be altered. Sukhomlinov was induced to cancel plans to raze some additional western forts; engineers were sent into Poland to repair the fortifications at Ivangorod and Warsaw.[136] Petersburg also decided to upgrade its stock of fortress artillery in the west, exchanging obsolete ordnance for improved models.[137]

Field forces earmarked for western operations also benefited. As another indicator of the shift in priorities, by the end of 1912 the most advanced field and mountain guns in Russia's arsenal had been concentrated in Europe, leaving only inferior and outmoded cannon for use by the Far Eastern forces.[138] Heightened tensions in Europe finally gave birth to the Big Program for defense expenditure. Approved by the Tsar in October 1913 and confirmed by the Duma early the following summer, the Big Program was designed to increase the army's size and firepower. The program envisioned expanding the peacetime army by 468,200 men, or almost 40 percent, by 1917. Those soldiers were to be employed chiefly to enlarge the infantry companies serving in the frontier zones from 120 to 200 men. The other important element in the program was the prescription for the overhaul of the entire Russian artillery arm. Weapons acquisitions, plus a reduction in the number of guns per artillery battery, would make possible a dramatic, nearly twofold increase in the number of batteries. The military districts of European Russia, possessing 451 batteries of various categories of ordnance prior to the reform, would have 887 batteries by the end of 1917. All of that, of course, would be very expensive. The War Ministry estimated that the Big Program would require a one-time outlay of 433 million rubles and a disbursement of 140 million for every year thereafter.[139]

Nor was the navy excluded from the defense spending bonanza. Noting the importance to Russia of the sea lanes of communication through the Baltic and Black seas, the Admiralty argued that if Russia did not rebuild its fleets, it might well be cut off from its allies should war come.[140] The naval construction program of 1912 provided for the building of two dreadnoughts and six light cruisers (plus several submarines and torpedo boats) in the Baltic.[141] Balkan crises and Turkish navalism also impelled the admirals to request the addition of three battleships, nine destroyers, and six submarines to the Black Sea squadron by

1918.[142] In March 1914 the Ministry of Marine unveiled a supplementary plan for the development of the Black Sea Fleet; the price tag was 102 million rubles.[143] The armed forces of Russia were by no means successful in getting everything they wanted. In particular, the Ministry of Finance could not refrain from sniping at the military budget. The army and the navy also remained bitter rivals in the struggle for appropriations. Still, army and navy outlays, which stood at 643 million rubles in 1909, had topped 965 million by 1913—a figure representing over 28 percent of all state expenditures.[144] Ultimately what made possible the brightening of the military financial picture was a general improvement in the fiscal health of the tsarist empire. Over the 1904–13 period, imperial revenues grew at twice the rate of the empire's population. Burgeoning apprehensions about the likelihood of war in Europe, in addition to skillful politicking by the admirals and generals, enabled Russia's armed forces to tap more deeply into those state resources.

Strategic Planning on the Eve of World War: A Collision of Insecurities

By 1912 the inevitability of war between the Triple Entente and the Triple Alliance was a subject of general discussion in the capitals of Europe. As Russian statesmen contemplated the impending conflict, they could take some comfort from their own military buildup. The deportment of their probable allies was also reassuring. The dispatches of Russian military attachés indicated that the French army had never been better prepared. France was, as well, increasingly confident of British aid when the war came. The French informed the Russians that it was almost certain that the English would support the war effort not only with their formidable navy but also with a Continental expeditionary force of at least six divisions, which might be enough to provide a margin of superiority over Germany.[145]

But Russia also had much to worry about on the debit side of the strategic ledger. In the first place, the Russian government believed that the war was most likely to begin as a result of a clash between Russia and Austria-Hungary. A January 1914 memorandum by Foreign Minister Sazonov provides an example of that thinking. It developed a scenario in which Austria opted for war as "the only exit from the unresolvable internal difficulties" of competing nationalisms.[146] Germany would automatically enter the conflict on Austria's side, hence the French alliance took on a renewed importance in Russian thinking. Without French assistance, Russia could not hope to prevail in such a one-sided struggle. Yet, as in the past, the only way Russia could be sure that the French would be there when it needed them was by convincing them that Russia was in a position to deliver early and powerful blows against Germany. In 1912 the Russians began a desperate effort to re-cement the French alliance. The Franco-Russian naval convention, signed in July of that year, was one manifestation. Another was the new cooperativeness Russia's representatives now showed in their meetings with officials from the *État-Major*. At the staff conversations of 1912 and 1913 the Russians tried to buy French good-will by promising to attack Germany with 800,000 men by the fifteenth day after the declaration of mobilization. At the 1913 conference Zhilinskii even insisted that within a year Russia would be able to launch an anti-German offensive by $M+13$.[147] The problem was that the defense reorganization of 1910 had placed constraints on Russia's ability to honor its pledges to France. The military reforms of 1910 complicated any quick forward response on Russia's part during a European military emergency. As we have seen, the eastward shift of the Russian army naturally entailed a slowdown in the rate at which Russia could concentrate forces in the western districts of the empire. Then, too, the original plan 19 had posited an initial Russian withdrawal; that assumption had informed the allocation of money for such purposes as the construction of strategic railroads.

In the past the Russian War Ministry had complained that its voice was excluded from the debate over railway development in the country. That had now changed. In 1908 Nicholas II appointed a special high commission for the study of railway affairs. Including War Ministry representatives, the commission had been ordered to evaluate the "fit" between present and projected railway lines and Russia's strategic needs. By working through the commission, the Ministry of War was able to acquire an unprecedented influence over railway construction.[148] Guided by the 1910 defense concept, however, the Ministry had flatly opposed investing in rail lines in the western regions of Poland, for those were expected to fall into the enemy's hands anyway. The result was that although Russia's entire rail net expanded from 61,000 to 73,000 versts from 1905 to 1914, the territories west of the Neman and south of the Belostok–Baranovichi line did not profit in the slightest. Reports from Warsaw and Kiev military districts on the very eve of the war declared that transportation resources in those areas were inadequate to the demands of modern war.[149] That grave situation was at least partly of the War Ministry's own making. By opting for the East—which was really what the strategic choice of 1910 had been about—the Ministry had undermined the army's ability to implement a rapid offensive against Germany. Owing to alliance considerations, the need for precisely such an offensive had been rediscovered.

Equally, however, the Russian military leadership felt that it still had to make provision for an offensive against the Austrians *as well as* against the Germans. Influential factions within the army (such as that led by General Alekseev of Kiev district) advocated aiming a strong initial blow at the Dual Monarchy.[150] The arguments they adduced for this were identical to those used fourteen years before. It was believed that Austria would be ready to attack Russia on the fifteenth day of the war. Russia's best response to that invasion would be a counterinvasion of Hungary; if Russia yielded ground to its Hapsburg enemy either involuntarily (through a defeat) or voluntary (by a defensive withdrawal), the result could be a Polish insurrection.[151] Various prominent men of state (such as Sazonov) had been recommending concessions to the Poles in part to cure them of their treasonous Austrophilism, but that advice had been disregarded.[152] Given the Russian persecution of their culture, language, and religion, millions of Poles had cause to despise the tsarist administration. Recognizing this, the General Staff feared that there would be a massive rebellion if Austrian forces managed to penetrate deep into Poland. That fear was the subtext of Zhilinskii's defense to the French of Russia's two-offensive strategy in the summer of 1912. As the Russian Chief of Staff explained to his French counterpart during their annual military talks, "Russia cannot expose herself to defeat at the hands of Austria. The moral effect would be disastrous. It is necessary for her to divide her forces to confront this power at the same time as Germany."[153] The "moral effect" that Zhilinskii had in mind was not chiefly the depression that such a defeat might cause among Russians, for he was even more concerned about the manic elation with which the Poles were likely to greet it.

If Russia's alliance policy compelled it to plan to attack Germany, it was its *nationality policy* that in the end made a simultaneous attack on Austria inescapable. An offensive against the Dual Monarchy was thus an unintended strategic consequence of the Russification of Poland. Although there were disagreements about the relative resources that should be devoted to each of those offensives, almost all Russian strategists understood their interrelationship.[154] To attack Austria alone would be to imperil the French alliance and was consequently unthinkable. To attack Germany alone was to risk the Austrian conquest of Poland. Still further, if Russia lost Poland it would in any case be incapable of sustaining offensive operations against the Germans, because its forces on the northwestern front would be threatened with encirclement. Despite the fact that mounting two offensives at once might be dangerous, the General Staff evidently felt that it would be still more dangerous not to make the attempt.

A final uncertainly afflicting Russia's generals was that they still did not possess reliable data about Germany's war plans. Intelligence about Austria was as abundant as ever. For years Redl had been Russia's most prized source in Vienna. Yet even after Austrian authorities caught the traitorous colonel and forced him to blow his own brains out in 1913, Austrian state secrets continued to make their way into Russian hands. Information on the Austrians was, if anything, too good, for it bred arrogance and false confidence in Petersburg.[155] But military intelligence concerning Germany remained maddeningly scanty, fueling Russian apprehensions.

To be sure, the French were traditionally of the view that they should be on the receiving end of the greatest German offensive thrust, and required formal Russian concurrence in this assessment at each of the annual meetings of the Chiefs of Staff. Indirect evidence tended to corroborate the French judgment. German war games pitting outnumbered defenders against invaders from the east were consistent with a massive attack on France.[156] So too was Germany's increasing investment in the fortifications of East Prussia.[157]

Yet the Russians were simultaneously suspicious of French motives and awed by German capabilities. It was in the French interest to minimize the military problems Russia would confront at the outset of a war so as to induce it to mount the largest possible offensive effort against Germany. It was true that many indicators pointed to the existence of a Schlieffen plan, but what if the safes in the German General Staff also contained a variant plan in which the east was the principle theater of the war? In light of their scary efficiency, was it not possible that the Germans might have two plans from which they could choose, depending upon circumstances? Even if that was improbable, the Russian military elite could not be sure it was not so. Russia's generals therefore concluded that it would be prudent for Russia to entertain the possibility of a German eastern option.[158] All these insecurities and political requirements shaped Imperial Russia's final prewar plan.

Plan 19 Altered

Plan 19 altered was essentially the plan with which Russia would take the field in August 1914. Approved in May 1912, it contained two variants, "A" and "G." "A," the automatic deployment, presupposed that Germany's strongest armies would march to the west. In that case sixteen Russian corps would be earmarked for operations against Austria and nine for use against Germany. The commander of the Austrian front would have the Third, Fourth, and Fifth Armies under his control. Those forces, including more than forty-five infantry divisions and seventeen cavalry divisions, were supposed to repel the anticipated Austrian invasion and then counterattack into Galicia in the direction of Riashev, Przemysl, Lemberg, and Mikolaev. Meanwhile the First and Second Armies (twenty-nine infantry divisions and nine cavalry divisions) would concentrate on the middle Neman, chiefly between Kovno and Grodno. They were then to invade East Prussia, passing around the Mazurian Lakes from the north and west respectively. The plan also required the formation of auxiliary armies to serves as reserves, guard the flanks, and observe the Rumanian frontier.[159]

Variant "G," in contrast, had to be specially ordered. Based on the presumption that Germany would attack Russia in strength, not merely defend against it, "G" estimated that Russia could initially have to confront as many as 132 Austrian and German divisions.[160] The "G" deployment consequently involved shifting the Third Army from the southern to the northern front. Although it did contain some optimistic prescriptions for an eventual Russian counterattack against Germany, in practical terms the plan implicitly countenanced the loss of Poland and an initial Russian defensive until reinforcements could be brought in from Siberia, Turkestan, and Transcaucasia.[161]

As has often been noted, Plan 19 altered was the product of committee work and compromise: it was elaborated and reworked in conferences of military district commanders throughout the year 1912. In the give and take of dispute, Alekseev's original proposal for a massive invasion of Austria had been diluted; forces that he wanted assigned to this operation had been reallocated to the East Prussian front.[162] It would, however, be incorrect to dismiss the plan as a freakish triumph of bureaucratic politics and special pleading over common sense. It would be even more perverse to argue that the defects of the plan somehow foreordained Russia's defeats in the opening campaigns of the war.[163] In the first place the plan was by no means a novel divergence from Russian strategic tradition. As we have seen, the defensist approach of the original plan 19 had been the real anomaly. In key respects 19 altered was a revision to principles that had guided Russian strategy since the time of Miliutin. Indeed, the double attack envisioned in the "A" variant replicated in broad outline the dual offensives initially mandated by plan 18 back in 1903. If the plan required Russia to stretch its military resources quite thin, that was not unprecedented either. Russia had to attack Germany to make sure France entered and stayed in the war. It simultaneously had to attack Austria in order to preserve its dominion over Poland. Both offensives therefore stemmed from an underlying anxiety and pessimism; anxiety and pessimism had had a venerable place in the Russian strategic tradition ever since the military implications of the Industrial Revolution had become apparent in the Crimean War.

The coexistence within 19 altered of two variants was in itself reminiscent of the dual-track war plans of the 1880s. Variant "G," of course, was the vestigial remnant of Danilov's original plan 19. The important point, however, was that Russia's defensive reorganization of 1910 supported variant "G," not the more likely variant "A." By transferring forces away from the periphery to the heartland, the Russian Ministry of War had effectively shifted its priorities from the defense of Europe to the defense of the Far East. When the changing course of international politics proved that the Ministry had been mistaken, it nevertheless had to live with the consequences of its earlier strategic choice. Whereas according to the war plan of 1899 thirty-four days would suffice for the total concentration of all of Russia's armies, plan 1912 altered scheduled forty days for the purpose.[164] In fact, the army's actual performance in August 1914 was somewhat worse even than that.[165] The retrogression in speed of concentration stemmed directly from the need to bring entire corps from the Moscow, Kazan, and Caucasus military districts to the western frontiers. The forces of the southwest (or anti-Austrian) front were most particularly discommoded by those delays. But the units involved in operations against Germany were also affected. If Russia honored its promise to France and invaded East Prussia on M+15, it would be attacking with armies in a weakened condition, armies that had not yet received their full complements of infantry and cavalry reinforcements. When divisions of the northwest front did begin to cross over onto German soil on August 3(16), 1914, they were in fact at less than full strength. It is true that this situation did not inevitably presage the annihilation of the Russian Second Army at Tannenberg—poor generalship and inadequate intelligence were far more important factors in the loss of that famous battle.[166] But it is equally true that deficiency in manpower scarcely conferred advantages on the Russians, either.

Russia's supreme commander, Grand Duke Nikolai Nikolaevich, described the invasion of East Prussia at the time as "a compulsory act, demonstrating our willingness to fulfill our alliance obligations to France."[167] "Alliance obligations" therefore mandated early attacks. But although Russia's initial offensives could easily have been more successful tactically and operationally, the fact that they were conducted prematurely and with under-strength forces did not augur well for the achievement of strategically decisive victories. The problem was in part of Russia's own making. The long shadow of the Manchurian war had induced the Ministry of War to opt for Asia in 1910. But by so doing, it had widened the gap between its capabilities and its military strategy for a western war. Russian disquiet over that gap grew in counterpoint with the rising tensions in Europe after 1911. Unease over the torpidity of its concentration of forces was also to play a large role in Russian decision-making during the July crisis that brought about World War I.

Russia and the Crisis of July 1914

On June 15(28), 1914, the Bosnian terrorist Gavrilo Princip assassinated Archduke Franz Ferdinand of Austria in Sarajevo. After some hesitation, the Austro-Hungarian government decided to use the incident as the pretext for a showdown with Serbia. Having requested and received full backing from its German ally on July 10(23), Vienna sent a note to Serbia accusing it of complicity in the murder.[168] The ultimatum made demands on Serbia that were incompatible with its continued sovereignty; it was, for example, supposed to tolerate an Austrian judicial investigation of the conspiracy on its own territory. Should Belgrade make any response short of unconditional acceptance of the note, Vienna would retaliate with a declaration of war.

Several motivations lay behind this Austrian bid to humble or destroy Serbia. By eliminating Serbia, Vienna hoped to smother the nationalist passions of its own south Slavic populations—passions that it believed would sooner or later endanger its own survival. At the same time, by changing the balance of power in the Balkans in its own favor, it would enhance its decaying credibility as a Great Power. On Germany's part, there was a desire to support the only reliable ally the Reich still had. Then, too, there was evidently a belief in Berlin that Russia could be bullied into doing nothing to help the Serbs, just as had happened in 1909.

Everything now hinged on how Russia would react to Austria's diplomatic aggression against its Serbian client. Russia had been aware for several weeks that Austria planned to take some action against the Serbs and had already attempted to neutralize it. Through Italian intermediaries it had cautioned Vienna on July 3(16) of its "unquestionable resolution" to defend Serbia if it was attacked.[169] The Russians were consequently all the more appalled when the text of the Austrian ultimatum became known. "C'est la guerre européenne!" Foreign Minister Sazonov exclaimed after the Austrian Ambassador told him of it.[170] On July 11(24), an emergency session of the Russian Council of Ministers resolved to try to persuade Austria to extend the twenty-four-hour time limit it had imposed for a Serbian response. If additional time could be found, it might be possible to organize a Great Power mediation of the crisis. The same meeting also adopted Sazonov's suggestion that the Ministries of War and Marine be authorized to seek the Emperor's permission for a mobilization of the Kiev, Odessa, Kazan, and Moscow military districts, should circumstances warrant it. The partial mobilization was supposed to serve both as an ostentatious warning to Vienna and as a gesture of reassurance to Berlin, since reservists were not to be called up in any districts abutting the German frontier.[171] Not a single member of the council was an enthusiast for war; all were acutely aware that Russia's military preparations were as yet incomplete. Yet the Ministers felt that Russia could not afford to appear weak. Indeed, a firm reply to Austria might be the best way to preserve the peace.[172]

In the memorandum he delivered to the Tsar the following day, Sazonov placed great stress on the injustice and unreasonableness of Austria's ultimatum. "The clear goal of this action, apparently supported by Germany, consists in completely destroying Serbia and breaching the political equilibrium in the Balkans."[173] Nicholas II evidently agreed, for he immediately approved all of the recommendations the Council of Ministers had made on July 11(24), including those that touched on the partial mobilization. If Austria attacked Serbia, Russia would announce that it was mobilizing, but only against the Dual Monarchy. In the meantime, the government made plans to put into effect the "ordinance on the period prior to mobilization" as of July 13(26). Various fortresses and ports were placed under martial law; troops at summer exercises were recalled to their barracks; officers on leave were summoned to their regiments.[174]

Although War Minister Sukhomlinov and the newly appointed Chief of Staff, Ianushkevich, did not at first object to a partial mobilization, the same was not true of all of their subordinates. While the Council of Ministers apparently viewed declaring a partial mobilization as a species of diplomatic signaling, technical experts in the General Staff worried about the impact it would have on the conduct of real war. Both the Quartermaster General, Danilov, and the head of the Staff's operations section, Dobrorol'skii, pointed out that a partial mobilization was fraught with risk. To attempt one might be utterly to disrupt general mobilization, should one become essential. Further, although a partial mobilization was technically possible, Russia's only concentration plan deployed forces against both Teutonic Powers. There had been absolutely no railroad preparation, for example, for a conflict with Austria alone. Finally, the partial mobilization left the Warsaw district untouched, out of concern for the feelings of the Germans. But the Warsaw district also had a common frontier with Austria-Hungary. An unmobilized Warsaw district would be defenseless against an Austrian assault on the left flank.[175]

On July 15(28) Austria declared war on Serbia, an act that committed the Russian government to hostilities with the Dual Monarchy at least. Once that had happened, partial mobilization lost all its military adherents. The entire military establishment was of the view that Germany would definitely intervene in a Russo-Austrian war. That being the case, the generals felt that Russia should implement a general mobilization at once. The staff prepared two draft mobilization orders for the Tsar's signature, one announcing a partial, the other a general mobilization. By the following day, as Austrian monitors began the bombardment of Belgrade, even Sazonov had become disenchanted with the idea of a partial mobilization. Count Portales, the German Ambassador, had informed him that if Russia did not halt military preparations of any kind, Germany would mobilize against it. Of this maladroit threat Sazonov wrote, "as we cannot fulfill Germany's desires, it remains for us only to speed up our armament and count on the true inevitability of war."[176] It had become clear to Sazonov that any Russian mobilization, whether partial or general, meant war with Berlin.[177]

In a meeting on July 16(29), Sukhomlinov, Sazonov, and Ianushkevich agreed on the need to pressure the Tsar into approving a general mobilization "in view of the small likelihood of escaping a war with Germany."[178] The Tsar gave in to the importuning of the Ministers and consented. But he almost immediately changed his mind and insisted on the restoration of the partial mobilization plan. He was apparently banking on his personal relationship with William II somehow to reestablish the European peace.

Funereal gloom enveloped the General Staff Building. On July17(30) the Tsar rebuffed several phone calls from his generals begging him to reconsider his decision. When Sazonov went off to see Nicholas later that afternoon, Ianushkevich implored him to persuade the Emperor to restore the general mobilization. If the Tsar agreed to do so, Ianushkevich wanted to know about it without delay. The Chief of Staff said he would then break the telephone that connected his office with Nicholas's palace so as to forestall any more imperial vacillation. Sazonov's arguments proved unexpectedly successful; he finally convinced Nicholas that there was no longer any chance to avoid war with Germany. A general mobilization would be proclaimed. Sazonov called Ianushkevich with the news, informing the latter that "you may now smash your telephone."[179] The mobilization began the following day, and on the day after that, July 19 (August 1), Germany declared war on Russia. Ironically, Vienna did not issue its own declaration of war on Petersburg for five more days.

In evaluating the reasons that Russia went to war in 1914, scholars have recently emphasized the important role memories of the Bosnian crisis played in the thinking of Russia's statesmen. Surely they are correct to have done so. In 1909 Russia had been forced to give way in the face of Austrian and German threats. The ministers of state believed that Russia could not afford yet another humiliation on that scale. Passivity in the face of the Austrian destruction of Serbia was not an option. If Russia did not respond to the provocation, it would vacate its position as a Great Power. The Russian Empire would be dishonored, and its prestige would dwindle away into insignificance. The internal consequences of such a fiasco might be incalculable. Even if worse came to worst and Russia went down in defeat, that would be better than skulking away in shame.[180]

But if the Bosnian crisis exerted a powerful influence on the behavior of Russia's civilian ministers in July 1914, historical experience also weighed heavily upon the minds of Russia's generals. Even if Germany had publicly proclaimed that it would tolerate a localized Russo-Austrian war, many of them would still have opposed the very concept of partial mobilization anyway. The war in Manchuria had taught the Russian military establishment to dread spontaneity and improvisation. The cumbrous and messy sequence of partial mobilizations in 1904 and 1905 had been attended by riots, transportation bottlenecks, and the thorough degradation of Russia's western defenses. There was every reason to suppose that a partial mobilization in the summer of 1914 would produce the same catastrophic side effects. What then would be the fate of the Russian Empire if Germany launched a sudden and treacherous attack? It was an article of faith among the generals that a partial mobilization doomed a general mobilization to failure.[181]

Some students of international diplomacy have charged that Russia's decision to mobilize by itself touched off World War I. If only the Russian government had had the wisdom to temporize and delay its military preparations, the argument goes, a negotiated solution might have been found.[182]

There is a kernel of truth in this analysis, for since Obruchev's time the Russian General Staff had maintained that mobilization was the equivalent of war. Russia's general mobilization was consequently a bellicose act directed at both Teutonic Powers. Even so, the Russian military had no incentive to postpone its call for mobilization. Austria's declaration of hostilities against Serbia on July 15(28) convinced Sazonov and all of Russia's military leaders that the great European war was at hand. Russia would now have to fight both Germanic Powers. That in turn meant that time was a precious commodity. For every hour that Russia postponed mobilization, it would pay a price in human blood on the battlefield; the speed with which Germany could mobilize far exceeded Russia's, as had been so in the 1870s. Still worse, owing to the defense reorganization of 1910 Germany now enjoyed an even greater superiority over Russia in speed of *concentration.* The sense of urgency felt by the military elite in the waning days of July was consequently intensified by the strategic choices that had been made as a response to the loss of the Russo-Japanese War.

How then did tsarist statesmen evaluate Russia's chances in the great continental war it had just entered? To be sure, few of them understood what World War I would actually be like. One exception was P. N. Durnovo of the Ministry of the Interior. In a famous February 1914 memorandum to the Tsar, Durnovo had advocated a rapprochement with Germany as the only way of preventing a long war, which would bring untold calamities down upon Russia.[183] Durnovo's was an isolated opinion, however, for in the main the Russian elite believed that the war would be over quickly; on no account would it last more than a year. That deluded view did not mean that high-ranking officials were confident of a triumphant outcome to the struggle. The national unity that the war occasioned, in addition to Britain's swift entry into the ranks of Russia's allies, did inspire a fleeting burst of optimism in some prominent statesmen. It was in such an elated mood that Sukhomlinov confided to his diary on July 27 (August 9) that "it seems that the German wolf will quickly be brought to bay: all are against him."[184] But the War Minister's good spirits were evanescent. He had been worried about Russia's prospects for victory prior to August 1914 and reverted to pessimism soon thereafter.[185]

Nor was Sukhomlinov alone. Key figures in the military elite were acutely aware that Russia was unready even for the sort of short-to-medium-length war it had been anticipating. Even though it was not necessarily inaccurate to describe Russia as better prepared for war in 1914 than at any other point in its recent history, it was simultaneously true that Russia's stocks of equipment and matériel were still below the targeted norms.[186] Those were supposed to be achieved only with the completion of the Big Program in 1917. The Russian General Staff consequently (and rightly) suspected that a prime motive in Berlin's drift toward war was the German desire to fight before Russia built up its power to its maximum extent.[187] Thus Russia was beginning the war with smaller supplies of weapons and munitions than its own planners had estimated would be needed. There was, for example, a shortfall of more than 300 million rifle cartridges.[188] What was true of bullets was also true of many other essential articles, from machine guns to rolling stock to capital ships.[189] During the July crisis the Minister of Marine insisted that the Russian navy was in no condition to vie with Germany's Baltic fleet; according to an eyewitness, it was "with heavy heart" that Admiral Grigorovich affixed his signature to the mobilization order.[190]

Material insufficiency was thus already perturbing Russian military elites even before the first battles of August and September proved that the pre-1914 estimates of wartime requirements had been preposterously low. But Russia's strategy itself was a source of discouragement at the very outset of the war. Since the 1870s, Russian strategies for western war had substituted magic for technology. Russian strategists had had very little choice, because the tsarist state had been unable to purchase the armaments, fortifications, or railroads that would underpin a technological approach to the question of defense. Although considerable strides had been made in military investment since 1910, the tsarist military knew that its adversaries (most particularly the Germans) still had technological superiority. Owing to technical inferiority and the iron logic of deployments, Russia's strategy for war in 1914 was still dependent on magic and miracle. For the strategy to work, the bravery, endurance, and leadership of Russia's army had to compensate for Russian economic, social, and technological backwardness. The problem was that many of the generals privately doubted that this was possible. World War I would demonstrate just how well-founded that doubt had been.

Strategies of Confidence and Strategies of Fear

Toward a Strategic Interpretation of the History of the Russian Empire

This book has examined the triangular relationship among Russian political objectives, strategy, and military potential over a period of three hundred years. In tsarist Russia as in other countries, war, diplomacy, society, and economy were bound together in complex systems. Only an investigation of these interrelationships can lay bare the role that military force and strategy played in the history of the Russian Empire.

That role was enormous. Good strategy contributed importantly to the rise of Russia, just as bad strategy prepared the way for Russia's decline and defeat. What made the strategies pursued by eighteenth-century Russia so strikingly successful? What made its late-nineteenth-century strategies so poor? We could answer these questions in part by pointing to the disabilities under which the statesmen of the later period labored. To an extent, late Imperial Russia was victimized by its own earlier successes, since one effect of those successes was to magnify both external and internal security threats to the state. Russia's expansion in the eighteenth and early nineteenth centuries enlarged the list of its potential foreign enemies, and by acquiring vast borderlands to the northwest, west, and southwest, Russia absorbed populations of millions of restive ethnic and religious minorities. The borderlands had to be heavily garrisoned and policed even in peacetime. If war came, there was the very real risk that Russia would find itself squaring off against a foreign aggressor while simultaneously combating an internal insurrection. Another constraint on its government after 1856 was that of relative technological and material inferiority. The Crimean War had illustrated that industrial development was an increasingly important component of military power. Russia's industry, transportation, and communications, however, lagged behind those of its chief European competitors.

Merely to observe that the security problems confronting the late Imperial regime were more severe than those the empire had faced in the past is not entirely satisfactory. The successes of the early period and the failures of the later one are best accounted for in terms of the interrelationship among *policy objectives, strategy,* and the *military system* derived from Russia's society and economy. From the reign of Peter the Great to that of Nicolas I, Russia's goals, strategy, and military system were congruent. Its goals were realistic and were pursued incrementally. In part because of the institutional context in which decisions were made, Russia crafted strategies that supported the attainment of those political objectives. Furthermore, Russia invented and sustained a military system that made the execution of its strategies possible. In the period after the Crimean War, however, distortions cropped up in the relationship among goals, strategy, and the military system. Often the tsarist state simultaneously pursued mutually exclusive goals or impulsively substituted one set of goals for another. The nature of late Imperial decision-making institutions militated against the rational coordination of policy. As a result, Imperial strategists frequently made choices that did not support state goals. Also, the state did not devise a military system consonant with the modern strategies that Russia's military leaders thought the empire needed, and as a consequence they developed strategies that were strange alloys of optimism and pessimism. Although the Ministry of War's plans included wildly optimistic operational assumptions, the overall strategic vision that drove the plans was overwhelmingly pessimistic. That overall strategy had profound implications for Russia's political objectives, for it influenced the way in which they were selected while sharply reducing the chance that they could be attained on a battlefield.

Throughout the seventeenth and eighteenth centuries, Russia entertained vast ambitions. In an age in which the only choice was to conquer or be conquered, Russia wished to neutralize its three most dangerous enemies—Sweden, Poland, and Turkey—

and then desired to expand at the expense of each. To achieve these goals would involve nothing less than a revolution in the status and political relations of all the countries of northern, eastern, and southern Europe. These daunting goals were pursued patiently, rationally, and consistently. The conciliar system of decision-making was significant. Originally adopted by Peter the Great, the conciliar approach was further reified by his successors, reaching its highest development in Catherine II's Council attached to the Imperial Court (*Sovet pri vysochaishchem dvore*). It was at these eighteenth-century war councils that strategy was matched to political objectives and harmonized with diplomacy.

Confident in the power of the empire, Russia's rulers, military leaders, and diplomatists worked closely throughout the century to advance the interests of their state. Foreign policy and war supported each other, for the elite understood that in view of the geographical position of the empire, Russia could be at least as well served by guile as by the sword. Most of Russia's wars were preceded by careful diplomatic preparation. The nation negotiated treaties and pacts to isolate a potential enemy, thereby ensuring that it would have to fight only one state at a time, often with allies' assistance. While its generals campaigned, its cabinets could guard against a widening of the war; military operations could be modulated to reassure other powers about Russia's intentions; compensation in the form of territorial awards could be used to purchase foreign acquiescence in Russia's conquests.

Undergirding Russia's entire effort in the eighteenth century was its military system. Seventeenth-century Muscovy had been locked into a mode of military power, with coherent strategies, clearly defined goals, and adequate human and material resources; but the problem had been how to tap into them. Peter the Great had solved that problem by narrowing the gap between the actual constraints on the exercise of authority and the limitless pretensions to power of the autocratic idea. He intensified the regime's demands on its population so as to produce a marginally sufficient military economy. His heirs had followed the same path, transforming Peter's manic improvisations in taxation and conscription into institutions. The amount of available revenue remained small when measured against the size of the military efforts Russia mounted, which is why Russian statesmen generally preferred to delay the order to march until foreign monetary assistance had been firmly guaranteed. But the eighteenth-century Russian state, while still needing respites for economic recovery after major struggles such as those with Sweden and Prussia, eventually was able shrewdly to exploit population growth, burgeoning trade, and industrial expansion to accumulate the money to finance protracted wars all by itself.

Serfdom was decisive in that process. Serfdom had been instrumental to the survival of even the pre-Petrine Russian state. Cash-poor Muscovy had maintained its force of cavalry servitors by rewarding them not with money but with populated land, but Peter and his successors found ways of extracting much more military power from the bondage of the Russian peasant than ever before. The unitary poll tax imposed on male peasants became the most important (and most reliable) source of state income. The very existence of serfdom made possible the command system of long-service conscription that produced the enormous infantry armies of the age. That system eventually even conferred operational and tactical advantages upon Russia's military leadership. By severing the ties of draftee so completely from his family and village community, eighteenth-century conscription virtually ensured the formation of a distinct military society. The small-group loyalty thereby engendered contributed to high morale in the ranks, something Russia's most gifted commanders turned to their benefit in battle. In the eighteenth century, then, diplomats, generals, and dynasts all came to agree that the military strength of Russia reposed in autocracy and serfdom. The former institution mobilized military resources, while the latter supplied them. It was thus precisely because Russia was so "backward," according to European standards, that it was so powerful.

Russia supplanted Sweden as the overlord of the southern Baltic coast, Poland was dismembered, and huge parcels of Turkey's domains in Europe came into Russian hands. The style of diplomacy and war that Russia developed during the eighteenth century was never seriously challenged until the Napoleonic Wars. Then Napoleon's defeat in 1812 reconfirmed the belief of the elite in the special excellences of Russia's entire approach to the problems of war and peace.

Russia's goals after the Napoleonic Wars were both more modest and more varied than those it had sought in the previous century. Once Nicholas I concluded that Russia was a satisfied power, the posture he assumed vis-à-vis Europe was largely defensive. Russia wanted to deter any attacks upon itself while preserving the status quo abroad. If that were not possible, it wished at a bare minimum to decelerate change in the interest of managing it. After 1856, maintaining the status quo remained desirable, but deterring attacks or repulsing those that could not be deterred became still more important. The Crimean War had revealed just how grotesquely inflated had been the autocracy's estimation of its power. In the aftermath of that war, the military leadership of the empire came to the view that power inhered in wealth and technological mastery. Russia's "backwardness" was no longer a benefit but a burden. Measured against the new standards, the nation was pitifully weak. If prior to 1800 Russian statesmen had been concerned about hiding the nation's strength from foreign eyes, after 1856 they took just as many pains to conceal its weakness. Russia's statesmen feared that if the empire was defeated in yet another major war, that war might well be its last, since the empire might collapse under the combined weight of foreign military pressure and internal unrest. Yet Russia had to respond to overt assaults on its honor and prestige even if that meant accepting war, since failure to do so would broadcast its weakness to the world. Thus, paradoxically the Russian Empire could be destroyed through fighting a war or through not fighting one.

Russia's rash imperialism contradicted its interest in tranquillity and self-defense. During the second half of the nineteenth century Russia added substantially to its holdings first in Central Asia and then in Manchuria. Unlike the meticulously plotted imperialism of the 1700s, that of the 1800s was usually either accidental or reactive. In Central Asia, border clashes produced punitive expeditions that could then result in unauthorized frontier "rectifications." And in Manchuria the grab for empire stemmed not from sober calculation about the profits and benefits of Pacific expansion, but from a deep-rooted fear that if Russia did not move to fill a vacuum of power it would be preempted by one of its most bitter rivals. In neither case was the later imperialism preceded by much in the way of advance planning. Then again, unlike their eighteenth-century predecessors, Russian statesmen of the late empire conspicuously failed to think through the problem of defending the new domains they had acquired. Whatever its motivations, Russia's imperialism had the gravest implications for the empire's security. Aggrandizement in Central Asia provoked a spiral of conflict with Great Britain. To cite but one example, Russia's grievances over the Panjdeh affair nearly provoked an attack upon the straits that could well have ignited a European war. And expansion into Manchuria both impaired the empire's western defenses and brought about a calamitous war with Japan.

Externally Petersburg saw enemies everywhere it looked after 1856. If Russia felt insecure on all its borders, how should it best allocate its military resources? Late Imperial institutional arrangements did not help Russia's government make prudent strategic choices. Government (and consequently strategy-making) during the nineteenth and early twentieth centuries was fragmented. The ministerial system Russia acquired in the early 1800s may have led to greater bureaucratic competence within individual departments, but at the cost of extraordinary governmental disunity. Since the Committee of Ministers was not empowered to coordinate state policies, ministers typically went their own way, hiding the affairs of their separate fiefdoms from the scrutiny of their colleagues, guarding their privilege of private report to the Tsar. Aside from the failed experiment with the Council of State Defense (1905–8), the only occasions when a real effort was made to connect military and diplomatic policies were when the Tsar summoned special conferences (*osobye soveshchaniia*). These, however, were *ad hoc* meetings to address specific crises—no substitute for routine consultation and interministerial collaboration. All too often at these conferences, crucial information that should long since have been the common property of every member of the government was reluctantly divulged. During a special conference in 1897, for example, Lamzdorff was astounded when it was finally explained to him why Russian military power was inadequate for a rapid seizure of the Bosphorus.

The ministries frequently worked at cross–purposes. The Minister of Foreign Affairs could take actions requiring military policies that were not necessarily those of the Minister of War. Such was the case in Izvol'skii's 1908 negotiations over Bosnia and Herzegovina. It was just as possible for the Ministry of War to embark on programs that subverted Russia's foreign policy, as Sukhomlinov did with the defense reorganization of 1910. Finally, the decisions of the Ministry of Finance could confound the expectations of generals and diplomats alike. Miliutin's entire scheme for the defense of Russia in Europe was invalidated when he was defeated by Reutern at the strategic conference of 1873. In short, whereas eighteenth-century strategy-making had been consensual, that of the later empire was conflictual.

The decentralization of threat analysis implicit in the military-district system also had bad results. Since the district commanders collected the bulk of the intelligence on which threat perceptions were based, at times they had an excessive influence on strategy-making. That influence was particularly conspicuous during the crafting of European war plans at the turn of the century and in the preparation for a possible war with Japan in the Far East. There was every reason for a commander to exaggerate the potential dangers that confronted his district. The military-district system conditioned him to think largely in terms of the security needs of the provinces under his control, not those of the empire as a whole.

The late Imperial regime's political objectives were often mutually exclusive. Its decision-making was incoherent owing to the structure of autocratic politics, while the military-district system routinely produced a maximization of threat perception. Nonetheless, Imperial strategists were the custodians of the prestige and security of the Russian state. They had to discriminate among threats on the basis of probability and seriousness. They usually arrived at a dominant paradigm of military vulnerability by projecting the experience of the immediate past on the future. Up until 1870, for instance, the Russian government chiefly feared a revival of the Crimean coalition: acting in concert, Britain and France would employ their superior navies to wreak destruction along Russia's extensive and sparsely defended coasts. German unification instilled the dread in the General Staff of a massive overland invasion accomplished before a sluggish Russia could mobilize itself to resist. Russia's treatment at the Congress of Berlin eight years later convinced the generals that Russia would never again be able to wage a localized war in Europe. A war localized at the start would sooner or later be transformed into a general war, no matter what dispute had originally provoked it. Russia would therefore have to fight for its survival against both Germany and Austria, at a bare mini-

mum. Russia's defeats in Manchuria in 1904–5 gave rise to the
nightmare of a belligerent Japan seizing all of Siberia between
the Pacific Coast and Lake Baikal. It is important to note that
none of these scenarios posited any intermediate outcomes between victory and cataclysm: the assumption was that if Russia
failed to thwart the schemes of its enemies, it would be either
utterly destroyed or so crippled that an eventual total collapse
would not be far away. Russian strategic planning for more than
fifty years was consequently conducted in an atmosphere permeated with emergency, even panic. This was fertile soil for the
growth of strategic pessimism within the Russian military elite.
The Russian Imperial General Staff affords us the unedifying (if
hardly unique) spectacle of an institution so frantic to avoid repeating its past mistakes that it overlooked the present and the
most likely contours of the future. The problem was that the
attempt to learn rigid lessons from the past usually produced still
more errors. Prior to 1877, Russia had prepared most assidu-
ously for war in Central Europe, only to stumble into an armed
conflict with Turkey. The strategic consequences of Manchurian
adventurism at the turn of the century forced an alteration, to
Russia's disadvantage, in the terms of the treaty of alliance with
France. After 1905, the reorientation of Russia's defense effort
toward Asia, which could not be entirely undone by 1914, was a
drag on the implementation of Russian strategy when World
War I broke out. Finally, Russia's interpretation of the "meaning"
of the Congress of Berlin helped ensure that the July crisis would
produce a general European war, not a localized one.

What, then, of the late Imperial military system? In the mid-
1820s tsarist statesmen were already beginning to understand
that serfdom was outliving its usefulness as the cornerstone of
military recruitment. To be sure, soldiers' *artels* continued to function as they were supposed to; the combat performance of Russia's troops remained high. But by the time of Nicholas I, the
demands on Russian military manpower even absent a major war
had outstripped the capability of the servile draft to deliver conscripts in sufficient numbers. The need to deter external aggression from any quarter, in addition to the burden imposed by the
insurrection in the Caucasus, compelled the Nicholaevan autocracy to support, over decades, the largest armies Russia had ever
seen. In the event of a true military emergency, how could a re-

cruitment system already straining to operate close to full capacity produce the quantity of troops large-scale war would demand? Based as it was on the essentially lifelong service of peasant recruits, the old Russian conscription system was incompatible with the formation of reserve cadres. The procedure for granting "unlimited furloughs" instituted by Nicholas in 1834 was a mere palliative, as the Crimean War conclusively demonstrated. Thereafter, redesigning the military recruitment system became a central issue of military reform.

Thirteen years after the emancipation of the Russian serfs in 1861, the tsarist state unveiled its law on the universal military service obligation: members of all estates and classes in the realm were technically liable to be drafted for short terms. The architect of the reform, D. A. Miliutin, hoped that the 1874 law would provide Russia with the necessary manpower without adversely affecting combat performance and morale. Miliutin expected his reform to substitute a new morale based upon patriotism and citizenship for the old morale that had been paradoxically engendered by the distinctiveness of military society. But his expectations were disappointed. Although Russian troops continued to distinguish themselves in battle and the Russian soldier's tolerance for suffering continued to amaze foreign observers, the reintegration of the army into civil society had some unintended side effects. The infantryman of the eighteenth century had been forced by the injustice of conscription to transfer his loyalty from his family to his comrades-in-arms. He had little choice, since he had no home to return to. Such was not the case after 1874. The barrier that had traditionally insulated the army from the mainstream of Russian life was broken down; the military now became permeable to influences from society on a scale previously impossible. Short-term recruits brought into the regiments all the social tensions that existed in the country at large. At the same time, the sense of common citizenship Miliutin had dreamed of as the source of motivation in his reformed army was never fully disseminated in the late Imperial period. Partially as a result, the army, once the unshakable buckler of tsarism, would now turn against it at critical junctures, for example, in 1905–6 and with even more explosive results in 1917. Ironically enough, as was so often the case in Russian history, reform undertaken to strengthen the regime would eventually imperil its continued survival. In his search for a new military system, Miliutin had forgone the advantages that "backwardness" brought to military morale without finding adequate substitutes for them.

The late Imperial period did witness some steady economic growth. At times even spectacular increases in output were achieved, as in 1885–1900 and 1906–14. But the tsarist government still found itself handicapped in its race to catch up with its richer European military competitors. Despite the fact that Russia's national income in 1913 was almost four times what it had been in 1861, twentieth-century Russia was actually poorer in relation to Germany than it had been fifty years previously.[1] Of course, by one crude measure Russia was not too badly off: it was usually able to afford supplies of modern armaments, though it often acquired such arms more slowly than its enemies. By 1914, Russia's arsenals possessed quick-firing artillery, magazine rifles, and machine guns; its fleets contained dreadnoughts and submarines; it had made its first explorations into the realm of military aviation. However, Russia's armed forces were still backward from the technical point of view, not in the least because, after the mid-nineteenth century, military technological adequacy inhered not merely in the possession of up-to-date weapons but also in the communication and transportation infrastructure that supported war. Although the exact pattern of the relationship between economic strength and military potential may have been but dimly perceived by the Russian military leadership, the generals were acutely conscious of what Russia's inferiority in roads and railways would mean if hostilities were to begin. In the opinion of the General Staff, by failing to invest enough in the transportation net, the Russian state was undermining military preparations for a successful defense of the empire. From the perspective of the Ministry of Finance, however, military complaints about underfunding were beside the point. It was not possible fully to meet the requirements of the army and the navy without neglecting other legitimate governmental interests. The simple truth was that the tsarist economy was not growing fast enough to permit the building of strategic railroads on anything like the scale envisioned by the Ministry of War.

Given the obsession with the German menace after 1870, the military elite could only view Russia's technological inferiority with alarm. Russian strategists assumed that Germany would hold the strongest cards in the event of a European war. Its population was better educated and more highly motivated than Russia's; its transportation network was clearly superior; and since Berlin would choose when the war was to begin, it would also enjoy the initiative. The tsarist government attempted to compensate for these German advantages in several ways. Russia created shadow commands to ease the transition from peace to war. It prepositioned thousands of troops in Poland to disrupt the timetable of the expected invasion. It crafted an alliance with France in order to make it inevitable that Germany would have to fight a two-front war. And it developed strategic plans that relied on magical élan and operational skill to offset its insufficiency in railroads and its poor logistics. When diplomacy proved inadequate to avert it, the great European war showed that these plans had been unrealistic and defective. Indeed, many of Petersburg's generals had expected as much prior to the July crisis of 1914. The premodern elements in Russian strategy and the underdevelopment of Russia's society and economy did not support the political objectives Russia would pursue when war came.

Two serious errors help to account for the mismatch between strategy and policy in late Imperial Russia. The first was psychological. Whereas Nicholas I had possessed an overweening faith in his military power, the elite of the late empire suffered from an equally excessive sense of military inferiority. Although eighteenth-century conquests had predisposed Russia in favor of perimeter defenses, it was untrue that the loss of Poland would automatically entail the collapse of the empire. Similarly, it was simply untrue that if Russia lost the first battles it would necessarily lose the entire war, but this mistaken assumption distorted Russian strategy. "Know the enemy and know yourself," wrote Sun Tzu, "[and] in a hundred battles you will never be in peril."[2] False self-perception, then, was one source of strategic failure.

The second error complemented the first. If the Russian government was so convinced of its military debility, it should have moderated its ambitions in accordance with that judgment. Yet the tsarist regime was reluctant to display any signs of weakness in its dealings abroad and was therefore reluctant to accept any diminution in Russia's international standing and prestige. This attitude led to an entirely avoidable overextension, which the tsarist state aggravated by means of its harebrained adventurism in Manchuria. The times demanded retrenchment, not expansion. In retrospect it is easy to say that any price Russia might have paid for peace in the summer of 1914 would have been worth it. In any event, if Russia believed there was no alternative to war, it would have been better to have taken the field with more confidence in its strategy than it had in plan 19 altered. The extravagant operational assumptions of that plan, like most of its predecessors, stemmed from the fact that it had been driven by fear.

The creation of a new military system based on industrial might was to be Stalin's achievement, but this system in its turn (like the entire nineteenth-century concept of Marxism itself) was beginning to show unmistakable signs of age by the 1980s. The nuclear arsenals of the two superpowers canceled each other out. Moscow's ability credibly to threaten NATO with a massive attack by its enormous tank armies was being eroded owing to the West's superiority in computers and electronics. Although traditionalist Soviet officers made the "magical" argument that élan, night operations, and even more rapid tempos of advance would prevent Western high-technology weapons from stopping a Soviet offensive, many other experts on the General Staff were dubious. The perceived need to restructure the economy and society in the interests of military efficiency clearly mobilized military support during the early stages of perestroika, just as it had fueled programs for reform after the Crimean and Japanese wars.

There are many other parallels between the history of Imperial Russia and that of the Soviet Union. Since the conclusion of the civil war, the Soviet leadership has had as much (if not more) cause to worry about the political and military reliability of the ethnic minorities than tsarist statesmen did in the nineteenth century. Certain features of the defensive plans the U.S.S.R. developed for war with Germany in the 1930s are strikingly reminiscent of Obruchev's optimal strategy of 1873. Stalin's military purges can partially be interpreted as the outcome of a struggle between "magicians" and "technologists." Then, too, the U.S.S.R.'s interest in military force as a instrument of intimidation during the cold war recalls the similar efforts of Nicholas I. The Soviet military doctrine of "defensive defense" unveiled under Gorbachev could readily be interpreted as a reversion to Russia's nineteenth-century military posture in Europe. Even Gorbachev's dramatic decision to cut the U.S.S.R.'s East European satellites adrift was foreshadowed by the thinking of those tsarist statesmen who wondered whether Russia might not benefit by relinquishing its position in Poland.

Yet the dissimilarities between the Soviet Union's current troubles and the strategic problems of the tsarist state are also notable. From 1600 to roughly 1830, Russian statesmen saw empire-building as one of the main purposes of military power. After the Crimean defeat, although there was sporadic interest in resuming expansion, the Russian government was chiefly concerned with hanging on to what it had already acquired. The remnants of the present Soviet government in Moscow would like to do the same, yet domestic woes may make this task impossible. Today the greatest threat to the existence of the U.S.S.R. is not external invasion but domestic nationalism. At present it appears that the decomposition of the Soviet Union as a centralized state is well under way. The question is, will the Soviet state pass from the scene by means of gradual decay or by violent explosion? It is in the interests of the Soviet state, the Soviet peoples, and the entire world that the former rather than the latter occur.

If a new, looser union is reborn, what role will centrally controlled military forces play in it? In any event, Moscow now confronts the prospect of using military force to manage the renunciation of empire—a challenge unprecedented in Russian history.

Notes

Introduction

1. For the most recent discussion of the "strategic culture" issue, see Colin S. Gray, *War, Peace and Victory: Strategy and Statecraft for the Next Century* (New York, 1990), pp. 44–78.
2. See Carl von Clausewitz, *On War.* Michael Howard and Peter Paret, ed. and trans. (Princeton, N.J., 1984), p. 128.
3. Even prior to the August 1991 coup Soviet military leaders were increasingly drawing direct parallels between the military tradition of the Imperial Russian state and the defense posture of the Soviet Union. For an example, see "Pozitsiia B. Kh. fon Miunikha v diskussii 1725 goda o sokrashchenii armii i voennogo biudzheta Rossii," *Voenno-istoricheskii zhurnal,* 1990, no. 8, pp. 3–7.
4. Borivoj Plavsic, "Seventeenth-Century Chanceries and Their Staffs," in Walter McKenzie Pintner and Don Karl Rowney, eds., *Russian Officialdom: The Bureaucratization of Russian Society from the Seventeenth to the Twentieth Century* (Durham, N.C., 1980), pp. 19–45. Dr. Plavsic makes a compelling case for the high quality of at least some Muscovite bureaucrats, but does not consider the disproportion between the size of the competent bureaucracy and the magnitude of the task of governing the immense Russian state.

1. Russian Military Weakness in the 17th Century

1. J. H. L. Keep, "The Regime of Filaret 1619–1633," in Michael Cherniavsky, ed., *The Structure of Russian History* (New York, 1970), pp. 334, 359.
2. C. Bickford O'Brien, *Muscovy and the Ukraine from the Periaslavl Agreement to the Truce of Andrusovo 1654–1667* (Berkeley, Calif., 1963), pp. 4–5.
3. S. M. Solov'ev, *Istoriia Rossii s drevneishikh vremen,* 5 (Moscow, 1961): 176.
4. E. E. Stashevskii, "Biudzhet i armiia," in M. V. Dovnar-Zapol'skii, ed., *Russkaia istoriia v ocherkakh i stat'iakh,* 3 (Kiev, 1912): 413–14.
5. E. Stashevskii, *Smolenskaia voina 1632–1634 gg.: Organizatsiia i sostoianie Moskovskoi armii* (Kiev, 1919), pp. 58–59.
6. On traditional Muscovite military institutions, see Richard Hellie, *Enserfment and Military Change in Muscovy* (Chicago, 1971), pp. 156–63, and Thomas Esper, "Military Self-Sufficiency and Weapons Technology in Muscovite Russia," *Slavic Review,* 28, no. 3 (June 1969): 185–89.
7. Michael Roberts, *Sweden as a Great Power 1611–1697: Government, Society, Foreign Policy* (London: 1968), pp. 134–37.
8. Thomas Barker, *Double Eagle and Crescent: Vienna's Second Turkish Siege in Its*

Historical Setting (Albany, N.Y., 1967), pp. 37–41; Jan Wimmer, "L'effort financier et militaire de la Pologne au XVIIe siècle," *Revue Internationale d'Histoire Militaire*, 1969, no. 28, pp. 434–38; Jerzy Teodorczyk, "L'armée polonaise dans la première moitié du XVIIe siècle," in Witold Bieganski *et al.*, eds., *Histoire Militaire de la Pologne: Problemes choisis* (Warsaw, 1970), pp. 95–99.

9. A. A. Novosel'skii, *Bor'ba Moskovskogo gosudarstva s Tatarami v XVII veke* (Moscow and Leningrad, 1948), pp. 5, 416–24, 430–33; Hellie, *Enserfment*, pp. 174–80.

10. Keep, "Regime," pp. 347–48; Hellie, *Enserfment*, p. 124.

11. O. L. Vainshtein, *Rossiia i tridtsatiletniaia voina* (Moscow, 1947), pp. 92–93.

12. A. N. Petrov, *Russkaia voennaia sila*, 2d ed., 1 (Moscow, 1892), 361, 401–2.

13. Stashevskii, *Smolenskaia voina*, pp. 55–56, 319.

14. Such negotiations were still the standard when Muscovy treated with foreign military experts decades later. Grigorii Kotoshikhin, *O Rossii v tsarstvovanii Alekseia Mikhailovicha* (St. Petersburg, 1906), p. 138; also Hellie, *Enserfment*, pp. 170–71.

15. Stashevskii, *Smolenskaia voina*, p. 319; Petrov, *Russkaia voennaia sila*, 1: 392.

16. Vainshtein, *Rossiia*, pp. 88, 151–63. Vainshtein, however, errs in arguing that Sweden was the instigator of the Smolensk war. Still more dubious is the thesis of B. F. Porshnev, *Tridsatiletniaia voina i vstuplenie v nee Shvetsii i Moskovskogo gosudarstva* (Moscow, 1976), that Muscovy was a full partner in the anti-Hapsburg coalition and consequently made war on Poland out of a concern for the balance of power in Germany.

17. Novosel'skii, *Bor'ba*, p. 423.

18. Stashevskii, *Smolenskaia voina*, p. 170.

19. Petrov, *Russkaia voennaia sila*, 1: 406–7.

20. Solov'ev, *Istoriia Rossii*, 5: 163.

21. *Zarys Dziejów Wojskowości Polskiej do roku 1864*, 1 (Warsaw, 1965): 458.

22. Stashevskii, *Smolenskaia voina*, p. 175; Petrov, *Russkaia voennaia sila*, 1: 400.

23. Tadeusz Korzon, *Dziejow Wojen i Wojskowości w Polsce*, 2d ed., 2 (Lwów, 1925), pp. 261–62.

24. *Zarys Dziejów Wojskowości*, p. 459; Korzon, *Dziejow Wojen*, p. 265.

25. Solov'ev, *Istoriia Rossii*, 5: 65.

26. On the problems of Sweden, Poland, and the Crimea, see Sven Lundkrist, "The Experience of Empire: Sweden as a Great Power," in Michael Roberts, ed., *Sweden's Age of Greatness* (New York, 1973), pp. 24–25, 34–35; Norman Davies, *God's Playground: A History of Poland*, vol. 1, *The Origins to 1795* (New York, 1984), pp. 454–68; O'Brien, *Muscovy and the Ukraine*, pp. 13–116; Emile Haumont, *La Guerre du Nord et la Paix d'Oliva 1655–1660* (Paris, 1893), pp. 269–94; B. H. Sumner, *Peter the Great and the Ottoman Empire*, (Hamden, Conn., 1965), pp. 12–14; Joseph von Hammer-Purgstall, *Geschichte der Chane der Krim unter Osmanischer Herrschaft* (Vienna, 1856), pp. 143–63.

27. S. K. Smirnov, *O posol'stve Il'ii Danilovicha Miloslavskago i d'iaka Leiontiia Lazorevskago v Turtsiia v 1643 godu* (Moscow, n.d.), p. 31.

28. V. A. Zorin, *et al*, eds., *Istoriia diplomatii*, 2d ed., 1 (Moscow, 1959), p. 302.

29. Max Immich, *Geschichte des Europäischen Staatensystems von 1660 bis 1789* (Munich, 1905), pp. 166–77.

30. Solov'ev, *Istoriia Rossii*, 7 (Moscow, 1962): 372; P. Pierling, *La Russie et le Saint Siège*, 4 (Paris, 1907): 106–7.

31. See for example, Paul Miliukov, *et al.*, *History of Russia*, trans. Charles Lam Markmann, 1 (New York, 1968): pp. 210–11. Miliukov describes the Polish peace as a success and the Crimean campaign as a "failure" without, how-ever, noting the direct relationship between the two. By contrast, G. K. Babushkina has emphasized the degree to which the campaigns were un-dertaken to serve Muscovite interests. "Mezhdunarodnoe znachenie Krym-skikh pokhodov 1687 i 1689 gg," *Istoricheskie zapiski*, 33 (Moscow, 1950): 158–59.

32. Dorothy M. Vaughan, *Europe and the Turk: A Pattern of Alliances 1350–1700* (Liverpool, 1954), p. 272.

33. Petrov, *Russkaia voennaia sila*, 1: 27.

34. Solov'ev, *Istoriia Rossii*, 7: 391.

35. L. G. Beskrovnyi, *et al.*, eds., *Istoriia SSSR* (Moscow, 1967), 3: 147–48.

36. M. C. Possett, ed., *Tagebuch des Generals Patrick Gordon während seiner Kriegsdienst unter den Schweden und Polen vom Jahre 1655 bis 1661 und seines Aussenthaltes in Russland vom Jahre 1661 bis 1699*, 2 (St. Petersburg, 1851): 171.

37. Possett, *Tagebuch*, pp. 174–75; *Istoriia SSSR*, 3: 148.

38. Solov'ev, *Istoriia Rossii*, 7: 406.

39. Possett, *Tagebuch*, p. 249; D. I. Bagalyi, *Ocherki iz istorii kolonizatsii stepnoi okrainy Moskovskago gosudarstva* (Moscow, 1887), p. 294.

40. Possett, *Tagebuch*, pp. 250–51; Petrov, *Russkaia voennaia sila*, 1: 389.

41. Possett, *Tagebuch*, pp. 252–54.

42. Solov'ev, *Istoriia Rossii*, 7: 407.

43. Possett, *Tagebuch*, pp. 257–59; Solov'ev, *Istoriia Rossii*, 7: 408; Petrov, *Russkaia voennaia sila*, 1: 389.

44. M. M. Bogoslovskii, *Petr I: Materialy dlia biografii* (Moscow, 1940), pp. 74–75.

45. For a discussion and critique of this trend, see Martin van Creveld, "The State of Military History Studies," *The Washington Quarterly*, 8, no. 1 (Winter 1983): 183–85.

46. See, for example, L. I. Babin, *F. E. Engels: Vydaiushchi'isia voennyi teoretik rabochego klassa* (Moscow, 1970), pp. 40, 57.

47. Bagalyi, *Ocherki*, pp. 285–86.

48. Teodorczyk, "L'armée polonaise", pp. 111–12.

49. Geoffrey Parker, *The Army of Flanders and the Spanish Road 1567–1659* (Cambridge, 1972), pp. 7–12; Geoffrey Parker, "The 'Military Revolution' 1560–1660—a Myth?" *The Journal of Modern History*, 48, no. 2 (June 1976): 203–6; Geoffrey Parker, *The Military Revolution: Military Innovation and the Rise of the West* (Cambridge, 1988), pp. 10–39.

50. Theodore A. Dodge, *Gustaphus Adolphus* (Boston, 1896), p. 42; William McNeill, *The Pursuit of Power: Technology, Armed Force and Society Since A.D. 1600* (Chicago, 1982), pp. 140–42.

51. Dodge, *Gustaphus Adolphus*, p. 35.

52. Hellie, *Enserfment*, p. 185; Joseph T. Fuhrmann, *The Origins of Capitalism in Russia, 16–17th Centuries* (Chicago, 1972), p. 109.

53. Thomas Esper, "Military Self-Sufficiency and Weapons Technology in Muscovite Russia," *Slavic Review*, 28, no. 3 (June 1969): 202, 205.

54. Petrov, *Russkaia voennaia sila*, 1: 396–97.

55. Howard L. Blackmore, *British Military Firearms 1650–1850* (London, 1961), p. 24.

56. Stashevskii, *Smolenskaia voina*, p. 170; Otton Laskowski, "L'art militaire Polonais au XVIe et au XVIIIe siècle," *Revue Internationale d'histoire militaire*, 1952, no. 12, p. 471; Jan Wimmer, "L'infanterie dans l'armée polonaise aux XVe–XVIIIe siècles," in Bieganski, *Histoire Militaire*, p. 37.

57. Teodorczyk, "L'armée polonaise," p. 113.

58. Petrov, *Russkaia voennaia sila*, 1: 495; Geoffrey Parker, *The Thirty Years War* (London, 1984), pp. 206–7.

59. Christopher Duffy, *Fire and Stone: The Science of Fortress Warfare 1660–1860* (London, 1975), pp. 136–43.

60. P. O. Bobrovskii, *Perekhod Rossii k reguliarnoi armii* (St. Petersburg, 1885), pp. 79–80.

61. L. J. D. Collins, "The Military Organization and Tactics of the Crimean Tatars During the Sixteenth and Seventeenth Centuries," in V. J. Parry and M. E. Yapp, eds., *War, Technology, and Society in the Middle East* (London, 1975), pp. 259–63.

62. Hammer-Purgstall, *Geschichte der Chane der Krim*, pp. 167–68.

63. George Gush, *Renaissance Armies 1480–1650* (Cambridge, 1975), pp. 11–12.

64. See McNeill, *Pursuit of Power*, pp. 126–42, for a particularly good account of the innovations of Maurice of Nassau in this regard. See also Hans Delbrück, *Geschichte der Kriegskraft im Rahmen der Politischen Geschichte*, 4 (Berlin, 1920): 178–91.

65. A good discussion of the importance of field fortifications in this period is provided in Hermann Meynert, *Geschichte des Kriegswesens und der Heerverfassungen in Europa*, 3 (Vienna, 1869; reprint: Graz, 1973): 100–101.

66. John Webster and Cyril Tourneur, *Four Plays* (New York, 1956), p. 69.

67. Teodorczyk, "L'armée polonaise," pp. 110–11. On the similarity of Muscovite and Polish tactics during the Smolensk war, see *Zarys Dziejów Wojskowości*, pp. 464–65.

68. Collins, "Military Organization and Tactics," pp. 265–71.

69. Collins, "Military Organization and Tactics," pp. 273–74; V. J. Parry, "La manière de combattre," in Parry and Yapp, *War, Technology and Society*, pp. 223–24; Thomas M. Barker, *The Military Intellectual and Battle: Raimondo Montecuccoli and the Thirty Years War* (Albany, N.Y., 1975), p. 117; Petrov, *Russkaia voennaia sila* (note 12 above), 1: 415; Teodorzcyk, "L'armée polonaise," p. 194; Linda Gordon, *Cossack Rebellions: Social Turmoil in the Sixteenth-Century Ukraine* (Albany, N.Y., 1983), pp. 80–81.

70. Martin van Creveld, *Supplying War: Logistics from Wallenstein to Patton* (Cambridge, 1977), pp. 6, 24–26, 37.

71. Petrov, *Russkaia voennaia sila*, 1: 41.
72. Petrov, *Russkaia voennaia sila*, 1: 393–94; Bobrovskii, *Perekhod Rossii*, pp. 72–73.
73. Stashevskii, *Smolenskaia voina*, p. 321.

2. Peter the Great & the Advantages of "Backwardness"

1. Dorothy Atkinson, "Society and the Sexes in the Russian Past," in Dorothy Atkinson, Alexander Dallin, and Gail Warshofsky Lapidus, eds., *Women in Russia* (Stanford, Calif., 1977), p. 26.
2. P. Dirin, *Istoriia Leib Gvardii Semenovskago Polka*, (St. Petersburg, 1883), 1: 175, 178.
3. There are numerous works on the Petrine reforms. See Paul Miliukov, *et al. History of Russia*, trans. Charles Lam Markman (New York, 1968), 1: 212–334; Vasili Klyuchevski, *Peter the Great*, trans. Liliana Archibald (New York, 1958); S. M. Troitskii, *Russkii absoliutizm i dvorianstvo v xviii v.*, (Moscow, 1974) pp. 47–118; John L. H. Keep, *Soldiers of the Tsar: Army and Society in Russia, 1462–1874* (Oxford, 1985), pp. 120–27; Claes Peterson, *Peter the Great's Administrative and Judicial Reforms: Swedish Antecedents and the Process of Reception* (Stockholm, 1979).
4. V. N. Latkin, *Lektsii po istorii russkogo prava* (St. Petersburg, 1912), pp. 198, 465–66, 469, 489.
5. On the "regular" state, see M. M. Bogoslovskii, *Oblastnaia reforma Petra Velikago 1719–27* (Moscow: 1902), pp. 12–23; V. I. Syromiatnikov, *Reguliarnoe gosudarstvo Petra Pervogo i ego ideologiia.* (Moscow, 1943); for the "haphazard" view see Klyuchevsky, *Peter the Great*, pp. 74–75. See also Marc Raeff, *The Well-Ordered Police State: Social and Institutional Change Through Law in the Germanies and Russia 1600–1800* (New Haven, 1983), pp. 215–21.
6. Klyuchevsky, *Peter the Great*, p. 265.
7. Miliukov, *History of Russia*, 1: 288–89, discusses the way in which peasant flight produced the curious phenomenon of declining census figures in Petrine Russia. Actually, of course, the population was increasing.
8. On Peter's ideology" and value system, see N. I. Pavlenko, "Petr I (k izucheniiu sotsialno-politicheskikh vzgliadov," in N. I. Pavlenko, ed., *Rossiia v period reform Petra I* (Moscow, 1973), pp. 40–102; on Menshikov, S. M. Troitskii, "Khoziaistvo krupnogo sanovnika Rossii v pervoi chetverti XVIII v," in Pavlenko, *Rossiia*, p. 228; on Shafirov, William E. Butler, introduction to P. P. Shafirov, *A Discourse Concerning the Just Causes of the War Between Sweden and Russia: 1700–1721.* (Dobbs Ferry, N. Y.: 1973), p. 25; on Gagarin, R. Wittram, *Peter I, Tsar und Kaiser* (Gottingen, 1964), 2: 108–10.
9. N. I. Pavlenko, *Ptentsy gnezda Petra* (Moscow, 1984), p. 21; N. N. Molchanov, *Diplomatiia Petra Pervogo* (Moscow, 1984), pp. 59–62.
10. Christopher Duffy, *Russia's Military Way to the West: Origins and Nature of Russian Military Power, 1700–1800.* (London, 1981), pp. 14–17; R. M. Hatton, *Charles XII of Sweden.* (London, 1968), pp. 151–57; E. I. Porfir'ev, *Petr I: Osnovopolozhnik voennogo isskusstva russkoi reguliarnoi armii i flota* (Moscow, 1952), pp. 122–24.

11. Golitsyn's letter of 23 August 1701 to F. A. Golovin is printed in N. Ustrialov, *Istoriia tsarstvovaniia Peter Velikago*, 4, pt. II, "Prilozhenie" (St. Petersburg, 1863): 202.

12. For a good brief account of these campaigns, see Pavlenko, *Ptentsy*, pp. 26–43; the most detailed treatment is to be found in Kh. Palli, *Mezhdu dvumia boiami za Narvu. Estoniia v pervye gody Severnoi Voiny 1701–1704* (Tallin, 1966).

13. E. V. Tarle, *Severnaia voina i shvedskoe nashestvie na Rossiiu* (Moscow, 1958), p. 68.

14. Hatton, *Charles XII,* p. 157, argues persuasively that Charles delayed the invasion of Saxony until 1706 in order to avoid offending the British and Dutch, who might have interpreted such a step as indirect support for Louis XIV of France.

15. Professor Dr. Ernst Carlson, comp., F. Mewius, trans., *Die eigenhandigen Briefe Konig Karls XII* (Berlin, 1894), p. 359.

16. See N. P. Mikhnevich, *Istoriia voennogo iskusstva s drevneishikh vremen do nachala deviatnadtsatogo stoletiia*, 2d ed. (St. Petersburg, 1896), p. 286; Tarle, *Severnaia voina*, pp. 55–56; Palli, *Mezhdu dvumia boiami*, p. 6; M. D. Rabinovich, "Formirovanie reguliarnoi russkoi armii nakanune Severnoi Voiny," in V. I. Shunkov, ed., *Voprosy voennoi istorii Rossii, XVIII i pervaia polovina XIX vekov* (Moscow, 1969), pp. 230–33.

17. A. Z. Myshlaevskii, *Petr Velikii: Voina v Finliandii v 1712–1714 godakh* (St. Petersburg, 1896), p. 473.

18. See R. Ernest Dupuy and Trevor N. Dupuy, *The Encyclopedia of Military History from 3,500 B.C. to the Present*, 2d rev. ed. (New York, 1986), p. 460, on the characteristics of the regular army.

19. B. H. Sumner, *Peter the Great and the Emergence of Russia* (New York, 1962), p. 58.

20. L. G. Beskrovnyi, *Russkaia armiia i flot v XVIII veke* (Moscow, 1958), pp. 22–23; Keep, *Soldiers of the Tsar*, pp. 103–4.

21. Miliukov, *History,* 1: 242–43; Ustrialov, *Istoriia,* 4, pt. 2: 489.

22. Beskrovnyi, *Russkaia armiia*, pp. 26–27.

23. Wittram, *Peter I,* 2: 9, says that 230,000 men were mobilized in fifty-three levies from 1699 to 1725. Keep, *Soldiers of the Tsar,* pp. 105–6, states that 138,000 men were enrolled from 1701 to 1709 and 153,000 more from 1713 to 1725. Miliukov, *History,* 1: 243, argues that 200,000 were drafted from 1700 to 1709. P. O. Bobrovskii, *Perekhod Rossii k reguliarnoi armii* (St. Petersburg, 1885), p. 177, estimates that 175,000 were called up between 1705 and 1709 alone. One reason for the confusion may be the tallying of labor drafts in with the totals for recruitment. Another may be the selective counting of irregular forces (Cossacks, Kalmyks, and so forth). Ustrialov, *Istoriia,* 4, prt. 2: 488–89. This summary figure was derived from adding the totals adduced in this text.

24. Beskrovny, *Russkaia armiia,* pp. 27–29. See also Gregory L. Freeze, *The Russian Levites: Parish and Clergy in the Eighteenth Century* (Cambridge, Mass., 1977), p. 36.

25. Mikhnevich, *Istoriia voennago iskusstva*, pp. 287, 290, 294; Tarle, *Severnaia voina*, p. 57; Wittram, *Peter I*, 2: 9.

26. A. Z. Myshlaevskii, *Severnaia voina na Ingermanlandskom i Finliandskom teatrakh v 1708–1714 gg. (Dokumenty gosudarstvennogo arkhiva); Sbornik voenno-istoricheskikh materialov*, 5 (St. Petersburg, 1893): 169–70.

27. Keep, *Soldiers of the Tsar*, pp. 107–8; Beskrovnyi, *Russkaia armiia*, p. 31.

28. Myshlaevskii, *Severnaia voina na Ingermanlandskom*, p. 308.

29. Ustrialov, *Istoriia*, 4, pt. 2: 95.

30. Myshlaevskii, *Petr Velikii*, "Prilozhenie," p. 70.

31. Bobrovskii, *Perekhod Rossii*, p. 174

32. Beskrovnyi, *Russkaia armiia*, p. 30.

33. Myshlaevskii, *Petr Velikii*, p. 23. See for example the eyewitness account of Peter Henry Bruce, *Memoirs of Peter Henry Bruce in the Services of Prussia, Russia and Britain* (Dublin, 1783; reprint: London, 1970), pp. 46–51.

34. Myshlaevskii, *Petr Velikii*, "Prilozhenie," p. 13.

35. Dirin, *Istoriia Leib Gvardii*, p. 167.

36. *Ibid.*

37. N. L. Rubinshtein, *Voennye ustavy Petra Velikogo: Sbornik dokumentov* (Moscow, 1946), p. 71.

38. B. T. Urlanis, *Voiny i narodnonaselenie Evropy* (Moscow, 1960), pp. 55, 58, 62, 335; c.f. Hatton, *Charles XII*, pp. 515–16.

39. Urlanis, *Voiny*, pp. 62, 335.

40. Porfir'ev, *Petr I*, pp. 59–61.

41. Bobrovskii, *Perekhod Rossii*, p. 175.

42. Myshlaevskii, *Petr Velikii*, "Prilozhenie," pp. 110, 147, 150.

43. V. N. Avtokratov, "Pervye komissariatskie organy russkoi reguliarnoi armii 1700–1710 gg.," in A. L. Sidorov, ed., *Istoricheskie zapiski*, 68 (Moscow, 1961): 162, 165–66, 174.

44. Pavlenko, *Ptentsy*, pp. 24–25.

45. Ustrialov, *Istoriia*, 4, pt. 2: 227, 292

46. *Ibid.*, pp. 292, 494.

47. Tarle, *Severnaia voina*, p. 290.

48. Myshlaevskii, *Severnaia voina na Ingermanlandskom*, p. 419.

49. Ragnhild Hatton, ed., "Captain James Jeffreyes's Letters to the Secretary of State, Whitehall, from the Swedish Army, 1707–1709," in *Historiska Handlinger del 35:1* (Stockholm, 1953), p. 37.

50. A. Z. Myshlaevskii, *Severnaia voina 1708 g. ot r. Ully i Bereziny za Dnepr* (St. Petersburg, 1901), p. 16.

51. Myshlaevskii, *Severnaia voina na Ingermanlandskom*, p. 77.

52. *Ibid.*, pp. 61, 66

53. Myshlaevskii, *Petr Velikii*, pp. 45, 109.

54. Pavlenko, *Ptentsy*, p. 37.

55. Bobrovskii, *Perekhod Rossii*, p. 159.

56. Ustrialov, *Istoriia*, vol., 4, pt. II, "Prilozhenie": 315, 395.

57. *Ibid.*, pp. 397–98

58. *Ibid.*, pp. 400, 401.

59. *Ibid.*, pp. 419–20.
60. Myshlaevskii, *Severnaia voina na Ingermanlandskom*, p. xx; *Perepiska i bumagi Grafa Borisa Petrovicha Sheremeteva, 1704–1722 gg.* (St. Petersburg, 1879), p. 139.
61. Myshlaevskii, *Petr Velikii*, "Prilozhenie," p. 36.
62. Rabinovich, "Formirovanie," pp. 224–25.
63. Ustrialov, *Istoriia*, 4, pt. II, "Prilozhenie": 429.
64. Myshlaevskii, *Severnaia voina 1708 g.*, p. 50; Rubinshtein, *Voennye ustavy*, pp. 60–61.
65. Myshlaevskii, *Severnaia voina 1708 g.*, pp. 51–52.
66. Dirin, *Istoriia Leib Gvardii* (note 2 above), pp. 170–71.
67. *Ibid.*, p. 171.
68. It might be objected that the sources on which we base these conclusions are selective or tainted, seeing as they come chiefly from printed documentary collections. But there is little reason to doubt this evidence: there are simply so many mutually corraborating accounts that document the persistence of the identical problems and identical abuses over the years. Further, many scholars who maintain that Peter did create the regular army concede every point I have made here, without, however, pondering their collective implications. Beskrovnyi, *Russkaia armiia*, p. 19, asserts that Peter founded the regular army, but confesses on page 33 that "the constant replenishment of the army with untrained recruits created many difficulties: it was necessary every year to teach the field army the basics of military service." Similarly Michael T. Florinsky, *Russia: A History and Interpretation*, vol. I (New York, 1953), notes on page 356 that the well nigh fabulous level of Petrine military casualties "represented the losses suffered not so much on the battlefield as from mass desertions and from the extraordinarily high mortality among the soldiers due to hunger, cold, and incredible living conditions." Yet he adds on the same page, apparently unaware of the contradiction, that "the concentration of the recruits in depots where they received some training before joining their regiments, and especially the protracted character of the war which for years kept men with the colors, led to the transformation of the militia into a regular army." Military service may be an education in itself, but one must survive it to profit from its lessons or impart them to others.
69. Florinsky, *Russia*, 1: 357.
70. E. V. Anisimov, *Podatnaia reforma Petra I: Vvedenie podushnoi podati v Rossii 1719–1728 gg.* (Leningrad, 1982), p. 278; Keep, *Soldiers of the Tsar*, pp. 139–40.
71. Porfir'ev, *Petr I*, p. 58.
72. Anisimov, *Podatnaia reforma*, pp. 22–30, esp. p. 30.
73. N. B. Golikova, *Politicheskie protsessy pri Petre I: Po materialam Preobrazhenskogo prikaza* (Moscow, 1957), pp. 257–58.
74. S. M. Troitskii, "Istochniki dokhodov v biudzhete Rossii v seredine XVIII v. (20-60-e-gody)," *Istoriia SSSR*, no. 3 (July–August 1957), pp. 177–78. Also see Anisimov, *Podatnaia reforma*, pp. 45–62, 233–38, 252–58, esp. p. 258.
75. Ustrialov, *Istoriia*, 4, pt. II, "Prilozhenie": 18. In a secret codicil to the treaty,

Peter also promised Augustus an additional payment of 20,000 rubles with which to bribe the Polish senate into a Russian alliance.

76. P. A. Miliukov, *Gosudarstvennoe khoziaistvo Rossii v pervoi chetverti XVIII stoletiia i reforma Petra Velikogo*, 2d ed. (St. Petersburg, 1905); Porfir'ev, *Petr I*, p. 55.
77. Anisimov, *Podatnaia reforma*, pp. 267, 280–82.
78. Porfir'ev, *Petr I*, pp. 49–50.
79. Wittram, *Peter I*, 2: 20–21.; R. C. Anderson, *Naval Wars in the Baltic 1522–1850* (London, 1910), p. 162.
80. A. A. Preobrazhenskoe, "Voennye postavki Nev'ianskogo zavoda nakanune poltavskogo srasheniia," in Shunkov, *Voprosy voennoi istorii*, p. 186.
81. E. V. Spiridonova, *Ekonomicheskaia politika i ekonomicheskie vzgliady Petra I* (Moscow, 1952), p. 146.
82. Beskrovny, *Russkaia armiia*, pp. 74–75; Porfir'ev, *Petr I*, p. 60; Myshlaevskii, *Severnaia voina na Ingermandlanskom*, pp xxv–xxvi.
83. Porfir'ev, *Petr I*, p. 60.
84. Beskrovnyi, *Russkaia armiia*, pp. 99–103.
85. Spiridonova, *Ekonomicheskaia politika*, p. 146, gives a total of two hundred. Wittram, *Peter I*, 2: 34, says 178 were opened. Miliukov, *History*, 1: 293, makes the point about dummy industrial establishments.
86. For a brief discussion, see Richard Pipes, *Russia Under the Old Regime* (New York, 1974), pp. 20–21.
87. Johann-Georg Korb, *Diary of an Austrian Secretary of Legation at the Court of Czar Peter the Great*, Count MacDonnell, ed. and trans. (London, 1863; reprint, London, 1968), p. 72.
88. M. I. Belov, "Rol' Petra I v rasprostranenii geograficheskikh znanii v Rossii," in Belov, ed., *Voprosy geografii Petrovskogo vremeni* (Leningrad, 1975), pp. 17–18; John Perry, *The State of Russia Under the Present Czar* (London, 1716; reprint, New York, 1967). pp. 1–8.
89. Robert E. Jones, "Getting the Goods to St. Petersburg: Water Transport from the Interior 1703–1811," *Slavic Review*, 43, no. 3 (Fall 1984): 417–19.
90. *Ibid.*, pp. 419–20.
91. G. D. Kapustina, "Guzhevoi transport v severnoi voine," in Shunkov, *Voprosy voennoi istorii*, pp. 157, 159, 161, 163–64. The calculations on food were made by me on the basis of data on page 161.
92. Pavlenko, *Ptentsy*, p. 26.
93. Kapustina "Guzhevoi transport," pp. 178–80.
94. Ustrialov, *Istoriia*, 4, pt. II, "Prilozhenie": 330.
95. Molchanov, *Diplomatiia*, p. 28.
96. David Chandler, *The Art of War in the Age of Marlborough* (New York, 1976), pp. 57, 115, 128; Gunnar Arteus, *Krigsteori och Historisk Forklaring*, vol. 2, *Karolinsk och Europeisk stridstaktik 1700–1712: Meddelanden från Historiska Institutionen i Göteborg* (Göteborg, 1972), pp. 121, 124; Hatton, *Charles XII*, p. 210.
97. Pavlenko, *Ptentsy*, pp. 29, 31; Porfir'ev, *Petr I*, p. 136.
98. Mikhnevich, *Istoriia voennogo iskusstva*, p. 295; Myshlaevskii, *Petr Velikii*, "Prilozhenie," p. 38.

99. *Pisma i bumagi Imperatora Petra Velikogo,* vol. 5, January–June, 1707 (St. Petersburg, 1907), pp. 41–42.

100. Myshlaevskii, *Severnaia voina na Ingermanlandskom,* p. xxiii; Arteus, *Karolinsk,* p. 123.

101. Hatton, *Captain James Jeffreyes's Letters,* p. 67.

102. Hatton, *Charles XII,* p. 281; Tarle, *Severnaia voina,* p. 294.

103. Pavlenko, *Ptensy,* pp. 73–79, Porfir'ev, *Petr I,* pp. 192–207; Duffy, *Russia's Military Way,* pp. 23–26.

104. Ustrialov, *Istoriia,* 4, "Prilozhenie": 236.

105. Porfir'ev, *Petr I,* pp. 135–40; Pavlenko, *Ptensy,* pp. 26–30.

106. *Doneseniia i drugiia bumagi chrezvychainago poslannika angliskogo pri russkom dvore Charl'za Vitvorta, i sekretaria ego Veisbroda s 1708 g. po 1711 g.: Sbornik Imperatorskago russkago istoricheskago obshchestva,* 50. (St. Petersburg, 1886): 298.

107. Perry, *State of Russia,* p. 45.

108. Myshlaevkii, *Petr Velikii,* p. 461; Chandler, *Art of War,* p. 20.

109. Bruce, *Memoirs,* pp. 318–19.

110. Mikhnevich, *Istoriia voennogo iskusstva,* pp. 299–300; Tarle, *Severnaia voina,* pp. 201–6.

111. Porfir'ev, *Petr I,* p. 269.

112. *Ibid.,* pp. 38–43; Molchanov, *Diplomatiia,* pp. 55–59.

113. Porfir'ev, *Petr I,* pp. 138–39.

114. M. Filmoshin, "Pervaia pobeda russkogo reguliarnogo flota," *Voenno-istorichkeskii zhurnal,* 8 (August 1984): 61–62.

115. Myshlaevskii, *Petr Velikii,* pp. 445–50; *idem, Severnaia voina na Ingermanlandskom,* p. v; Porfir'ev, *Petr I,* pp. 234–35.

116. Bruce, *Memoirs,* pp. 234–36.

117. E. P. Podiapol'skaia, "Voennye sovety 1708–1709 gg.," in L. G. Beskrovny, ed., *Poltava: K 250-letiiu poltavskogo srazheniia—Sbornik statei* (Moscow, 1959), pp. 113–14.

118. Ustrialov, *Istoriia,* 4, "Prilozhenie": 391–93.

119. Myshlaevskii, *Petr Velikii,* p. 468.

120. Ustrialov, *Istoriia,* 4, "Prilozhenie": 448.

121. Myshlaevskii, *Severnaia voina 1708 g.,* p. 19–31, "Prilozhenie," pp. 3–10.

122. Ustrialov, *Istoriia,* 4, "Prilozhenie": 93–94.

123. Myshlaevskii, *Severnaia voina 1708 g.,* "Prilozhenie," pp. 3–4.

124. Molchanov, *Diplomatiia,* p. 227.

125. The best modern work on the colleges is Peterson, *Peter the Great's Administrative and Judicial Reforms.*

126. Gustave Adlerfeld, *Histoire Militaire de Charles XII, Roi de Suede,* 1 (Amsterdam, 1740): 81.

127. Tarle, *Severnaia voina,* pp. 184–85, paints an exceptionally unsavory picture of Charles as strategist, quoting the famous remark attributed to him in 1708 ("Jag har ingen dessein": I have no plan) as evidence. Yet even Hatton, *Charles XII,* pp. 238–39, otherwise sympathetic to the king, berates him for his fuzzy planning.

128. Tarle, *Severnaia voina,* pp. 94–95; Porfir'ev, *Petr I,* p. 148.

129. Ustrialov, *Istoriia,* 4, "Prilozhenie": 448.

130. G. Iu. Gerbilskii, "Russko-polskii soiuz i Zholkovskii strategicheskii plan," in Beskrovny, ed., *Poltava*, pp. 77, 87.
131. Ragnhild Hatton, *George I: Elector and King* (Cambridge, Mass., 1978), pp. 235–42.
132. Whitworth describes this in *Doneseniia*, pp. 485 ff. It is also discussed in Myshlaevskii, *Petr Velikii*, p. 14.
133. *Pisma i bumagi*, 5: 61.
134. A good example is Mikhnevich, *Istoriia voennogo iskusstva*, p. 286.
135. *Doneseniia*, p. 296.
136. Adlerfeld, *Histoire militaire*, 3: 274.
137. *Zhurnal ili podennaia zapiska blazhennyia i vechnodostoinyia pamiati Gosudaria Imperatora Petra Velikago s 1698 goda dazhe do zakliucheniia Neishtatskogo Mira: Napechatan s obretaiiushchikhsia v kabinetnoi arkhive spiskov, pravlennykh sobstvennoiu rukoiu ego Imperatorskago Velichestva* (St. Petersburg: 1770), p. 157.

 Gerbilskii, "Russko-pol'skii soiuz," p. 78, denies that this was Sheremet'ev's idea, but he is contradicted by most other scholars. See N. Ustrialov, "Petr Velikii v Zholkieve 1707 g.," *Drevniaia i novaia Rossiia*, 2, no. 1 (1876): 7; B. S. Telpukhovskii, *Severnaia voina 1700–1721: Polkovodcheskaia deiatelnost' Petra I* (Moscow, 1946), p. 58. The Prussian ambassador who attended the meeting explicitly identified Sheremet'ev as the originator of the idea. Bobrovskii, *Perekhod Rossii*, pp. 178–79.
138. Bobrovskii, *Perekhod Rossii*, pp. 178–79.
139. Cited in Pavlenko, *Ptentsy*, p. 60; Myshlaevskii, *Severnaia voina 1708 g.*, p. 16.
140. *Pisma i bumagi*, 5: 5.
141. *Ibid.*
142. Adlerfeld, *Histoire Militaire*, 3: 212–13.
143. *Doneseniia*, p. 57.
144. Hatton, *Captain James Jeffreyes's Letters*, p. 61, says that by this point the army was living on what it could find buried underground.
145. Tarle, *Severnaia voina*, p. 208.
146. *Ibid.*, p. 289; also, Adlerfeld, *Histoire Militaire*, 4: 17.
147. Tarle, *Severnaia voina*, p. 299. Of course, Charles was reinforced prior to Poltava by approximately ten thousand Zaporozhan cossacks loyal to Mazeppa. But these light calvary forces were of little use in a formal battle of the type Poltava was and these men themselves were feeling the effect of the food shortages.
148. Mikhnevich, *Istoriia voennogo iskusstva*, pp. 301–2, 304; Porfir'ev, *Petr I*, pp. 192–93.

3. Russian Imperialism & Military Power in the 18th Century

1. Raymond H. Fisher, *Bering's Voyages: Whither and Why* (Seattle, 1977), pp. 138, 155.
2. Christopher Duffy, *Russia's Military Way to the West: Origins and Nature of Russian Military Power, 1700–1800* (London, 1981), p. 47; G. A. Nekrasov,

Rol' Rossii v evropeiskoi mezhdunarodnoi politike 1725–1739 gg. (Moscow, 1976), p. 227.

3. E. V. Anisimov, *Rossiia v seredine XVIII veka: Bor'ba za nasledie Petra* (Moscow, 1986), p. 131.

4. F. Ia. Polianskii, ed., *Istoriia narodnogo khoziaistva SSSR: Kurs lektsii* (Moscow, 1960), p. 146.

5. In 1743 Russia forced Sweden to accept Adolf Frederick of Holstein, uncle to the future Russian Empress Catherine II as crown prince of the realm. Dominique Maroger, ed., *The Memoirs of Catherine the Great* (New York, 1955), p. 72; Russia's "rights" with respect to the Ottoman Empire's Christian subjects were secured by means of the treaty of Kuchuk Kainardzhi in 1774. M. S. Anderson, *The Eastern Question* (London, 1966), pp. xi–xii; Russian mediation of the war of the Bavarian Succession (also known as "the Potato War" of 1778–79) is treated in Isabel de Madariaga, *Russia in the Age of Catherine the Great* (New Haven, 1981), pp. 379–81; the Armed Neutrality of 1780 was a combination of northern states that challenged British right to blockade the ports of Spain and France. Piers Mackesy, *The War for America, 1775–1783* (Cambridge, Mass., 1965), pp. 377–78;

6. See, for example, Isser Woloch, *Eighteenth-Century Europe: Tradition and Progress, 1715–1789* (New York, 1982), pp. 26–30, where the "waxing" of Russian power is rather too patly connected to the success of political absolutism in the empire and its failure in neighboring states.

7. William Richardson, *Anecdotes of the Russian Empire* (London, 1784; reprint: New York, 1970), pp. 74–75.

8. John Francis Gough, trans., *The Private Letters of Baron de Vioménil on Polish Affairs* (Jersey City, 1935), p. 119.

9. See Paul Kennedy, *The Rise and Fall of the Great Powers: Economic Change and Military Conflict From 1500 to 2000* (New York, 1987), pp. 94–95;119–20, for an explanation of the growth of Russia in this period heavily weighted toward economic factors.

10. For a statement of this position, see Edward Vose Gulik, *Europe's Classical Balance of Power* (New York, 1967), pp. 11–51. Note in particular p. 39, where Gulik dismisses Russia's eighteenth-century conquests as minor and of little significance for the balance of power.

11. M. S. Anderson, *Europe in the Eighteenth Century 1713–1789* (London, 1961), p. 163.

12. Alfred Ritter von Arneth, ed., *Joseph II und Katharine von Russland: Ihr Briefwechsel* (Vienna, 1869), pp. 3–4.

13. Stanford J. Shaw, *Between Old and New: The Ottoman Empire Under Sultan Selim III 1789–1807* (Cambridge, Mass., 1971), p. 46.

14. Norman Itzkowitz and Max Mote, annot. and trans., *Mubadele: An Ottoman–Russian Exchange of Ambassadors* (Chicago, 1970), p. 119.

15. *Arkhiv Gosudarstvennago Soveta*, 1, pt. 1, *1768–96 gg.* (St. Petersburg, 1869): 530, 574; Shaw, *Between Old and New*, p. 37.

16. Francis Ley, *Le Maréchal de Münnich et La Russie au XVIIIe siècle* (Paris, 1959), p. 87.

17. On the barrier, see Nekrasov, *Rol' Rossii*, pp. 216–17, and Michael F. Met-

calf, *Russia, England and Swedish Party Politics 1762–1766* (Totowa, N.J., 1977), p. 2. On French policies generally, see David Lerer, *La Politique Française en Pologne sous Louis XV, 1733–1772* (Toulouse, 1930), pp. 35–61, and Arthur M. Wilson, *French Foreign Policy During the Administration of Cardinal Fleury 1726–43* (Cambridge, Mass., 1936), pp. 249–65. As Wilson notes (p. 249), French support for Stanislas was in all likelihood totally insincere since France's true goal, eventually achieved, during this "War of the Polish Succession" was not the installation of Louis's father-in-law in Warsaw but rather the reversion to France of the Duchy of Lorraine.

18. A. Baiov, *Russkaia armiia v tsarstvovanie Imperatritsy Anny Iovannovny: Voina Rossii s Turtsiei v 1736–1739 gg, Kampaniia 1739* (St. Petersburg, 1906), p. 15; General Christopher Hermann von Manstein, *Contemporary Memoirs of Russia from the Year 1727 to 1744*, ed. David Hume (London, 1856), pp. 299–300.

19. M. N. Bogdanovich, *Pokhody Rumiantseva, Potemkina i Suvorova v Turtsii* (St. Petersburg, 1852), p. 80. For a contemporary insight into French policy, see *Memoirs of the Baron de Tott on the Turks and the Tartars, Translated from the French by an English Gentleman at Paris Under the Immediate Inspection of the Baron*, vol. 2 (Dublin, 1785).

20. *Memoirs of Baron de Tott*, 2: 126, 148.

21. *Ibid.*, 2: 126; Barbara Jelavich, *St. Petersburg and Moscow: Tsarist and Soviet Foreign Policy 1814–1974* (Bloomington, Ind., 1974), p. 21; John M. Sherwig, *Guineas and Gunpowder: British Foreign Aid in the Wars with France, 1793–1815* (Cambridge, Mass., 1969), pp. 5–6.

22. As, for example, occurred at the Peace of Jassy in 1792. See Shaw, *Between Old and New*, p. 67.

23. For a favorable assessment of Frederick's activities, see Heinrich von Srbik, *Deutsche Einheit: Idee und Wirklichkeit von Heiligen Reich bis Königgratz* (Munich, 1940), pp. 98–102, 104. For a less favorable interpretation, see Gerhard Ritter, *Frederick the Great*, trans. Peter Paret (Berkeley, Calif., 1968), pp. 71–85.

24. Baiov, *Russkaia armiia*, p. 263; Manstein, *Contemporary Memoirs*, p. 235; Melchior Vischer, *Münnich, Feldherr, Ingenieur, Hochverräter* (Frankfurt-am-Main, 1938), p. 425.

25. On this "diplomatic revolution," see R. Waddington, *Louis XIV et le Renversement des Alliances* (Paris, 1896), pp. 527–29, and Walter Dorn, *Competition for Empire* (New York, 1940), pp. 292–316.

26. L. Jay Oliva, *Misalliance: A Study of French Policy in Russia During the Seven Years War* (New York, 1964), pp. 105, 113, 134, 177; Herbert H. Kaplan, *The First Partition of Poland* (New York, 1962), p. 127.

27. Arneth, *Joseph II*, pp. 79–80.

28. Joseph was most especially alarmed by the Russian seizure of Ochakov, which he believed would preclude the early negotiation of a peace. He noted in a letter of February 1789 to his Chancellor, Kaunitz: "The taking of Ochakov is most propitious for the continuation of the war, but not for making a peace, since the Russians will never desire to return that city and the Turks will never agree to cede it." See Arneth, *Joseph II*, p. 325.

29. Madariaga, *Russia in Age of Catherine the Great,* p. 403.
30. On Münnich's approach to Ukrainian security, see Ley, *Le Maréchal de Münnich,* pp. 63–64; on the situation after 1739, see Baiov, *Russkaia armiia,* pp. 30–32.
31. John P. LeDonne, "Outlines of Russian Military Administration 1762– 1796, Part I: Troop Strength and Deployment," *Jahrbücher für Geschichte Osteuropas* 31, no. 3 (1981): 329–30. I want to thank Professor LeDonne for providing me with a copy of this article.
32. S. M. Troitskii, *Finansovaia politika russkogo absoliutizma v XVIII veke* (Moscow, 1966), p. 230.
33. John P. LeDonne, *Ruling Russia: Politics and Administration in the Age of Absolutism 1762–1796* (Princeton, N.J., 1984), pp. 278–80, 294, 303.
34. N. M. Korobkov, ed., *Fel'dmarshal Rumiantsev: Sbornik dokumentov i materialov* (Moscow, 1947), p. 71.
35. Colonel Maslovskii, *Russkaia armiia v semiletniuiu voinu, Vypusk I: Pokhod Apraksina v Vostochnuiu Prussiiu* (Moscow, 1886), p. 8; F. von Stein, *Geschichte des Russischen Heeres von Ursprunge desselben bis zur Thronbesteigung des Kaisers Nikolai I Pawlowitsch* (Hannover, 1885), p. 127.
36. Maslovskii, *Russkaia armiia,* p. 131.
37. See A. Kochubinskii, *Graf Andrei Ivanovich Osterman i razdel Turtsii: Iz istorii vostochnago voprosa—Voina piati let (1735–1739)* (Odessa, 1899), p. 159; *Arkhiv Gosudarstvennago Soveta,* 1, pt. 1: 2, 497.
38. S. M. Troitskii, *Russkii absoliutizm i dvorianstvo v XVIII v. Formirovanie biurokratii* (Moscow, 1974), pp. 172–73.
39. David L. Ransel, *The Politics of Catherinian Russia: The Panin Party* (New Haven, 1975), p. 38.
40. *Arkhiv Gosudarstvennago Soveta,* 1, pt. 1: 461.
41. While only in his twenties, Potemkin lost his left eye owing to the incompetence of a physician called in to attend him. See George Soloveytchik, *Potemkin* (New York, 1947), p. 51.
42. [N. P. Mikhnevich], *Stoletie voennago ministerstva,* vol. IV, *Glavnyi shtab: Istoricheskii ocherk* (St. Petersburg, 1902), p. 193.
43. Korobkov, *Fel'dmarshal Rumiantsev,* p. 69.
44. P. Dirin, *Istoriia Leib Gvardii Semenovskago polka,* 1 (St. Petersburg, 1883): 261.
45. F. Ia. Polianskii, ed., *Istoriia narodnogo khoziaistva SSSR: Kurs lektsii* (Moscow, 1960), p. 147.
46. On Eighteenth-Century agriculture generally, see Michael Confino, *Domaines et Seigneurs en Russie vers la Fin du XVIIIe Siècle* (Paris, 1963), pp. 113– 30, and Arcadius Kahan, *The Plow, the Hammer and the Knout: An Economic History of Eighteenth Century Russia* (Chicago, 1985), pp. 13, 45–49.
47. Jerome Blum, *Lord and Peasant in Russia from the Ninth to the Nineteenth Century* (Princeton, N.J., 1961), pp. 328–29; Arcadius Kahan, "Natural Calamities and Their Effect upon the Food Supply in Russia (An Introduction to a Catologue)," *Jahrbücher für Geschichte Osteuropas,* neue folge, 16, no. 4 (September 1968): pp. 372–73.

48. E. V. Anisimov, *Podatnaia reforma Petra I* (Leningrad, 1982), pp. 282–83; M. M. Bogoslovskii, *Istoriia Rossii XVIII veka 1725–1796* (Moscow, 1915), p. 21.

49. Walther Mediger, *Moskaus Weg nach Europa: Der Aufsteig Russlands zum Europäischen Machtstaat im Zeitalter Friedrich des Grossen* (Braunschweig, 1952), pp. 143–44.

50. Troitskii, *Finansovaia politika* (note 32 above), p. 213.

51. James F. Brennan, *Enlightened Despotism in Russia: The Reign of Elisabeth 1741–1762* (New York, 1987), p. 147.

52. *Ibid.*, pp. 150–56, 247.

53. Troitskii, *Finansovaia politika*, pp. 230–31.

54. John T. Alexander, *Autocratic Politics in a National Crisis* (Bloomington, Ind., 1969), pp. 14–15.

55. *Ibid.*, p. 15; Troitskii, *Finansovaia politika*, pp. 248–49.

56. *Arkhiv Gosudarstvennago Soveta*, 1, pt. 2: 72.

57. N. Iu. Dubrovin, ed., *Sbornik voenno-istoricheskikh materialov* 3 (St. Petersburg, 1893): 21.

58. Maslovskii, *Russkaia armiia*, p. 30.

59. Manstein, *Contemporary Memoirs*, p. 55.

60. Maslovskii, *Russkaia armiia*, p. 32.

61. R. C. Anderson, *Naval Wars in the Baltic 1522–1850* (London, 1910), p. 207; B. H. Sumner, *Peter the Great and the Emergence of Russia* (New York, 1962), p. 181; Maslovskii, *Russkaia armiia*, p. 8.

62. A. K. Il'enko, *Stoletie Voennago Ministerstva 1802–1902: Glavnyi Shtab—Istoricheskii ocherk—Komplektovanie vooruzhennykh sil v Rossii do 1802 g.*, part 1, book 1, section 1 (St. Petersburg, 1902), p. 110.

63. P. K. Fortunatov, ed., *Materialy po istorii russkoi armii: P. A. Rumiantsev—Dokumenty*, vol. 1, *1756–63* (Moscow, 1953), p. 212.

64. Baiov, *Russkaia armiia*, pp. 70–71.

65. Maslovskii, *Russkaia armiia*, p. 92.

66. *Arkhiv Gosudarstvennago Soveta*, 1, pt. 2: 76.

67. Mediger, *Moskaus Weg nach Europa*, p. 327.

68. Troitskii, *Finansovaia politika*, p. 247. The text of the memorandum is available in *Arkhiv Kniazia Vorontsova*, 4 (Moscow, 1872): 174–78: see particularly p. 176.

69. David M. Griffiths, "The Rise and Fall of the Northern System: Court Politics in the First Half of Catherine II's Reign," *Canadian Slavic Studies*, 4, no. 3 (Fall 1970): 551.

70. Cited in Walter J. Gleason, *Moral Idealists, Bureaucracy, and Catherine the Great* (New Brunswick, N.J., 1981), p. 109.

71. Anisimov, *Podatnaia reforma*, p. 284; Troitskii, *Finansovaia politika*, pp. 227–28.

72. See Duffy, *Russia's Military Way*, p. 57, and Oliva, *Misalliance*, p. 4.

73. [A. Turgenev], *La Cour de la Russie il y a Cent Ans 1725–1783: Extraits des Dépêches des Ambassadeurs Anglais et Français* (Berlin, 1858), pp. 130–33; Herbert Kaplan, *Russia and the Outbreak of the Seven Years War* (Berkeley, Calif., 1968), p. 16.

74. On the fiscal situation in 1756, see the report of P. I. Shuvalov in "Protokoly

Konferentsii pri Vysochaishem dvore," vol. 1, 14 March 1756–13 March 1757, *Sbornik Imperatorskago Russkago Istoricheskago Obshchestva*, 136 (St. Petersburg: 1912): 514–20; Shuvalov wrote that "the war is beginning and there is no capital," p. 514.

75. [Mikhnevich], *Stoletie*, 4: 191. This aborted proposal, of course, foreshadowed the famous military colonies of Alexander I.

76. Korobkov, *Fel'dmarshal Rumiantsev*, p. 78; also Iu. R. Klokman, *Fel'dmarshal Rumiantsev v period Russko-Turetskoi voiny 1768–1774 gg.* (Moscow, 1951), pp. 191–92.

77. See David R. Jones, "The Soviet Defense Burden Through the Prism of History," in C. Jacobson, ed., *The Soviet Defense Enigma: Estimating Costs and Burdens* (Oxford, 1987), p. 156; Kahan, *The Plow*, p. 337

78. The savagery of East European war in the eighteenth century was noted by Albert Sorel in 1898. See Albert Sorel, *L'Europe et la Revolution française* (Paris, 1898), 1: see also Anderson, *Eastern Question*, pp. 134–35.

79. Richardson, *Anecdotes*, p. 72.

80. Bogdanovich, *Pokhody Rumiantseva*, pp. 161–62; See also John L. H. Keep, *Soldiers of the Tsar: Army and Society in Russia, 1462–1874* (London, 1985), p. 215, for a discussion of the circumstances in which Russian troops were prone to show this sort of cruelty.

81. Anisimov, *Rossii v seredine*, p. 119. Slightly different casualty figures can be found in Duffy, *Russia's Military Way*, p. 90; Christopher Duffy, *The Army of Frederick the Great* (London, 1974), p. 90; and G. G. Frumenkov, "Rossiia i semiletniaia voina," *Voprosy Istorii*, 1971, no. 9, p. 114. As perhaps befits a nationalistic-minded Soviet scholar, Frumenkov interprets Zorndorf as a Russian victory. Duffy, with more justice, characterizes it as "an indecisive slaughter."

82. See [Ernst Münnich], *Rossiia i russkii dvor v pervoi polovine XVIII veka: Zapiski i zamechaniia gr. Ernsta Minikha* (St. Petersburg, 1891), p. 50.

83. See Baiov, *Russkaia armiia*, p. 59.

84. For a fascinating account of the consequences of climate and terrain for campaigns on the periphery of Russia, see the 1951 report prepared for the U.S. Army by a group of German generals: *Terrain Factors in the Russian Campaign* (Washington, D.C.: CMH Pub. 104-5, 1986).

85. [Münnich], *Rossiia i russkii dvor*, p. 74.

86. Fortunatov, *Materialy*, p. 45.

87. Bogdanovich, *Pokhody Rumiantseva*, p. 57.

88. Klokman, *Fel'dmarshal Rumiantsev*, p. 158.

89. Count A. Lanzheron, "Russkaia armiia v god smerti Ekateriny II," pt. 1, *Russkaia starina*, 83 (March 1895): 161.

90. Sergei M. Soloviev, *History of Russia*, vol. 35, *The Rule of Empress Anna*, trans. and ed. Richard Hantula (Gulf Breeze, Fla, 1982), p. 51.

91. A Russian officer who served as ADC to General Gustav Biron corroborated Paradies's depiction of the Russian supply column: "We marched very slowly: frequently something broke down in the baggage train, or there was some minor damage to the harness with the result that the entire army had to stop. Consequently it wasn't possible to advance 500 paces

without pausing for half an hour or more. Thus even during the shortest marches it was impossible to arrive at camp before four or five o'clock in the evening; in addition, the soldier was debilitated by the sunstroke and bad food, while the animals, being in harness all day, were exhausted and suffered no less." A. Kochubinskii, *Graf Andrei Ivanovich Osterman i razdel Turtsii: Iz istorii vostochnago voprosa, voina piati let (1735–1739)* (Odessa, 1899), pp. 159–60.

92. Frumenkov, "Rossiia i semiletniaia voina", p. 112.

93. *Arkhiv Kniazia Vorontsova, Kniga sed'maia: Bumagi gosudarstvennago kantslera grafa Mikhaila Larionovicha Vorontsova* (Moscow, 1875), p. 442.

94. Stein, *Geschichte*, p. 110. Stein's fascination with organizational statutes and administrative minutiae often palls, but he reveals a keen understanding of the importance of logistics.

95. Baiov, *Russkaia armiia*, pp. 57–58.

96. Anisimov, *Rossiia v seredine*, p. 125.

97. Manstein, *Contemporary Memoirs*, pp. 113–16.

98. [Münnich], *Rossiia i russkii dvor*, p. 61.

99. Solov'ev, *Rule of Empress Anna*, p. 33.

100. Brennan, *Enlightened Despotism*, p. 244, is *very* wide of the mark when he derisively writes of Apraksin's "irrational obsession with a shortage of forage."

101. Fortunatov, *Materialy*, p. 161.

102. Frumenkov, "Rossiia i semiletniaia voina," p. 113; for a different view of Gross Jägersdorf, emphasizing the muddled character of this battle, see Duffy, *Russia's Military Way*, p. 78–81.

103. Fortunatov, *Materialy*, p. 261.

104. *Arkhiv Gosudarstvennago Soveta*, 1, pt. 2: 78.

105. In a gloomy note about the prognosis for the 1770 campaign against Turkey, Count Zakhar Chernyshev cast a glance back at Münnich's Turkish war in which, he said, "every year entirely ruined armies returned to our frontiers," Dubrovin, *Sbornik*, p. 322.

106. Baiov, *Russkaia armiia*, p. 237.

107. Manstein, *Contemporary Memoirs*, pp. 170–71. Manstein also notes: "In the same manner are their bands chosen; so that one may easily judge of the quality of their military music." Manstein was, of course, writing about the 1730s. In fairness I should add that later in the century several noted commanders made honest and laudable efforts to upgrade the medical services.

108. *Ibid.*, p. 59; on this occupation, see also Troitskii, *Finansovaia politika*, p. 228.

109. Manstein, *Contemporary Memoirs*, p. 133.

110. [Münnich], *Rossiia i russkii dvor*, "Zamechanie," p. 151.

111. Manstein, *Contemporary Memoirs*, p. 133,

112. Baiov, *Russkaia armiia*, p. 3.

113. Duffy, *Russia's Military Way*, p. 53.

114. Manstein, *Contemporary Memoirs*, p. 246; see also B. Ts. Urlanis, *Voiny i narodnonaselenie Evropy* (Moscow, 1960), p. 55.

115. Anisimov, *Rossiia v seredine*, p. 115.

116. Klokman, *Fel'dmarshal Rumiantsev*, p. 114.

117. Carl von Clausewitz, *On War*, Michael Howard and Peter Paret, ed. and trans. (Princeton, N.J., 1976), pp. 119–21.

118. David Chandler, *Marlborough as Military Commander* (New York, 1973), p. 130.

119. J. Colin, *L'Education Militaire de Napoleon* (Paris, 1901), pp. 70–72; Thomas M. Barker, *The Military Intellectual and Battle: Raimondo Montecuccoli and the Thirty Years War* (Albany, N.Y., 1975), pp. 61–63.

120. Baiov, *Russkaia armiia*, pp. 48–50.

121. Maslovskii, *Russkaia armiia*, pp. 14–15.

122. V. A. Aleksandrov, *Sel'skaia obshchina v Rossii (xviii–nachalo xix v.)* (Moscow, 1976), pp. 245, 273–76. Aleksandrov, an outstanding Soviet ethnographer, has produced in this study the best assessment to date of the impact of military conscription on the village in the eighteenth century.

123. See Keep, *Soldiers of the Tsar*, pp. 144–66, for a meticulous and judicious assessment of the "informality and arbitrariness" of the recruitment system.

124. A. N. Petrov, *Vtoraia turetskaia voina v tsarstvovanie Imperatritsy Ekateriny II 1787–1791*, vol. 1, *1787–1789* (St. Petersburg, 1880), p. 89.

125. Keep, *Soldiers of the Tsar*, p. 222.

126. *Arkhiv Kniazia Vorontsova*, 3 (Moscow, 1871): 521.

127. This procedure was *required* by Saltykov's recruiting statute of 1757. See Il'enko, *Stoletie*, p. 109.

128. Petrov, *Vtoraia turetskaia voina*, p. 90. He added, however, that the officers often squandered the money they had received.

129. For two examples of this style of criticism see [Mikhnevich], *Stoletie*, p. 153 (where Münnich's Prussian-inspired drill of 1731 is attacked), and A. I. Gippius, *Stoletie voennago ministerstva: Glavnyi shtab—Istoricheskii ocherk: Obrazovanie (obuchenie)voisk*, pt. 1, book 2, section 3 (St. Petersburg, 1903), pp. 42–43, 50, 60–61, 73, for similar comments.

130. Maslovskii, *Russkaia armiia*, p. 70.

131. These details are derived from the memoirs of Count Langeron, a French officer who served for years as a regimental commander in the late-eighteenth-century Russian army. See Graf A. Lanzheron, "Russkaia armiia v god smerti Ekateriny II," pt. 2, *Russkaia starina*, 83 (March, 1895): 151–52.

132. Mediger, *Moskaus Weg nach Europa*, pp. 325–26.

133. See William C. Fuller, Jr., *Civil-Military Conflict in Imperial Russia, 1881–1914* (Princeton, N.J., 1985), Ch. 3, 5, and 8.

134. However, as John Keep suggests, it would be a mistake to see the guards chiefly as praetorians. "The Secret Chancellery, The Guards and the Dynastic Crisis of 1740–41," *Forschungen zur Osteuropäischen Geschichte* (Berlin, 1978), 25: 178.

135. On this topic generally, see D. A. Korsakov, *Votsarenie Imperatritsy Anny Iovannovny* (Kazan, 1880), especially pp. 240–78.

136. See Tibor Szamuely, *The Russian Tradition* (London, 1974), p. 128.

137. Brennan, *Enlightened Despotism*, p. 29.

138. This was the view of Britain's Ambassador to St. Petersburg; see [Turgenev], *La Cour*, p. 209.

139. Ransel, *The Politics of Catherinian Russia*, p. 1.

140. A representative example of this interpretation can be found in Paul Dukes, *The Making of Russian Absolutism, 1613–1801* (London, 1982), pp. 117–18. In another work, *Catherine the Great and the Russian Nobility* (Cambridge, 1967), Professor Dukes adopts the concept of dyarchy to explain Catherine's reign. The Empress's freedom of manuever was constrained by her need to "appease" the nobility of her realm. See pp. 249–51.

141. Frumenkov, "Rossiia i semiletniaia voina," pp. 107–8.

142. See Kaplan, *Russia and the Outbreak of the Seven Years War*, pp. 47–48, for an acid critique of the Konferentsiia. In Kaplan's words, this institution dealt with "the large and the small, the important and the incidental . . . the principles of alliances and the salaries of diplomats . . . the export policy of the whole Empire and the complaints of individual merchants . . . the entire financial structure of the country and funds for Kalmyk soldiers' caftans."

143. Maslovskii, *Russkaia armiia*, pp. 165–66; Anisimov (relying on Maslovskii), *Rossiia v seredine*, p. 111; The text of the Instruction can be found in *Arkhiv Kniazia Vorontsova*, 3 (Moscow, 1871): pp. 508–29. For a good example of these contradictions, see especially p. 525.

144. [Mikhnevich], *Stoletie*, pp. 173–74, offers another criticism of the baleful impact of the Konferentsiia on Russian strategy.

145. Madariaga, *Russia in Age of Catherine the Great*, p. 206.

146. Ransel, *Politics of Catherinian Russia*, pp. 134, 197

147. [Münnich], *Rossiia i russkii dvor*, p. 56.

148. On Vorontsov's relation to Bestuzhev generally, see Oliva, *Misalliance*, p. 6; for this particular episode, see Kaplan, *Russia and the Outbreak*, pp. 41–44.

149. [Turgenev], *La cour*, p. 119.

150. See the report of the British Ambassador, Sir Charles Hanbury-Williams, from September 28, 1758, in *ibid.*, p. 149

151. Frumenkov, "Rossiia i semiletniaia voina," p. 112–13; Anisimov, *Rossiia v seredine*, p. 112.

152. Oliva, *Misalliance*, p. 16.

153. *Arkhiv Kniazia Vorontsova*, 12 (Moscow, 1877): 75, for a letter of P. V. Zavadovskii to S. R. Vorontsov (January 27, 1792) condemning the ascendancy of Zubov: "Not one of the former favorites, including even the all-powerful Prince Potemkin, ever had such a wide sphere" of activity.

154. Dukes, *Making of Russian Absolutism*, p. 118.

155. Bogoslovskii, *Istoriia Rossii*, p. 132; Stein, *Geschichte*, p. 129. Brennan, *Enlightened Despotism*, p. 236, provides a reason for this hatred, however incredible and ridiculous. Russo-Prussian relations, he says, began to fall apart in 1746, when Frederick II rejected Elizabeth's demand for the return of the "giant soldiers" lent to Berlin by Peter I and Anna.

156. Michael T. Florinsky, *Russia: A History and an Interpretation* (New York, 1967), 1: 479–80.

157. [Turgenev], *La Cour,* p. 312.

158. Kaplan, *First Partition of Poland,* p. 189.

159. Anisimov, *Rossiia v seredine,* p. 113.

160. According to an eyewitness to these events; see [Andrei Bolotov], *Zhizn' i prikliucheniia Andreia Bolotova: Opisannye samim im dlia svoikh potomkov,* ed. A. V. Lunacharskii, 2 (Moscow and Leningrad, 1931; reprint: Cambridge, Mass., 1973): 30–31.

4. Russian Imperialism and Military Power in the 18th Century

1. E. I. Druzhinina, *Kiuchuk-Kainardzhiiskii mir 1774 goda* (Moscow, 1955), presents a multicausal explanation of Russian imperialism, but also places great stress on the quest for markets. See pp. 54–65. R. J. Kerner's *The Urge to the Sea* (Berkeley, Calif., 1942), which seeks to explain Russia's expansion in terms of river systems, portages, and trade routes, at least in part implicitly adopts an economic explanation.

2. Alton S. Donnelly, *The Russian Conquest of Bashkiria 1552–1740: A Case Study in Imperialism* (New Haven, 1968), pp. 60–63, 170–71.

3. Quoted in Herbert Kaplan, *Russia and the Outbreak of the Seven Years War* (Berkeley, Calif., 1968), p. 55.

4. Marc Raeff, "In the Imperial Manner," in Marc Raeff, ed., *Catherine the Great: A Profile* (New York, 1972), p. 199. See also *Vysochaishiia sobstvennoruchnyia pis'ma i poveleniia blazhenoi i vechnoi slavy dostoinoi pamiati Gosudaryni Imperatritsy Ekateriny Velikiia k pokoinomu generalu Petru Dmitrievichu Erapkinu i vsepoddanneishiia ego doneseniia v trekh otdeleniiakh sobrannyiia i s Vysochaishago dozvoleniia v perachi izdanniia kollezhskim sovetnikom Iakovom Rostom* (Moscow, 1808), pp. 246–47, 258–59. I am indebted to Professor Robert Jones for this reference.

5. Joseph Schumpeter, *Imperialism and Social Classes* (London, 1951), p. 59, writes of the reign of Louis XIV that "the belligerence and war policy of the autocratic state are explained from the necessities of its social structure rather than from the immediate advantages to be derived from conquest." In other words, Schumpeter is arguing that Louis XIV engaged in expansionist wars neither to enhance his own *gloire* nor to further a geopolitical strategy. Rather, he waged war in order to appease the ruling class of France—its military nobility. This theory is also akin to the not entirely tongue-in-cheek formulation that the purpose of British rule in India was to "provide outdoor relief to the ruling classes."

6. John P. LeDonne, *Ruling Russia: Politics and Administration in the Age of Absolutism, 1762–1796* (Princeton, N.J., 1984), p. 82; also see p. 25.

7. The quoted phrases are from Paul Dukes, *The Making of Russian Absolutism 1613–1801* (London, 1982), pp. 117–18.

8. Raeff, "In the Imperial Manner," p. 198, explicitly warns against this style of interpreting Russian imperialism: "It is easy in restrospect to view these events [Russia's eighteenth-century expansion] as a working out of conscious designs; ideological tenets and consistantly purposeful actions. But

such a view is too much of a rationalization and it harbors the danger of anachronistic judgment."

9. David Griffiths, for example, sees the First Partition of Poland as the largely accidental outcome of a mushrooming sequence of Russian miscalculations. As he narrates it, (1) Stansislas Poniatowski wanted to implement political reforms in Poland; (2) Petersburg was willing to accept these (provided there existed a "reliable pro-Russian party in Warsaw") and told the Poles so; (3) Prussia, however, objected, causing Russia to renege on its promises; (4) this, in turn, caused the angry Poles to rise in insurrection; (5) Russia's attempt to suppress the uprising with military force alarmed the Ottomans into declaring war; (6) thus leading to Russian victories and the eventual dismemberment of the Polish state to keep Austria and Prussia contented. David M. Griffiths, "The Rise and Fall of the Northern System: Court Politics in the First Half of Catharine II's Reign," *Canadian Slavic Studies,* 4, no. 3 (Fall 1970): 554–55.

10. See John Gallagher and Ronald Robinson, "The Imperialism of Free Trade," *The Economic History Review,* 2d ser., VI, no. 1 (1954): p. 3.

11. Thomas Garrigue Masaryk, *The Spirit of Russia,* trans. Eden Cedar and Paul Cedar (London, 1968), 1: 41.

12. For discussion and criticism of this style of interpretation, see Adam Ulam, "Nationalism, Panslavism, Communism," in Ivo J. Lederer, ed., *Russian Foreign Policy: Essays in Historical Perspective* (New Haven, 1962), pp. 39–41.

13. See Theodore von Laue, "Problems of Modernization", in Lederer, *op. cit.,* p. 79.

14. *Sbornik Imperatorskago Russkago Istoricheskago Obshchestva,* 51 (St. Petersburg, 1880): 9.

15. Robert Howard Lord, *The Second Partition of Poland* (Cambridge, Mass., 1915), p. 500.

16. The characterization of Potemkin's party is LeDonne's. See LeDonne, *Ruling Russia,* p. 62.

17. See Elizabeth L. Eisenstein, "Who Intervened in 1789?" in Ralph W. Greenlaw, ed., *The Social Origins of the French Revolution: The Debate on the Role of the Middle Classes* (Lexington, Mass., 1975), p. 203.

18. LeDonne, *Ruling Russia,* pp. 24, 26, 59.

19. *SIRIO,* 19 (St. Petersburg, 1876): 288 (Robert Gunning to the Earl of Suffolk, July 13[24], 1772).

20. N. Iu. Dubrovin, ed., *Sbornik voenno-istoricheskikh materialov* (St. Petersburg, 1893), pp. 305–9, 322–28; *SIRIO,* 51: 9–11; Isabel de Madariaga, *Russia in the Age of Catherine the Great* (New Haven, 1981), p. 189.

21. LeDonne, *Ruling Russia,* pp. 64, 65. For Bezborodko's biography (and his relationship with Rumiantsev), see *Russkii biograficheskii slovar',* 2 (St. Petersburg, 1900): 634–39.

22. See Robert E. Jones, "Opposition to War and Expansion in Late Eighteenth Century Russia," *Jahrbücher für Geschichte Osteuropas,* 32 (1984) no. 1: 38–41.

23. *Arkhiv Gosudarstvennago Soveta,* 1, pt. 1, *1768–96 gg.* (St. Petersburg, 1869): 60.

24. *Ibid.*, pp. 143–44 (Meeting of January 24, 1774).

25. Robert E. Jones, *The Emancipation of the Russian Nobility 1762–1785* (Princeton, N.J., 1973), offers a strong critique of the concept of "dyarchy" under Catherine. His chief contention is that the state emancipated the nobility not as the price of keeping a usurping sovereign in place, but rather in order to use the local nobility to assist in the task of keeping order in provincial Russia.

26. The quotation is from David Ransel, *The Politics of Catherinian Russia: The Panin Party* (New Haven, 1975), pp. 100–101.

27. Ransel himself admits that Catherine used the Panins; see *ibid.*, p. 139.

28. See Kaplan, *Russia and the Outbreak*, pp. 50–54.

29. None was so mistaken as the British Ambassador, Hanbury-Williams, who reported to London in August 1755: "In a word all that has been given up until now is to buy the support of Russian troops, but this this last sum, if given, will buy the Empress." [A. Turgenev], *La Cour de la Russie il y a Cent Aus 1725–1783: Extraits des Dépêches des Ambassadeurs Anglais et Français* (Berlin, 1858), p. 129. Unfortunately, the Empress was not for sale. For other examples of the limits of foreign influence on Russia's external policies, see E. V. Anisimov, *Rossiia v seredine XVIII veka: Bor'ba za nasledie Petra* (Moscow, 1986), pp. 87, 97–98, and Walther Mediger, *Moskaus Weg nach Europa: Der Aufsteig Russlands zum Europäischen Machstaat im Zeitalter Friedrich des Grossen* (Braunschweig, 1952), p. 298.

30. Walter J. Gleason, *Moral Idealists, Bureaucracy, and Catherine the Great* (New Brunswick, N.J., 1981), pp. 161–62; See also Griffiths, "Rise and Fall of Northern System", p. 568: "The question inevitably arises if the various groupings with their respective systems gave impetus to the empress and her foreign policy, or if the groupings were simply reflections of the empress's policies and acted as her agents. It would seem that the latter was true."

31. *Arkhiv Gosudarstvennago Soveta*, 1, pt. 1: 45. With regard to the Crimea, the Counsel noted the desirability of a Crimean Khanate independent of Turkish suzereinty. Such a state would have to accept Russian garrisons and would have to cede at least one harbor to Russia. But Catherine was not satisfied with this and added that "it is no less essential for us to have the passage from the Sea of Azov into the Black Sea in our hands."

32. Carl von Clausewitz, *On War*, Michael Howard and Peter Paret, ed. and trans. (Princeton, N.J., 1976), pp. 585–86.

33. *Entia non sunt multiplicanda*, that is, the concept that we may dispense with the unnecessary facts or, put another way, the simpler the explanation, the more likely it is to be correct.

34. Ransel, *Politics of Catherinian Russia*, pp. 115–16.

35. See L. Jay Oliva, *Misalliance: A Study of French Policy in Russia During the Seven Years War* (New York, 1964), pp. 169, 179.

36. Bestuzhev also believed that Osterman's policies were the authentic continuation of those of Peter the Great. See Anisimov, *Rossiia v seredine*, p. 98; also Michael T. Florinsky, *Russia: A History and An Interpretation*, 1 (New York, 1953): 466–67.

37. A point also made by Zakhar Chernyshev in the secret memorandum of 1763 to which we have already referred: *SIRIO*, 51: 9.

38. See Madariaga, *Russia in Age of Catherine the Great*, p. 192; and Michael F. Metcalf, *Russia, England and Swedish Party Politics 1762–1766* (Totowa, N.J., 1977), pp. 38–39. Of course, Panin could not know that Russia was on the cusp of a demographic explosion that would increase its population nearly fourfold between 1750 and 1850. See Richard Pipes, *Russia Under the Old Regime* (New York, 1974), p. 13.

39. Mediger, *Moskaus Weg Nach Europa*, p. 597.

40. On Russia's justifiable fears of possible Prussian encroachment into the Baltic, see G. G. Frumenkov, "Rossiia i semiletniaia voina," *Voprosy Istorii*, 1971, pp. 108–9; Kaplan, *Russia and the Outbreak*, pp. 3–4; Mediger, *Moskaus Weg Nach Europa*, pp. 224–25. Indeed, one of the chief points that Mediger develops in this brilliant (if all too little known) book is that Russia's clash with Prussia was not the result of the machinations of Petersburg courtiers, but rather was a consequence of Russia's pursuit of her own national interests. See in particular, p. 597.

41. Colonel Maslovskii, *Russkaia armiia v semiletniuiu voinu, Vypusk I: Pokhod Apraksina v Vostochnuiu Prussiiu* (Moscow, 1886), p. 118, for a description of Russia's outrage at the Prussian violation of the treaty of Breslau (1744).

42. *Arkhiv Kniazia Vorontsova*, 2 (Moscow, 1871): 19.

43. The first quotation is from *ibid.;* the second is from Anisimov, *Rossiia v seredine*, p. 99.

44. *Arkhiv Kniazia Vorontsova*, 2: 20.

45. Frumenkov, "Rossiia i semiletniaia voina," p. 108.

46. David L. Ransel, "The 'Memoirs' of Count Münnich," *Slavic Review*, 30, no. 4 (December 1971): 849–50.

47. Donnelly, *Russian Conquest of Bashkiria*, pp. 52–53, 170.

48. Alan W. Fisher, *The Russian Annexation of the Crimea 1772–1783* (Cambridge, Eng., 1970), p. 36.

49. Maslovskii, *Russkaia armiia*, p. 132.

50. A point first made by B. H. Sumner. See Norman Itzkowitz and Max Mote, *Mubadele: An Ottoman–Russian Exchange of Ambassadors* (Chicago, 1970), p. 36. See also Raeff, "Imperial Manner," p. 201, for an argument about how Russia's quest for security in the south was the motive of both of Catherine the Great's wars with Turkey.

51. A. Kochubinskii, *Graf Andrei Ivanovich Osterman i razdel Turtsii: Iz istorii vostochnago voprosa—Voina piati let* (Odessa, 1899), pp. 211–12, 217.

52. V. V. Pruntsov, *Polkovodets P.A. Rumiantsev* (Moscow, 1946), pp. 14–15.

53. *Arkhiv Gosudarstvennago Soveta*, 1, pt. 1: 501.

54. Francis Ley, *Le Maréchal Münnich et la Russie au XVIIIe siècle* (Paris, 1959), p. 70.

55. Oliva, *Misalliance*, p. 179.

56. *SIRIO*, 51: 9.

57. *Arkhiv Gosudarstvennago Soveta*, 1, pt. 2: 907.

58. Madariaga, *Russia in Age of Catherine the Great*, pp. 200–203, 430–32, 445–46. The Russian intervention of 1792 was directed against the absolutist

constitution of May 1791. In a remarkable foreshadowing of language that would be heard from future generations of Soviet diplomats, Russia's ambassador to Warsaw explained that "the incursion of the forces of her majesty is not war, but fraternal assistance, in a neighborly fashion, for the reestablishment of liberty and legal rule." See Nikolai Kostomarov, *Poslednie gody Rechi-Pospolitoi* (St. Petersburg, 1886), 2: 69.

59. See for example, the letter of Count P. V. Zavadovskii to S. R. Vorontsov (January 27, 1792) in *Arkhiv Kniazia Vorontsova,* 12 (Moscow, 1877): 77.

60. A very capable and meticulous scholar, Robert Howard Lord, who conducted exhaustive research in the archives of Vienna, Berlin, and St. Petersburg prior to World War I, concluded that the Second Partition was *not* forced on a reluctant Catherine the Great by Prussia; rather, it was "the consummation of the Empress' secret plans and ambitions." See Lord, *Second Partition of Poland,* pp. xvi, 498–99.

61. See the perhaps overly schematic but still stimulating discussion of the problem of strategic effectivness by Alan R. Millet, Williamson Murray, and Kenneth H. Watman, "The Effectiveness of Military Organizations," in Allan R. Millet and Williamson Murray, eds., *Military Effectiveness,* vol. 1, *The First World War* (Boston, 1988), pp. 2–21.

62. See N. P. Eroshkin, *Ocherki istorii gosudarstvennykh uchrezhdenii dorevoliutsionnoi Rossii* (Moscow, 1960), pp. 107–8.

63. In an interesting investigation of the socio-economic profile of Russia's mid-century diplomats, S. M. Troitskii discovered a very large representation among them of men from the lower ranks of society, leading him to conclude that the doors to a diplomatic career were increasingly opening to men of ability rather than birth alone. See S. M. Troitskii, "Russkie diplomaty v seredine XVIII v.," in V. T. Pashuto, ed., *Feodal'naia Rossiia v vsemirno-istoricheskom protsesse* (Moscow, 1972), pp. 398–406.

64. For an example, see A. Baiov, *Russkaia armiia v tsarstvovanie Anny Ivanovny: Voina Rossii s Turtsiei v 1736–1739 gg., Kampaniia 1739* (St. Petersburg, 1906), pp. 122–23.

65. See for example, *Arkhiv Kniazia Vorontsova,* 3: 508–29.

66. P. K. Fortunatov, *Materialy po istorii russkoi armii: P. A. Rumiantsev—Dokumenty,* vol. 1, *1756–63* (Moscow, 1953), p. 523.

67. Christopher Duffy, *Russia's Military Way to the West: Origins and Nature of Russian Military Power, 1700–1800* (London, 1981), p. 93.

68. See, for example, the rescript to A. B. Buturlin of September 28, 1760, in *Arkhiv Kniazia Vorontsova,* 7 (Moscow, 1875): 441–43.

69. *Arkhiv Gosudarstvennago Soveta,* 1, pt. 1: 5–7.

70. *Ibid.,* pp. 8–10, 462, 497.

71. Baiov, *Russkaia armiia,* p. 1.

72. G. A. Nekrasov, *Rol' Rossii v evropeiskoi mezhdunarodnoi politike 1725–1739 gg.* (Moscow, 1976), p. 273.

73. See Gleason, *Moral Idealists,* p. 162, for Nikita Panin's assessment of the ideas of "the madman" Orlov in this regard.

74. Raeff, "Imperial Manner", p. 201, argues convincingly that the Greek Proj-

ect was actually a species of anti-Turkish propaganda; by contrast, Madariaga, *Russia in Age of Catherine the Great*, pp. 381 ff., seems to assume that the project was a driving force in Russian foreign policy.

75. See Stanford J. Shaw, *Between Old and New: The Ottoman Empire Under Sultan Selim III 1789–1807* (Cambridge, Mass., 1971), p. 21.
76. Ley, *Le Maréchal Münnich*, p. 151.
77. Christopher Hermann von Manstein, *Contemporary Memoirs of Russia from the Year 1727 to 1744*, ed. David Hume (London, 1856), p. 335.
78. Oliva, *Misalliance*, p. 137.
79. Oliva characterizes the Franco-Russian relationship during the Seven Years War in the following manner: "Russia . . . had taken advantage of French misfortunes to move into the French vacuum in Eastern Europe and to keep France tied to a continental war which served Russian purposes but destroyed France." *Ibid.*, p. 169.
80. See, for example, *Arkhiv Gosudarstvennago Soveta*, 1, pt. 1: 646–48, for a discussion of the ways in which Austria might be used by Russia as a shield in the event of a surprise Prussian attack.
81. Baiov, *Russkaia armiia*, p. 20; Nekrasov, *Rol' Rossii*, pp. 245–46, 265–66, 284. Indeed, Russia's policy in Sweden during this period is the central theme of Nekrasov's entire book.
82. Fortunatov, *Materialy*, p. 519.
83. See, for just one of many examples, *Arkhiv Gosudarstvennago Soveta*, 1, pt. 1: 137.
84. *Ibid.* pp. 142–43.
85. *Ibid.*, p. 647 (meetings of December 14–16, 1788).
86. *Ibid.*, p. 648. Joseph II's correspondence with Catherine the Great reveals that he was himself at this time terrified at the prospect of a Prussian alliance with Turkey. See Arneth, *Joseph II*, p. 331.
87. M. N. Bogdanovich, *Pokhody Rumiantseva, Potemkina i Suvorova v Turtsii* (St. Petersburg, 1852), pp. 206–7.
88. A. V. Suvorov, *Pis'ma*, ed. V. S. Lopatin, (Moscow, 1986), pp. 205, 608. But then, Suvorov never really understood the international political context of Russia's wars. Indeed, he rarely even made an effort to do so. As he wrote in November of 1790, "Je n'être point [sic] dans la politique des Cabinets."
89. *Arkhiv Gosudarstvennago Soveta*, 1, pt. 1: 859, 864–65, 874.
90. See for example, *Arkhiv Gosudarstvennago Soveta*, 1, pt. 1: 559, for the Council's concern about the effect that Polish "stubbornness" was having on Russian grain requisitions during the Second Turkish War.
91. *Ibid.*, 1, pt. 1: 7.
92. Herbert Kaplan, *The First Partition of Poland* (New York, 1962), pp. 131–41.
93. It is usually argued that Austria's unilateral incorporation of Spitz into the kingdom of Hungary in the winter of 1770 paved the way for the First Partition. In Berlin, the King's brother, Prince Henry, was also a keen partisan of partition. See *Ibid.*, pp. 131, 136. Count Panin apparently initially considered relinquishing some of Russia's Turkish gains to stave off the partition, but eventually he, too, supported it. In any event, since the

Turkish war had discredited his northern system his influence was on the wane; he could no longer speak with authority about Russia's foreign policy. See Griffiths, "Rise and Fall", pp. 556–57; Ransel, *Politics of Catherinian Russia*, pp. 197 ff.

94. *Arkhiv Gosudarstvennago Soveta*, 1, pt. 1: 906–7.

95. See Madariaga, *Russia in Age of Catherine the Great*, pp. 434–36, 448–50; Lord, *Second Partition*, pp. 153 ff, 497–98; Kostomarov, *Poslednie gody*, vol. 1, pp. 303, 502, and vol. 2, pp. 11,15–16, 146, 631–632.

96. Galibert, a French officer in the service of the Polish Confederacy, wrote an extremely interesting account of the Russian siege of Cracow (February–April 1772) that gives us insight into the sort of fare the hungry defenders of fortresses came to relish. In his diary entry for the week of March 22 he notes his gratitude for the party the commandant of the fortress had recently given for his officers: The "commander gave us a lovely meal; after several plates of horse meat, he served us a warm patty, composed of a stewed cat, seven rooks and eighty sparrows." John Francis Gough, trans. *The Private Letters of Baron de Vioménil on Polish Affairs* (Jersey City, 1935), p. 218.

97. Bogdanovich, *Pokhody Rumiantseva* (note 87 above), p. 115.

98. Christopher Duffy, *The Army of Frederick the Great* (London, 1974), p. 128.

99. *Ibid.*, p. 128.

100. Anisimov, *Rossiia v seredine*, p. 132.

101. See Madariaga, *Russia in Age of Catherine the Great*, pp. 390, 394; Bogdanovich, *Pokhody Rumiantseva*, p. 10; A. N. Petrov, *Vtoraia turketskaia voina v tsarstvovanie Imperatritsy Ekateriny II 1787–1791*, vol. 1, *1787–1789*, p. 81.

102. Dubrovin *Sbornik*, p. 325.

103. Fisher, *Russian Annexation*, p. 32.

104. Bogdanovich, *Pokhody Rumiantseva*, pp. 7–8.

105. *Ibid*, p. 166.

106. Iu. R. Klokman, *Fel'dmarshal Rumiantsev v period Russko-Turetskoi voiny 1768–1774 gg.* (Moscow, 1951), p. 157.

107. Dubrovin, *Sbornik*, p. 322. In his "Opinion on the Forthcoming Campaign of 1770," Zakhar Chernyshev provided an accurate depiction of the Turkish enemy, who, he said, "has with him from 80,000 to 100,000 light cavalry, who does not enter into battle, but flees, and who can, by means of delays or the seizure of transport, reduce an opposing army to utter destruction."

108. A. Z. Myshlaevskii, ed., *Sbornik voenno-istoricheskikh materialov*, vol. XI, *Vsepoddanneishiia doneseniia Gr. Mininkha*, pt. II (St. Petersburg, 1899), p. 332.

109. Duffy, *Russia's Military Way*, p. 52.

110. Sergei M. Soloviev, *The History of Russia*, vol. 35, *The Rule of Empress Anna*, trans. and ed. Richard Hantula (Gulf Breeze, Fla., 1982), p. 29.

111. Münnich's letter in the original German is reproduced in Melchior Vischer, *Münnich, Feldherr, Ingenieur, Hochveräter* (Frankfurt-am-Main, 1938), p. 412.

112. Myshlaevskii, *Sbornik voenno-istoricheskikh materialov*, XI: 330.

113. Baiov, *Russkaia armiia,* p. 113.
114. Klokman, *Fel'dmarshal Rumiantsev,* pp. 86–87, 113, 129, 154, 157–158.
115. Petrov, *Vtoraia turketskaia voina,* 1: 81–82; vol 2, *1789–1791 gg.* (St. Petersburg, 1880), pp. 177–79, 181, 187, 189.
116. Philip Longworth, *The Art of Victory, The Life and Achievements of Generalissimo Suvorov 1729–1800* (London, 1965), pp. 184–89.
117. S. M. Troitskii, *Finansovaia politika Russkogo absoliutizma v XVIII veke* (Moscow, 1966), p. 215; F. Ia. Polianskii, *Istoriia narodnogo khoziaistvo SSSR: Kurs lektsii* (Moscow, 1960), p. 146.
118. Polianskii, *Istoriia narodnogo khoziastva,* p. 158.
119. See Arcadius Kahan, "Continuity in Economic Activity and Policy During the Post-Petrine Period," in Michael Cherniavsky, ed., *The Structure of Russian History* (New York, 1970), pp. 195, 203.
120. A. Romanovich-Slavatinskii, *Dvorianstvo v Rossii* (Kiev, 1870), pp. 213, 225–44; Jones, *Emancipation of the Russian Nobility,* pp. 282–83.
121. Polianskii, *Istoriia narodnogo khozhiastva,* p. 154.
122. *Ibid.,* p. 154.
123. See James F. Brennan, *Enlightened Despotism in Russia: The Reign of Elisabeth 1741–1762* (New York, 1987), p. 180 and Paul Dukes, *Catherine the Great and the Russian Nobility* (Cambridge, Eng., 1967), p. 239.
124. Troitskii, *Finansovaia politika,* p. 230; Brennan, *Enlightened Despotism,* pp. 148–50.
125. Polianskii, *Istoriia narodnogo khoziastva,* p. 160.
126. Troitskii, *Finansovaia politika,* p. 214; and Dukes, *Making of Russian Absolutism,* p. 168.
127. *Arkhiv Gosudarstvennago Soveta,* 1, pt. 2: 83–85. At issue was an investigation of privately held factories that produced cloth for the army's needs.
128. This resulted in large measure from the increasing complexity of the budget and the expansion in outlays for the support of the court, central, and local administration. Troitskii, *Finansovaia politika,* pp. 242–43.
129. For Münnich's biography see Ley, *Le Maréchal de Münnich,* and Vischer, *Münnich.*
130. For an example, see Klokman, *Fel'dmarshal Rumiantsev,* pp. 23–24.
131. See P. Dirin, *Istoriia Leib Gvardiia Semenovskago polka* (St. Petersburg, 1883), p. 260; [Ernst Münnich], *Rossiia i russkii dvor v pervoi polovine XVIII veka: Zapiski i zamerhaniia gr. Ernsta Minikha* (St. Petersburg, 1891), p. 29.
132. *Ibid.,* p. 52.
133. Nekrasov, *Rol' Rossii* (note 72 above), p. 295.
134. See Manstein, *Contemporary Memoirs,* p. 308. Münnich's colleague, the Irish General Lacy, shrewdly distanced himself from court intrigue. Awakened at bayonet point during the night of the coup of 1741 and asked to which party he belonged, he is said to have responded without hesitation: "To the ruling party." See Brennan, *Enlightened Despotism,* p. 31.
135. Der Prinz Eugen der Russen . . . Er war der wahre Held des russichen Reiches . . . der Bewahrer der staatlichen Macht." See Vischer, *Münnich,* p. 7.
136. See LeDonne, *Ruling Russia,* p. 309.

137. For details of Rumiantsev's biography see: Pruntsov, *Polkovodets P.A. Rumianstev,* pp. 3–18, and Fortunatov, *Materialy,* pp. vii–xviii.

138. Fortunatov, *Materialy,* is a good illustration: "Rumiantsev was an authentic innovator of Russian military art. He was a follower of the military school of Peter the Great; and he broke with the antiquated provisions of the regulations in issues of training the troops and conducting battle." P. xviii.

139. For Rumiantsev's interest in hygene, see *ibid.,* pp. 22–23, 116; also N. M. Korobkov, ed., *Fel'dmarshal Rumiantsev: Sbornik dokumentov i materialov* (Moscow, 1947), p. 77.

140. Suvorov was constantly falling down—tumbling, on various occasions, into the Vistula, from the back of his horse, and down the steps of monasteries, and so on. See Longworth, *Art of Victory,* pp. 51, 86.

141. For eye-popping details about the eccentricities of Suvorov, including his constant boozing during battle, see the memoirs of Langeron, who served under him: Count A. Lanzheron, "Russkaia armiia v god smerti Ekateriny II," pt. 1, *Russkaia starina,* 83 (March 1895): 156 ff.

142. See Suvorov, *Pis'ma,* pp. 253 ff (letter of July 1793 to Alexandre Karatshay, whose father, an Austrian cavalry commander, had served with Suvorov during the Second Turkish War).

143. Suvorov has been the subject of an enormous literature. Nineteenth-century Russia's future reforming War Minister D. A. Miliutin established his scholarly reputation with a six-volume treatise on the campaign of 1799, a campaign that also served Karl von Clausewitz as the subject for a book. For his life, in English, see Longworth, *Art of Victory.* In Russian, a laudatory popular biography that unconsciously provides insight into the meaning of the Suvorov cult is Oleg Mikhailov, *Suvorov* (Moscow, 1973). The most significant piece of recent scholarship is the superbly edited and annotated edition of Suvorov's letters that appeared in Moscow in 1986: Suvorov, *Pis'ma.*

144. Duffy, *Frederick the Great,* p. 91.

145. *Ibid.,* pp. 89–91; on the persistence of these practices, see Gunther Rothenburg, *The Art of Warfare in the Age of Napoleon* (Bloomington, Ind., 1978).

146. A. I. Gippius, *Stoletie Voennago Ministerstva: Glarnyi shtab—Istoricheskii ocherk: Obrazovanie (obuchenie) voisk* vol. I, bk, II, pt, III (St. Petersburg, 1903), pp. 42–49.

147. Pruntsov, *Polkovodets P.A. Rumiantsev,* p. 108.

148. Baiov, *Russkaia armiia,* p. 232; Manstein, *Contemporary Memoirs,* p. 252.

149. See Pruntsov, *Polkovodets P. A. Rumiantsev,* pp. 97–98; Klokman, *Fel'dmarshal Rumiantsev,* p. 169; [N. P. Mikhnevich], *Stoletie Voennago Ministerstva,* vol. IV, *Glavnyi shtab: Istoricheskii ocherk* (St. Petersburg, 1902), p. 175.

150. Suvorov, *Pis'ma,* pp. 139, 144.

151. Baiov, *Russkaia armiia,* p. 296–99.

152. Duffy, *Russia's Military Way,* pp. 69–72. The quotation is from page 72. The Shuvalov howitzer, with its oval barrel, was supposed to fire "a shower of deadly canister parallel with the ground at about the height of a man." p. 70. For other general remarks on improvements in the artillery

during the Seven Years War, see Anisimov, *Rossiia v seredine*, p. 121, and Frumenkov, "Rossiia i semiletniaiia voina," p. 115.

153. Klokman, *Fel'dmarshal Rumiantsev*, p. 101.
154. For one such assessment see Bogdanovich, *Pokhody Rumiantseva*, p. 99.
155. Petrov, *Vtoraia turetskaia voina*, p. 91. On eighteenth-century Russia's emphasis on artillery, see also Hew Strachan, *European Armies and the Conduct of War* (Boston, 1983), pp. 32–33.
156. See Manstein, *Contemporary Memoirs*, pp. 101–2. Manstein, who is largely favorable toward Münnich, nonetheless berates him for beginning his first campaign without having made a thorough reconnaissance of the theater of war.
157. [Ernst Münnich], *Rossiia i russkii dvor v porvoi polovine XVIII veka: Zapiski i zamechaniia gr. Ernsta Minikha* (St. Petersburg, 1891), pp. 57–58. See also Duffy, *Russia's Military Way*, which on page 50 tells of Münnich's "increasingly self contained system of supply."
158. See Korobov, *Fel'dmarshal Rumiantsev*, p. 149; Petrov, *Vtoraia turketskaia voina*, pp. 84–85, 89; Fortunatov, *Materialy*, p. 395.
159. *Arkhiv Kniazia Vorontsova*, 2 (Moscow, 1871): 492.
160. See Duffy, *Army of Frederick the Great*, pp. 154–55, and Archer Jones, *The Art of War in the Western World* (Urbana, Ill., 1987), pp. 267–72, 307–8.
161. Duffy, *Russia's Military Way*, p. 88, and Jones, *Art of War*, p. 302.
162. Duffy, *Russia's Military Way*, p. 51; Bogdanovich, *Pokhody Rumiantseva*, p. 8; Kochubinskii, *Graf Andrei Ivanovich Osterman*, pp. 475–76.
163. Fortunatov, *Materialy*, p. xviii.
164. *Ibid.*, p. xvi.
165. Duffy, *Russia's Military Way*, p. 175.
166. Bogdanovich, *Pokhody Rumiantseva*, p. 279.
167. Duffy, *Russia's Military Way*, p. 170; [Mikhnevich], *Stoletie Voennago Ministerstva*, IV: 172; A. A. Komarov, "Razvitie takticheskoi mysli v russkoi armii v 60–90-kh godakh XVIII v.," *Vestnik Moskovskogo Universiteta*, series 8, *Istoriia*, 1982, no. 3, p. 61. On Jägers generally, see Peter Paret, *Yorck and the Era of Prussian Reform 1807–1815* (Princeton, N.J., 1966). In this fine work, Professor Paret is, however, far too dismissive of the eighteenth-century Russian army. See pp. 202–3.
168. Fortunatov, *Materialy*, pp. 403–4; Jones. *Art of War*, pp. 309–11, 313–14.
169. Longworth, *Art of Victory*, pp. 312–13.
170. Kochubinskii, *Graf Andrei Ivanovich Osterman*, p. 475.
171. Klokman, *Fel'dmarshal Rumianstev*, pp. 29–30.
172. *Ibid.*, pp. 90–94.
173. *Ibid.*, p. 97; Bogdanovich, *Pokhody Rumiantseva*, pp. 28–37.
174. Ley, *Le Maréchal de Münnich*, p. 63.
175. Korobov, *Fel'dmarshal Rumiantsev*, p. 263, reproduces a letter Rumiantsev wrote Potemkin on the subject of the *chevaux* in the winter of 1787.
176. Pruntsov, *Polkovodets P. A. Rumiantsev*, p. 95.
177. Suvorov, *Pis'ma*, p. 144.
178. Petrov, *Vtoraia turetskaia voina*, II: 33–34.
179. See "Nauka pobezhdat," in Suvorov, *Pis'ma*, p. 397.

180. For some interesting reflections on the ways in which the legend of Suvorov helped to distort Russian military thinking in the late nineteenth and early twentith centuries, see Walter Pinter, "Russian Military Thought: The Western Model and the Shadow of Suvorov," in Peter Paret, ed., *Makers of Modern Strategy from Machiavelli to the Nuclear Age* (Princeton, N.J., 1986), pp. 354–75.

181. Baiov, *Russkaia armiia*, p. 232; Bogdanovich, *Pokhody Rumiantseva*, p. 8.

182. Bogdanovich, *Pokhody Rumiantseva*, p. 18.

183. *Ibid.*, p. 31; Korobov, *Fel'dmarshal Rumiantsev*, p. 185.

184. Longworth, *Art of Victory*, pp. 93, 143.

185. V. I. Ignatov, *Russkie istoricheskie pesni: Khrestomatiia.* (Moscow, 1970), pp. 192–93.

186. Komarov, "Razvitie takticheskoi mysli," pp. 58–60; see also Gippius, *Stoletie voennago ministerstva*, II, pt. I, section III: 65–75.

187. In *Russia as a Great Power 1709–1856: Reflections on the Problem of Relative Backwardness, with Special Reference to the Russian Army and Russian Society,* Keenan Institute for Advanced Russian Studies, Occasional Paper, no. 33 (Washington, D.C., 1978), Professor Walter Pintner argues that the Russian army did not in fact exploit operational innovations or imaginative tactics in the eighteenth century; in his view, the Russian army fought more or less as its European opponents did. Professor Pintner, however, concentrates almost exclusively on the Seven Years War and overlooks the Turkish Wars in his analysis. See pp. 48–53.

188. See Clausewitz, *On War,* pp. 187–89.

189. A. K. Il'enko, *Stoletie Voennago Ministerstva 1802–1902: Glavnyi Shtab—Istoricheskii ocherk—Komplektovanie vooruzhennykh sil v Rossii go 1802 g.,* ed. D. A. Skalon, pt. 1, bk. I, section I (St. Petersburg, 1902), p. 92.

190. N. P. Mikhnevich, "Vvedenie," *Stoletie Voennago Ministerstva: Glavnyi Shtab—Istoricheskii ocherk,* ed. D. A. Skalon, IV (St. Petersburg, 1902): 165.

191. Maslovskii, *Russkaia armiia v semiletniuiu voinu,* p. 16.

192. John L. H. Keep, *Soldiers of the Tsar: Army and Society in Russia, 1462–1874* (London, 1985), p. 292.

193. Manstein, *Contemporary Memoirs,* p. 170.

194. Lanzheron, "Russkaia armiia," p. 154.

195. Baiov, *Russkaia armiia,* p.232.

196. Manstein, *Contemporary Memoirs,* p. 243.

197. F. von Stein, *Geschichte des Russischen Heeres von Ursprunge desselben bis zur Thronbesteigung des Kaisers Nikolai I Pawlowitsch* (Hannover, 1885), pp. 98, 130.

198. *Ibid.,* p. 131.

199. M. Lyons, ed., *The Russian Imperial Army: A Bibliography of Regimental Histories and Related Works* (Stanford, Calif., 1967), p. vii.

200. Pruntsov, *Polkovodets P. A. Rumiantsev,* p. 12; Frumenkov, "Rossiia", p. 118.

201. William Richardson, *Anecdotes of the Russian Empire* (London, 1784; reprint: New York, 1970), p. 49.

202. Klokman, *Fel'dmarshal Rumiantsev,* p. 107.

203. Bogdanovich, *Pokhody Rumiantseva,* p. 46.

204. Longworth, *Art of Victory*, pp. 166–68; for the exploit of Father Trofim Egorovich Kutsinskii, see Suvorov, *Pis'ma*, p. 611.
205. Suvorov, *Pis'ma*, p. 397.
206. George Bernard Shaw, *The Man of Destiny*, in *Complete Plays with Prefaces*, 1 (New York, 1963): 699.
207. [Münnich], *Rossiia i russkii dvor*, p. 61.
208. Petrov, *Vtoraia turetskaia voina*, 2: 187–88.
209. Kostomarov, *Poslednie gody*, 2: 632–33.
210. Suvorov, *Pis'ma*, p. 397.
211. Petrov, *Vtoraia turketskaia voina*, 2: 179.
212. Suvorov, *Pis'ma*, p. 397.
213. Keep, *Soldiers of the Tsar*, pp. 208–10, makes much of the soldiers' belief "in a religious Utopia" and is doubtless right to do so. But that belief cannot alone account for the superior combat performance of the Russian army. After all, prior to the Enlightenment millions of people in scores of countries were sustained by an identical belief, yet did not necessarily evince sterling martial qualities as a result.
214. Manstein, *Contemporary Memoirs*, pp. 170–71, says that many soldiers died during the Turkish War of the 1730s because they refused to eat meat on Orthodox fast days. I should note that more than ninety days in the year were so designated by the Orthodox calendar used at the time.
215. Duffy, *Army of Frederick the Great*, p. 55.
216. If only because the modern concept of nationalism was very much the invention of bookish intellectuals in late-eighteenth- and early-nineteenth-century Europe. See Peter Burke, *Popular Culture in Early Modern Europe* (New York, 1978), pp. 3–22, for some stimulating ideas on this subject.
217. Keep, *Soldiers of the Tsar*, p. 160.
218. Keep, for one, confesses himself perplexed by this. "On the whole the Russian soldier remained a submissive cog in the vast machine of which he formed part—remarkably so, in view of the deprivations and injustices to which he was subjected and the lack of any effective procedure for settling grievances." *Ibid.*, p. 227.
219. See L. N. Pushkarev, "Soldatskaia pesnia—istochnik po istorii voennogo byta russkoi reguliarnoi armii xviii–pervoi poloviny xixv," in V. I. Shunkov, *Voprosy voennoi istorii Rossii xviii i pervaia polovina xix vekov* (Moscow, 1969), p. 428.
220. V. A. Aleksandrov, *Sel'skaia obshchina v Rossii (xviii–nachalo xix v.)* (Moscow, 1976), p. 290. Indeed the sorry plight of the soldier's wife was a staple theme in Russian folklore.
221. Charles François Philibert Masson, *Secret Memoirs of the Court of St. Petersburg, Particularly Towards the End of the Reign of Catherine II and the Commencement of That of Paul I* (London, 1895), p. 289.
222. Aleksandrov, *Sel'skaia obshchina*, pp. 290–91.
223. Lanzheron, "Russkaia armiia," 83 (April 1895): 148–49.
224. For more on the *artels*, see Keep, *Soldiers of the Tsar*, pp. 178–79; Dietrich Beyrau, *Militär und Gesellschaft im Vorrevolutionären Russland* (Cologne, 1984), pp. 347–52. Beyrau, however, concentrates on the economic di-

mension and has more to say about the *artels* of the nineteenth century than those of the eighteenth.

225. Elise Kimerling, "Soldiers' Children 1719–1856: A Study of Social Engineering in Imperial Russia," *Forschungen zur Osteuropäischen Geschichte*, 30 (Berlin, 1982): 63, 71, 88, 102. Of course, the official estimate of the number of people in this class, 12,000 in 1797, for instance, was grotesquely low. What the government seems to have done is to have counted the numbers of people of this class either enrolled in special state-sponsered schools or receiving maintenance of some kind from other state institutions.

226. Lanzheron, "Russkaia armiia," pt. 3, *Russkaia starina*, 83 (May 1895): 190–91.

227. Dirin, *Istoriia*, p. 273.

228. Aleksandrov, *Sel'skaia obshchina*, pp. 292–93.

5. The Baleful Consequences of Victory

1. N. Dubrovin, ed., *Otechestvennaia voina v pis'makh sovremennikov (1812–1815 gg.)* (St. Petersburg, 1882), pp. 87, 96.

2. *Ibid.*, p. 106.

3. "Depesha grafa Zhozefa de-Mestra Sardinskomu Koroliu o nashei otechestvennoi voine 1812 goda," *Russkii arkhiv*, 1912, no. 1, p. 47. In the letter of justification he wrote Alexander I about the abandonment of Moscow, Kutuzov said that the loss of that city was actually Barclay's fault, for withdrawing from Smolensk. See *Izvestiia o voennykh deistviiakh Rossiiskoi armii protiv Frantsuzov 1812 goda* (St. Petersburg, 1813), p. 75.

4. *Memoires inedits de l'Amiral Tchitchagoff: Campagnes de la Russie en 1812 contre La Turquie, L'Austriche et La France* (Berlin, 1855), p. 85. General Sir Robert Wilson, *Narrative of Events during the Invasion of Russia by Napoleon Bonaparte and the Retreat of the French Army 1812*, ed. Herbert Randolph (London, 1860), pp. 318–19, 356–57; Michael Glover, *A Very Slippery Fellow: The Life of Sir Robert Wilson 1777–1849* (Oxford, 1977), pp. 109–10,

5. Such as the impressive statues of Barclay and Kutuzov sculpted by Orlovskii in 1837 for the colonnade of the Kazan Cathedral in St. Petersburg.

6. Both tsarist historians and Soviet historians to this very day refer to the war of 1812 as the *Otechestvennaia voina*, or Fatherland War.

7. John T. Alexander, *Catherine the Great: Life and Legend* (New York, 1989), pp. 296–97.

8. On Paul I's love of Prussia and servile emulation of its military practices, see A. V. Predtechenskii, *Ocherki obshestvenno-politicheskoi istorii Rossii v pervoi chetverti xix veka* (Moscow, 1957), p. 48. Also see John L. H. Keep, "The Russian Army's Response to the French Revolution," *Jahrbücher für Geschichte Osteuropas*, 28 (1980), no. 4: 506–9.

9. On these events, see Norman E. Saul, *Russia and the Mediterranean, 1797–1807* (Chicago, 1970), pp. 39–60, and Andrei A. Lobanov-Rostovsky, *Russia and Europe 1789–1825* (Durham, N.C., 1947), pp. 20–26.

10. James J. Kenney, Jr., "Lord Whitworth and the Conspiracy Against Tsar

Paul I: The New Evidence in the Kent Archive," *Slavic Review*, 36, no. 2 (June 1977): 216–19.

11. See Patricia Kennedy Grimsted, *The Foreign Ministers of Alexander I: Political Attitudes and the Conduct of Russian Diplomacy, 1801–1825* (Berkeley, Calif., 1969).

12. L. G. Beskrovnyi, *Russkoe voennoe iskusstvo v xix veke* (Moscow, 1972), p. 93.

13. Predtechenskii, *Ocherki*, pp. 37–38. See also M. F. Zlotnikov, *Kontinental'naia blokada i Rossiia* (Moscow, 1966), pp. 150, 354–56.

14. S. B. Okun', *Ocherki istorii SSSR: Konets xviii–pervaia chetvert' xix veka* (Leningrad, 1956), pp. 162–65.

15. See Beskrovnyi, *Russkoe voennoe iskusstvo*, p. 90.

16. N. I. Kazakov, "Taina russkoi strategii v Avstro-Frantsuzskoi voine 1809 g.," *Istoriia SSSR*, November–December 1969, no. 6, p. 69. Kazakov is less than convincing, however, when he argues that despite what he may have told Vienna, Alexander actually intended to prosecute the war as a zealous French ally.

17. Despite the many loopholes in the continental system, which ranged from smuggling to special exemptions granted by Napoleon himself, it did result in shortages of grain and bullion in Great Britain. The latter made it particularly difficult for Britain to defray the costs of the peninsular war or to encourage potential antagonists to Napoleon with monetary subsidies. See John M. Sherwig, *Guineas and Gunpowder: British Foreign Aid in the Wars with France, 1793–1815* (Cambridge, Mass., 1969), pp. 232–33, 263.

18. See A. K. Dzhivelegov, S. P. Melgunov, and V. I. Pichety, eds., *Otechestvennaia voina i russkoe obshchestvo*, 3 (Moscow, 1912): pp. 67–71. See also Michael Josselson and Diana Josselson, *The Commander: A Life of Barclay de Tolly* (Oxford, 1980), pp. 78, 84.

19. Russia was able to persuade the new Swedish King, the former Marshal Bernadotte, to sign the alliance by agreeing to the Swedish annexation of Norway. See V. V. Roginskii, *Shvetsiia i Rossiia: Soiuz 1812 goda* (Moscow, 1978), pp. 73, 83.

20. Richard K. Riehn, *1812: Napoleon's Russian Campaign* (New York, 1990), p. 50.

21. Armand de Caulaincourt, *With Napoleon in Russia, The Memoirs of General de Caulaincourt, Duke of Vicenza*. ed. George Libaire (New York, 1935), p. 45. George Nafzinger, *Napoleon's Invasion of Russia* (Novato, CA, 1988), p. 114.

22. N. K. Shil'der, *Imperator Aleksandr Pervyi, Ego zhizn' i tsarstvovanie*. vol. 3 (St. Petersburg, 1905), pp. 100–101.

23. On the strategic plan of Phull, see Friedrich von Smitt, *Zur Näheren Aufklärung über den Krieg von 1812* (Leipzig, 1861), pp. 474–75.

24. Caulaincourt, *With Napoleon*, p. 78.

25. Josselson and Josselson, *Commander*, p. 118.

26. In a letter to his sister dated September 18, 1812, Alexander explained the appointment of Kutuzov as follows: "At Petersburg I found everybody bent on old Kutuzov being given the chief command and that was the general cry. My knowledge of the man made me against it at first, but when, in his letter of August 5th, Rostopchin [the governor-general of

Moscow] informed me that all Moscow wanted Kutuzov to command, considering Barclay and Bagration both incapable of the post . . . I could no do otherwise than yield to the general wish and appointed Kutuzov." *Scenes of Russian Court Life, Being the Correspondence of Alexander I with his Sister,* trans. Henry Havelock (London, n.d.), p. 112.

27. Eugene Tarle, *Napoleon's Invasion of Russia, 1812,* trans. G. M. (New York, 1942), pp. 168–72.
28. On Napoleon and the prisoners at Borodino, see Caulaincourt, *With Napoleon,* p. 99; Tarle, *Napoleon's Invasion,* p. 200; and Count Phillipe-Paul de Segur, *Napoleon's Russian Campaign,* trans. J. David Townsend (Cambridge, Mass., 1958), p. 83.
29. N. P. Mikhnevich, "Fili," in Dzhivelegov *et al., Otechestvennaia voina,* 4: 31–32.
30. A. P. Ermolov, *Zapiski Alekseiia Petrovicha Ermolova* (Moscow, 1863), p. 184. Ermolov attended the Fili conference, and his memoirs are the best source we have concerning it.
31. For the text, see *Izvestiia o voennykh deistviiakh,* pp. 74–75.
32. The burning of Moscow has long been a matter of controversy. At the time, the French were convinced that responsibility for the fires lay almost exclusively with Rostopchin. See Caulaincourt, *With Napoleon,* p. 121; Segur, *Napoleon's Russian Campaign,* p. 115; M. de Fezensac, *The Russian Campaign, 1812,* trans. Lee Kennett (Athens, Ga., 1970), pp. 40–41. For their part, many Russians both at the time and ever after have blamed French looters for the conflagration. S. B. Okun', *Istoriia SSSR: Lektsii,* pt. 2 *1812–1825* (Leningrad, 1978), pp. 39–41; Tarle, *Napoleon's Invasion,* p. 236. On pre-planned acts of military arson, see P.A. Zhilin, *Otechestvennaia voina 1812 goda* (Moscow, 1988), pp. 188–94.
33. Caulaincourt wrote that a drive on Petersburg was "impracticable in view of the state of our artillery and cavalry, while Kutuzov was so close to us with a well-organized army and numerous cavalry." Caulaincourt, *With Napoleon,* p. 134.
34. The Surgeon General of Napoleon's army, Baron Larrey, estimated that had the supplies in Moscow been carefully preserved and husbanded, they could have sufficed the troops for six months. Unfortunately, even if that had been done, the Grand Armée would probably have required an eight-month rather than a six-month supply of food before the opening of the campaign season in 1813. Baron Dominique Jean Larrey, *Surgical Memoirs of the Campaigns of Russia, Germany and France,* trans. John C. Mercer (Philadelphia, 1832), p. 46. Another veteran, Fezensac, derided the possibility of wintering "in a ravaged town where we had starved in the month of October." Fezensac, *Russian Campaign,* p. 46.
35. Segur, *Napoleon's Russian Campaign,* p. 134.
36. *Ibid.,* pp. 190–91.
37. Cited in David G. Chandler, *The Campaigns of Napoleon* (New York, 1966), p. 858.
38. Denis Davydov, *Dnevnik partizanskikh deistvii 1812 g.* (Leningrad, 1985), p. 161.

39. Larrey, *Surgical Memoirs*, pp. 82–83.
40. Larrey noted that the coldest days were December 8–9, 13–15; *ibid.*, p. 78.
41. Riehn, *1812*, pp. 143. For German opinion on this score, see *Terrain Factors in the Russian Campaign* (Washington, D.C., Center for Military History Publication 104-5, 1982), pp. 58–59.
42. For a variation on this interpretation, see Martin van Creveld, *Supplying War: Logistics from Wallenstein to Patton* (Cambridge, Eng., 1977), pp. 65–68.
43. G. Fabry, ed., *Campagne de 1812: Documents Relatifs a l'Aile Gauche* (Paris, 1912), p. 30; see also G. Fabry, ed., *Campagne de Russie (1812)*, 2 (Paris, 1900): 56.
44. Caulaincourt, *With Napoleon*, p. 86.
45. Ermolov, *Zapiski*, p. 242.
46. G. Fabry, ed., *Campagne de Russie (1812)*, 5 (Paris, 1903): 151.
47. Larrey, *Surgical Memoirs*, p. 54; Fezensac, *The Russian Campaign*, pp. 69–70.
48. For Napoleon's view of Alexander, see Mack Walker, ed., *Metternich's Europe* (New York, 1968), pp. 96–97.
49. Caulaincourt, *With Napoleon*, p. 48.
50. *Ibid.*, p. 6.
51. Shil'der, *Imperator Aleksandr Pervyi*, 3: 117.
52. Quoted in Curtis Gate, *The War of the Two Emperors: The Duel Between Napoleon and Alexander—Russia 1812* (New York, 1985), p. x.
53. Dubrovin, *Otechestvennaia voina*, pp. 23–24.
54. Zhilin, *Otechestvennaia voina*, p. 214.
55. S. B. Okun', *Istoriia SSSR: Konets xviii–nachalo xix v. Lektsii*, pt. 1 (Leningrad, 1974), p. 5.
56. Dzhivelegov *et al.*, *Otechestvennaia voina*, 3: 72. Keep, "Russian Army's Response," p. 501, provides higher figures, apparently the result of including those who served in the territorial reserves, or *opolchenie*.
57. Zhilin, *Otechestvennaia voina*, pp. 216, 222.
58. V. I. Assonov, ed., *V tylu armii: Kaluzhskaia guberniia v 1812 godu—Obzor sobytii i sbornik dokumentov* (Moscow, 1912), pp. 35–36; "Kutuzov v 1812 godu. Istoricheskaia kharakteristika D. P. Buturlina," *Russkaia starina*, October 1894, p. 197.
59. Dzhivelegov *et al.*, *Otechestvennaia voina*, 3: 82.
60. Dubrovin, *Otechestvennaia voina*, pp. 444–45; after the loss of Moscow, Wilson wrote that "the reinforcement and provisioning of the assembling army was one of the most extraordinary efforts of national will ever made." Wilson, *Narrative of Events*, p. 194.
61. "Kutuzov v 1812," p. 194.
62. Zhilin, *Otechestvennaia voina*, pp. 254; Tarle, *Napoleon's Invasion*, p. 346; S. A. Kniaz'kov, "Partisany i partizanskaia voina v 1812-m godu," in Dzhivelegov *et al.*, *Otechestvennaia voina*, 4: 209.
63. Kniaz'kov, "Partisany," 4: 215.
64. "Kutuzov v 1812 godu," p. 197; Ermolov, *Zapiski*, pp. 206–7.
65. Caulaincourt, *With Napoleon*, p. 149.
66. Fezensac, *Russian Campaign*, p. 48.
67. The Russians reported the capture of eight generals, three hundred offi-

cers, 21,170 soldiers, and 209 guns during the four days of fighting. See *Izvestiia o voennykh deistviiakh*, p. 257.

68. Larrey, *Surgical Memoirs*, p. 69.
69. Fabry, *Campagne de 1812*, pp. 185–86.
70. Caulaincourt, *With Napoleon*, p. 288.
71. Tarle, *Napoleon's Invasion*, pp. 46–47.
72. Josselson and Josselson, *Commander*, p. 41.
73. V. V. Pugachev, "K voprosu o pervonachal'nom plane voiny 1812 g.," in *1812 god: K stopiatidesiatiletiiu otechestvennoi voiny—Sbornik statei* (Moscow, 1962), p. 34.
74. Fabry, *Campagne de Russie*, 2: 87.
75. *Memoires inedites*, p. 3; Shil'der, *Imperator Aleksandr*, 3: 88.
76. Dubrovin, *Otechestvennaia voina*, pp. 86–87.
77. *Ibid.*, pp. 95–96, 98.
78. Pugachev, "K voprosu," p. 34.
79. Dubrovin, *Otechestvennaia voina*, pp. 89–90.
80. See for example the letter of July 30 (August 11), 1812, in *ibid.*, pp. 66–68; the quotation is on page 66.
81. Shil'der, *Imperator Aleksandr*, 3: 122.
82. A similar point was made by Stalin shortly before the battle of Stalingrad. In his order 227 of June 28, 1942, Stalin noted that it was not possible to retreat indefinitely. "A complete stop must be put to all talk about . . . our having plenty of territory, our country being great and rich, our having a large population and always plenty of grain. Such talk is false and harmful, it weakens us and strengthens the enemy, because, if we do not stop retreating we shall be left without grain, without fuel, without metal, without raw materials, without factories and mills." S. M. Shtemenko, *The Soviet General Staff at War 1941–1945*, Book I, trans. Robert Daglish (Moscow, 1985), pp. 102–3.
83. Tarle, *Napoleon's Invasion*, pp. 269, 352, 409.
84. Zhilin, *Otechestvennaia voina*, p. 16.
85. *Dnevnik Aleksandra Chicherina 1812–1813*, trans. M. I. Perper (Moscow, 1966), p. 142.
86. Davydov, *Dnevnik*, p. 24.
87. Shil'der, *Imperator Aleksandr*, 3: 101.
88. Tarle, *Napoleon's Invasion*, pp. 269–70.
89. Zhilin, *Otechestvennaia voina*, p. 12.
90. *Ibid.*, p. 16.
91. *Ibid.*
92. Davydov, *Dnevnik*, p. 9.
93. See for example, Dubrovin, *Otechestvennaia voina*, p. 69.
94. Hans Rogger, *National Consciousness in Eighteenth-Century Russia* (Cambridge, Mass., 1960), pp. 1–4, 276–77.
95. For another example, see *Khronika nedavnei stariny: Iz arkhiva Kniazia Obolenskago-Neledinskago-Meletskago* (St. Petersburg, 1876), pp. 134–36.
96. Fabry, *Campagne de Russie*, 2: 32 (letter from Pajol to Davout of July 19).
97. Zhilin, *Otechestvennaia voina*, p. 262.

98. J.-J. E. Roy, *Les Français en Russie: Souvenirs de la Campagne de 1812 et de deux ans de captivité en Russie* (Tours, 1856), p. 23.
99. Wilson, *Narrative*, p. 256.
100. Zhilin, *Otechestvennaia voina*, pp. 260–62.
101. V. P. Alekseev, "Narodnaia voina," in Dzhivelegov *et al.*, *Otechestvennaia voina*, 4: 227–29.
102. Ermolov, *Zapiski*, p. 242.
103. Caulaincourt, *With Napoleon*, p. 163.
104. Beskrovnyi, *Russkoe voennoe iskusstvo*, p. 115.
105. See, for example, Tarle, *Napoleon's Invasion*, p. 250.
106. Davydov, *Dnevnik*, pp. 56–69.
107. Tarle, *Napoleon's Invasion*, p. 285.
108. Ermolov, *Zapiski*, p. 240.
109. Even Tarle admits this. See *Napoleon's Invasion*, p. 353.
110. Dzhivelegov *et al.*, *Otechestvennaia voina*, 3: 74–75.
111. Tarle, *Napoleon's Invasion*, p. 264.
112. Davydov, *Dnevnik*, p. 172.
113. *Khronika nedavnei stariny*, p. 137.
114. "Zapiski Soldata Pamfila Nazarova v inochestve Mitrofana 1792–1839 g.g.," *Russkaia starina*, 22 (1878): 530–33, 538.
115. Fabry, *Campagne de Russie (1812)*, 5: 110–12 (intelligence report to Napoleon of July 13).
116. Assonov, *V tylu armii*, p. 18.
117. Dubrovin, *Otechestvennaia voina*, p. 68.
118. Assonov, *V tylu armii*, p. 97.
119. *Ibid.*, p. 115.
120. *Ibid.*, pp. 116–18, 120.
121. For one example, see *ibid.*, p. 111.
122. Davydov, *Dnevnik*, pp. 54–55; Dzhivelegov *et al.*, *Otechestvennaia voina*, 4: 210.

6. The Policy and Strategy of Nicholas I

1. for an extremely sympathetic interpretation of the Holy Alliance, see Francis Ley, *Alexandre Ier et sa Sainte-Alliance* (Paris, 1975), p. 296; also see H. G. Schenk, *The Aftermath of the Napoleonic Wars: The Concert of Europe—An Experiment* (New York, 1967), pp. 38–41.
2. Harold Nicolson, *The Congress of Vienna: A Study in Allied Unity 1812–1822* (New York, 1961), pp. 171–79; Henry A. Kissinger, *A World Restored: Metternich, Castlereigh and the Problems of Peace 1812–22* (Boston, n.d.), pp. 154–55. The Polish dispute, which revolved around Alexander's attempt to make Poland a large Russian satellite state, was so heated that the entire Congress almost broke down. A compromise achieved by dint of threats of war resulted in the creation of a Polish kingdom smaller than Alexander had aimed at, the retention by Prussia and Austria of some of their Polish territories, the establishment of Cracow as a "free city," and compensation for Prussia in Saxony.

3. Peter Quennell, ed. and trans. *The Private Letters of Princess Lieven to Prince Metternich 1820–1826* (New York, 1938), pp. 53, 295, for the diametrically opposed views of Princess Lieven and Capo d'Istria.

4. W. Bruce Lincoln, *Nicholas I: Emperor and Autocrat of the All the Russias* (Bloomington, Ind., 1978), pp. 109–10, notes that, in contrast to Alexander I, Nicholas I was concerned about the West only "insofar as it posed a threat to the domestic tranquility of Russia."

5. N. K. Shil'der, *Imperator Nikolai Pervyi: Ego zhizn' i tsarstvovanie.* 2 (St. Petersburg, 1904): 563.

6. Nicholas accepted Russian annexation of the mouth of the Amur, the result of the monomaniacal and self-interested actions of N. N. Murav'ev, not because he wished for more territory but because he feared that Russia would lose prestige if he repudiated it. See Hugh Seton-Watson, *The Russian Empire, 1801–1917* (Oxford, 1967), pp. 296–97.

7. Prince Shcherbatov, *General-Fel'dmarshal Kniaz' Paskevich: Ego zhizn' i deiatel'nost'* 4 (St. Petersburg, 1894), "Prilozhenie": 145–46.

8. Lincoln, *Nicholas I*, pp. 126–27.

9. Shil'der, *Nikolai Pervyi*, 2: 554.

10. Constantin de Grunwald, *Tsar Nicholas I*, trans. Brigit Patmore (London, 1954), p. 191, for the conversation with Barante of January 1836.

11. A. L. Narochnitskii *et. al.*, eds, *Vneshniaia politika Rossii xix i nachala xx veka*, 2d series 1815–1830, 6 (14) (Moscow, 1985): 398.

12. F. Martens, comp., *Recueil traités et conventions conclus par la Russie avec les Puissances Étrangerès publié d'order du Ministère des Affaires Etrangerès*, 4, pt. 1 (St. Petersburg, 1878): 440.

13. "Otchety ministerstv za dvadtsatipiatiletie tsarstvovaniia Imperatora Nikolaia I," *Sbornik Imperatorskago Russkago Istoricheskago Obschchestva* (afterwards *SIRIO*) 98 (St Petersburg, 1896): 291.

14. *Ibid.*, 292.

15. The confusion extended to Nicholas and Konstantin as well, for each brother initially swore allegiance to the other. Nicholas was apparently uncertain about the legality of Konstantin's removal from the line of succession. On Decembrism generally, see Anatole G. Mazour, *The First Russian Revolution* (Berkeley, Calif., 1937), pp. 85 ff; Marc Raeff, ed., *The Decembrist Movement* (Englewood Cliffs, N.J., 1966), pp. 11, 15–16, 20, 27; John L. H. Keep, *Soldiers of the Tsar: Army and Society in Russia 1462–1874* (Oxford, 1985), pp. 256–57; also very important is the article by W. Bruce Lincoln, "A Reexamination of Some Historical Stereotypes: An Analysis of the Career Patterns and Backgrounds of the Decembrists", *Jahrbücher für Geschichte Osteuropas*, 24 (1976), no. 3: 357–67. Here Professor Lincoln suggests that the majority of the participants in the movement may not have been as motivated by liberal and radical ideologies as commonly supposed. He also demolishes the myth that the typical Decembrist was an officer whose service abroad from 1813 to 1822 had familiarized him with social and political conditions in Western Europe. As he demonstrates, the bulk of the Decembrists actually had had no foreign service.

16. See, for example, his comments to the French ambassador La Ferronnays of

January 1826: "This insurrection should not therefore be compared with those of Spain and Piedmont. Thank God, we aren't there yet and I hope that we never get there." Nicholas P. Wakar, "Les rapports de l'ambassade de France à Saint-Peterbourg, sur la conjuration des Décembristes", *Le Monde Slave*, December 1925, no. 12, p. 449. On Nicholas's view of Decembrism as international conspiracy, see M. Polievktov, *Nikolai I* (Moscow, 1918), p. 61; for a more recent treatment, Lincoln, *Nicholas I*, p. 109.

17. "Otchety ministerstv", p. 293. On the relation between foreign revolution and potential domestic subversion, see also Baron von Haxthausen, *The Russian Empire: Its People, Institutions and Resources*, trans. Robert Faire, 2 (London, 1856): 272.

18. A. de Nesselrode, ed., *Lettres et Papiers du Chancelier Comte de Nesselrode 1760–1850*, 7 (Paris, 1908): 237.

19. Shcherbatov, *Paskevich*, 6 (St. Petersburg, 1899): 284.

20. *Ibid.*, 4: 94.

21. Nesselrode, *Lettres et Papiers*, 8 (Paris, n.d.): 57 (letter of Nesselrode to Meyendorff, October 24, 1840).

22. Most of the intelligence collected does not, however, appear to have been of a very high order, consisting mostly of printed information about the French order of battle. For examples, see TsGVIA, f. 440, op. 1, d. 258 (French forces in 1837), and TsGVIA, f. 440, op. 1, d. 260 (French forces in 1839).

23. Nesselrode, *Lettres et Papiers*, 11 (Paris: n.d.): 115.

24. Shcherbatov, *Paskevich*, 3: 24. "Prilozhenie," 9–10; Lincoln, *Nicholas I*, p. 114.

25. Nesselrode, *Lettres et Papiers*, 7: 152.

26. Grunwald, *Tsar Nicholas*, pp. 106–7; Shil'der, *Nikolai Pervyi*, 2: 563.

27. cited in N. S. Kiniapina, *Vneshniaia politika Rossii pervoi poloviny xix veka* (Moscow, 1963), pp. 184–85.

28. Grunwald, *Tsar Nicholas*, pp. 110–11.

29. for an example, derived from the confession of M. Bestuzhev, see Raeff, *Decembrist Movement*, p. 50.

30. On Nicholas's opinion about the baleful consequences of foreign travel, see Wakar, "Les rapports", p. 454; the decree on surveillance is in Narochnitskii *et al. Vneshniaia politika*, p. 391,

31. *En passant* we should note that the brutality of the regime's repression was from time to time counterbalanced by incompetence and even comedy. While under police supervision in Novgorod province in the early 1840s, Aleksandr Herzen was assigned to a post in the governor's office in which one of his official duties was countersigning police reports about his own political reliability. See Alexander Herzen, *My Past and Thoughts: The Memoirs of Alexander Herzen*, ed. Dwight Macdonald, trans. Constance Garnett (New York: 1973), p. 271. On the political police, see also Sidney Monas, *The Third Section: Police and Society in Russia Under Nicholas I* (Cambridge, Mass., 1961), p. 132.

32. See Seton-Watson, *Russian Empire*, pp. 275–78.

33. See the bizarre memorandum of A. B. Lobanov-Rostovskii on this subject,

submitted to Nicholas I in March 1849: TsGAOR, f. 978, op. 1, d. 43, "O vneshnei politike Rossii v Evrope i v Azii," II: 3–5, 8.

34. Narochnitskii *et al.*, *Vneshniaia politika*, p. 391, and S. B. Okun', *Istoriia SSSR 1812–1825 gg.* (Leningrad, 1978), p. 102.

35. Kiniapina, *Vneshniaia politika*, pp. 118–21.

36. Kiniapina, *Vneshniaia politika*, p. 155.

37. Lincoln, *Nicholas I*, pp. 145–46.

38. Martens, *Recueil*, 4, pt. 1: pp. 449, 453, 461; Shcherbatov, *Paskevich*, 5 (St. Petersburg, 1896): 97–98.

39. Shcherbatov, *Paskevich*, 5: 93 (letter of Paskevich to Nicholas of January 24 [February 6], 1833).

40. Nesselrode, *Lettres et Papiers*, 8: 58 (letter of Nesselrode to Meyendorff, October 24, 1840).

41. Shcherbatov, *Paskevich*, 4, "Prilozhenie": 145. Emphasis in the original.

42. Kiniapina, *Vneshniaia politika*, p. 145.

43. Grunwald, *Nicholas I*, p. 87.

44. Shcherbatov, *Paskevich*, 4, "Prilozhenie": 91, 93 (quote is from a letter of Nicholas to Paskevich of September 10 [22], 1831, and appears on page 93.)

45. *Ibid.*, 5: 93.

46. Lincoln, *Nicholas I*, p. 287.

47. TsGAOR, f. 722, op. 1, d. 169 ("Ob"iasnitel'naia zapiska N. F. Paskevicha Kn. Warshavskogo, 'K istorii voiny protiv Miatezhnikov v Vengrii v 1849 g.' "), l. 1.

48. I. V. Bestuzhev, "Krymskaia voina 1853–56," in L.G. Beskrovnyi, ed., *Stranitsy boevogo proshlogo* (Moscow, 1968), p. 259; also Paul W. Schroeder, *Austria, Great Britain and the Crimean War: The Destruction of the European Concert* (Ithaca, N.Y., 1972), pp. 41–42. I find myself in disagreement with two more recent interpretations that assert that Nicholas's purpose was really to provoke the Turks into a shooting war. See Ann Pottinger Saab, *The Origins of the Crimean Alliance* (Charlottesville, Va., 1977), pp. 13–14, 155, and David Wetzel, *The Crimean War* (Boulder, Colo., 1985), pp. 44, 48. In a letter to Paskevich of May 17(29), 1853, Nicholas made it clear that he still hoped the Turks would capitulate after the occupation of the principalities. See A. M. Zaionchkovskii, *Vostochnaia voina 1853–1856 gg. v sviazi s sovremennoi ei politicheskoi obstanovki*, 1, "Prilozhenie" (St. Petersburg, 1908): p. 437.

49. TsGAOR, f. 722, op. 1, d. 197, ("Materialy otnosiashchaisia k podgotovke russkoi-turetskoi voiny 1853–55 g.g.") ll. 213, 215.

50. *Reskripty i pis'ma Imperatora Nikolaia I k Knziaiu Menshikovu za vremia Sevastopol'skoi oborony* (St. Petersburg, 1908) (letter of Nicholas to Menshikov of October 9 [21], 1853), p. 6.

51. "Perepiska Imperatora Nikolaia Pavlovicha s Velikim Knizaem Tsesarevichem Konstantinom Pavlochichem, 1830–1831 gg," *SIRIO*, 132 (St. Petersburg, 1911): 56; "Otchety ministerstv", pp. 306–7.

52. Kiniapina, *Vneshniaia politika*, p. 158.

53. William's son was married to Nicholas's sister, Anna Pavlovna; see Polievktov, *Nikolai I*, p. 118.

54. Shil'der, *Nikolai Pervyi*, p. 564. Nicholas's strategic note of 1830: "If France and England unite to fall on Holland, we will protest for we cannot do any more, but at least the name of Russia will not be sullied by complicity in such an act."

55. Kiniapina, *Vneshniaia politika*, p. 136.

56. Shcherbatov, *Paskevich*, 3, "Prilozhenie": 1

57. *Ibid.*, 4: 9, 4 "Prilozhenie": 16.

58. Baron Helmuth von Moltke, *The Russians in Bulgaria and Rumelia in 1828 and 1829* (London, 1854), p. 475.

59. Shcherbatov, *Paskevich*, 6: 323.

60. TsGAOR, f. 722, op. 1, d. 197, l. 30.

61. *Ibid.*, ll. 209, 241.

62. This consideration also reinforced Nicholas's decision to limit military operations to the mere occupation of Wallachia and Moldavia. *Ibid.*, ll. 209, 211–13, 215–16, 241.

63. TsGVIA, f. 400, op. 4, d. 445, l. 74.

64. Moltke, *Russians in Bulgaria*, pp. 272–74.

65. Shcherbatov, *Paskevich*, 4: 20.

66. *Ibid.*, 4: 42.

67. *Ibid.*, 4: 47.

68. *Ibid.*, 6: 298, 313. (The quotation, from a letter of July 13 [25], 1849, appears on page 313.)

69. TsGAOR, f. 722, op. 1, d. 214 (letters about the military situation during the Crimean War), l. 91.

70. *Ibid.*, d. 197, l. 118.

71. For some representative comments, see John Sheldon Curtiss, *The Russian Army Under Nicholas I, 1825–1855* (Durham, N.C., 1965), pp. 46–47; Nicholas Riasanovsky, *Nicholas I and Official Nationality in Russia, 1825–1855* (Berkeley, Calif., pp. 8–11); Lincoln, *Nicholas I*, p. 164.

72. Polievktov, *Nikolai I*, p. 62.

73. Wakar, "Les rapports" pp. 448–49. See Nicholas to La Ferronnays, January 5, 1826: "I must repeat to you that this was by no means a military insurrection," p. 449.

74. "Gr. A. Kh. Benkendorf o Rossii v 1827–1830 g.g.," *Krasnyi arkhiv*, 37 (1929): 151.

75. Curtiss, *Russian Army*, pp. 51–52.

76. Shcherbatov, *Paskevich*, 4, "Prilozhenie": 110.

77. Riasanovsky, *Nicholas I*, pp. 10–11.

78. *Stoletie Voennago Ministerstva: Glavnyi shtab*, vol. iv, pt. 2, bk. 1, section 2, *Istoricheskii ocherk: Komplektovanie voisk v tsarstvovanie Imperatora Nikolaia I* (St. Petersburg, 1911), p. 4; Lincoln, *Nicholas I*, p. 230.

79. Douglas Porch, *Army and Revolution: France 1815–1848* (London, 1974), p. 63; Gunther E. Rothenberg, *The Army of Francis Joseph* (West Lafayette, Ind., 1976), p. 15.

80. Haxthausen, *Russian Empire*, 2: 305.
81. *Ibid.*, 2: 292–93.
82. Joseph Cánski, *Tableau Statistique Politique et Moral du Système Militaire de la Russie* (Paris, 1833) p. 267. On page 268 he goes on to explain the relatively low rates of desertion from the Russian army in terms of the allegiance of soldiers to their units and each other.
83. Haxthausen, *Russian Empire*, 2: 334–35. See also John S. Maxwell, *The Tsar, His Court and His People*, (New York, 1848), p. 269.
84. Polievktov, *Nikolai I*, pp. 324–25.
85. Daniel Reichel, "La position du général Jomini en tant, qu'expert militaire á la cour de Russie," *Actes du Symposium 1982*, Service historique, Travaux d'histoire militaire et de polémologie, 1 (Lausanne, 1982), 64–65. Jomini had served with Napoleon's army, 1805–13. After the conclusion of the Napoleonic wars, he joined the court of Alexander I of Russia as an informal military adviser. After Alexander's death he exerted no less influence on his successor. During the Turkish war of 1828–29, for example, he accompanied Nicholas to Izmail in the capacity of a military confidant. Indeed, it was at Nicholas's suggestion that Jomini wrote his most famous book, *The Summary of the Art of War*. See John Shy, "Jomini," in Peter Paret, ed., *Makers of Modern Strategy from Machievelli to the Nuclear Age* (Princeton, N.J., 1986), pp. 152–53.
86. "Otchety ministerstv," p. 334; Keep, *Soldiers of the Tsar*, p. 327. ·
87. Haxthausen, *Russian Empire*, 2: 338. See also *Entsiklopedicheskii slovar'*, pub. Brokgauz & Efron, 30 (St. Petersburg, 1895): 941.
88. On the colonies in general, see Keep, *Soldiers of the Tsar*, pp. 284–86. Richard Pipes, "The Russian Military Colonies, 1810–1831," *Journal of Modern History*, 22 (1950): 205–19; Mikhail Semevskii, ed., *Graf Arakcheev i voennyia poseleniia 1809–1831* (St. Petersburg, 1871).
89. Semevskii, *Graf Arakcheev*, p. 183.
90. Shcherbatov, *Paskevich*, 3, "Prilozhenie": 127–33, on the chronology of Russian conquests in the Caucasus. On the origins of the 1826–28 Persian war, see Kiniapina, *Vneshniaia politika*, pp. 131–33.
91. Anthony L. H. Rhinelander, *Prince Michael Vorontsov, Viceroy to the Tsar* (Montreal, 1990), pp. 126–28; J. Milton Mackie, *Life of Schamyl* (Boston, 1850), pp. 179–85, 252–57; D. A. Miliutin, *Vospominaniia* (Tomsk, 1919; reprint: Newtonville, Mass., 1979), pp. 181–89, 191–92, 292–93.
92. Alexander did so against the advice of some of his leading statesmen. The Corsican-born Pozzo di Borgo, for one, wrote Alexander a famous letter in October 1814 in which he warned the Tsar against resurrecting a Polish state, arguing that it would pose a chronic threat to Russia. See TsGAOR, f. 828, op. 1, d. 1332 (letters of Pozzo di Borgo, Stein, and Karamazin on the Establishment of Poland), l. 2. Capodistrias was also opposed to the Polish state. See Patricia Kennedy Grimsted, *The Foreign Ministers of Alexander I. Political Attitudes and the Conduct of Russian Diplomacy, 1801–1825* (Berkeley, Calif., 1969), p. 242.
93. See R. F. Leslie, *Polish Politics and the Revolution of 1830* (London, 1956).
94. Nesselrode, *Lettres et papiers*, 11: 74.

95. TsGAOR, f. 722, op. 1, d. 602 (memorandum of Michael Podogin to Nicholas I and a response to it by Nesselrode, summer, 1854), l. 19.

96. Shcherbatov, *Paskevich*, 4: 39.

97. A. J. P. Taylor, *The Struggle for Mastery in Europe 1848–1918* (London, 1954), p. 54.

98. TsGAOR, f. 828, op. 1, d. 1339 (letters of Nesselrode to Gorchakov about the Austrian demands, August 1854), l. 1.

99. See René Albrecht-Carrie, *A Diplomatic History of Europe Since the Congress of Vienna* (New York, 1958), p. 73.

100. TsGAOR, f. 722, op. 1, d. 602, l. 28.

101. M. S. Anderson, *The Eastern Question 1774–1923* (London, 1966), p. 118. Saab, *Origins*, pp. 14–15.

102. Wetzel, *Crimean War*, p. 94.

103. Moltke, *Russians in Bulgaria*, p. 248.

104. Beskrovny, *Stranitsy boevogo proshlogo*, p. 267; Saab, *Origins*, p. 92.

105. Shcherbatov, *Paskevich*, 4, "Prilozhenie,": 12–14, for an example of Nicholas's intervention in operational decision-making during the Polish war of 1831. For later examples from the Crimean War, see *Reskripty*.

106. *Reskripty*, p. 11.

107. Grunwald, *Tsar Nicholas I*, p. 89.

108. Moltke, *Russians in Bulgaria*, pp. 114, 137, 216, 229.

109. Rhinelander, *Prince Michael Vorontsov*, pp. 147–49; "Shamyl' ", *BE*, 77: 129.

110. Miliutin, *Vospominaniia*, p. 297.

111. For example, see his letter to Menshikov of September 30, 1854, in which he attempted to hearten the defenders of Sevastopol by demanding that they emulate the glorious heroes of 1812. *Reskripty*, p. 35.

112. Moltke, *Russians in Bulgaria*, pp. 25–26; Shil'der, *Nikolai Pervyi*, p. 544.

113. Cánski, *Tableau Statistique*, p. 110. Canski's book, which is undeservedly obscure, is extraordinary not least because it is the work of a former Polish officer who knew the Russian military system of the time from the inside.

114. Shcherbatov, *Paskevich*, 4, "Prilozhenie,": 76.

115. Beskrovnyi, *Stratnitisy boevogo proshlovo*, pp. 260, 268; Curtiss, *Russian Army*, pp. 326–28.

116. Shil'der, *Imperator Nikolai Pervyi*, p. 85.

117. Moltke, *Russians in Bulgaria*, p. 271.

118. Roderick E. McGrew, *Russia and the Cholera 1823–1832* (Madison, Wisc., 1965), pp. 102–5.

119. Mackie, *Life of Schamyl*, p. 180.

120. Miliutin, *Vospominaniia*, p. 232.

121. "Otchety Ministerstv," 98: 372.

122. *Ibid.*, p. 374. This fact does not, however, justify V. G. Verzhbitskii's conclusion that 65–70 percent of all soldiers in the army, on average, became seriously ill enough every year to require medical attention. Verzhbitskii has confused numbers of cases with numbers of soldiers. V. G. Verzhbitskii, *Revoliutsionnoe dvizhenie v russkoi armii 1826–1859* (Moscow, 1964), p. 37.

123. "Otchety Ministerstv," 98: 328, 374.
124. *Ibid.*, p. 317.
125. This is described by Maxwell; see *The Czar*, p. 268.
126. Haxthausen, *Russian Empire*, 2: 309.
127. Beskrovnyi, *Stranitsy boevogo proshlogo*, p. 260.
128. See Chapter 7 for a more complete discussion.
129. On this subject, see the discussion in Keep, *Soldiers of the Tsar*, pp. 327–29.
130. Ellis Kimerling Wirtschafter, *From Serf to Russian Soldier* (Princeton, N.J., 1990), pp. 22–23.
131. Moltke, *Russians in Bulgaria*, p. 24.
132. Polievktov, *Nikolai I*, p. 331.
133. "Otchety Ministerstv," 98: 336.
134. N. Kutuzov, "Sostoianie gosudarstva v 1841 godu; Zapiska N. Kutuzova podannaia Imperatoru Nikolaiu I 2 aprelia 1841," *Russkaia starina*, 85 (1898): 525.
135. Wirtschafter, *From Serf to Russian Soldier*, pp. 34–35, for the best treatment of this issue. Verzhbitskii, *Revoliutsionnoe dvizhenie*, p. 39, notes that Third Section data for 1842 indicated that only one third of furloughed soldiers were involved in agriculture. Most of these, presumably, were state peasants.
136. Kutuzov, "Sostoianie," p. 526.
137. Verzhbitskii, *Revoliutsionnoe divzhenie*, p. 39.
138. John Shelton Curtiss, *Russia's Crimean War* (Durham, N.C., 1979), pp. 469–70.
139. Wirtschafter, *From Serf to Russian Soldier*, pp. 90–95, provides the most sophisticated and satisfying discussion of this issue.
140. Cánski, *Tableau Statistique*, pp. 220–21.
141. Verzhbitskii, *Revoliutsionnoe dvizhenie*, p. 37.
142. Miliutin, *Vospominaniia*, p. 87.
143. See the horrific description of one such punishment in "Bumagi N. A. Mobelli," in V. Desnitskii, ed., *Delo Petrashevtsev*. 1 (Moscow and Leningrad, 1937): 250–52.
144. *Ibid.*, pp. 242–43.
145. Kutuzov, "Sostoianie," pp. 523–24; for more commentary, see Wirtschafter, *From Serf to Russian Soldier*, pp. 28–29.
146. Polievktov, *Nikolai I*, p. 329.
147. Arakcheev's morals may also have rubbed off on his associates. His mistress, the low-born Anastasiia Fedorovna Minkina, was notoriously cruel to her domestic staff; in 1825 her cook slit her throat. See Semevskii, *Graf Arakcheev*, p. 6.
148. *Ibid.*, pp. 9–11, 190–91.
149. Keep, *Soldiers of the Tsar*, pp. 301–2; Verzhbitskii, *Revoliutsionnoe divizhenie*, pp. 120–21. For an eyewitness account, see P. P. Kartsov, *Iz proshlogo: Lichnaia i sluzhebnyia vospominaniia*, pt. 1 (St. Petersburg, 1888), pp. 5–20.
150. *Stoletie*, 4, pt. 2, bk. 1, section 2: 50–54.
151. Walter McKenzie Pintner, *Russian Economic Policy Under Nicholas I* (Ithaca, N.Y., 1967), pp. 30–31, 127.

152. Polievktov, *Nikolai I,* p. 333; TsGVIA, f. 400, op. 4, d. 445, l. 74.
153. See Theodore Ropp, *War in the Modern World* (New York, 1962), pp. 161–64.
154. For a discussion of sea power during the early years of the reign, see A. S. Grishinskii, V. N. Nikol'skii, and N. L. Kladko, eds., *Istoriia russkoi armii i flota,* 9 (St. Petersburg, 1913): 180–235.
155. Polievktov, *Nikolai I,* p. 337.
156. TsGAOR, f. 722, op. 1, d. 190 (letters of Konstantin Nikolaevich to N. N. Murav'ev about the defense of Kamchatka and the Far East, 1854–55), l. 1.
157. A. P. Khrushchov, *Istoriia oborony Sevastopolia: Zapiski Generala-Ad"iutanta Aleksandra Petrovicha Khrushchova* (St. Petersburg, 1888), p. 157.
158. *Reskripty,* pp. 38, 40.
159. Schroeder, *Austria, Great Britain and the Crimean War,* p. 24.
160. Anderson, *Eastern Question,* p. 122–23.
161. Schroeder, *Austria, Great Britain and the Crimean War,* pp. 57–60.

7. From the Treaty of Paris to the Congress of Berlin, 1856–78

1. TsGAOR, f. 828 (A. M. Gorchakov), op. 1, d. 1362.
2. *Ibid.,* l. 3
3. *Ibid.*
4. TsGAOR, f. 722 (Konstantin Nikolaevich), op. 1, d. 604, l. 6
5. TsGAOR, f. 828, op. 1, d. 1362, l. 3
6. For an exhaustive study of the peace process, see John Shelton Curtiss, *Russia's Crimean War* (Durham, N.C., 1979), pp. 472–527.
7. A. J. P. Taylor, *The Struggle for Mastery in Europe 1848–1918* (London, 1954), p. 85.
8. On Gorchakov's ill health, see, for example, TsGAOR, f. 828, op. 1, d. 221 (letters from January 5, 1858, to December 21, 1860), l. 50, and TsGAOR, f. 828, op. 1, d. 224 (letters from January 8, 1867, to December 22, 1869), ll. 20, 51. Gorchakov had known A. S. Pushkin as a fellow student at the Imperial lycée. For all of his adult life he bored his companions at dinner parties with his oft-told reminiscences of the great poet.
9. TsGAOR, f. 828, op. 1, d. 221, l. 60.
10. Henry John Temple, Viscount Palmerston. British Foreign Secretary 1830–41 and 1846–51; Home Secretary 1852–55; Prime Minister for most of 1856–65. Regarded in St. Petersburg as an inveterate enemy of Russia.
11. TsGAOR, f. 828, op. 1, d. 221, l. 56. (letter of August 26, 1860). Alexander II scribbled the words "This is completely true" next to this passage.
12. P. A. Zaionchkovskii, *Voennye reformy 1860–1870 godov v Rossii* (Moscow, 1952), p. 63.
13. TsGAOR, f. 828, op. 1, d. 221, l. 18.
14. Among works on the Great Reforms, see Count G. Dzhanshiev, *Epokha velikikh reform,* 2d ed. (St. Petersburg, 1907), a classic of prerevolutionary liberal historiography; Daniel Field, *The End of Serfdom: Nobility and Bureaucracy in Russia 1855–1861* (Cambridge, Mass., 1976); P. A. Zaionchkovskii,

Otmena krepostnogo prava v Rossii (Moscow, 1963); Daniel T. Orlovsky, *The Limits of Reform: the Ministry of Internal Affairs in Imperial Russia, 1802–1881* (Cambridge, Mass., 1981); Richard Wortman, *The Development of a Russian Legal Consciousness* (Chicago, 1976); Gregory Freeze, *The Parish Clergy in Nineteenth-Century Russia: Crisis, Reform, Counter-Reform* (Princeton, N.J., 1983); and W. Bruce Lincoln, *In the Vanguard of Reform: Russia's Enlightened Bureaucrats 1825–1861* (DeKalb, Ill., 1982), an important work on the bureaucratic origins of reform.

15. Barbara Jellavich, *St. Petersburg and Moscow: Tsarist and Soviet Foreign Policy, 1814–1974* (Bloomington, Ind., 1974), p. 134.

16. See N. S. Kiniapina, *Vneshniaia politika Rossii vtoroi poloviny xix veka* (Moscow, 1974), pp. 14–27, for an excellent short treatment of Franco-Russian relations in this period.

17. See his account of his diplomatic activity in TsGAOR, f. 730, op. 1, d. 544 (N. P. Ignat'ev collection), ll. 6, 116, 145.

18. TsGAOR, f. 828, op. 1, d. 1457, l. 70 (letter to Novikov in Vienna of April 24, 1872).

19. TsGAOR, f. 828, op. 1, d. 1362, l. 56.

20. The first quotation is from *Ibid.*, l. 10, and the second from *Osoboe pribavlenie k opisaniiu russko-turetskoi voiny 1877–78 g.g. na balkanskom poluostrove*, Vypusk I, *ves'ma sekretno* (St. Petersburg, 1899), p. 63.

21. TsGAOR, f. 828, op. 1, d. 1362, l. 10.

22. *Ibid.*, l. 4.

23. See L. I. Narochnitskaia, *Rossiia i voiny Prussii v 60 godakh xix v. za ob"edinenie Germanii "sverkhu"* (Moscow, 1960), p. 65.

24. TsGAOR, f. 828, op. 1, d. 1362, l. 7.

25. V. V. Mavrodin and Val. V. Mavrodin, *Iz istorii otechestvennogo oruzhiia: Russkaia vintovka* (Leningrad, 1981), pp. 28–29.

26. See Curtiss, *Russia's Crimean War*, pp. 324–25.

27. L. G. Beskrovnyi, *Russkaia armiia i flot v xix veke* (Moscow, 1973), p. 343.

28. TsGVIA, f. 400, op, 2, d. 677 (rules for recruitment, 1867), l. 32.

29. See Curtiss, *Russia and Crimean War*, pp. 188–89; Zaionchkovskii, *Voennye reformy*, pp. 18–19.

30. A. V. Fedorov, *Russkaia armiia v 50–70-kh godakh xix veka. Ocherki* (Leningrad, 1959), p. 38, discusses the War Ministry report of November 1867 that developed this scenario.

31. TsGVIA, f. 400, op. 3, d. 175, l. 3 (letter of General Kotsebu, Commander of Odessa Military District, to Alexander II, December 16, 1868).

32. TsGAOR, f. 677, op. 1, d. 345 (note by D. A. Miliutin on the development of Russia's armed forces, December 9, 1870), l. 3.

33. A. M. Solov'eva, *Zhelezhnodorozhnyi transport Rossii vo vtoroi polovine xix v.* (Moscow, 1975), pp. 80, 83.

34. TsGVIA, f. 400, op. 4, d. 565 (strategic military roads, 1800–1888), l. 171; a verst equals about five-eighths of a mile.

35. TsGVIA, f. 400, op. 3, d. 371 (correcting military maps, 1874–75), ll. 1, 2, 17, and *passim*.

36. TsGVIA, f. 400, op. 2, d. 2484, l. 23.

37. Zaionchkovskii, *Voennye reformy*, p. 49.

38. TsGVIA, f. 400, op. 2, d. 1472 (war preparations, 1870), ll. 7, 16, 41, 142.

39. See Maurice Pearton, *The Knowledgeable State: Diplomacy, War and Technology Since 1830* (London, 1982), pp. 96–99. For some interesting reflections on the degree to which railroads had (and had not) actually facilitated the Prussian victories, see Dennis E. Showalter, *Railroads and Rifles: Soldiers, Technology and the Unification of Germany* (Hamden, Conn., 1976), pp. 52–59; and Martin van Creveld, *Supplying War: Logistics from Wallenstein to Patton* (New York, 1977), pp. 89–108. Also Larry H. Addington, *The Blitzkrieg Era and the German General Staff, 1865–1941* (New Brunswick, N.J., 1971), pp. 8–10.

40. P. A. Zaionchkovskii, ed., *Dnevnik D. A. Miliutina*, vol. 1, *1873–1875* (Moscow, 1947), p. 216.

41. TsGVIA, f. 400, op. 3, d. 371 (report of Commander of Orenburg Military District for 1865), l. 15.

42. R. F. Leslie, *Reform and Insurrection in Russian Poland 1856–65* (London, 1963), p. 224.

43. TsGVIA, f. 400, op. 3, d. 435 (data on troop mobilization, 1876), ll. 3, 4.

44. Narochnitskaia, *Rossiia i voiny Prussii*, p. 22.

45. He was also, apparently, the originator of the concept of "artificial glasnost," that is, the practice of using publicity to build support for controversial governmental policies. See TsGAOR, f. 722, op. 1, d. 192, ll. 21–22.

46. On Konstantin Nikolaevich, see Lincoln, *In Vanguard of Reform*, pp. 141–48; see also Jacob Kipp, "The Grand Duke Konstantin Nikolaevich and the Epoch of the Great Reforms, 1855–1866," Ph.D. dissertation, Pennsylvania State University, 1970, pp. 25–51, 272–86.

47. See Nik. Zherve, *Graf D. A. Miliutin: Biograficheskii ocherk* (St. Petersburg, 1906), pp. 11–12, 20. Zaionchkovskii, *Voennye reformy*, one of the greatest of Soviet historical works, is devoted to Miliutin's career as a War Ministry reformer. In English, see Forrestt A. Miller, *Dmitrii Miliutin and the Reform Era in Russia* (Charlotte, N.C., 1968). On the background to the reforms, see also E. Willis Brooks, "Reform in the Russian Army, 1856–61," *Slavic Review*, 43, no. 1 (Spring 1984): 63–82.

48. On Obruchev's involvement with revolutionary work, see Franco Venturi, *Roots of Revolution: A History of Populist and Socialist Movements in Nineteenth-Century Russia*, trans. Francis Haskell (New York, 1966), pp. 268–69; Adam Ulam, *In the Name of the People: Prophets and Conspirators in Prerevolutionary Russia* (New York, 1977), pp. 130–31; V. A. D'iakov, *Osvoboditel'noe dvizhenie v Rossii 1825–1861 gg.* (Moscow, 1979), pp. 240–44; and N. Makeev, *N. G. Chernyshevskii—redaktor "Voennogo sbornika"* (Moscow, 1950), pp. 25, 41, 54.

49. For some remarks on Obruchev's early career, see Peter Jakobs, *Das Werden des französisch-russischen Zweibundes, 1890–1894* (Weisbaden, 1968), pp. 32–35.

50. The rest were armed with either Karlés or Krnks. On rifles in general, see Mavrodin and Mavrodin, *Iz istorii*, pp. 54, 68, 76; Beskrovnyi, *Russkaia armiia i flot*, pp. 300–310; Joseph Bradley, *Guns for the Tsar: American Technol-*

ogy and the Small Arms Industry in Nineteenth-Century Russia (Dekalb, Ill.,
1990), pp. 104–26.

51. On artillery, see Beskrovnyi, *Russkaia armiia i flot*, pp. 346–47; and G.E.
Peredel'skii, ed., *Otechestvennaia artilleriia: 600 let* (Moscow, 1986), pp. 54–
55.

52. On the districts, see Miller, *Dmitrii Miliutin*, pp. 52, 54–55, 69; Zaionchkovskii, *Voennye reformy*, pp. 84–85, 95. The districts were Warsaw, Vilna,
Kiev, Odessa, Petersburg, Moscow, Finland, Riga, Khar'kov, Kazan, Caucasus, Turkistan, Orenburg, Western Siberia, and Eastern Siberia.

53. See William C. Fuller, Jr., *Civil–Military Conflict in Imperial Russia, 1881–
1914* (Princeton, N.J., 1985), pp. 7–8.

54. TsGVIA, f. 400, op. 4, d. 77, ll. 63.

55. Fuller, *Civil–Military Conflict*, pp. 10–11.

56. TsGAOR, f. 677, op. 1, d. 345 (notes by Miliutin on military reform, 1870),
ll. 7–9, 18.

57. TsGAOR, f. 722, op. 1, d. 192 (note on activity of Konstantin Nikolaevich as
Minister of Marine until January 1858), l. 35.

58. *Ibid.*, l. 37.

59. Kipp, "Grand Duke Konstantin Nikolaevich," pp. 230–32, 245–58.

60. Fedorov, *Russkaia armiia*, p. 38.

61. TsGVIA, f. 400, op. 3, d. 175, ll. 5–6.

62. L. M. Shneerson, *Franko-prusskaia voina i Rossiia* (Minsk, 1976), p. 10.

63. See, for example, Count Kutaisov's note of 1875 advocating privateering.
TsGAOR, f. 677, op. 1, d. 454.

64. See N. A. Khalfin, *Prisoedinenie srednei azii k Rossii* (Moscow, 1965), pp. 420–
24, for an explanation of the Central Asian conquests that stresses the
Russian government's "responsiveness" to the interests of its bourgeoisie.

65. See Hugh Seton-Watson, *The Russian Empire, 1801–1917* (Oxford, 1967),
pp. 442–43. See also Dietrich Geyer, *Russian Imperialism: The Interaction of
Domestic and Foreign Policy, 1860–1914,* trans. Bruce Little (New Haven,
1987), pp. 88–90. In my view, Geyer makes far too much of the psychological component behind Russia's conquests in Central Asia. In his opinion,
Russian imperialism both in central Asia and elsewhere can be understood
best as psychic compensation for the status anxiety of the Russian elite.
There is something to this, of course. As he shows, at times even a frustrated Miliutin could speak of this or that Russian annexation as an answer
to England or a challenge to Europe. Yet the weakness of this explanation
is its *a priori* assumption that Russian expansion was irrational—an assumption that unduly belittles the strategic imperative.

66. TsGVIA, f. 400, op. 2, d. 288 (Orenburg Report for 1865), ll. 17–18.

67. TsGAOR, f. 828, op. 1, d. 1457, ll. 205–6 (Gorchakov to Brunnov, August
30 [September 11], 1872).

68. Described by Cherniaev's sympathetic American biographer, David Mc-
Kenzie, in *The Lion of Tashkent: The Career of General M. G. Cherniaev* (Athens, Ga., 1974), pp. 83–91.

69. TsGAOR, f. 828, op. 1, d. 226, l. 67 (Gorchakov to Alexander II, March 13,
1873).

70. See Shneerson, *Franko-prusskaia voina*, pp. 193–206.
71. TsGAOR, f. 828, op. 1, d. 1457, ll. 209, 215 (Gorchakov letter to Alexander II of August 28 August [September 9], 1872, reporting on his conversations with Bismarck and Andrassy).
72. According to Count Osten-Saken, a Russian Foreign Ministry Official who had attended the Berlin meeting. See *Arkhiv Vneshnei Politiki Rossii* (hereafter AVPR), f. sekretnyi arkhiv ministra, op. 467, d. 271/272, l. 15. For a general treatment of the Berlin meeting, see William L. Langer, *European Alliances and Alignments, 1871–1890* (New York, 1950; reprint: New York, 1964), pp. 21–26.
73. AVPR, f. sekretnyi arkhiv ministra, op. 467, d. 110/119, l. 4; on the "War in Sight" Crisis of 1875 in general, see Langer, *European Alliances,* pp. 45–54; Jellavich, *St. Petersburg and Moscow,* p. 160.; Kiniapina, *Vneshniaia politika,* pp. 134–38.
74. Langer, *European Alliances,* p. 45.
75. Kiniapina, *Vneshniaia politika,* p. 134.
76. I was unfortunately unable to consult this memorandum (TsGVIA, f. VUA, d. 78854) while in Moscow. For much of what follows, I have relied on the exhaustive summary provided in Zaionchkovskii, *Voennye reformy,* pp. 280–304.
77. *Ibid.,* p. 280.
78. *Ibid.*
79. Zaionchkovskii, *Voennye reformy,* p. 284.
80. Among the lines proposed were ones between Moscow and Warsaw; Warsaw and Brest; Kursk–Kiev–Brest; and Khar'kov–Kremenchug–Volochissk. See TsGVIA, f. 400, op. 3, d. 911, l. 1; also TsGAOR, f. 828, op. 1, d. 1366 (opinion of Finance Minister Reutern on the War Ministry proposal, 1873), l. 4; and Zaionchkovskii, *Voennye reformy,* p. 285.
81. Zaionchkovskii, *Voennye reformy,* pp. 286–87; TsGAOR, f. 828, op. 1, d. 1366, l. 4.
82. TsGAOR, f. 828, op. 1, d. 1366, l. 4.
83. In retrospect it is clear that Berlin sought no war with Russia in the 1870s or the early 1880s. Bismarck's policy was, after all, predicated on peace with Russia. Even the most rabid militarists were opposed to such a war, both because of the difficulty they had in imagining how such a war could be brought to an end and because they saw no benefits to Germany from victory. In April 1879 Moltke wrote: "The Russians are unpleasant neighbors. They have absolutely nothing that one could take from them after a victorious war. They have no money and we do not need land." See D. von Schmerfeld, *Graf Moltke: Die Deutschen Aufmarchpläne 1871–1890* (Berlin, 1920), p. 80.
84. *Ibid.,* pp. 77–78, 87.
85. AVPR, f. sekretnyi arkhiv ministra, op. 467, d. 76/83 (Obruchev memorandum of January 29, 1880), l. 7.
86. Zaionchkovskii, *Voennye reformy,* p. 274.
87. *Ibid.,* p. 304.
88. TsGAOR, f. 828, op. 1, d. 1366, l. 4.

89. TsGVIA, f. 400, op. 3, d. 911, op. 2 (Russian railroads, 1870–89), l. 2

90. TsGAOR, f. 828, op. 1, d. 1366, ll. 6–8.

91. TsGAOR, f. 828, op. 1, d. 1365 (War Ministry–Finance Ministry dispute over the German–Russian defense expenditure comparisons, 1872–73), contains the Finance Ministry's rebuttal and the War Ministry's response.

92. *Ibid.*, l. 75, contains all of the cited quotations.

93. Fuller, *Civil–Military Conflict*, p. 60.

94. Zaionchkovskii, *Dnevnik Miliutina*, 1: 119.

95. In his sadly still unpublished doctoral dissertation, Peter von Wahlde discusses the two groups under the names of "Academics" and "Nationalists." This distinction, although valid for military *theoretical* thought, is in my view not entirely adequate when applied to practical strategy-making. What Wahlde has done is to apply the categories "Slavophile" and "Westernizer" to Russian military thinking. Slavophiles/nationalists believe that there is an authentically and peculiarly Russian art of war, while Westernizers/academics deny this, asserting that military science is not dependent on nationality or ethnicity, but is rather unitary and universally valid over time and culture. Yet in the practical world of the general staff, it was possible for a strategist to be both a "Slavophile" and a technologist, like V. A. Sukhomlinov, or a "Westernizer" and a magician, like Nikolai Nikolaevich the younger, simultaneously. See Chapter 8 of this book. Another reason I prefer my categories to Wahlde's is that arguments between technologists and magicians are by no means unique to Russia. See Peter von Wahlde, "Military Thought in Imperial Russia," Ph.D. dissertation, Indiana University, 1966, pp. 100–115.

96. M. I. Dragomirov, *Ocherki* (Kiev, 1898), p. 139. On Dragomirov, see also Wahlde, "Military Thought," pp. 120–29; G. P. Meshcheriakov, *Russkaia voennaia mysl' v xix veke* (Moscow, 1973), pp. 198–201, 216–17; and Fuller, *Civil–Military Conflict*, p. 6.

97. TsGVIA, f. 400, op. 3, d. 911, l. 2.

98. TsGVIA, f. 400, op. 3, d. 388 (troop dislocation, 1874–76), l. 1.

99. [V. A. Sukhomlinov], *Vospominaniia Sukhomlinova* (Moscow and Leningrad, 1926), p. 17.

100. AVPR, f. sekretnyi arkhiv ministra, op. 467, d. 76/83, ll. 8–9.

101. TsGVIA, f. 400, op. 3, d. 435 (material of the committee on collecting data of troop mobilization, 1876), l. 9.

102. *Osoboe pribavlenie*, Vypusk IV, *Soobrazheniia kasaiushchiesia plana voiny* (St. Petersburg, 1901), p. 2.

103. R.W. Seton-Watson, *Disraeli, Gladstone, and the Eastern Question: A Study in Diplomacy and Party Politics* (New York, 1972), pp. 73–74, 80.

104. TsGAOR, f. 677, op. 1, d. 677 (note of Saburov on Austro-Russian treaties), l. 1.

105. On the diplomatic antecedents of the Russo-Turkish war, see M. S. Anderson, *The Eastern Question 1744–1923* (London, 1966), pp. 178–93; B. H. Sumner, *Russia and the Balkans 1870–1880* (Hamden, Conn., 1962), pp. 137–289; and Richard Millman, *Britain and the Eastern Question 1875–1878* (Oxford, 1979), pp. 87–273.

106. Zaionchkovskii, *Dnevnik Miliutina*, 1: 195.

107. TsGVIA, f. 400, op. 3, d. 488, l. 134 (War Ministry to Ministry of Ways and Communications, November 12, 1876).

108. *Osoboe pribavlenie*, Vypusk IV, pp. 40 ff.

109. *Ibid.*, pp. 11–22.

110. *Ibid.*, Vypusk VI, *Dokumenty iz sekretnykh bumag g-ad. Miliutina* (St. Petersburg, 1911), pp. 195, 199 (note of February 7, 1877).

111. *Ibid.*, Vypusk I, pp. 90–91.

112. *Sbornik materialov po russko-turetskoi voine 1877–78 gg. na Balkanskom poluostrove*, Vypusk 22, "Prilozhenie" (St. Petersburg, 1899), p. 365.

113. *Osoboe pribavlenie*, Vypusk I, p. 95 (additional explanation to D.A. Miliutin by Obruchev concerning the note of February 13, 1877).

114. *Ibid.*, Vypusk IV, p. 29.

115. *Ibid.*, vypusk IV, pp. 31–38.

116. *Ibid.*, Vypusk IV, p. 81. Obruchev's 1880 version of Russian war objectives is defended, albeit unconvincingly, by L. G. Beskrovnyi in *Russkoe voennoe iskusstvo xix v.* (Moscow, 1974), pp. 309–10.

117. *Osoboe pribalenie*, Vypusk IV, p. 29.

118. *Ibid.*, Vypusk VI, p. 199.

119. See Nikolai Nikolaevich's letter to Alexander II of March 4, 1877, in *ibid.*, Vypusk IV, pp. 22–26.

120. *Ibid.*, pp. 38–39.

121. Forty thousand Rumanian troops and seven thousand Bulgarian militiamen fought on the side of Russia during the war; see Konstantin Kosev and Stefan Doinov, *Osvoboditelnata voina 1877–1878: Bolgarskata natsionalna revoliutsiia* (Sofia, 1988), p. 118.

122. On Gurko and the Shipka pass, see Colonel Epauchin, *Operations of General Gurko's Advance Guard in 1877,* trans. H. Havelock (London, 1900). Dragomirov, who was himself badly wounded at Shipka Pass, did try to put his theories into practice during the Russo-Turkish war. Wanting to encourage his troops to use cold steel, he issued them only sixty cartridges each prior to any battle and informed them that he would be hugely displeased with any man who returned with fewer than thirty. See D. A. Skalon, *Moi vospominaniia 1877–1878 gg.,* 1 (St. Petersburg, 1913): p. 145. Skalon, who served as Nikolai Nikolaevich's personal adjutant during the war, is a good source for both colorful anecdotes and high-level politics.

123. AVPR, f. sekretnyi arkhiv ministra, op. 467, d. 29/30, l. 62. (Material on the Peace with Turkey, 1878)

124. *Osoboe pribavlenie*, Vypusk VI, p. 267.

125. See George Hoover Rupp, *A Wavering Friendship: Russia and Austria 1876–1878* (Cambridge, Mass., 1941), pp. 451–54, 464; Nicholas Der Bagdasarian, *The Austro-German Rapprochement, 1870–1879* (London, 1976), p. 225.

126. AVPR, f. sekretnyi arkhiv ministra, op. 467, d. 29/30, l. 74.

127. S. L. Chernov, *Rossiia na zavershaiushchem etape vostochnogo krizisa 1875–1878 gg.* (Moscow, 1984), p. 73.

128. On the Western Powers and the Congress, see W. N. Medlicott, *The Congress of Berlin and After: A Diplomatic History of the Near East Settlement 1878–1880,* 2d ed. (Hamden, Conn., 1963).

129. Rostunov, *Russko-turetskaia voina 1877–78 g.g.* (Moscow, 1977), p. 257.

130. See A. Kornilov, *Kurs istorii Rossii xix v.*, pt. 3 (Moscow, 1918), pp. 211–17.

131. Bismarck once explained the Dual Alliance with the following analogy: "If one were going through a wood with a dear friend who exhibited signs of madness, one did very well to put a revolver in one's pocket, but one could be very friendly all the same." Bagdasarian, *Austro-German Rapprochement*, p. 301.

132. This was an argument originally made by Engels himself. See V. A. Zolotarev, *Russko-turetskaia voina 1877–78 gg. v otechestvennoi istoriografii* (Moscow, 1978), pp. 17–18; L. I. Narochnitskaia, *Rossiia i natsional'no-osvoboditel'noe dvizhenie na Balkanakh 1875–1878 gg.* (Moscow, 1979); A. L. Narochnitskii et al., eds., *Rossiia i natsional'no-osvoboditel'naia bor'ba na Balkanakh 1875–1878* (Moscow, 1978).

133. Rostunov, *Russko-turetskaia voina*, p. 258. Peter von Wahlde, "Dmitrii Miliutin: Appraisals," *Canadian Slavic Studies*, 3, no. 2 (Summer 1969): 401.

134. Zaionchkovskii, *Voennye reformy*, pp. 356 ff., represents the war as a severe test that Russia did not entirely pass. N. I. Beliaev, *Russko-turetskaia voina 1877–78 gg.* (Moscow, 1956), pp. 55, 434–38, emphasizes tactical failings. For a contemporary criticism of inadequacy of the reforms by an officer who served during the war, see Skalon, *Moi vospominaniia, 1: 11.*

135. Beskrovnyi, *Russkaia armiia i flot*, p. 310. Turkeys' rifles had been manufactured in the United States by the Providence Tool Company of Rhode Island.

136. Fedorov, *Russkaia armiia*, p. 172.

137. Beliaev, *Russko-turetskaia voina*, has the most thorough discussion of tactical issues; see pp. 44–50.

138. Skalon, *Moi vospominaniia*, p. 5.

139. Beskrovnyi, *Russkoe voennoe iskusstvo*, p. 315.

140. Beliaev, *Russko-turetskaia voina*, p. 411. In other words almost five illnesses were reported for each soldier serving in the army of the Caucasus.

141. J. H. Anderson, *Russo-Turkish War 1877–78 in Europe* (London, 1911), p. 103. Contributing to this problem was the army's fatal delay in disposing of the corpses of thousands of men and animals who had perished in the last months of the winter. See TsGVIA, f. VUA, d. 7854, (field commandant's department 1877–78), l. 5.

142. See TsGVIA, f. 400, op. 3, d. 551 (military measures in the aftermath of the Turkish war), ll. 42, 121–22, 159, 242–44.

143. Rostunov, *Russko-turetskaia voina*, p. 257.

144. *Ibid.*, p. 63.

145. Donald W. Mitchell, *A History of Russian and Soviet Sea Power* (New York, 1974), p. 182.

146. N. Monasterev and Serge Teretschenko, *Histoire de la Marine Russe*, trans. Jean Perceau (Paris, 1935), p. 205; Beskrovnyi, *Russkoe voennoe iskusstvo*, p. 313.

147. TsGVIA, f. 400, op. 4., d. 57 (note on the defense of Finland, 1878), ll. 3–4, 6, 58.

8. Alliances, Squandered Opportunities, & Self-Inflicted Wounds

1. TsGVIA, f. 400, op. 3, d. 551 (military measures after the Turkish war), l. 42.
2. TsGAOR, f. 568, op. 1, d. 52 (memorandum by V. N. Lamzdorff "Political Conditions in Europe After the Congress of Berlin"), l. 2.
3. AVPR, f. sekretnyi arkhiv ministra, op. 467, d. 110/119 (report of Bismarck's conversation with the French Ambassador in Berlin, November 14, 1879), l. 5. Bismarck was obviously making a smirking allusion to Alexander's relationship with his mistress, the Princess Catherine Dolgorukaia. About almost no other subject was the Tsar as touchy as about this.
4. TsGAOR, f. 568, op. 1, d. 52, ll. 15–16, 23.
5. *Ibid.*, ll. 25–26.
6. See William L. Langer, *European Alliances and Alignments, 1871–1890* (New York, 1950; reprint, 1964), pp. 171–211; Barbara Jelavich, *St. Petersburg and Moscow: Tsarist and Soviet Foreign Policy*, 1814–1974 (Bloomington, Ind., 1974), pp. 192–96; A. J. P. Taylor, *The Struggle for Mastery in Europe 1848–1918* (London, 1954), pp. 267–71.
7. TsGAOR, f. 568, op. 1, d. 52, l. 27. The quoted phrase comes from the resolution of the December 1879 meeting of the council.
8. AVPR, f. sekretnyi arkhiv ministra, op. 467, d. 146/150 (instructions to Ambassadors in Vienna and Berlin), l. 3.
9. *Ibid.*, l. 5.
10. William C. Fuller, Jr., *Civil–Military Conflict in Imperial Russia, 1881–1914* (Princeton, N.J., 1985), p. 49.
11. AVPR, f. sekretnyi arkhiv ministra, op. 467, d. 76/83, l. 15.
12. TsGAOR, f. 568, op. 1, d. 89 (Charykov note on Anglo-Russian conflict over India and Afghanistan, 1881–83), l. 4.
13. See Aaron L. Friedburg, *The Weary Titan: Britain and the Experience of Relative Decline 1895–1905* (Princeton, N.J., 1988), pp. 224–25, 215, 234.
14. On the Stoletov mission, see N. S. Kiniapina, *Vneshnaia politika Rossii vtoroi poloviny xix veka* (Moscow, 1974), pp. 264–65; Sir Robert Ensor, *England 1870–1914* (London, 1968), pp. 62–63; David Gillard, *The Struggle for Asia 1828–1914: A Study in British and Russian Imperialism* (London, 1977), pp. 136, 139.
15. Gillard, *Struggle for Asia*, pp. 140, 143.
16. TsGAOR, f. 568, op. 1, d. 90 (journal of the Special Conference of December 1884), l. 9.
17. TsGAOR, f. 568, op. 1, d. 91 (Russian–Afghan clash in the Kush region, March 1885), l. 5.
18. *Ibid.*, l. 11.
19. TsGVIA, f. 400, op. 4, d. 584 (preparations for Black Sea operations, 1885–95), ll. 4, 7–8.
20. Ironically enough, British military planners did not place much credence in their own capability of inflicting harm on Russia through an exclusive use of naval power. In fact, after 1892 the British Admiralty took the view that Russia was strong enough to force the straits any time it wished. See

Friedberg, *Weary Titan,* pp. 216, 217; Samuel R. Williamson, Jr., *The Politics of Grand Strategy: Britain and France Prepare for War, 1904–1914* (London, 1990), p. 16.

21. TsGAOR, f. 543, op. 1, d. 67 (reports of I. S. Dolgorukov, 1882–84), l. 1.
22. Katkov also frequently warned the Emperor about German intentions in his private correspondence. See, for example, TsGAOR, f. 677, op. 1, d. 477 (Katkov to Alexander III, May 11, 1887, on the need to limit German influence in the Balkans), ll. 1, 9–10.
23. The Bulgarian mess is the centerpiece of George Kennan, *The Decline of Bismarck's World Order: Franco-Russian Relations 1875–1890* (Princeton, N.J., 1979), Chapters 5–17.
24. See the report of Russia's military attaché in Paris of March 5, 1887, in TsGVIA, f. 440, op. 1, d. 193, l. 40.
25. TsGVIA, f. 428, op. 1, d. 197 (military preparations in Austria-Hungary, 1887), ll. 7, 9, 14, 16, and *passim.*
26. *Ibid.,* ll. 21–22.
27. *Ibid.,* ll. 59–64, 91, 92, 109, 121, 227.
28. TsGVIA, f. 428, op. 1, dd. 122–25.
29. *Ibid.,* d. 167.
30. TsGAOR, f. 568, op. 1, d. 53 (Lamzdorff's review of the foreign policy of Alexander III, 1894), l. 2.
31. See Beck's letter of December 1, 1887, in Edmund von Glaise-Horstenau, *Franz Josefs Weggefährte: Das Leben des Generalstabschefs Grafen Beck—Nach seinem Aufzeichnungen und hinterlassen Dokumenten* (Vienna, 1930), p. 299.
32. TsGVIA, f. 428, op. 1, d. 205 (defense attaché reports from Vienna, 1891), l. 87.
33. TsGVIA, f. 428, op. 1, d. 197, l. 47.
34. Fuller, *Civil-Military Conflict,* pp. 49, 60.
35. TsGVIA, f. 400, op. 3, d. 911 (strategic railroads, 1888–89), ll. 1–3, 5–7, 21.
36. TsGVIA, f. 400, op. 4, d. 565 (strategic roads, 1830–1904), ll. 108, 172.
37. AVPR, f. sekretnyi arkhiv ministra, op. 467, d. 76–83, l. 12 (Obruchev to Giers, October 27, 1883)
38. TsGVIA, f. 400, op. 4, d. 445 (papers of the Operations Section of the Main Staff on Russia concentrations in the west, 1880–1903), l. 68.
39. *Ibid.,* ll. 68–69.
40. AVPR, f. sekretnyi arkhiv ministra, op. 467, d. 76–83, ll. 13,15.
41. TsGVIA, f. 400, op. 4, d. 445, ll. 78.
42. Fuller, *Civil–Military Conflict,* p. 15; *Obzor deiatel'nosti voennogo ministerstva v tsarstvovanie Aleksandra III 1881–1894* (St. Petersburg, 1903), appendix, "Mobilizatsionnaia gotovnost' voisk," p. 10.
43. TsGAOR, f. 568, op. 1, d. 52 (report of Orlov on conversation with Bismarck), l. 7.
44. AVPR, f. sekretnyi arkhiv ministra, op. 467, d. 76/83, l. 12 (Obruchev to Giers, October 27, 1883).
45. TsGVIA, f. 400, op. 4, d. 13 (material on the defense of the western territories, 1901 and previously), l. 83.

46. *Ibid.*, d. 3 (rear areas under plan 17, 1893), ll. 1–2.
47. *Ibid.*, d. 436 (rear areas of the armies, 1900–1905), ll. 39, 171, 213.
48. William C. Fuller, Jr., "The Russian Empire," in Ernest R. May, ed., *Knowing One's Enemies: Intelligence Assessment Before the Two World Wars* (Princeton, N.J., 1984), p. 106.
49. TsGVIA, f. 428, op. 1, d. 197, l. 175 (on the mission of Colonel Romanenko).
50. *Ibid.*, l. 219.
51. TsGVIA, f. 400, op. 4, d. 277 (information on Afghanistan 1892–1904), l. 1. This particular mission did not pan out all that well. The political agent, F. A. Fel'dman, wrote that he had paid two different agents 200 and 300 rubies respectively for their efforts, and complained that "the sums, of course, are very small but all the same they are too high by comparison to the results we achieved" see. l. 2.
52. *Ibid.*, d. 266 (secret report on nationalities within the Austro-Hungarian Empire, 1901–3), ll. 37, 56.
53. Bakhmeteff Archive, Columbia University, A. M. Nikolaev Collection, part 3, 5, BAR 306.2.2, file 36, "Instruction to Military Attachés, 1880," p. 3.
54. TsGVIA, f. 428, op. 1, d. 208 (Austrian military preparations, 1893), l. 185.
55. On intelligence in the late 1880s and 1890s, see *ibid.*, d. 205 (information from Zuev in Vienna, 1891), ll. 17a–17b; TsGVIA, f. 400, op. 4, d. 260 (Austrian war plans of 1891–1903), ll. 55 ff., 64, 80, 82–83, 113–15.
56. TsGVIA, f. 400, op. 4, d. 445, l. 81.
57. *Ibid.*, d. 260, ll. 64–65.
58. *Ibid.*, d. 445, l. 74.
59. *Ibid.*, l. 76.
60. *Ibid.*
61. *Ibid.*, ll. 77–82
62. *Ibid.*, l. 78; this passage is also quoted by A. M. Zaionchkovskii. *Podgotovka Rossii k imperialisticheskoi voine: Ocherki voennoi podgotovski i pervonachal'nykh planov po arkhivnykh dokumentam* (Moscow, 1926), p. 35.
63. On the French approach in 1879 after the Congress of Berlin, see TsGAOR, f. 568, op. 1, d. 52, l. 1; on approaches in 1887, including offers of intelligence collaboration, see TsGVIA, f. 440, op. 1, d. 193 (reports on the condition of the French army, 1882–87), ll. 48–49.
64. Rene Albrecht-Carrié, *A Diplomatic History of Europe Since the Congress of Vienna* (New York, 1958), pp. 209, 212–13.
65. AVPR, f. sekretni arkhiv, op. 467, d. 146/150 (secret instructions to ambassadors, 1884), l. 5.
66. TsGAOR, f. 568, op. 1, d. 52, l. 27.
67. "A monarchical, strong, and prosperous France would be in our interests and in those of the normal equilibrium of Europe," the 1884 instructions to Orlov on the eve of his departure for Berlin concluded. This was, of course, more wishful thinking than policy guidance. AVPR, f. sekretnyi arkhiv ministra, op. 467, d. 146/150, l. 6.
68. TsGAOR, f. 543, op. 1, d. 67 (reports of Dolgorukov from Gastein and Berlin, 1882–84), l. 6.

69. TsGVIA, f. 440, op. 4, d. 264 (the French maneuvers of 1879), ll. 12, 14–15.
70. On the influence of the nonrenewal of the Reinsurance Treaty on the Emperor, see AVPR, f. sekretnyi arkhiv, op. 467, d. 146/150 (instructions to ambassadors, 1895), l. 15. The instruction to Osten-Saken, Ambassador-designate to Berlin, given here provides a capsule summary of the Ministry of Foreign Affairs' version of the origins of the Franco-Russian alliance. On the Franco-Russian alliance in general, see also George F. Kennan, *The Fateful Alliance: France, Russia, and the Coming of the First World War* (New York, 1984). This beautifully written book, an intricate and detailed study of Franco-Russian negotiations in the early 1890s, nonetheless offers several interpretations with which I disagree. I also have a problem with contradictions in the text. Kennan argues, for instance, that Alexander was relieved by the lapsing of the Reinsurance Treaty (p. 34) but later (p. 68) identifies that event as one of "the decisive factors shaping the Tsar's readiness in principle, to pursue the project of a genuine alliance with France." See also Peter Jakobs, *Das Werden des französisch-russischen Zweibundes, 1890–1894* (Weisbaden, 1968), pp. 44–45.
71. AVPR, f. sekretnyi arkhiv ministra, op. 467, d. 133/138 (correspondence on the Franco-Russian alliance), l. 13.
72. Larry H. Addington, *The Blitzkrieg Era and the German General Staff, 1865–1941* (New Brunswick, N.J., 1971), p. 12–14.
73. After the signing of the Franco-Russian alliance, this interpretation of the designs of the Triple Alliance also became a staple at the Russian Foreign Ministry. The secret instructions to Osten-Saken, drafted by the Foreign Minister and approved by the Emperor in 1895, contained the sentence: "We now know that the Triple Alliance plans for war against us and envisions taking Poland away from us." See AVPR, f. sekretyni arkhiv ministra, op. 467, d. 146/150, l. 14.
74. *Ibid.*, d. 133/138, ll. 1, 4–17.
75. *Ibid.*, l. 20 (the French draft military convention), and l. 21 (the explanatory note by General Boisdeffre, Chief of the French General Staff).
76. *Ibid.*, d. 373 (material on the Franco-Russian alliance; Giers to Alexander II, August 22, 1891), l. 31.
77. *Ibid.*, l. 44. Kennan provides an English translation of this document in *Fateful Alliance*, pp. 264–68; see also the discussion in Jakobs, *Das Werden*, pp. 115–16.
78. AVPR, f. sekretnyi arkhiv ministra, op. 467, d. 373, l. 45
79. *Ibid.*
80. *Ibid.*, l. 48.
81. It will be noted, once again, how my interpretation of the military rationale for the Franco-Russian alliance differs from that of George Kennan. Ambassador Kennan, who includes a partial translation of the Obruchev memorandum as an appendix to his *Fateful Alliance* (pp. 264–68), is dismayed by the fact that it appears to accept war as inevitable, and further apparently says nothing either about war causation or war objectives. He views it as seminal document in European military history, a manifesto promoting unlimited war in Clausewitz's sense. "Now, as one sees from

Obruchev's paper, victory was to be either total or overwhelmingly decisive; and it was, in this sense, regarded as an objective in itself. The idea now is that you would defeat your opponent—his armies and his people—so decisively that his will would become crushed or insignificant; your will, correspondingly, would become supreme. Total war, in other words, and total victory," pp. 161–66 (quote from page 164). In my view, Ambassador Kennan's reading of this text is mistaken on several counts. First, since he is unaware of the despair at the Russian War Ministry over the deterioration of the military balance, he depicts Obruchev's insistence on simultaneous mobilization, general war, and so on, as symptoms of belligerance. In fact, Obruchev's sole concern was the defense of Russia. As I have shown, the memorandum of the summer of 1892 was the logical outgrowth of his thinking about what would be necessary to secure that defense. Thus, Obruchev's demand for immediate mobilization, which Kennan sees as an "arrogant" command to the diplomats to abstain from spoiling the plans of the military, was actually nothing of the kind. Given his belief in the decisiveness of mobilization speed, Obruchev was saying that if Germany mobilized, war had already begun, and the diplomats had already failed in their attempts to avert it. That being the case, they should do nothing that would reduce Russia's chances of victory. As for Obruchev's disregard for the putative objectives of the war, this once again stemmed from a concern for defense, not from truculence. Nowhere, and at no time, did Obruchev recommend aggression by Russia against the Teutonic Powers. His unchanging assumption was that the war would result from German or Austrian aggression. Russia's objective, therefore (and the only objective that military leaders could properly entertain), would simply be to defend itself. Yet the most bizarre misreading of the memorandum occurs when Kennan represents Obruchev as a proponent of total victory, as promoting the end of the Hohenzollern and Hapsburg dynasties. Obruchev speaks of the war as ending with a general European conference of the powers—that is, negotiations, not unconditional surrender. Further, this conference would be attended by representatives of "the sides" involved, clearly implying that the defeated parties will have stable governments with whom it will be possible to negotiate. Obruchev is not prophesying the Paris Peace Conference of 1918 here; rather he is thinking back to the Congress of Berlin. Far from advocating the end of the Hohenzollerns or the Hapsburgs, he is exclusively concerned with the Romanovs. The German and even the Austrian empires might well survive defeat in a general European war. However, Obruchev had his doubts about whether Russia could.

82. On Giers's objections, see AVPR, f. sekretnyi arkhiv ministra, op. 467, d. 133/138, l. 22 (Giers to Vannovskii, May 13, 1892), l. 24 (Giers to Alexander III, May 18, 1892), d. 373, l. 53 (Giers to Alexander III, June 4, 1892), l. 58 (Giers to Alexander III, August 1, 1892), ll. 67–68 (Giers to Alexander III, August 7, 1892).

83. AVPR, f. sekretnyi arkhiv ministra, op. 467, d. 133/138, ll. 31–32 (Giers to Alexander III, September 1893, with a copy of the note of Boisdeffre).

84. *Ibid.*, l. 35–36.

85. The Moltke concept in the event of a European war had been for Germany to stand on the defensive against France while launching an offensive against Russia. By contrast, the famous Schlieffen plan posited a holding action in the east and a massive attack in the west. Addington, *The Blitzkrieg Era*, pp. 12–14. On the domestic context of the bill, see Gordon A. Craig, *Germany 1866–1945* (New York, 1978), pp. 235–38, 257–58. On the strategic context, Taylor, *Struggle for Mastery*, pp. 338–40.

86. My reading of material in AVPR, f. sekretnyi arkhiv ministra, op. 467, d. 133/138, d. 373 leads me to differ, once again, with George Kennan, who argues (*Fateful Alliance*, pp. 219–220, 230) that Alexander III had decided to approve the military convention prior to receiving Vannovskii's letters.

87. Any student of the Franco-Russian alliance must be grateful to V. N. Lamzdorff, whose contemporary memoranda, preserved in Foreign Ministry Archives, represent an ongoing chronicle of the negotiations. See AVPR, f. sekretnyi arkhiv ministra, op. 467, d. 373, ll. 52, 56–57, 78, 110.

88. George Kennan. This in a nutshell is the thesis of his *Fateful Alliance*.

89. TsGAOR, f. 543, op. 1, d. 668 (memorandum of Sergei Popov, dated Vevey-la-Tour, September 5[17], 1896), ll. 1, 5, 12–13, 14, 16, 18–19, 27. On Nicholas II and public opinion, see TsGAOR, f. 568, op. 1, d. 63 (notes of Lamzdorff for 1903), l. 10. "Speaking of the undesirability of war in general, the minister [Lamzdorff] reminded His Majesty of those consequences which the war of 1877–78 had in the area of revolutionary propaganda. At that time public opinion had influenced the decision taken by the government. The weakness and inconsistency of the government was exploited by leaders of the advanced parties 'and all of this led to the 1st of March' [the date on which Alexander II was assassinated], noted the Tsar," (meeting between Lamzdorff and Nicholas II, February 11, 1903).

90. TsGAOR, f. 568, op. 1, d. 53 (secret overview of the foreign policy of Alexander III, 1894–95), l. 6.

91. AVPR, f. sekretnyi arkhiv ministra, op. 467, d. 133/138, l. 37 (Vannovskii to Giers, 1893).

92. M.E. Falkus, *The Industrialization of Russia, 1700–1914* (London, 1977), p. 64.

93. See John P. McKay, *Pioneers for Profit: Foreign Entrepreneurship and Russian Industrialization, 1885–1913* (Chicago, 1970), p. 26. For discussions of the problems with this figure, see pp. 29–32. See also the most important new work on tsarist economic development: Peter Gatrell, *The Tsarist Economy 1850–1917* (London, 1986), pp. 226–28.

94. McKay, *Pioneers*, p. 32.

95. This point is developed with considerable sophistication in Gatrell, *Tsarist Economy*, pp. 207–14.

96. Paul Kennedy, *The Rise and Fall of the Great Powers: Economic Change and Military Conflict from 1500 to 2000* (New York, 1987), pp. 210–11, 242. See also Paul R. Gregory, *Russian National Income 1885–1913* (Cambridge, 1982), pp. 154–59.

97. Gatrell, *Tsarist Economy*, p. 43; Fuller, *Civil–Military Conflict*, p. 49.

98. On military finance in the 1880s and 1890s generally, see Fuller, *Civil–Military Conflict*, pp. 47–74.

99. See A. Kersnovskii, *Istoriia russkoi armii, ch. III (1881–1917 gg.)* (Belgrad, 1935), pp. 512, 530.

100. On this crisis see Gillard, *Struggle for Asia,* pp. 155–56; AVPR, f. 133 (chancellery, 1892), op. 470, d. 47, ll. 91–93, particularly l. 93, with the conclusion of the special conference of August 25, 1892, on this subject.

101. TsGAOR, f. 568, op. 1, d. 58 (private notes of Lamzdorff on his weekly reports to the Emperor, 1897), ll. 36, 40–41.

102. AVPR, f. sekretnyi arkhiv ministra, op. 467, d. 160/162 (Ministry of Foreign Affairs–Ministry of War Correspondence, 1898), ll. 2–3.

103. "The outcome of the great war confronting us against a European coalition must of course be decided on the banks of the Vistula or Oder on the one hand and on the Rhine on the other. Whatever successes we might obtain in the remaining secondary theaters, the conditions of the peace treaty will be determined by victory or defeat on our western frontier" (Cherniaev to Vannovskii, December 14, 1892), TsGVIA, f. 400, op. 4, d. 480 (reports on Turkestan, 1892–1902), l. 39.

104. *Ibid.,* l. 24, 47–48 (quote from l. 24).

105. *Ibid.,* d. 26 (report of the Commander of Turkestan Military District for 1900), ll. 3–9.

106. Andrew Malozemoff, *Russian Far Eastern Policy 1881–1904* (Berkeley, Calif., 1958), pp. 62–67.

107. Shumpei Okamoto, *The Japanese Oligarchy and the Russo-Japanese War* (New York, 1970), pp. 48–49.

108. See Jellavich, *St. Petersburg and Moscow,* pp. 230–32.

109. TsGAOR, f. 568, op. 1, d. 58 (notes by Lamzdorff for his weekly foreign policy briefings to the Tsar, 1897), l. 7,17–18; see also "Proekt zakhvata Bosfora v 1897 goda," *Krasnyi arkhiv.* 1 (Moscow, 1922): 153–54.

110. Malozemoff, *Russian Far Eastern Policy,* pp. 131–44.

111. TsGAOR, f. 568, op. 1, d. 62 (Lamzdorff's notes on his weekly foreign policy briefings to the Emperor, 1901), l. 18 (May 15, 1901).

112. For an example of this sort of thing, by an extremely sympathetic American observer, see Albert J. Beveridge, *The Russian Advance* (New York, 1903), p. 15: "Russia's far-sighted and patient policy, which has always looked ahead and considered the needs of the Russian people a century beyond the immediate moment . . ."

113. Jellavich, *St. Petersburg and Moscow,* pp. 232–37, touches on most of these explanations. For an interesting interpretation combining economics and psychology, see Dietrich Geyer, *Russian Imperialism: The Interaction of Domestic and Foreign Policy 1860–1914,* trans. Bruce Little (New Haven, 1987), pp. 186–19. On page 192 the seizure of Port Arthur is described as "compensation for the Bosphorus expedition that never happened." For an exhaustive review of the economic side of Russia's Asian imperialism, see B. A. Romanov, *Russia in Manchuria (1892–1906),* trans. Susan Wilbur Jones (New York, 1974), pp. 62–93.

114. TsGAOR, f. 601, op. 1, d. 1199 (letters of Wilhelm II to Nicholas II), ll. 9–10.

115. John Albert White, *The Diplomacy of the Russo-Japanese War* (Princeton, N.J., 1964), pp. 37–44, 63–64; Malozemoff, *Russian Far Eastern Policy,* pp. 184–

86; TsGAOR, f. 543, op. 1, d. 185 (manuscript by A. A. Abaza on Russian Far Eastern Policy, 1896–1904), ll. 4–6.

116. TsGAOR, f. 601, op. 1, d. 716 (telegrams to and from Nicholas II about the seizure of Port Arthur), l. 1.

117. Andrew Marshall Verner, "Nicholas II and the Role of the Autocrat During the First Russian Revolution," Ph.D. dissertation, Columbia University, 1986, pp. 66–67.

118. See *Ibid.*, pp. 154 ff.

119. Malozemoff, *Russian Far Eastern Policy*, pp. 46–48.

120. Geyer, *Russian Imperialism*, pp. 187–91, 193. Richard Pipes, *The Russian Revolution* (New York, 1990), pp. 12–13.

121. "Proekt zakhvata Bosfora", pp. 153–54.

122. TsGAOR, f. 568, op. 1, d. 58, ll. 17–18.

123. *Ibid.*, l. 42 (weekly report of July 1, 1897).

124. "Proekt zakhvata Bosfora," pp. 161–62.

125. TsGAOR, f. 543, op. 1, d. 173 (memorandum of Prince Vol'konskii, December 1897), ll. 3, 27.

126. TsGAOR, f. 568, op. 1, d. 58, l. 71 (report to Nicholas II of November 27, 1897).

127. *Ibid.*, d. 59 (notes of Lamzdorff on his weekly reports to the Emperor, 1898), l. 1; on the Navy's lack of interest in Port Arthur, see also Malozemoff, *Russia's Far Eastern Policy*, pp. 100–101.

128. TsGAOR, f. 601, op. 1, d. 720, ll. 1–3.

129. Geyer, *Russian Imperialism*, p. 210.

130. TsGVIA, f. 400, op. 4, d. 60 (materials on the conference of January 25, 1903, about a potential withdrawal from Manchuria), ll. 21–22.

131. TsGAOR, f. 543, op. 1, d. 170 (memoranda on Mongolia, Japan, and Manchuria in the Tsarskoe selo palace archives, 1900–1903), ll. 11, 17, 20, 34.

132. TsGAOR, f. 568, op. 1, d. 65 (notes by Lamzdorff on his weekly reports to the Emperor, 1904), l. 7 (February 10, 1904).

133. TsGVIA, f. 165, op. 1, d. 602 (report by War Minister A. N. Kuropatkin, 1900), l. 31.

134. TsGVIA, f. 400, op. 4, d. 56 (notes of the Main Staff on naval matters, 1903), ll. 26–27.

135. *Ibid.*, d. 62 (report by V. V. Sakharov on the strategic situation in Pacific Asia, March 17, 1901), ll. 1–2.

136. [Voenno-istoricheskaia komissiia po opisaniiu Russko-iaponskoi voiny], *Russko-iaponskaia voina 1904–1905 gg.* 1 (St. Petersburg, 1910): 183, 193.

137. *Ibid.*, 1: 171, 176, 180–82, 187, 192, 196–97, 207–8, 214, 233, 246, 248–49.

138. TsGAOR, f. 543, op. 1, d. 185, l. 58.

139. TsGVIA, f. 400, op. 4, d. 56, l. 31.

140. I have consulted two copies of the report. TsGVIA, f. 165, op. 1, d. 602, contains Kuropatkin's copy, along with his working drafts. TsGAOR, f. 601, op. 1, d. 445, is Nicholas II's copy, with marginal comments by S. Iu. Witte.

141. TsGVIA, f. 165, op. 1, d. 602, l. 20.
142. *Ibid.*, l. 22.
143. *Ibid.*, ll. 39–40.
144. *Ibid.*, ll. 25–26, 31.
145. *Ibid.*, l. 35
146. *Ibid.*, l. 41,
147. *Ibid.*, l. 47.
148. TsGVIA, f. 400, op. 4, d. 546 (communications between the Army and Navy Main Staffs, 1903), l. 1.
149. *Ibid.*, d. 56, l. 27.
150. TsGAOR, f. 543, op. 1, d. 67 (1903 report on War Ministry activities from 1898 to 1903), l. 97.
151. *Ibid.*, l. 98.
152. AVPR, f. sekretnyi arkhiv ministra, op. 467, d. 162/164, (proposed negotiations on quick-firing artillery, 1898), ll. 6–7. For the ultimately decisive objections of Lamzdorff, see TsGAOR, f. 568, op. 1, d. 59, ll. 12–14.
153. Dan L. Morrill, "Nicholas II and the Call for the First Hague Conference," *Journal of Modern History*, vol. 46, no. 2 (June 1974).
154. TsGVIA, f. 400, op. 4, d. 433 (basic guidelines for deployments in the west, 1899–1904), ll. 4–5.
155. TsGVIA, f. 165, op. 1, d. 602, l. 19.
156. TsGAOR, f. 543, op. 1, d. 67, l. 97.
157. TsGVIA, f. 400, op. 4, d. 21 (secret report of Warsaw military district, 1900), l. 85.
158. *Ibid.*, d. 77 (notes on reports of the commanders of military districts, 1898–99), ll. 3, 5.
159. *Ibid.*, d. 3 (rear regions under plan 17), l. 20.
160. *Ibid.*, d. 50, (retrospective report on western defense, 1898–1902), l. 30.
161. *Ibid.*, d. 23 (report of Odessa district for 1900), l. 18.
162. *Ibid.*, l. 18.
163. *Ibid.*, d. 77, ll. 1–2.
164. *Ibid.*, d. 50, l. 91.
165. *Ibid.*, ll. 91–92.
166. TsGVIA, f. 400, op. 4, d. 441 (intelligence data about Austria-Hungary, 1901), ll. 3, 10, 70, 83, 115; for data from 1902 and 1903, see *ibid.*, d. 56, l. 5.
167. *Ibid.*, d. 16 (journal of the conference on western defense, 1901), l.32.
168. *Ibid.*, d. 30 (proposals for increasing the size of the Russian army in the 1904–8 budgetary period), l. 124.
169. *Ibid.*, d. 50, l. 22.
170. *Ibid.*, ll. 91–92.
171. This is one of the main theses of Douglas Porch's excellent work, *March to the Marne: The French Army 1871–1914* (London, 1981), pp. 90–99.
172. See the report of the Main Staff April 22, 1903: "The military weakness of France as a consequence of the transition to the two-year term of service; the struggle of parties in parliament, part of whose deputies want to turn the French army into a militia; the unsuccessful reforms of General An-

dré; the potential involvement of the army in the political battle; the·
adhesion of officers to different parties—all of these enfeeble our ally
and increase the likelihood of an attack on Russia, which might have to
stand alone again." TsGVIA, f. 400, op. 4, d. 50, l. 92.

173. *Ibid.*, d. 445 (new concentrations on the western frontier, 1902–3), l. 61.
174. *Ibid.*, ll. 61–63.
175. AVPR, f. sekretnyi arkhiv ministra, op. 467, d. 133/138, l. 46 (copy of note by Nicholas to Perier, November 11, 1894).
176. TsGAOR, f. 601, op. 1, d. 1199, l. 18.
177. TsGAOR, f. 568, op. 1, d. 69, l. 55.
178. AVPR, f. sekretnyi arkhiv ministra, op. 467, d. 373, l. 131.
179. *Ibid.*, l. 144–46.
180. *Ibid.*, d. 374 (Foreign Ministry correspondence on the Franco-Russian alliance, 1901–1913), l. 154–55.
181. *Ibid.*, d. 373, l. 147.
182. *Ibid.*, d. 374, l. 155.
183. *Ibid.*, d. 373, l. 147.
184. *Ibid.*, d. 374, l. 164 (draft of letter of Nicholas II to Delcassé, May 15, 1901).
185. See TsGVIA, f. 400, op. 4, d. 23 (Odessa District report for 1900), l. 3.
186. *Ibid.*, d. 56, l.19 (Main Staff report of March 19, 1903).
187. *Ibid.*, d. 433, l. 40.
188. "The decisive character the coming struggle of the peoples will assume, the enormous tension of all forces that Russia will have to exert, absolutely demands that we be capable and ready not only to ward off blows, but to deliver blows that will carry the struggle onto the territory of the enemy in order there to seek the conclusion of the war and the attainment of its final ends." (1903 note by Colonel Alekseev, subsequently Nicholas II's Chief of Staff in World War I), *ibid.*, d. 50, l. 41.
189. *Ibid.*, d. 13 (special conference on the defense of the west), ll. 183–87; quotations from l. 187.
190. *Ibid.*, ll. 188–89, 211.
191. *Ibid.*, d. 16, ll. 87, 90.
192. *Ibid.*, d. 28 (mobilization issues, 1901), l. 116.
193. *Ibid.*, d. 16 (journal of the Special Conference on Western Defense, 1901), l. 34.
194. *Ibid.*, d. 50, ll. 35–36, and d. 453 (secret instructions to front commanders), ll. 1–2, 5.

9. The Quest for Exits

1. See F. I. Bulgakov, *Port-Artur: Iaponskaia osada i russkaia oborona ego s moria i suchi,* 1 (St. Petersburg, 1905): 31, 91–93.
2. TsGAOR, f. 568, op. 1, d. 65 (Lamzdorff notes for 1905), l. 6 (February 10[23], 1904).
3. [Voenno-istoricheskaia komissiia po opisaniiu russko-iaponskoi voiny], *Russko-iaponskaia voina 1904–1905 gg.* 1 (St. Petersburg: 1910): 181.

4. TsGVIA, f. 400, op. 4, d. 60 (materials of the Operations Section of the Main Staff on issues of Far Eastern defense), ll. 24–25.
5. *Russko-iaponskaia voina,* 1: 192.
6. TsGVIA, f. 280, op. 1, d. 3 (A. F. Rediger memoirs), l. 390.
7. See Bruce Menning, *Bayonets Before Bullets* (Bloomington, Ind., 1992), Chapter 5.
8. M. Kazakov, "Izpol'zovanie rezervov v russko-iaponskoi voine, 1904–1905 gg.," *Voenno-istoricheskii zhurnal* 13, no. 4 (April 1971): 47–48.
9. TsGAOR, f. 543, op. 1, d. 159 (journal of the Conference of February 28, 1905), l. 2.
10. For one important contemporary evaluation of the war in this sense, see Julian S. Corbett, *Some Principles of Maritime Strategy* (London, 1911), pp. 75–81.
11. TsGAOR, f. 568, op. 1, d. 66, l. 2.
12. On the request of Admiral Rozhdestvenskii, see TsGAOR, f. 568, op. 1, d. 66, l. 10; also TsGAOR, f. 543, op. 1, d. 676 (Foreign Ministry note of 1904 on using the Black Sea Fleet in the Far East), ll. 3, 6.
13. TsGAOR, f. 543, op. 1, d. 160 (supplies for the Manchurian army, March 1905), ll. 1–2.
14. For some interesting comments on this process, see A. A. Kizevetter, *Na rubezhe dvukh stoletii: Vospominaniia 1881–1914* (Prague, 1929), pp. 354–56, 370–72.
15. These eventually resulted in the call-up of more than a million men. See L. G. Beskrovnyi, *Armiia i flot Rossii v nachale xx v.: Ocherki voenno-ekonomicheskogo potensiala* (Moscow, 1986), p. 11.
16. TsGAOR, f. 543, op. 1, d. 160, l. 42, 44.
17. TsGVIA, f. 400, op. 4, d. 472 (changes in western deployments caused by the Manchurian war), l. 4.
18. V. A. Sukhomlinov, *Vospominaniia Sukhomlinova* (Moscow and Leningrad, 1926), p. 94.
19. TsGAOR, f. 400, op. 4, d. 276 (intelligence information on Austria), ll. 2, 4; TsGVIA, f. 400, op. 4, d. 275 (additional intelligence information on Austria), ll. 1–2. On Colonel Redl, see Istvan Deak, *Beyond Nationalism: A Social and Political History on the Hapsburg Officer Corps, 1848–1918* (New York, 1990), pp. 144–45; Ian D. Armour, "Colonel Redl: Fact and Fantasy," *Intelligence and National Security,* 2, no. 1 (January 1987): 170–83
20. TsGAOR, f. 543, op. 1, d. 160, ll. 45–54.
21. TsGVIA, f. 400, op. 4, d. 335 (intelligence reports about Japan, 1904–5), ll. 16, 40, 53, 193. Russia had agents with the Japanese field forces in China and also back in the Japanese home islands themselves.
22. TsGAOR, f. 568, op. 1, d. 66, l. 9.
23. AVPR, f. sekretnyi arkhiv ministra, op. 467, d. 237/238 (material on peace negotiations with Japan, January–August 1905), ll. 37–40. The quotation is found on l. 40.
24. Witte had been chosen as plenipotentiary with a view to placating the Americans, since it was hoped that his liberal reputation might help to win U.S. sympathy over to Russia. Originally, Nicholas II had intended to send

his Ambassador to Italy, Murav'ev. See TsGAOR, f. 568, op. 1, d. 66, ll. 29–30; also S. Iu. Vitte, *Vospominaniia*, 2 (Moscow, 1960): 393–97, 426–32.

25. K. F. Shatsillo, *Rossiia pered pervoi mirovoi voinoi (vooruzhennye sily tsarisma v 1905–1914 gg.)* (Moscow, 1974), pp. 13–14; L. Martov, P. Maslov and A. Potresov, eds., *Obshchestvennoe dvizhenie v nachale xx-go veka*, 2, pt. 1 (St. Petersburg, 1909): 30–32.

26. William C. Fuller, Jr., *Civil–Military Conflict in Imperial Russia, 1881–1914* (Princeton, N.J., 1985), pp. 129–30, and Chapter 5.

27. On this subject, see John Bushnell, *Mutiny amid Repression: Russian Soldiers in the Revolution of 1905–1906* (Bloomington, Ind., 1985), pp. 100–108, 204 ff.

28. Fuller, *Civil–Military Conflict*, pp. 225–26.

29. Indeed, military observers throughout the world generally viewed the Russo-Japanese War as proof that offensive action remained necessary despite the lethality of such new weapons as the machine gun and the quick-firing artillery piece. See Michael Howard, "Men Against Fire: The Doctrine of the Offensive in 1914," in Peter Paret, ed., *Makers of Modern Strategy from Machiavelli to the Nuclear Age* (Princeton, N.J., 1986), pp. 518–19.

30. On the "military renaissance" after 1905 and the politicization of Russian officers in general, see Fuller, *Civil–Military Conflict*, pp. 196–207.

31. See TsGAOR, f. 543, op. 1, d. 49 (note by V. V. Sakharov on the Council of State Defense, September 1, 1905), l. 3.

32. *Ibid.*, ll. 1–2, 7.

33. Fuller, *Civil–Military Conflict*, p. 195.

34. TsGVIA, f. 544, op. 1, d. 1333 (note on the reform of the Nicholas Academy of the General Staff), ll. 20–27.

35. TsGVIA, f. 1, op. 1, d. 70264, ll. 7–9, 12–13, 17.

36. TsGVIA, f. 1, op. 2, d. 165, l. 6.

37. Beskrovnyi, *Armiia i flot*, p. 193.

38. TsGVIA, f. 400, op. 2, d. 7494, l. 35.

39. A. A. Polivanov, *Iz dnevnikov i vospominanii po dolzhnosti voennago ministra i ego pomoshchnika 1907–1916 gg.*, 1 (Moscow, 1924): 39.

40. Shatsillo, *Rossiia pered pervoi mirovoi voinoi*, p. 37.

41. Polivanov, *Iz dnevnikov*, p. 49.

42. TsGVIA, f. 1, op. 1, d. 70264, l. 23.

43. Fuller, *Civil–Military Conflict*, pp. 160–66.

44. TsGVIA, f. 400, op. 3, d. 2947 (material on Persia, 1907–10), l. 162.

45. Lamzdorff later wrote that the Kaiser had "a certain influence over our impressionable monarch." See TsGAOR, f. 568, op. 1, d. 66, l. 36.

46. On the Björkö treaty, see [Aleksandr Izvol'skii], *Recollections of a Foreign Minister*, trans. Charles Louis Seeger (New York, 1921), pp. 27–73; Fritz Fischer, *War of Illusions: German Policies from 1911 to 1914*, trans. Marion Jackson (New York, 1975), pp. 51–52; Gordon A. Craig, *Germany 1866–1945* (New York, 1978), pp. 321–22; Prince von Bülow, *Memoirs of Prince von Bülow*, trans. Geoffrey Dunlop, 2 (Boston, 1931): 164–65.

47. See TsGAOR, f. 559, op. 1, d. 17 (reports of B. N. Evreinov to A. P. Izvol'skii, 1906), ll. 1–2.

48. See AVPR, f. sekretnyi arkhiv ministra, op. 467, d. 377 (the Franco-Russian alliance, 1900–1913), ll. 203, 209–10.
49. *Ibid.*, l. 185.
50. [Izvol'skii], *Recollections*, p. 58; Craig, *Germany*, pp. 320–21; Bülow, *Memoirs*, 2: 220–31.
51. AVPR, f. sekretnyi arkhiv ministra, op. 467, d. 377, ll. 175–81.
52. Risto Ropponen, *Die Kraft Russlands: Wie Beurteilte die Politische und Militärische Führung der Europäischen Grossmächte in der Zeit von 1905 bis 1914 die Kraft Russlands* (Helsinki, 1968), pp. 229–30.
53. TsGAOR, f. 653, op. 1, d. 21 (note of A. F. Rediger on the General Staff's mobilization plan), ll. 1–2.
54. S. Pashuto, ed., "K istorii anglo-russkogo soglasheniia 1907 g.," *Krasnyi arkhiv*, 69–70 (Moscow, 1935): 37.
55. At a special conference on the Persian question (November 30, 1907), Izvol'skii told his colleagues that upon taking up his duties he had been horrified to acquaint himself "with certain plans, the breadth of whose designs produced upon me an impression of something fantastical. Such were the plans for the subordination of Tibet, for the construction of a military port on the Persian gulf, extension of a railroad to the latter, and so forth." Plans of this kind, he hinted, should be left to molder in the archives. TsGVIA, f. 400, op. 3, d. 2947, l. 164. See also Pashuto, "K istorii," p. 26.
56. In his memorandum on his meeting with the Tsar on July 19, 1906, Lamzdorff recorded that Nicholas "grimaced" when a possible agreement with Britain was mentioned. See TsGAOR, f. 568, op. 1, d. 66, l. 36.
57. Pashuto, "K istorii," p. 26.
58. "Anglo-russkoe sopernichestvo v Persii," *Krasnyi arkhiv*, 1/56 (Moscow, 1933): 61.
59. Pashuto, "K istorii," p. 27.
60. Firuz Kazemzadeh, *Russia and Britain in Persia, 1864–1914* (New Haven, 1968), pp. 497–99; Ropponen, *Die Kraft Russlands*, p. 46.
61. Pashuto, "K istorii," p. 37.
62. TsGVIA, f. 400, op. 3, d. 2947, l. 383.
63. *Ibid.*, ll. 383–84, 387; Kazemzadeh, *Russia and Britain*, p. 529.
64. On this episode, see Serge Sazonov, *Fateful Years 1909–1916* (London, 1928), pp. 66–67; Ropponen, *Die Kraft Russlands*, p. 47.
65. For the text of the proposed agreement between Austria and Russia, see AVPR, f. kantseliariia, 1908 god, op. 470, d. 204 (secret negotiations with Austria), ll. 87–88. For the telegram of September 4[17], ll. 11b. Bernadotte E. Schmitt, *The Annexation of Bosnia 1908–1909* (New York, 1970), pp. 20–21.
66. AVPR, f. kantseliariia, 1908 god, op. 470, d. 204, l. 3.
67. *Ibid.*, l. 8.
68. *Ibid.*, l. 34 (Izvol'skii telegram of September 11[24].
69. *Ibid.*, l. 36.
70. *Ibid.*, l. 36. The Kadet (or Constitutional Democratic) Party favored radical political and social reform. The Octobrists, by contrast, were a party of the right, hawkish on defense issues.

71. *Ibid.*, l. 89 (telegram of V. N. Kokovtsov to Izvol'skii, September 20 [October 3], 1908).
72. *Ibid.*, ll. 107–8.
73. *Ibid.*, l. 95 (for Charykov's remark on the press), ll. 67 ff. (for representative press clippings); TsGAOR, f. 601, op. 1, d. 755 (Bosnian crisis), l. 1.
74. TsGAOR, f. 601, op. 1, d. 755, l. 13.
75. TsGVIA, f. 400, op. 3, d. 3169 (military intelligence material on the Bosnian Crisis), ll. 1, 27, 30, 35, 39, 49.
76. TsGAOR, f. 601, op. 1, d. 755, l. 24.
77. I. I. Astaf'ev, *Russko-germanskie diplomaticheskie otnosheniia 1905–1911 gg.* (Moscow, 1972), p. 172.
78. AVPR, f. sekretnyi arkhiv ministra, op. 467, d. 271/272, ll. 2, 5, 12 (correspondence on German rumors of Russian neutrality).
79. D. C. B. Lieven, *Russia and the Origins of the First World War* (New York, 1983), p. 36; Schmitt, *Annexation*, pp. 194–95.
80. TsGAOR, f. 601, op. 1, d. 755, l. 25–26.
81. William C. Fuller, Jr., "The Russian Empire," in Ernest R. May, ed., *Knowing One's Enemies: Intelligence Assessment Before the Two World Wars* (Princeton, N.J., 1984), p. 99.
82. Sazonov, *Fateful Years*, p. 33.
83. *Un Livre Noir: Diplomatie d'avant Guerre d'après les Documents des Archives Russes*, 2 (Paris, n.d.): 332, for Sazonov's memorandum about Potsdam.
84. *Ibid.*, p. 336.
85. TsGAOR, f. 543, op. 1, d. 185, l. 168.
86. TsGAOR, f. 601, op. 1, d. 750 (Unterberger report of February 9, 1909), ll. 1–2. Also see *ibid.*, l. 1 (Unterberger report of February 22, 1907). The Peace of Portsmouth did in fact touch off massive rioting in Tokyo. See Shumpei Okamoto, *The Japanese Oligarchy and the Russo-Japanese War* (New York, 1970), pp. 211–13.
87. TsGAOR, f. 601, d. 470 (Unterberger report of October 17, 1909), ll. 3–4.
88. A. N. Kuropatkin, "Zapiski," *Krasnyi arkhiv*, 8 (Moscow and Leningrad, 1925): 85; *idem, Zadachi russkoi armii* (St. Petersburg, 1910), 2: 272, and 3: 250–57.
89. TsGAOR, f. 555, op. 1, d. 246, ll. 3–4, 6 (the quotation is from l. 3).
90. TsGVIA, f. 400, op. 3, d. 1647, l. 1.
91. *Ibid.*, l. 12.
92. *Ibid.*
93. *Ibid.*
94. *Ibid.*, ll. 13, 15.
95. *Ibid.*, l. 12.
96. Menning, *Bayonets Before Bullets*, Chapter 6.
97. Menning, *Bayonets Before Bullets*, Chapter 6, provides the best and most comprehensive account of these developments in English. See also Norman Stone, *The Eastern Front, 1914–1917* (New York, 1975), pp. 30–31.
98. TsGAOR, f. 555, op. 1, d. 244 (Sukhomlinov's report of December 1909), l. 7.
99. A. M. Zaionchkovskii, *Podgotovka rossii k imperialisticheskoi voine* (Moscow, 1926), pp. 107, 112.

100. *Ibid.*, p. 85.
101. V. N. Kokovtsov, *Out of My Past: The Memoirs of Count Kokovtsov*, trans. Laura Matveev. (Palo Alto, Calif., 1935), p. 230.
102. TsGAOR, f. 555, op. 1, d. 244, l. 4.
103. *Ibid.*, l. 6.
104. *Ibid.*
105. Zaionchkovskii, *Podgotovka rossii*, p. 160–62.
106. TsGAOR, f. 555, op. 1, d. 210 (Vitner memorandum of February 10, 1909), l. 1.
107. *Ibid.*, l. 3.
108. *Ibid.*, l. 2.
109. *Ibid.*
110. *Ibid.*, l. 6.
111. *Ibid.*, l. 7.
112. Zaionchkovskii, *Podgotovka rossii*, p. 142.
113. *Ibid.*, pp. 198–99, 211, 225–27.
114. *Ibid.*, p. 226.
115. TsGVIA, f. 400, op. 3, d. 1695 (deployment changes, 1909–10), ll. 510, 573; TsGAOR, f. 543, op. 1, d. 59 (reports of Sukhomlinov about the new deployment, 1910), ll. 1–3.
116. Kokovtsov, *Out of My Past*, p. 254.
117. V. A. Apushkin, *General-ot-porazhenii V. A. Sukhomlinova* (Leningrad, 1925), p. 34.
118. M. Grulev, *Zapiski generala evreia* (Paris, 1930), p. 249.
119. Fuller, *Civil–Military Conflict*, pp. 240–42.
120. Zaionchkovskii, *Podgotovka Rossii*, pp. 149, 217.
121. Stone, *Eastern Front*, pp. 30–31.
122. *Materialy po istorii franko-russkikh otnoshenii za 1910–1914 gg: Sbornik sekretnykh diplomaticheskikh dokumentov* (Moscow, 1922), pp. 700–703; S. Dobrorol'skii, "Strategicheskie plany storon k nachalu mirovoi voiny," *Voennyi sbornik*, 2 (Belgrade, 1922): p. 62.
123. Pertti Lutinen, *French Information on the Russian War Plans, 1880–1914*, Societas Historica Finlandiae, Studie Historica, 17 (Helsinki, 1984): 128–29.
124. TsGAOR, f. 543, op. 1, d. 674 (note of Prince Mikhail Andronnikov and Sergei Sharapov about their mission to France, 1911), l. 5.
125. AVPR, f. sekretnyi arkhiv ministra, op. 467, d. 377, l. 337.
126. Kokovtsov, *Out of My Past*, p. 321.
127. Michael Boro Petrovich, *A History of Modern Serbia 1804–1918*, 2 (New York, 1976): 594–96.
128. Sazonov, *Fateful Years*, p. 83.
129. *Materialy po istorii franko-russkikh otnoshenii*, pp. 631, 649; Liman von Sanders, *Five Years in Turkey* (Annapolis, 1927), pp. 57–8.
130. On the Liman von Sanders affair, see *Materialy*, p. 688; I. V. Bestuzhev, "Bor'ba v Rossii po voprosam vneshnei politiki nakanune pervoi mirovoi voiny (1910–1914)," *Istoricheskie zapiski*, 75 (Moscow, 1965): 71–74; Sazonov, *Fateful Years*, pp. 120–25.
131. A. S. Silin, *Ekspansiia germanskogo imperialisma na blizhnem vostoke nakanune pervoi mirovoi voiny 1908–1914* (Moscow, 1976), p. 128.

132. I. A. Khol'msen, "Na voennoi sluzhbe v Rossii," mimeograph (New York, 1953), Khol'msen collection, Bakhmeteff Archive, Columbia University, p. 54.
133. Silin, *Ekspansiia*, p. 130.
134. AVPR, f. sekretnyi arkhiv ministra, op. 467, d. 326/330 (Black Sea naval balance), l. 1 (note by Bazili of July 1, 1913).
135. Zaionchkovskii, *Podgotovka rossii*, p. 395; AVPR, f. sekretnyi arkhiv ministra, op. 467, d. 326/330, l. 1.
136. A. V. von Shwartz, "Vospominaniia," in Alexander Pronin, ed., *Russian Emigré Archives* (Fresno, Calif., 1973), 3: 165.
137. TsGVIA, f. 1, op. 2, d. 171, l. 30.
138. *Ibid.*, l. 29.
139. on the Big Program, see A. Zhilin, "Bol'shaia programa po usileniiu russkoi armii, *Voenno-istoricheskii zhurnal*, 16, no. 7 (June 1974): 92–94; Shatsillo, *Rossiia pered pervoi mirovoi voinoi*, pp. 100–101; Zaionchkovskii, *Podgotovka rossii*, pp. 92–93; TsGVIA, f. 1, op. 1, d. 173 (War ministry report for 1913), l. 3.
140. TsGAOR, f. 543, op. 1, d. 123/128 (naval questions, 1911–13), ll. 11–13. (report of Rear Admiral Prince Lieven, Chief of the Naval General Staff, of January 30, 1912).
141. Lieven's report, cited above, was the official justification for the program.
142. V. A. Emets, *Ocherki vneshnei politiki Rossii 1914–1917* (Moscow, 1977), pp. 27–28.
143. AVPR, f. sekretnyi arkhiv ministra, op. 467, d. 326/331 (project for the naval development of the Black Sea, March 17, 1914), ll. 9–10.
144. Fuller, *Civil-Military Conflict*, pp. 222–27.
145. E. Adam, ed., "K istorii vozniknoveniia mirovoi voiny," *Krasnyi arkhiv*, 34 (Moscow and Leningrad, 1929): 175–76 (report of Major General G. I. Nostits to Ia. G. Zhilinskii, January 4 [17], 1912).
146. TsGAOR, f. 543, op. 1, d. 675, l. 3.
147. AVPR, f. sekretnyi arkhiv ministra, op. 467, d. 377, ll. 374, 382.
148. TsGVIA, f. 400, op. 3, d. 1625, l. 118.
149. Beskrovnyi, *Armiia i flot Rossii*, p. 117; Zaionchkovskii, *Podgovtka Rossii*, p. 132.
150. On Alekseev as an Austro-centric strategist, see Jack Snyder, *The Ideology of the Offensive: Military Decision Making and the Disasters of 1914* (Ithaca, N.Y., 1984), pp. 169, 174–79.
151. Iu. N. Danilov, *Rossiia v mirovoi voine 1914–1915 gg.* (Berlin, 1924), p. 86.
152. TsGAOR, f. 543, op. 1, d. 675, ll. 4, 5
153. AVPR, f. sekretnyi arkhiv, op. 467, d. 377, l. 374.
154. Even General Alekseev, who in 1912 proposed an overwhelming attack on Austria, nonetheless advocated detaching six corps for offensive operations into East Prussia. Zaionchkovskii, *Podgotovka Rossii*, p. 237. Snyder, *Ideology of the Offensive*, p. 174, incorrectly describes those forces as "a defensive screen."
155. On intelligence about Austria after Redl's suicide, see E. Adamov, ed., "K

voprosu o podgotovke mirovoi voine," *Krasnyi arkhiv,* 64 (Moscow and Leningrad, 1926): 88 ff.; Fuller, "Russian Empire" pp. 116–17.

156. Fuller, "Russian Empire," p. 114.

157. Danilov, *Rossiia v mirovoi voine,* p. 88.

158. *Ibid.,* p. 88.

159. Zaionchkovskii, *Podgotovka Rossii,* pp. 256–61, 271–75.

160. *Vostochno-prusskaia operatsiia: Sbornik dokumentov* (Moscow, 1939), p. 69.

161. *Ibid.,* pp. 262–65; Danilov, *Rossiia v mirovoi voine,* p. 103; N. N. Golovin, *Iz istorii kampanii 1914 goda na russkom fronte,* 1 (Paris, 1936): 43–51. On plan 19 altered, see also I. I. Rostunov, *Russkii front pervoi mirovoi voiny* (Moscow, 1976), pp. 92–95.

162. Snyder, *Ideology of the Offensive,* pp. 175–82.

163. This point of view was advanced *ex post facto* by General N. N. Golovin. See Nicholas Golovine, *The Russian Campaign of 1914: The Beginning of the War and Operations in East Prussia,* trans. A. G. S. Muntz (London, 1933), pp. 71–73.

164. TsGVIA, f. 400, op. 4, d. 445, l. 84; Zaionchkovskii, *Podgotovka Rossii,* p. 266; Snyder, *Ideology of the Offensive,* p. 172.

165. Dobrorol'skii, "Strategicheskie plany," pp. 62–63. This was so because I and II Siberian Corps did not arrive in the theater of war until October 1 [14], 1914—that is, more than sixty days after the declaration of mobilization.

166. David R. Jones makes this point effectively. See "Imperial Russia's Forces at War," in Allan R. Millet and Williamson Murray, eds., *Military Effectiveness,* vol. 1. *The First World War* (Boston, 1988), p. 288.

167. TsGAOR, f. 601, op. 1, d. 556 (dispatches of Nikolai Nikolaevich to Nicholas II), l. 2.

168. V. R. Berghahn, *Germany and the Approach of War in 1914* (New York, 1973), pp. 188–89; Andreas Hillgruber, *Germany and the Two World Wars,* trans. William Kirby (Cambridge, Mass., 1981), pp. 30–31.

169. *Mezhdunarodnye otnosheniia v epokhu imperializma,* 3d series, 4 (Moscow, 1931): 296–97.

170. James Joll, *The Origins of the First World War* (London, 1984), p. 12.

171. The report of this meeting was published in *Mezhdunarodnye otnosheniia,* 3d series, 4: 33–35; the original text is in AVPR, f. 133 (kantseliariia), 1914, op. 470, d. 383, ll. 2–4.

172. K. A. Krivoshein, *A. V. Krivoshein (1857–1921): Ego znachenie v istorii Rossii nachala xx veka* (Paris, 1973), pp. 200–201.

173. *Mezhdunarodnye otnosheniia,* 3d series, 4: 64.

174. Sergei Dobrorol'skii, "O mobilizatsii russkoi armii v 1914 godu", *Voennyi sbornik,* 1 (Belgrade, 1921): 101. On German reactions to these steps, see Ulrich Trumpener, "War Premeditated? German Intelligence Operations in July 1914," *Central European History,* 9, no. 1 (March 1976): 70.

175. Lieven, *Russia and the Origins,* p. 145; Dobrorol'skii, "O mobilizatsii," pp. 100–103.

176. *Mezhdunarodnye otnosheniia,* 3d series, 4: 210.

177. Marc Trachtenberg, *History and Strategy* (Princeton, N.J., 1991), pp. 84, 94–95.
178. *Ibid.*, p. 214.
179. *Ibid.*, p. 257.
180. This argument is most ably made by D. C. B. Lieven. See Lieven, *Russia and Origins*, pp. 140–50.
181. On the widespread acceptance of this idea within the General Staff, see Dobrorol'skii, "O mobilizatsii," pp. 96–97.
182. L. F. C. Turner, "The Russian Mobilisation in 1914," in Paul M. Kennedy, ed. *The War Plans of the Great Powers 1880–1914* (Boston, 1979), pp. 252–66. "From the purely military point of view, there was no immediate necessity for the Russian mobilisation order. Russia had introduced 'The Period Preparatory to War' on 26 July and had thus gained several days' advantage over Germany, who was not to proclaim *Kriegsgefährzustand* until the 31st. The Austrian partial mobilisation of eight army corps on 25 July was in no sense a direct threat to Russia; on the contrary, the more the Austrians committed themselves to the Balkans, the weaker their position would be in Galicia, where their northern frontier would be vulnerable to a Russian attack."
183. Frank Alfred Golder, *Documents of Russian History 1914–1917*, trans. Emanuel Aronsberg (Gloucester, Mass., 1964), pp. 3–23.
184. I.A. Blinov, ed.,"Dnevnik Generala Sukhomlinova," in *Dela i dni.* vol. 1 (Petersburg [sic] : 1920), p. 221.
185. On Sukhomlinov's views prior to the war, see Fuller, "Russian Empire," p. 110–11; also *idem., Civil–Military Conflict* pp. 257–58.
186. [Sukhomlinov], *Vospominaniia Sukhomlinova*, p. 224.
187. Holger H. Herwig, "Imperial Germany," in May, *Knowing One's Enemies*, pp. 94–95.
188. Beskrovnyi, *Armiia i flot*, p. 85.
189. *Ibid.*, p. 81.
190. Dobrovol'skii, "O mobilizatsii", p. 106.

10: Strategies of Confidence and Strategies of Fear

1. Peter Gatrell, *The Tsarist Economy, 1850–1917* (New York, 1986), pp. 31–32.
2. Sun Tzu, *The Art of War*, trans. Samuel B. Griffith (New York, 1963), p. 84.

Archival Materials

Tsentral'nyi Gosudarstvennyi Voenno-Istoricheskii Arkhiv (TsGVIA), Moscow [Central State Archive of Military History]
    f. 1 Chancellery
    f. 165 A. N. Kuropatkin
    f. 428 VUA (Military-Education Archive)
    f. 432 VUA (Military-Education Archive)
    f. 400 Main Staff
    f. 440 VUA (Military-Education Archive)
    f. 544 Archive of the Nicholas Academy of the General Staff
    f. 831 Military Council
    f. 2000 Main Administration of the General Staff
    f. 2003 General Headquarters, World War I
Tsentral'nyi Gosudarstvennyi Arkhiv Oktiabr'skoi Revoliutsii (TsGAOR), Moscow [Central State Archive of the October Revolution]
    f. 543 Archive of the Palace at Tsarskoe Selo
    f. 555 A. M. Guchkov
    f. 559 A. P. Izvol'skii
    f. 568 V. N. Lamzdorff
    f. 577 A. A. Neratov
    f. 601 Nicholas II
    f. 677 Alexander III
    f. 722 Marble Palace
    f. 730 A. P. Ignat'ev
    f. 828 A. M. Gorchakov
    f. 978 A. V. Lobanov-Rostovskii
Arkhiv Vneshnei Politiki Rossii (AVPR), Moscow [Archive of the Foreign Policy of Russia]
    f. 133, op. 470 Chancellery
    f. sekretnogo arkhiva ministra, op. 467 [Secret Archive of the Minister]

Index